Architecture and the Right to Heal

Architecture and the Right to Heal

Resettler Nationalism in the Aftermath of Conflict and Disaster

Esra Akcan

DUKE UNIVERSITY PRESS

Durham and London

2 0 2 5

Printed in the United States of America
on acid-free paper ∞
Project Editor: Livia Tenzer
Designed by A. Mattson Gallagher
Typeset in Minion Pro and Real Head Pro
by Westchester Publishing Services

Library of Congress Cataloging-in-
Publication Data
Names: Akcan, Esra author
Title: Architecture and the right to heal :
resettler nationalism in the aftermath of
conflict and disaster / Esra Akcan.
Description: Durham : Duke University
Press, 2025. | Includes bibliographical refer-
ences and index.
Identifiers: LCCN 2025004827 (print)
LCCN 2025004828 (ebook)
ISBN 9781478032571 paperback
ISBN 9781478029243 hardcover
ISBN 9781478061465 ebook
Subjects: LCSH: Architecture and society |
Architecture and climate | Nationalism and
architecture | Common good
Classification: LCC NA2543.S6 A3965 2025
(print) | LCC NA2543.S6 (ebook) | DDC
720.1/03—dc23/eng/20250411
LC record available at https://lccn.loc.gov
/2025004827
LC ebook record available at https://lccn.loc
.gov/2025004828

Cover art: Cappadocian spaces. Photo: Esra
Akcan, 2018.

In the memory of my father,
and to my grandmother and mother,
who endured this history

Contents

Acknowledgments

When I started *Architecture and the Right to Heal* in 2017, there was no global pandemic, no recent earthquake in Turkey, no active war in Gaza or Sudan, and yet the historical forces at the root cause of almost all of these conflicts and disasters had been unfolding. Many individuals and institutions helped me conduct this research. The book was undertaken with residential fellowships and research grants at the Radcliffe Institute for Advanced Studies at Harvard University, the Canadian Center for Architecture in Montreal, the Mui Ho Center for Cities Research Grant at Cornell-AAP, and the Mellon-funded Migrations Grant at Cornell University. Additional funding was provided from my Michael A. McCarthy Professorship (2019–24) research budget and the Institute for Comparative Modernities at Cornell University. I am indebted to these institutions for their financial support without which none of the travel for fieldwork or archival research would have been possible, and to the anonymous reviewers for these grants who trusted me even when the idea was in its premature stages. And, of course, I thank my cofellows and research fellows whose intelligence and own research in arts and academic disciplines quite different from mine inspired and motivated me to find my own place in the universe.

This research was conducted on sites and archives in Canada, Egypt, Greece, Iran, Iraq, Sudan, Turkey, the United Kingdom, and the United States. I am indebted to all the librarians and staff who steward the documents in the archives whose list you will find in the bibliography. I would like to extend additional thanks to the individuals who guided me through the documents and places much beyond my expectations, and without whose help you would not be able to read the following pages. Let me list them in alphabetical order of countries where I met them.

In Canada, as I was conducting research at the Canadian Center for Architecture (CCA) for *Abolish Human Bans*, I stumbled across hints that prompted me to look further for *Architecture and the Right to Heal*. Among them, I am most proud of embarking on research about the brilliant but previously unacknowledged Sudanese architect Abdel Moneim Mustafa. After my research in Sudan, I made the connection with Moneim Mustafa's office and the CCA, which culminated in the digitalization of the architect's drawings and their placement in Wikimedia Commons for public use. In addition to the individuals in Sudan listed below, I would like to thank, on behalf of us all who are interested in architectural knowledge, Martien de Vletter, Albert Ferré, and Rafico Ruiz. Little did we know back then that this initiative to preserve architectural drawings beyond the norms of colonial collecting would gain additional urgency, given the war that exploded in Sudan shortly after. As I watched the fragmented videos broadcasted by war journalists, I wondered if the drawings or the buildings that I photographed a couple years earlier still stood. To this day, I do not know the answer to this question.

In Egypt, Balsam Abdul-Rahman stepped in enthusiastically to guide me through the Hassan Fathy papers and other materials during my limited time in the Rare Books and Special Collections Library at the American University in Cairo.

In Greece, I cannot thank enough Giota Pavlidou at the Doxiadis Archives, whose broad knowledge about Constantinos Doxiadis and the documents in the collection has been guiding scholars tremendously. Additionally, Giota helped me navigate all the other archives in Athens with kindness, good will, and pleasant demeanor. I would also like to thank Barbara Kontogianni at the Center for Asia Minor Studies for their generosity with the permissions to publish images, in addition to all the other archives in Athens. Ioanna Theocharopoulou's and Şükrü Ilıcak's moral support and tips in traveling around Greece and in understanding different urban layers of neighborhoods in Athens were matchless (in addition to their own scholarship, of course). Finally, my heartfelt gratitude goes to one of my Airbnb hosts, Kostas, who accompanied me through the entire Evia island, and worked his magic to enter the churches and houses of Nea Sinasos and Nea Prokopi—not to mention his tips for all the other marvels along the coastal villages.

In Iran, what would I have done without the wonderful Yaser Parsa and Sepideh Khabiri, and Anbar Fereshteh Oreizi, who made these contacts? While I ended up including only one project intended for but never implemented in Tehran, the site visits to similar projects across many cities in Iran allowed me to have a better understanding. I would also like to thank Pamela Karimi for her welcoming and encouraging comments about my work, and Nader Ardalan for his responsiveness and generosity in image permissions.

In Iraq, I would like to thank my colleagues Saba Sami and Mohammed Kassim for their time and willingness to share during my visit to Baghdad, and Caecilia Pieri for facilitating my introduction to Iraqi colleagues. I hope the publications that came out of these encounters, and the collaborations we have cultivated since then, pay due tribute to your generosity. I cannot wait to continue these partnerships. I also thank Zaydoon Munir for giving image permissions for his father Hisham Munir's work.

In Sudan, I have a very long list of individuals whom I am indebted to. My colleague Salah Hassan at Cornell University has not only been an inspiration with his scholarly work and institution building skills, but also a vital support in my introduction to networks. Migdad Bannaga accompanied me to all buildings designed by Abdel Moneim Mustafa, and I am forever grateful. Additionally, I would like to thank Adil Mustafa Ahmad for sharing his ideas and own experience about architecture and architectural education in Khartoum; the Technocon office for making Moneim Mustafa's drawings available; Amira Swar-El-Dahab, Osman M. El Kheir, and Elamin Osman for their intellectual hospitality and knowledge; Ilham Abdalla Tagelsir Ali for her help in Khartoum; and the Mansour Khalid, Bedridi Suleyman, Mahmood Abdelrahim, and Haj Al-Safi families for their hospitality and opening their houses. Once I started publishing about Sudan, Suha Hasan, Mohieldin Gamal, and Mai Abusaleh reached out as they were establishing a Docomomo chapter in Sudan, and the Modern Sudan Collective. Their work for the documentation and preservation of modern architecture continues to inspire me. As I was writing the manuscript, the war displaced almost all of these individuals, and foreclosed the possibilities we had imagined—a case in point for the wounds created by historically and globally inflicted conflicts and disasters that this book tries to expose and to heal.

In Turkey, it is impossible to list all the individuals who prepared me for this book, including my grandparents and parents who lived through this history and planted seeds of curiosity in my mind with real-life stories that they told in passing. Even though I deliberately did not turn this research into an autoethnography, trace family lineages, or seek DNA tests, I assume a piece of me can be found on the lands that this book covers from West Asia to Northeast Africa and to Southeast and Northeast Europe, given the mass and family migrations that took place due to the international treaties, compulsory or voluntary displacements, and slave trades that this book records during the long dissolution of the Ottoman Empire and the emergence of successor states. For the particular research that went into this book, I can hardly give due acknowledgment to Aslı Özbay, who generously shared her work and introduced me to key actors in Cappadocia, including those who opened doors of closed churches, chapels, mosques, museums, cisterns, and hotels. Cappadocia is very lucky to have you, Aslı. I am indebted to all Saturday Mothers in Istanbul, and especially Maside Ocak, Sebla Arcan, and Aylin Tekiner, who inspire me with their human rights activism, their integrity, and their artwork, and who helped me in reaching visual documents of their movement. I would like to thank Mehmet Kentel for his help in researching Istanbul Research Institute's Collection, and Aslıhan Günhan for the documents on Sudan in Ottoman Archives. Finally, I am grateful to Ayfer Mertler and Hatice Küçükakyüz for their incredible generosity during my research in Zeytinburnu Municipality's archives. Even though they may be disappointed with some of my criticism of the municipality's policies, I like to think they would appreciate this book. On a personal level, I can't express enough my indebtedness to Aybars Aşçı, a migrant from Turkey to New York like me, for years of friendship that always reminded me of what really matters.

In the United Kingdom, I would like to thank the entire staff of the Archives and Special Collections of Durham University, and especially Francis Gotto, whose tips in searching through the Sudan Archives led to marvelous discoveries. He also helped me get permissions for images that are being published here for the first time.

In the United States, I am indebted to the archivists and librarians of the Frances Loeb Special Collections, and numerous Gropius collections at Harvard University; and of those in the Architectural Archives of the McHarg Center at the University of Pennsylvania. I would especially like to extend my thanks to William Whitaker for his tips in searching the McHarg collection that led me to the understanding of a very complex international project.

At Cornell University, I officially consulted experts for this book, including Magnus Fiskesjö, who advised me on the Uyghur refugees from China in Turkey; and Amanda Rodewald and Christopher Dunn, who guided me in matters related to wildlife biology and botanical studies. A feedback structure was established with the support of a generous Mellon grant so that the intellectual labor for this expert consultation gets compensated. This structure acknowledges the need for more collaboration between humanities scholars and scientists to bear on issues of the designed environment, both architectural and natural, in settlements with more-than-human residents. I thank all the scientists and academics who helped me understand the complexities of architecture in its relation to other disciplines. My talented and hard-working research assistant Farzana Hossein drew the speculative maps of Zeytinburnu for chapter 3; and Ronishka Sabu Nalpathil helped in formatting the bibliography. Needless to say, my students at Cornell University gave priceless feedback when I presented parts of this work in seminars. I would like to thank all the faculty and doctoral students at the History of Architecture and Urban Development (HAUD) PhD program, who were erudite, careful, and stimulating commentators, and especially my primary doctoral advisees Salvatore Dellaria, Lara Fresko, Filip Galic, Aslıhan Günhan, Eun Jeong Kim, Gökhan Kodalak, Michael Moynihan, Elizabeth Muller, Ana Ozaki, Sergio Preston, Ecem Sarıçayır, Priyanka Sen, Alican Taylan, and Asya Ece Uzmay for the opportunity to think together. I cherish the feedback and conversations with Cornell colleagues after I made presentations on this book, including, again in alphabetical order, Begüm Adalet, Leslie Adelson, Caitlin Blanchfield, Iftikhar Dadi, Naminata Diabete, Seema Golestaneh, Maria Gonzalez-Pendas (special thanks to you, Maria), Saida Hodzic, Pamela Karimi, Lori Khatchadourian, Farzin Lotfi-Jam, Fouad Makki, Natalie Melas, Mostafa Minawi, Susan-Buck Morss, Viranjini P. Munasinghe, Caroline O'Donnell, Aziz Rana, Rachel Beatty Riedl, Suman Seth, Deborah Starr, Ashley Stockstill, Eric Tagliacozzo, Chantal Thomas, Wendy Wolford, and others. These faculty and students continue to inspire me with their talent, brilliance, commitment, and research. My heartfelt thanks to Andrei Marmor, who had to sit through listening and responding to hours of doubt, and who accompanied me to some of the site trips in Athens and Cappadocia, where we sometimes ended up finding no trace of the buildings I had promised to visit.

I shared some parts of this book's work in progress in departmental lectures, conference papers, and publications, and I thank my colleagues who invited me or accepted my application to these venues. They include, in alphabetical order, Annemarie Adams, Hoor al Qasimi, Angela Andersen, Daniel Barber, Basile C. Baudez and Aaron Shkuda, Victoria Beard, Sibel Bozdoğan, Peter Christensen, Sheila Crane, Iftikhar Dadi, Mohieldin Gamal, Reto Geiser, Berin Gür and Neşe Gürallar, Elie Haddad, Salah Hassan, Steffen Haug, Jocobe Huet, Ruba Kana'an, Farhan Karim, Vladimir Kulic and Amit Srivastava, Enno Maessen, Reinhold Martin, Conor Moynihan and Jamie DiSarno, Maria Luisa Palumbo, Spyros Papapetros, Petros Phokaides and Fatina Abreek-Zubiedat, Panayiota Pyla, Sonia S. Ralston, Pari Riahi, Sean Roberts and Radha Dalal and Jochen Sokoly, Avinoam Shalem, Ufuk Soyöz, Martino Stierli, Alican Taylan and Elisa Iturbe, Ipek Türeli, Jim Williamson, Meejin Yoon, and Claire Zimmerman. Your trust in my work in progress led to valuable feedback and gave me the wherewithal to situate it in multiple fields.

At Duke University Press, I owe a lot to the four anonymous blind reviewers of the manuscript, whose praise gave me self-confidence and motivated me to become more ambitious about the book's relevance and impact. I feel blessed to be working with the legendary editor Ken Wissoker, who always moves manuscripts in the right directions and never publishes a book that is short of excellent. My deepest gratitude goes to my careful, responsible, and patient editors, Kate Mullen and Livia Tenzer, my copyeditor, Zubin Meer, and graphic designer, A. Mattson Gallagher, and my indexer, Diana Witt, who transformed words and images on a personal computer screen into an artwork for many to share. Unless otherwise indicated, all translations are mine, and I thank again those who helped me access documents in several languages.

Introduction

This book explores architecture's role in healing after conflicts and disasters by discussing buildings and spaces in relation to transitional justice and energy transition. It locates spaces of political and ecological harm, and makes a call to repurpose them as healing places where violence and violations are confronted and accountability and reparations are instituted. While working on the manuscript in the past few years, I frequently came back to the premise that started this research: To insist on imagining the future is sometimes the only resistance against the destructive powers in times of crisis. How reversible is damage due to state or social violence? How does a postdisaster society accomplish justice? As professions of futurity, architecture and planning are involved in healing, but they have also been historically responsible for building a world where a majority of the human population lives in unjust and disaster-prone environments. The book therefore critically examines the causes of and opportunistic responses to crises that foreclose the right to heal, and at the same time demonstrates architecture's potential for a meaningful reckoning and repair. As chapters proceed from the healing of an individual to that of a rural community, an urban district, the world, and the earth, they demonstrate that sudden shocks have deep roots in history and trace the real cause of present wounds to intertwined processes where colonizing empires dissolved into industrializing and purist nation-states and later became integrated into the neoliberal world order.

Architecture is sometimes an offender, at other times a healer in conflicts and disasters. Many of us must have experienced or imagined, at least once, what it means to watch one's home burn down in a fire, to be evacuated from one's flooded house with a rescue helicopter above the roof, to return to the rubble of one's neighborhood after a civil war, or to wait for days for rescue workers in the dark void of a collapsed building after an earthquake while dying slowly with a sense of abandonment by inhaling toxic dust. A pandemic and three wars took place during the time that I worked on this book on lands that relate to it. News outpoured frequently about the hottest year and the hottest day in history as well as climate refugees. After the disastrous earthquake that hit Turkey and Syria on February 6, 2023, as I was writing this book, I kept being haunted by a self-made video that circulated on social media. It showed a family, trapped in a claustrophobic alcove of a collapsed building, who sent love and apologies to their friends outside, unable to move even minimally, next to their lifeless child who they did not include in the camera's frame to spare us from seeing the deceased body. Less than a year later, the voices and images of those trapped in Gaza shook the world, as well as my immediate university campus environment, due to the military violence that the International Court of Justice described as a plausible genocide, and the United Nations Special Rapporteur reported as an actual one. We feel not only pain but also collective guilt and anger coming face to face with such accounts, because deep down we know that many conflicts and disasters could have been avoided through better planning and architecture, not to mention better theories, governments, and policies.

There is considerable literature on the reconstruction of cities after international wars and attacks, but transitions after internal social-, state- or business-led aggressions are not explored. There are ample journalistic essays on state violence and climate change, but they do not trace the interconnected historical causes of traumas or theorize right to heal as a simultaneous struggle toward social, global, and environmental justice. Connected to one another both conceptually and episodically, each chapter of *Architecture and the Right to Heal* brings new archival and on-site research to an unknown story about an ongoing struggle toward healing on lands at the intersection of Afro-Euro-Asia (ex-Ottoman lands referred to as "Middle East," "northeast Africa," and "Balkans") while also referring to similar examples around the world.

Architecture and the Right to Heal substantiates the argument that seemingly singular and isolated shocks have deep roots in intertwined history. Chapter 1, "Enforced Disappearance," tells the story of a mother whose child did not return from state custody; chapter 2, "Partition," follows two rural communities that were subject to forced mass migration; chapter 3, "Collapse," focuses on an urban district where residents lost their houses due to civil wars, state demolitions, and earthquakes; chapter 4, "Climate Disaster," discusses famine, flood, sandstorm, and other catastrophes; and chapter 5, "Extinction," discusses architects' responses after realizing the terminal loss of animals. Each chapter illustrates that these traumatic conflicts and disasters are in fact caused by much longer and entangled processes, commonly referred to as colonization, nationalization, capitalization, and industrialization.

The book suggests and elaborates on the concept of *resettler nationalism* to come to terms with these seemingly benign but actually violent historical processes on the lands that it covers throughout the long twentieth century.

Architects were frequently complicit in serving ruling powers including governments, businesses, and ethnic or economic elites in maintaining their control and advantage over the environment at the expanse of natural and social fabrics. Healing is a long and often incomplete process that erases the damaging impacts of these processes of command over individuals, communities, and nature. Beyond the limits of the debates over "the past torn and the past restored," or the journalistic essays that describe state violence, natural disasters, or international hypocrisy ahistorically, *Architecture and the Right to Heal* demonstrates that a more extensive and layered spectrum of social, global, and environmental issues may be addressed through architectural history. Each type of conflict and disaster calls for a discussion on related architectural programs—housing is implicated in healing after mass displacement and earthquakes; memorials matter for repairing state violence; master plans and campuses are implicated in climate disasters; gardens, parks, and ruderal landscapes matter for preventing the loss of biodiversity.

While "right to heal" reflects conceptual ambitions, the book's historical contribution foregrounds the transition of the Ottoman Empire into post-imperial national orders after European colonization throughout the twentieth century. I aim to write the global history of modernism in architecture in higher resolution and to highlight the historical layers on lands that are still excluded from current narratives. Part of my reason for choosing this focus was my dissatisfaction with the formulaic global history of the recent years, which has created a simplified narrative about the colonization and decolonization of the world based mostly on the history of British, French, and Spanish colonization. While correcting earlier accounts and exposing the entanglement of modernity, capitalism, and coloniality, this history excludes large sections of the globe. It ignores differences between lands before and after they were colonized by the European imperial powers, and the political and ecological harms of modernity's other dark sides that were reliant on or followed colonialism, such as national partitions, religious divides, and ethnocentrism. The British Empire's post-Ottoman interests, such as colonies and mandates in today's Cyprus, Egypt, Iraq, Jordan, Palestine, and Sudan, and targets of intervention such as Greece, Turkey, and the Balkans provide good examples in order to trace the intertwined history of colonization, nationalization, and carbonization or, to put it in other words, to show the explanatory power of resettler nationalism in global history. Racist constructs of European Orientalism against the Ottomans and extractive economies of industrial capitalism, on the one hand, and the rising racist and classist tensions among the Muslim and non-Muslim *millets* and *unsurs* of the Ottoman Empire, on the other hand, converged with major consequences on the built environment. This book discusses the long dissolution of the Ottoman Empire at the geometric center of Africa, Asia, and Europe, when culturally and religiously mixed populations were divided during the making of the modern world order. This history at the intersection of Afro-Euro-Asia demonstrates that modernity partitioned this land into three continents and built physical and imaginative borders between and within them.

Healing as a Matter of Rights

Healing is used as an umbrella term in this book, which encompasses but differs from *repair, restoration, reparation,* or *restitution.* As distinct from mechanistic or financial metaphors such as repair and reparation, *healing* refers to the improvement of human and nonhuman organisms. Healing takes place not only due to the actions of responsible institutions but also through self-improvement. Healing foregrounds architecture's worldmaking abilities, but it does not always involve repair or restoration. It sometimes means choosing not to repair. The phrase *right to heal* acknowledges healing as a human and nonhuman species right, and identifies individuals and institutions that hold the responsibility to deliver this right. Healing as a matter of rights alludes to both a lengthy and intertwined process of struggle toward social, global, and environmental justice, and an extended definition and practice of rights that fosters international solidarity. This book starts and ends with an advocacy on the expansion and implementation of human and nonhuman species rights. Chapters in between discuss the aftermath of the Ottoman Empire's dissolution by offering the idea of resettler nationalism as a framework to explain the political and ecological harms of the period. All chapters demonstrate how healing (or the lack thereof) manifests in different situations, after distinct types of traumas, and how it may take diverse forms.

There is a recent momentum in the world to reckon with the injustices of the past, including those of military regimes, apartheids, civil wars, colonialism, and slavery—and a growing anxiety over and backlash to reparations. The term *reparations* originally referred to monetary compensations paid to countries after wars and to individuals after legal procedures. Recent discussions call for broadening this nomenclature of diplomacy and law, and for searching for ways to implement not only material compensations but also nonmaterial restitutions. This book responds to this call for finding more approaches that invite societies to take accountability for political and ecological harms of the past. In this sense, *reparations* means justice achieved retroactively. *Architecture and the Right to Heal* foregrounds the accentuated role of history writing in matters of justice, while not using the term *justice* monolithically. Instead, it foregrounds the distinctions between penal and nonpunitive forms of justice, as well differences within nonpunitive or restorative justice. For instance, distributive justice seeks to close the present gaps in a society, such as income gaps, education gaps, or incarceration gaps by allocating current resources more evenly, but right to heal is invested in tracing the historical causes of this gap much more precisely and bringing justice against past violations of fairness for a better justification of redistribution. As Ta-Nehisi Coates, whose essay "The Case for Reparations" brought new momentum to the idea of Black reparations, would say, one cannot close an achievement gap without closing the injury gap.[1] These discussions on reparations call for a more holistic approach to justice to be achieved retroactively, and to healing through justice. This book elaborates on a prolonged and delayed notion of transitional justice for this healing process—a sphere in human rights and international law that was officially recognized in the first decade of the twenty-first century.

But what exactly is "human" and what exactly are human rights? I do not take the concept of "human" lightly. A new and expanded practice of human rights first needs to confront and overcome the definition of the "human," which, as Sylvia Wynter warned, had been constructed as if it is synonymous with "Man" (i.e., "Western" and "white") during European colonial modernity. In Wynter's words, "Our present struggles with respect to race, class, gender, sexual orientation, ethnicity, struggles over the environment, global warming, severe climate change, the sharply unequal distribution of the earth resources . . . are all differing facets of the central ethnoclass Man vs. Human struggle."[2] Building on the work of Wynter, Christina Sharpe, Katherine McKittrick, and others, part of my intention is to trace the real cause of sudden social conflicts and environmental disasters to the historical process that is predicated on this association between human and "Man" and to argue that healing depends on their deassociation.

I do not take the concept of "human rights" lightly either. Despite its omnipresent use in daily language, the definition of human rights as a concept remains unresolved. Ever since human rights crystallized with eighteenth-century peoples' revolutions around the world, it has implicitly become a reference point in discussions about space. The concept of human rights has received its own share of suspicion and reproach from authors at different ends of the political spectrum. The far-right press portrays human rights as an alibi to protect criminals.[3] Jeremy Bentham ridiculed the foundational premise of human rights that all human beings are born free—perhaps to be expected from the inventor of the panopticon who attempted to discipline bodies through an architectural device—and rebuked the idea that natural and inalienable rights should be distinct from legal rights because, he claimed, that would be an invitation to anarchy.[4] Karl Marx famously opposed human rights for their egoistic preoccupations that protect individuals instead of political communities, and for reducing the definition of the "true" human being into a bourgeois individual.[5] Despite Marx's initial objections, however, nowhere has the concept of human rights been more acknowledged in architectural and urban theory than in left-wing circles. Henri Lefebvre's "The Right to the City"[6] has served as a guide to reflect on architecture's relation to uneven development in the capitalist city, and to turn the city into a platform of revolutionary transformation.[7] As early as Olympe de Gouge's and Mary Wollstonecraft's appeals, feminist critique has exposed the hypocrisy of gender discrimination in the initial declarations that advocated for the rights of "man and citizen."[8] Another common critique of the current human rights regime has been the assertion that the concept is a Western invention and therefore its universalization is an imperialist expansion—an accusation that Amartya Sen defined as cultural critique.[9] The worst scandals of human rights history happened when Western superpowers used human rights as an excuse for military intervention that destroyed cities and buildings in order to serve other interests. Discussions continue on the possible distinctions between human rights as a moral issue aiming to define basic universal ideas about human dignity, and as a matter of international law identifying the legitimate international response to a state government that is deemed to be violating those rights.[10] Hannah Arendt, Giorgio Agamben, and others have exposed the limits of the continuing attachment between human and citizenship rights in protecting refugees and their housing.[11]

With some of these fallacies corrected but others left unresolved, the concept of human rights continues to be relevant today in architectural theory for moral commitment to rectify injustice and ensure equality, or political action to protect human dignity, enable participatory democracy, and foster progressive change, or still, to build empathy for the oppressed. Despite numerous challenges from skeptics and authors with different philosophical convictions, "the claim to 'natural rights' has never been quite defeated," as Margaret MacDonald summarized: "It tends in some form to be renewed in every crisis in human affairs, when the plain citizen tries to make, or expects his leaders to make, articulate his obscure, but firmly held conviction that he is not a mere pawn in any political game, nor the property of any government or ruler, but the living and protesting individual."[12]

Even though the topic of human rights is relevant for architecture, not to mention multiple other social sciences and humanities fields,[13] it has been overwhelmingly perceived as a legal matter administered by the United Nations (hereafter UN) after the second half of the twentieth century. The perception of human rights as an exclusively legal and governmental matter assumes that there should be a responsible institution whose duty is to deliver human rights, and operates as if something could be defined as a human right only if it can be combined with a correlating obligation. This may be important in the legal implementation of human rights, but it has tapered down the epistemological, ethical, and cultural discussions about the topic. Narrowly speaking, the legal debate on human rights has paid attention to architecture only in relation to the right to housing. Ever since the first deliberations at the UN that resulted in 1948's Universal Declaration of Human Rights, there has been international discord over what constitutes a human right. Housing has been one of them.[14] Even though the UN admits that the situation of housing around the world is dire, housing in particular or architecture in general has not necessarily become a top priority for human rights. Preventing discrimination, forced evictions, and war crimes involving the unjustified destruction of housing have come to be the only legal human rights considerations when it comes to architecture.[15] This book urges us to cast a wider net, not necessarily as a legal but cultural discussion: Chapter 1 discusses how the recent human rights conventions of the twenty-first century may open new potentials for architecture's relevance; chapter 5 advocates for the recognition of species' rights beyond humans.

Recovering from the contested history of human rights and building on the corrections of the definition of "human" as a concept, *Architecture and the Right to Heal* suggests that healing from conflict and disaster is contingent on the local and international solidarity movements and institutions that expand and protect human and species rights. The examples in the following chapters give evidentiary support that this process has already started. A familiar and justified critique of the human rights regime and the international organizations such as the UN is their originary Eurocentrism and the hierarchical structure between nation-states. However, I qualify this critique by referring to a global history of human rights that gives due acknowledgment to all its makers. Historically, the concept of human rights has been mobilized and improved in several episodes of anticolonial, antiracist, feminist, anti-slavery, and antiapartheid struggles, and continues to expand with grassroots activism taking place with actors and in countries outside "the West," like the ones exemplified in chapter 1. This chapter explores the relation between physical space and right to truth as a foundational concept of transitional justice. Indirectly recognized by international law and the UN, the right to truth oversees the right of relatives to know the truth about individuals who had been subject to state violence and human rights violations in the past, which have been obscured due to denial of accountability and distortion of facts in official narratives. Chapter 1 discusses truth and the recognition of suffering as a prerequisite of healing.

The Global South played a foundational role in the emergence of transitional justice. As elaborated further in chapter 1, the accountability for abuses in the past came to the forefront of human rights movements with the grassroots protests in South America and South Africa since the 1980s, and culminated in a new UN human rights convention (adopted in 2006) on the protection from enforced disappearance. The field continues to expand to account for other historical crimes. In July 2021, UN Special Rapporteur Fabian Salvioli issued a report that suggests transitional justice mechanisms to examine the human rights violations committed during colonial times.[16] Building on international law scholars of transitional justice such as Ruti Teitel and Pablo De Greiff, I reflect on the multiple, conciliatory, and long-term goals that go much beyond monetary compensations and material reparations, but include the role of architectural history and design in harm recognition and reconciliation.[17] This book identifies several measures for the right to heal, not only prosecutions, reparations, and repatriations, but also truth-telling, institutional reforms, memorials as official apologies, adequate housing and city services, and other artistic and educational steps for nonrecurrence and "never again" movements.

The discussion on transitional justice as a new sphere of human rights in chapter 1 helps crystallize ideas about the healing of the human, both individual and communal (bonded or imagined communities of a town or a nation-state). Additionally, I carry the problematization of the concept of "human" to the final chapters on the healing of the planet. The book's structure moves from the healing of the individual to that of the communal and the planetary. Recently, scholars such as Bram Büscher and Robert Fletcher, William Cronon, Donna Haraway, Emma Marris, and Anna Lowenhaupt Tsing have unsettled the nature/culture and human/nonhuman division, suggesting that environmental problems can only be addressed by leaving behind the mainstream epistemology that separates humans from other species in "nature," and by acknowledging that all are part of the same ecosystem. Similarly, I scrutinize in chapter 5 the constructed definition of the "human" to imagine a new understanding that potentially heals the damaged relation between humans and nonhumans.[18]

The history outlined in this book makes a case for the need to conceptualize the relational logic between the wounds of capitalism, colonization, nationalization, and carbonization. Several authors have inspired this conclusion. Ann Laura Stoler's foundational volume *Imperial Debris* reveals the multiple aftermaths of imperialism as sedimented violence.[19] *Architecture and the Right to Heal* demonstrates sedimented violence caused by not only competitive imperialism and nation-state formation but also the carbonizing industrial capitalism that motivated the nineteenth-century British colonization of Ottoman lands in northeast Africa and West Asia. Adding to the traditional Marxist labor history by evaluating the impact of industrial capitalism on climate change, Andreas Malm shows the cumulative effect of carbon emissions, which means that carbon's impact in causing climate change is augmented with the passage of time, and that each carbon emission harms future victims even more so than the present ones.[20] In other words, debris and sedimentation that postcolonial scholars discuss in relation to imperialism are also fitting concept metaphors for carbonization. The final chapters of this book discuss the relations between dominant politico-economic convictions and climate change, by building on Malm, Naomi Klein, Ashley Dawson, and T. J. Demos, among others.[21]

I join a group of authors who reveal the relations between multiple oppressive forces of history. Lisa Lowe demonstrates the intertwined history between the settler colonialism on Indigenous lands, the slavery of African peoples, and the exploitation of Asian immigrants; Rinaldo Walcott alludes to the pitfalls of denying the relations between different episodes of white violence in delivering freedom to Blacks; and Max Liboiron exposes environmental degradation and settler colonial violence as twin problems.[22] These authors bring us face to face with the fact that the wounds in North America can only be addressed with the writing of global intertwined history. I build on these ideas, albeit with caution, because their untranslated transportation to a book on lands previously part of the Ottoman Empire— where some slaves were white and where competitive imperialism and nationalist violence complicated the domination dynamics—runs the risk of epistemic imperialism. Instead, this book adds to these debates on North America by exposing the missing "other" in these formulations. It returns to authors such as Edward Said, who analyzed the transformation of European Orientalism into North American area studies that continues to dictate the mainstream foreign policy decisions and the "clash of civilizations" ideology.[23] The Middle East—whose definition is quite vague but usually refers to the Ottoman lands in West Asia and Africa during and after their transition from the imperial regime—has continued to be construed as the ultimate "other" of the West for almost the entire timespan covered in this book and today. I demonstrate this process of "othering" by visiting historical episodes during British colonization, the partitions after the Ottoman Empire's dissolution, the failure of postimperial nation-states in delivering freedom, and the rise of American power, soft and military.

Each chapter focuses on one type of traumatic experience and on a relatively small group of victims, but shows that these wounds have been long in the making through globally connected events. Giving a name to conflicts and disasters as a matter of human *and* political rights is a prerequisite of healing. A mother may mourn in isolation over her child who never returned from state custody, but it is only when this trauma is named as enforced disappearance that it can be identified as a human rights violation, gain public visibility, and become a social movement. A community may be deported from one land and resettled in another, but it is only when this forced migration is named as partition that its perpetrators can be identified as national leaders and diplomats of international institutions. A society may conceive an earthquake or a famine as God's will, but it is only when this building failure or food insecurity is named as human-made urban or climate disaster that one can identify its root causes and see it as injustice rather than misfortune. All of us can mourn the extinction of a charismatic animal, but it is only when international institutions and nation-states recognize and ratify the rights of nature and rights of nonhuman species that humans might reverse the alarming rates of mass extinction. A chain of conflicts and disasters that extends to the entire book shows that a mother's right to mourn is also a society's right to heal from state violence; a village community's right to heal from enforced migration also involves struggle against xenophobia and violent transgressions of international law; a city's struggle to recover from deadly earthquakes is the same struggle to avoid economic crashes; a country's right to feed its population is also its right to heal from colonization and environmental extraction; another country's right to heal from global war is also the world's right to recover from global warming; and the planet Earth's species' right to live is also the nations' struggle to live together. This structure is a demonstration of the intersectionality of social, global, and environmental justice, and that one cannot confront climate change and mass extinction—harms against nature—without understanding harms against peoples and communities.

Resettler Nationalism

Of all the migration stories that I heard in passing from my grandparents while growing up in Turkey, the most unbelievable was that of a grand-aunt who had lived on a distant island on the Danube River, an island so small that it was forgotten in an international treaty and accidentally remained part of the Ottoman Empire until it submerged under the waters. At first, I thought this story of a small, sunken island that grown-ups did not care enough to remember was a fairy tale. I realized only later that it used to be a real place: Adakale was indeed forgotten in the Berlin Treaty of 1878, and it did indeed sink under the Danube's waters due to a Romanian-Yugoslav cobuilt hydraulic plant, which forced its remaining habitants to emigrate in 1967. Such displacements and desertions were hardly unique in my family and many around me whose great-grandparents migrated during the transition of the Ottoman Empire into different nation-states. This book foregrounds the stories of these migrants either as part of communities that were displaced and resettled on new lands or as experts who contributed to the built environment of new nation-states. It suggests the concept of resettler nationalism to come to terms with this transition.

Though not exclusively, *Architecture and the Right to Heal* focuses on a few post-Ottoman lands that became independent nation-states either directly during the empire's dissolution or after the British colonization. The long dissolution of the Ottoman Empire triggered countless incidents at the geometric center of Afro-Euro-Asia that eventually divided this land into three continents and numerous nation-states. For instance, al-Idrisi's world map of the year 1154 CE famously depicted the continents we call Africa, Asia, and Europe as one continuous and connected landmass (figure I.1). In the nineteenth century, the Ottoman Empire still extended to parts of the three continents as one entity, before they were perceived as divided in the twentieth. This process brought significant population movements into the Ottoman Empire,[24] including, according to rough estimates, the 500,000 Tatars who moved to Ottoman lands between 1789 and 1800; 400,000 Crimeans between 1860 and 1864; 1 million North Caucasian Muslims who sought refuge in the empire between the 1850s and World War I; 1.5 million people from the Balkan countries after the 1877–78 Ottoman-Russian War, when thousands of

Armenians moved in the other direction to Russia; and 640,000 more people during the Balkan War of 1912–13. Justin McCarthy prepared a map showing the forced displacements of 5 million Muslims and 1.9 million Christians between Ottoman and neighboring lands from 1770 till 1923 (figure I.2).[25] These population movements significantly altered the cultural, social, and built environments of the lands of departure and arrival. They turned the Ottoman state into an "empire of refugees" in Vladimir Hamed-Troyansky's words, and many parts of the empire into "refugee countries," such as the modern city of Amman that was founded as a consequence of the arrival of north Caucasian refugees.[26] The ethnic and religious homogenization of post-Ottoman Turkey is a case in point of resettler nationalism: While in 1870, there were 2.3 million Armenians, 2.1 million Greeks (*Rum*), and 4 million Arabs within the borders of the Ottoman Empire, these numbers dropped to 65,000, 120,000, and 135,000, respectively, within the borders of the Republic of Turkey in 1927.[27] As a consequence of these forced mass migrations that continued well into the late twentieth century, "the age of co-existence" on the lands of the Ottoman Empire, in Ussama Makdisi's terms, was replaced with what I name the age of resettler nationalism.[28] Today, there are still unresolved territorial claims over the lands that were once the Ottoman Empire: Armenia, Israel, Kosovo, Northern Cyprus, and Palestine continue as states with limited recognition at the UN. Uncertainties due to armed conflicts are continuing in Iraq, Israel/Palestine, Syria, and Sudan. As I was writing, I read the news about the destructions of Gaza and Sudan, including the buildings in Khartoum that are portrayed in this book and that I had visited a couple of years earlier.

The transition of the Ottoman Empire into a postimperial order that triggered these episodes of mass migration also polarized the world as a conflict between "Islam" and "the West." *Architecture and the Right to Heal* writes the complicated and layered history of this divide between the major world events that fortified it, namely, between the Balkan War (1912–13) and the Islamic Revolution in Iran (1978–79) that coincided with the rise of neoliberalism. Population transfers and migration of refugees or families continued during much of this timespan. Those that are addressed in the following pages include the 1915 Tehcir (relocation) law with significant consequences on the non-Muslims, especially Armenians, of the Ottoman Empire; the 1919 Greek-Bulgarian population transfer convention; the 1923 Greek-Turkish Exchange of Populations Treaty; the 1950 Bulgarian decree to expel Muslim Turks; the 1953 Yugoslav migration agreement that lifted the prohibition to leave the country; the 1964 Turkish decree to expel Christian

Figure I.1
Al-Idrīsī, world
map, 1154 CE.

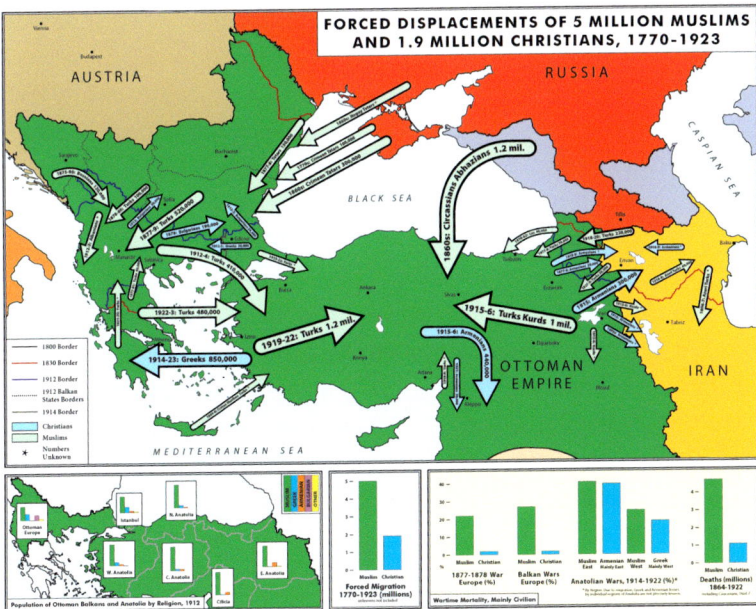

Figure I.2 Forced displacements of 5 million Muslims and 1.9 million Christians during the dissolution of the Ottoman Empire. Map by Justin McCarthy.

Greeks; the 1974 war in Cyprus as a result of which many families in both Turkey and the Greek islands were forced to emigrate; and the 1989 Bulgarian decree to expel Muslim minorities. Moreover, Kazak, Afghan, Uzbek, Uyghur, and other Central Asian refugees and asylum seekers from the Soviet Union and China migrated to Turkey from the days of the first military invasion of Xinjiang in 1949 till today. In February 2025, US President Donald Trump suggested a similar resettlement plan for Gaza.

This book shows that the diplomatically supported compulsory population transfers and the forced mass or family migrations throughout this period have created urban debris that is still visible and usually still in need of healing. For instance, I look at the afterlife of buildings and entire villages that were completely abandoned despite being located in striking landscapes. Chapters 2 and 3 write the urban history of modern Athens and modern Istanbul as refugee-arrival cities. They discuss the aftermath of these population movements by tracing the experience of those who were displaced because of an ideology that emerged as if it was a remedy to ethnic violence—an ideology I term *resettler nationalism*. I offer resettler nationalism as a concept with more explanatory power than those used in established histories and popular media. Much like settler colonialism, resettler nationalism relies on the mass migration of peoples and causes forced dislocations and dispossessions. However, unlike established and popular history that casts nationalism as an anticolonial idea, this book demonstrates the wounds of resettler nationalism. By *resettler nationalism*, I refer to the double ideology of religious rift and national fault line that stirred race-based nationalist and religious sentiments, escalated ethnic violence, and eventually caused mass dispossessions.

Architecture and the Right to Heal identifies the root cause of social conflicts and environmental disasters as resettler nationalism while it converged with European industrialist colonization, authoritarian states, and capitalism. These include enforced disappearance (chapter 1), forced mass migration (chapter 2), civil war (chapter 3), dispossession and poverty (chapters 2 and 3), slum development (chapters 2 and 3), death in earthquakes (chapter 3), pollution (chapter 3), racial urban segregation (chapter 4), sandstorm, flood, and famine (chapter 4), and the inability to respond to ecocide (chapter 5). Moreover, resettler nationalism perpetuated partition along perceived ethnic, religious, and racial lines and hindered cosmopolitan ethics. By criticizing resettler nationalism, I seek to disassociate *cosmopolitanism* in a multireligious and multilingual society from its pejorative nineteenth-century connotations, when the word was scorned due to the rise of ethnocentrism outlined in this book. Instead, cosmopolitan ethics could become a prerequisite for a new culture of welcoming and peace to come.[29]

I have selected the Ottoman imperial capital, and cities to its south, north, east, and west as case studies in order to discuss resettler nationalism as a major cause of conflicts and disasters. This section of the introduction overviews the historical events during this transition as a background for buildings and spaces discussed throughout this book, as well as the current scholarship about this transition to clarify the book's contributions.

In the south, Khartoum in today's Sudan provides an understudied but telling example.[30] Modern Sudan is curiously absent from the scholarship on both "African" and "Islamic architecture." The history of Khartoum unsettles the conceptualization of Africa as a separate and singular continent whose nations gained independence after being colonized by Western European powers. One of my historiographical aims is to put the neglected Ottoman Empire into the histories of Africa and to see the competitive imperialisms and extractive economies as well as the layered postcolonial struggles on these lands. A map in the Ottoman Archives dated 1883–84 indicates a fortressed settlement in Khartoum, across the river from Omdurman (Ümmü Derman), the Tutti Island, and Halfaya (today's Khartoum North, see figure 4.1).[31] The first fortified urban settlement in Khartoum is traced to 1821 and accredited to Mehmet Ali Paşa's conquest (also known as Muhammad Ali), after which the city became the capital of the Ottoman Sudan province during the time locally named as the *al Turkiya* period. Most relevant for this book is the fact that Mehmet Ali connected southeastern Europe and northeastern Africa during the late Ottoman Empire in multiple ways. Born in 1770/71 in Kavala in today's Greece as a descendant from a Turkish family who did not speak Arabic, Mehmet Ali used to earn his living in the tobacco trade before he became the Ottoman governor in today's Egypt—a post he held for four decades—when he served the Ottoman authority in regaining order and power in North Africa after the French invasions. A modernizer of many towns in today's Egypt, his rule also made an impact on his hometown in the Balkans, as Kavala became the beneficiary of the taxes collected after he stopped rebellions on behalf of the Ottoman rule.[32] In addition to Egyptian Ottomans, Greek, Kurdish, and Armenian Ottoman administrators and builders were part of Governor Mehmet Ali's inner circle.[33] During the reign of Ismā'īl Bāshā of Ottoman Egypt (1863–81, also known as Khedive Ismail), British representatives were also added to the high military and civil officials, such as General Charles George Gordon, who left an important imprint on Khartoum. The time of Khedive Ismail is characterized by the struggle against the slave trade that was finally abolished with the 1877 Anglo-Egyptian Slave Trade Convention, and infrastructure projects including railways, river transportation lines, and telegraph systems.

Understudied until recently, Ottoman Africa has raised questions about the competitive imperialisms of the nineteenth century. The industrial-colonial ambitions of the European powers affected the Ottoman Empire intensely, as British, French, and Italian militaries took hold of the Ottoman lands in Africa and the "Middle East," and as their economic power affected the remaining cities of the empire due to the rise of capitalism. I build on historians such as Selim Deringil and Mostafa Minawi, who treat the Ottomans in Africa as both colonizer and colonized as well as traditional imperialists who tried to maintain competitiveness in the new European colonial order while having to fight against it. While local subjects had agency, governing and negotiating power under customary Ottoman rule, the situation changed by the late nineteenth century under Abdülhamid II's regime.[34] Ottoman intellectuals aspired to insert themselves into the modern world order so as to be part of perceived advanced civilization, on the one hand, and yet they held anti-imperialist sentiments against European Orientalism, on the other hand. In Deringil's words, the ruling elite of the late Ottoman Empire in a world now ruled by Britain, France, and Germany "adopted the mindset of their enemies, the arch-imperialists, and came to conceive its periphery as a colonial setting."[35] Against the established narrative that the Ottoman Empire was an inward-looking and defensive state after the Ottoman-Russian War of 1877–78, Minawi studies the Ottoman Empire's rigorous, albeit failed, participation in the Scramble for Africa during the Berlin Conference of 1884–85.[36] The Mahdist state took over the rule in Sudan after the uprising against Ottoman Egypt led by Muhammad Ahmad ibn'Abdallah, who claimed himself as the expected religious leader Mahdi (1881–85). The Mahdist imperial rule for the spread of Islam continued after his untimely death with his son, Khalifa Abdallah, till 1898.[37] Mahdi settled his headquarters with a mosque and housing complex in Omdurman across the river from Khartoum, which was a small village at the time, but grew into a large town with the migration of peoples from multiple directions in Africa during the Mahdist rule.

After the Battle of Omdurman of 1898, the rule was transferred from the Mahdi regime (1886–98) to the Anglo-Egyptian Condominium (1898–1956). Despite the name of the condominium, absolute civil and military powers were combined under the sovereign British governor-general (until 1924) who reported to London's Foreign Office through the British representative in Cairo, which had been under British colonization since 1882. The balance of powers changed over the course of the twentieth century with the rise of Egyptian and Sudanese nationalism, and the British interests after World War I that sought to eliminate Egypt's involvement in Sudan, on the one hand, and to contain the growth of Sudanese national consciousness, on the other.[38] Eve Troutt Powell defines the Anglo-Egyptian Condominium as a "triangle of colonialism marked by Great Britain, Egypt and Sudan" and analyzes Egyptian politicians, intellectuals, and authors within the psyche of the "colonized colonizer." She posits her explanation of the Sudanese colonization as a necessary nuance to the established framework of imperialism that conceives the global history of modernity and colonization as a binary between the West and the rest.[39] The following pages in this book also complicate this picture as a polygonal equation by discussing not only architects and planners of British colonial forces but also Greek-Ottoman builders in Africa. They also trace the post-Ottoman and local professional networks into the years of independent Sudan.

While Khartoum's urban and architectural history exposes the north–south divide of the modern world order, the east–west divide that materialized during the transition from imperial to national order has been no less impactful. I focus on the Balkan regions such as Athens, Skopje, and Evia Island on the west side of the European border, and Istanbul, Cappadocia, Baghdad, and Tehran (even though Tehran was never part of the Ottoman Empire) on the east side to discuss this divide in this book. Among the wars and insurgencies that caused the eventual end of the Ottoman Empire, the Balkan War (1912–13) has come to be the most unforgettable for the founders of the nation-states that emerged out of the empire. In the First Balkan War of the autumn of 1912, which lasted for six weeks, the Ottoman Empire fought a loose coalition from Bulgaria, Greece, Montenegro, and Serbia; in the Second Balkan War of the summer of 1913, which lasted for four weeks, these states fought each other for the ownership of lands that were no longer Ottoman territory after the first war. Many see World War I, which started less than a year later, as the continuation of the Balkan War, and the conflict that culminated in the collapse of Yugoslavia in 1991 as its reemergence.[40]

The historians of Great Powers immediately construed the Balkan War as justice restored. In 1914, only one year after the ceasefire, Jacob Gould Schurman wrote, "The expulsion of Turks from Europe was long ago written in the book of fate. . . . A little clan of oriental shepherds, the Turks had in two generations gained possession. . . . What happened, however, was the revolt of subject provinces and the creation out of the territory of European Turkey of the independent states. . . . There is historic justice in the circumstance that the Turkish Empire in Europe met its doom at the hands of the Balkan nations themselves."[41] Schurman posited the Balkan War as a natural extension of the Greek War of Independence for which "Powers now recognized that nothing but intervention could save Greece for European civilization."[42] He did not only interpret the Balkan War as the fight between civilization and barbarism or the Christian-Muslim rift. Following the common Western perception of the relation between race, nation, and territory at the time, he also regarded it as a "race" war: The Ottoman Empire had failed to accommodate the alleged racial distinctions among the Balkan states and the "ties of blood and language."[43] The British colonialists regarded the Ottoman towns and cities as the unnatural mixing of different races that needed to be unmixed for a stable world order. Lord Curzon famously described the Greek-Turkish partition as the "unmixing of peoples." In Isa Blumi's words, "Cast in these terms, living under the Ottoman Empire was a tragic story of Oriental 'enslavement' of essentially 'white' European Christians whose national ambitions could only be served when they lived in distinctive enclaves from 'others' not of their denomination."[44]

Assuming "mixed" religions and languages in multicultural societies would unavoidably break into pieces, and instead of tracing the precise history of the emergence of ethnic violence that forecloses cosmopolitan ethics, the established historiography wrote the Balkan War as the final evidence of modern nation-state's inevitability. Atrocities against civilians and forced migrations were normalized, even glorified, as the unavoidable human cost in the name of nationalism, struggle against guerrilla warfare and invasion, or liberation from despotism, rather than ethnic cleansing or demographic engineering.[45]

The double ideology of religious rift and national fault line not only determined the borders in Europe but also stirred race-based nationalist and religious sentiments and escalated ethnic violence within the remaining borders of the Ottoman Empire as well. Even though the Ottoman Empire had already been losing ample territories in Central Europe and North Africa, it is indeed curious that the ejection from the Balkans made a devastating mental impact on a group of intellectual and military leaders commonly known as the Young Turks and founders of the Republic of Turkey. Erik Jan Zürcher points out that 82 percent of the ruling members of the early republic were migrants from the West, and that 41 percent of them were born on lands lost to the Ottoman Empire during the Balkan War. This means that the Republic of Turkey was founded and ruled for its first twenty-three years by Balkan refugees, including the founder Mustafa Kemal Atatürk from Salonica, and the director of refugee resettlement, Şükrü Kaya from Kos, both in today's Greece.[46] Scholars have argued that the Balkan migrants consequently turned to Anatolia as their homeland and cultivated the idea of Turkishness as race-based nationalism.[47] Many authors, novelists, and poets of the time contributed to the sense of loss and insecurity that they associated with the loss of lands in the Balkan War.[48] For example, the novelist and activist Halide Edip Adıvar wrote in her memoirs that the Balkan War "intensified nationality in Turkey, . . . the feeling that in order to avoid being exterminated, the Turks must exterminate others."[49] The race-based nationalism after the Balkan War replaced the Young Turks' short-lived ideas about Ottomanism (the parliamentary governance of a multicultural society with mechanisms of representation, conflict resolution, and cohabitation).[50] The move from diverse Ottomanism to Turkish nationalism with the adaptation of Anatolia as the territorial core could not have been an instant process for everyone, but it was effective.[51] Scholars including Fuat Dündar and Taner Akçam demonstrate that the leadership around Committee of Union and Progress (CUP) consequently participated in Anatolia's demographic engineering and the Armenian genocide.[52] In scholars Ümit Kurt and Doğan Gürpınar's words, "The Balkan Wars were the turning point in the rise of an anti-liberal, anti-cosmopolitan pessimist culture, as well as a new radical and ethnic Turkish nationalism."[53]

Those traumatized by the Balkan War were not limited to the founders of the Turkish Republic. In an extensive study about the immediate debates following this war, Eyal Ginio has analyzed the memoirs, press articles, novels, poems, monuments, photographs, and postcards produced by Turkish-, Arabic-, and Ladino-speaking communities from Istanbul to Salonica to Plovdiv and to Cairo.[54] There was indeed a wide range of responses. While many expressed themselves with apocalyptic words, their topics included such various and at-times competing themes as Ottoman decline, military weakness and repair, European colonization, the atrocities against and the suffering of Ottoman refugees, the building of national and patriotic awareness, the similarity of the Balkan defeat to the expulsion of the ancient Israelites from their lands, the failure of Ottomanism, the betrayals of Ottoman non-Muslims, the restoration of the Ottoman Empire and Islam in Europe, irredentism and revenge, the disappointments with European hypocrisy in the face of atrocities against Muslims, the building of a stronger national economy with Muslim capitalists by diminishing the leadership of non-Muslim entrepreneurs, and many more.

In addition, the Balkan War sparked trends of Islamism in and out of the Ottoman Empire. There was a strong reaction to the perception of Islamic civilization as inferior and the maltreatment of Muslim subjects in the Balkan states.[55] The Balkan War stirred up the use of Islamic motifs and the call to solidarity of the Islamic *ümmet* (community). Referring to it as a new episode in the aggression of Crusaders was a common metaphor. The trope of Crusaders and the sentiment that the Ottoman Empire was the only fortress that protected Muslims against European colonization echoed in the Egyptian and Indian press as well, and Egyptian Red Cross and its Indian counterpart poured aid into Istanbul.[56] It is generally accepted that the populist rise of Islamism after the nineteenth century within the borders of the Ottoman Empire was not unconnected to the cycles of wars in the Balkans and European colonization around the world.[57]

The next episode in resettler nationalism was the Exchange of Populations Treaty of 1923, administered by the League of Nations, which is discussed at length in chapter 2. The exchange treaty mandated the compulsory migration of all Christian "Greeks" in today's Turkey to Greece and all Muslim "Turks" in Greece to Turkey (see figure 2.2). It also legitimized the refugee status of those who had already moved between lands due to wars before 1923. Even though the precise numbers have been disputed, the treaty affected close to 2 million people. Greece's Muslim population decreased from approximately 20 percent to 6 percent as a result, while Turkey's non-Muslim population decreased from roughly 20 percent to 2.5 percent due to the sum of population transfers, massacres, and wars. Thus the partition and population transfers between Europe and Anatolia at the end of World War I marked the irreversible dividing of the Christian and Muslim communities of the Ottoman Empire. The Exchange Treaty also served as a model for future compulsory population transfers instituted by the UN as the League of Nations' successor, such as the partition of India and Pakistan in 1947, and the Partition Plan for Palestine adopted on November 29, 1947. While this book is not suggesting to flatten out the differences between these specific cases, it joins a group of scholars who work toward a more connected picture of the global history of partitions, ethnic cleansings, and forced migrations during the transitions from colonial/imperial to national orders. I hope that the methodological insights of this book might be relevant for other internationally administered resettler-nationalist policies.[58]

The story of resettler nationalism is also one of dispossession—a term whose extensive use to refer to different world events has raised questions about conceptual clarity. I have decided to employ this word by building on

Robert Nichols's discussion of dispossession as a core term of critical theory that mediates criticism of capitalism and settler colonialism.[59] Nichols disassociates the theory of dispossession in settler colonial contexts from the unprovable claims to "first occupancy" and from reliance on possession that goes against the moral aims of the critique. Dispossession is predicated on the conceptualization of land as property and involves theft through the very act of instituting a property regime that benefits the white settlers or creates unfair primary accumulation in a capitalist order. Any partition of land is indeed a making of property and territory along which comes a dispossession. Nichols brings together Marxist and Indigenous studies that concern geographies that are different from the ones in this book, and yet this theory of dispossession resonates considerably well here. The making and transition of property regimes during the dissolution of the Ottoman Empire involved processes that also generated seizures of land and possessions that were far from fair.[60] Chapters 2 and 3 write histories of dispossession that occurred both instantly through the expulsion of communities from their lands by turning their homes and farms into exchangeable commodities, and over long stretches of time through the unofficial occupation of land followed by property legalization.

It is indeed possible to trace similar patterns of thinking among the re-settler nationalists then and now. In a mirror image of the Greek nationalists who see the "Asia Minor Disaster" of 1922–23 as the expulsion of Greeks from their exclusive ancient homeland, the Turkish nationalists see the Balkan War of 1912–13 as the "final episode in the tragedy of Turkish migration" when they "had to leave the lands they [their nomadic and sedentary ancestors] considered home for at least 450 at most 1400 years."[61] I acknowledge the trauma of forced emigration but criticize the entitlement to exclusive ownership of land and the anticosmopolitanism in such agendas. I am also cognizant of the fact that the critical decolonial scholarship written in the last two decades has been weaponized for the advance of other oppressive ideologies, such as the neo-Ottoman imperial fancy combined with political Islam in Turkey. The reign of Abdülhamid II has become the political symbol of the Islamic Right who praise the sultan's anticolonial policies as a way of holding on to the territorial, educational, and cultural relevance of the Ottoman Empire in Europe without confronting his oppressive decisions.[62] This neo-Ottoman nostalgia and the equally common Ottoman abjection are the two opposite ends of a spectrum. I use *Ottoman abjection* here as an umbrella term to refer to the dismissal, trivialization, suppression, denial, or subconscious forgetting of facts about the Ottoman Empire while explaining modern architecture throughout the late nineteenth and twentieth centuries. I also refer to the lack of acknowledgment of the local struggles that were connected—by way of opposition or solidarity—to Ottoman citizenship and subjectivity. This book distances itself from these ideas by providing a critical history of the resettler-nationalist patterns of thinking as part of a longer history of the post-Ottoman nation-state era. Rather than taking sides with either of the national or religious official historiographies, I speak politically outside the polar narratives by writing the people's history of architecture under resettler nationalism (more on this below).

The chapters below show the architectural reverberations of the long-lasting patterns of thinking both immediately after these markers of resettler nationalism and their aftermaths that extend to the present. Chapter 1 alludes to the enforced disappearance of Armenian and Kurdish intellectuals as part of the resettler-nationalist ideology. Chapter 2 explores the intertwined histories of dispossession, transportation, and resettling of two communities in today's Greece and Turkey, one departing from and the other arriving in the same Cappadocian village due to the enforced population exchange of 1923. As an example of struggle toward healing, it analyzes a rare group of architects and residents who restitute the erased memory of expelled communities. Chapter 3 traces the hundred years of Istanbul's Zeytinburnu district as the arrival space both of Balkan refugees from Greece, Bulgaria, and Yugoslavia and of Uygur, Kazak, Azeri, and other Central Asian refugees from China and the Soviet Union. It follows the transformation of refugee settlements to slum developments as a reflection of capitalist urbanization, and the subsequent transformation of these illegal houses into legal but earthquake-vulnerable buildings as a result of the government's negligence while it was advancing Turkish-Islamist cultural agendas. Chapter 4 comments on the continuities between settler colonialist and resettler-nationalist logic by contrasting British colonization and postcolonial struggles in Sudan's capital, Khartoum, and cotton plantations in its countryside, Gezira. Parts of chapters 4 and 5 discuss the continuing impact of Ottoman professional networks after the empire's dissolution and the work of architects who were subject to population exchange, including the prolific Greek architect Constantinos Doxiadis in Sudan. Chapter 5 exposes the roadblocks to healing from planetary disasters of the twenty-first century in a world divided into nations. Established accounts of British colonization, of nation building, and of midcentury modernization are challenged when one writes the global history of architecture by registering the impact of Ottoman succession.

The research for this book prompted me to think about the definition of perpetrator and victim, or offender and healer, in a much longer spectrum of history. Perhaps the real distinction in these examples is the one between those who divide and those who connect. The dividers in the following pages include the leaders who did not allow for self-governance; the competitive and opportunistic imperialist forces that perpetuated race-based categorizations; the authors who insisted on the nation-state's inevitability and the unmixing of peoples; the ethnoreligious demographic engineers who exerted genocide or cultural extinction with the pretext of saving their own nation and faith; and the architects who were complicit with the dividers' ideologies. These victors of history bring to mind Walter Benjamin's Angel of History, and make one suspect that there might indeed be no document or monument of history that is not at the same time a document of violence.[63] The connectors in these episodes, on the other hand, include those who could not be exterminated by history's victors: the migrants who carried their memories and cultural artifacts from their departure places and hybridized them with those in their arrival places; the builders who crossed the borders of partition; the architects who used building materials to empower migrant economy; the refugees from the Balkans, Central Asia, or Anatolia who remembered fondly the days when they coexisted in solidarity with their neighbors of a different faith; the first responders to earthquakes and wildfires; and the ordinary citizens who sent food, supplies, and blood to the other side of the border in order to ease the suffering of the grandchildren of those that their own grandparents once shared citizenship with. Architecture as the debris of erased peoples is indeed a connector between those who stayed and those who were expelled.

Climate Determinism, Consciousness, and Reparations

"The division of the global ecosystem into nation states is ecocidal," as Franz Broswimmer warns against the harms of nationalism on the environment.[64] The final two chapters of this book suggest that the process set in motion by resettler nationalism is one of the root causes of climate change and mass extinction. The planetary healing cannot be conceived without the communication, agreement, and solidarity between nation-states. As disappointed as multiple generations are with the hypocrisy, passivity, and bureaucratic cumbersomeness of the UN, the struggles against climate change and biodiversity loss would be unthinkable without this institution since the UN

Conference on the Human Environment in Stockholm in June 1972. Coming back to the discussion on healing as a matter of rights, the recognition of the rights of future generations and species beyond humans at the UN is part of the struggle for planetary healing.

In his article "Geology of Mankind" (2002), where he is usually credited with coining the term *Anthropocene*, Paul Crutzen identified the built environment as one of the five causes that made humans a geological force on the planet and put an end to the 11,700 years of the Holocene.[65] On the one hand, my book joins the work of scholars like Dipesh Chakrabarty who call for new approaches to the discipline of history writing as a result of the realization that we live in the age of Anthropocene, namely, that humans have become a geological force that causes climate change.[66] On the other hand, it also joins the work of Donna Haraway, T. J. Demos, and others who find the term *Anthropocene* insufficient, even a dangerous misnomer, for not showing the responsibility of dominant nations in climate change.[67] The undifferentiated category of the "human" as an entire species fails to come to terms with the bigger responsibility and accountability of dominant rulers and businesses than countries and communities who were not decision-makers but who are now the most vulnerable to climate disasters. I resist gothic literary representations or utopian architectural engineering projects that capitalize on horror, monstrosity, and apocalyptic moods.[68] Instead, I analyze climate disasters and mass extinction as the result of political and economic decisions that are deceptively seen benign or unavoidable. Those who suggest dark imaginaries or utopian, geoengineering-type solutions are, for the most part, authors and architects of the global elite, whereas climate disaster has become part of the everyday experience of the Global South and the global poor—a condition Rob Nixon warns against in one of the first books on climate change and cultural representation.[69]

One may misleadingly infer from the data on the built environment's responsibility in causing climate change that architects have not paid attention to climate. To the contrary, however, there is hardly any other criterion as ordinary and as omnipresent as climate in architectural design. From Vitruvius to guidebooks of corporate environmentalism, references to environmental regulation and considerations of the sun and wind, heat and cold, rain and snow have been regular inputs for designers of buildings around the world. This does not mean there has been a univocal approach to climate. The challenge for architectural historians today, therefore, is to evaluate architecture's role in climate justice by writing about climate in the history of architecture in such a way that architecture's role in the history of climate (climate change) is also revealed.

Established architectural historians have provided a large spectrum of definitions for climate, ranging from a criterion to be controlled to one that inspires difference. In his book *Architecture of the Well-Tempered Environment*, Reyner Banham wrote the entire history of modern architecture as a chain of technological inventions that control the climate in order to "provide comfort and well-being of humans," and one that moves toward hermetically sealed buildings that can be reproduced anywhere.[70] The telos of modern architecture, seen in this light, is a seamless closed interior, a perfect artificial environment, in the name of human comfort, which is made possible with climate-management fixtures. The realization of the environmental crisis with the 1972 UN Conference did not change Banham's mind. "Rather than calling for more efficient air-conditioning, the call was for the abandonment of air conditioning all together, no matter who might suffer," he said, while expressing his disappointment with the rising interest in traditional modes of construction.[71] In contrast, for Kenneth Frampton, thinking with rather than against climate was one of the criteria for "critical regionalism," which he suggested as a movement to resist the homogenization of the world and the erasure or trivialization of cultural heritage in a given location.[72]

Recently, Daniel Barber has written the history of Western modern architecture by foregrounding the facade as the mediator between the interior of a building and the climate of its exterior.[73] The facade mitigates, mediates, or negotiates with the climatic conditions outside. Barber has collected ample examples of shading devices, brise-soleil, screens, and other ways of controlling the sun's entry into the building, which amounts to a thick set of evidence that demonstrates midcentury modernists' attention to climate. Against the perception of Le Corbusier as the mastermind of sealed interiors—given the architect's fascination with engineers and machines to live in—Barber claims "climatic modernism followed from him," after the brise-soleil proved the adaptability of the modernist architectural language in the Global South.[74] By drawing attention to "climatic modernism," Barber also made a call to architects and scholars to engage more consciously with climate in the age of environmental crisis.[75]

Architecture and the Right to Heal contributes to this scholarship but takes issue with many historians' soft antagonism toward climatic modernism's complicity with colonialism and resettler nationalism. Climate has indeed served as a proxy for nation and race for much of the modern and colonial period. At the height of the European colonial power and the age of energy transition into carbon-based technologies, architecture in the ex-Ottoman lands was mobilized to sustain the British Empire's industrial capitalist power. Chapter 4 analyzes the precise moments when climate served as an ideological tool to exert power and reify racial segregation, in order to distinguish between climate determinism for the sake of the perpetuation of hierarchies, as opposed to climate consciousness for the sake of sustainable architectural practices and climate debt (not loan) for the sake of reparations. Climate determinism frames humans in essential identity categories according to the climates of the lands that they come from—that is, climate acts as a proxy for race and nation—whereas climate consciousness means envisioning the racial justice and planetary healing that would arise if climate is duly employed in professions such as architecture. Climate reparation aspires for a just energy transition by giving dues to those who have been subjugated because of climate determinism in the past.

I have chosen Sudan as a focus to discuss the right to heal from climate disasters. Chapter 4 shows the relation between colonization and climate disasters such as sandstorms, floods, and famines, and reveals implicit criticisms formulated by independence-era figures, including architects who were descendants of the Ottoman professional networks. It traces the cause of climate disasters to climate determinism, and shows the connections between colonization, carbonization, and creation of agrarian monocultures whose slow violence in causing climate disasters and mass extinction is being realized today. It demonstrates both the continuities and the discontinuities between the colonial and nation-state periods, and excavates latent ideas about climate consciousness so that healing from climate determinism may start. Climate determinists imagined Africa and the Middle East as hostile climates and maintained the Orientalist conviction against the Ottoman lands that the locals needed European civilizing technologies. The hierarchy constructed between moderate and tropical climates, north and south, Europe and its colonies, "white" and "native," affected architecture to such an extent that cooling for "white comfort" became a major design goal and thus produced the residential typology, urban morphology, and plantation logic in European colonies during the age of industrial capitalism. By joining architectural historians such as Jiat-Hwee Chang, Ana Ozaki, and Ola Uduku, who discussed "tropical architecture" in the context of southeast Asian colonies, Brazil and Portuguese African colonies, and West African postcolonial architecture, respectively, I discuss the problematic implementation of tropical architecture in Sudan.[76] By building on scholars such as Victoria Bernal, Judith Shklar,

Christian Parenti, Sven Beckert, and Jenny Edkins, I look at an intersection between architecture and water infrastructure, which reveals that famine is a historically caused injustice rather than the misfortune of a natural disaster.[77] Looking at the Gezira plantations in Khartoum's southern countryside discloses how architecture helped in the creation of cotton monocultures during colonization, whose harms on biodiversity and attempted remedies are discussed further in chapter 5. This final chapter analyzes two early historical episodes where a variant of the word *Anthropocene* was coined much before its common use today, and where the garden metaphor was used for planetary healing against extinction in projects located in Sudan and Iran but undertaken by international teams of architects.

The lands that concern this book complicate the established history of climate and architecture beyond Sudan and Iran.[78] Discussions include confronting the colonial history of climatization; race-based imperial urbanism and the dismissal of local wisdom in climate control; politics of climate-specific modernism during colonial times, and its difference, if any, from midcentury climate responsive architecture during independence; environmentalist concerns following the UN Conference of 1972 in Stockholm; production of ignorance on passive heating and cooling techniques as air-conditioning became the norm; and the entanglement of global warming and global wars for the extraction of oil.

The relation between modern architecture and the sun gets complicated when viewed from this perspective. Bruno Taut's work in Turkey provides a strong falsification against the general perception that interwar modernists paid attention to solar orientation but dismissed climatic differences. Taut's book *Mimari Bilgisi* (Knowledge of architecture, 1938) was an early criticism of homogenization through modernization, for reasons of not only cultural imperialism but also climate imperialism.[79] He objected to the claims that attributed a universal significance to a form of expression that originated from a limited region. Even the most successful building would melt or freeze in a different climate. The deadly mistake of modernism was to ignore this fact, an argument Taut illustrated with the drawing of a morphing zeppelin as it tours around the world. Taut's complicated theory of climate—which sometimes bordered on climate determinism[80]—was as geopolitical as it was functionalist. Far from merely considering the securing of human comfort through the careful organization of sunlight and wind, he was equally concerned with his colleagues' moods in Japan and Turkey that he found "melancholic" and "tormented" due to the hierarchies imposed by colonial modernity. Taut realized that environmental problems were inseparable from social and geopolitical ones, and suggested a climate-conscious modernism to sustain difference around the world. Elsewhere, I have argued that Taut's interest in climate carried him to a call for cosmopolitan architecture as a prerequisite for perpetual peace. To distance himself both from importing modernism from Europe and from reactionary nationalism taking command in countries such as his native Germany, Taut theorized "climate" as a matter of not only architectural design but also international solidarity.[81]

The perceived benefits of the sun changed over time, especially during the transition from colonial to postcolonial eras. "It has been shown that the greatest enemy of white men in the tropics is the sun," W. H. McLean said as one of the town planners of British Khartoum and British Palestine, summarizing a very common perception at the time.[82] As demonstrated comprehensively in chapter 4, British architects and residents were on a mission to block the sun during their settlement in Sudan. When one compares colonial climatization of the early twentieth century with the advocacy for solar energy today, one would indeed be surprised by the relative standing of the sun. The sun was the "enemy of the white man" during the British colonization in the Global South, but it was the North Star for interwar modernists who considered light and orientation as their main design criteria. Modern sanatoriums were designed with the premise of the healing powers of the sun. The sun was the major renewable energy resource for the solar house scientists of the 1950s, until it was replaced with oil infrastructures during the Cold War era. The scientific and commercial success of the solar house in the 1950s, albeit brief, crystallized the status of the sun as a friend of the state-of-the-art and technologically advanced home.[83] The sun enjoyed renewed attention as a major energy resource after the 1973 oil crisis. The *Sorry, Out of Gas* exhibition and the accompanying catalogue brings together a myriad of creative architectural designs using the sun, wind, and earth as alternative energy resources when some members of the Organization of Petroleum Exporting Countries (OPEC) imposed an embargo against the United States during the 1973 Arab-Israeli War.[84]

The feeling of cool and warm must have also changed over time, especially after air-conditioning became the norm. The dissemination of air-conditioning after the 1980s as a fossil fuel–dependent technology put a hiatus to passive climate control in design that had enjoyed a momentum with midcentury modernism.[85] The design and construction of the University of Baghdad (1954–81) is a perfect example demonstrating both the midcentury modernist attention to climatic difference and the transformation from passive to air-conditioned climate control. A British mandate following the Ottoman Empire (as were Sudan and Palestine), Iraq provides significant albeit underacknowledged episodes for the global history of modern architecture. During the British mandate (officially 1917–32, but continued till 1958, given the British-established Kingdom), the government buildings were designed by military engineers with personnel who had served British colonization in India.[86] After the 1951 agreement that diminished British control in oil revenues, and after the 1958 Revolution, a group of architects in Iraq wanted to take matters into their own hands and to replace the British mandate's cultural symbolism with another that would come out of their collaboration with international architects.[87] As a result, Walter Gropius, a name strongly associated with established modernism as the director of Bauhaus in Germany, and the director of the Harvard Graduate School of Design at the time, received the commission for the University of Baghdad.

Elsewhere, I have demonstrated that the encounter between Iraqi, American, British, and German architects, scholars, rulers, elites, and policymakers resulted in an architectural language with passive climate control techniques in the University of Baghdad (figure I.3). The campus is composed of free-standing clusters with ample green spaces in between, which seems, at first sight, to be at odds with the tight urban fabric associated with traditional Baghdad neighborhoods. The exposed reinforced concrete buildings with modular facades recall the aesthetic of industrialization. However, the architects of the campus—Gropius and The Architects Collaborative (TAC) in Boston and Hisham Munir in Baghdad—paid special attention to climatic differences and passive climatization, by referencing what they called "the old Baghdad houses." Buildings were placed close to each other in their own clusters in order to provide maximum shade as in traditional urban fabric. The ramps and covered streets-in-the-air provided a network of shaded spaces. Extensive cantilevers created shadows beneath; deep set-back facades protected the interior from the sun's rays. In gender-specific dormitories, the buildings created a courtyard with an L-shaped street circling two sides of the square cluster so that outdoor spaces were shaded and rooms had correct orientation and privacy. Vertical screens with bricks were meant to cast shade on inner walls and protect them from excessive sun, like the windows of *ursi* rooms in traditional houses. Courtyards and water fountains replicated the climate control techniques of *tarma* houses in Baghdad. The roofs were to be irrigated with a vaporized water sprinkler system, which the team associated with the local custom of pouring water to cool down in dry heat. An air-cooling system would be placed in window openings to drip water and allow the prevailing wind to blow inside, like the *bagdir* openings in traditional

Figure I.3 Walter Gropius and TAC, and Hisham Munir, University of Baghdad, Baghdad, 1954–81. Perspective drawing of the Engineering Library, 1960. Courtesy Zaydoon Munir.

houses. I traced the choice of these passive cooling techniques to episodes of learning from the local wisdom, both past and contemporary. Namely, the invention of a new midcentury modernist vocabulary that emphasized sun-protected surfaces and shaded outdoor spaces, covered walkways, sun-shading devices at the facade, courtyards, and umbrella roofs—often credited to powerful men such as Gropius, Oscar Niemeyer, and Le Corbusier—was actually the result of a multidirectional and multinational translation process with many agents in Baghdad.[88]

The British Orientalist scholars treated Baghdad's history as nothing but a broken link between the ancient glory of al-Mansur's Round City and the British Empire. Everything in between, including the "old Baghdad houses" built during the Ottoman Empire, was treated as a decline.[89] Namely, the University of Baghdad's design team chose an inspiration that went against the grain of the British historiography. The team developed these passive climate control techniques by hybridizing local wisdom and high modernist aesthetics in a context, ironically, invested in American soft power so that the American-Iraqi oil deals would not be disrupted by the Iraqi popular revolution of 1958. William Polk, the director of the Middle Eastern Studies at Harvard, a consultant to the US State Department, and a scholar in Gropius's team, worked hard for the continuation of the project when it faced cancellation, because, he said, "What, in effect, do we want from the Middle East? . . . . At the present, the answer seems to me to be sufficient peace to prevent a world war and a sufficient flow of oil."[90] Polk was never dishonest about the fact that his motivation in continuing diplomatic and professional relations with Iraq was the US interest in oil, not necessarily climate responsive design.

The midcentury climate consciousness—an example of which came out of the multinational collaboration in Baghdad—was short-lived because of the rise of oil-dependent air-conditioning after the 1980s. Air-conditioning enables what Barber calls "a planetary interior," the ability to have a thermally controlled interior at any season, anywhere in the world. Ironically, the world got hotter by cooling itself.[91] The Iraqi government commissioned Gropius's office TAC, after the architect's death, for an extension to the University of Baghdad in 1981 as part of a new development leap. Ironically, the new project amplified air-conditioning in lieu of passive climate control techniques, at a time when references to cultural identity had become the norm in architectural discourse. The drawings that had been named "Chilled Water Distribution" in the 1960 version were now readjusted to reflect the advanced HVAC systems. The new design for the Fine Arts buildings did not employ the passive cooling techniques of the midcentury version.[92] Air-conditioning units were installed over time all around campus, between or under brise-soleil and shading devices, making facades a forest of boxes that blew cold air inside while dripping water outside (figure I.4).

Iraq holds an additional symbolic place in global history due to the unjustified US-led invasion of this country in 2003. The US-led reconstruction after this assault has failed all transitional justice standards. Judging from the economic and ecological waste spent on Iraq's conflict and postconflict eras,[93] it would not be surprising to hear that the US military is a bigger polluter than 140 other countries today.[94] While reconstructing the country after occupation, US companies ignored the passive cooling techniques that had been developed during midcentury architecture in Iraq. They imported concrete materials and labor, disregarding Iraq's own advanced reinforced concrete industry that had produced some of the world's most noteworthy brutalist buildings. Iraq's reconstruction exposes a tendency that extends much beyond the thinking patterns of military intervention. The dominance of fossil fuel–dependent architectural technologies in the interest of oil and coal companies is a blatant example of "agnotology" in architecture. In *Agnotology: The Making and Unmaking of Ignorance*, the editors define *agnotology* not simply as ignorance but as the active production of nonknowledge.[95]

Figure I.4 Walter Gropius and TAC, and Hisham Munir, University of Baghdad, Baghdad, 1954–81. The image shows shaded common spaces and added A/C units. Photograph: Esra Akcan, 2018.

Much like oil companies that concealed Indigenous peoples' knowledge of land, or much like climate-change deniers during the Cold War who equated regulations with communism and claimed global warming was a lie to abolish capitalism, the producers of desire for fossil fuel–dependent appliances and construction methods in architecture foreclosed the advancement of passive heating and cooling techniques and the use of renewable energy. Agnotology is the conscious manufacturing of ignorance, the suppression of knowledge production, and the disenfranchisement of existing wisdom. The discontinuation of traditional and midcentury passive cooling techniques in favor of air-conditioned climate control in the University of Baghdad is a typical example. Chapters in this book demonstrate how similar types of climate agnotology are responsible for climate disasters.

Climate agnotology, in the sense of the trivialization and dismissal of climate-conscious architecture in favor of luxury and fuel-dependent climatization technologies, also invites discussions on climate adaptation. Recent debates differentiate between adaptation and mitigation as two distinct ways of responding to climate change. While the former involves changing projects to get ready for the rising temperatures and sea levels, the latter advocates changing policies to prevent climate change. Both are clearly necessary, but climate activists rightly caution against climate adaptationists for igniting a climate fatalism of sorts that sees global warming as an unavoidable fait accompli. What is often overlooked in this discussion, however, is the low-carbon architectural practices that have long served as climate adaptation techniques before fossil fuel–dependent technologies took over. Part of chapter 5 reveals the ideas of a multinational group of architects who theorized architecture as the most effective medium for humans to adapt to their environment. Pardisan, a park in Tehran, Iran, and a collaboration between Ian McHarg, Eskandar Firouz, Nader Ardalan, Laleh Bakhtiar, Charles Eames, and Buckminster Fuller among others, sought to fight the extinction of the Persian lion while exhibiting world architectures as a matter of climate adaptation. It is partially the erasure of these passive climate adaptation techniques that has brought the carbonization of the environment and climate change. Architecture has a long, albeit obliterated, history of climate adaptation that can be remobilized along with climate mitigation.

Trivialization of climate-conscious architecture also invites us to question ideas that posit dry cities or interiors with moderate temperatures as signs of progress. Modernism globalized Western standards of living and dictated a narrow definition of progress to other parts of the world. While colonial architects who worked with climate-determinist ideas construed dryness and moderate temperature as modern norms of civilization and progress, they also eradicated long-standing ways of living with water or heat in communities that did not necessarily codify wetness or hotness as an inferior condition. It was the imperial mindset that imposed dryness and moderate temperatures as universal norms, and thereby devised climate engineering systems for the Global South that intervened in the planetary ecosystem.

Case studies can be multiplied. Scrutinizing the relation between climate and architecture in the context of the post-Ottoman British colonies before World War II and in the context of US soft power during the Cold War in chapters 4 and 5, this book concludes that healing from resettler nationalism and from climate disaster are connected. When one comes face to face with the interrelated history of state violence against peoples and human violence against nature, one realizes that the successes of transitional justice and energy transition depend on each other. Acknowledging the convergence of carbonization and colonization due to climate determinism, as well as the links between global war and global warming, I hope, fosters a call for climate reparations that the first industrializing nations of the Global North owe to the Global South.[96]

There are ample episodes in the past when societies turned to architecture in order to heal after conflicts and disasters. Pandemics provide a good example. The nineteenth-century cholera outbreak exposed the liability of water-distribution systems and eventually brought the improvement of sanitary infrastructure in London; it necessitated the update and extension of underground sewage system in Paris; and fostered the removal and transfer of existing cemeteries to the outskirts in Istanbul. Fires motivated orthogonal and wider city streets so that emergency technologies could reach disaster areas, as well as indoor plumbing and fire-escape regulations in buildings. The garden-city as a settlement model employed in modified forms around the globe—from Germany to Japan, from Turkey to Uganda—was devised partially with the conviction that the re-establishment of human contact with nature in industrial times would prevent contemporary public health hazards. Interwar and midcentury public housing were designed around the world with hygiene and health priorities in mind, as freestanding building blocks in open space were meant to provide ample sun, air, and greenery to all habitants. Architects with early twentieth-century modernist design sensibilities advocated minimal, unornamented, and functional spaces and surfaces partially because they were easy to clean. Architecture was believed to cure tuberculosis in sanatoriums with large balconies that were open to sun and air flow.

The list can be expanded. However, most of these solutions did not pay enough attention to, and even constructed, the socioeconomic, ethnic, and global inequalities, and discriminatory and disciplinary structures. To refer to a classic book, Michel Foucault's *Discipline and Punish* analyzed how plague prevention during the end of the seventeenth century evolved into panopticism, where the modern prison as an architectural type serves as a metaphor for surveillance society.[97] The modernization and sanitization of Paris under the Baron Haussmann was famously brutal in destroying the city fabric and displacing the poor. Today, many world cities are segregated along class and racial lines, and push disenfranchised populations to zones with worse environmental conditions and fewer healthcare opportunities compared to affluent neighborhoods. Modern planning and architectural design that invented sanitary cities also produced ruthless inequalities.

One of the major intentions of *Architecture and the Right to Heal* is to write the architectural history of conflicts and disasters from the viewpoint of the wounded, and devise mechanisms to do so in the absence of conventional documents. Methodologically, this extends my previous book *Open Architecture* that gave voice not only to architects and policymakers but also to immigrant residents of an urban renewal initiative. Oral history was my preferred method in writing *Open Architecture*, because an oral historian refrains from representing an entire ethnicity or group, and adds the name of the underrepresented individual to history. Rather than saying "a Muslim migrant," or reducing migrants to numbers and percentages, I used the preferred names of the individual migrants to give credit to their agency in making our cities. Many researchers in current conflict zones conclude their studies with a similar request from refugees: "See me"—as a human being, as an individual. In this approach, architectural history does not end when the building leaves the hand of the architect. Oral history extends the narrative by combining the time of a building's design with the time of a specific occupation. The contingency and partiality that result from this specific amalgam of the two time periods acknowledge the necessarily open and unfinished nature of architectural history.

Architecture and the Right to Heal extends this method of architectural history writing to a past where conducting oral history is no longer possible. It tells the story from the viewpoint of both designers and habitants of architectural spaces; from the perspective of peoples, rather than merely planners, architects, and policymakers. Even where oral history is not within reach, it is possible to write the people's history of architecture by excavating this voice in literatures, ad hoc interviews, archives of ethnographic works, family photographs, and diaries. Chapter 1 foregrounds the voices of mothers whose children have been subject to enforced disappearance. Chapter 2 tells the history of nation formation by focusing on the memoirs, photographs, and belongings of two expelled migrants and their communities. Chapter 3 quotes extensively from the memoirs of refugees and exchanged migrants who settled in Istanbul. Chapter 4 writes the urban history of Khartoum with family photographs and declarations of previously colonized individuals. Chapter 5 contests the premise that planetary healing requires hyperopic and top-down environmentalism, and acknowledges the role of nonhuman actors in healing the cities that humans built. All chapters thereby challenge the preconceptions of the knowing subject in architectural studies.

In his book *A People's History of the United States*, Howard Zinn shows that the past written from the perspective of Indigenous peoples, slaves, women, members of the working class, and migrant laborers overthrows myths of great men and national glory, but still highlights the most meaningful struggles in the United States.[98] In *Architecture and the Right to Heal*, such a bottom-up history proves to significantly transform existing narratives as well. For example, in chapter 2, the people's history of the Exchange of Populations Treaty exposes a big contrast between the declarations of state agents and the experiences of those involved. Reading migrant testimonies on both sides of the European border, and tracing architectural histories, this chapter characterizes this foundational decision in nation formation as a trauma imposed on these lands. Against the official historiographies of nation-states that identify partitions as tough but necessary solutions to the problem of ethnic conflict, aided by state-sponsored architecture, this chapter writes partition's architectural history from the ground up. This leads to a reconceptualization of the partition as the rift between the rulers and the peoples, and not the rift between the two communities. This history from below guides us to a transformative de-polarization and a new solidarity between actors of the previously polarized communities. Moreover, chapter 3 unsettles the current scholarship on slum development. By uncovering the past from the memoirs of refugees and migrants, it traces the birth of squatter settlements in Turkey to early resettler nationalist ideology, rather than to midcentury urbanization. While analyzing the British colonization in Sudan from the viewpoint of climate change, chapter 4 refrains from a very common and convenient method in architectural history that writes the colonial history, critically or not, only with the documents in the colonizer's archive, and therefore from the viewpoint of the colonizer. This book advocates the postcolonial view that the responsibility to analyze colonialism critically also brings the responsibility to write the (previously) colonized people's history of architecture to be excavated from beyond colonial and military archives. To that end, this chapter brings the history of colonial violence and independence struggles together, and raises the voice of those who criticized colonial planning and architecture from the viewpoint of local residents. Additionally, chapter 4 revises the established accounts about the era of developmentalist modernization. It does so by registering the role of the Ottoman Empire's dissolution in the history of modern architecture and by following the work of architects who were citizens of the new Ottoman successor states.

In his book *The Last Ottoman Generation*, Michael Provence exposes the historiographical shortcomings of writing different national histories of countries that came out of the Ottoman Empire. Such histories not only maintain uncritically the Western epistemologies of the "national idea," but also obscure these lands' commonalities till the mid-twentieth century. Provence follows the careers of officers who were educated in the Ottoman military schools and took posts in Ottoman province capitals such as

Damascus, Beirut, Adana, and Salonica, and who later built the resistance against European mandates in Ottoman successor states and, eventually, participated in the governance of independent nations.[99] While Provence's book compiles a history of military and government personnel, *Architecture and the Right to Heal* looks instead at the makers of cities, buildings, and spaces. The following chapters trace the work of architects from Ottoman lands who migrated into new nations during the empire's dissolution, including those from Alexandria, Asenovgrad, Giresun, Istanbul, Karpathos, Kavala, Sinasos, and others. Tracing the post-Ottoman professional networks reveals unexpected connections that unsettle dominant area studies categories and current academic compartmentalization. For example, Greek builders, as well as merchants, moneylenders, shipbuilders, jewelers, artisans, and farmers, had established themselves in Sudan and North Africa during Mehmet Ali's rule.[100] Chapter 4 reveals the continuing Greek presence in Khartoum much after the end of the Ottoman Empire, and its impact on the architectural profession during the independence period as an example of the dissemination of post-Ottoman professional networks. It shows that the established accounts on the relation between European coloniality and midcentury developmentalism are challenged when history is written by registering the dissolution of the Ottoman Empire.

As a result of this research, art historical categories such as the "Islamic city and architecture" appear in a new a light. In her overview of the changing frameworks in the historiography of the "Islamic city," Giula Annalinda Neglia draws attention to the 1920s when art historical interest shifted from the monuments to the urban fabric of the Ottoman Empire. Scholars started suggesting common attributes of the "Islamic city," which they derived from studies of a few cities, but extended to an entire imagined "Islamic world."[101] Scholars in France, Germany, Italy, the United Kingdom, and the United States pursued a range of methods for freezing a definition for the "Islamic city." They employed morphological analyses and descriptions of as-found physical features on the ground or religion-based speculations about how and why these cities developed historically. Only in the 1980s, the field questioned in a self-reflective way whether there was anything that could be actually named an "Islamic city" and suggested alternative nation-based terms.[102] However, the term and the field continued to exist, and the alternative names did not terminate but were prone to create new identity-based essentialisms. Till the mid-1980s, the late Ottoman era was overwhelmingly portrayed as a period of decline and was identified with a lack of progress (lack of infrastructure, lack of modernism, etc.)—a narrative that subconsciously validated

British colonial historians cited in this book. These historians of the colonial and mandate periods had glorified ancient Iraq and Sudan, and claimed that only European colonizers could save them from decline due to the Ottoman rule and could bring them back to "civilization." It was only in the mid-1980s that the Ottoman-era modernization started receiving a closer look in Western academia, and diversified after the integration of scholars and works from the region.[103] *Architecture and the Right to Heal* builds on the work of scholars who have written on late Ottoman cities, but foregrounds these cities' cosmopolitan and post-Ottoman histories in a way that exposes their national and religious homogenization during this time, both socially and epistemologically. The naming and historiography of the "Islamic city" is premised on the compartmentalization of the world and of the scholarship with the ideology of resettler nationalism that this book criticizes. *Architecture and the Right to Heal* unsettles the category of the "Islamic city," by adding previously unstudied settlements to scholarship and by demonstrating their shared history with cities in Africa and Europe.

Timelines and Itineraries of the Book

A book on healing from sedimented violence and historical debris requires a specific consideration of time and space to account for the unfolding of events and arguments. The five chapters are organized thematically so that each concentrates on a shock, but *Architecture and the Right to Heal* creates a forward momentum to show that sudden traumas have deep roots in history and are connected globally. The book starts with one woman's story looking for justice in the present-day Istanbul. Tracing threads of this story of transitional justice and energy transition from one chapter to the next carries the readers as far back as the late nineteenth century, and takes them to locations in Anatolia, Southeast Europe, Northeast Africa, and West Asia, and by extension to similar struggles around the world.

There are two timelines in the book. This enables the simultaneous discussion of the overarching global challenges of our present time and the detailed historical events unfolding at the geometric center of Afro-Euro-Asia during the twentieth century. The first timeline focuses on unknown historical episodes to which the book brings new archival research and fieldwork. The chapters tell textured stories of architectural artifacts and spaces with a narrative that starts from and returns to Istanbul via stops in Cappadocia, Evia, Athens, Khartoum, Gezira, and Tehran. When migrants and travelers to these regions are included, the geography extends to Baghdad, Cairo,

Kavala, Salonica, and Skopje in the Ottoman lands and successor states, and to China, Japan, and the Soviet Union in the East, as well as to Argentina, Chile, the United Kingdom, and the United States in the West. The book starts at the end of this timeline—the coup d'état in Turkey in 1980—but the narrative carries the readers from the dissolution of the Ottoman Empire and the upsurge of British colonialism on these lands at the end of the nineteenth century to the rise of a new West-Islam divide and of neoliberalism in 1980. The narrative does not unfold in chronological order but recounts chronological markers such as the British colonization of Sudan following the Ottoman Empire (1898), the enforced disappearance of Armenian intellectuals in Istanbul (1915), the British mandate in Iraq following the Ottoman Empire (1917), the cycles of migration between the Balkans and Anatolia (1912–89), the Greek-Turkish partition (1923), the independence of Sudan and Iraq from the British rule (1956 and 1958), the rise of American soft power and collaborations in the Middle East (ca. 1960), the Islamic Revolution and the fall of the Shah's regime in Iran (1978–79), and the coup d'état in Turkey that increased state violence against Kurdish minorities among other things (1980). The intention is not to tell a complete and causal history but to focus on architectural episodes that take place during the modern restructuring of the world.

The second timeline is what might be termed our present age from roughly the 1980s onward. Namely, the first timeline carries the reader from the end of the nineteenth century to the beginning of the second timeline. Chapter 1 ("Enforced Disappearance") discusses the ongoing struggles toward healing from human rights violations and state violence; chapter 2 ("Partition") looks at present-day architects and habitants who seek healing from the continuing wounds of the international world order and nation formation; chapter 3 ("Collapse") confronts the aftermath of civil war, earthquakes, and market crashes in neoliberal cities as related events; chapter 4 ("Climate Disasters") discusses the role of architecture in climate change; and chapter 5 ("Extinction") comments on contemporary conservation debates that aim to preserve nature by striking the right balance between the built and the unbuilt environment. Chapters move from individual to societal to planetary healing. Each chapter has its own conclusion; all together they suggest a new ethic of cosmopolitan, democratic, and bottom-up healing, which imagines in the horizon the extension of human and species rights, a broadened and holistic notion of justice and reparations, and the elimination of national partitions and of human/nonhuman divisions.

1 Enforced Disappearance

On March 21, 1995, Hasan Ocak was taken into state custody and never came back. When his relatives searched for him in police stations, they always got the same reply that he had never been there. His mother, Emine Ocak, was detained for nineteen days because she shouted in court asking for his whereabouts. While family and friends were continuing a sit-in for his release, they found a photograph of his tortured body in the Forensic Office,[1] and learned that his corpse was discovered in a forest and buried in the cemetery for unknown people in Altınşehir. On May 19, the family took his dead body out and reburied it in Gazi Cemetery, albeit not without some censorship on his gravestone inscriptions.[2] The next Saturday, on May 27, his mother and siblings made their first weekly demonstration at Istanbul's Galatasaray Square together with five families in the same situation.[3] They called themselves Saturday Mothers, referring to the Mothers of Plaza de Mayo in Argentina, who visited them on one of those Saturdays on May 13, 1998. Similar episodes in Argentina and Chile continued to serve as reference points, as graffiti circulated on walls and symbolic gravestones with Hasan Ocak's portrait.[4] As the Saturday Mothers' determination to meet at the Galatasaray Square grew, so did the police violence.[5] As weeks passed by, more "Mothers" came to demonstrations; Hasan's mother aged but his younger sister and brother took active roles; some of the mothers died, but the families' newborn children joined; and then came other human rights activists (figure 1.1).

Hasan Ocak is one of the tens of thousands around the world who has not returned from state custody, and this chapter is about those left behind. The "Saturday Mothers" of Turkey—a growing group of mothers, fathers, sisters, brothers, wives, husbands, children, grandchildren, aunts, and uncles, as well as human right defenders and citizens in solidarity—have been asking for the whereabouts of the 1,353 individuals (of whom a majority are Kurdish or left-wing) who have disappeared since 1980 in Turkey, by protesting at Istanbul's Galatasaray Square every Saturday since May 27, 1995 (figure 1.2).[6]

Figure 1.1 Hasan Ocak's relatives protesting at Galatasaray Square, Istanbul, 1995–ongoing. Courtesy Maside Ocak.

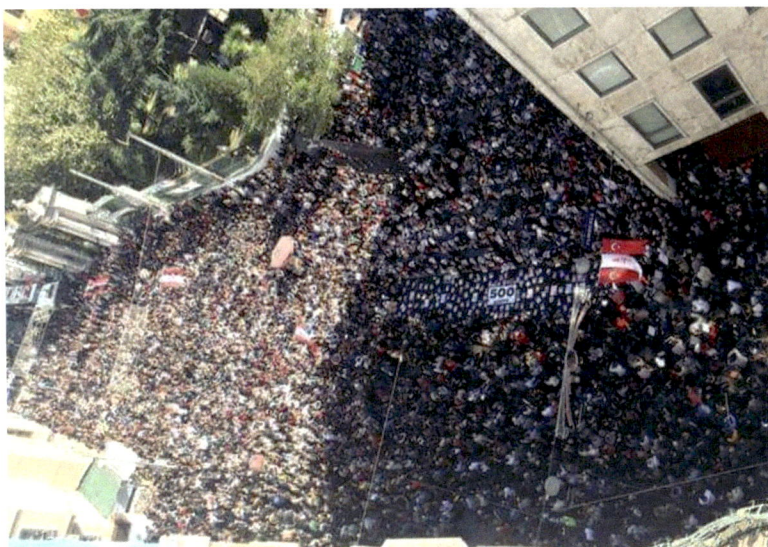

Figure 1.2 Saturday Mothers' five-hundredth meeting at Galatasaray Square, September 24, 2016. Courtesy Maside Ocak.

This social movement invites discussions on human rights, feminism and gender, the psychoanalysis of mourning, and memory. With this chapter, I would like to add a spatial and visual studies perspective, by analyzing works of art, architecture, and urbanism from the framework of transitional justice. What does it mean to be subject to violence and murder by one's own state and police force—namely, by institutions that are meant to protect their citizens in the modern world order? There is a considerable literature on healing after the trauma inflicted by international wars, but what about internal aggressions such as state violence? I would like to amplify the moments where a social movement intersects with a city and architecture, and how this intersection contributes to the human rights debate and transitional justice. The chapter explores the place of the new conventions of human rights in a healing process, and in reckoning with prolonged and unresolved cases of injustice. It does so by demonstrating the role of architectural programs and physical spaces, such as urban squares, cemeteries, museums, and memorials.

Right to Truth and Transitional Justice

Hasan Ocak's case is a typical example of what is now named as enforced disappearance. And the state's denial of accountability is a violation of the right to truth. Both are recognized as crimes in international law since 2006, through a convention signed by ninety-eight countries and ratified by sixty-two as of January 2020.[7] Enforced disappearance has long been a common act of military juntas and oppressive governments, such as the Night and Fog directive of the Nazi regime as the first officially recognized example. This chapter traces back the history of enforced disappearance on the lands concerning this book to the deportation of Istanbul's Armenian intellectuals in 1915. Even though enforced disappearance existed for a long time, the UN and Amnesty International have warned that the practice actually increased and spread over the world after 1980, with systematic cases in Argentina, Chile, China, East Germany, Guatemala, Iraq, Russia, Spain, Sri Lanka, the United States, and many others. In August 2014, the UN Working Group reported 43,250 unresolved cases of disappearances in eighty-eight different states.[8]

Those subject to enforced disappearance expose how modern states turn bodies into what Giorgio Agamben called "bare life" (*homo sacer*), in the sense that states hold the power to deprive citizens of their political rights and push them outside the realm of protection by their own governments. While denying citizenship rights, state violence simultaneously throws bodies out

of the realm of rights and makes them stateless. Ever since its first declaration, natural and civil rights, birth and nationhood, have been collapsed
into each other, making citizenship the necessary condition of many human
rights and statelessness the condition or excuse for the denial of said rights.[9]
Moreover, turning humans into bare lives gives those states "necropower," as
Achille Mbembe coined the term: it gives statecraft a deadly license, a pre-
sumed "right to kill" with impunity.[10]

Protection against enforced disappearance has been defined as a human
right only in 2006, and it is still in the process of recognition. It invites discussion on the underacknowledged role of human rights in architectural
theory. "Right to truth" entered the official lexicon with this recent human
rights convention. After the adoption of the Universal Declaration of Human
Rights in 1948, the UN Human Rights Commission continued to add new treaties that are open to member states' ratification. Initially, the first two covenants
(also known as the International Bill of Rights) aimed to resolve the ideological split between the Cold War's superpowers that prevented including all
rights under one treaty. As the number of member states increased during
the decolonization processes of the 1960s and in response to several social
movements around the globe, the UNHRC added new conventions, such as
the ones on the elimination of racial discrimination and of discrimination
against women as well as the conventions against torture and on the rights of
the child. One of the two new treaties adopted in 2006 was the International
Convention for the Protection of All Persons from Enforced Disappearance,
which also defines a right to truth.[11]

The history of transitional justice is tightly related to enforced disappearance. The accountability for past abuses came to the forefront of human
rights movements with the grassroots protests against enforced disappearance, such as the one by Mothers of Plaza de Mayo starting in 1977. When
Raúl Alfonsín became the president of Argentina after the end of the military dictatorship in 1983, he instituted the National Commission on the
Disappearance of Persons that officially identified 8,960 names and led to
the president's formal apology in 1989. However, civil society organizations
such as the Mothers of Plaza de Mayo insisted that there were at least thirty
thousand disappeared people.[12] Enforced disappearance proved to be a
characteristic crime in many countries in transition whose postconflict
commissions tried to institute a "never again" policy, including in Chile, El
Salvador, South Africa, and others.[13] The concept of transitional justice entered the lexicon of international law as new nations emerged out of the end
of Cold War, and with conflicts in Yugoslavia and Rwanda.[14] The official UN

Definition for transitional justice, released in 2004 when Kofi Annan was secretary-general, reads: "The full range of processes and mechanisms associated with a society's attempts to come to terms with a legacy of large scale past abuses, in order to ensure accountability, serve justice and achieve reconciliation."[15] In addition to the UN, the foundational and operational role of regional courts has been particularly important, such as the Inter-American Court of Human Rights, European Court of Human Rights, and African Court of Human and People's Rights.[16] Transitions from military regimes, civil wars, genocides, and apartheids, as well as reparations to heal from the sediments of colonization and slavery, can indeed be topics of the multidisciplinary field of transitional justice.[17]

The Saturday Mothers of Turkey make three specific demands: to know what happened to their relatives under state custody, to see perpetrators punished, and to find the disappeared or remains of their bodies so that they can bury their dead. Over the years, they have also shown solidarity with other atrocities in the country's history. Namely, the Saturday Mothers appeal for truth, justice, and a space for their relatives, and by extension a moral and institutional reform for the broader society.

These requests fall squarely on the goals, mechanisms, and steps theorized by transitional justice scholars. For instance, in one of the first comprehensive books on the subject, Ruti Teitel categorizes the forms of transitional law as criminal, historical, reparatory, administrative, and constitutional justice.[18] Pablo De Greiff defines the four goals of transitional justice as recognition, civic trust, reconciliation, and democratization, while he identifies several measures such as criminal prosecutions, truth-telling, reparations, and institutional reform to achieve these goals.[19] After interviews and field research with the relatives of the disappeared in Turkey's Şırnak and Cizre, the Truth, Justice and Memory Center in Turkey came up with four suggestions: trials, truth commissions, compensation programs, and institutional reforms.[20]

The right to truth is one of these goals that oversees the right of relatives and society to know the truth about state brutality and human rights violations in the past, which have been obscured due to the denial of responsibility and distortion of facts in official national histories. Truth and recognition of suffering is a prerequisite of healing. As Michael Ignatieff puts it, "The new human rights culture has been accompanied by the global diffusion of the psychoanalytic ideas about the healing power of truth."[21] Far from being resolved however, the right-to-truth claims have often injected a dilemma into the healing process, because truth commissions that were established during transitional periods often secured amnesties to perpetrators in return for collaboration. Truth, in other words, was revealed at the expense of criminal justice.[22] Truth commissions are not trials, but semi-official mechanisms that are instituted to bring some form of justice after massive, systematic, or historical crimes that cannot be tried in criminal courts, because previous regimes that had authorized these crimes during their rule have secured impunity or amnesties for themselves. After Argentina, truth commissions have been instituted or suggested in several countries in the process of confronting not only enforced disappearance but also other forms of state violence, such as the healing from the "Bloody Sunday" of 1972 in Ireland or justice and rights protection in East Timor.[23] Currently, truth and reconciliation commissions are being instituted in Belgium and Canada to reckon with legacies of violence during colonialism and against Indigenous communities, respectively.

A history of transitional justice might indeed be written by showing the dilemma between truth and criminal justice, and the historical struggles in different countries to minimize it. The Truth and Reconciliation Commission during South Africa's transition from the apartheid regime is a case in point. Beginning with public hearings in 1996, the TRC heard testimonies from two thousand and compiled written reports from twenty-three thousand people, but it was not left unchallenged (figure 1.3). For instance, Steve Biko's family protested that his enforced disappearance was not punished due to the amnesty granted in return for perpetrators' collaboration. The court rejected the family's appeal with a declaration that it would not have been possible to attain a "peaceful transition to a democratic society" otherwise.[24] The defendants of the truth commission also argued that the decision reflected the local conception of justice in South Africa, which synched better with forgiveness, harmony, and peace than criminal justice. It was the best of possible options, and still therapeutic for victims.[25] Conversely, in Argentina, the right-to-truth movement and protests against impunity for the previous military regime eventually led to a new form of trial that is specific to this country. The trials for truth in Argentina were somewhere between truth commissions and classical criminal trials, where the judge's mission was "declarative rather than punitive." The judge was not a historian, but allowed for the "legal recognition of the factual truth."[26]

Transitional justice is unresolved also because subsequent regimes were usually far from perfect themselves, and *their* truths and *their* justices were also partial. In many cases, results were compromising or even flawed, reparations functioned as whitewashing devices, financial compensations were symbolic,

Figure 1.3 A scene from the Truth and Reconciliation Commission, South Africa, ca. 1996–2003. Courtesy Pumla Gobodo Madikizela.

and institutional reforms such as purges and vetting gave unfair advantages to new regime supporters.[27] As Pablo De Greiff puts it, transitional justice takes place in "a very imperfect world." If democracy and reconciliation are the final goals, one "despot's truth commission will need to be followed by another truth commission."[28]

Moreover, the assumption of the "objectivity" and "universality" of international law is rightly debated, and the framework to reconcile the international and place-based justice systems remains undertheorized.[29] A comparative ethnographic and sociological study in transitional Bosnia, Rwanda, Iraq, and Uganda has revealed that conceptions of justice among communities vary; societies respond to violations differently; methods that they use to find justice differ; reconciliation means forgiveness in some countries but punishment in others; there is no direct correlation between victimhood and the desire for war crime trials; individual opinions about justice in a given country are skewed according to nationalist and ethno-centric ideologies and depend on social and economic factors and change over time.[30] Gayatri Spivak also formulates a critique of the potential colo-niality of human rights activism and proposes to rectify it through a "sutur-ing" educational program that revises both Western and local structures.[31] When the same measures and steps are applied universally, international law becomes ignorant of domestic practices and sabotages the fulfillment of human rights. When perceived as a toolkit that can be applied anywhere without translation, transitional justice forecloses a society's right to heal.

In the context of the unfinished struggles toward right to truth, the imperfect conditions of transitions, and the unreconciled international and national laws, transitional justice needs to be conceived as a continually evolving, self-reflective, and open platform, where societies formulate new forms of justice and peace-building steps. World communities may need to find other transitional justice steps, in addition to truth commissions, criminal prosecutions, truth trials, reparations, financial compensations, purges, vetting, institutional and constitutional reforms, official apologies, and memorialization.

In this literature, art and architecture usually get referenced for their role in forward-looking prospective justice, rather than retrospective and corrective mechanisms such as truth commissions and trials.[32] Memorials and museums about atrocities may not be able to compensate for the past, it is suggested, but they can become forms of apology used to build more just societies in the future. While this is certainly important, I would argue that the Saturday Mothers reveal a much larger role, including for architectural history, in right to truth: An alternative history of the public square where Mothers demonstrate every week will prove that urban spaces and social movements build each other.

An Alternative History of the Galatasaray and Taksim Squares

Countless interviews with relatives of the disappeared in Istanbul and Kurdish majority towns have shown that they cannot grieve their losses without conventional mourning rituals, or face the facts without learning the truth about the whereabouts of bodies.[33] Berfo Kırbayır, who died at the age of 105, left the front door to her house open every night after 1980 hoping that her son Cemil would return.[34] Hasan Ocak's mother kept his belongings and bed untouched, and prohibited anyone from using his room.[35] Depriving citizens of their political rights and turning them into bare lives, state violence simultaneously throws their relatives out of the sphere of social mourning. Reading Sigmund Freud's seminal text "Mourning and Melancholia" critically, we may ask how much ordinary forms of mourning could work for subjects who have been excluded from the socially constructed definition of the "normal."[36] Melancholy, the inability to have closure in grief, is not a pathological response, as it would have been deemed in normative Freudian psychoanalysis, but the only option left to relatives, which they have fought back by turning perpetual grief into activism. Mourning *and* protesting in one of the busiest public spaces of Istanbul have helped them to live with ungrievable death. Every week, the relatives brought red flowers to the urban square that they would have otherwise taken to cemeteries.

Sharing pain and vulnerability in urban space proved to be an effective form of resistance.[37] Yet the Galatasaray Square has not only served as a symbolic cemetery and a public demonstration site. It has also become something like a truth commission of transitional periods, even though the state did not admit accountability. Truth commissions do not have juridical power, but they enable public recognition of truth about past crimes, empower victims and survivors as basic sources of evidence, and give perpetrators an opportunity to diminish the burden of guilt. In Teitel's words, countries "begin the long and necessary process of healing the wounds of the past" through truth commissions.[38] During my interview with Maside Ocak and Sebla Arcan, who were among the initiators of the Saturday Mothers movement, both women emphasized that it would not have been possible for the relatives or the public to realize that enforced disappearance had been a systematic state policy unless new "mothers" and witnesses kept showing up in the public square to tell their own stories. Even though many individuals were lost in regions with a Kurdish majority, Istanbul's Galatasaray Square became the meeting point where relatives exercised their right to truth.[39] Some moved to Istanbul to be able to join the protests that received good media coverage. Many had already migrated here to escape the conflict in the eastern areas.[40] Testimonies of perpetrators spread by word of mouth in such get-togethers, such as the one by Yıldırım Beğler, who confessed that he participated in the gendarme forces that burned bodies in boilers or threw them out of helicopters.[41] Beğler identified these actions as a "professional job," just like the National Socialist Adolf Eichmann, whose trial has carried Hannah Arendt to notice that the darkness in the bureaucrat who dutifully follows orders is the most commonplace and therefore the most dangerous of all evils.[42]

Additionally, the Galatasaray Square also became a platform for prospective justice. In interviews, some relatives suggested that their public visibility prevented the state from committing further crimes, and that the number of enforced disappearances decreased over time.[43] Those who survived state custody came to the Saturday meetings and declared that the police spared them because they knew their mothers would join the movement.[44] In short, the Saturday Mothers' struggle for visibility in public space not only remained a cry to be seen, but also evolved into a truth-telling and corrective platform. No wonder the government tried to relocate the demonstration to the obscure Kazlıçeşme area and to block it with increasing police violence. Meeting at the Galatasaray Square had been banned on the seven-hundredth week, on August 25, 2018, pushing the mothers to a narrow street in front of the Human Rights Association.[45] As I was writing and editing this chapter in 2020–21, the trial against forty-six members of the Saturday Mothers for peacefully protesting was still ongoing.

The coupling of a social movement with a specific public space transformed gender-specific stereotypes as well. In some of the earliest academic articles, feminists criticized the Saturday Mothers for perpetuating the idea of womanhood as motherhood. This association maintained the identification of woman with her dependence on man, the argument warned, and the media coverage of suffering mothers doubly victimized them as powerless women.[46] Sometimes the name "Saturday People" is used to undo gender-specificity. However, this critique does not take into account that the Mothers transformed the traditional image of maternity over time.[47] With a dogged determination for almost thirty years, despite police beatings and detentions, the Mothers were mournful and peaceful, but they can hardly be described as passive or obedient. Appearing as human rights defendants in urban space, they falsified any perception that confined a woman's place to the private realm as a caretaker of men, and resisted any political or social calculation to domesticate her. Looking retroactively, the movement's association with motherhood served a strategic purpose. It is possible that the Saturday Mothers persisted as long as they did, in a context where many other protests were blocked, because their activism was initially trivialized as a group of weeping women with a personal cause. The state's failure to see the Mothers' revolutionary role in the early years and the reluctance to ban them from mourning publicly might have contributed to the social movement's success.[48]

From the perspective of transitional justice, "mother" is an appropriate metaphor for the struggle against enforced disappearance, because state modernization establishes a contract with relatives over the protocols of burial. No burial can take place without state permission, which at the same time makes the state responsible for informing its citizens about their deceased relatives. The state controls, classifies, guides, and keeps track of dead bodies, but the authoritarian state also pushes them out of the burial protocol. Consequently, relatives, like mothers, are eligible to be claimants of enforced disappearance cases in the sphere of international law. Additionally, the Saturday Mothers detached the concept of maternity from its patriarchal biological association, and showed that a sibling, partner, child, grandchild, or any citizen in solidarity can be the "Mother" of the deceased whose rights were violated. They simultaneously called the state apparatus to transform itself with values of care and love that had been associated with motherhood. Another aspect that the Saturday Mothers of Turkey share with their muse, Mothers of Plaza de Mayo in Argentina, is their ability to revolutionize and socialize maternity. In her book *Revolutionizing Motherhood*, Marguerite Guzman Bouvard explains how unexpected but also transformative it was to observe mothers subverting tyranny in Argentina. "The mothers have subverted the concept of motherhood as merely biological, however, and stepped out of their roles as passive and private persons. In so doing, they also challenged the conservative Catholic heritage that provided support for the political system. . . . As such they have transformed themselves from women seeking to protect the sanctity of the mother-child bond within the existing political system to women wishing to transform the state so that it reflects maternal values."[49]

In sum, the city square built the social movement, but also vice versa. The Galatasaray Square takes its name from the Galatasaray Lycee, whose establishment as an institution dates back to 1481, and whose reformed version opened in 1868 in one of the earliest Ottoman state buildings in today's Taksim-Beyoğlu district. In an exhibition showcasing over five hundred years of the Galatasaray school and square, three of the exhibition's ten contemporary artists inserted the Saturday Mothers into the long canonic history of the area.[50] In his piece *Cumartesi* (Saturday), Barış Göktürk transformed a typical class photo into a blurred image composed of a collage of Mothers holding portrait photographs of the disappeared in front of the school's gate. The artist reproduced images from the past twenty-five years on Xerox paper, reminiscent of street fliers and posters, and transitioned them on silk surface. The choice of this medium resulted in layered images that blurred each other and mirror images that inverted the names of the disappeared, making them partially illegible. For the artist, the making of this "pictorial fog" was also a matter of personal healing. Remembering his early encounters with the demonstration, he said, "I can see, but I am also blinded by the weight of it all. I am a teenager. I can't come to terms with it. I walk on. It is a Saturday. It is every Saturday. I know this and I don't know it at all."[51] Göktürk questions himself for his failure to *actually see* the Saturday Mothers. He inhabits the role of the bystander, a group of quite diverse people joined in their hostility against the "other," or silence in the face of violence against the "other." For years, we resisted to see what could not be unseen and what the Saturday Mothers really showed. Shortly after their demonstration was

Figure 1.4 Barış Göktürk, *Cumartesi* (Saturday), mixed media, 311 × 597 cm, 2018. Saturday Mothers left red flowers under the work at the *School Square Galatasaray* exhibition, Pera Museum, Istanbul, 2018.

banned in its associated public space in 2018, a group of the Saturday Mothers visited the exhibition and left their red flowers under Göktürk's work—the flowers that they would have brought to the Galatasaray Square every week, and that they would have otherwise taken to cemeteries (figure 1.4).

Göktürk's work also reminds us the power of the portrait photograph, through which the disappeared appears in the city (figure 1.5). Reports by human rights organizations expose that regimes learned the apparatus of enforced disappearance from one another.[52] So did the resistance. Over the years, the portrait photograph in the public space has consistently proved its power as a form of transnational solidarity. Mothers of Argentina came up with creative performances to make the disappeared appear in public space using silhouettes and masks (figure 1.6).[53] The most common form has been the portrait photograph with the victim's name on it, and a question about the whereabouts, which jumped between Argentina, Turkey, Mexico, Colombia, Chile, Iran, El Salvador, and many places. Some demonstrators use state ID photographs, appropriating the disciplinary power's visual field to a subversive effect. The portrait photographs in public protests expose the intrinsic ungrievability of the disappeared. Many authors who theorized photography, from Walter Benjamin to Susan Sontag, commented on the photograph's role in freezing time. In periods of transitional justice, time is also suspended because it affects the living and the living-dead differently. Nothing exemplifies this better than an anecdote of a Saturday Mother: when she held up the portrait photograph of her husband who disappeared in his twenties thirty years ago, someone asked her if she was looking for her son. She had aged, but her husband's portrait photograph had not.

The photo and audio installation *On the Wall* by Aylin Tekiner brings the audience face to face with this fact (figure 1.7). Tekiner turns the camera away from the public square to domestic spaces where "Mothers" keep the memories of the disappeared. The audience puts the still image on the wall into time throughout the duration of the audio. Time passes for those in the living world but is frozen for those in the disappeared. "The eleven-year-old me still waits on that stair," Gülbahar Alpsoy says, remembering the day she watched her father being taken away. The overwhelming presence of the portrait photograph is noticeable in the pictures, whether in size, placement, or relation to other objects. Many relatives make a connection between the portrait and the missing grave. "Our graves are the melancholic photographs on our walls," Alpsoy continues, whereas İkbal Eren explains that they did not dare to put his brother Hayrettin's photograph up for the last thirty-four years, because that would have meant to admit his death.[54]

The portrait photograph as evidence in grassroots truth commissions and standing in for the missing body in the suspended time brings up my next topic: the cemetery. Over the years in the Saturday Mothers movement, as hopes that the disappeared would return dwindled, the motto of the movement became "We want our bones and to bury our dead," a request that reappeared in countless transitional justice cases across the world: Bones were found years later under bridge piers or resurfaced on lakeshores; bones were excavated from pits or revealed in truth commissions when perpetrators confessed; in Mexico, animal bones were sent to families to claim that the migrants had died in accidents.[55] The missing graves of the disappeared raise the question that Judith Butler asked: "What makes a grievable life?" Why does the state apparatus consider some lives mournable, but others so unmournable that it denies them graves?[56] To discuss this question, I would like to draw attention to the place of architectural history in the right to truth. The physical environments can indeed be treated as primary sources of history and evidences in truth-telling.

If we zoom out of the Galatasaray Square to its surroundings from Kasımpaşa to Taksim, and compare old and new maps, it would be clear

Figure 1.5 Saturday Mothers use portrait photographs during protests. Photo: Ali Öz.

Figure 1.6 Mothers of the Plaza de Mayo protest, Buenos Aires, ca. 1987–88. Photo: Gerardo Dell'Orto.

Figure 1.7 Aylin Tekiner, *On the Wall*, photo and audio installation, Depo Gallery, Istanbul, 2014. Courtesy the artist.

that in Istanbul, it was not only the people but also the graveyards that disappeared. Istanbul has long been acknowledged as the land of cemeteries. Edhem Eldem mentions the abundance of cemeteries and other architectural symbols of death as the city's identifying character during the Ottoman Empire. With the religious conviction that a grave could be reserved for only one body, cemeteries soon spread both inside and outside the city walls and became a main urban element that Islamicized Istanbul after its conquest by the Ottoman Empire.[57] During the second half of the nineteenth century, the Galatasaray Square was part of the sixth district of the Istanbul Municipality, which had relative autonomy due to the protections granted to non-Muslim *millets* as a result of European capitulations. A map analysis reveals the disappearance of the Muslim Small Cemetery (Küçük Kabristan/Petit Champs des Morts) during Pera's transformation from a land of grapes and graves to a city of elite households and hotels, during the Ottoman Empire's integration into capitalism. Comparing the maps of the Sixth District prepared by B. D'Osotya in 1858–60 (figure 1.8) and by Cervati Frères & Fatzea in 1882 (figure 1.9) reveals that parts of the "Le Petit Cimetière Turc" were replaced with buildings and divided by streets. As Mehmet Kentel researched, the emerging forces of modernization and urbanization during this time involved the destruction of city walls, the opening of wider streets, the expropriations of land, the emergence of a new cosmopolitan elite, and the construction of modern infrastructure. In this context, the edges of the cemetery were in constant pressure due to the rising land prices. Following the cholera epidemic of 1865 and the perceived health hazard of graves, a wall was built around, changing the cemetery from a public passageway and recreational area into a border that separated the wealthy Pera from the poor Kasımpaşa. When the Tünel, the world's second subway, was constructed between 1873 and 1875, the graveyard of the Galata Mevlevi Lodge was expropriated, and the debris that came out of the excavation for the subway was dumped on the Small Cemetery (figure 1.10). The subway's engineer, Eugene-Henri Gavand, made the argument that the straightening of the cemetery's steep slope on the street level would increase the land values and thus be beneficial for the real estate market.[58] A new life started over the totally covered Muslim graves, and the area came to be known for its best views in town that attracted tourists to canonic hotels. The city theater was built and later destroyed on the landfill that replaced the cemetery.[59] If Frank Gehry's design for a cultural center (2005) is constructed, its basement will dig nine floors deep, so that cars will replace the bones as the final act of the graves' total obliteration.

The Large Cemetery (Büyük Kabristan/Grand Champs de Morts), on the other hand, the second cemetery around today's Taksim and Gezi Park, used to be the site of non-Muslim cemeteries. After the cholera epidemic and pressured by real estate, a new land law in 1869 mandated that all graves be relocated to the outskirts of the city. While the Catholic and Protestant graves were relocated without much controversy to today's Feriköy, there was some public dissent over the Greek Orthodox one, but the municipal authorities successfully negotiated with the Greek Patriarch for the relocation of the cemetery and its graves to a larger site.[60] The map of the Sixth District prepared by C. Stolpe in 1858–61 (see figure 1.8) clearly shows the Greek cemetery at the entrance of today's Istiklal Street, and the Catholic and Protestant cemeteries to the north of the Ottoman Military Artillery (replaced today with the tail end of the Gezi Park). The same district's map by Cervati Frères & Fatzea in 1882 (see figure 1.9) no longer shows these cemeteries, but identifies the Greek cemetery site as the church and its garden, and the Catholic and Protestant cemetery sites as the Taksim Garden (Jardin du Taksim). Yet the Armenian Cemetery remains in both maps. Following a few attempts to expropriate the Armenian Surp Agop cemetery and its church since 1855, the negotiations had remained unresolved when World War I broke out. After the Ottoman Empire dissolved, the Turkish Republic confiscated the land in 1939, through unjustified "legal" means by manipulating the

Figure 1.8 Galatasaray School/Square (*center*), Small Cemetery (*top*), and Large Cemetery (*bottom right*), Istanbul. B. D'Osotya, Plan Général de Galata, Pera et Pancaldi, 1858–60. Sinan Genim Collection-IAE.

transition between imperial and national property regimes and denying the Armenian Patriarch lawful ownership of the land. Such dispossessions of Armenian property whose owners had been deported, exiled, or murdered was part of the denial statecraft and the continuing climate of impunity. The Gezi Park and Intercontinental Hotel (originally built as a Sheraton) stand today on the older site of the relocated Catholic and Protestant cemeteries, while the Divan and Hyatt Hotels as well as a series of modern buildings stand on the older site of the confiscated Armenian Cemetery. Revealing the history of the eight-year-long court case that resulted in the dispossession of the Armenian community in 1939, Tamar Nalci and Can Dağlıoğlu write, "Only after confrontation and official apology, perhaps we can finally bury our dead."[61]

It is not a coincidence that both the Saturday Mothers and the legal historians of the Armenian Cemetery conclude their words with the same request: to bury their dead. Throughout their thirty years of demonstration, the Saturday Mothers have shown solidarity with the victims of other historical atrocities and have been joined by other activists. Even though the

PLAN GÉNÉRAL
DE
GALATA, PERA ET PANCALDI,
— 6ME CERCLE DE CONSTANTINOPLE —
de
O. D'OSTOYA
1858–1860

Saturday Mothers' members are specifically looking for their relatives who disappeared since the 1980 coup d'état, they have drawn attention to similar episodes of state violence throughout the history of the Ottoman Empire and the Turkish Republic. For instance, at their 679th meeting, on March 31, 2018, they argued that the murder of Turkish intellectual and poet Sabahattin Ali in 1948 was a typical example of enforced disappearance.[62] To give another example that fits the topic of disappearing cemeteries, at their 683rd meeting, on April 28, 2018, the Saturday Mothers memorialized the approximately 250 Armenian intellectuals in Istanbul who were subject to deportation and eventually to enforced disappearance on April 24, 1915 (figure 1.11).[63] This was one of the many episodes of demographic engineering as a main mechanism of resettler nationalism during the dissolution of the Ottoman Empire that this book confronts.

The reason that authorities are so threatened by mothers of the disappeared around the world must be because the mothers powerfully reveal an intrinsic truth about the nation-state apparatus. They expose how states exploit their dead in the name of the physical, economic, or ideological victory of one group over the other. That is also why the Saturday Mothers movement is more than a search for personal grieving.

A mother's right to mourn is also a society's right to heal.

BEFORE

AFTER

Figure 1.9 (above)
Galatasaray School/
Square (*center*),
Small Cemetery (*top*),
and Large Cemetery
(*bottom right*),
Istanbul. Cervati
Frères & Fatzea,
Plan de Péra, 1882.
Sinan Genim
Collection-IAE.

Figure 1.10 (left)
Before and after views
of Istanbul's Small
Cemetery, showing
changes made ca.
1860–90. Top: M. C.
"Kasımpaşa," Getty
Collection. Bottom:
"Tepebaşı," Selahattin
Giz Collection.

Figure 1.11 Saturday Mothers' 683rd Meeting, memorializing 250 deported Armenian intellectuals, April 28, 2018, Galatasaray Square. Courtesy Maside Ocak.

Memorials and Transitions to Come

After truth and justice, the Saturday Mothers' third public demand is a space for the remains of their relatives. In this chapter, I argued against the narrowing down of architecture's role to designing memorials. Instead, the history of today's Beyoğlu and Taksim shows the explanatory power of spatial analyses in truth-telling about past violations. In this part, I would like to continue suggesting that architectural scholarship can take more proactive roles in transitional justice by engaging in the accountability debates at earlier stages. Transitional justice memorials reveal architecture's role in prospective justice. They are different from war and heroism memorials, as they come to terms with internal violence—with actions of states that violate the rights of citizens whom they claim to protect. However, architects are usually excluded from the decisions over the need, site, representatives, and narrative of memorials, only to be brought in at the last stage to design the physical environment. Let me make a case for a more proactive role by discussing transitional justice memorials from the perspective of site, form, program, funding, and procedure.

As there are no official memorials for the Saturday Mothers as of today to contemplate, I will comment on the memorials to come that commemorate the truth to be discovered about the bones to be found of the humans who have disappeared. Of course, all the temporary installations and performances that the Mothers have already constructed every Saturday at the Galatasaray

Square and in their homes are grassroots memorials. And yet official apologies and memorials have an additional meaning in transitional justice and the closure of grief, precisely because they are declarations of accountability, despite their potential contradictions that will be discussed below.

Let me start with the location. During my meeting with the Saturday Mothers, we discussed possible locations for memorials, and a provisional list emerged.[64]

- The Galatasaray Square

- Buildings where the disappeared were taken from their homes into police custody, each to be marked with a public plaque

- Regarding Sansaryan Han, the building built as an Armenian school but turned into a police precinct that became Istanbul's most violent torture space, where well-known intellectuals, artists, and activists from Nazım Hikmet to Deniz Gezmiş were detained; the Saturday Mothers would like to see the repurposing of this building into an apology museum, rather than a proposed five-star hotel[65]

- The cemeteries of Altınşehir, Gazi, Kasımpaşa, Feriköy, and Gayrettepe or any place where the bodies of the disappeared or their bones have been found, reburied, or hoped to be buried when found.

This list envisions healing spaces in both found and constructed locations—namely, both spaces where the trauma happened and the symbolic spaces that would be associated with healing by virtue of the memorial. Unlike those that prompted Robert Musil's critique that there is nothing as invisible as a monument, transitional justice memorials are no longer sculptures of a handful of heroes on pedestals but complex conceptions of sites, where sculpture, architecture, landscape, design, earth-art, performance, and educational programs might be combined. There are mixed opinions about locations that repurpose torture spaces. While such spaces strongly reveal historical violence, they may also perpetuate trauma rather than heal it. The location of the Memory Park in Argentina (inaugurated in 2001, incomplete) at the former torture chamber of Buenos Aires raised concerns for this reason.[66] Conversely, in Chile, exposing and appropriating the violation spaces became a major transitional step, such as the uncovering of the Villa Grimaldi as a secret police torture center in 1998, which led to the creation of one of the most internationally known memorials.[67]

An additional concern is the fact that torture spaces tend to be in isolated locations, and using them as healing spaces impairs the visibility of the accountability debate in public media, especially if they are not accompanied by other platforms of transitional justice, such as public programs, temporary exhibitions, and additional memorials. A familiar critique of memorials is their participation in forgetting and whitewashing despite their opposite intention, and the choice of location is not a trivial factor in the contribution of built form during transitions. A frozen singular site is more likely to trivialize atrocities than multiple sites that are constantly animated with educational and art programs. The number and accessibility of Holocaust memorials and museums all over the world are more likely to disseminate the necessary reminder "never again" (for all peoples) than a single frozen memorial in an isolated location. In Chile, multiple memorial sites emerged mostly with the determination of local communities, such as one in rural Paine that houses dozens of memorial mosaics completed by the relatives of the disappeared.[68] In Santiago there are memorials at the State University of Technology, Víctor Jara Stadium, the National Stadium, Patio 29 (a grave site), and Londres 38 and Villa Grimaldi (detention centers), among other locations, in addition to the approximately 250 plaques in the city to the victims of Pinochet.[69] The fact that President Patricio Aylwin made the official apology for the disappearances, following the truth commission's report, in the National Stadium gives additional relevance to stadium memorials as spatial markers of transition. The Space for Memory Institute of Argentina estimated about two hundred sites of memory in Buenos Aires alone.[70]

The second consideration is the physical design and form of the memorial. Andreas Huyssen has drawn attention to the synchronized growth of memorials and the human rights debate after the 1990s.[71] The booming of transitional justice memorials around the world would confirm this assessment. From a formal standpoint, these memorials have shaken architecture's confidence in monumentality. Modern monumentality has been a long and periodically rising topic in architecture.[72] While the historical antagonism between modern architecture and monumentality was summarized in Lewis Mumford's well-known motto of 1938, "If it is a monument it is not modern, if it is modern it is not a monument,"[73] less than a decade later, such influential critics as Sigfried Giedion and Elizabeth Mock argued for the need to reestablish the civic representational value of architecture by erecting modern monuments. Even though monuments had been the very tools of totalitarian regimes, they were necessary to commemorate the dead and pay tribute to a society's values. Hence, they said, it should have been possible to erect monuments to democracy.[74]

In comparison, the debate since the 1990s about memorials and monumentality sought new forms of commemorative imagination. It was realized that official state monuments had manipulated collective memory by overemphasizing and stabilizing the dominant voice and thus by taking part in cultural repression. One of the most recognized turning points in the United States was the Vietnam Veterans Memorial in Washington, designed by Maya Lin (1980–82).[75] In sharp contrast to the neoclassical scale and representational strategies of the surrounding monuments on the Washington Mall, Lin's memorial is hardly visible from a distance. The gesture of inscribing on the walls more than 58,000 names of men and women who died in the war makes it a memorial to individuals, rather than to an official narrative symbolized in the sacrifice of the unknown soldier. The memorial is complete only with the individuals filling up the space between the two wings when they look for the names of their dead relatives. The names of the dead resist their own erasure and disappearance in the name of authority, as would have been the case in state memorials to unknown soldiers. In the United States, commemorating minority memories soon became common practice in the wake of Maya Lin's success. A walk on the Washington Mall is sufficient to make one realize that a memorial has become one of the most recognized mediums of self-representation and struggle for public visibility.[76]

Writing names of individuals on walls has proven to be an effective commemorative mode for victims of torture and enforced disappearance as well. Just as the graphic combination of a portrait photograph, a name, and a question jumped like a meme from country to country in public demonstrations against enforced disappearance, the wall of names appeared in transitional justice memorials in the United States, Argentina, Bosnia, Chile, Uruguay, and other countries (figure 1.12). During the design of the Monument to the Victims of State Terrorism in Argentina, designed by the Baudizzon-Lestard-Varas Studio, with Claudio Ferrari and Daniel Becker (2007) in the Memory Park of Buenos Aires, it was a matter of controversy to decide which names to write on the wall. Acknowledging those who disappeared after 1969, as opposed to 1976, would change the level of accountability for the inner structures of the state. With the momentum toward memorialization in 2007, a new law secured the inscription of all names that were revealed by the truth commission, but designers nevertheless left twenty-one thousand slabs empty in the overall memorial, gesturing to the higher number suggested by the Mothers of Plaza de Mayo and other human

Figure 1.12 Walls of names in transitional justice memorials around the world. *Clockwise from top left*: United States (Vietnam Veterans Memorial, photographed by Esra Akcan, ca. 2005); Chile (Memorial for the Disappeared, photographed by Paul Lowry, 2009); Bosnia (Srebrenica Massacre Memorial, photographed by Michael Büker, 2009); Argentina (Memory Park in Buenos Aires, photographed by Marcelo Brodsky, 2007).

rights organizations.[77] The University of Virginia (UVA) Memorial to Enslaved Laborers in the United States designed by Höweler + Yoon and Mabel Wilson also gestures toward the need for further research and exploration by leaving empty spaces in the wall of slave names.

In Germany, a countermonumental turn in public art took place with Holocaust memorials. No other country but Germany has a longer history of memorialization that reckons with its past crimes, where the discipline of architectural history took on active roles. Germany has also served as a model for the elaboration of transitional justice mechanisms, both due to its past crimes and reparations. In an agreement reached in 1952, West

Germany approved to make restitutions and monetary reparations to the Jewish victims of Nazism. The memorable image of Willy Brandt kneeling down in a dramatic apology in Warsaw in 1970 has sparked debates on reparations. While East Germany refused accountability in 1952, claiming it did not bear moral or historical responsibility for the crimes of the Nazis, the state agreed to reverse this policy in 1988. After the dissolution of East Germany and the two Germanys' reunification, authorities discussed reparations for property seized by communists for the past four decades. The late Cold War debate on memorials and monumentality increasingly claimed to have put an end to the assumed connection between authority and monumentality, between the will to power and the will to leave traces. Holocaust memorials struggled to get over Theodor Adorno's challenge to the writing of "nonbarbaric" poetry after Auschwitz. This challenge was legitimately taken into consideration in some literary and cinematographic representations of the Holocaust, which refrained from claiming that the victim's actual experience could be represented or re-enacted in a particular medium. Erecting monuments or memorials to Holocaust victims presented its own set of problems: Given both the historical and etymological relation between monuments and memory (*monumentum* derives from *monere*, "to remind," in Latin), and given also the association of monumentality with power, grandeur, prestige, and glory, how could one commemorate the Holocaust with a monumental expression? As the basic tool of the totalitarian regimes to freeze their own figure of victory, did not monumentality itself take part in cultural repression by disseminating and stabilizing official memories? Or, to follow Horkheimer and Adorno, if the Holocaust was a major scar on the face of modernity, raising a serious concern about its inherent inability to confront otherness and difference, how could one continue to use conventional monumental practices to represent the Holocaust memories?[78]

After the 1990s, artists commemorated traumas with countermonumental forms in response to this challenge. For example, Jochen Gerz and Esther Gerz conceived their Disappearing Monument against Fascism in Harburg (1986–91) as a twelve-meter pillar that was gradually lowered as citizens of the city signed their names on it to indicate their rebellion against fascism. This interactive countermonument was designed to vanish eventually, challenging the very notion of permanence and stability that is usually attributed to traditional monuments. The pillar's complete disappearance marked the symbolic defeat of fascism.[79] Daniel Libeskind Studio and Peter Eisenman both used countermonumental formal strategies, in their different ways for the Berlin Jewish Museum (1988–2001) and Memorial to the Murdered Jews of Europe in Berlin (2004), respectively, such as the spatial and programmatic void, the lack of visible entrance, the lack of a privileged viewpoint, or the uncanny interchangeability between the formal associations of the rational and the irrational.[80]

Against those who claim that the Holocaust is not comparable to any other atrocity—an objection that appears periodically during escalations in Israel-Palestine conflict—architects of memorials have learned from one another. Intertextuality between the apology memorials speaks to the importance of transnational solidarity. In addition to the wall of names, the Memorial for Peace and Justice ("Lynching Memorial," 2018) that reckons with slavery and racism in the United States, designed by MASS Design, references Eisenman's Holocaust memorial by creating a forest of studs. While this forest rises from the ground in the Berlin memorial, it is suspended from the roof in the Alabama one (figure 1.13). At the UVA memorial to enslaved laborers, Höweler + Yoon and Wilson make a reference to Maya Lin's memorial in Washington in their choice of scale, material, and the wall of names.

Memorials to enforced disappearance also employ countermonumentality as a formal strategy to avoid the paradox of criticizing atrocities with heroic monumental conventions. Countermonuments are critical because they can still make us remember, yet through an intentionally nonmonumental representation, because they refute form, scale, and aesthetic assumptions of traditional monuments but not the necessity to commemorate. The winning competition design for the Monument to the Victims of State Terrorism of Argentina in Memory Park by Baudizzon-Lestard-Varas Studio with Ferrari and Becker creates a cut on land as a metaphor of a wound into which visitors enter. They walk on the zigzag path underground along a wall on which the names of the disappeared are inscribed. The visitor slowly reaches the river that symbolizes all the waters where bodies of the disappeared were dumped into. This is not an arbitrary reference. Some mothers wished their ashes would be thrown into these waters so that they could reunite with their children (figure 1.14).[81]

Countermonuments bring visitors face to face with victims' experience rather than victors' propaganda, and memorials to the Rwanda genocide have added a new layer to the presence of the index of violence in memory sites. Unlike memorials that use replicas or represent traumas through mediated experiences, the Kigali Genocide Memorial Center (2004) displays actual human remains and the bones of dead bodies (figure 1.15). Nothing could possibly bring the visitor closer to the presence of the slaughters when churches, schools, and public spaces were covered with dead bodies.[82] The

Figure 1.13 Intertextuality in transitional justice memorials. *Top*: MASS Design, Memorial for Peace and Justice ("Lynching Memorial"), Montgomery, Alabama, 2018. *Bottom*: Peter Eisenman, Memorial to the Murdered Jews of Europe, Berlin, 2004. Courtesy MASS Design; photo: Esra Akcan.

Figure 1.14 Baudizzon-Lestard-Varas Studio, with Claudio Ferrari and Daniel Becker, Project for Memory Park, Argentina, 2007.

Rwanda genocide memorial takes its power from the architecturalization of the index of violence.

Third, I would suggest the program as another consideration of transitional justice commemorative spaces, even though their function in taking accountability for the past abuses is self-evident. Let's hypothesize that additional research, education, and art programs that keep healing spaces informative, social, and active and that turn accountability into a constantly self-reflective open process are more meaningful steps in the struggles toward justice than frozen and isolated memorials. In *Exhibiting Atrocity*, Amy Sodaro points out the insufficiency of memorials alone to heal wounds from past atrocities and analyzes the memorial museum as a new program, such as the National Museum of Memory in Colombia, the United States Holocaust Memorial Museum, the House of Terror in Budapest, the Kigali Genocide Memorial Center, and the Museum of Memory and Human Rights in Chile. These museums usually put the victims' experience at the center and emphasize both historical archives and emotional journey.[83]

Despite their role in healing, transitional justice memorials and museums are prone to many unresolved contradictions, such as whitewashing liability, freezing the transition, and derailing the progress toward equality and peace. One of the dilemmas generates from the state sponsorship of memorials. The Mothers of Plaza de Mayo refused a state-sponsored memorial

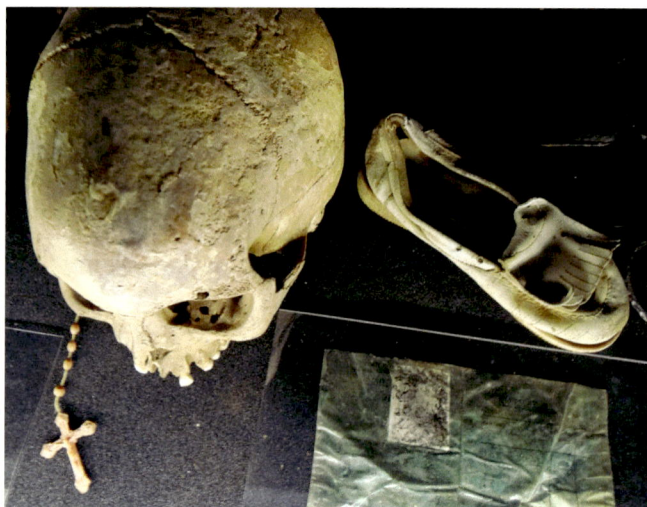

Figure 1.15 Skull and belongings of genocide victims, Kigali Genocide Memorial Center, Kigali, Rwanda. Courtesy of Adam Jones via a Creative Commons Attribution–Share Alike 3.0 Unported license: https://creativecommons.org/licenses/by-sa/3.0 /deed.en.

because they conceived it as a step toward releasing the state from its accountability for future steps. In Nancy Gates-Madsen's words, the mothers "resist any memorializing impulse sponsored by those whom they view as having contributed to the culture of amnesia and injustice. . . . For them, any permanent installation will tend to fix memory at a certain point in time, precluding continued progress or further understanding."[84] In Chile, it has been the human rights organizations, individual activists, victims' families, trade unions, and student centers that undertook the memorialization initiative, until the government instituted a second official truth-telling procedure in 2004, which many scholars still find ambivalent or carried out by mid-level bureaucrats rather than executives.[85]

Opportunism to whitewash the current governments notwithstanding, the lack of state funding throws these memorials into the market economy, if they were to reach a broader public than their immediate communities. This condition creates its own contradictions. Andreas Huyssen warns about the commodification of Holocaust memory as a new form of forgetting.[86] Apology memorials erected after the end of dictatorships in Argentina and Chile were co-opted to the "memory market" as an extension of the simultaneous neoliberalization of the world in the 1990s. In a context where memory groups reject government support and need to survive in the market economy, trauma sites get integrated into the tourism industry, the "never again" motto turns into a logo, and memorialization becomes a brand.[87] The Memory Park of Argentina, originally proposed by family members of the disappeared and a group of students at the National College of Buenos Aires, evolved so that it would commemorate other atrocities, with seventeen sculptures planned but only three completed by the first opening in 2001.[88] Many have seen this multiplication as a necessary step to fund the park by attracting more visitors. However, historians reveal that the completion and management of the park periodically faced drawbacks because of the ambiguities in its funding structure.[89] Commercialization not only lets the state get away from its financial burden, but also cheapens the transitional justice process by turning trauma into a commodity that needs to sell well.

If the state is not involved in memorials to the victims of enforced disappearance, the result is not an apology, and memorialization is left to its own devices in a neoliberal world. If the state is too involved, it dictates the message in its own partiality and in "a very imperfect world." Many memorial museums freeze history writing and disseminate a version of the past that is convenient for present rulers. For these reasons, societies need to find ways so that the state is involved in the funding of the construction and management of transitional justice memorials, while the narrative is democratized by involving many groups including those who had been most affected. In the meantime, critical historiography needs to endure so that justice and peace building become a continually updated process.

Another contradiction of transitional justice memorials is the implied ranking of suffering due to unequal monetary resources, space, and scale granted to different memorials, whether by the state or the market economy. Nothing but the visual presence of Holocaust memorials at the expense of other victims exposes this contradiction better. While the Holocaust to the Murdered Jews of Europe fortunately takes up vast space at the center of unified Berlin in proximity to the Reichstag and Brandenburg Gate, other Nazi victims such as the Roma and homosexual populations hardly get commemorated in the same vein. The collective memory debate in Germany has often been competitive, as if different groups of victims need to compete with one another in their struggle over scarce resources, and as if recognizing and taking accountability for the oppression of one group would take away these rights from another. While the Holocaust has often been declared unique among genocides and the Nazis among perpetrators, it can and it has served as a model for the mobilization of other material and moral reparations in unexpected places of the world. The confrontation with the Holocaust has sometimes helped and at other times impaired the articulation of other horrors and the recognition of other victims. Moreover, the early Holocaust memory debate actually took shape in dialogue with the antiracist and anticolonial struggles of intellectuals such as Hannah Arendt, W. E. B. Du Bois, and Charlotte Delbo, as scholar Michael Rothberg convincingly analyzes.[90] Andreas Huyssen also traces the beginnings of this memory discourse and the growing awareness of the Holocaust to the decolonization and the civil rights movements.[91] The relations between the Holocaust memory, xenophobia, and the reception of Muslim immigrants in Germany after the 1970s have been no less complex and changing. Many immigrants compared racism against them to antisemitism, such as the neo-Nazis' deadly attacks in Mölln (1992) and Solingen (1993), and many Middle Eastern immigrants took the German-Jewish trope as a model for their own cooperative unions, associations, and demands for rights.[92] In literary studies, Leslie Adelson analyzes Holocaust consciousness and accountability in German-Turkish immigrant literature after Germany's reunification.[93] Esra Özyürek draws attention to the fact that the situation changed around 2000, when "the interconnected commitments of European leaders to fight anti-Semitism became one of the grounds for legitimizing racialization of immigrants, and singling out the Muslims as the main contemporary anti-Semites."[94] Holocaust memorials in immigrant neighborhoods such as Berlin's Kreuzberg failed to triangulate German, Jewish, and immigrant memories, even though many intellectuals drew connections between historical and contemporary discriminations against the Jewish and Muslim populations.[95] Zafer Şenocak's words best summarize this situation: "In today's Germany, Jews and Germans no longer face one another alone."[96] Only recently in 2015, the official deliberations started for a consensus over the history of and an apology for the German pre-Nazi genocide in southwest Africa.[97]

The exclusionary practice in the selective inclusion of victims brings me to the topic of identity politics in transitional justice memorials. On the one hand, most conflicts are due to ethnic and racial discriminations, and truth-telling needs to expose this racialization processes if societies are ever to confront their mistakes. On the other hand, the final goal of transitional justice is perpetual peace building to put an end to conflicts. Transitional justice is a delicate reconciliation, after which all involved parties shake hands in peace, so to speak. Any action or memorial that fuels conflicts by reversing and constructing a new hierarchy between groups or by planting seeds of violence through identity politics, or by confusing equality with revenge, or by using the word "victim" as a synonym of the "good" is bound to distort this final intention. When the Saturday Mothers demand justice, they do not ask it only for themselves alone but in solidarity with other victims of atrocities, which makes them a possibly exemplary social movement in memorialization as well.

In this context, we might ask how the architecture discipline could give a forward momentum to transitional justice today, whether through historical analyses of buildings and settlements to improve truth-telling or memorials designed before state acknowledgment. Memorials can indeed start the process of transitional justice rather than conclude it. For example, as Valentina Rozas-Krause shows, the first plaque at Tanforan Assembly Center to commemorate the interned 110,000 Japanese and Japanese Americans during World War II was placed before the official apology in 1981, which was followed by the reparations that were granted with the Civil Liberties Act of 1988. In other words, it was the memorial that started the process of transitional justice, and demanded apology and reparation, rather than the other way around.[98] Similarly, the Chicago Torture Justice Center, which "seeks to address the traumas of police violence and institutionalized racism through access to healing and wellness services, trauma-informed resources, and community connection," has initiated the design of a memorial.[99] The Chicago Torture Justice Memorials group selected a project designed by Patricia Nguyen and John Lee, and asked the mayor for the money and land to construct it.[100]

Memorials to come also imply transitions to come.

Conclusion: Globalizing and Localizing Human Rights

Today, the memorialization debate and the transitional justice framework are giving a new momentum to healing from prolonged and unresolved cases of injustice such as colonization and slavery. During the summer of 2020, several Confederate and military monuments were toppled or removed during the Black Lives Matter protests in Virginia and Alabama, as well as in Boston, Bristol, Antwerp, and other cities. This new episode of upheaval in the continuing debate around monuments also sparked discussions on accountability and the right to truth. For instance, during these protests, Angela Davis proposed transitional justice mechanisms, including a truth and reconciliation commission, to reckon with the historical damages caused by slavery and its continuing racist legacy.[101] Shortly after the toppling of the statue of King Leopold II in Antwerp in the summer of 2020, Belgium instituted a sort of a truth and reconciliation commission in the form of a parliamentary special commission, meant to scrutinize Belgium's colonial past and to discuss reparations to ex-colony Congo.[102] In the sphere of diplomacy and international law, transitional justice offers a broader and more holistic framework for colonization reparations, and one that can deal in legal terms with the passage of time between official colonization and today. Reparations and restitutions to bring justice to the residual inequalities caused by authoritarian regimes, slavery, and colonization need to be at the forefront of contemporary human rights activism.

Even before the recent spark of the debate around Confederate monuments, Ta-Nehisi Coates and the UN Working Group Report of Experts on People of African Descent had already used the transitional justice language to give a new push to the Black reparations debate.[103] Unlike remedial or distributive justice that opts to close the present gaps (income gap, education gap, and incarceration gap) by allocating present resources slightly more evenly, transitional justice is invested in tracing the historical causes of this gap much more precisely and bringing justice to past violations. Recently, scholars in the transitional justice field have made the case that in the major US transition periods, such as the Reconstruction and civil rights eras, equity has been sought through ahistorical distributive justice and has thus remained less effective than possible.[104] Instead, transitional justice procedures might move toward fairer reparations, including monetary redress, and have a better chance at preventing backlash (as seen in statements such as "affirmative action is reverse racism" or as evidenced in the cancellation of diversity and inclusion initiatives in 2025). As Robert Meister wrote in one of the earliest anthologies on transitional justice in 1999, the United States is a country "still in transition from its history of slavery" and, we should add, settler colonization.[105] Needless to say, apart from the debate over the Confederate monuments and where to place them, if they are to be kept at all, the question about what gets preserved and memorialized as a "historical place" is a major part of this discussion, giving yet more evidence for architecture's central role. Out of the 95,214 properties listed in National Register of Historical Places, only 2 percent are related to African American history, 0.42 percent to women's history, 0.14 percent to Latino heritage, 0.10 percent to "Asian" history, and 0.03 percent to LGBTQ history.[106]

Evidence abounds. The Saturday Mothers movement is exemplary as a grassroots healing struggle that is also pushing for transitional justice to come. However, Turkey itself is a cautionary example that the transitional justice measures will fail when imposed from above by international organizations and manipulated by nation-states. During the reconstitution of democracy to put an end to the military junta that started with the 1980 coup, and as a result of its application to full membership into the European Union in 1987, Turkey is supposed to have gone through transitional justice measures, even though few citizens would recognize it as such. In 1995, the European Court of Human Rights ruled against Turkey and called the country to address its past. Enforced disappearance was one of the most important tests of this transition. In 1998, Amnesty International released a report about the Saturday Mothers.[107] As a response, the Turkish parliament launched a study on the disappearances, but this proved to be a move to please the international community, rather than to answer the demands of relatives. In 2002, the UN special rapporteur for disappearances, Francis Deng, was finally allowed in the country, and reported a high number of disappearances. In 2004, a committee to oversee the compensation laws to families was instituted as a response to pressure from the European Union and UN— there were about 1,500 cases pending in European Court of Human Rights at the time, and the court had ruled in one hundred to three hundred cases against Turkey since 1995.[108] In 2011, Prime Minister Recep Tayyip Erdoğan met representatives of the Saturday Mothers,[109] but this proved to be another disingenuous tactical step rather than a consequential transitional justice measure, as the Mothers have received even more police violence and lawsuits since then, and their meeting at the Galatasaray Square has been banned. Turkey has still not signed the UN convention against enforced disappearance despite the pressure from its human rights organizations, such as IHD (İnsan Hakları Derneği—Human Rights Association) and Yakay-Der (Yakınlarını Kaybedenlerle Yardımlaşma ve Dayanışma Derneği—Association in Solidarity with Those Who Lost Relatives), which have helped the Saturday Mothers.[110]

A similar process took place for other episodes of historical violence. As a founding member of the UN in 1945, and a party of the European Conventions on Human Rights and Fundamental Freedoms since 1954, Turkey signed many of the UN human rights conventions in the 1960s, but did not ratify them till the first decade of 2000s.[111] As a response to the European Union's demands to improve political pluralism and human rights and to rectify the Turkish-Greek relations as well as the Cyprus question, the government undertook several steps during the first decade of the twenty-first century, including the confrontation with the mandatory population exchanges with the Balkans (chapter 2). However, most transitional justice measures, large or small, have been foreclosed or manipulated with tactical steps if they were to question the "Turkishness" of the land and people.

In Anja Mihr's assessment, "the government only allowed top-down, strategically and tactically measured transitional justice process, controlling the narrative, the memorials, trials and reparations for the sole purpose of maintaining domestic stability under control of AKP."[112] Despite a few exceptions, this was true for the minor steps that concerned art and architecture. When the Ministry of Culture restored the Armenian Church of Akdamar as a museum, it publicized this as a demonstration of "Turkish tolerance" rather than a confrontation with past crimes. The *Statue of Humanity* (*İnsanlık Anıtı*) by sculptor Mehmet Aksoy that was begun in Kars in 2009 as the first Armenian-Turkish reconciliation memorial was destroyed in 2011 soon after the prime minister characterized it as a "freak." With its monumental scale that captured the landscape and could be observed from a distance, this memorial had sought to communicate with both sides of the border as an artistic call to peace, but was deemed ugly by the Turkish ruler. After the 2016 coup attempt, the government has employed the transitional justice toolkit, including purges and memorials, to consolidate power under the guise of democracy and to penalize democratic opposition and civil rights organizations that had nothing to do with the coup but criticized the ruling power.

To conclude, the story of the Saturday Mothers as a prism to look at historical state violence around the world has prompted me to acknowledge the necessity to both globalize and localize transitional justice, and to keep it as a continually open and self-reflective platform. A familiar and justified critique of the human rights regime and the international organizations such as the UN is their originary Eurocentrism and the hierarchical structure between nation-states. However, this critique needs to be qualified with several considerations. The common belief that human rights was "invented in the West" is ungrounded, because there was a network of people's revolutions in the eighteenth century when the concept of human rights emerged. "Non-Western" revolutions contributed to this process and constituted some of the major chronological markers, such as the Haitian Constitution of 1805 that abolished slavery.[113] The claim that only the Western philosophical tradition prepared the theory of human rights sounds offensive to many ears, as if values such as human fulfillment, dignity, and equality could not be found in Confucian, Hindu, Buddhist, Islamic, and many other world teachings.[114] Historically, the concept of human rights has been mobilized and improved in several episodes for anticolonial, antiracist, feminist, antislavery, and antiapartheid struggles. Today, the assumption that the torch of human rights is carried by "Western" nations is also ungrounded, as the United States, for one, has only signed five out of eighteen of the UN's additional human rights conventions.[115] The grassroots struggles and the writing of the international conventions to bring justice to historical crimes discussed above constitute a case in point that human rights activism and international legislation today are taking place with actors and in countries outside "the West." The global history of human rights needs to be written, first and foremost, by giving due acknowledgment to all its makers.

By globalizing transitional justice, I mean the struggles to have all states sign the international human rights conventions (even though this would be far from sufficient) while making the UN truly cosmopolitan. It is the *local* human rights associations and actors, such as the ones recorded in this chapter, who demand this global reach and carry out these struggles against their governments that refuse to participate in international law. Examples cited in this chapter point to the fact that struggles for transitional justice in general, and reparations in particular, have sometimes blocked but at other times learned from each other. One group's struggle for the recognition of pain could actually inspire and guide another's. It could help devise mechanisms of truth-telling, confrontation, and nonrecurrence, including survival testimonies, the naming of crimes, memorials, educational programs, repatriation protocols for cultural heritage objects, compensation norms, and "never again" movements. Globalizing transitional justice debates would allow us to see if and how a comparative analysis and dialogue can build solidarities, identify double standards, if any, and work toward overcoming them.

By localizing transitional justice, I mean the need to translate between international and local justice systems, because transitions have a chance to be effective only if they are participatory and bottom-up. The failure of top-down international pressures on Turkey is a case in point. Conceiving international and local justice, or UN and grassroots activism, as competitive struggles sabotages the protection of peoples. Instead, much could be achieved through complementary processes. A recent example of this, even if symbolic, was the mobilization of one of the eighteen UN conventions, the Convention on the Rights of the Child (1990), for the fight against climate change, when sixteen child petitioners including Greta Thunberg presented an official complaint over the violation of this convention in 2019.[116] With its devices to analyze space and give physical shape to human rights activism, architecture can take a proactive role in globalized, localized, and open transitional justice platforms.

A mother's right to mourn is also the world's right to heal.

2 Partition

When members of architect Aslı Özbay's team discovered a sunken communal space under piles of debris during the retrofitting of a group of Cappadocian buildings in the first decade of the twenty-first century, they came face to face with the long history of erasures that has shaped the environment in Anatolia and the Balkans to this day. The village was deserted, and many of the houses were either totally destroyed or left barely standing (figure 2.1). Once the team accidentally came across the void during construction in 1999, they kept removing the debris for two years until they reached the ground. What they found was an ancient Byzantine church, which had been used with minor changes as a caravanserai and a candle-oil workshop (Bezirhane) in the Seljuk and Ottoman times, until the village was abandoned and turned into a dumping area. Cappadocia, in south central Turkey, is a very special place due to its natural geography, formed in a geological process of volcanic eruptions and erosions that started millions of years ago. The "fairy chimneys" used as monasteries and ornamented with outstanding iconic paintings, as well as the built environment composed of rock-cut houses and vertical subterranean cities in tuff-stone caves, have uplifted emotions for many generations. How, you may ask, could a Byzantine church and an entire abandoned village be hidden in such a striking landscape? This chapter explores the intertwined stories of two communities, one departing from and the other arriving at the same village in Cappadocia, as a result of an international treaty signed in 1923. It weaves together the life and work experiences of Seraphim Rizos and Süreyya Aytaş, who, respectively, departed from and arrived in this Cappadocian village due to the treaty; and the architects Nikos Zoumboulidis and Aslı Özbay, who, respectively, were born there and came to live and work there. By connecting the story of this village to thousands of others that were affected by the same international pact, it makes a case for the harms of and struggles to heal from resettler nationalism.

Partitions and compulsory mass migrations have drawn the borders of modern countries, while simultaneously establishing ethnoreligious

Figure 2.1 A deserted village in Cappadocia. Uçhisar, ca. 2000. Photo: Aslı Özbay.

homogenization as a mandatory condition for the inauguration of nation-states. The cycle of wars, treaties, and state-sponsored dispossessions between Europe and Anatolia after the Ottoman-Russian War of 1877–78, continuing with the Balkan War and World War I and throughout the twentieth century, changed the demographic composition of these lands significantly. As one example, the 1923 "Exchange of Populations" (*Antallagi* in Greek, *Mübadele* in Turkish) between Greece and Turkey was in effect a partition that segregated the Muslim and the Christian communities of the Ottoman Empire, after it formally ended in 1922. The following pages concentrate on the dispossession, transportation, and resettling during and immediately after this compulsory mass migration, and ask how, if at all, the official and professional discourses of land settlement and architecture acknowledged the violence on which they were predicated. The chapter exposes a big contrast between the declarations of state agents and the experiences of those compelled to move. Reading migrant testimonies on both sides of the Aegean Sea and tracing architectural histories, I characterize this partition as a trauma imposed on these lands from which they are still trying to heal. Rather than assuming to stay neutral or taking sides with either the Greek or the Turkish official historiographies, I argue that it is possible to speak politically outside the polar narratives by disclosing this partition's architectural history from below. In other words, architectural history from the ground up may guide us to a transformative depolarization and a new solidarity between actors of the previously polarized communities. I suggest that the diplomatically supported compulsory population exchanges and the forced mass migrations of the twentieth century, taking place around the world, have created urban layers whose residues are still visible and still in need of healing. I discuss the aftermath of these population movements by tracing the experience of those who were displaced because of an ideology that emerged as if it were a remedy to ethnic violence—an ideology that I term *resettler nationalism*.

Phase 1. Dispossession: The Migration to End All Migrations

ARCHITECTURE AS AN INTERNATIONAL DISPOSSESSION ENGINE

In the aftermath of World War I, and as another international recognition of the new nation-states that came out of the Ottoman Empire, the Convention Concerning the Exchange of Greek and Turkish Populations was signed on January 30, 1923, as an annex to the Treaty of Lausanne, negotiated under the auspices of the League of Nations.[1] This "Exchange of Populations Treaty" mandated the compulsory migration of all Christian "Greeks" (*Rum*) in today's Turkey to Greece, and of all Muslim "Turks" in Greece to Turkey. It also legitimized the refugee status of those who had already moved between lands due to wars before 1923. Even though the precise numbers have been under dispute, the treaty affected close to 2 million people (figure 2.2). Numbers vary in accounts, and yet Greece's Muslim population decreased from roughly 20 percent to 6 percent as a result, while Turkey's non-Muslim population decreased from 20 percent to 2.5 percent due to the sum of wars, massacres, and population transfers.

Many called the Exchange of Populations a repatriation rather than a displacement. Fridtjof Nansen—the chief negotiator in 1923 and the League of Nations High Commissioner for Refugees—had won the Nobel Peace Prize for his work to "resettle, repatriate and provide aid to refugees."[2] The histories of this compulsory mass migration have been written separately from the nationalist perspectives of Greece and Turkey. In Greece, it was named the Asia Minor Disaster (i.e., the end of the Megali Idea, or the departure of Greeks from Anatolia), but cast as a success story of resettlement and Hellenization. In Turkey, Christian peoples' heritages were turned into relics and erased from public memory as if they had never lived on these lands, but the Lausanne Treaty was celebrated as bringing decolonization and victory in the War of Independence (i.e., freedom from Western capitulations during the Ottoman Empire and the post–World War I foreign occupation).[3] On both sides of the Aegean Sea, the statesmen characterized the population exchange as a cure to a problem rather than the cause of trauma; as an agreement that brought stability and peace to a region rather than one that unjustifiably and perpetually ripped people apart; as the end of war rather than the beginning of a new struggle and need for healing. To this day, some scholars define the international decision as a "necessary evil, the most humanitarian of logistically viable options,"[4] while others define it as a "segregation justified through racialized discourses of incommensurable differences."[5]

The Subcommittee of the Exchange of Prisoners and Populations in Lausanne decided to implement an irreversible and compulsory mass migration rather than employ the existing international laws of minority protection that were in effect in Europe at the time, or rather than regulate voluntary transfers and give individuals the right to self-determination, as was the case for other borders in Europe after World War I.[6] They divided the exchangeable populations residing in thousands of villages and cities across Anatolia, the Black Sea, Thrace, Macedonia, and east and west of the Aegean Sea into two purified categories, which assumed the exact alignment of religion, nation, and territory, regardless of the actual diversity of peoples and whether there were hostile or peaceful relations on the ground. To institute an ethnoreligious partition between lands meant exerting violence, not only because it enforced dispossession and migration on peoples but also because it ignored the diversity of social bonds. Many communities did not fit neatly into the flattened-out categories of the diplomats, including Albanians in Greece, Turkish-speaking Orthodox Christians of Cappadocia, Macedonian-speaking Muslims of the Thessaloniki (Salonica) region, Christian Orthodox Arabs, and the Orthodox Greeks who followed the Patriarchate in Damascus or in Kayseri, rather than the one in Constantinople/Istanbul. Many communities categorized as Greek according to the treaty spoke Turkish, and vice versa. Some of them said they had never heard of a country called Greece.[7]

Despite these inconsistencies, the languages, cultures, social norms, and individual attributes of these two religiously identified groups were considered so untranslatable between each other that the international powers must have deemed that these communities could continue on only after total separation. In effect, the statesmen thought homogenization was a mandatory principle for nation-states, and they simultaneously solidified it as an international norm of the twentieth century. The contradiction in this—that compulsory transfers such as slave trades and enforced dislocations had made much of the world's history but were now supposed to be violations of modern ethical standards—must have escaped the decision-makers. Another paradox was the division of peoples in relation to their religions in order to

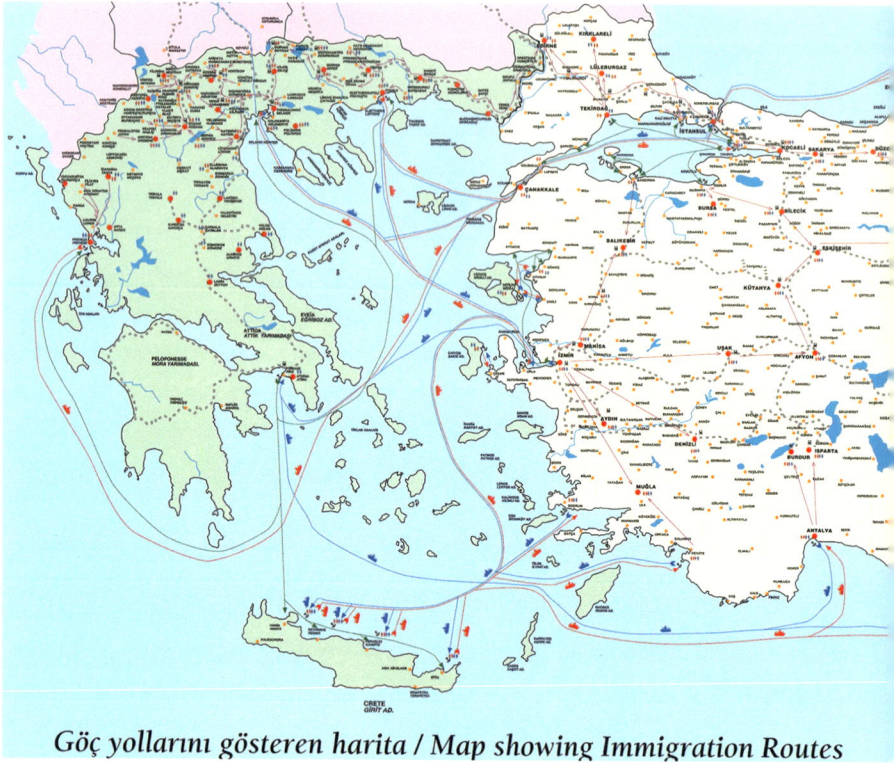

Göç yollarını gösteren harita / Map showing Immigration Routes

Figure 2.2 Map of migration routes between Greece and Turkey mandated by the Exchange of Populations Treaty of 1923. LMV Archives.

constitute a world order that was premised on the secular nation-state. The exchange treaty served as the legal formalization of a modern forced mass displacement of unprecedented magnitude, regulated by international law.

Surely, this was not the first time people voluntarily or involuntarily migrated. As a matter of fact, the Ottoman Empire managed a territory that cut across one of the five major nomadic areas of the world and resettled communities for centuries. As Reşat Kasaba overviews, the early to mid-Ottoman state structure integrated the nomadic tribes to help with the movement of goods and establish lines of communication. Moreover, migration was a major Ottoman policy in settling newly acquired territories, as either a form of punishment or an incentive by giving tax exemptions, which forced or encouraged both nomadic tribes and sedentary households to move. "The

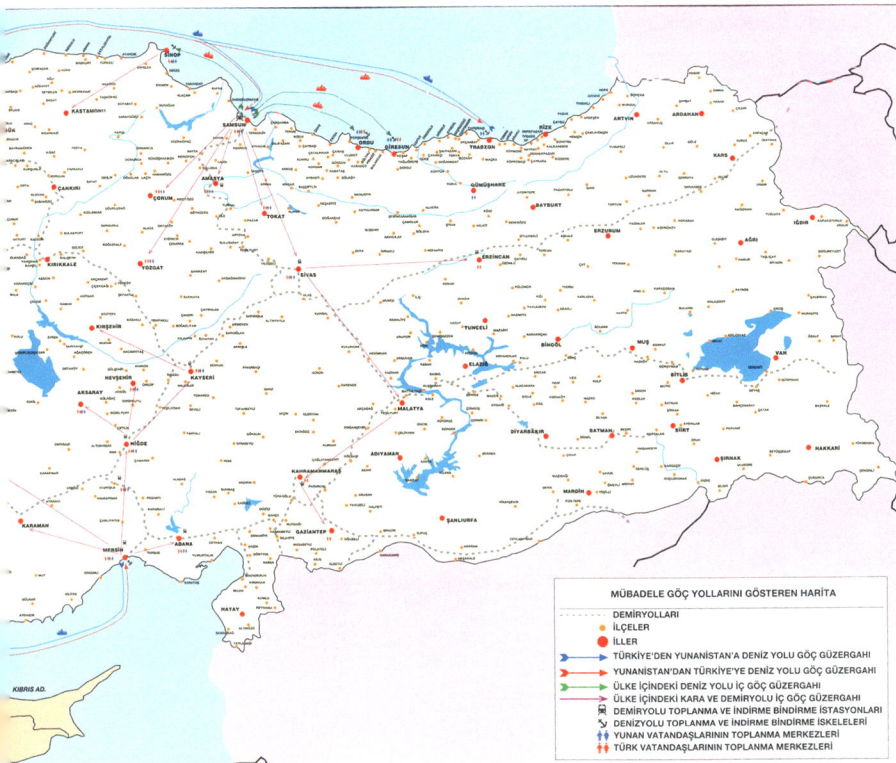

MÜBADELE GÖÇ YOLLARINI GÖSTEREN HARİTA
- - - - - DEMİRYOLLARI
● İLÇELER
● İLLER
→ TÜRKİYE'DEN YUNANİSTAN'A DENİZ YOLU GÖÇ GÜZERGAHI
→ YUNANİSTAN'DAN TÜRKİYE'YE DENİZ YOLU GÖÇ GÜZERGAHI
→ ÜLKE İÇİNDEKİ DENİZ YOLU İÇ GÖÇ GÜZERGAHI
→ ÜLKE İÇİNDEKİ KARA VE DEMİRYOLU İÇ GÖÇ GÜZERGAHI
🚊 DEMİRYOLU TOPLANMA VE İNDİRME BİNDİRME İSTASYONLARI
⚓ DENİZYOLU TOPLANMA VE İNDİRME BİNDİRME İSKELELERİ
👥 YUNAN VATANDAŞLARININ TOPLANMA MERKEZLERİ
👥 TÜRK VATANDAŞLARININ TOPLANMA MERKEZLERİ

superimposition of the long distance migrations onto the local movements created a highly fluid social environment throughout the territory, especially in Anatolia, where it became difficult to distinguish between the arriving, staying and departing tribes between the eleventh and fourteenth centuries."[8] The empire slowly transformed from a mobile and fluid to a sedentary society, starting with decrees to settle nomadic tribes during the seventeenth century and continuing with citizenship and immigration regulations during the nineteenth century, in an age when cosmopolitan sentiments transformed into ethnically pure nationalist ones. The "imagined communities" that came out of the Ottoman Empire, to use Benedict Anderson's famous definition of "nations," were not independent from Western ideas about the perceived modernization of the world through the construction of nation-states.[9] The Greek War of Independence (1821–29) had already led to the formation of modern Greece. During the making of the nation-states in the Balkans, 3.5 million people had already been subject to migration in multiple directions between 1912 and 1923 (see chapter 3).[10]

Against this background of centuries-long migrations and hybridizations, Lord Curzon, who coordinated the Lausanne conference, defined the 1923 population exchange as "the unmixing of peoples." As a British imperialist in India, Curzon was no stranger to dividing peoples based on his perceived ideas about religion and race, and he had already partitioned Bengal in 1905.[11] In other words, the 1923 treaty was arguably modeled on the ideas of the British imperialists in India; and, in turn, it served as a model for the UN's partition of India and Pakistan as well as of the partition plan for Palestine during the formation of Israel, both dating to 1947, or twenty-four years later. The 1923 treaty mandated the migration to end all migrations in Southeast Europe and West Asia.

Architecture holds a probing place in this population transfer. The exchange treaty made a clear distinction between the "movables" and the "immovables." Article 8 of the treaty reads: "Emigrants shall be free to take away with them or to arrange the transport of their movable property of every kind, without being liable on this account to the payment of any export or import duty or any other tax." Article 9 reads: "Immovable property, whether rural or urban, belonging to the emigrants, or to the communities, and movable property left by these emigrants or communities shall be liquidated in accordance with the following provisions by the International [Mixed] Commission."[12] Emigrants were free to carry or transport their "movable property," but "immovable property" had to be "liquidated." No wonder that the entire enterprise was called an "exchange," and that Nansen considered the negotiations as a technical problem involving economic matters, calling all else "folkish romanticism."[13] Namely, architecture had to be commodified so that its exchange value could be transported as the prerequisite of resettler nationalism.

The international contract reveals both the racial capitalist framework in nation building and architecture's mobilization for dispossession. As discussed in the introduction, I use the word *dispossession* here by building on and adding to Robert Nichols's critical theory that mediates between critique of capitalism and of settler colonialism.[14] Similarly, I do not use the word with claims to "first occupancy" or to validate the idea of possession, but to discuss the harms of conceptualizing land (and architecture) as property as well as the disenfranchisements that take place during the institutionalization of a property regime. Any partition of land is indeed a making of property and territory along which comes an often-unfair distribution. The making and transition of property regimes during the dissolution of the Ottoman Empire generated seizures of land and belongings that can hardly be categorized as fair exchanges. On the one hand, the exchange treaty relies on the identification of architecture as an immovable and commodifiable asset that could be given and taken away by the state so that peoples could be segregated in relation to the perceived racial and religious categories of a "nation." To claim that a contract can displace and resettle populations without violating their rights or dignity means to claim that lands, homes, workshops, and religious and community spaces are nothing but exchangeable goods. An international treaty that assumes masses of people can be justifiably ripped apart from their living spaces and resettled in others conceptualizes architecture as a landless, placeless machine, a commodified property, whose qualities can be carried and reproduced smoothly anywhere. On the other hand, the treaty relies on the unjustified assumption that there would be a fair exchange during the liquidation of immovables at a forced moment after military conflicts and through a process determined by an international committee. The majority of clauses in the Exchange of Populations Treaty outlined the provisions that regulated how such a liquification was to be made. However, these provisions proved to be prone to countless disputes and messy transactions.[15] Some migrants sold their underpriced properties before leaving; others were promised compensation of equal wealth, as if this was easy to calculate under postconflict conditions. Eventually many migrants became poorer and were forced to accept direr living conditions, as the history of architecture from below in the following pages demonstrates. In the hands of the international committee, architecture became a dispossession engine.

THE CONTRAST

There was a big contrast, however, between the declarations of state agents and the experiences of those involved. The more I traced the dispossession, transportation, and resettlement paths from the perspective of enforced migrants, the more I came to identify this "exchange" as state violence and international-law viciousness rather than diplomacy and peace. One can already sense the hints of this contrast in the visual documents of the period. Iconic photographs taken during the League of Nations meeting in Lausanne stand in stark contrast to the lesser known images of the population exchange. At the League of Nations, a group of men representing the participating countries—Britain; France; Greece; Italy; Japan; the Kingdom of Serbs, Croats and Slovens; Romania; the Soviet Union; Turkey; and the United States—in ironed official attire look at the camera to declare the new international order that would regulate territories in the Balkans and Anatolia thereafter.[16] As their entitled looks confirm, the participating diplomats must have perceived the peace treaty as a resolution to long-overdue problems.

The experiences of those who were subject to this population exchange, however, differed significantly from the visual and verbal traces left behind by the diplomats, as well as the celebratory official histories of the polarized nation-states. It would be useful to know that individual testimonies of enforced migrants reached the public only around the year 2000. The Center for Asia Minor Studies (CAMS) in Athens identified 2,163 settlements subject to exchange in Asia Minor (Anatolia) and conducted research on 1,375 of them by interviewing 5,051 migrants ("informants" in the center's parlance) under the directorship of the folk music scholar Melpo Merlier.[17] While the musicological research had started as early as 1930, the ethnographic archive was undertaken between 1948 and 1970. However, these individual testimonies were published and translated only by the end of the century.[18] Moreover, the center's activity was perceived as a biased unscientific collection composed of peaceful stories and reflective of a "bourgeois interest in oral folk" and the "amateur pastime of an educated lady of leisure."[19] In Turkey, the individual testimonies of migrants started being collected only at the very end of the twentieth century and were published as works of literature rather than oral history because of the perceived unpreparedness of the public for the facts.[20] The Foundation of Lausanne Treaty Emigrants actively compiled individual recollections after its establishment in 2001.[21] I use these migrant testimonies and archival photographs as evidences of a counternarrative to the official accounts of international law and national historiography.

The protagonists of this chapter, Seraphim Rizos and Süreyya Aytaş, both fell into the treaty's indeterminate categories. Rizos's community resided in the Cappadocian town of Sinasos (today's Mustafapaşa, in its Turkish name)[22] and it was made up of Turkish-speaking Christians who wrote in the Greek alphabet, known as Karamanlı.[23] His father, Nikolaos Rizos, was the author of *Kappadokika* (1856), which was one of the first books to draw attention to both Cappadocian Orthodox culture and their script, and which became a frequent reference for those subject to exchange after they settled in Greece.[24] The nationality of Karamanlıs indeed became a matter of competition during the dissolution of the Ottoman Empire between those who claimed they were Turkish Christians and those who claimed they were Greeks who had to adopt Turkish language during the Ottoman rule. This rivalry even materialized as the establishment of the Turkish Orthodox Christian Patriarchate under Papa Eftim, as distinct from the other Christian denominations as well as the Patriarchate in Istanbul.[25] The status of Karamanlıs was a matter of dispute during the deliberations in Lausanne, as the Turkish delegation wanted to keep them exempt from the exchange at one point, just like the Greeks of Istanbul and Muslims of Thrace who continued their residency in Turkey and Greece, respectively. The number of Turkish-speaking Orthodox Christians of Anatolia has been under dispute and varies between 140,000 and 500,000 in different sources.[26]

Ironically, soon after Turkish-speaking Greeks left Sinasos, the people of Aytaş's village, Jerveni (in the Kastoria region of Macedonia), were brought in, even though they did not know a word of Turkish but spoke a special Macedonian dialect. In her grandfather's recollection, they found themselves dropped in the village square after a two-month-long tough journey. The locals who saw their miserable condition brought some food, but when they thanked them in their own language, the locals started screaming "these are foreigners, these are infidels," causing a fight on that very first day.[27]

Rizos's and Aytaş's families had somewhat different experiences before departing their hometowns. Rizos testified to mutually supportive and friendly relations in Sinasos: "The Turks in our area showed no joy in our Exchange. . . . . The profound reasons why Muslim people did not want us to leave were, in my view, these: Our same everyday needs of life, the same sorrows and the same joys, our common sun and sky, our common mother earth, had slowly but surely, imperceptibly, brought us closer to one another. . . . . When famine began to bedevil our village during the war, . . . fifty of our Turks' impoverished children ate in our soup kitchen . . . When later, I went to Niğde to ask for state aid, [our request was granted.] The inspector . . . said to me 'I thank you very much, Seraphim Efendi. We shall never forget your gesture.'"[28] Migrants from Aytaş's hometown Jerveni spoke of a happy existence that deteriorated with the Balkan War: "My childhood was very nice . . . But then everything went upside down. All of us used to gather in one house in fear. The news was always bad. They said they would kill all the Muslims. . . . [We heard] thirty-five of us were trapped by bandits on the road, and killed. One of them watched a friend beheaded and survived by faking his own death."[29]

Similarly, the oral histories in both Greece and Turkey revealed mixed reminiscences of the multiethnic life before the Lausanne Treaty. Those who participated in the Balkan War (1912–13) or the Greek-Turkish War (1919–22), and the civilians who lived in the conflict areas, narrated killings and beatings, destructions and lootings, imprisonments and escapes,[30] while others testified to peaceful and supportive relations between the groups that the treaty separated. Many blamed an anonymous group of bandits rather than their neighbors when there was a conflict. In any event, almost everyone spoke of being traumatized and criticized the resettlement. In their testimonies, ex-Cappadocians overwhelmingly spoke of a friendly coexistence rather than a brutal civil war. "When we learned about the exchange," Kalistenis

Mustakidu said, "we were very surprised. Could this be possible? Could an entire village be sent to Greece?. . . . The Turks from the neighboring villages kept pouring in, telling us not to leave, with tears in their eyes."[31] Sofia Devletoğlu spoke of a Mr. Süleyman who unlocked the door to let her take her valuables, then under state custody, and replace them with junk so that she did not lose her wealth.[32] Such stories remind us of the importance of mid-level bureaucrats who showed some resistance rather than absolute obedience to state's orders, and who could avoid the "banality of evil," to evoke Hannah Arendt's explanation of the spread of fascism.

Phase 2. Transportation: Sailing for a New Life?

THE LAST SIGHT

Just before his enforced migration, Rizos decided to make a photo album of the buildings that were defined as "immovables" in the exchange treaty. Cappadocia, the most attractive tourist destination in contemporary Turkey, is geographically very special, and who can blame Rizos for wanting to capture the images of his town one last time? Not owning a camera, he asked the wealthier Pantazidis sons from the neighboring village of Prokopi/Ürgüp for help; they photographed the surrounding villages in June and July 1924 (figure 2.3; see also figure 2.14).[33] Rizos also made a book with these images, amounting to nothing short of a comprehensive history of the residents, arts, religion, governing structure, education system, crafts, farming, everyday life, customs, and songs and dances of this stunning land. As he was speaking of the dwellings and chapels carved into geological formations, he wrote, "They were veritable fortresses, cut in enormous sandstone rocks. Their doorways, tall as the height of man and half a meter deep, were set high up on precipitous surfaces of the rocks. . . . You went into a large rock-cut cavern. At the far end you made out other doorways, that communicated with caves one after another and very often one on top of the other. High up on the ceiling you saw another hole, which communicated with another chain of hideouts."[34] Rizos spoke of his own house in a rock-cut set of buildings surrounded by vineyards and apricot trees: "The greater part of my family house was hewn from an enormous trapezoidal rock. . . . The rock was fifty meters high, in some places abrupt and precipitous, and in others with gentle slopes, terraced, planted and with rock-cut houses" (see figure 2.26). Then he went on to tell every single detail about their grape-pressing installations, cisterns, ovens, terraces, the storage of grapes and dried leaves, all rock-cut in their own ways. Acknowledging the delicate craftsmanship of the Turkish

Figure 2.3 Seraphim Rizos, with Pantazidis sons, Cappadocian village. From Sinasos album, 1924.

Kufu family of stone-carvers, he continued: "The hewing of the bathroom is so fine and beautiful that it immediately draws your attention and you realize that it is the work of an artisan devoted to his job. Perhaps it is also due to the more precise tools. You think it is a work of art, that it has been carved" (see figure 2.31).[35]

The Sinasos photo album was not only a farewell to one's home, but it was also a eulogy to a town that was about to lose its residents and even its name. As the last sight before evacuation, it is unique in the visual catalog of the Greek-Turkish population exchange. However, there are ample real or imagined verbal descriptions of enforced migrants' final looks at their hometowns before deportation: those who traveled backward in the carriage in order to see the last tip of the minaret disappear, those who put the luggage on the ground to have a good look and waved goodbye with their hats, or those who watched the land from the ship until it became the flat horizon.[36] Lazaros Takadopoulos, the teacher of Sinasos and the secretary of the Exchange Committee, was the last Greek to leave town. On October 2, 1924, he sent a telegram to Istanbul: "Today, the last of us who remained in Sinasos are also leaving . . . Sinasos. My dearest homeland. I address to you my last goodbye."[37]

The photographs in Rizos's Sinasos album stand in stark contrast to the disciplinary photographs of the institutions that were established to oversee the international treaty's biopolitical intervention. The dislocation, transportation, temporary accommodation, and relocation of hundreds of thousands of people, along with their belongings and animals, who came from countless cities, towns, and small villages across the lands, was a massive management challenge. The Mixed Commission of the League of Nations (established in September 1923) implemented the convention, mediated between the two governments, and supervised the liquidation of immovable and movable properties. In Greece, the international Refugee Settlement Committee (RSC), coordinated by the League of Nations, took over the task from the Refugee Relief Fund and oversaw the process after November 1923. In Turkey, following a long tradition of commissions that have been settling refugees since the 1877–78 Ottoman-Russian War,[38] the Ministry of Exchange, Reconstruction, and Resettlement, founded in October 1923, settled exchange migrants until its tasks were transferred to the Ministry of Interiors in 1924.[39]

Even though the League of Nations was supposed to be a neutral third party, the RSC's first president, Henry Morgenthau—the former US ambassador in Istanbul—clearly upheld the Western glorification of the Greeks as his own ancestors while simultaneously fostering racism against their "others": He wrote:

Moved to profound pity as I was, it would not have been unnatural to think of these people [Greek refugees] only as objects of charity— poor wretches like the poverty-stricken hordes of India, to be *governed* back toward subsistence, rather than *guided* back to their natural independence and self-sufficiency. . . . To an American's eyes these Greeks were not hapless dependents, but equals, the worthy descendants of a glorious ancestry, the capable brothers of one of the ablest and most enterprising of modern peoples. . . . And they are not, as in Turkey for example, the brilliant exceptions at the top of a stolid mass. They are rather, as in America, the best representatives of a race of intelligent, ambitious, energetic people, evolved by competition with worthy competitors into acknowledged leadership.[40]

This quotation exposes the stark Western/non-Western divide in RSC president Morgenthau's racist mind between those superior races who deserved independence and sovereignty, like the Greeks and Americans, and those who were allegedly incapable of self-governance and had to be governed, like Indians and Turks.

The migration officers made systematic collections of full-body and portrait photographs of the displaced individuals, and produced IDs using the camera to register, regulate, and control human bodies in a way similar to how photography had already been employed for colonial and imperial purposes.[41] Military and commercial ships carried the migrants between Greece and Turkey.[42] Photographs taken in port cities and on ships that show masses of bodies being regulated between lands are in sharp contrast to the ones that came out of the slick spaces in Lausanne, but they do not necessarily serve a different purpose (figure 2.4). They imply the magnitude of the event and its technical difficulty, but do not portray the deaths, dispossession, pauperization, or the loss of property. They must have been intended to present the exchange as a solution to a problem, a necessity, a repatriation carrying masses to their new healing homes after conflict and a tough journey. But photographs always have the power to subvert their captions and the intentions of their commissioners. For instance, some taken onboard ships during the exchange show mothers sitting on deck, forced to carry their newborn babies on a multiweek journey toward multiyear temporary accommodation. When the camera zooms in on faces among the masses of bodies, the resulting photographs show trauma and anger rather than enthusiasm for a peaceful and stable life with fellow nationals. They indeed put a human face to international law and nation formation (figure 2.5).

The sight of arriving migrants must have raised a tiny bit of doubt in the minds of the international community who were tasked with finding them new homes. Upon seeing a ship's arrival in Greece, the RSC's president, Morgenthau, was appalled that seven thousand people were crowded into a ship meant for two thousand:

> A more tragic sight could hardly be imagined. . . . They were packed like sardines upon the deck, a squirming, writhing mass of human misery. They had been at sea for four days [many traveled much more than that]. There had not been space to permit them to lie down to sleep, there had been no food to eat, there was no access to any toilet facilities. For those four days and nights, many had stood on the open deck, drenched by an autumn rain, pierced by the cold night wind, and blistered by the noonday sun. They came ashore in rags, hungry, sick, covered with vermin, hallow-eyed, exhaling the horrible odor of human filth—bowed with despair.[43]

Figure 2.4 Transportation of exchanged individuals during the Greek-Turkish partition, 1924. CAMS Archives.

Figure 2.5 The camera zooms in to show the faces of exchanged individuals during transportation, 1924. Union of Smyrneans.

At the time, there were only a couple public critics of the exchange per se, such as Pierre Fauchille, who in 1925 wrote, "Populations cannot be treated as a herd of animals where somebody can negotiate control over them."[44]

Years later, migrant testimonies filled in the gaps in these photographs and written accounts. In addition to the last sight before deportation, the transportation itself made a series of inerasable marks in practically every migrant's memory. For instance, among Rizos's community, four hundred Karamanlı women and children were detained in the Haydarpaşa Train Station in Istanbul waiting for the results of the Lausanne conference to see if they would be allowed to stay home. They were among the two hundred thousand Greeks who, while waiting for the results, were stranded in refugee camps in Istanbul, where an epidemic broke out and killed more than 1,400 people.[45] Rizos's neighbors, the Turkish-speaking Orthodox Christians of Prokopi (Ürgüp), walked on foot to Ulukışla, took the train to Mersin, and from there traveled by ship to the Greek port of Piraeus in a journey that lasted a month. After staying in quarantine for days, they lived in tents between 1925 and 1927, when sixty of them died due to malaria, to be eventually relocated to the town of Nea Prokopi.[46] Aytaş's family left Jerveni for Thessaloniki in July 1924, and spent thirty-five days at sea on two different ships while being transported to Mersin, from where they were taken first to Ulukışla, then to Niğde, then to Ürgüp, before walking to Mustafapaşa (Sinasos). They started as 480 people, but lost 120 to epidemics on the way.[47] Flu, tuberculosis, and malaria were the common diseases during the exchange, killing at least 20 percent of the migrants, according to the League of Nations (but the actual numbers must be higher).[48]

Almost everyone remembers that the dead bodies were thrown into the sea during transportation. From slaves being traded across the Atlantic to refugees crossing the Mediterranean, the image of the dead falling down into waters from ships that carried them to enforced new homes looms in distant and recent memory. Is it possible to tell this incident from a victim's viewpoint, given the impossibility for the conventional documents to represent the experience of the dead under the depths of the sea? Christina Sharpe devises ways to do so, and writes what might have happened to the dead bodies who were thrown into the ocean during the transatlantic slave trade. Combining poetic images with scientific evidence, she writes:

Once in the water that thrown overboard person would have experienced the circular or bobbing motion of the wake and would have been carried by that wake for at least a short period of time. . . . And then there were the sharks that always traveled in the wake of slave ships. . . . What happened to the bodies? By which I mean, what happened to the components of their bodies in salt water? . . . the atoms of those people who were thrown overboard are out there in the ocean even today. They were eaten, organisms processed them, and those organisms were in turn eaten and processed, and the cycle continues.[49]

During the Christian-Muslim partition, the ships crossing the Aegean Sea made a similar mark in migrants' memory. Parents hid their children's death until they could not hide the smell; Aytaş's relatives remember that one mother jumped into sea with her deceased baby.[50] Fiction writers have been particularly moved by such facts and have written stories about migrants who kept looking for lands "where the fish did not eat dead babies."[51]

Phase 3. Land Settlement and Demographic Engineering

Disasters that produce shock effects in communities have usually generated two-phased architectural responses. First, there are the emergency relief spaces in the acute phases, such as medical treatment and mass quarantine locations, and "temporary" shelters after disasters that caused displacement. Sometimes this phase is so long that it confines entire generations to a state of emergency. Second, there are the presumably "permanent" solutions purporting to turn life back to the "new normal," many of which have fallen short of making true reforms or have constructed inequalities and discriminations in their subsequent societies.

ATHENS AS A REFUGEE ARRIVAL CITY

Athens served as the arrival city for the exchanged migrants from Turkey to such an extent that the temporary settlements from this time made impacts on its urban development throughout the twentieth century. Some of the residues of these arrival zones are still detectable both physically and morphologically. Migrant builders and craftsmen of the Ottoman Empire had already taken fundamental roles in the founding phase of Athens as the modern Greek capital.[52] The bureaucrats and architects of resettlement after the compulsory population transfer were also among those who forcibly migrated. Architect and engineer Constantine Sgoutas—a native of Istanbul—is reported to have built about twenty thousand dwellings in five settlements in

Athens by employing refugees who made up 90 percent of the workforce.[53] Leonidas Bonis, Kleon Krantonellis, and Patroklos Karantinos, born in Giresun, Kavala, and Istanbul, respectively, built some of the most well-known modernist icons of Greece, such as the Attika building and House in Plaka, both in Athens, and the Archaeological Museum in Thessaloniki.[54] Of all the people who settled in Greece as a result of the 1923 population exchange, none other than architect Nikos Zoumboulidis from Sinasos fits the story of this chapter better. Educated as an architect in Istanbul and Berlin, he designed some of the finest buildings in Athens and Nea Sinasos, as well as the architectural identity of the National Bank of Greece, with branches all over the country, as discussed below.[55] Another is Apostolos Doxiadis, who had arrived in Athens when Greece signed an exchange convention with Bulgaria during the dissolution of the Ottoman Empire in 1919, as a result of which fifty-three thousand people left Greece and thirty thousand left Bulgaria. Apostolos Doxiadis became the Greek Minister of Refugees, Social Welfare, and Public Health in 1922, and took an important role in re-settling the exchanged populations arriving from Turkey that this chapter records.[56] His son, Constantinos Doxiadis, who was also "exchanged" with the 1919 agreement, would become the world-influential planner and architect whose career spanned the entire Global South and North America and whose work in Ottoman successor states will be discussed in chapters 4 and 5.

The Greek-Turkish population exchange officially started on November 10, 1923. As a result of the arrival of approximately 1.2 million "exchanged" individuals, one in every four people in Greece was an immigrant waiting for resettlement. In Greece, the international Refugee Settlement Committee (RSC) identified 786,431 refugees who had already arrived before the Lausanne Treaty. By March 1923, 533,240 of them were receiving daily funds for food and medication from the Refugee Relief Fund, which was supported by international organizations such as the Red Cross and Near East Relief.[57] The refugees in Greece were camping in emergency relief spaces, including on the slopes of the Acropolis and in school buildings, public baths, and railway stations. Of all the existing public spaces that were appropriated for the crisis, the Athens Opera House was the most striking, where each family camped in one of the theater boxes (figure 2.6).

The migration bureaucrats in Athens functioned by applying racial categories that planted seeds of discrimination within the new society. A commentator remarked: "The streets of Athens were transformed by the surging multitude that now invaded them. . . . Strange dialectics of Greek assailed the ear. The eye was caught by outlandish peasant costumes from interior

Figure 2.6

Migrants temporarily settled in the theater boxes of the Opera House of Athens, 1923. Courtesy Henry Morgenthau.

Asia Minor."[58] Morgenthau identified the migrants arriving from Turkey as people whose "virtues" were blocked because of their "enforced association with inferior peoples" and because their "destiny has been wrapt up for centuries, with those of the backward Turks."[59] Even to this day, historians describe the migrants with stereotypical tropes of Western Orientalism that look down on them: "Their identity was Greek, but they spoke many languages . . . and had strange ways of thinking, and alien ways of both cultivation and of doing business."[60] A 1926 League of Nations report categorized the migrants arriving in Greece based on their departure places with striking stereotypes, even though it insisted on their racial purity: "Among those brothers by race, there is a complete identity of feeling, aspirations and national and religious traditions, but, having lived in different countries and districts, they differ in character, temperament and mentality." Those arriving from inner Anatolia who were "living in the midst of Turks and Kurds, had characteristics of Asiatic peoples being backward, submissive and timid." Cappadocians were "serious and reflective, hardworking and energetic, enterprising and practical." Those from Smyrna were "true Ionians in their individualism." Pontus showed great variety "from the rough heavy and dull-witted type to the subtlest of Greeks." Those from Kars were "industrious and supple-minded," from Tiflis "less civilized."[61] As the founding scholar of the Greek-Turkish exchange, Renée Hirschon, assessed, these stereotypes had long-lasting reverberations in Athens and discriminated neighborhoods along class and ethnic lines.[62] The authors of the international report must have missed the contradiction that they were dividing into separate essential categories a group of people whom they were eager to identify as one race that needed to be unmixed from other races. The League of Nations report exposed the incongruity of the entire exchange enterprise that was instituted by the league itself.

Makeshift sheds were constructed around Athens in Kokkinia, Kaisariani, Nea Smyrna, Neos Kosmos, Vyronas, and Nea Ionia, which later became permanent neighborhoods. These were "tents pieced out of burlap bags, or huts extemporized out of the ubiquitous five-gallon Standard Oil cans" according to the RSC records.[63] Period photographs confirm that the shelters were initially constructed from fragile materials such as cloth tents and tin roofs. They were built on ad hoc street patterns that organized their community relations, rather than on grid plans that characterize official camps. Soon after, wooden constructions replaced huts and tents when refugee aid supplied more permanent materials (figure 2.7). For example, as an arrival zone for exchanged migrants, Nea Smyrna initially emerged with one- to two-story sparsely placed houses, but soon flourished into a wealthy neighborhood with the construction of a school, a church, a cinema, villas, a large four-story orphanage, and a canonic municipal building well before the 1950s.[64]

Dourgouti in Neos Kosmos was one of the earliest settlements for ex-Ottoman migrants. Named as the "labyrinthine settlement of Armenians" in old maps, and home to Armenians who arrived in 1914 from the Ottoman Empire and founded the Armenian Catholic Church in 1925 here, as well as home to exchanged migrants who arrived from Turkey with the 1923 treaty and to internal migrants who moved in throughout the midcentury, Dourgouti grew into a large district composed of informally built single-story wooden houses, finished with ad hoc materials, along nonorthogonal streets.[65] The movie *Magiki Polis* (*The Magic City*), directed by Nikos Koundouros, provides an unmatched visual documentation of the informal district in 1954, which has since then been completely rebuilt. As the camera moves through

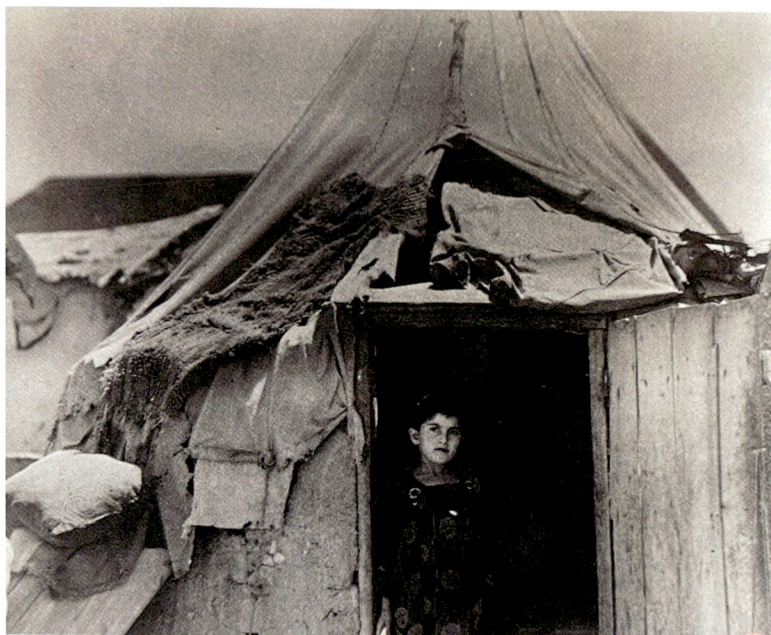

Figure 2.7 Cloth and wood tent at a temporary settlement for refugees and exchanged migrants in Athens, 1922–23. CAMS Archives.

the dense, narrow streets, the viewer watches the contrast between modern Greece and this refugee neighborhood, as well as the solidarity between migrants in their modest interior spaces: women collect water from wells and dry laundry on verandas and balconies, children play in streets, and cats and dogs wander peacefully among humans.[66] Dourgouti was also the target of official housing operations. Located here were Italika, one of the first formal migrant housing complexes, composed of twenty-four single-story houses in six rows, and funded with war reparations from Italy administered by the League of Nations, and the still-standing canonic social housing complex of the 1930s that integrated refugees (see figure 2.13). In 1965, with the slogan "Death to shacks," Prime Minister George Papandreou started the process of this urban fabric's erasure and laid the foundations of the larger, taller multifamily buildings that make up Dourgouti today.[67]

As another arrival zone of exchanged migrants in Athens, Kaisariani was initially built in an informal way as a refugee relief space but then grew into a large neighborhood with many urban functions. Today, some of the "refugee" (πρόσφυγας) houses still stand in the neighborhood next to five- to six-story or higher multifamily apartment buildings (figure 2.8). The original

Figure 2.8 Kaisariani neighborhood in Athens, ca. 1925 and 2022. CAMS Archives; photo: Esra Akcan, 2022.

houses of migrants are low-rise structures on smaller plots of land with red tile roofs, worn-out walls covered with graffiti, and aging door and window frames. Sometimes they constitute a row on a street; at other times they stand isolated in stark contrast to taller new buildings that are located in adjacent lots. Some of these houses are vacated, but many are still occupied. A few of them have been upgraded with new red tiles, larger glazing, and verandas.

Some have been appropriated as art spaces and restaurants with large shop windows. While these physical remnants of the partition are still visible in today's Athens, a hidden layer also manifests itself in the urban morphology. Parts of Kaisariani are made of narrower urban blocks as a sediment of the refugee arrival zones. Chapter 3 discusses the same condition in Istanbul. These urban districts prove the enduring debris of postdisaster settlements in world cities.

Urban and architecture historians have pointed out that many of the neighborhoods originally built as temporary refugee arrival and emergency spaces remained as "unfinished shabby structures and a culture of political dissent" well into the 1960s.[68] Eventually, scholars calculated that 350,000 migrants were settled in Athens, almost doubling the city's population. While the above-mentioned areas were initially built as temporary solutions but continued as informal settlements, the official settlement operation added regular housing with more durable materials. By 1929, the RSC had built 27,343 houses in 125 urban quarters, in addition to the nine thousand already built by the government.[69] After another Greece-Turkey treaty in 1930, the two governments agreed to freeze the process of property liquidation, which meant that the migrants could not receive their remaining payments, causing much spite and political negotiation for years to come.[70] Master planning of Athens as the new "Royal Seat and Capital City" had become one of the most productive policies since 1834.[71] However, as a result of the separation of Town Planning and Refugee Settlement offices due to the urgency and magnitude of the housing shortage, city officials put existing master plans on hold and allocated areas that had been reserved for public health and green space as new refugee zones. In Alexandra Yerolympos's words, the result was "uncoordinated and unsustainable, . . . [the] aspiration to produce urban plans that would combine developmental goals and modern spatial and functional requirements within a reformist approach was never fulfilled. The modern Greek city was thus turned into a home-owner refugee settlement . . . which scars the Greek landscape up to the present day."[72]

RESETTLEMENT AND AGRICULTURE

Specifically tasked with the permanent resettlement and integration of migrants into the production chain, the RSC prioritized agricultural settlements. Many communities were settled in new villages after living for years in the temporary tents described above. It is reported that by 1928, the RSC had created two thousand rural settlements all over Greece, and settled 578,824 people on farmlands (8,668 were settled by the government).[73] Morgenthau remembers how he and other Greek officials, including A. Doxiadis, worked on the financing of refugees' temporary accommodation and new constructions. They took loans internationally, including from the Bank of England, and negotiated the legal property status of *çiftliks* (farms) that had been left empty by the departure or absence of Turkish landowners.[74] Rizos's community of Sinasos was among those settled on rural land. They were relatively fortunate in self-determination, as they managed to select their location with the help of their connections in Athens and Istanbul. During the investigation process, they rejected five different locations because of the lack of public transport, long distance to harbors, marshy and unhealthy lands, proximity to the Albanian border, or "the alien customs and language of the inhabitants."[75] Finally, they selected the island of Evia (Euboea), where 450 hectares of land was expropriated to be given to their migrant community in conjunction with the refugee settlement procedures. Their village was named Nea (New) Sinasos in 1940, just as many towns and urban neighborhoods in today's Greece are named in reference to the departure place of the migrants who arrived with the Exchange of Populations. Their neighboring community from Prokopi (Ürgüp) settled in Nea Prokopi where the Ottoman Ahmet Ağa's *çiftlik* was expropriated.[76]

On the other side of the Aegean Sea in Turkey, due to the immigrants arriving during and after the war, the officials estimated that 1.5 million people were homeless.[77] Arriving migrants were temporarily accommodated in hostels that were retrofitted from vacated artilleries and charity foundations.[78] If one were to assume the successful application of a seventeen-point hostel regulation issued in November 1923, each family had its own private space; everyone slept on beds and nobody on wood or earth; all rooms were heated, lit, secured, and in healthy condition; there was running water and sanitary staff; a doctor awaited in large hostels; and a gendarme was on duty. The local community brought food to the migrants every day who stayed for a maximum of three days.[79] However, records on the ground painted a much grimmer picture, reporting on migrants being dragged from place to place before getting settled in their permanent places, families being separated and sent to wrong towns, and some giving up their rights to housing and compensation out of despair.[80]

All over the land in both countries, some immigrants were settled in houses vacated by emigrants. In Aytaş's village in today's Greece, for instance, the two exchanged populations overlapped due to the gap between departure and arrival times. In an interstitial time and as a hybrid solution between temporary and permanent housing, her grandparents' generation shared their houses with Greeks arriving from Sinop in today's Turkey for six months. When Süreyya Aytaş conducted her interviews in the 1990s, she found that some neighbors mentioned mutual hostility and fear, whereas others spoke of living in isolated rooms but helping each other with cooking. Even though a large number of communities were living in peace together before the exchange, the new living situation brought controversy rather than peace. Aliye Özbay remembers becoming a foreigner in her own house and complains that the newcomers cooked her chickens, which were her source of income.[81] Their village was not unique. Other testimonies also mention the inappropriate matching of home-shares. Three migrant families from Turkey were brought into Mustafa Acar's house who were craftspeople and had no clue about farming. "Rather than feeding the animals and getting produce, they kept killing and eating the animals."[82]

These mismatching stories during the temporary housing stage were only a prelude to a much more permanent state apparatus. The long-term relocation of migrants involved two questions about the built environment: on which lands to settle the migrants in the new national geography, and into which houses? In Turkey, the government quickly identified ten regions and settled communities arbitrarily.[83] Craftsmen were sent to farms; tobacconists were brought to Samsun and Bolu, but given lands whose soil was unsuitable for tobacco; those in need of grape farms and olive orchards were mixed up; farmers who had arrived with their cows and mules in Kayseri were given urban houses and had to share their apartments with their farm animals;[84] migrants who settled in Greek vineyards cut the trees as they did not know the fruit was edible.[85] As a result, some former Greek towns such as Levissi/ Kayaköy were completely abandoned and soon became ruins, because the newly settled communities did not have the means or know-how to sustain their livelihood in those locations (figure 2.9).

Moreover, the League of Nations' Mixed Commission was supposed to oversee the liquidation of migrants' property, but many complained about getting much less than their former property's value in their new lands. In one of the earliest scholarly assessments in 1940, Mihri Belli used the league's documents and calculated that the Exchange of Populations had exploitative economic impacts on both communities and countries.[86] Testimonies from the ground confirm this fact. The existing building stock of abandoned and forcibly vacated houses was to be distributed to the treaty's migrants as well as to political and disaster refugees, veterans, and migrants arriving from elsewhere.[87] A 1915 regulation had allowed the settlement of Balkan War migrants (*mühacir*) in forcibly vacated Armenian villages.[88] However, in the

Figure 2.9 Abandoned houses in Levissi/Kayaköy, Turkey. Photo: Esra Akcan, 2018.

war-torn and postgenocide context, there was no reliable account of vacated and abandoned property. Empty Greek and Armenian houses, especially the wealthy ones, were not necessarily distributed to migrants or refugees, but seized by government officials and opportunist locals.[89] For example, when Aytaş's village got "exchanged" and arrived in Sinasos/Mustafapaşa upon the departure of Rizos's family, only one hundred of the six hundred abandoned houses were left for them, according to official records. The rest were occupied by locals.[90] The architect Arif Hikmet Koyunoğlu mentioned that countless houses deserted by "exchange" emigrants were being sold for underpriced amounts, but he refused to buy one of those houses that were dispossessed "with tears on their walls."[91] It should be plausible to trace the precise roots of economic inequality in the upcoming years in Turkey to the state-controlled but half-legal and uneven distribution of property during the resettlement process of the inaugural years.[92]

These mistakes did not go unnoticed in the Parliament: the Deputy Esat Bey criticized the "misery injected on the migrants due to the government's mistakes of settling people from plains to mountains, and mountains to plains."[93] Historians who use state records as their sources have explained these missettlement cases as understandable glitches in the institutional chaos of a nation-building process in a war-torn land. The numbers to be resettled were so immense, time so short, survey of existing stocks so unreliable, and resources so slim that most migrants were settled arbitrarily in rural lands that they did know how to cultivate.[94] This is partially true, and the government must have known that nobody would benefit from the failed economic integration of the migrants. However, it is also important to realize that the new Turkish state was quick to turn land settlement into a tool for demographic engineering.

First coined by Milica Zarkovic Bookman in 1997, who explained inter-ethnic conflicts as the "demographic struggle for power,"[95] the term *demographic engineering* can be defined as the "intentional pursuit by ethnic groups in conflict of strategies aimed at increasing their demographic strength either as an end in itself—thus ensuring the group's presence, persistence and proliferation—or as a means to military or political power."[96] Its methods abound, including affecting fertility rates, manipulating push and pull factors of migration, population transfers, deportations, immigrant bans, resettlements, ethnic cleansing, selective tax policies, and renaming locations. It is possible to identify this state apparatus in several countries, including the Ottoman Empire/Turkey, Russia, China, the United States, and Israel, some of them being quite foundational in the determination of national borders and core majority groups.[97] Fuat Dündar suggests that the resettlement mechanisms after the Exchange of Populations Treaty in 1923 can be traced back to the demographic engineering of the late Ottoman Empire. Both Abdülhamid II and the nationalist Ittihat ve Terakki (Committee of Union and Progress) quite intentionally carried Turkification policies by manipulating the land and intervening in the migration and settlement of ethnic groups including Greek, Bulgarian, Armenian, Jewish, Assyrian, and Kurdish populations during the final years of the empire. Dündar argues that the Turkish nationalists used methods such as economic boycott, settlement of Turkish migrants in Ottoman-Greek towns, changing names of places (starting in 1915), exposure of Greek nationalist violence across the Aegean Sea, and persuasion of Ottoman-Greeks for departure as forms of national and personal revenge.[98] The late Ottoman state prepared master plans and regulations to locate homogenous groups of war migrants (*mühacir*) in villages and urban districts that would be constructed according to the perceived characteristics of an "Islamic neighborhood." These projects envisioned houses around a central mosque as the essential element of Muslim settlements, to be followed in time with shops, school, fountain, and a central square.[99]

The Exchange of Populations Treaty was an episode in demographic engineering managed by international law. And both nation-states continued devising other mechanisms thereafter. Rather than settling exchanged migrants in concentrated areas, they dispersed them across the land. This might seem reasonable given the vacated villages and distribution of urban-rural systems, but much more was at stake. During the international discussions, it was suggested to agglomerate the minorities in specifically set-up zones, but the Turkish delegates rejected the proposal as a threat to security.[100] In 1934, an additional Settlement Law (no. 2510) was instituted in Turkey to manage a new wave of population transfer from the Balkans, which amplified the existing assimilation policies.[101] The new law was introduced in the Parliament as follows: "Turkification of language is among the greatest devices for assuring the future of the Turkish race. . . . This is our aim."[102] The law divided the country into three zones: two of them differentiated the habitable and inhabitable areas due to sanitary and security reasons, and a third zone clearly marked places set aside for the relocation of populations so as to ensure the assimilation of all nations into "Turkish culture." The Kurdish majority zones in East Anatolia, such as Diyarbakır, Dersim, Elazığ, and Ağrı, were particular targets, and some Balkan migrants were located there.[103] In summary, the state extended the demographic engineering mechanisms that had already been initiated during the late Ottoman Empire and had been put in place with an international treaty, and turned the expulsion of Greeks from Anatolia into one of the many state apparatuses of Turkification.

The exchange treaty amplified rather than put an end to ethnocentrism, not only in Turkey but in Greece as well. As a result of the exchange, the Muslim population in Drama dropped from 79 percent to zero percent followed by Cailaria from 76 percent, Kavala from 69 percent, Kilkis from 66 percent, Langada and Pravi from 60 percent, Cozani and Serres from 40 percent, which all dropped to zero percent.[104] A similar process with the one in Turkey took place in Greece with the looting and seizure of vacated houses. Anastasia Karakasidou demonstrates that Muslim properties in Macedonia were forcibly dispossessed already before the war. After the Lausanne Treaty, Muslim landowners had to transfer their properties to local Christians under coercion; powerful Greek elites took over large vacated lands using their social standing and taking advantage of the ambiguous legal status of Muslim properties; and the RSC appropriated abandoned Ottoman *çifliks* for resettling exchanged populations such as those from Cappadocia's Prokopi/Ürgüp.[105]

Phase 4. The New House: Architecture to Heal Displacement?

Finally, there was the question of the physical site and architectural design of the planned settlements, both urban and rural. The homogeneity of state solutions in modern housing in both countries and their similarity to each other are indeed striking.

In Greece, the RSC employed grid-iron site plans and devised standardized units for both rural and urban typical houses to be repeated all across the country. The rural type was one-story single or double houses elevated from the ground and finished with sloped roofs (figure 2.10); the urban type was one- or two-story double houses, and sometimes multifamily housing blocks with up to seven families. While one-story houses were built of brick, pebbles, and straw, two-story ones were of masonry and fired bricks.[106] Sometimes the RSC constructed entire settlements but sometimes provided only plots of land. Sometimes it commissioned private companies, such as the ten thousand units constructed by the Sommerfeld-Dehatege company in Macedonia, out of wooden or concrete frames with brick or stone infill and tiled roof.[107] Regardless, the RSC houses were characterized by their monotonous uniformity, which, to some, was an implementation of the modernist housing principles toward public health and social equality. An author characterized Kokkinia in Athens with ten thousand units as follows: It has "well-built dwellings following all the rules of hygiene. . . . Kokkinia is simply a dream. Constructed with an appreciation of plastic beauty. Its town planning has made it a masterpiece. Roads one and a half kilometers long—both parallel to one another and perpendicular. To the little birds flying above, the little houses must look like lines of little soldiers. What a beautiful sight."[108]

In reality, however, it was only with residents' additions and appropriations that these homogenized neighborhoods found life. Among the urban settlements, Yerania (a neighborhood in Kokkinia) has been the subject of one of the most comprehensive ethnological studies on immigrants in Greece from Turkey. As the last RSC-built housing in Athens, it was as homogenous as any other standardized plan and built from prefabricated panels rather than stone. By 1927, 276 uniform structures had been erected for 552 families. Composed as twin houses circling a porous central green area divided into plots of gardens, each unit was 4 × 9.5 meters, with two rooms, one kitchen, and a washroom. The wooden construction frame was filled with asbestos panels on the external facade, and with thin partition walls inside. In her ethnographic research, Hirschon showed how residents significantly modified

Figure 2.10 Typical rural house designed by the Refugee Settlement Commission (RSC) for exchanged migrants in Greece, 1925. CAMS Archives.

these RSC houses, by combining units, adding spaces, efficiently using level differences, and appropriating streets into community spaces where they bonded in solidarity to fight discrimination and poverty.[109] Today, Kokkinia (named Nikaia since 1940) continues to host mixed residential types, ranging from one-story, one-room, older structures to seven-story, newer, and more luxurious apartment buildings. Narrow streets in some parts, such as those around Giannitson Street, are not fit for cars and appropriated as pedestrian spaces that generate a different urban sociality. Covered with plants in vases, supplied with ample urban furniture and diverse artifacts, and a home to happy wandering cats, these streets are like open-air museums of horticulture and crafts (figure 2.11).

A few architects sought to design better quality housing in contrast to the normative and standardized RSC and state-built housing units in both countries. In today's Nikaia, Athens, collective housing rises as a unique urban fabric from the regular street pattern, by virtue of its identifiable site plan with dead-end public streets that extend to gardens inside city blocks. While the dwellings on the ground floor of the stucco-covered stone buildings have separate entrances, two external stairs carried by wooden buttresses are placed symmetrically along the side facades in order to give access to the two streets-in-the-air on the long facades of each building. Despite the unkept state of the buildings today, they provide a rare and creative example in the

Figure 2.11 Street view in Nikaia (formerly Kokkinia), Athens. Photo: Esra Akcan, 2022.

typological dictionary of collective housing. Another but wealthier exception is Nea Philadelphia, a neighborhood in Athens, erected by the migrants from Turkey with some financial aid from the state.[110] With a garden city–type site plan, it is composed of circular tree-lined and flowered streets radiating from common urban areas, and freestanding, two-story, single-family houses with balconies. The only memorial to the Greek-Turkish population exchange stands in one of its urban junctions today, erected in 1990 thanks in no small part to the initiatives of Filio Haidemenou (figure 2.12).[111] In the 1930s, migrant housing projects were constructed with multifamily building blocks that followed the design principles of the simultaneously produced public housing programs in Germany and France.[112] The canonic examples include Ambelokipi Refugee Housing, designed by Dimitris Kyriakos and Kimon Laskaris in 1933–35, a version of which is located in the Ottoman migrant settlement Dourgouti (figure 2.13),[113] and housing in Nea Philadelphia designed by Aris Konstandinis in 1955.[114]

On the other side of the Aegean Sea in Turkey, the Ministry of Exchange, Reconstruction, and Resettlement also planned typical village projects on grid-iron site plans, much like the contemporaneous worker settlement towns around the world that were regarded as rational, affordable, efficient, and hygienic. The Rural Law (no. 442) came into effect on March 18, 1924, which defined regulations for the health, hygiene, and rational planning of typical

Figure 2.12 Monument to the Exchange of Populations, detail, Nea Philadelphia, Athens, 1990. Photo: Esra Akcan, 2018.

Figure 2.13 Refugee Housing in the former Dourgouti neighborhood of Athens, built ca. 1934. Photo: Esra Akcan, 2022.

villages. Every village would have a village square, a room for the Council for Elders, a school, and a small mosque (*mescit*); some streets would be paved and all kept clean; ruined buildings were to be restored; living spaces and stables would be separated in village houses; there would be in-house and public toilets, underground sewage, and clean water systems; and the graveyards would be placed outside the settlement.[115] The Ministry also devised standardized plans for "affordable housing" with single-story two-roomed units of 36 m², and slightly bigger "village housing" of 65 m² with an additional kitchen and *sofa* (veranda), in 1924 and 1925. Two or four affordable units were placed together in rows for efficiency purposes.[116] These were lower budget as well as much more subdued and straightforward designs than the unrealized typical village projects that had been designed for the migrants of the Balkan War during the last stages of the Ottoman Empire. The latter were composed of larger single or double houses with covered *sofas*, large gardens protected by walls at eye-level, and a shack at the end of the garden for storing equipment and crops.[117] Eventually sixty-nine model villages from scratch were constructed with varying degrees of success in placement, site plan, construction materials, and sizes.[118] For example, Çobanisa (Manisa) was designed on a grid-iron system with common buildings at the center and 146 twin houses of 70 m², constructed with cement floor, stone walls, wooden ceiling, and tiled roof. Arif Hikmet Koyunoğlu designed İkizceoba and Karacaoba villages (in Bursa), which had common village squares and radial street patterns, elevated houses with wooden frames, stone/brick infills, and concrete floors.[119]

Just as in Greece, professional architects in Turkey became increasingly interested in the problem of modern settlement and affordable housing as part of the contemporary international discourse on residential modernism. After the 1930s, they had a direct access to these debates, because most of the key figures of collective modern housing theory and practice had escaped from Nazism and were exiled in Turkey at the time, including Bruno Taut and Martin Wagner from the Berlin Public Housing program. Margarete Schütte-Lihotzky from the Frankfurt Public Housing program, designer of the worldwide-adopted Frankfurt Kitchen, prepared typical village school plans in Turkey for a variety of climatic conditions and sizes, as part of the government's village enlightenment policy.[120] During this housing debate, some architects produced paper projects about ideal villages and model rural houses. Burhan Arif and Behçet Ünsal repeated the grid-iron settlement plans and introduced their projects with texts that promoted housing as a "rational" architectural technology. Both put much more emphasis on common buildings, larger farmlands, and gardens than the government-issued projects.[121] Kazım Dirlik and Abidin Mortaş suggested relatively nonordinary schemes rather than grid-iron plans: the former turned Ebenezer Howard's garden-city diagram into an actual circular city; the latter proposed L-shaped houses circling large courtyards.[122] All put emphasis on common buildings, such as the school, mosque, grocery store, and squares for social gatherings. Abdullah Ziya drew attention to climatic differences and proposed large, steep roofed houses for the rainy Thrace villages.[123] However, these were too little, too late, and they did not move beyond the narrow circles of the profession. Moreover, architects folded the issue of model villages and affordable houses into their nationalist and often paternalistic concerns about teaching the masses how to become "modern, Western and Turkish." The coeditor of *Arkitekt*, Mortaş, introduced model villages with the following words: "We must not forget that the villager is also a person of the age. No matter how simple their life and needs might be, an educated, art-loving, and comprehensive intellect must outline a program for the villager."[124] In the pages of the nationalist *Ülkü* magazine and the newly founded nationalist *Yapı*, the design of villages was promoted as one of the highest ranks of "building for the people."[125]

One would look in vain, however, for projects or essays that confront the trauma of compulsory mass population transfer or its toll on the society. The discourse of modernism in architecture hid the underlying conditions of violence that predicated it. It not only turned a blind eye to the religion and race-based discriminatory worldview that caused displacement and dispossession, and hence created the demand for new land settlement and housing in the first place, but also advanced the erasure of religious and cultural pluralism.

NIKOS ZOUMBOULIDIS FROM SINASOS: MORE NATIONALISM OR MORE HEALING?

Architects of the time as well as architectural historians thereafter have evaluated these state-built homogenized immigrant housing projects as second-rate. In Turkey, the editor of the main professional magazine *Arkitekt*, Zeki Sayar, criticized the government for not involving architects enough in the country's immigrant settlement programs for exchanged migrants.[126] In Greece, Alexander Tzonis and Alcestis Rodi summarized the perception of the RSC and state-built refugee housing as "emergency undertakings free from architectural ambitions and seen as transitional shelters only."[127]

These were not unfair exaggerations. Seraphim Rizos's community, for one, had left the extraordinary natural and built Cappadocian landscape of Sinasos and was settled in Nea Sinasos, where families were placed in small, standardized, rectangular units on a grid-iron site plan. The orderly and parallel streets were supposed to reflect rational and efficient site-planning principles (figure 2.14). A white marble pyramidal monument at the entrance of Nea Sinasos signals that this is a government-built, modern, and planned village. The inscription "Sinasos" on the retaining wall at the entrance communicates the name of the town where the habitants have been displaced from. The village is settled on a valley and two hills, surrounded by olive trees and farms—a quite different climate and landscape from Cappadocia. One can see the Aegean Sea at a distance only from the street at the highest altitude. The implementation of the generic grid-iron site plan on a hilly landscape culminated in streets with steep slopes that are challenging to walk even on a dry day.

Many residents have modified the original units of the planned village by adding new spaces, pergolas for outdoor seating, upper floors, and pitched roofs with tiles (figure 2.15). Gardens with lemon and orange trees, maintained with care, bring a major improvement when compared with the photographs of the settlement during its construction. A few remaining but deserted original houses whose cheap prefabricated construction materials have been taken over by nature expose the contrast between the state-built units and the residents' agency. In one house, for instance, the residents have literally wrapped the original unit with several new structures from all sides.[128] When one compares Rizos's own house in Sinasos with those built originally in Nea Sinasos, one comes face to face with a lifeless, generic environment, miles away, both physically and emotionally, from the spacious and unique houses in Sinasos that had been carved into exceptional rocks and exquisitely ornamented by talented tuff-stone artisans (see figures 2.3, 2.14, 2.15, 2.23, 2.26, 2.31). To someone who knows the history of the Muslim-Christian partition at the crossing of Asia and Europe, Nea Sinasos reflects the impoverished world of dispossession.

The only exception in Nea Sinasos is the church designed by Nikos Zoumboulidis in 1925–34. It stands out in the village with its central location, large front square, stone walls, perfect geometric design, clock tower, dome on an octogonal base, and fountain in a garden. Black, white, and red rough stones are bound together with designed metal work. One can tell that the church is a source of both melancholy and pride for the habitants, as the inscription above its gate confirms that the edifice was built by the residents

FROM

TO

Figure 2.14 Comparison of environs of Sinasos/Mustafapaşa, Turkey (*top*), and Nea Sinasos, Greece (*bottom*), 1924. From Seraphim Rizos, with Pantazidis sons, Sinasos album; contemporary photo: Esra Akcan, 2022.

FROM

TO

Figure 2.15 Comparison of Sinasos/Mustafapaşa, Turkey (*top*), and Nea Sinasos, Greece (*bottom*), ca. 2020. Photos: Esra Akcan.

from Sinasos after they arrived due to the Asia Minor Disaster. Inside, the contrast becomes even stronger. A dense group of expensive objects, icons, jewelery, golden and silver ornate boxes, hagiographs of saints, and framed paintings fill in the space, which have been carried from Sinasos during deportation with the legal status of "movables" under the jurisdiction of the Lausanne Treaty. A comparison between the wealth hidden in these valuable objects from Sinasos and the relative poverty made visible in the Nea Sinasos houses is yet more evidence of the dispossession through partition. Wall paintings with Christian symbols leave no surface neglected in the Nea Sinasos church, but the most indicative is the large mural that covers the entire vaulted surface of the entrance wall with a depiction of the Saint Nikolaos Monastary and courtyard in Sinasos. It is an impecably accurate depiction of its referent, considering that it must have been painted from memory and one photograph in Rizos's 1924 Sinasos album (figure 2.16). Designing this church soon after being exchanged from Sinasos, Zoumboulidis, who is also credited as the hagiographer,[129] made a successful career as the architect of several church projects in Athens and Montreal.[130]

The contrast between the churches and the houses of the Cappadocian migrants in Greece is even more visible in the nearby village Nea Prokopi. In addition to icons and small objects, the Prokopians carried a monumental bell and, more phenomenally, the relic of Saint John the Russian from their hometown in the tough journey that lasted for two years.[131] The relic of the saint's body now lies in the large church with the same name, and the bell stands on three pillars outside on the square. A major reference point for matters of identity, the monumental building fosters religious tourism in Nea Prokopi.

Of all the architectural exceptions and unrealized intentions in housing, the most fitting for this chapter is a project by Zoumboulidis from Sinasos. Philothei, or the "Garden city of the National Bank Employees" in Athens (1936–37), was advertised as a garden city in the periphery of the town. It promised fresh air, open space, healthy accommodations, and houses in generous plots of green. Taking its cue from an existing river, the site plan is conceived as a radial street system providing surprising vistas and pleasant green-lined paths as in early garden cities. Rather than a monumental building to solidify hierarchy, the center of the area is reserved for a park through which the river flows. A church is placed on a hill at a peripheral rather than a commanding location. Also designed by Zoumboulidis, the church differs from the stone-walled, monumental, and cruciform examples commonly used in Greece. Approached diagonally from the garden after

Figure 2.16 Nikos Zoumboulidis, Church of Nea Sinasos, Greece, 1925–34. Mural with depiction of Saint Nikolaos Monastery of Sinasos (*top*) and external view (*bottom*). Photos: Esra Akcan, 2022.

passing through a designed gate, without any monumental or ceremonial promenade, the small building with a modest height is hidden behind trees on all sides. With nonornamented white stucco facades, arcade on a side wall, flat bell tower, and vaulted interior painted blue and golden, it looks like a white marble sculpture placed on a paved square in a dense garden of trees.

The broader Psychiko area, where Zoumboulidis's project for the garden city is situated, was intended as affordable cooperative housing that would have prevented arbitrary urban development. In the current economic

Figure 2.17 *Left*: Nikos Zoumboulidis, the architect's own house in Philothei, Athens, 1934, with Minoan-style columns. *Right*: Minoan columns at Knossos archeological site, Crete, ca. 1700 BCE. Photos: Esra Akcan, 2024.

context, however, Philothei could be completed only with the financial support of the National Bank, which eventually provided wealthy villas for its employees, failing to sustain the social housing ideals of the original program.[132] Among these freestanding houses in gardens, Zoumboulidis's own house (1934, now a kindergarten) stands out with its brown rough-stone facades, play of cubic volumes, and red and blue Minoan columns. Minoan columns are found in remaining structures of the ancient civilization on Crete and other Aegean islands, such as at the Knossos archaeological site. Zoumboulidis was unique in reviving these columns openly and expressively in his buildings.[133] With inverted diminution, where the diameter of the striking red columns gets narrower toward the bottom, and colorful disk-like column capitals, the "Minoan columns" not only found a modern life with Zoumboulidis's projects but also served as an alternative source of reference for a Greek identity, different from neoclassicism. Just as at the Knossos archaeological site (the accuracy of which was later debated, due to interventionist reconstruction policies), red-brown rough stone and Minoan columns are bounteously used in the Philothei house, accompanied with red beams over windows and blue window frames and shutters that complete the color palette (figure 2.17).

A few steps away from this house stands the Malamatinou Residence. On its facades are embedded specifically designed niches filled with custom-made Kütahya tiles. These tiles, with their striking light blue, navy blue, and red flowery motifs, are used as a cornice just below the roof, in two carved arches above windows, and in two circular plates on the facade (figure 2.18). In a nearby building, Kütahya tiles with a pastel brown-green color palette are used in a cornice that circumnavigates the entire building with multiple corners. Visible from a distance, the use of Kütahya tiles in otherwise non-ornamented houses gives the most identifiable character to both of these houses. Taking their name from the Armenian ceramics and tile workshop in the Anatolian town of Kütahya (Κοτύαιον in ancient Greek, Cotyaeum in Latin) in today's Turkey, these tiles were used in mosques, churches, and other monumental buildings throughout the Ottoman Empire. Artifacts from the original workshop were brought to Greece as "movables" under the jurisdiction of the exchange treaty, many of which are held today in the Benaki Museum in Athens, as part of its large collection from Asia Minor (see figure 2.24).

Zoumboulidis prepared the logo of the Greek National Bank with Kütahya tiles, and used them in all branches of the National Bank, including the buildings in Athens, Florina, Samos, Ionnia, Kozani, and Preveza. The National Bank in Athens (1923–25), in particular, owes its iconic reputation in no small part to these tiles, which are used bounteously in its facade (figure 2.19). Zoumboulidis preferred navy and light-blue abstract wavy patterns for this building, rather than flowery motifs. Most significantly, the tiles were produced in the new workshop established in Neo Faliro (a suburb of Athens near Piraeus), which employed exchanged migrants from Turkey.[134]

Zoumboulidis's use of historical references from Kütahya and Crete in the design of new buildings raises a discussion about labor and architectural memory. At first sight, such gestures might be interpreted as contradicting both the architect's otherwise abstracted forms and the dominant values of European modernism, where ornament and historical references were perceived as outdated. However, such an interpretation would disregard Zoumboulidis's situatedness in the dissolution of the Ottoman Empire. Both Kütahya and Crete were, until a few years earlier, part of the Ottoman Empire, of which he was a citizen. Their Greek and Turkish residents were subject to the same 1923 Exchange of Populations Treaty as Zoumboulidis's home-towners from Sinasos. By using Kütahya tiles in the design of his buildings all around modern Greece, Zoumboulidis was not only making a symbolic gesture but also helping the employment of refugees in the new Neo Faliro

Figure 2.18 Kütahya tiles on the facade of the Malamatinou Residence in Philothei Garden City, Athens, designed by Nikos Zoumboulidis, ca. 1936–38. Photo: Esra Akcan, 2022.

Figure 2.19 Nikos Zoumboulidis, National Bank, Athens, using Kütahya tiles on the facade, 1923–25. Photo: Esra Akcan, 2022.

workshop in Athens. Increasing the demand for refugee labor enabled the continuation of their craft. At a time when most exchanged migrants were becoming poorer, Zoumboulidis's decision sought to enable their economic improvement by valorizing and honoring their labor and craft.

Making explicit references to ancient Minoan columns in new buildings, rather than using the typical symbols of neoclassical architecture that had been mobilized for the construction of Athens as the capital of the newly independent Kingdom of Greece (as of 1832), raised curiosity for locals then, as it does for historians today. The use and abuse of ancient Greek architecture associated with the Athenian Parthenon in the fabrication of the white supremacist view of European and Aryan identity needs no further discussion. By not using neoclassicism to bolster national identity, Zoumboulidis might as well have been taking a position against the classical revival that was slowly being manipulated by the fascist regimes of Europe at the time. This search for a distinct architectural representation was also consistent with Zoumboulidis's community of Turkish-speaking Orthodox Greeks from Anatolia, who kept themselves at a distance from Hellenization and continued cultivating another cultural identity. After a textual analysis of Karamanlı literature and periodicals, including *Anatoli*, to which Rizos contributed, scholars Foti and Stefo Benlisoy conclude that the Cappadocian Greeks maintained their distinct cultural, lingual, and at times political identity up to the time of the partition. On the one hand, they struggled against the perception of their language, cultural creations, and customs as inferior to those of the Greeks of Istanbul, which motivated their production of narratives that conceived of Anatolian Christians as a distinct yet integral part, even the origin, of Greek civilization. On the other hand, they struggled against the European missionaries and criticized the Istanbul Patriarch for not showing them enough support. A similar dilemma persisted in their relation to emerging Greek nationalism as well, which went as far as establishing a Turkish Orthodox church. Even at the beginning of the twentieth century, the Cappadocian Greeks of the Ottoman Empire did not participate in the longings of Greek nationalists or feel attached to the Kingdom of Greece. They kept speaking Turkish despite the ubiquity of Hellenization policies in Greek schools of the Ottoman Empire.[135] Intellectuals who felt attached to Greek nationalism emerged in Karamanlı literature sporadically only in the 1910s and, according to some historians, changed the course of the merging of Muslim and Christian communities on these lands.[136]

The transition, in other words, from a religion-based imagined community to a nation-based imagined community was not smooth for the residents of Cappadocian towns like Sinasos. Zoumboulidis's refusal to position himself concurrently in the language of either neoclassicism or modernism and his search for alternatives in Crete and Kütahya appear in a new light when situated in the context of these historical forces before and after the Christian-Muslim partition. Using Kütahya tiles as ornaments and Minoan columns as historical references need not be read as a rejection of modernism. For Zoumboulidis, it might as well express a longing for a lost land by building a connection to it through architecture. It might as well be a gesture to work through melancholy, a refusal to forget, an aspiration to hold on to the memories of a place from which he and more than a million others had been expelled. This is a way of engaging with the past and the "nation," but one that is completely different from the neoclassical revivalism that had been mobilized for Eurocentric purposes. It also creates a distance from the language of efficiency and standardization in the state-built modernism of resettler nationalism.

To conclude this section: Did the repatriation claims of the exchange treaty heal the alleged conflict between the Christian and Muslim communities, and did architecture help (if we assume that it could)? The national authorities and international community at the time were content with the results of resettlement in both countries. Jacques Ancel, a professor at the

Figure 2.20
Life in Turkish rural settlements, as promoted by the state journal *La Turquie Kemaliste,* 1938.

École des Hautes Études Internationales, said: "Those miserable Turkish hamlets are now replaced by large cheerful villages. . . . What a miracle."[137] In a similar propagandistic tone on the other side of the Aegean Sea, the Turkish government's official publication *La Turquie Kemaliste* introduced rural settlers with large, possibly staged photographs of smiling and happy women (figure 2.20).[138] Once again, the testimonies from the ground were quite different. It is very doubtful that the compulsory population transfer improved the quality of life of a majority of exchanged migrants. Many complained about discrimination due to language difficulties, among other things. The Cappadocians had left extraordinary environments of fairy chimneys and cave chapels adorned with colorful icons, which are now World Heritage Sites and tourist destinations. Their houses were constructed of turf-stones by talented masons and carved into extraordinary volcanic structures. In their testimonies, many ex-Cappadocians complained about their new conditions and increased poverty. "I could not get used to it," Sofia Devletoğlu said. "The floor was earth, the roof was tile. . . . Is it easy to leave a house like a palace and come here to live in the cold among rats and cockroaches?"[139] Even though they moved into wealthier houses that they eventually appreciated, Aytaş's family was not initially fond of the houses in Sinasos/Mustafapaşa either. "The house we came into was very big, very glamorous. I still remember my astonishment. . . . The house was made of stone and rock, something very unfamiliar to us. . . . All the rooms were hewn into a rock. . . . We used to go up to the roof made of earth and look around. There were a lot of large houses here, but the weather was unfamiliar, and there were no trees or greens. In our town, the trees were taller than minarets, here there were rock caves taller than minarets."[140] Many immigrants who came to Cappadocia from Greece were surprised at the flat roofs and earth surfaces, as they had "come from lands where even the chicken cages had tiled roofs."[141]

Did the Exchange of Populations Treaty enable postconflict healing as it claimed it would? Not to trivialize the immense challenge of settling millions, or to erase the nonnormative struggles of some architects—but I have concluded that the authorities in both countries treated land settlement as a top-down demographic engineering device, and its architecture as a technical problem in a postdisaster setting, failing to notice the trauma of enforced mass population displacement, or refusing to confront the cultural complexity of their task. The standardized and typified housing units placed in equally homogenized grid-iron settlement plans were meant to serve the Turkification and Hellenization policies of their respective governments. Both countries drew from the debate over standardization and industrialization that was becoming a universalizing phenomenon at the time. As a result, ironically, housing in both countries was almost the same, regardless of the climatic or historical differences and despite the fact that their residents had been partitioned due to their religions. Peoples were separated and dispossessed because of a conviction about the untranslatability of their cultures into each other, and then moved into standardized houses that were exactly the same as each other's (figure 2.21).

Decades Later: Aslı Özbay and Healing Through Retrofitting

Let's return to the opening scene of this chapter. When the architect Aslı Özbay's team discovered a sunken church under the piles of debris during the retrofitting of a group of Cappadocian buildings in the first decade of the twenty-first century, they came face to face with the long history of erasures that has shaped these lands to this day. Countless churches and mosques all

Figure 2.21 Settlements of "exchanged" migrants, ca. 1925. *Top*: Muratlı Immigrant Village, Turkey. *Bottom*: Movroneri Immigrant Village, Greece. *La Turquie Kemaliste,* 1938; CAMS Archives.

over Anatolia and the Balkans, Thrace, Macedonia, and along the Aegean Sea and the Black Sea remained empty and were left to decay after the population exchange. The Christian-Muslim partition implemented more far-reaching consequences on architecture than religious spaces alone, because an entire set of houses, gardens, agricultural lands, schools, and community spaces had been dispossessed. Özbay's team, consulted by Turgut Cansever at the time, was working in a village that had been completely deserted after being identified as a disaster zone due to the threat of falling rocks in 1968.[142] Özbay, who had previously worked as an architect and served at top posts in the Chamber of Architects in the capital city of Ankara, decided to live permanently in Cappadocia, because the architectural design, renovation, and construction in this unique environment requires her constant presence.

In the meantime, the Greek-Turkish conflict had periodically reemerged for much of the rest of the twentieth century. After partitions, nationalist narratives are sustained during subsequent decades by stimulating periodic conflicts and fueling more xenophobia into state declarations and school textbooks as well as state-sponsored art and journalism, so that the public never questions the decision to forcibly displace people from their homes or to tear them apart from their lands and livelihoods. To reinforce resettler nationalism further, the minority rights of the descendants of the remaining 111,200 Greeks in Istanbul constantly deteriorated with the harsh tax Law of Capital Levy (1942–44),[143] the beatings of non-Muslims and the destruction of their property during the pogrom of September 6–7, 1955,[144] the abandonment of the friendship agreement and the expulsion of Istanbul Greeks in 1964, and the closure of the Theological Seminary (connected to the Ecumenical Throne) in 1971 that caused additional abandonment of minority schools, including the iconic seminary building in Istanbul's Heybeliada island. The ever-expanding Turkification ideology constantly diminished the Greek minority's educational, cultural, and property conditions, giving them incentives to leave.[145] The decree of March 16, 1964, terminated the residence of twelve thousand Greek passport-holders in Istanbul (a population of approximately forty thousand with their relatives), who were soon expelled from the city and allowed to carry only twenty kilograms of belongings or twenty-two US dollars with them. The Cyprus controversy exploded into a war in 1974, and Nicosia still stands as the last divided city of Europe. Many of the Greeks who were deported from or left Istanbul during the Cyprus controversy are known to have settled in Athens's Palaio Faliro district, where they created a lively community along the shore.

Despite the complaints of the migrants who experienced the partition, only a couple of scholars wrote critically about it till recently. In one of the earliest critical assessments in 1940, the Turkish citizen Mihri Belli identified this exchange as the economic exploitation of both countries in the interest of Western capitalist powers, and made a call to reunify the two shores of the Aegean Sea. He suggested to critically address the causes of this tragic event, which, in his assessment, included the oppressive "theocratic and imperialist Ottoman Regime" that in turn motivated the Greek minority to act like "spies in the interest of the foreign imperial occupation."[146] Nonetheless, the progressives of both communities had shared interests and could unite in solidarity against world powers, Mihri concluded in 1940, after which he went to Greece to fight in the civil war against the anticommunist regime where he was tasked with mobilizing the remaining Turkish-speaking minorities in Thrace.[147]

In Anatolia and along the Turkish shore of the Aegean Sea, photographs of the ex-Greek and newly resettled towns circulated in the media without any reference to historical violence, as if the compulsory population transfer of 1923 was a secret everybody knew but stayed silent about. New architectural projects ignored the violent past and appropriated estates from former Greek residents. Even abandoned towns, such as Levissi/Kayaköy where the history of violence is self-evident, attracted architectural education programs and tourist development that romanticized its ruins (see figure 2.9). To this day, most of these initiatives are aesthetically drawn to the formal and geometric qualities of the town and its unique relation to topography. Some commentators even identify the village's abandonment after the population exchange as the reason that the place could sustain its original architectural fabric, beauty, and genius loci.[148] The deserted village has been defined as "an architectural laboratory," a school to teach architectural form, an open-air museum, a site for a technopark, a ruin-park for architectural tourism, but rarely a site for a program where societies would confront their violent history self-critically.[149] The only exception came from the archaeologists who declared Levissi/Kayaköy as a "town of Greek-Turkish Peace and Friendship" in 1988.[150]

In this context Aslı Özbay and Baran Idil prepared the Conservation Public Works Plan for Mustafapaşa (Sinasos) in 2004. A survey of slowly deteriorating houses showed that the village was under threat of complete collapse just like other abandoned towns. The architects extended the heritage site from the well-known tourist destinations of geological formations to the village, and thereby added the existing houses and new construction under the purview of a Preservation Committee.[151] Following this plan, in 2006 Özbay and Aytaş organized a week-long workshop and prepared the brochure *Mustafapaşa'yı Korumak İçin Bilmemiz Gerekenler* (What we need to know to preserve Mustafapaşa), which they distributed to local habitants.[152] The brochure emphasized the importance of local participation to implement the conservation plan, and outlined the protection process step by step. Using the photographs from Rizos's 1924 Sinasos album to show the village's nonruined state, the two women thus promoted the preservation of the buildings' character before the population exchange. They identified the do's and don't's, plausible retrofit programs, low-budget and technically applicable

Figure 2.22 Aslı Özbay and Süreyya Aytaş, pages showing Mustafapaşa before and after partition, from the brochure *Mustafapaşa'yı Korumak İçin Bilmemiz Gerekenler* (What we need to know to preserve Mustafapaşa), 2006.

Figure 2.23 A restored mansion in Sinasos/Mustafapaşa, exterior view (*left*) and interior (*right*). Photo: Esra Akcan, 2018.

means, so that buildings would be preserved and retrofitted (figure 2.22). Mansions in Sinasos/Mustafapaşa were now restored and retrofitted with state funding (figure 2.23). Unlike the conventional archaeological and cultural heritage discourse that looks down on locals as uneducated masses who obstruct scientific excavations and heritage protection, Özbay and Aytaş's initiative was a bottom-up project that involved both professional architects and the local population. Preserving the buildings of expelled populations and preventing their slow disappearance is an important step in confronting the historical violence of partition.

Özbay and Aytaş's practice both benefited and differed from Turkey's transitional justice measures of the first decade of 2000s (see chapter 1). In 1995, the European Court of Human Rights had ruled against Turkey and called the country to address its past. This resulted in the acknowledgment of the need to improve political pluralism and human rights as well as Greek-Turkish relations. As a response, the government took or allowed some transitional justice steps during the early 2000s, such as the confrontation of and reconciliation with the mandatory population exchange. As part of the transitional justice initiatives, the Foundation for Lausanne Treaty Emigrants launched a couple of projects after its establishment in 2001. Among them was the Common Cultural Heritage program that organized two conferences and two exhibitions about the Greek-Turkish population exchange as well as the decaying Greek and Turkish buildings in Mustafapaşa and Crete, respectively. A team of authors, NGOs, art historians, and architects from Greece and Turkey, including Özbay and Aytaş, shared their historical research and personal experiences during these conferences. They went sightseeing to the demolished churches, mosques, baths, and houses in both places, and discussed possible action items. They issued a declaration to study, protect, and restore what they now called the common cultural heritage.[153] The Saint Nikolaos Monastery of Sinasos/Mustafapaşa was restored as the first church to be preserved by the Turkish government in 2009.

GOING BACK OR MEMORY INDUSTRY?

Going back was a common trope both in migrant testimonies of the twentieth century and in the short-lived transitional justice initiatives of the early twenty-first century. There are ample stories in migrant testimonies about the desire to go back and see one's old house for one last time—which was not possible in the early years due to travel bans. Some purposefully did not get married with the hope that they would go back; others discreetly traveled to their hometowns; some looked down at their villages from a hill but were unable to walk down; others got frozen at the doorstep but carried back a bag of soil or a bottle of water to their new homes.[154] Zoumboulidis visited his hometown Sinasos in 1957 and wrote a letter to Rizos from there. The letter mentions that everybody remembers Rizos, that his house is "just as he left it." Zoumboulidis's own house, however, no longer existed. "Next year, we will come here together," he wrote to Rizos.[155] To our knowledge, Rizos was never able to go back to Sinasos; he passed away in 1969. The Nea Sinasos Association organized tours to Sinasos in the early years of 2000s, so that migrants' children and grandchildren could visit their relatives' houses. The Foundation of Lausanne Emigrants also coorganized a reunion tour where forty-two evenly distributed citizens from Greece and Turkey between the ages twenty-three and ninety-six were funded to travel to the other side of the Aegean Sea.[156]

The short-lived memory boom in the first decade of the twenty-first century crystallized as exhibitions, museums, and house museums. Among these, Aytaş appropriated part of her house (now turned into hotel) as a museum of the population exchange, where she exhibits the belongings, photographs, and documents that her family brought from Greece—things that the Lausanne Treaty had categorized as "movables" (figures 2.24 and 2.25). One of the original houses in Nea Sinasos is also appropriated as a museum to commemorate the population exchange.

On a more institutional level, the *Relics of the Past* exhibition at the Benaki Museum in Athens and the Population Exchange Museum in Çatalca, on the outskirts of Istanbul, both opened in 2010.[157] The *Relics of the Past* exhibited the iconic objects that had arrived in Greece after being transported in about 250 crates that contained 2,833 precious objects. These objects had been taken into state custody and stored in Athens's Byzantine Museum. Other objects had been buried in secret places and brought later after international agreements, such as the treasures of the Soumela Monastery. After the transportation of the enforced migrants, the two governments had gone back and forth trying to make a deal about their remaining properties. Eventually in 1930, the governments signed the Treatise of Friendship and Commerce to solve the unresolved issues for the liquidation of properties, as a result of which the remaining values were transferred to respective governments. In the spirit of this "friendship" agreement, the Greek government made an appeal to the Turkish government, and the Exchange Fund financed the journey of a Soumelite monk who dug up the treasures and transported them to Greece.[158] While the exhibition at the Benaki Museum included such objects, it necessarily excluded the vessels, icons, and books that had been deliberately and ceremonially burned by their Greek communities before their departure from Turkey. Ioanna Petropoulou has interpreted burial and burning as two modes of deliberate destruction. She posits, "One could argue that it is not just fear that dictates these acts of virtual self-immolation, but an ineffable sense of finality. We realize that they

Figure 2.24 "Movables" of the Exchange of Populations Treaty exhibited in museums in Greece and Turkey. *Left*: textiles in the Population Exchange Museum, Çatalca, Istanbul. *Right*: Kütahya ceramics in the Benaki Museum, Athens. Photos: Esra Akcan, 2018, 2019.

Figure 2.25 Süreyya Aytaş's house turned into the Jervini Cave Hotel and house museum, Sinasos/Mustafapaşa. Photo: Esra Akcan, 2018.

are doing two contradictory things: the burials embody the hope of return, while the conflagrations mark a definitive rupture. . . . It was an idiosyncratic balancing act in the face of tragedy."[159]

Unlike the *Relics of the Past* exhibition in Athens that featured objects kept in state archives, the Population Exchange Museum in Istanbul includes objects that were donated by families of individuals who had been subject to forced migration. It includes documents of everyday life, such as light furniture, kitchenware, textiles, legal papers, and jewelry, that were carried across the seas with the migrants. These objects are displayed with accompanying testimonies and oral histories of actual migrants. As in the exhibition in Athens, these remaining objects represent only a fraction of the migrants' everyday life and domestic culture before they were forced to leave behind their belongings. Despite some good intentions, the memory initiatives under the patronage of the Turkish government and the European Union throughout the early 2000s did not necessarily build the stepping stones for perpetual peace.[160] Most accountability measures, large or small, were foreclosed or manipulated if they were to question the "Turkishness" of the land and the people (see chapter 1). Moreover, these measures were prone to undeniable contradictions. For example, how could one turn a blind eye to the contradiction that Turkey's peace-building steps with the historically expelled "Greeks" as an ethnic group were taking place simultaneously with its racialization and displacement of other non-Muslim, non-Sunni, and non-Turkish groups?

Despite their confrontation with the wounds and traumas of the population exchange, both the Athens and Istanbul exhibitions maintained the official, polarized historical narratives of the Asia Minor Disaster and the War of Independence in Greece and Turkey, respectively. In both, objects from each population continued to remain separated and presented as testimonies to the burnished national cultures of their respective countries, but not to the shrinking life of modern-day Greece and Turkey due to the departure of migrants. The focus was on the lost hometowns and arriving nationals, but not on departing neighbors or the lost sense of living together. In other words, the residues of resettler nationalism triumphed over the possibility of cosmopolitan ethics. Even in the most progressive reunions of recent years, authors defined the exchange as a painful but unavoidable wound, which could be healed only with time, as if coexistence was unthinkable due to untranslatable differences.[161] However, the exchange treaty had not only taken away their hometowns from the deported migrants. It had also eliminated the possibility of a cosmopolitan existence both for the migrants who departed and for the locals who were left behind.

Figure 2.26 Seraphim Rizos's pre-expulsion house in Sinasos turned into the Seraphim Cave Hotel in Mustafapaşa. Courtesy Seraphim Cave Hotel.

PREDICAMENTS OF TOURISM AND RETROFITTING

Rizos's old house in Sinasos is now a hotel in Mustapaşa (figure 2.26). Aytaş, too, retrofitted her house as a small hotel and house museum (see figure 2.25). Among the most common retrofitting programs in the region, hotels take the first rank; but tourism is a double-edged sword. It is an important source of revenue for the region, perhaps the only economic means for Mustafapaşa to fight its poverty, but it is prone to destroying the physical and social landscape.

In this context, Aslı Özbay and Baran Idil's conservation plan for Mustafapaşa took the challenge of devising physical planning initiatives that would encourage sustainable and local rather than investors' tourism. Özbay's architectural practice stands out because she participates in the tourism industry and memory boom, but at the same time holds a critical distance with her uncompromised approach to architectural retrofitting. In addition to her work in Sinasos/Mustafapaşa, her retrofitting of buildings in Uçhisar, such as the Argos Hotel on a neighboring slope, reveals another layer in the already daunting task of preservation after traumatic partitions. As an expensive hotel catering to rich clients, Argos Hotel differs from hotels in Mustafapaşa/Sinasos that are owned and managed by local habitants such as Aytaş. Nonetheless, Özbay's practice differs from that of the chain hotels located in modern parts of the Cappadocian cities, which organize daily tours to tourist destinations and thereby turn volcanic tuff-stone buildings into relics. Her approach also differs from that of the Club Med that was the first hotel that adapted volcanic structures located in the unique Cappadocian landscape. Despite the innovative uses of tuff stone and creative appropriation of the aesthetics of the existing environment in the interior decoration, this luxury hotel carved a large, imposing building into the geological formations (figure 2.27). Instead, Özbay states that she "refrains from creating large blocks, and when necessary assimilates them into the existing architectural fabric" (figure 2.28).[162]

Özbay's retrofitting involves two distinguishable stages: the reconstruction of the ruined houses on the ground and the recovery of the Byzantine subterranean caves that are discovered during construction. Her team members rely on a historical photograph taken before the town's abandonment as their guide, like those in Rizos's Sinasos photo album. The team has renovated the existing buildings and added new designs into the decayed urban fabric in a piecemeal fashion in nine phases over a course of twenty years. Unlike conventional restoration projects that imitate the past *mot à mot*, as if history has not left aging marks or even destroyed buildings, the team takes a freer transformative approach in the design of surfaces and building elements. This approach reminds the viewer of the passage of time while not obliterating the previous users of the town (figure 2.29).

The recovery of the subterranean caves requires months of careful removal of debris that had been piled up since the village's abandonment. At each stage, the architects need to do research to find out the previous and often-changing uses of the space over centuries. In addition to the Byzantine church that they retrofitted as an event space, Özbay's team members discovered a subterranean water cistern, another candle-oil workshop, and a chapel that was probably used as a monastery at one point in time, which they retrofitted as a wine cellar, a museum, and another event space, respectively (figure 2.30). Özbay finds the role of architects to be quite foundational for the healing process: "This is not an archaeological site. It is an area with rock-cut cave dwellings that were still used and changed till fifty years ago. As architects who unearth these living spaces that have been turned into trash dumping areas in the twentieth century, we are the ones who see them first, draw them first and speculate on their uses for the first time. Our profession is responsible for preserving sensitively and understanding what we find, and

Figure 2.27 Club Med, Uçhisar, Cappadocia, built in 1964. Photo: Esra Akcan, 2018.

Figure 2.28 General view of Uçhisar, Cappadocia, with the Argos Hotel, retrofitted by Aslı Özbay. Photo: Esra Akcan, 2018.

Figure 2.29 Aslı Özbay et al., Argos Hotel, Uçhisar, Cappadocia, 1996–2017. Photo: Esra Akcan, 2018.

sharing them with historians and social scientists."[163] The unique nature of this environment necessitates the simultaneous innovation of drawing techniques, surveying methods, and construction tools at each stage. The retrofitting process has also served for the education of new turf-stone masons and the revival of a centuries-old craft (figure 2.31).

As part of her attempts to turn the Cappadocian settlements into economically independent towns rather than extractive investor tourism destinations, Özbay also led the Women's House (Kadın Evi) initiative. Her office restored and retrofitted an old school as a compound where local women take and give classes in crafts, cooking, and self-development. They also produce and sell their artifacts as well as agricultural produce, and manage a restaurant for tourists.[164] In addition to its contribution to sustainable tourism, this initiative has become a basic place for local women's empowerment.

Conclusion: Whose Rift Is Partition?

Did partitions heal postconflict societies, as modern statesmen claim? Peoples were separated because of their alleged incommensurable differences, but consequentially resettled in modern housing that was exactly the same, erasing the plurality and coexistence of prepartition times. Resettlement projects

Figure 2.30 Aslı Özbay et al., subterranean space retrofitted as a museum, Argos Hotel, Uçhisar, Cappadocia, 1996–2017. Photo: Galip Hasan Temur, 2018.

Figure 2.31 Craftsmanship in Cappadocian houses. *Top*: anonymous; *bottom*: Aslı Özbay. Photos: Esra Akcan, 2018.

for the "exchanged" migrants followed the modernist planning and housing practices that were evolving globally at the time, but without paying sufficient attention to the intergenerational social, cultural, and international wounds that the partition had caused and would perpetuate. The diplomats at the League of Nations and national authorities of the Exchange of Populations Treaty conceived land as an ethnoreligious category but resettlement as a modernizing technology that served the homogenizing ideologies of nation building, the erasure of the history of pluralism, and the foreclosure of a truly cosmopolitan ethic. After the shock of partition—which caused epidemics, deaths, abandonment, and slow destruction of cultural heritage—there could at least have been a more complex and nuanced layer of response in order to identify and critically confront the cause of these disasters. This chapter has argued that the real cause of disasters during the Greek-Turkish population exchange was not necessarily the rough transportation conditions, the epidemics, the state of emergency, the subpar conditions of temporary settlements, or the environmental threats such as falling rocks. The real cause of disasters was resettler nationalism, which the international treaty served by strengthening socially constructed racial and religious identity as an international norm of the idea of the nation-state. The Exchange of Populations Treaty perpetuated partition and foreclosed cosmopolitan ethics. A critical history of partition, therefore, needs to disassociate the term *cosmopolitan* from its pejorative nineteenth-century connotations, which led to its being scorned due to the rising ethnonationalism outlined in this chapter, and reclaim cosmopolitan ethics as a prerequisite for a new culture of welcoming and peace to come.[165]

The partition between Europe and Asia, "the West" and "Islam," continues to have far-reaching consequences today. In 2020, the conversion of Istanbul's Hagia Sophia—built in the 530s CE as a Byzantine church, then converted to a mosque in 1453, and then to a museum in 1935—back into a mosque opened the wounds yet again, and strengthened the current Turkish government's ever-expanding Islamization and Turkification policy (see chapter 3). The Hagia Sophia had been unique as a museum dedicated to the art and architecture of multiple cultures and religions, while, after the population exchange, countless churches and mosques continued to be neglected. Still serving as a mosque at the time of the exchange, the Hagia Sophia was not officially affected, and yet the friendship agreement of 1930 gave way to consequential changes. The Byzantine remnants in the Hagia Sophia began to be revealed in 1931, and the Christian symbols and mosaics that had been covered with plaster over time during the building's use as a mosque were restored before the building opened as a museum in 1935. Amid the hatred, xenophobia, and intolerance of the twentieth century, the Hagia Sophia had survived as a museum. Additionally, during its life as a museum, the edifice could have been made a symbol of accountability and transitional justice in the face of state violence and imperial ambitions—a potential that no longer exists. It could have served as an acknowledgment that respect for multicultural art and architectural heritage should take priority over nationalist sentiments. The museum could have been an invitation to lasting international friendship, so that no religion erases the other with military or soft power.[166]

Moreover, the 1923 partition line between Greece and Turkey evolved into the border between today's European Union and non-EU countries—the border where refugees from Syria and Afghanistan are being agglomerated today, risking their lives to cross and dying on the way. It became one of the borders where "global apartheid" is executed, as Catherine L. Besteman aptly coined the term while defining the worldwide mechanisms with which countries of the "West" and "Global North" control the mobility and labor of people from elsewhere in order to perpetuate their own prosperity.[167]

Above all, the Christian-Muslim partition was an example of a very common but misguided way that world authorities deal with conflict: responding to divisions with more divisions, to polarization with more polarization, to conflict with more conflict, to armed and military violence with more military violence, while, instead, transitions after conflicts and peace building require very different steps. Against the official historiography that identifies partitions as tough but necessary solutions to a problem, aided by state-sponsored architecture, in this chapter, I have retold the story of partition from the perspective of architecture from the ground up in order to make a gesture toward those different steps. Instead of emphasizing the religious and nationalistic sentiments that informed and perpetuated the divide, as does the official historiography, I differentiated those who defended partition and those who would not have done so, if only they had been able to determine their own futures. Far from the deceptive argument about being neutral to polar sides, this is a reconceptualization of the partition as the rift between the rulers and the peoples, not the rift between the two communities.

Common disasters such as earthquakes and wildfires continue to connect the peoples of today's Greece and Turkey, even though civil wars, international treaties, and nationalist policies have been dividing them for two centuries. When I visited Nea Sinasos for research for this book in January 2022, a wildfire in the summer of 2021 had burned down the forests of the island of Evia, Greece, where the village sits. I myself was arriving from another wildfire in Marmaris, Turkey, where we had almost been evacuated from our house. The two fires on the two shores of the same sea had been set ablaze simultaneously due to the climate change that affects both countries. I had checked the NASA map of fires several times a day to see the spread of the fire on both coasts, and watched the news showing the evacuation of villages on Evia, including Nea Sinasos. As we drove through Evia island, my host, Kostas, frequently cried in pain as he looked at the gray, leafless trees and the ash-covered ground, and repeated, "Our island was so beautiful, with great pine forests and mountains, and now we have nothing." Even though I rehearsed the deceptive conciliation that forests grow back in a decade, I could not help but remember the same anxiety and grief that I had witnessed on the face of farmers and beekeepers during the wildfire that I had just endured in Turkey.

My personal experience was by no means unique. In the summer of 1999, two major earthquakes hit Istanbul and Athens with twenty-one days in between.[168] The two disasters sparked an unexpected sense of solidarity and mutual aid in the two neighboring countries on both a civil and official level. Hostilities had periodically intensified in the last century, but the ministries, mayors, and ambassadors of both countries facilitated rescue teams that were the first to arrive on site on the other side of the border. Food and blood donations from ordinary citizens poured out in both directions. The mayor of Istanbul met the mayor of Athens personally on the tarmac when the latter visited the Turkish earthquake zone. Newspapers and broadcasting channels reported daily on the Greek-Turkish solidarity in a series of events that came to be known as "earthquake diplomacy."[169] The forced migrants and descendants of the 1923 Greek-Turkish population exchange said that they were so heartbroken because of their lost homeland's suffering during the 1999 earthquakes that they decided to participate in the eventually unsuccessful transitional justice processes that I discussed above. Like the concurrent wildfires that burn forests down on both sides of the geopolitical divide, the 1999 earthquakes created a shared wound in the collective memory of the two countries. Chapter 3 explores more deeply the historical causes and continuing aftermaths of this earthquake damage by focusing on a refugee arrival district in Istanbul, as a counterpart of Athens discussed in parts of this chapter.

3 Collapse

Collapse signifies the sudden loss of one's home and lifeworld. Collapse could be the demolition of a building due to an earthquake, a fire, an explosion, a government decree, or a civil or state-sponsored war. It could also mean the loss of one's assets in a market crash. Collapse is the utmost traumatic experience of modern times. Like all disasters, collapse prepares itself slowly, slyly, and hiddenly, but happens suddenly. It hurts people disproportionately and shakes its immediate victims incurably. This chapter discusses collapse in modern cities as the deadly convergence of resettler nationalism and industrial capitalism. It traces how these seemingly unavoidable and benign historical forces caused civil war, mass migration, xenophobia, urban negligence, and real estate greed that turned some world cities into ticking time bombs for disasters. It unearths ideas that create a loop of repetition between collapse and manipulations in the name of healing. Architecture is implicated in collapse as both an offender and a healer.

On August 17, 1999, a major earthquake with a magnitude of 7.6 hit Istanbul's environs.[1] According to the official numbers, 17,127 people died (some estimates are as high as 45,000), when approximately 20,000 buildings collapsed and more than 120,000 were damaged beyond repair, leaving hundreds of thousands of people homeless. As a modern popular saying in Turkish goes, it is not the earthquake but the building that kills.[2] Survivors and corpses were excavated for days out of the rubble of what used to be reinforced-concrete structural beams and columns, and brick infill walls.

Historically, earthquakes have shaken humanity's sense of justice. Is it a misfortune or an injustice that some die in earthquakes while others remain less affected? The earthquake in Lisbon in 1755 had raised this question for Immanuel Kant, Jean-Jacques Rousseau, Voltaire, and others who asked whether this disaster was God's will or a human wrongdoing.[3] In her book *The Faces of Injustice*, Judith Shklar calls the 1755 Lisbon earthquake one of the "many birthdays" of the modern age, given the intellectual skepticism it raised about the phrase "act of God," which had become an "excuse for avoiding legal liabilities."[4] Shklar theorizes on the distinction between misfortune and injustice as a vital fault line in political philosophy: "Is it, for example, a misfortune or an injustice to be a woman? What about famines? Unemployment? Poverty? To a great extent, our answer to such conundrums will depend on what we know or choose to believe to be inevitable and unalterable. . . . It does not follow that a powerful sense of injustice will always incline us to see avoidable human conduct and wrongdoing in all disasters, but it will move us, as it moved Kant, to come down hard on those causes of human misery for which we are undeniably and solely responsible, like war."[5]

Death in an earthquake raises the question about the difference between natural and human-led disasters, inevitability and intentionality, misfortune and injustice. So does a market crash in the capitalist world order. According to capitalism's proponents, budgetary collapses are to be expected and taken naturally within the logic of this economic system. However, many businesses profit from disasters and intentionally produce "disaster capitalism," as Naomi Klein coined the term to demonstrate the fabrication and opportunistic use of war, disaster, and other types of crises in order to implement and gain revenues from the neoliberal world order.[6] This chapter discusses collapses due to earthquakes and capitalist urbanism together, not as divine misfortunes or natural crises but as human-led injustices. Earthquake-damage prevention and repair might be a topic of seismic and civil engineering, but it is also a topic of architecture's relation to justice.

It is architecture that kills in earthquakes and other urban disasters, but it is also architecture that victims turn to after collapse in order to find new homes. First response to disasters has stayed within the purview of humanitarian practice, and raised limited interest among professional architects. A few exceptions include postdisaster reconstructions led by Japanese architects Kenzo Tange in Skopje, Toyo Ito in Tohoku, and Shigeru Ban in Kobe.[7] As if urgency and perceived temporariness are extraneous for the concerns of steady and long-lasting buildings, few architects have let humanitarian work inform their architectural practice.[8] The false distinction between a state of emergency and a state of normalcy obscures the long-lasting impacts of postdisaster buildings and their continuing relevance as urban layers. Against the perception of refugee camps as distant spaces outside the legal contracts of citizenship, architectural historian Anooradha Iyer Siddiqi discusses these settlements as locations of design, construction, spatial imagination, and urbanism. She historicizes the Dadaab refugee camp as a culmination of the colonial-partition logic, as a sedentarization tool of land settlement, as a space where the history of humanitarian architecture unfolded, and as a result of the UN's role in constructing the spatial language of emergency relief shelters. She also shows postdisaster settlements as places where refugees make worlds for themselves by constructing self-governance and their own dwellings.[9] While Siddiqi's book elaborates on the complex layers of urbanity in refugee camps, this chapter reciprocally demonstrates the enduring debris of refugee settlements in urban environments—which, in the case of Istanbul, were also the most vulnerable to earthquakes.

The following pages trace the urban development of a migrant district in Istanbul by demonstrating how three modes of collapse and manipulation in the name of repair changed it from a land of greenery, cemeteries, and agriculture to a land where multistory buildings collapse with no apparent cause. One way to understand environmental change is by imagining oneself as an urban stroller in a time capsule. This chapter reveals the contrasts between the imaginary strolls one would take in Istanbul's borough Zeytinburnu in 1919, 1969, 1999, and 2019, and demonstrates the sea changes due to the collapses that migrants experienced over a course of a hundred years. I have also prepared abstract maps of the land during these four periods, based on earlier maps, historical information, and some level of speculation where precise documents could not be found (map 3.1). The chapter is framed in relation to three types of collapses that carry the reader from the Balkan War as one of the major episodes of resettler nationalism at the beginning of the twentieth century to the Islamic-capitalist urban renewal under the guise of earthquake prevention at the beginning of the twenty-first century. Civil war, state demolition, and earthquake, examined here together as three modes of collapse, all produced refugees—conflict or disaster refugees—in the sense of those who lost their homes as a result of collapse and whose worlds built in the aftermath of collapse shaped modern cities as they stand today. I argue that the collapses brought about by the civil war, the state demolition, and the earthquake constituted a cycle of repetition that was in fact caused by the convergence of capitalist urbanization and resettler nationalism and its heir Turkish-Islamist cultural ideology.

Collapse 1: Civil War and Resettler Nationalism (1912–1950)

The long dissolution of the Ottoman Empire created countless conflict refugees at the geometric center of Afro-Euro-Asia that was eventually divided into numerous nation-states and three continents. Among them, the Balkan

War (1912–13) has come to be one of the most unforgettable. The Balkan War is usually regarded as the first all-European conflict of the twentieth century, one of the deadliest civil wars due to ethnic conflict and the first modern warfare due to mass murder, advanced weapons, and impact on entire civilian populations who fought to the point of exhaustion. It drew the borders of the Balkan states, established the Albanian state, and almost entirely eliminated the Ottoman Empire's presence in Europe. Many see World War I, which started less than a year later and culminated in the Exchange of Populations Treaty (see chapter 2), as its continuation, and the conflict that culminated in the collapse of Yugoslavia in 1991 as its reemergence.[10]

In the canonic architectural history of modern architecture, the Balkan War is mentioned, if at all, as a time when the founder of the avant-garde Futurist movement, Filippo Marinetti, worked as a war correspondent. The artist had already demonstrated his thirst for war and inspiration from violence when he covered the Ottoman-Italian War for Libya where he wrote *Words in Freedom*.[11] The Balkan War also makes an appearance in Pablo Picasso's cubist collages when he used newspaper clips about it as canvas materials. However, the urban and architectural history of Southeast Europe and West Asia was shaped by the aftermath of the Balkan conflicts much beyond that. The Balkan War continues to occupy historians who have different views about its cause, legitimacy, and impact on the modern world order. Even the naming of the region is convoluted: while the Ottoman subjects referred to it as *Rumelia*, the ancient name *Macedonia* re-emerged on maps and the modern European word *Balkan* appeared in publications after the nineteenth century. Whether one identifies it as a civil war or a war of national independence, this armed violence caused the collapse of countless homes. International reports confirm that all sides committed atrocities on civilians. Villages were burned and looted, civilians from all nations and religions were killed, tortured, raped, and forced from homes. Numbers of casualties vary in sources and are hard to fix, but the updated calculations identify 32,000 Bulgarians killed, 110,000 wounded, and 34,000 dead from disease; 36,550 Serbians killed and 55,000 wounded; 7,762 Greeks killed and 42,800 wounded; and 3,076 Montenegrins killed and 7,563 wounded. The Ottoman deaths are estimated to be more than one hundred thousand, with a majority due to large cholera and dysentery epidemics.[12] The same year, in 1912, a big earthquake hit the west of Istanbul and the Marmara Sea that left 83,633 people homeless and destroyed 313 churches and mosques.[13]

Map 3.1 The evolution of Zeytinburnu, Istanbul. *Top row*: ca. 1919 and ca. 1969. *Bottom row*: ca. 1999 and 2019. Maps prepared by Esra Akcan and Farzana Hossain, based on earlier maps, historical information, and some level of speculation where precise documents could not be found.

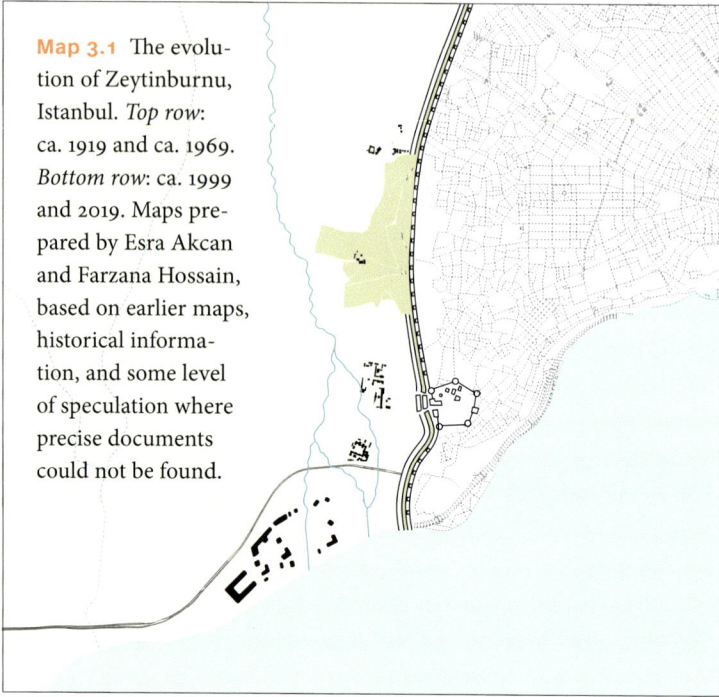

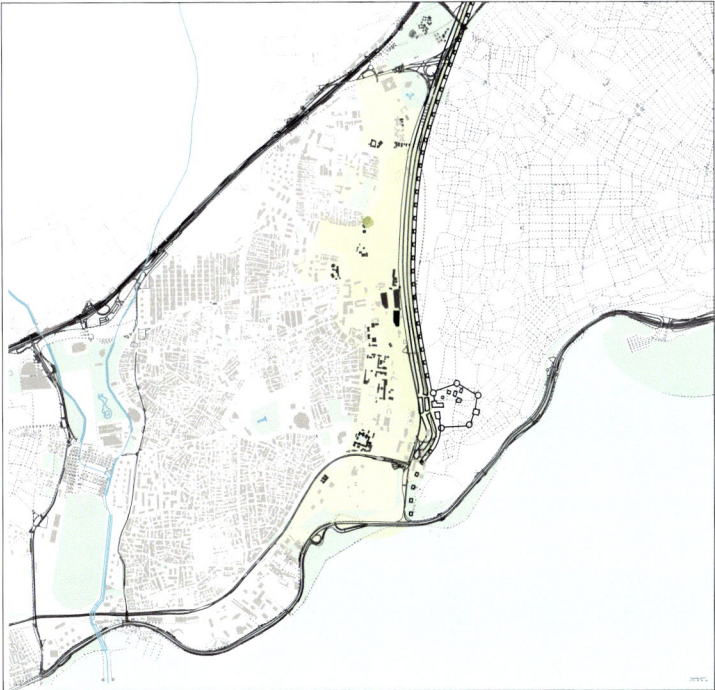

Mass migration was the major outcome of these armed conflicts that irreversibly transformed human settlements on these lands.[14] The cycle of wars and treaties starting with the Ottoman-Russian War of 1877–78 and continuing with the Balkan War and World War I changed the demographic landscape significantly. The precise number of refugees escapes modern bureaucracies of data-collecting, but the best estimates expose the scope of this collapse. Between the first Balkan War in 1912 and 1922, 3.5 million people are calculated to have been subject to forced migration.[15] Prior to the Balkan War, the Muslim population in the region was 51 percent; by its end, 62 percent of Muslims had been either killed or evicted from these European territories.[16] The percentage of Muslims in the Bulgarian Principality had already fallen from 40 percent to 9.1 percent due to the events following the 1878 Treaty of Berlin; 120,000 people emigrated from the relatively small state Montenegro in 1913–15; when Salonica surrendered to Greek forces in 1912, it sent half of its 50,000 refugees away to Ottoman lands;[17] people switched from being citizens to refugees as cities changed hands; some refugees were prohibited from entering cities where they sought shelter because authorities were concerned over the exhaustion of supplies; thousands died from the epidemics in refugee camps; and the list goes on.

The state-sponsored compulsory migrations between and within Rumelia and Anatolia continued well after the Balkan War till 1989: With the 1919 Greek-Bulgarian convention concerning minorities, 30,000 Greeks forcibly left Bulgaria and 53,000 Bulgarians left Greece; the 1923 Greek-Turkish Exchange of Populations Treaty affected close to 2 million people (see chapter 2); the Bulgarian governmental decree on August 10, 1950, expelled around 250,000 people to Turkey; the Yugoslav president Tito's free migration agreement of 1953 lifted the prohibition of movement as a result of which tens of thousands settled in Turkey between 1954 and 1960. Due to these state-sponsored migrations, 1,204,205 people must have migrated from Balkan countries of Europe to Turkey between 1923 and 1960, amounting to approximately 6 percent of the arrival country's overall population.[18] The Turkish government's decree on March 16, 1964, deported around forty thousand Greek-associated minorities (twelve thousand Greek passport-holders and families) from Istanbul to Greece allowing them to take minimal belongings; and approximately 350,000 Turkish-associated minorities were subject to forced emigration from Bulgaria to Turkey in May 1989.

As outlined in the introduction, the established nationalist histories have written the Balkan War as the founding moment of the respective countries in southeastern Europe and Anatolia. The historians of the so-called Great Powers construed it as historic justice and the liberation of Europeans from "Orientals." Assuming mixed religions and languages in multicultural societies would unavoidably break into pieces, and instead of tracing the precise history of the emergence of ethnic violence that forecloses cosmopolitan ethics, the established historiography wrote the Balkan War as the final evidence of modern nation-state's inevitability. Atrocities against civilians and forced migrations were normalized, even glorified, as the unavoidable human cost in the name of nationalism, struggle against guerrilla warfare or invasion, or liberation from despotism, rather than ethnic cleansing or demographic engineering. The double ideology of religious rift and national fault line not only determined the borders in Europe but also stirred race-based nationalist and religious sentiments, and escalated ethnic violence within the remaining borders of the Ottoman Empire. A large number of historians argued that the defeat in the Balkan War and ejection from Rumelia made a devastating mental and political impact on the group of intellectual and military leaders, commonly known as the Young Turks and founders of the Republic of Turkey, who did not refrain from multiple forms of demographic engineering for their own ethnic victory afterward. Moreover, scholars have attributed the rise of Islamism during the late nineteenth century to the conflicts in the Balkans as well. There was a strong reaction to the perception of Islamic civilization as inferior and the maltreatment of Muslim subjects in the Balkan states that were gaining autonomy under Ottoman suzerainty or independence. Many commentators interpreted European ambition for colonization as a major cause of collapses during the Balkan War. Referring to it as a new episode in the aggression of Crusaders was a common metaphor. Revenge and irredentism were also frequent emotions in the Ottoman publications. This chapter exposes critically the reverberations of these long-lasting patterns of thinking including European colonialism, ethnic nationalism, and Islamism as they shaped the urban history of Istanbul where refugees of the Balkan conflict settled. Against this background, I look at the consequences of this armed violence for the migrants it created. I prioritize the written memoirs of these migrants who settled in Istanbul and endured new collapses over the records of war correspondents, state archives, or nationalist and Islamist elites. I am less interested in telling the history of the Balkan War from the viewpoints of its military, insurgent, or ruling powers on either side, and more interested in the collapses experienced by its civilian victims. This story accounts for the debris of the historically produced ethnic conflicts and resettler nationalism in cities.

War historians mention in passing the refugee influx in arrival cities, but hardly trace the story beyond that. The Ottoman Mühacirin Komisyonu (Refugee Commission or Administrative Commission for Muslim Migrants), established in 1860, had directorates in each territory and settled refugees after the Crimean War (1853–56), the Caucasus War (1817–64), the Ottoman-Russian War (1877–78), and the Balkan War (1912–13).[19] According to some sources, the Ottoman state settled 667,760 refugees in 1878, mostly in Hüdevandigar, Edirne, Kosovo, Sivas, and Salonica (Thessaloniki), and 297,548 refugees in 1913 mostly in Aydın and Edirne (a much smaller number than 413,922, calculated as Muslim refugees during the Balkan War—others must have been left to their own devices).[20] These offices distributed resources and negotiated with both the central administration and existing residents, who could be frustrated with sharing their local assets. Many local authorities found themselves in need of raising funds for new immigrants. For instance, the population in the city of Salonica doubled after the resettling of the 1878 refugees, which accelerated the tearing down of the city walls, and gave rise to officially created and organically developing neighborhoods.[21] The city of Kosovo has famously been on the front line of the tensions as a result of the mass population transfers and may still be suffering from the debris of this period.[22] In chapter 2, I discussed the urban development of Athens as a result of the influx of refugees from today's Turkey after the 1923 Exchange of Populations Treaty.

Istanbul was an arrival city of resettler nationalism only indirectly. The Ottoman Empire placed 2,594 people here immediately after the Balkan War,[23] which amounts to less than 1 percent of the officially resettled refugees in 1913, and much less than the estimated number of displaced people. Istanbul received only 0.2 percent of the population settled by the Ottoman institutions after 1878. The Republic of Turkey resettled only forty thousand exchanged migrants after the 1923 Greek-Turkish Exchange of Populations here, and most of them in the far outskirt borough of Çatalca.[24] As the previous chapter demonstrated, a great majority of exchanged migrants were settled on rural lands—a decision that fits the resettler-nationalist logic after the Balkan War and the conception of Anatolia as the new territorial core of the new republic.

Istanbul was rather the transit city for refugees in all directions during the entire set of conflicts and, I will argue, home to those who rebuilt a life for themselves outside the state's formal settler operation—who resettled informally, so to speak. When around 2 million Muslims left Russia and the Balkans during the Ottoman-Russian War, and when the entire Circassian and Chechen populations in Thrace and Macedonia were displaced to Anatolia and Arab lands, their first stop was Istanbul.[25] Istanbul remained a first stop for war refugees, who significantly increased the city's overall population and changed its Muslim inhabitants from 51 to 81 percent between 1882 and 1914. These war refugees did not confine themselves to refugee camps.[26] In 1912, at least one hundred thousand refugees arrived in this city, and more than twenty thousand were on the way,[27] a daily reminder to the residents that the war had approached the imperial capital. Two commissions were responsible for the accommodation of these migrants, and 14,856 of them were settled in 3,709 mosques and schools.[28] They brought stories of conflict and collapse, and memories of lost homes. For instance, Fatma Iclal wrote about her hometown Salonica with melancholy, and referred to herself as an orphan, quoting her student's letter from this city: "We are now coerced to spend our time in a world of bewitched slavery in despair and in misery that only a while ago we used to label as the city of freedom. . . . This is so because all our existence is engulfed by this tremendous non-existence."[29] Waiting for the results of the wars before the 1923 Exchange of Populations Treaty, two hundred thousand Greeks (*Rum*) were stranded in temporary settlements in Istanbul.[30]

No other district in Istanbul but Zeytinburnu provides a better example to illustrate the debris of this ethnic violence and resettler nationalism, as well as the alleged remedies that created more collapse. Located to the west of the historical peninsula, immediately outside the city walls, Zeytinburnu was the urban refugee camp par excellence. When existing mosques, schools, and military barracks proved impossible to accommodate the Balkan refugees, the Ottoman state decided to provide temporary building materials for constructing temporary shelters outside the city walls for those who were expected to be settled in Anatolia after a short stay.[31] Compared with the ubiquitous scholarly and touristic publications on Istanbul's historical city inside the city walls and the Pera District outside the coastal city walls, scholarly interest on Zeytinburnu is scant. Most publications were recently undertaken by its local municipality, aiming to reverse this negligence. If one has to think of a spatial metaphor for Zeytinburnu before 1980, one could call it the underpaid sweatshop of a lucrative business. Longtime Istanbulites often referred to it as "the other side of the city walls"[32] or the *gecekondu* (slum) neighborhood. In their memoirs, migrants who settled unofficially in Zeytinburnu mention they were ashamed of disclosing their home addresses.[33] When the government tried to reduce participation in the Saturday Mothers movement, it attempted to relocate the demonstration to Kazlıçeşme in Zeytinburnu (chapter 1). Established historians still write about this district with contempt as the smelly area where unurbanized migrants commit homicide daily.[34]

Located on the Via Egnatia connecting ancient Rome to ancient Constantinople, the area outside the famous Gilded Gate of the city's land walls (built by Theodosius II in the fifth century) had served as the threshold to enter Istanbul/Constantinople since the Byzantine period.[35] The famous seventeenth-century Ottoman explorer Evliya Çelebi, who is known for his ornate but exaggerated writing style, mentions it as the Roman quarantine zone where everyone was held for seven days before being admitted to the city.[36] Most importantly for today's Turkish-Islamist ideology, Zeytinburnu was the land where Mehmet II placed his army tents and fought the war of conquest in 1453, against the city walls' three lines of defense. After Istanbul became part of the Ottoman Empire, these walls lost their function, but continued to serve as the border across which another world started. The dead bodies moved from inside the walls to the necropolis situated here. In the words of a contemporary traveler, "A never-ending caravan of coffins could be seen along the routes leading to cemeteries" during the plague of 1812.[37] In his book published in Greek in 1851, Skarlatos Byzantios, who unusally gives equal praise to Byzantine and Ottoman monuments, speaks of this area as the "other" of both, one that "besmirches" a "pleasant vista," due to the "tent camps set up by Athinganoi at various spots along the land walls, . . . exercis[ing] their usual crafts and lead[ing] a life of utmost degredation."[38] A late nineteenth-century photograph by Guillaume Berggren also shows people living in cloth tents outside the city walls (figure 3.1). During the Balkan War, five refugee-shelter zones were spread along the city walls in this area, which also became the epicenter of the 1912 cholera epidemic.[39] Ottoman Greeks waiting for the negotiations of the 1923 Lausanne Conference were treated in the Greek Hospital here.[40]

With a long history as the transit space for travelers, conquerors, and refugees, and having become an "other" in Istanbul's collective subconscious, Zeytinburnu had been turned into the arrival zone of both international and rural-to-urban migrants by the mid-twentieth century. For instance, in her memoirs, Nurten Yenal, whose grandparents were refugees from Salonica during the Balkan War, narrates that she and her father laid their cloth tent in Zeytinburnu as they could not afford to live anywhere else. Remembering this district from his family's refugee days, the father bought the tent

Figure 3.1 Guillaume Berggren, *Zeytinburnu, Istanbul,* at the end of the nineteenth century.

from the Sümerbank factory in the area. A week later there was another tent nearby.[41] Assuming children can trust the family history communicated to them by their parents, Şemsettin Loklar's family had escaped from Üsküp (Skopje) in 1911–12, and started animal farming in the Çırpıcı Meadow of the district—an occupation he remembers continuing as a kid.[42] Üzeyir Üzüm's grandfather came from Manastır (Bitola) in 1917 and traded his land with *Rum* (Greek) owners to become one of the first settlers.[43] Turgut Soner speaks about his great-uncle who moved into one of the three houses in the Tepebağ neighborhood in 1924 after being exchanged with the Exchange of Populations Treaty of 1923, and slowly brought his entire family from Rumelia.[44] Fikret Dalbeler was born in Zeytinburnu in 1938, after his parents were expelled from Greece due to the same treaty and got the land from a non-Muslim family.[45]

A STROLL IN ZEYTINBURNU IN 1919

If one were to take a walk in Zeytinburnu during the time that the Balkan migrants started moving here, one would notice only a few buildings rising from the meadows, and olive, grape, and mulberry trees. Period maps, such as the ones by Byzantios in 1851 and C. Stolpe in 1869, as well as late nineteenth-century photographs show empty lands bordered by the city walls and buildings around religious centers. These centers for multiple religions and communities located side by side put cosmopolitan existence to a test during the Ottoman Empire. Starting the stroll from the Topkapı Gate and walking south toward the sea, one would see the Merkezefendi Center composed of several buildings and tombs—the oldest dervish lodge (tekke) in the district dating back to the 1550s, extended and renovated in 1886. The religious establishment was also a center for healing; travelers mention its curing spring water.[46] According to Evliya Çelebi, the center had attracted five hundred houses by the early seventeenth century, most of which must have disappeared by the twentieth century, because the Balkan migrants called the area Beşevler, naming it after the five houses that they built.[47] The Yenikapı Mevlevi Lodge was located a little to the southwest of the Merkez-efendi Center—the second oldest complex in Istanbul for what is commonly known as whirling dervishes (the first being the Galata Mevlevi Lodge), built in 1598, burned in 1906, but restored by the well-known architect of the time, Mimar Kemalettin, who redesigned it according to the rising nationalist style in 1913 (figure 3.2).[48] By the time migrants arrived, both Muslim complexes had been stripped of their religious functions due to the Republican Law of 1925, and the Mevlevi lodge was repurposed as a student hostel.

To the south of these buildings lies one of the most significant structures of the Greek Orthodox faith, the Balıklı Complex, comprising the Monastery of the Life-Giving Spring and Panagia Pege Church, the oldest structure in the area that is included in all traveler, architectural-history, and tourist guide books (figure 3.3). Built in the mid-fifth century by Leon I, but destroyed and rebuilt several times due to earthquakes, wars, and vandalism, it was and is a bearer of several miracle myths: the blind are said to be healed after drinking its spring water; stones left over from the building of Hagia Sophia are said to have been used for its first restoration; Murat II is said to have stayed there when he besieged Constantinople in 1422; and a fish is said to have jumped out of the frying pan there during the city's conquest in 1453. The church and the holy spring were repaired by Nikodimos of Derkos (Terkos) with Ahmed III's permission in 1726–27, and by the architect of the time Hadji Komninos Kalfa under Selim III in 1793.[49] All of the Greek patriarchs of Istanbul have been buried in its rear courtyard since 1842 (see figure 3.9). The complex collapsed several times, because it was the target of religious and nationalist controversy throughout the ongoing nationalization of Turkey. For instance, the church was demolished in retaliation for the Greek

Figure 3.2 Yenikapı Mevlevihane (Dervish Lodge) in Zeytinburnu, Istanbul, built in 1598, burned in 1906, and renovated by Mimar Kemalettin in 1913. The building is now part of Fatih University. Photo: Esra Akcan, 2019.

Revolution on March 21, 1821. Finding it in rubble when he visited in 1825, Byzantios remembers: "Tears flowed from my eyes, as I retreated in some corner and recalled hundreds of memories pertaining to that place." When the church was rebuilt over its old foundations to be reopened in 1835, probably with original stones kept in the Turkish graveyard by Architect Markis during the reign of Mahmud II, Byzantios continued, "Twenty-four years had passed when I once again visited the shrine and gently as ever, but instead of the ruins, I saw a church standing magnificent. . . . I was unable to withhold my tears. But these were tears of joy, reverence and national pride."[50] The donations for reconstruction were collected with a call in the Karamanlı language (spoken in Turkish and written in the Greek alphabet, this language was also used by Greeks of Cappadocia; see chapter 2).

If one continued walking south, one would come across two large, architecturally impressive medical complexes: the Balıklı Greek (*Rum*) Hospital and Surp Pırgiç Armenian Hospital. Founded as two small wooden structures to treat plague patients in 1753, the Greek Hospital expanded several times on twenty-four acres of land and was renovated after the 1894 earthquake, in order to give specialized services in durable buildings in gardens (see figure 3.21). With some of the best doctors in the city, and administered and

Figure 3.3 Holy spring at the Monastery of the Life-Giving Spring and Panagia Pege Church in the Balıklı Greek (*Rum*) Complex, Zeytinburnu, Istanbul, 5th–21st centuries. Photo: Esra Akcan, 2021.

funded by the Greek community, the complex included a psychiatry clinic, the Greek orphanage, a residential satellite where mental health patients lived with their families, and a barn for cows to produce milk, among other pavilions. Eight buildings on another thirty-five acres were added in 1904.[51] During times of conflict, the hospital treated soldiers and epidemic victims from all over the war zones. It became a military base during World War I and the base of the Greek Red Cross and Near East Relief after the defeat of Ottomans in this war, treating refugees in transit and Ottoman Greeks stranded before the exchange. The Armenian Hospital, on the other hand, was constructed approximately two hundred meters away and opened in 1834. Designed by the period's most important architects Garabed Amira Balyan and Ohannes Amira Serveryan, it accommodated both medical and spiritual programs, including a church, a school, a poorhouse, and an orphanage that became home to children from Anatolia after the 1915 genocide.[52]

Reaching the southern end of the stroll, one would see the first factories of the Ottoman Empire and the Republic of Turkey. Most consequently for the migrants to come, the area along Zeytinburnu's Marmara Sea coast—often referred to as Kazlıçeşme—had been an industrial zone from the beginnings of Ottoman industrialization until recently. Immediately after the Ottoman conquest, tanneries (leather-making workshops) and slaughterhouses were built along the sea with Mehmet II's orders. They gave Zeytinburnu its reputation for bad smell. Travelers and historians recount the fresh dog feces used in leather production, making it necessary to feed thousands of dogs in the area, and encouraging children to collect dog feces from the streets and rush them to leather workshops.[53] Historian Namık Erkal has reconstructed the details of this area throughout the Ottoman era, which was a zone for fatteners, butchers, stringers, tanneries, pastrami-makers, candle makers, soap makers, glue makers— all producing unwanted smells and keeping away intruders from the city gate.[54] The leather industry expanded and remained a lucrative business in the area till the late twentieth century, producing commodities that were sold at the Grand Bazaar nearby and assisting the growth of the textile industry.

In addition to leather production, the southern area had turned into a heavy industrial zone after the nineteenth century. Cannon production had already begun in the military complex since the 1700s. The first iron factory started operation in 1846 as part of the project to establish an imperial industrial complex (Fabrika-i Hümayun). In travelers' words, "the promontory of Zeytinburnu is dominated by the towering, marble white chimney of the Foundry, clearly visible to the boats that sail by, where the iron . . . is processed into various casts."[55] With industrialization under Abdülhamid II's patronage, factories for gunpowder, weaponry, and cartridges as well as a gas factory and more were added.[56] Starting in 1872, the railway tracks from Florya to Sirkeci passed through Zeytinburnu, dividing the sea from the land. A monumental military hospital was built with a classical architectural layout in 1890, serving the wounded workers during the production of weapons and soldiers during the Balkan War and World War I (figure 3.4).[57] Scholars Önder Küçükerman and Jülide Edirne Erdinç identify Zeytinburnu as the birthplace of industrial design in the Ottoman Empire, due to the availability of empty and flat lands outside the city walls that proved a suitable space for large factories, and the animal farming that boosted leather production, as well as the watery ground for agriculture that helped the cotton plantations and textile factories.[58] The weapons and symbols of

Figure 3.4 Ottoman Military Hospital, 1890, Zeytinburnu, Istanbul. The building was converted into the Zeytinburnu Municipality Building and Museum, 1984–2019. Photo: Esra Akcan, 2019.

the first Ottoman industrial design were produced here and displayed in international fairs such as the Istanbul Public Exhibition of 1863 and the Paris Exhibition of 1867.[59]

Apart from these scattered religious landmarks, and medical and military industrial complexes, a stroll in Zeytinburnu in the early twentieth century would pass through acres of cemeteries covered with trees, including large Muslim, Greek, Karamanlı, Armenian, and Syriac cemeteries, where Istanbulites, war victims, and epidemic fatalities were buried (figure 3.5). Of particular note was the agricultural land (*bostan*) that extended all along the city walls, where farmers cultivated land for almost fifteen centuries. The rest of the lands to the west of these buildings and north of the industrial zone were meadows, orchards, farms, and vineyards that had been the agricultural and leisure (*mesire*) land during the late Ottoman Empire. Of particular note are the meadows, where Easter, Christmas, and Muslim festivals, wedding parties, horse races, and archery contests as well as light comedy and fairs used to take place. Çırpıcı Meadow appears in documents and texts as a land of joy, entertainment, drinking, and free play between women and men, as well as prohibitions on such behavior. There were streams running through the meadow and wells that had been dug by the German army during World War I.[60]

Figure 3.5 Armenian Cemetery, Zeytinburnu, Istanbul. Photo: Esra Akcan, 2019.

Collapse 2: State Demolition and Capitalist Urbanism (1950–1999)

RESETTLER NATIONALISM AND INFORMAL CITIES

As forced migrants from the Balkans settled on lands outside the city walls, Zeytinburnu made a name for itself as the birthplace of Turkey's informal urban development: the *gecekondu*. According to 1949 statistics, 3,218 of Istanbul's 5,000 *gecekondu* buildings were located in Zeytinburnu.[61] Balkan migrants continued settling here informally in the 1950s and 60s, such as those who moved from Bulgaria after their expulsion on August 10, 1950.[62] The migrants from Yugoslavia throughout the 1950s were not settled by the state, and 57 percent of them are known to have made their homes in Istanbul.[63] Migrant solidarity enabled the informal urban development. Enver Nehir remembers his three-day-long train ride from Yugoslavia to an unknown situation, when his family coincidentally stumbled into his father's distant relative upon arrival. "In those days, migrants went to the train station daily to see if one of their relatives or friends arrived [from Europe] in Istanbul, and took them to the neighborhood."[64] The population of Zeytinburnu increased from 17,585 to 117,000 between 1955 and 1965 as new migrants built new *gecekondu* houses. Literally translated as "landed at night," usually translated in scholarship as "slums," "squatter settlements," or "shantytowns," and comparable to those in Sao Paolo, Lima, Mumbai, or Karachi, *gecekondu* settlements expose the hidden corruptions of industrial capitalism.

These houses were built rapidly as one- to two-room shelters but expanded as families grew, by using ad hoc materials available nearby and on lands that did not belong to habitants. During the early 1960s, 60 percent of Ankara's and 45 percent of Istanbul's population lived in *gecekondu* houses, although these numbers are unreliable due to the very illegality of the phenomenon. The Turkish law devised a definition for these informal settlements in 1966: "buildings erected against the legal planning and building construction regulations, on lands and lots that belong to others, without the consent of the owner."[65] *Gecekondu* houses have been perceived as either urban wounds or the outcome of a popular solution to housing crises; as testimony of modern corruption or niches of self-help; as temporary structures that will disappear once immigrants are integrated into the city; or as the Global South's perpetual urbanization mode.[66]

Established scholarship attributes *gecekondu* development to urban-to-rural migration following the mechanization of agriculture and industrialization. However, I infer from the evidence above that the cross-border population movements during and after the dissolution of the Ottoman Empire constituted the primary reason for the emergence of these settlements. Slum development, in other words, is a debris of resettler nationalism. In 1960, there were immigrants from sixty-seven different cities in Zeytinburnu, and the population who migrated from out of Turkey outnumbered those born in the country, with 36.7 percent of them from Bulgaria, 25.5 percent from Yugoslavia, 18.1 percent from Greece, and 14.3 percent from Romania.[67] Many of these numbers (except Greeks) compare concurrently with the immigrant percentages in the rest of Turkey.[68] These percentages stayed the same in Zeytinburnu till the 1970s, when 51.8 percent of residents were born outside Turkey.[69] In other words, just as in Athens, Istanbul's first informal settlements were residues of refugee camps. They constituted the debris of ethnic cleansing and the collateral result of the resettler-nationalist logic.

ESCAPE FROM SOVIET UNION AND CHINA

In addition to the Balkan migrants, Zeytinburnu has been an arrival city for Kazak, Afghan, Uzbek, Uyghur, and other Central Asian refugees and asylum-seekers from the Soviet Union and China. As scholar Magnus Fiskesjö explains, China's cultural oppression of Uyghur identity goes back to 1945, when poets were killed for their language. In the 1950s, refugees fled after the military invasion and the imposition of the Chinese rule on the Xinjiang region. Uyghur mass flight in the 1960s may be attributed to the Maoist Cultural Revolution and communist homogenization. While the situation worsened through the 1990s, it has reached genocidal dimensions after 2017, when Uyghur identity is criminalized and cultural heritage erased.[70] Today, journalist reports and victim testimonies allege that the Chinese government detains Uyghur Muslims in camps of forced assimilation and identity conversion.[71] The first wave of Uyghurs and Kazaks arrived in Zeytinburnu after China's military invasion of Xinjiang in 1949 (members of the diaspora who reject the Chinese rule call the area East Turkistan).[72] One of them, Hızırberk Gayretullah, who later became the editor of the *East Turkistan Magazine* published by the Association of Migrants from East Turkistan, remembers the attack on their convoy as they crossed the border to India before they took asylum in Turkey.[73] Ilyaz Saka, who later became a consultant to the mayor of Zeytinburnu Municipality and Hatice Küçükakyüz's parents—who is now the director of urban development in the same institution—also arrived with the first wave in 1952.[74] Another wave escaped in 1961, including Hamit Göktürk, who later compiled the writings of Ilham Tohti—a writer whose life in prison has become a symbol of the violation of Uyghurs' human rights in Chinese detention camps.[75] Of their escape, Göktürk remembers: "It felt like the rocks would fall down on us. I remember crying in fear due to the bad state of the road and the horror of the environment."[76] They walked to Afghanistan, searched for Kirgiz Turks for two months on foot, and camped for years before they could be resettled in "Turkistan Houses" in Kayseri in 1965—public housing that had already been demolished by the time I visited in 2019. Yusuf Kulca, who later founded a charity organization for homeless children, arrived in 1969 along with two hundred families after a two-month journey with the UN's oversight. Having left his mother behind, they stayed in a hostel in Zeytinburnu that had been repurposed from an existing building, before he was sent to an orphanage, leaving his father in the Zeytinburnu Turkistan House.[77]

Turkish-speaking migrants of Central Asia escaped to Zeytinburnu from the Soviet Union as well. Ali Çağrı, for one, arrived from Afghanistan in 1982 via a refugee camp in Pakistan with thousands of Afghan refugees who were exiled due to the Soviet occupation. Even though the Turkish government settled them in eastern cities, he came back to Zeytinburnu to work in the leather industry—a skill he had acquired during the process.[78] Landing in the Zeytinburnu hostel as their first stop for asylum, many refugees returned to this district when they could not make a living in other towns where the Turkish government settled them officially.[79] Many mention their leather workshops in houses where the entire family worked together. Many take pride in their contribution to the

Turkish economy through the leather industry.[80] There are no reliable numbers for those who escaped from the former Soviet Union, Afghanistan, or China outside the legal asylum process, but a few anthropological and oral history studies confirm that the Central Asian migrants chose Zeytinburnu due to their relatives who already lived here. Linguistic and cultural familiarity, availability of employment in the leather industry, sociocultural networks, and active civil society organizations helped men and women advance their political causes and pass their residential and food culture to the next generations.[81] Zeytinburnu was the arrival district for a long chain of migrations from both east and west.

CAPITALIST URBANIZATION MAKES RENTAL BABIES

Memoirs and family photographs of early *gecekondu* residents who moved to Zeytinburnu from the Balkans, Central Asia, and other cities of Turkey reveal a textured architectural and urban history of this district in the second half of the twentieth century (figure 3.6).[82] Many dramatically mention the muddy ground, which was so thick and prone to suctioning that they lost their boots in it (figure 3.7). You could not walk on Zeytinburnu's unpaved paths without changing your shoes at the border where the planned formal city ended and the informal one started. Once you entered the district, you would see that the *gecekondu* houses were placed in gardens, two or three of which sometimes shared a courtyard. Upon first arrival in Istanbul, many migrants stayed with relatives for the first days, but soon "encircled an area" (*çevirmek*) on unbuilt land with stones to construct their own houses. The more friends arrived from hometowns, the more clusters densified. Hatullah Yeniyol remembers how his family's house number kept changing as new houses were added between the existing ones on the same street.[83]

Collapse took the form of state demolition in the mid-twentieth century, rather than the civil war that the victims had escaped from. The locals used the pseudonym "the greens" (*yeşiller*) for the state's gendarme forces who frequently pulled their houses down. Almost all residents were subjected to this, and either watched the municipal officers demolish their houses or came back from work to a pile of debris. Consequently, they designed architectural and social tactics to prevent state demolition. Sometimes they secretly gathered at night in groups of hundreds and built ample houses on empty flat land they had selected before.[84] Other times, they made sure to use lime as mortar rather than cement in between briquettes, because it was hard for officers to break the briquettes that way.[85] Mehmet Ali Vatansever describes the construction of his and others' *gecekondu* houses upon their arrival in Zeytinburnu from Yugoslavia:

Figure 3.6 Family photograph of Besim Sadıker in Zeytinburnu, ca. 1950. Zeytinburnu Oral History Project.

Figure 3.7 *Gecekondu* (squatter) houses in Zeytinburnu, ca. 1965. Zeytinburnu Municipality Archives.

Everyone used to encircle an area to their liking; it did not matter if it belonged to a foundation or not. Three to five families used to get together. The operation did not take place in daylight due to the gendarme forces. We used to hide the construction materials in the [Armenian and Greek] Kazlıçeşme cemeteries, as these cemeteries had tall grass.

After five o'clock, we carried the briquettes, bricks, sand, and wood to build the houses. It was important to finish the roof and to put a cradle with a baby inside the house, because the gendarme forces could not demolish houses that had babies in them. But where would you find that many babies? There were babies for rent. For instance, my sibling was a rental baby.[86]

This single memory-image demonstrates the impact of resettler nationalism on an entire lifespan: the dead in unattended non-Muslim cemeteries whose relatives could no longer visit their graves are accompanied by the babies of conflict refugees who had to be rented out as a tactic to prevent state demolition. Despite the alleged illegality of *gecekondu* settlements, the government and its arms controlled home construction for their own benefit. Ahmet Dildar mentions that it was impossible to sustain a *gecekondu* house unless one bribed the gendarme forces.[87] Cemal Aslan remembers that their house was demolished nineteen times, before his father quickly finished construction during a weekend and paid a fee to the municipality as if the house had always been there.[88] Houses did not collapse during the days of election campaigns, making it easier to build and move in at that time, because the government did not dare to lose votes.[89]

Contrary to the common perception, it was not amateurs but building masters (*usta*) who oversaw the construction with the request and help of residents.[90] Some residents paid a fee to the masters, others benefited from the gift economy. Enver Sertel exchanged the radio that he had brought from Macedonia for the construction fee of his house,[91] while Mehmet Zeynel gave the refrigerator he had carried from Skopje in exchange for a *gecekondu*.[92] These transactions are reminiscent of the 1923 Exchange of Populations Treaty that had made a distinction between movables and immovables to be recognized by international law. Leaving immovables behind caused unquantifiable harms to the memories and economic status of exchanged migrants, while movables became reminders of old life and museum objects (see chapter 2). The distinction between movables and immovables reappeared in other operations of resettler nationalism. The movable artifacts that migrants carried while crossing national borders turned into exchangeable possessions to acquire immovable real estate in places of arrival. Circulating between hands, these movable artifacts continued to connect Rumelia and Anatolia despite the official border that had been drawn between them.

Memoirs of first *gecekondu* residents reveal exploitation and pollution as wounds of industrial capitalism. Leather workshops and factories expanded in the first years of the republic. Zeytinburnu was identified as an industrial zone with a governmental ruling on April 27, 1947, and as a heavy industrial zone on August 4, 1949. The number of *gecekondu* houses increased from 18,000 in 1954 to 26,000 in 1957. Between 1955 and 1973, 325 new factories and workshops were constructed in the area, which accelerated the population increase.[93] Almost all *gecekondu* residents remember their poverty despite the fact that they easily found jobs in one of the nearby factories with help from relatives. Many women worked at home for long hours, sewing and knitting for the textile industry to make ends meet.[94] A survey conducted for a sociological study in 1974 confirms that migrants continued feeling poor.[95] As a Balkan refugee Fikret Dalbeler summarizes, "Migration means poverty."[96]

Child labor was ubiquitous during these decades.[97] A Balkan migrant, Bahriye Bahtır, remembers that factory directors used to visit *gecekondu* houses door to door to find workers and recruit young children in the 1940s and early 1950s.[98] Sebahattin Sönmez confirms that "there was no single child who did not collect scrap or sold rusk. You had to; there was no money. . . . All children worked."[99] Adil Çalışkan remembers his first days after migrating from the Balkans:

> I did not know Turkish. I started work at eight o'clock in the morning and finished at eleven o'clock in the evening, and returned home with the train. I was eleven years old. I was very petite and felt sleepy. I arrived at home at midnight and woke up at 6. My parents had brought a jar of marmalade from our hometown in Rumelia. . . . I ate that marmalade every day at the [twenty-minute] lunch break during work for a year.[100]

Established scholarship often portrays *gecekondu* residents as rural migrants who were unable to urbanize and integrate into the subtleties of Istanbul's metropolitan culture.[101] Zeytinburnu refugees confirm that they were occupied simultaneously with industrial and agricultural activities. Almost all residents mention cow farming; some fed thirty to forty goats at a time; others had large goats, sheeps, chickens, and dogs.[102] As Besim Sadıker confirms, every migrant coming from Rumelia was already skilled in agriculture and continued farming activities in their gardens.[103] Those expelled from Bulgaria in 1950 had arrived almost exclusively from villages.[104] Mehmet Alpay reiterates that he lived exactly like his father and grandfather in a Rumelian village.[105] Ayşe Ceylan from central Anatolia describes her experience as "coming from one village to another village."[106] As a matter of fact women who fed cows in the garden and made yogurt from milk earned more money than their husbands in the factory.[107] Cengizhan Mutlu mentions his discomfort with the "socialized and noble" lifestyle of urbanized Istanbul, which prompted him to move to Zeytinburnu.[108] Almost everyone remembers eating from cherry, sour cherry, plum, and other fruit trees in their own gardens, as well as from the wild berry trees that covered the entire landscape (*dutluklar*).

The truth is, industrial capitalists and Istanbul's elite benefited from the unurbanized existence of *gecekondu* settlers that they looked down on. One might wonder why half the residents in big cities lived in illegal houses across Turkey—a country known for the militant ways of its rulers. Was it because of negligence, miscalculation, or a conscious choice that successive Turkish governments did not prevent the growth of *gecekondu* settlements? Was the state helpless in the face of urbanization and modernization and its own citizens who settled on lands that did not belong to them? Why did the state demolish *gecekondu* houses as a mechanism of social control, rather than instituting a policy for a planned city and formalized housing? Why did it create an endless loop of repetition between collapse and rebuilding? Why was Zeytinburnu allocated as a heavy industrial zone but with no prospect of building public housing for industrial workers? Can it be that the state turned a blind eye to the *gecekondu* settlements' long-term harms in order to allocate the country's resources elsewhere? As self-built solutions to the workers' housing shortage, "*gecekondu* not only provided cheap labor for industry," as scholar Ilhan Tekeli explains, "but also reduced the resources allocated to urbanization, which could be transferred to industrialization."[109] In other words, *gecekondu* was a problem from the viewpoint of urban planners, but it was an opportunistic solution from the viewpoint of industrial capitalists. It made urbanization a cheaper expense in the state's budget. Some may argue that this Global South or Third World way has saved urban residents from the top-down regulations of formal state housing. However, calling these settlements "informal cities" for this reason rather than "slums" obscures the hidden harms of uneven capitalist development.

The movie *Çark* (Wheel) directed by Muzaffer Hiçdurmaz and shot on location provides a stark depiction of buildings in Zeytinburnu's industrial zone in 1987, before the tanneries and factories gradually moved out of the area due to the workers' strikes that started days after the movie (figure 3.8).[110] Hordes of men, women, children, and disabled workers (many actors were chosen from real-life workers) arrive at the Kazlıçeşme train station in the morning. The day is dark, and the air is covered with smoke coming out of the factory chimneys. Buildings are high, and streets are narrow and blocked with piles of animal remains and unused skins. Arriving at the zone for the first time and obviously disturbed by the sight and smell, a worker asks: "What kind of a place is this? This is worse than a slaughterhouse." It is like a "graveyard of the living," one comments; but all commercial shoes, belts, and coats are produced here, another states.[111] The workers in leather workshops are employed without insurance in unkept buildings with low ceilings, exposed pipes, and peeling wall paint. They work in crowded conditions, squeezed in between old machines, and subject to the punishing watchful eye of the midlevel boss. Leather production on an industrial scale is a smelly, muddy, and polluted business without necessary sanitary regulations. The industrial zone is just next to the sea, but the workers can hardly see even a glimpse of the blue waters. A child worker dies after being caught up in one of the machines. As the workers try to carry the blood-covered corpse of the child on their shoulders out of the industrial zone, they are blocked by police forces at every exit and threatened with being charged with illegally organizing a march and unauthorized absenteeism if they do not go back to their factories immediately. For about eight minutes, the camera follows the group as they try to find a way out of the narrow, labyrinthine, muddy, decaying, and blocked streets of Zeytinburnu's industrial zone. Finding no exit, the group lays the child's dead body on the ground of an urban square and puts their clothes on the deceased in a symbolic attempt to organize his funeral.

Zeytinburnu residents remember their hybrid life with industrial and agricultural activities fondly today with a hint of nostalgia. However, long-term infrastructural, economic, and sanitation problems hardly made this district a better alternative to formalized housing. In addition to low wages and lack of formal housing, the industrial economy in Zeytinburnu caused high levels of pollution with no accountability for residents' health. In a questionnaire in 1974, 89 percent of residents said their health conditions were poor due to the insufficiency of their houses.[112] Ali Yerli remembers

Figure 3.8 Aerial view of the industrial zone and tanneries of Zeytinburnu, Istanbul, ca. 1980. Zeytinburnu Municipality Archives.

that roofs were covered with white dust coming out of the cement factory's chimney, and that it was impossible to wear a white shirt as it would have been covered with black coal dust when one walked by the train station near the factories.[113] Fahriye Efeoğlu remembers that flat meadows became the city's waste dumping area, where residents collected scraps of wool, thread, and fabric "like ants in the trash."[114]

There was no water or electricity in the houses till the 1970s, and residents carried polluted limey water from the eight artesian wells and 174 fountains nearby.[115] This created yet another symbolic border between "uncivilized" Zeytinburnu and "civilized" Istanbul. In 1948, the government had issued a report where the artesian water wells and fountains of Istanbul were deemed "uncivilized" due to polluted water and waterborne diseases. The leadership thereby prepared master plans to construct a connected underground pipe network, but delays in integration to this infrastructure signaled negligence and continued existing hierarchies. As Asya Ece Uzmay writes, "Ad-hoc solutions like precarious mobile water carriers, artesian wells, fountains, and cesspools gave authorities the freedom to not take responsibility of these neighborhoods."[116] Even though there are no official numbers, pollution in the air and water caused diseases in Zeytinburnu, including the 1970 cholera outbreak that must have spread here from its epicenter in Sağmalcılar.[117]

A doctor by profession, Zeytinburnu resident Muzaffer Çavuşoğlu asserts that bronchitis was common in families who lived near the cement factory, and indeed "leather and cement factories spread disease."[118] Despite the fact that the biggest hospitals of the city were located in Zeytinburnu, nonmedical healers treated diseases at home.[119] At other instances, residents sought help at distant hospitals, because the Balıklı Greek and Surp Pırgiç Armenian hospitals only treated non-Muslim Istanbulite communities at that time.[120] The ambulances could not enter the neighborhood and the sick bodies had to be carried on shoulders.[121]

In her book *Pollution Is Colonialism*, Max Liboiron resists the definition of pollution as a healable environmental damage or a side effect, but exposes its root cause as settler-colonial mentality and extractive relation to land, which disregarded the Indigenous wisdom in North America. Modern science calculates pollution with measures such as critical load, tolerance dose, carrying capacity, or assimilative capacity that denotes the amount of permissible contaminant. However, the definition of pollution as a threshold beyond which the environment is considered harmed creates the misconception of nature as resilient and self-healing. It allows settler colonialists and industrialists to pollute the land until its maximum permissible level.[122] Similarly, pollution conceived as a side effect of industrial progress obscures and perpetuates the inequalities and harms caused by capitalist urbanization. In Zeytinburnu, the dual ideologies of resettler nationalism and capitalist urbanization turned migrants into industrial workers who breathed polluted air and drank contaminated water as if this was the price nations were willing to pay to heal from underdevelopment. While pollution is caused by settler colonialism in the context of post-Columbian Americas, as Liboiron convincingly argues, it is caused by resettler nationalism in the context of post-Ottoman Afro-Euro-Asia.

RESETTLER NATIONALISM IS DISPOSSESSION

The state policy for *gecekondu* areas swung between demolition and legalization between 1953 and 1980 in Turkey. Assuming that illegal construction would be superseded, the amnesty law of 1953 legalized previously built houses all over the country. As a result, the land in Zeytinburnu was sold to *gecekondu* residents between 1954 and 1959.[123] And yet, *gecekondu* construction did not come to an end either here or in the rest of Turkey. Those who arrived in Zeytinburnu after the 1960s bought the official title deed of the land, but still built illegal houses on these properties. Amnesty laws kept coming in 1963, 1966, and 1976 that legalized previously built houses.

It did not escape the public that these amnesty laws were granted especially before elections, and that the political parties used *gecekondu* legalization as a campaign tool.[124]

Who really owned the land that the migrants had unofficially settled on? In other words, whose land was the state selling to the migrants of resettler nationalism? The answer is complicated due to the residues of the Ottoman Empire's property regimes, its late integration into capitalism, and the dispossessions due to its dissolution. As discussed in the introduction and chapter 2, I do not use the word *dispossession* here with "first occupancy" claims or to validate the idea of possession, but as a process that shows the transformation of land into property and the disenfranchisements that take place during the institutionalization of a property regime. During the Ottoman Empire's classical period, farmers cultivated the agricultural land and paid taxes, but they could not claim this land as their private property. All land except those affiliated with a Muslim *vaqf* (foundation) or a non-Muslim foundation belonged to the state.[125] This started changing in the nineteenth century, and the Ottoman land regime had five categories that did not concurrently fit the European ones. State property increased after the dissolution of the Ottoman Empire when non-Muslim populations were exterminated or expelled, resulting, in many instances, in the de facto transfer of their land to the state. Two-thirds of Turkey's territory still belonged to the state at the end of the twentieth century, a situation that changed with the rise of neoliberalism.[126]

There were unresolved accounts about the previous owners and stewards of land in Zeytinburnu, before the state sold the land to *gecekondu* residents. Writing in 1974, Faik Akçay speculated that three-quarters of the land belonged to the Greek community.[127] Other historians argue that most of the area had belonged to Bezm-i Alem Valide Sultan and Sultan Beyazit-ı Veli Khan Endowments. In 1880, the Armenian community applied to design an Armenian neighborhood in this area, and their request was granted even though the construction never materialized. The land was registered in the name of Priest Agop from the Armenian Church, who sold some of the property to Armenian, Greek, and German individuals after the cancellation of the construction plans before 1914.[128] After Priest Agop's death, the rest of the land was eventually considered state property in an act of dispossession that was quite common for this period.

The Greek Patriarch and community had also received titles for land since the times of Beyazit II. The Balıklı Greek Hospital secured the large area on which it stands as the property of the Greek Patriarch and community with a title deed of 1837. After the Law on Foundations of 1936, when the Turkish state got a hold of much land from Ottoman *vaqfs* with the aim of dispossessing Islamic religious foundations and secularizing Turkey, the Greek Hospital's land was also expropriated. When the foundation took the decision to court, the Supreme Court of Appeals found the expropriation legitimate in 1971, claiming that it was not legal for non-Turkish persons to purchase land. This decision violated minority rights, as Istanbul Greeks were indeed citizens of Turkey. In 1975, the court admitted the mistake but held on to the position.[129]

After the amnesty law of 1953, the state sold one square meter for three liras to the *gecekondu* residents. Private owners sold it for 75–80 kuruş (cents) after realizing the existence of houses on their property whose dwellers would have been difficult to evict. There were countless confusions during the process, as the same house could be located on land whose parts belonged to an individual, a *vaqf*, and the municipality simultaneously.[130] This is to be expected due to the unresolved histories of property regimes and dispossession during the dissolution of the Ottoman Empire, and lawless decisions thereafter. In any event, starting in 1954, the Turkish state sold Zeytinburnu's lots to migrant settlers, some of which had been dispossessed or taken by deceit from the Islamic and Greek foundations, as well as exiled or murdered Armenian landowners. While refugees and rural migrants legitimately tried to make a life for themselves in arrival cities after being dispossessed themselves, land was turned into a mechanism of capitalization and dispossession within the ideology of resettler nationalism. Below, I show how this process continued during neoliberalism in the shape of wealth transfer to the Turkish-Islamist elite as the heir of resettler-nationalist ideology.

RESETTLER NATIONALISM HINDERS COSMOPOLITAN ETHICS

In their memoirs, Zeytinburnu residents speak fondly of their life in a district with migrants from different parts of the Balkans, Central Asia, and Turkey. Comments on solidarity, good neighborly relations, the absence of crime, monetary and material gifts, and lack of discrimination overflow in oral history documents.[131] Besim Sadıker says his family had no relatives or friends in Zeytinburnu when they migrated from Rumelia. When the state forces demolished their first *gecekondu* house, other Rumelian migrants who were complete strangers helped them build a new one.[132] Many residents characterize Zeytinburnu as a "cosmopolitan" neighborhood, using this word itself or others to that effect, such as a "mosaic" or an agglomeration of different cultures.[133] Burhan Eraslan characterizes living in a migrant district as "Zeytinburnu's biggest fortune at the time. People learned each other's culture, and lived together peacefully (*kardeşçe yaşamak*)."[134] For others, Zeytinburnu residents "bonded tight because they all shared the same destinity," and "complemented each other."[135] After the 1966 earthquake in Varto, Muş, victims were brought to Zeytinburnu, and residents shared their houses and food despite the fact that they did not speak one another's language.[136] Refugees from China, such as Abdulvahab Kılıç and Abdülfettah Malkoç, also underline multiculturalism with appreciation and solidariy between neighbors—people from seventy-two nations lived in Zeytinburnu, the latter speculates.[137]

Some insist there was "no discrimination," "no racism," or "no othering," either between different hometowners or migrants from different nations or between Muslims and non-Muslims.[138] Yet, one cannot help but notice many comments that contradict these assessments. Oral histories confirm that a majority fasted as a requisite of the Muslim faith, but those who did not observe fasting felt the pressure to hide it.[139] Zeytinburnu increasingly became a devout neighborhood, and voted for Islamist parties.[140] Even though migrants claim they were race-blind and did not pay attention to the place of origin, they refer to each other with their national identities. Sporadic comments give a sense of each other's perception. The migrants from Greece were very poor,[141] those from Yugoslavia did not know Turkish at first, those from Turkistan were so hardworking that they worked on their private sewing machines all night till dawn,[142] those from Giresun paid attention to same-city marriage.[143]

It was common to visit one another without notice and share migration stories.[144] It should not escape us that these stories were usually about violence and discrimination against Muslims and Turks, rather than the crimes of the Ottoman Empire or the Republic of Turkey.[145] Those who came from Yugoslavia after the free migration agreement explain their choice by referring to Turkey as their "motherland because it was Muslim."[146] In Kefayet Sertel's words, "I am so glad our parents brought us here; look what happened after we left. Look what happened in Bosnia, in Kosovo, in Macedonia."[147] Refugees from China and Soviet Union mention similar reasons, such as Abdülhak İren[148] and Reşide Yüksel. The latter says they took asylum in Turkey because they "belonged to the same religion and spoke the same language."[149] Only a few acknowledge, however, the previous Greek and

Armenian owners and remaining Greek residents of the district.[150] Even then, some mention feeding their farm animals in the Armenian Cemetery because of its abundant herbs, but without a sense of grief over the missing relatives that would have visited those graves.[151] Only a couple, like Yusuf Yonucu, acknowledge multireligious upbringing: "Our neighborhood was just adjacent to a city that had been the center of the Roman Empire, and three empires, and religions. It was impossible for us not to appropriate from those cultures. . . . With such a multicultural heritage, it is impossible to become a violent or discriminatory person. . . . For this reason, nobody was discriminated or 'othered' here due to their ethnicity or identity."[152]

One could only wish this was the majority viewpoint. Despite their high moral ground, these comments obscure the continuing hierarchies and instances of violence against the non-Muslim and non-Turkish citizens, fueled by the Turkification ideology of resettler nationalism. For instance, none of the residents mentions the expulsion of Istanbul Greeks in 1964. Only a couple mention the pogrom of September 6–7, 1955,[153] and Istanbul's "loss and impoverishment"[154] due to the event, when a mob attacked, destroyed, burned, and looted Greek and other non-Muslim businesses, religious spaces, schools, and houses, in retaliation to a state-sponsored lie that Atatürk's house had been bombed in Thessaloniki. The events of September 6–7 are remembered today for the monstrous destruction in the Pera District, but the non-Muslim buildings in Zeytinburnu were also attacked. The Balıklı Holy Spring and Church complex was smashed, and the sarcophaguses of the deceased Patriarchs in the church's rear courtyard were vandalized (figure 3.9).[155] The growth of racism against Istanbul Greeks who had been exempt from the 1923 exchange treaty (till 1964) coincides with the period when Zeytinburnu expanded as a *gecekondu* neighborhood and residents were granted their title deeds. Additionally, during this time, a highway network constructed in the 1950s under the Menderes government surrounded Zeytinburnu with the London highway (later E5) and the coastal highway from Florya.[156] This highway brought city services, but it also caused the erasure of non-Muslim heritage. During its construction along the city walls between Topkapı and Yedikule, the Karamanlı cemetery was removed. The tombstones with Karamanlı script—the written language of Cappadocian Greeks (chapter 2)—were carried to the Balıklı Greek complex, where they were repurposed as courtyard pavement.[157]

The removal of Karamanlı cultural heritage from Zeytinburnu during highway construction is a fitting metaphor of resettler-nationalist

Figure 3.9 Vandalized sarcophaguses of the patriarchs in the Monastery of the Life-Giving Spring and Panagia Pege Church at the Balıklı Greek (*Rum*) Complex, Zeytinburnu, Istanbul, 1955.

urbanization. The midcentury Turkification was also an ideology of wealth transfer. Scholars have shown that the state-sponsored development of a Turkish middle class is intricately connected to the long-term ideology of Turkification, which used policies such as wealth tax and labor camps to erode the wealth of non-Muslim entrepreneurs.[158] A 1928 pamphlet lists factory owners in Zeytinburnu's industrial zone as Greek, Armenian, and Jewish businessmen, but the situation started changing in the 1950s.[159] After the defeat in the Balkan War, a common objective of the Turkish nationalists was the establishment of a stronger economy with Muslim capitalists by diminishing the leadership of non-Muslim entrepreneurs.[160] From the viewpoint of Turkish nationalists, the leadership had belonged to the cronies of European imperialists during the integration of the Ottoman Empire into finance capitalism, and that had to be changed. In the following decades, Zeytinburnu's industrial zone became a testing ground for the right-wing parties that ruled Turkey for much of the post-1950 period in implementing an economic policy that aimed to make a Muslim and Turkish capitalist class and to put an end to the domination of non-Muslims. The same replacement was true for residential zones, as I discuss in the next section.

Collapse 3: Earthquake and Turkish-Islamic Cultural Ideology (1999–Present)

THE 1999 EARTHQUAKE, NEOLIBERAL URBANIZATION, AND JAPANESE EXPERTISE

The ever-expanding *gecekondu* settlement, the industrial zone, and the new highway network discussed in the previous section irreversibly changed Zeytinburnu from what it had been at the end of the Ottoman Empire and the first years of the republic. A stroll in Zeytinburnu during the 1960s to the 1980s would have been quite different from one in the 1920s. The Greek and Armenian religious and medical complexes and the Ottoman-Islamic foundations no longer rose as the main structures in the landscape, and some were now hidden behind new structures. The meadows and orchards were completely replaced by *gecekondu* houses in gardens that were now legalized. The leather and other factories created a polluted, dense urban fabric with narrow streets without sufficient sanitation or regulation. The same stroll in 1999 would have been even more striking because of its difference from the one at midcentury. Most strikingly, all the single-story *gecekondu* houses in gardens were now replaced by five- or six-story (or higher) multi-family apartment buildings that filled up the entire lots and eliminated the previous gardens. The Greek, Armenian, and Ottoman-Islamic foundations were now dwarfed by these taller and larger apartment buildings made out of reinforced concrete. As evident from the 1999 earthquake, these multistory apartment buildings were also prone to collapse (figure 3.10).

How did this happen? The transformation of the refugee and migrant settlements into legal but earthquake-prone real estate constitutes yet another episode in the long chain of collapses. This conversion of *gecekondu* houses to multistory and multifamily apartment buildings that increased Zeytinburnu's population to 250,000 by 2000 is a typical example of neoliberal urbanization after 1980. Turkey's violent military coup in 1980 coincided concurrently with the neoliberalization of the world that is usually traced to the Washington Consensus in the same year. Another series of updated amnesty laws in 1983 and 1984 made it easier to apply for license, increased allowable construction area, and thereby turned *gecekondu* legalization into a lucrative opportunity for slum profiteers. Larger and taller buildings were now constructed lot by lot by individual developers on the existing irregular urban fabric of the previous *gecekondu* settlements, without proper inspection of ground or construction. Amnesty law was now no longer a justified empowerment of the urban poor but a new urban development strategy.

Figure 3.10 Apartment buildings built after the 1980s, Zeytinburnu, Istanbul. Photos: Esra Akcan, 2021.

When this process opened *gecekondu* zones to real estate investment, the *gecekondu* owners in Zeytinburnu (and elsewhere) gave their lands and houses to individual developers in exchange for modern apartments in new buildings. Zeytinburnu's first settlers admit that the process made them richer, albeit disproportionately.[161] However, the actual winners were the middle-class constructors and real estate developers. The dispossession of non-Muslim properties and their distribution to Turkish entrepreneurs via conflict refugees was thus complete. On some level, this policy was an economic structure that enabled upward class mobility and decolonization as many Turkish nationalists considered capitulation to European powers as a form of capitalist colonization. But it was also an authorization for corruption: The resulting buildings are defenseless in the face of an earthquake. It is a well-known "secret" that many developers took advantage of the lack of official control to increase their profits, and cheated on the structural strength of the steel and the quality of sand hidden inside the poured concrete, making buildings vulnerable to earthquakes.[162]

As part of healing after the deadly 1999 earthquake, Zeytinburnu was selected as a pilot district for future earthquake damage prevention. The 1912 and 1999 earthquakes whose epicenters were to the west and east of Istanbul alarmed this metropolis that the next earthquake on the same fault line will be closer and deadlier. The Istanbul Metropolitan Municipality employed the Japan International Cooperation Agency (JICA) for a thorough report on Istanbul's vulnerability and preparedness for the next earthquake. Turkey's turn to Japan was not surprising, given Japan's long history of assistance to developing countries in disasters between 1945 and 1999.[163] The Japan Society of Civil Engineers prepared the damage and casualty report after the 1999 earthquake.[164] Shigeru Ban was one of the first respondents, appropriating the Paper Log houses he had devised after the Kobe disaster in Japan in relation to the conditions in Turkey, by using standard sizes of plywood and inserting shredded wastepaper into the paper tubes for more insulation.[165]

Japanese architects had already built a reputation for postearthquake reconstruction, including in cities from where many immigrants of Zeytinburnu came from, such as Skopje, Macedonia. Following an invited competition, the UN commissioned Kenzo Tange for a plan for Skopje after the 1963 earthquake with a generous UN Special Fund (figure 3.11). Skopje, or Üsküp, as Muslim migrants called it, would have become unrecognizable to many who emigrated from there if the Tange Team's project was built in its entirety. The team proposed a megastructure that managed the private vehicular, public rail, public vehicular, and pedestrian traffic to assist the development of the city and connect its parts. Composed of a City Gate ("a transformer" of scale and speed) and a City Wall ("a vessel" containing the existing and new structures), and fitting well with Tange's and Metabolists' ideas at the time, the report explained the adaptations and modifications to occur in time within the framework of the megastructure. The jury found many ideas respectable, but criticized the scale and the fact that some existing buildings and housing would not be preserved properly.[166] Kenzo Tange Team's project has been recognized as one of the most extensive international collaborations that brought together experts from both the First and Second Worlds of the Cold War in a nonaligned country. It has been praised as a crossroad that made Skopje the "City of Solidarity" and the focus of the UN's attention.[167] Those who advocate that big disasters should prompt brand new beginnings and large gestures received it favorably. However, the project also raises questions as part of a chain of urban policies that had marginalized the Ottoman heritage and eradicated Muslim houses in Skopje since the Balkan War. It maintained the subsequent regimes' treatment of minorities that had caused the desertification of Muslim neighborhoods and exodus to Turkey.[168]

The Japan International Cooperation Agency had been and continues to be deployed very often in disasters around the world.[169] In an extensive, ten-chapter report submitted to the Istanbul Municipality in December 2002, JICA thoroughly analyzed Istanbul's earthquake vulnerability and

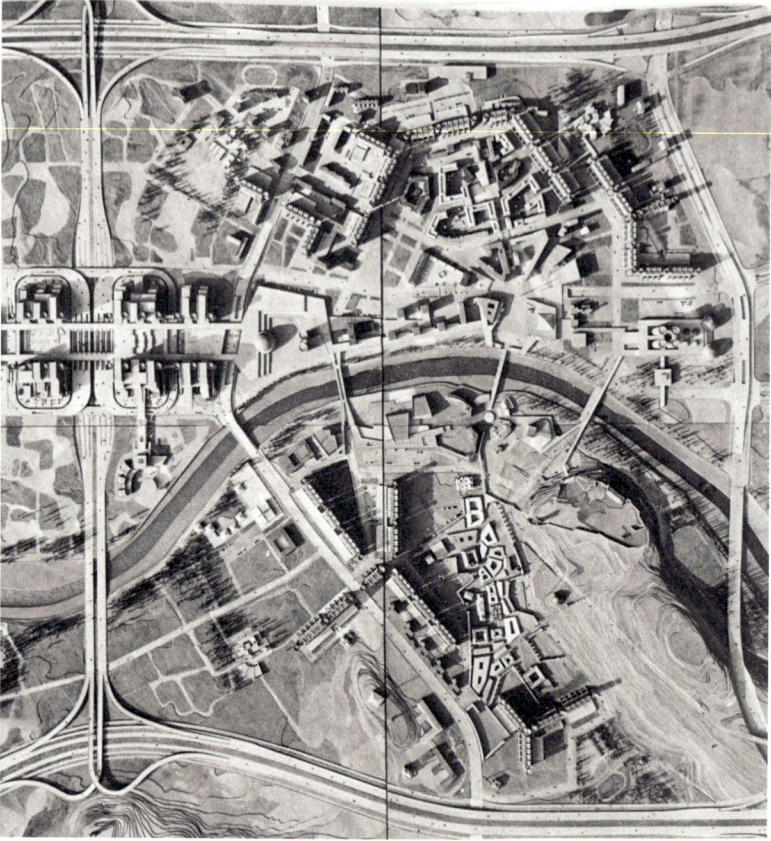

Figure 3.11 Kenzo Tange Team, postearthquake plan for Skopje, Macedonia. UN Special Fund, 1963.

preparedness from geological, geotechnical, seismic, legal, institutional, and social angles, such as disaster management, evacuation routes, availability of postdisaster first-response areas, and the role of civil society organizations (figure 3.12).[170] Zeytinburnu ranked high in vulnerability and low in preparedness. For instance, the report predicted 4,629 deaths and 6,785 severe injuries in Zeytinburnu in the next earthquake, which amounted to 1.9 percent and 2.8 percent of the district's overall population. This was a much higher number than the average expected for Istanbul (0.8 percent deaths and 1.4 percent injuries), which was already too high.[171] Researchers unanimously diagnosed the inadequate quality of reinforced concrete construction as one of the biggest liabilities. "Architects have been left out of the inspection procedures,"[172] they warned. All schools and probably other

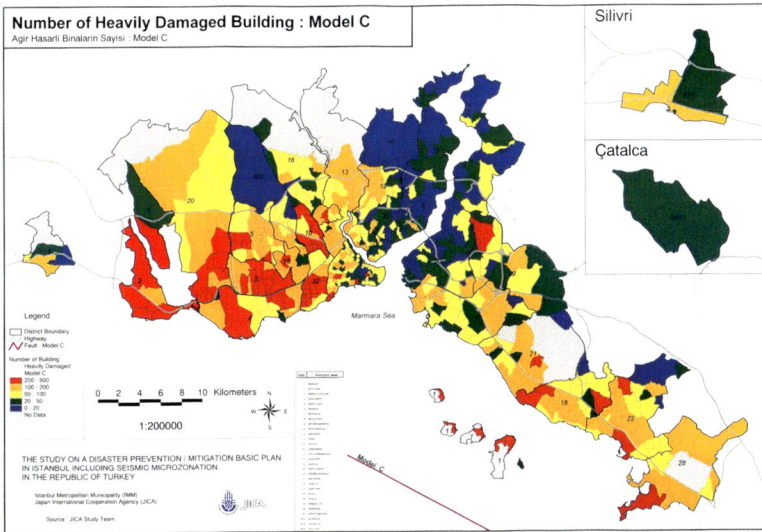

Figure 3.12 Japan International Cooperation Agency, "Number of Heavily Damaged Building[s]" expected in Istanbul in the next earthquake. From a report after the 1999 earthquake, prepared in December 2002.

public buildings were at risk, large fires were to be expected, and there were no sufficient unbuilt open areas for agglomeration after disaster.

As a result, Zeytinburnu was identified as the first pilot zone for "urban renewal in reference to earthquake" ("deprem referanslı kentsel dönüşüm"). The municipality governed by the Islamist Justice and Development Party (AK Party, hereafter), which took office partially as a consequence of the 1999 earthquake, was supposed to identify buildings prone to damage and replace them with state-sponsored housing.[173] In 2013, fourteen years after the earthquake, the government-affiliated construction company KIPTAS finally finished a housing project in the vulnerable Sümer neighborhood to the west of the district. Negotiating with 250 current families that used to reside in twenty-five buildings, the urban reconstruction project resettled them in a typical social housing compound.

The prime minister and head of the AK Party, Recep Tayyip Erdoğan, made the grand opening on February 23, 2013, along with the Zeytinburnu Municipality's Mayor Murat Aydın from the same political party. The latter did not miss the opportunity to promote this undertaking as a "modern Robin Hood who takes from the rich and gives to the poor," so that "houses are no longer our coffins."[174] This was quite an overstatement even for the standards of political propaganda. The twenty-five buildings replaced with state-sponsored housing amounted to only 0.46 percent of the 5,334 buildings expected to collapse in a possible earthquake in Zeytinburnu.[175] Moreover, the small percentage of "lucky" residents were resettled in their new homes fourteen years after the previous earthquake. Instead, as the next section demonstrates, the same company constructed luxury apartments in gated communities on sites reserved for earthquake mitigation. Moreover, the AK Party government and the Zeytinburnu Municipality shifted their attention and resources to a "cultural project," as if in a subconscious retaliation of Kenzo Tange Team's postearthquake scheme for Skopje. Using its own regulations of 2004 and 2005 that gave extreme powers to evict residents in *gecekondu* and other settlements,[176] the regime built high-end museums and religious centers to glorify its ancestors and to minimize the cosmopolitan heritage of the area.

THE 1999 CULTURAL VALLEY PROJECT

The same year as the earthquake in 1999, the newly elected mayor of Zeytinburnu Municipality, Murat Aydın, embarked on an ambitious "Cultural Valley" project, in order to "construct an identity that would improve the sense of belonging for those who live in the district."[177] The mayor approached the established architect Turgut Cansever for guidance, who submitted his report in May 2000 (figure 3.13).[178] The municipality declared to have chosen Cansever by virtue of his approach to architecture "as a matter of morals, and therefore religion."[179] Known for his competent buildings whose abstract and modernized forms were inspired by Islamic paintings and theological principles, as he explained at the time,[180] Cansever prioritized the preservation and valorization of the historical buildings in Zeytinburnu. "In that way," he said, "the next generations will not be deprived of reaching the wisdom that has been left to extinction in the depths of history."[181]

The most striking and consequential decision in Cansever's report was the renaming of Zeytinburnu as the "conquest area" (*fetih alanı*). Referring to Mehmet II's conquest of Istanbul (then Constantinople) in 1453 as the chronological marker that divides history into a "before" and "after," Cansever insisted:

> The most important task is to revive the historical fabric in this area where the important war of conquest took place, and to meet every contemporary need by showing respect to this sublime heritage. It is necessary to arrange the area with memories of the conquest war, the

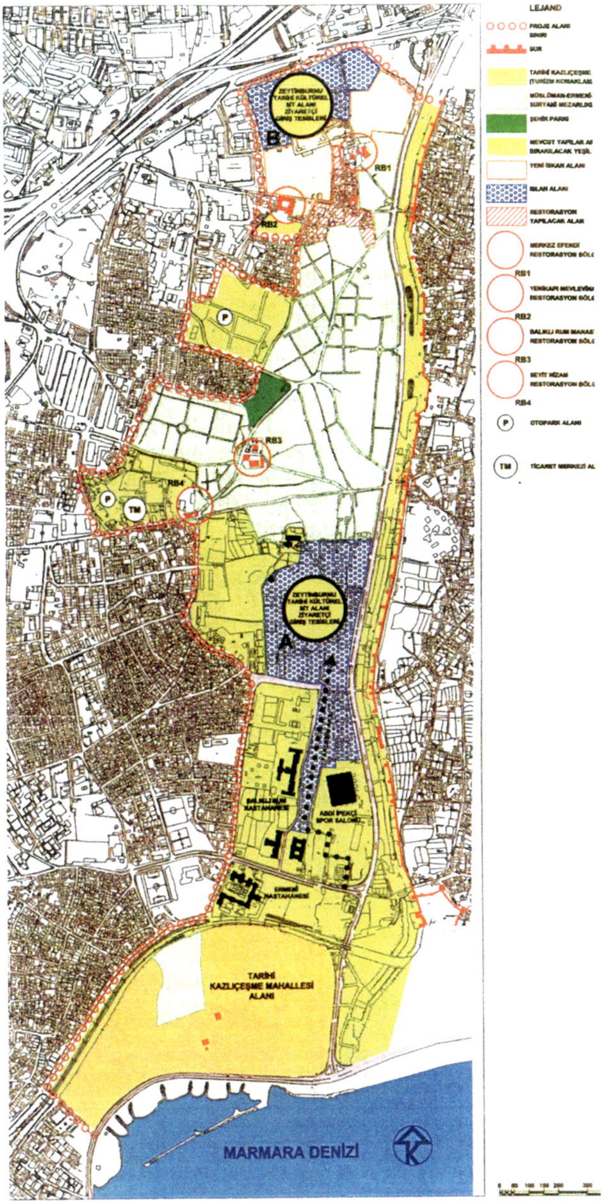

Figure 3.13 Turgut Cansever, plan for Zeytinburnu Cultural Valley project, Istanbul, 2000.

coffeehouses outside the city walls, the roads that reached the city gates after lines of defense, and the small squares that were the meeting places of those who entered and exited the city. When the project area is arranged with the architectural design and urbanism approach that it deserves, people who pass through the narrow but sublime city gates will find themselves in a wide-open area and will come face to face with the historical war of conquest . . . in all its stunning intensity.[182]

As scholar Jenny White and architectural historians Bülent Batuman and Berin Gür show, the political leaders and intelligentsia of Turkish-Islamist circles have recently valorized the Ottoman conquest of Istanbul in 1453 as the victory of Islam over Christendom, and are using ceremonies and architectural symbols to reify this meaning and to rewrite the conquest as the founding moment of the current Turkish nation.[183] The reconversion of Hagia Sophia from a museum into a mosque in 2020, where conquest narratives poured out during the opening ceremony, was the widest-reaching broadcast of this reconstructed architectural heritage to national and international audiences. As this chapter reveals, Cansever's Zeytinburnu Cultural Valley project of 1999 was its earliest architectural indicator.

To exhibit the "conquest area in all its stunning intensity," Cansever identified artifacts of Ottoman cultural heritage and proposed to remove all structures that had been built around them in the time of the Republic of Turkey. He selected four mosques, four dervish lodges, five fountains, eleven "examples of civil architecture" (that included the Balıklı Greek Complex and the Greek and Armenian hospitals), the city walls, and cemeteries for preservation, and proposed to add buildings that would serve as visitor centers.[184] All the rest would be cleared. Cansever's office and the municipality legitimized this clearance with the need for earthquake prevention and evacuation. "The buildings had lost their foundations, their columns were removed, and they lacked structure. Approximately 92 percent of Zeytinburnu would be unusable [after an earthquake]. . . . People were working in unnecessary services in a very valuable area that could have become a significant place for urbanism and international visitors. They had to be transported to their real places."[185]

Thus entered Feruz Kutsal, the chief security officer (*zabıta müdürü*) in Zeytinburnu Municipality who was put in charge of demolition. Describing himself as "the Conqueror's grandson," and starting with the restaurants that sold alcohol, he "cleaned" all of the houses, retail shops, peddlers, workshops, garages, and teahouses around the mosques and dervish lodges, or on the site of the projected buildings, despite protests, brawls, and lawsuits.[186] This included the remaining Armenian and Greek grocery store and bakery that were the oldest businesses in the area and nice childhood memories for residents.[187] Collapse had now taken the form of state demolition in the name of extinguishing anything that stood in the way of monumentalizing the conquest of Istanbul as the origin of Turkish-Islamic culture.

Following Cansever's call to write the history of the area "before and after the conquest,"[188] the municipality construed the Cultural Valley as a historiographical project as well.[189] It funded high-quality books, which the mayor introduced as "the history of [a] 'locality' that had been left behind by the Renaissance."[190] The ambitious publication program contributed significantly to knowledge, but many authors produced either a tone-deaf or a cultural imperialist account of the past. When reporting on the orphans in the Armenian Hospital or the decreasing number of patients in the Greek Hospital, for instance, the articles did not mention the events of 1915, the Exchange of Populations Treaty of 1923, or the expulsion of Istanbulite Greeks of 1964.[191] When introducing a 1,614-page book that "read the geography of Islam" through gravestones, recording the Arabic script, decoration, and stone on every Muslim grave in the area, the author referred to an anecdote in which a Western historian was lectured about the relative size of Armenian and Muslim graveyards. "Cemeteries construct an important argument in showing the real owners of the land and country (*vatan*)," the author Süleyman Berk remarked as if the smaller size of an Armenian Cemetery in comparison to the Muslim could serve as an evidence for the denial of genocide.[192]

Indeed, the Cultural Valley project intended to make exactly the same argument as this necropolitan history. It aimed to overwhelm the entire landscape with the size and scale of Turkish-Islamic artifacts. In the next two decades, tax money poured in for the preservation of selected buildings and the construction of new monuments that acted out the revenge of the Balkan War defeat and completed the dispossession on a symbolic level.

A STROLL IN ZEYTINBURNU IN 2019

A stroll in Zeytinburnu in 2019 would demonstrate the extent of the "cultural renewal" undertaken according to the Cultural Valley project, after Zeytinburnu's designation as an urban renewal zone for earthquake prevention. Starting from the north and walking south toward the sea, one would notice a cluster of new buildings in the area that was designated as the Visitor Center in Cansever's sketch. The first is the Panorama 1453 History Museum, which

Figure 3.14 Painted panorama of the conquest of Istanbul (then Constantinople) by Mehmet II in 1453. Hilmi Şenalp (architect), Haşim Vatandaş (painter), and Özkul Eren (designer), Panorama 1453 History Museum, Zeytinburnu Cultural Valley, Istanbul, 2003–9. Photo: Esra Akcan, 2019.

reenacts the conquest of Istanbul and the defeat of the Roman Empire, built between 2003 and 2009 according to the plans of architect Hilmi Şenalp, painter Haşim Vatandaş, and designer Özkul Eren, in the tradition of the eighteenth-century painted panoramas located in circular buildings.[193] The walkway to the rotunda is filled with maps and panels of history lessons, including detailed, step-by-step explanations of the war of conquest, and assertions that the Prophet Mohammed had foretold Muslims' conquest of Istanbul. Once entering the rotunda, the visitor is supposed to be transported to a war scene and immerse herself in the experience, which is augmented by dramatic lighting and loud epic sounds of cannons and screaming soldiers. The panoramic painting depicts a victorious scene at the site of the conquest, with flags, cannons, swords, fires, and soldiers who fight on foot or on horses. The majestic Theodosian walls are crumbling, and Ottoman soldiers are pushing the third line of defense. Apart from these walls and a small fountain, the conquest area, Zeytinburnu, is unbuilt, but instead filled with Sultan Mehmet's soldiers and war machines (figure 3.14).[194] The Panorama 1453 museum started a fashion in AK Party circles, who reenacted the conquest scene with architectural models and exhibited them in the city's most prestigious and previously secular cultural buildings.[195]

The Cultural Center of the Turkish World (Türk Dünyası Kültür Merkezi) is located to the north as part of the same compound, and accessed

through a wide park over the highway junction with public transportation stops. In his report, Cansever had proposed to carry out historical research so that the original location of Mehmet II's headquarters and the tent of conquest could be identified.[196] Sure enough, in a few years, and shortly after the convenient removal of the Topkapı Intercity Bus Station from the area in 1994, the Istanbul Municipality claimed that this site was the location of the original conquest headquarters. The leadership then built small museums representing the cultures of Azerbaijan, Kazakhstan, Uzbekistan, Kirgizstan, Turkmenistan, Tatarstan, the Turkish Republic of Northern Cyprus, and the "Turkish Presence in the Balkans" there (figure 3.15). This is a public history operation that manipulates the suffering of refugees and asylum-seekers from the Balkans, China, and the Soviet Union to claim an exclusively Turkified and Islamified heritage in Istanbul. In an emulating retaliation against traditional World Expos aimed at reversing the geopolitical hierarchy they constructed by paying scant attention to the Ottoman Empire and Muslim culture, each pavilion in the Zeytinburnu complex contains history panels, books, carpets, building photographs, furniture, domestic artifacts, clothing, and, if relevant, information about the post-Soviet nationalization and modernization projects. The pavilions also display photographs of each country's president shaking hands with the Turkish President Erdoğan. There are wall texts in large fonts, stating sentiments such as "Azerbaijan Turkey: One Nation, Two States" or "You started living on Anatolia, we [Uzbekistan] stayed in our ancestors' land. Despite the distance between us, our hearts have never departed." Of particular note are the two large, impressive, colorfully carpeted and decorated tents, gifted by the republics of Kirgizstan and Kazakhstan to

Istanbul Municipality and Erdoğan himself, respectively (figure 3.16). By the 2000s, the Central Asian population of Zeytinburnu had reached approximately 16.4 percent of the district;[197] and Fifty-Eighth Street had become the commercial and cultural center with ample civil society organizations and restaurants. In her anthropological study of Zeytinburnu's Uyghur migrants and asylum-recipients in 2015, Yasemin Çakırer Özservet concluded that the district "has a special character that welcomes migrants, not all but of a specific kind—those who have Turkish origins. It is not possible for migrants who do not have Turkish roots to be integrated into the social networks, no matter where they come from."[198] There are ample examples that support this conclusion in the publications on Zeytinburnu. Passionate statements about Muslim and Turkish suffering and Turkey's hospitality in giving asylum are coupled with hateful speech against Kurdish and Armenian citizens of Turkey. Migrants who frequently use the legally unrecognized term *East Turkistan* to refer to their hometowns in China or to name their civil society organizations and shops, react vehemently to the word *Kurdistan*, or disdain that international powers recognize the Armenian but not the Uyghur genocide.[199] This is not to say that there is a lack of self-criticism. An asylum-recipient from China, Yusuf Kulca, criticizes the ubiquity of identity-based civil society organizations, and instead calls on migrants from China and the ex-Soviet Union to establish human rights–based migrant movements.[200] In this context, the state-built Cultural Center of the Turkish World in Zeytinburnu is an architectural way of reifying identity-based immigration policy, as well as the Turkification and Islamification of Istanbul under the guise of hospitality and integration.

Continuing south on the stroll, one would arrive at the renovated Merkez Efendi Complex, a priority in the Cultural Valley project, whose buildings are now connected with an urban design that includes a large terrace paved with shiny white marble and surrounded with a U-shaped canopy that overlooks the city (figure 3.17). Close by is another building in the form of a vaulted canopy, designed by Cansever's daughter, Emine Öğün, and Mehmet Öğün. Relying on Evliya Çelebi's account that there were houses surrounding the Merkez Efendi Dervish Lodge, and partially following Cansever firm's proposal to build an "Ottoman neighborhood" in the area,[201] the municipality renovated and reconstructed several buildings in accordance with the typology of the "Turkish house."[202] The new complex creates traditional Ottoman-looking streets and integrates the renovated tomb, *hamam* (Turkish bath), harem (women's quarter), and three renewed large mansions (figure 3.18). The "Ottoman Neighborhood" leads smoothly to the

Figure 3.15 Architectural model of the Cultural Center of the Turkish World. Zeytinburnu Cultural Valley project of 1999, Istanbul. Photo: Esra Akcan, 2021.

Figure 3.16 Tent gifted by the Republic of Kirgizstan for the Cultural Center of the Turkish World, Zeytinburnu Cultural Valley, Istanbul. Photo: Esra Akcan, 2019.

Figure 3.17
Urban renewal of the Merkez Efendi Complex, Zeytinburnu Cultural Valley project of 1999, Istanbul. Photo: Esra Akcan, 2019.

Figure 3.18
"Ottoman Neighborhood" created for the Zeytinburnu Cultural Valley project of 1999, Istanbul. Photo: Esra Akcan, 2019.

renovated Yenikapı Mevlevi Lodge complex, now repurposed as part of the Fatih University. Public performances of whirling dervishes regularly take place here (see figure 3.2).

Walking south along the cemeteries, one would come across the "Garden of Healing Plants" (Tıbbi Bitkiler Bahçesi), another new addition to the district that opened in 2005. The municipality built this garden as a material counterpart of the medical festival in the memory of Merkez Efendi's healing paste (*mesir macunu*). Seven hundred healing plants from Anatolia and tropical climates have been transported into Zeytinburnu's Garden of Healing Plants, where some are replanted outside and others are kept inside a greenhouse that regulates the climate (figure 3.19). In the accompanying catalogue that introduces each plant's origin and healing capacities, the authors criticize the side effects of Western medicine and the biopirating through which the medicine industry makes millions out of traditional seeds without giving due financial or symbolic acknowledgment to the caretakers of these plants. To create a reliable guide for those interested in healing through natural plants, but somewhat in a self-contradicting manner, the book promotes following the tradition of Western colonial botanical gardens.[203] In a district of human migrations, the Garden of Healing Plants creates a controlled environment of migrant species. At the same time, however, it perpetuates the divide between Western and Eastern, modern and traditional medicine in a neighborhood previously known for its Greek and Armenian hospitals. The Islamic religious leader Merkez Efendi's traditional healing paste is mobilized to build a showcase that follows the colonial tradition of botanical gardens and participates in an urban renewal project—one that aims to retaliate for the past with the Turkish regime's aspiration to become a new imperial power.

Even though they are next to each other and even though both make a claim to traditional healing methods, there is no access between the Garden of Healing Plants and the Balıklı Complex. Tourists who visit the Monastery of the Life-Giving Spring and Panagia Pege Church in the Greek Orthodox Complex no longer mix with Zeytinburnu's local residents. The sarcophaguses of the deceased Patriarchs that had been vandalized during the events of September 6–7 in 1955 have been restored, and the tombstones with Karamanlı script that had been saved from highway construction still pave the front courtyard. Nuns from Greece still take fellowships to spend time in the Balıklı Complex, and religious services still continue in the church. And yet these happen in a sealed environment. "Tourists and communities come with buses, spend time and leave with the same buses without stepping into the neighborhood," says Ayfer Mertler, who works in the Zeytinburnu

Figure 3.19 Garden of Healing Plants, opened in 2005. Zeytinburnu Cultural Valley, Istanbul. Photo: Esra Akcan 2019.

Municipality and whose parents had migrated from Greece.[204] The same is true for the funeral and church services in the nearby Armenian Cemetery. A rare addition is the Balıklı Armenian Church, only visible upon entering the Armenian Cemetery, commissioned by Sarkis Gövderelioğlu and designed by architect Yetvart Şahbaz in 1985. As one of the few newly built Armenian churches in Turkey after 1915, it combines modern formal gestures with traditional symbols, such as the continuous surface that folds the pitched roof into the side wall, acute angular fenestration, and bell towers (figure 3.20).

To the west of the Balıklı Greek Complex and next to the cemeteries, a new mosque has been built to complement the restored Seyyid Nizam tomb, designed by architect Aydın Yüksel and constructed in 2013–14. Following Cansever's report that called for the recognition of the Baghdad-born religious leader Seyyid Nizam, the new mosque, the existing tomb, and the auxiliary structures complement the historiographical project to revive his memory.[205] Walking farther south through the cemeteries, one would pass the buildings of the Greek Hospital, located in large green spaces, and the Armenian Hospital behind its gates. By now the clientele of the hospitals is different. After a restoration in 1991, the Greek Hospital started treating any patient, and the only section that remained exclusively for Greeks was the Seniors' house (or nursing home).[206] A fire broke out in this building

Figure 3.20 Yetvart Şahbaz, Balıklı Armenian Church, Zeytinburnu, Istanbul, 1985. Exterior view (*left*) and interior (*right*). Photos: Esra Akcan 2019.

on August 4, 2022, precisely when I was writing these pages, traumatizing the seniors who already felt deserted due to the expulsion of their extended families and relatives (figure 3.21). Taking the stroll in the Cultural Valley, one would see at a distance the city walls, a stretch of which has been restored, the remaining slice of the *bostan* (farmland) along those walls, where farmers cultivated agricultural land for fifteen centuries, several fountains, and some newly constructed university buildings. Finally, one would reach the old Ottoman military hospital in the now removed industrial zone (see figure 3.4). Late Roman and early Byzantine mosaics were discovered during the restoration of this building, when it was being repurposed by the municipality in 1984. Extended excavations, conducted until 2019, located a burial chamber, sarcophagus, and skeletons.[207] The building has now been adapted partially as a museum displaying the mosaics—a gentle reminder of what lies beneath this all.

Apartment buildings built between 1980 and 2000 in the inlands of the district still overwhelm the land despite their vulnerability to earthquake. A notable exception is the cluster of buildings in the geometric center of the area, where the new tall municipal building and its distinct mosque on the entrance piazza are located. A large shopping mall is situated nearby, as well as the District Administration and Center for Art and Culture, a newly designed Square of July 15 in commemoration of the failed coup against

Figure 3.21 Balıklı Greek (*Rum*) Hospital, Zeytinburnu, Istanbul, burning. The complex was built in 1753, expanded in 1894, restored in 1991; the Seniors' house caught fire on August 4, 2022.

Erdoğan in 2016. Needless to say, all these well-funded and recently constructed buildings are daily reminders of the Turkish-Islamic regime's current wealth and triumph.

Moreover, Zeytinburnu is now surrounded by large gated communities. They are constructed with the same market enthusiasm, crony procedures, and resulting aesthetics that changed Istanbul during its neoliberal development supported by the Islamist AK Party regime.[208] The leather factories in the industrial zone had been gradually demolished when the leather production moved to Tuzla in the 1990s. The old industrial zone has become prime real estate, and gradually gets occupied by skyscrapers and luxury Cando buildings with gorgeous views of the Marmara Sea. The neoliberal building boom has also spread to the areas that had been designated as earthquake-mitigation zones. The municipal construction company KIPTAS is constructing luxury apartment buildings in the Sümer neighborhood—an earthquake-prevention zone in the Zeytinburnu borough (figure 3.22).[209]

Conclusion: More Culture or More Collapse?

The architects and policymakers of the Cultural Valley took pride in Zeytinburnu's cosmopolitanism given the different religions and cultures that had coexisted in this district for centuries.[210] And yet they embarked on an ambi-

Figure 3.22 Luxury housing in Zeytinburnu's zone reserved for "urban renewal in reference to earthquake." Photo: Esra Akcan, 2019.

tious project that trivialized and concealed the non-Turkish and non-Muslim architectural remnants and relics. With every single decision, the Cultural Valley was meant to remind people of the Ottoman conquest of Istanbul and thereby to create a hierarchy in their minds. Fighting the relative negligence of Ottoman buildings, religious leaders, and industrial design in the area, historians unearthed documents and published volumes of books, but did not reach out to the Greek or Armenian community members to tell their own stories of the holy spaces, hospitals, or cemeteries. The demolitions and preservation projects brightened the Muslim Ottoman structures. The newly constructed museums and exhibition spaces, additions to religious complexes, gardens, botanical parks, and urban designs underlined Muslimness and Turkishness. One has feelings of déjà vu on hearing the metaphors used to promote the Cultural Valley and realizing how they match the ones that immediately followed the defeat in the Balkan War. Revenge and regaining honor, reversing the affluence of non-Muslims and the poverty of Muslims, and the mobilization of Muslim refugees from Rumelia for the purposes of nationalism were common concerns among the Ottoman publications immediately following the Balkan War.[211] Generations have learned about the Balkan War in textbooks as an "incident that robbed the Ottomans of their European territory which they had 'chivalrously' conquered and 'justly' ruled for centuries."[212] Absorbing the sequence of resettler nationalism, industrial capitalism, and Turkish-Islamic cultural supremacy, the Cultural Valley project culminated in a hierarchically conceived assimilation of "other cultures" into Istanbul. This was conquest culture posing as cosmopolitan existence and cultural imperialism posing as peaceful leadership.

On May 6, 2021, a five-story building collapsed in Zeytinburnu.[213] There was no earthquake, no explosion due to a civil war, no state demolishing the building. Built in 1995 but without a license, the building fell down with no apparent cause (figure 3.23). This incident is not only a reminder of what could happen in the upcoming earthquake, but also an alarm that collapse could take place anytime due to years of negligence, real estate greed, and the corruption of the construction industry. A sociological study in Zeytinburnu in the 2010s found out that adoption of earthquake-risk mitigation was very low (30 percent) among residents, and fatalistic emotions that identify earthquake damage as God's will were overwhelming.[214] A report in 2019 exposed that the number of evacuation routes and postdisaster agglomeration areas have actually decreased in Istanbul since the 1999 earthquake, despite all the expert advice to do precisely the opposite, and despite the twenty years that should have been utilized for earthquake mitigation.[215] Moreover, journalists found out that the government manipulated the bidding law that had been reserved for earthquake emergencies and used the tax money that had been collected for earthquake preparedness in order to carry out large scale projects that profited its supporters.[216]

The government-affiliated construction company KIPTAS carries out luxury housing projects not only in the earthquake-prevention zones of Zeytinburnu but also other *gecekondu* areas where migrants from the Balkans had settled. In the Venezia Mega Mall and Housing Complex in Gaziosmanpaşa, for example, the residential blocks and towers overlook a shopping mall that is a miniaturized mock-up of the city of Venice, Italy. They form a monumental fortress that separates the locals outside from the luxury compound's residents and shoppers inside. Residents live among the replicas of Venetian canals, cruise in gondolas, and eat in restaurants located on a miniature of Piazza San Marco (figure 3.24).[217] As a matter of fact, the Venezia Mega Mall and Housing Complex exposes the scale and intensity of a common crony capitalist urbanism, because many other housing compounds of this kind served as a tool that produced neoliberal wealth and channeled it to the AK Party supporters. A study in 2008 found out that a considerable majority (approximately 70 percent) of the construction bids for state-sponsored buildings had been channeled to companies whose stakeholders were mem-

Figure 3.23 A building in Zeytinburnu that collapsed on May 6, 2021, with no apparent cause.

bers of the party itself, its allies, or those associated with political Islam.[218] In Zeytinburnu, the government spent the resources that could have been allocated for the protection of residents from earthquakes on the Cultural Valley, which was designed to establish the supremacy of the Turkish-Islamic monuments over all else that had existed in the district. More culture brought more collapse.

One may wish that Zeytinburnu was an exception, but the laws and government policies were nationwide and impunity for corruption was contagious. As I was writing, a disastrous earthquake hit southeastern Turkey and Syria on February 6, 2023. The official death toll in Turkey was reported as 50,096, but the real number must be four or five times higher, when one accounts for the missing bodies trapped inside multistory collapsed buildings. Coming back to the opening question of this chapter: Is death in collapse a misfortune or an injustice? The 2023 earthquake should spark anger and frustration because a majority of these deaths could have been prevented. It exposed that not much has been learned from previous disasters. On the contrary, the hidden violence of a corrupt construction industry had escalated and the ruling government had turned earthquake-mitigation measures into an instrument of wealth transfer. Under the rule of crony capitalism of the 2000s, the illegal settlements became a "legitimate" market, and legality became a slippery ground. The "lawful" was determined less by the law

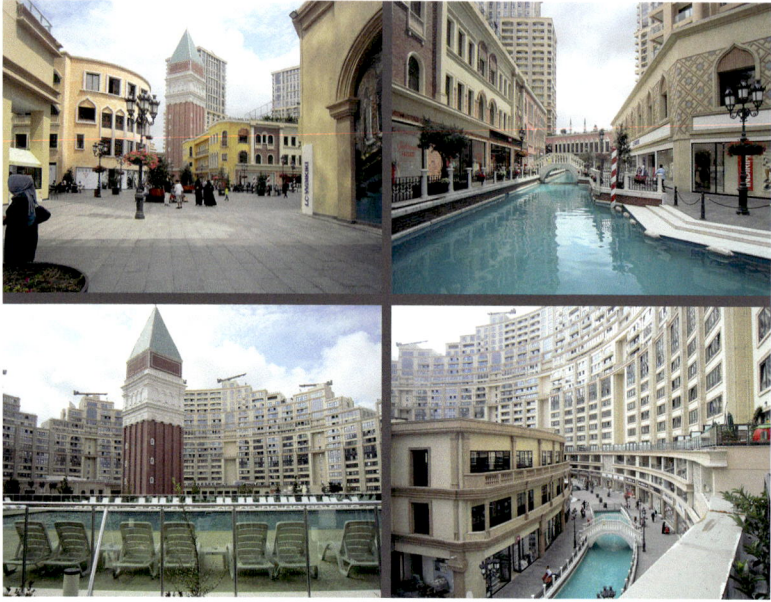

Figure 3.24 Venezia Mega Mall and Housing Complex, Gaziosmanpaşa, Istanbul. Photos: Esra Akcan, 2016.

and more by the authority, who was not held accountable for earthquake disasters.[219]

Murder with buildings and collapse in modern cities is the deadly convergence of geologic hazards and architectural priorities. Forced migration, uneven urban development, negligence, and real estate greed turned these cities into ticking time bombs for disasters. If one ever wonders why some buildings stand firmly while others kill tens of thousands in an earthquake, the answer is not because some people were unfortunate, or because there is no science to prevent collapse, but because authorities and developers did not value experts, discredited scholarship, and prioritized profit over human life. The real cause of disaster was hardly the earthquake itself, but the corrupt construction industry backed up by the ruling elite. One can only hope that this will be the last incident, and that this earthquake will put an end to the loop of repetition. One can only hope that the accountability measures and reparations will, this time, bring institutional and moral reform so that such a disaster will never happen again. Just as it is the case for the Saturday Mothers and the Armenian grandchildren discussed in chapter 1 who seek proper transitional justice measures for the enforced disappearance of their relatives, we may only then be able to truly mourn and bury the dead who disappeared in earthquakes.

The conflicts and disasters exposed by an urban district such as Zeytinburnu are not limited to civil war, earthquake, and state demolition in the name of capitalist urbanization. Midcentury urban development in Zeytinburnu is a typical example of what Mike Davis discussed in his book *The Planet of Slums*. In follow-up articles, Davis and Ashley Dawson have pointed out the impossibility of climate change mitigation and energy transition today without incorporating slum settlements that overwhelm cities of the Global South.[220] Sustainability studies for a few wealthy buildings would indeed be negligible unless their findings could be translated to the housing of the global poor and vice versa. In other words, social conflicts and climate disasters are so intertwined that it is required to think global, social, and environmental justice together. The planet of slums is also a planet of climate change and food insecurity. For instance, the only farming land (*bostan*) that has remained in Istanbul today is in Zeytinburnu along the city walls. This shrinkage accounts for a big loss, when compared to the gardens and grasslands that sustained the residents' food supplies before the neoliberal turn. Zeytinburnu's transformation is also an example of the gradual exclusion of green and agriculture from the metropolis, the loss of biodiversity, and the increasing distance food needs to travel today, which has made our planet an unsustainable web of urban-rural networks. The next chapters discuss climate disasters such as famine, flood, sandstorm, and extinction by writing the history of British colonization and soft power on Ottoman lands and successor states, and by tracing the work of architects and planners of the dissolving Ottoman Empire, including Constantinos Doxiadis, who was "exchanged" as a child during the forced population movements in the aftermath of the Balkan War.

4   Climate Disaster

The conflicts and disasters connected to climate change need no enumeration. As I was writing this book, news poured out frequently about the hottest year and the hottest day in history, and the millions of climate refugees who were displaced due to flooding or desertification.[1] This chapter traces the cause of climate disasters to climate determinism, and shows the connections between colonization, carbonization, and creation of agrarian monocultures. It does so in order to differentiate climate determinism from climate consciousness and climate reparations. As defined in the introduction, climate determinism frames humans in essential identity categories according to the climates of the lands that they come from, whereas climate consciousness envisions the racial justice and planetary healing that would arise if climate is duly considered in architecture. To that end, this chapter analyzes the precise moments when climate determinism served as an ideological tool to exert power for the sake of the perpetuation of hierarchies, as opposed to climate consciousness for the sake of the sustainability of life in the planet. It points to the need for climate reparations that would restore justice by giving dues to those who have been subjugated because of climate determinism in the past.

By *climate determinism*, I mean an ideology that uses climate as a proxy for race and nation, and sets a hierarchy between civilizations in relation to the perceived amenability or hostility of climates. Climate determinism has long shaped Euro-American notions of beauty and artistic superiority. In one of the earliest and most influential texts of art history as a discipline, in 1763, Johann Winckelmann unambiguously claimed that it was the moderate climate that enabled the ancient Greek man and women to perfect their bodies with outdoor sports and therefore it was climate that inspired the ancient Greek sculptors and architects to immortalize the figures and proportions of perfect human bodies.[2] Beyond the neoclassical assumptions of beauty and interest in archaeological excavations, this type of climate determinism had consequences on the lands that concern this book.

Acknowledging the convergence between colonization, carbonization, and the creation of agrarian monocultures requires admitting the differentiated responsibility of humanity in climate change. In 1825, the same year when Thomas Telford finished constructing the world's first suspension bridge in England, which daringly displayed the technological possibilities of the Industrial Revolution, Britain accounted for 80 percent of the global emissions of carbon dioxide from fossil fuels. The energy transition to fossil fuels and the resulting economy that depended on the continuous growth of production and carbon dioxide emissions is largely responsible for making humanity a major geophysical force on the planet. And yet the fossil economy was barely endorsed by all of humanity or even by all sections of industrializing Britain, but it was "a form of power exercised by some people against others" as the author of *Fossil Capital*, Andreas Malm, demonstrates in detail.[3] Ever since, countries and peoples that did not have much agency in deciding about this energy transition suffered the most from it. The extractive economies in the colonies accelerated, and companies dumped their fossil-fuel combustion into colonized and poorer countries. This book joins scholars who come to terms with the social and economic hierarchies of the age of climate change, and analyzes environmental disasters as geopolitically caused conflicts to evaluate architecture's role in climate justice.

Khartoum in today's Sudan—a city at the confluence of the Blue Nile and White Nile—and the cotton plantations in its countryside are a thought-provoking example to demonstrate how climate determinism shaped colonial urban and agricultural planning, as well as colonial architecture while planting seeds of environmental disasters such as famines and sandstorms. The era of early independence in Sudan also presents ignored-but-telling examples where a network of citizen and foreign architects envisioned correctives to colonial-era decisions. In other words, Sudan's climate disasters and architectural attempts to prevent them fittingly demonstrate the distinction between climate determinism and climate consciousness. This land is at the crossroads of currents caused by the British colonization in Africa, the dissemination of Ottoman professional networks, and the pilgrimage between West Africa and Mecca. The fact that modern architecture in Sudan features neither in books about "British colonization" or "Ottoman architecture" nor in those about "African architecture" or "Islamic architecture" is a testimony to the weakness of categories and territorial compartmentalization in current scholarship. Despite the ubiquity of books on the architecture of British colonization in the Americas, Africa, and South and East Asia, Sudan is curiously absent. The Ottoman Empire is also missing in the standard histories of colonization and decolonization of Africa, which often treat the continent as a separate and singular land. This chapter not only rectifies this condition through new archival research, but also analyzes British colonization from the perspective of climate change and compares it with the independence era by registering both postcolonial and post-Ottoman subjectivity. The section "The Sun" traces the "tropical architecture" debate in urban planning and architecture of Khartoum by carrying the reader from the Ottoman and the British to the Sudanese eras, and anchors this discussion on the veranda as a climatization space. The section "The Water" adds more layers to the same historical timeline by analyzing the role of architecture in the cotton plantations of Khartoum's southern countryside. The impacts of the British mandate and American soft power during the dissolution of the Ottoman Empire and the independence eras in other Ottoman successor states such as Cyprus, Egypt, Iraq, Jordan, and Palestine provide comparable examples. So do histories of colonization in South and East Asia due to the architectural and planning epistemology that the British Empire shaped and disseminated throughout.

The Sun: Friend or Foe?

CLIMATE AND IMPERIAL URBANISM

The relation between modern architecture and the sun gets complicated when viewed from the perspective of colonial history. A good testimony to the sun's changing status in architecture is Khartoum, a city fraught with the militaristic and segregation policies of its colonial master plan.[4] A map dated 1883–84 at the Ottoman Archives (Istanbul) indicates a fortressed settlement in Khartoum, across the river from Omdurman (Ümmü Derman), the Tutti Island, and Halfaya (today's Khartoum North) (figure 4.1).[5] The British War Office's 1884 map also identifies a fortressed Ottoman settlement that guarded a governor's palace and gardens, arsenal, and military barracks, as well as German, French, Austrian, and Italian consulates along the Blue Nile, and a mosque, markets, tombs, and "native huts" inland.[6] Travelers of the second half of the nineteenth century report a population of sixty thousand.[7]

Upon conquest in 1898, Britain's General Kitchener laid out a new master plan for Khartoum, which replaced the fortressed Ottoman settlement with a gridded-street layout and defined large blocks cut diagonally with large avenues. In addition to the street layout, the plan identified the location of the palace, cathedral, post office, war office, and Gordon College along the

Figure 4.1 Area
around Khartoum,
Sudan, 1883–84.
The map shows the
Ottoman fortressed
settlement Chartum
(Khartoum) across
the river from
Umderman
(Omdurman).
Ottoman Archives,
Istanbul.

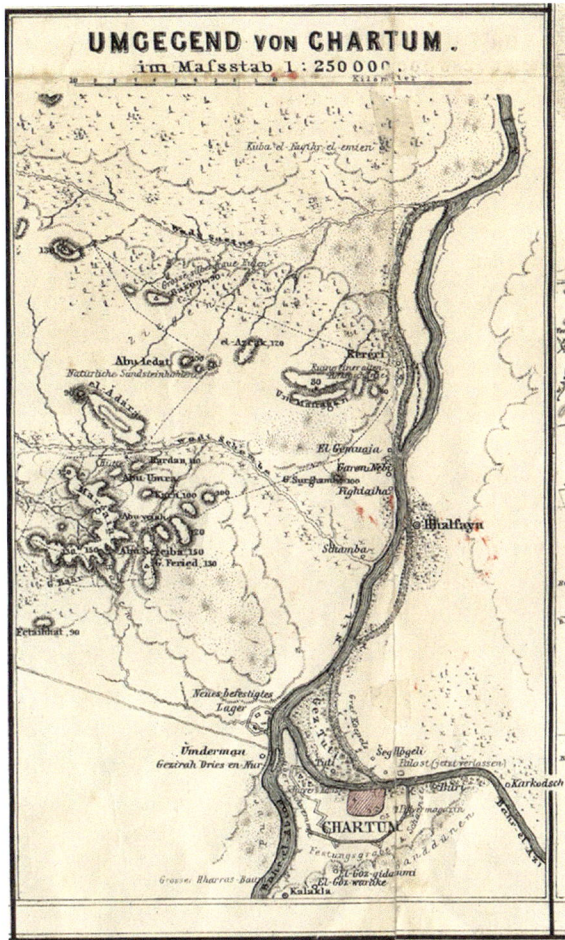

Blue Nile; a zoological and botanical garden to the west of the town; and
Ottoman and British military barracks along the periphery. Even though
the Ottoman city plans marked the threat of floods and avoided settlement
to the west of the city along the White Nile, Kitchener's plan neglected this
climate wisdom and extended the same gridded pattern to the flooding
zones.[8] In 1905, Colonel Stanton suggested to excavate a flood canal, raise
the grounds, and build a stone-faced embankment wall along the White Nile
to prevent flooding, but this was not carried out due to cost.[9] After the construction of the Blue Nile Bridge to the east of the town, the railway reached
Khartoum in 1909.

In 1912, Municipal Engineer W. H. McLean extended the master plan
under the direction of Kitchener with similar street patterns (figure 4.2),

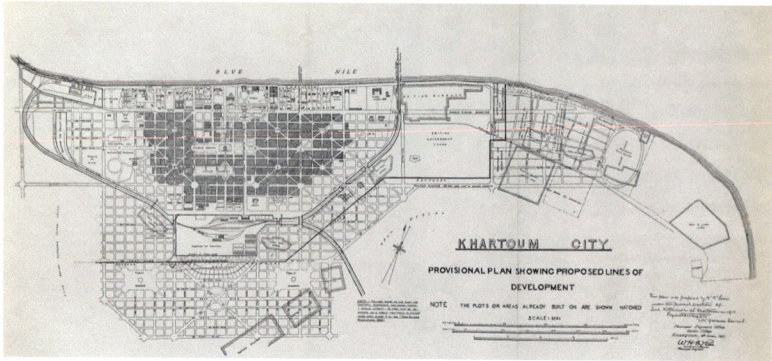

Figure 4.2 W. H. McLean, "Khartoum City: Provisional Plan Showing Proposed Lines of Development," 1912. This was an extension of the British General Kitchener's 1898 master plan for Khartoum.

explaining the origins of the colonial grid as a military invention that posited the British Empire as the heir of the Roman Empire: "It is interesting to take this 'grid-iron' plan, which was doubtless the design initiated by that great soldier Alexander, and to note its similarity to the plan of Khartoum, which, more than two thousand years later, was initiated by that great soldier of the late Lord Kitchener."[10] To justify their colonial ambitions, McLean and his successor, Governor Edwin Geoffrey Sarsfield-Hall, relied on the Orientalist accounts of travelers such as those by George Melly, John Petherick, and Sir Samuel Baker, written in the 1850s and 1860s.[11] In Petherick's assessment, Ottoman "Khartoum—a general fault in Soudan—is most irregular; there are but a few commodious thoroughfares, the generality of the streets being tortuous and narrow."[12]

The British War Office's 1884 report also described Ottoman Khartoum as a town with "dirty," "treeless," "narrow" streets and mud houses "cemented with cow-dung and slime," in a way to justify occupation as a harbinger of civilization.[13] These exact words were soon picked up by the official history of Khartoum.[14] Ignoring the modernization projects of the Ottoman Empire—a common feature of colonization by European great powers—and repeating travelers' and military accounts, Khartoum's planner McLean described the Ottoman Khartoum as a "miserable, filthy and unhealthy" town composed of "primitive houses" and "impassable streets," which "remained in ruins until the reconquest of the country by Lord Kitchener in 1898."[15] The British occupation of Sudan is yet another case that confirms Edward Said's foundational work that showed the causal and mutual relation between

Orientalism and colonization.[16] Racist constructs about "Orientals"—in this case, the Ottomans and Muslims—that were activated in travelogues, history books, and literary and visual representations motivated the colonizers to assume themselves as agents who bring civilization to allegedly uncivilized lands. While advocating for the British occupation of Ottoman lands, McLean's and Sarsfield-Hall's intellectual muse, Sir Samuel Baker, had summarized this reciprocal relation between culture and imperialism crisply in his travelogue, which included Sudan. "The explorer is the precursor of the colonist; and the colonist is the human instrument by which the great work must be constructed—that greatest and most difficult of all undertakings—the civilization of the world."[17]

This chapter demonstrates that climate served as a proxy for race, and that climate determinism shaped the decisions of urban planning and architectural typology in Khartoum's colonial setting. It shows that it was the colonialists who identified, often misguidedly, the modern spatial norms of climatization, and critically analyzes the obliteration of equally or more effective climate adaptation know-how during the process of what is now often called *climatic modernism.*

The first step was urban segregation based on climate. Kitchener and McLean segregated local and British habitants by placing their buildings in different urban fabrics and on opposite banks of the river, and justified this difference with the alleged racial adeptness to climatic conditions. McLean clearly stated, "As a general rule, it is well, if possible, to segregate the population, as the epidemics to which all tropical cities are liable can be so much more easily dealt with."[18] He maintained the Orientalist author Baker's views that industrial civilization depended on moderate climate: "The natural energy of all countries is influenced by climate; and civilization being dependent upon industry, or energy, must accordingly vary in its degrees according to geographical position. The natives of tropical countries do not progress: enervated by intense heat, they incline rather to repose and amusement than to labour."[19]

The term and expertise on *tropical architecture* has colonial origins, and had been used intensively during the British colonization in South and Southeast Asia. McLean clearly expressed the need for proficiency in tropical architecture in order to protect the British citizens, whom he differentiated from "natives" due to their skin color: "It has been shown that the greatest enemy of white men in the tropics is the sun, and that the effect of tropical light on such men is injurious, causing nervous and other diseases. The native of tropical regions being highly pigmented is protected naturally from the harmful rays of sun, so that he is in perfect adjustment with his environment."[20]

McLean thus proposed to segregate the "white" and "native" people "so that zones may be arranged as far as possible to the requirements of the various sections of the population," and that "Europeans live in houses so arranged as to be exposed to the prevailing winds . . . surrounded by gardens or open spaces to permit the free circulation of air," even though "the natives can live comfortably in much more crowded circumstances."[21] This premise about human difference and European comfort in a perceived tropical climate resulted not only in the racial segregation of populations in Omdurman and Khartoum, but also in the latter's construction with wide streets on a grid-iron plan and large urban blocks that produced very low density.

This history gets more complicated when a historian registers the dissolution of the Ottoman Empire. The term "native" that McLean categorically differentiated from the "white" was in fact very convoluted in Ottoman Khartoum. McLean segregated the urban zones of these two groups based on his climate-deterministic convictions about their different abilities to adapt to the sun. However, when municipal officers proceeded to implement this master plan, they discovered that many communities did not fit into the flattened categories. Even as a town of seventy thousand people when the British took over, Khartoum had been an extremely diverse Ottoman province. Different communities continued to have their separate religious buildings, schools, and community centers during the British rule. According to the 1934 census, of the 6,754 "foreigners" in Khartoum, only 428 were British (in addition to the British garrison). The colonial category of the "foreigner" included the Ottoman *millets*: Greeks (highest number), Egyptians, Cypriots, Yemenis, Syrians, and Armenians, many of them in numbers higher than the British.[22] The perceived distinction between Omdurman and Khartoum as the towns of locals and foreigners, respectively, also needs qualification. Omdurman had become a growing center of the Mahdi movement, after the Mahdi revolt against the Ottoman Egypt in 1885 until the Anglo-Egypt Condominium's takeover in 1898. A municipal report of the mid-1930s conveyed the town's population as 111,000 people "composed of a large variety of African races and non-African natives" with almost no "Europeans."[23] Considering that most "natives" of Omdurman—in colonial nomenclature—settled here during and after the Mahdi regime from the Sudan province and West Africa, one can safely assume that many of the migrating Ottomans must have arrived in the region earlier than the perceived locals. Reporting in 1947, the British nutritionist Geraldine Mary

Culwick was puzzled that the tensions of Ottoman diversity were *not* (but I should say *not only*) color-based contentions. "You can't imagine what a mixture of peoples and tongues it is, and absolutely no color bar at all. I gather there are pretty rigid social distinctions of class in Khartoum. But nowhere dependent on color."[24] This experience on the ground created a disjoint in Culwick's perception of race as a color line as well as her perception of the white-native dichotomy that she received from the British colonial mindset.

McLean had the British colonial settlers in mind when he diagnosed the sun as their "enemy in the tropics." However, the census carried out during Sarsfield-Hall's rule exposed the incongruity of "white" and "native" as the only two colonial categories of race—not that they were justified when divided into two races. Even then, the municipal officers never truly confronted the conceptual challenges that the diversity on the ground should have evoked. As a result, they invented new demographic categories to calibrate their Orientalist and color-based biases with census statistics, such as "better-class natives," "native laboring classes," "non-African natives," and "non-European foreigners," all of which appeared arbitrarily in official documents and master plans that implemented social hierarchies and forcibly moved some communities to segregate the city neatly.

In 1929, Governor Sarsfield-Hall extended Kitchener and McLean's master plan under the jurisdiction of the Khartoum Town Planning Committee with clearly marked zones to be segregated in relation to race, class, and level of urbanity (figure 4.3).[25] A zone was reserved for "Europeans and persons occupying houses of a European pattern and living."[26] Houses in this zone would be located in large plots of land of five hundred square meters minimum, and "segregated as far as possible from houses of native type, in which they could live their lives in accordance with European standards, unaffected by the noises, odors and crudities of native method of existence."[27] These European houses were to be constructed of red brick with plinths and provide separate zones for servants. The plan legalized the destruction of "native" houses and stables in this area to make room for European residences.[28] Another zone inside the railway ring adjacent to shops and workshops was reserved for "houses of a second-class quality." Other zones included a "suburb for occupation by better class natives," and a "native cantonment outside the town but accessible to it, for occupation by the native laboring classes."[29] The new cantonment was intended as a "model native settlement . . . in which natives can live their own lives in accordance with native standards but under improved public health conditions."[30] The government did not sell land but granted squatter rights here,[31] thereby blocking upward-class mobility for the

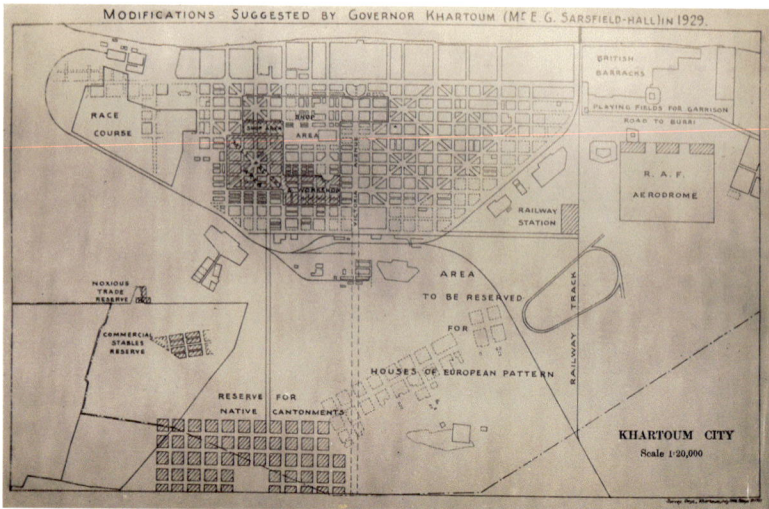

Figure 4.3 Edwin Geoffrey Sarsfield-Hall, "Modifications Suggested by Governor [of] Khartoum," 1929. This extended Kitchener's and McLean's master plans for Khartoum of 1898 and 1912, respectively. E. G. Sarsfield-Hall Collection, Sudan Archive Durham (SAD 679/1/18). Copyright. Reproduced by permission of Durham University Library and Collections.

non-British workers. Areas for those "engaged in noxious trades" (the report gives no further clarification but illegal slavery may be implied) and "owners of animals" were pushed out of the town.[32] The separation of Khartoum into zones identified according to the British categories of race under Ottoman Empire is a perfect demonstration of the continuities between settler colonialism and resettler nationalism. Khartoum's master plan was a harbinger of the post–World War I world order that relied on the perceived necessity to "unmix peoples" of the Ottoman Empire. The borders that divided the colonial city with racial categories were simultaneously being mapped onto the planet's territory as borders that divided nations.

Sarsfield-Hall showed climatic reasons as excuses for the high expenditure of infrastructural services in Khartoum's wide avenues. "Houses have had, for instance, to be sited facing north and south to catch the prevailing breezes and wide thoroughfares have had to be provided to allow for the free access of air to buildings, the provision of unusually wide thoroughfares necessitating the adoption of unusually spacious layouts and involving increased expenditure on roadmaking, lighting, draining, etc." (figure 4.4).[33] The British rule Europeanized health and leisure spaces by building public gardens, football grounds, tennis lawns, race courses, polo grounds, and golf courses.[34] Given the alleged diseases expected in tropical climates, which was a recurring theme of British colonization,[35] the government considered public health as the central mission of city planning.[36] Municipal works installed piped water so that old wells would be gradually disused,[37] and regulated the *suq* (public markets) so that concrete stalls were built for vegetable sellers, zinc-topped tables for butchers, and metal cages for poultry.[38] To the governor's surprise, the rain water drainage was much more challenging in Khartoum than in Omdurman where water flew naturally—a local wisdom in settling that he did not care to admit.[39] A "double-bucket system" was used for sewage, where non-British sanitation workers collected the buckets filled with urine and feces, and replaced them with clean buckets once daily for private and twice for public buildings.[40] Camel- or horse-drawn lorries carried these piles of feces-filled buckets to a light railway, with which they were transported and dumped out of town (figure 4.5). The government decided to neglect and leave the native cantonment to its own devices as it was deemed too "impractical" and "expensive" to install and maintain this sewage system there. The twenty to thirty thousand "natives of lower classes" used earth bunkers on the outskirts of this cantonment for their defecation, and the feces were removed and buried by non-British women sweepers (figure 4.6).[41] Regardless, Governor Sarsfield-Hall was confident about the civilizing impact of his team's work:

> The closest attention has been paid to public health considerations since the earliest days of re-occupation, and, as a result, Khartoum, Khartoum North and Omdurman, which were formerly unhealthy fever stricken centers of evil reputation, are now numbered amongst the healthiest towns of the world.[42]

> There is something almost European about modern Khartoum with its airy spaciousness, its greenery, its Clubs and football grounds, its up to date shops and stores, its garages, its cinematograph theatre, and its electric tramway. It is difficult to realize that it is really a remote African town which came into existence less than 40 years ago.[43]

Across the river, Omdurman's governance presented a problem for the British officials, where houses surrounded the central area with a big mosque, Khalifa's (Mahdi's successor) residential complexes, and janissaries' barracks. Just as he did for the Ottoman Khartoum, Governor Sarsfield-Hall

Figure 4.4 Aerial view of Khartoum showing large avenues and the Kitchener Memorial Medical School in the foreground, built in 1924.

judged Omdurman with demeaning words as a "dervish town." It was, in his eyes, "a maze of squalid mud houses crowded together with no regard for health, sanitation or any other public consideration; . . . a vast labyrinth of filthy mud hovels."[44] One can read in between the lines that Omdurman's residents resisted British colonizers' ways. Determined to employ the same city planning measures as they did in Khartoum, the colonial officers tried to open spacious, straight avenues in Omdurman, but were confronted with resistance when the locals claimed private property. The governor admitted: "Unless all such claims were to be summarily disregarded, and unless complete demolition of all existing buildings was to be decreed, it was impossible to make an entirely new and symmetrical layout for Omdurman and to raise an entirely new City on the ruins and debris of the old city as was done in Khartoum."[45] He complained about the lack of macadamized streets, and of private and public gardens due to gravelly soil, as well as the continuing use of wells for water supply. Despite the large number of expropriated lands (thousands of plots, according to the governor) and the opening of large streets, Omdurman preserved its urban character throughout the colonial times and till today (figure 4.7).

Figure 4.5 (left) Photographs showing Khartoum's "double-bucket system" for sewage. From "Municipal Works under Governor Sarsfield-Hall, Khartoum, Sudan," 1936. E. G. Sarsfield-Hall Collection, Sudan Archive Durham (SAD 679/1/41–43). Copyright. Reproduced by permission of Durham University Library and Collections.

Figure 4.6 (right) One of the sweepers for the handling of defecation in the cantonments. From "Municipal Works under Governor Sarsfield-Hall, Khartoum, Sudan," 1936. E. G. Sarsfield-Hall Collection, Sudan Archive Durham (SAD 679/2/37). Copyright. Reproduced by permission of Durham University Library and Collections.

Figure 4.7 Aerial view of Omdurman, Sudan, ca. 1928–32. E. G. Sarsfield-Hall Collection, Sudan Archive Durham (SAD 684/4/9). Copyright. Reproduced by permission of Durham University Library and Collections.

Eventually, the British colonial engineers' conviction about the necessity of wide straight boulevards on a grid due to perceived climatic reasons created a striking contrast between the urban fabric of Khartoum and Omdurman, constructing a racist distinction between the modern civilized new and the traditional uncivilized old. The colonial Khartoum was meant to provide thermal comfort for the "Europeans" and "better-class natives" in a harsh climate, while Omdurman was perceived as a town for "natives" who were accustomed to the current climate and could therefore continue living in the urban fabric that differed from that of Khartoum (compare figures 4.4 and 4.7).

Despite the centrality of climate as the main criterion of urban planning, the British planners ignored the most important weather events that hit Khartoum and its countryside quite often. Heavy rains flooded some areas and made streets unusable as evidenced in photographs of the time.[46] Moreover, frequent *haboob,* or sandstorms, created piles of dust and sand that overwhelmed practically every building. In 1909, the Iraqi-born Ottoman traveler Muhammed Mihri had described Sudan's storms dramatically as winds strong enough to blow stones into the air and knock down trees and boats on the Nile, and as weather events that appeared at the horizon as giant red and black clouds piled on each other, which approached to hit one's face like fire and make one feel suffocated.[47] A photograph by Karakashian Brothers capturing the *haboob* of July 1933 over Khartoum shows dark and dense clusters of sand clouds approaching the city, at least twenty-five times higher than the height of a common building. The handful of people in the wide avenues seem to be rushing to find a shelter in one of the single-story buildings. One can predict that the city scene captured in this photograph will be totally invisible a few minutes later as the sand blows into the streets and gardens. One can imagine the day will turn into night for residents waiting for the storm's end inside their houses with closed windows and doors (figure 4.8).[48] C. A. E. Lea did not fail to notice the dust and sand dunes that buried a district commissioner's house after the *haboob* of October 31, 1935, which had to be removed by manual labor.[49] Civil Secretary James Angus Gillan photographed the day after the *haboob* on February 18, 1938, when piles of sand formed mountains as high as the houses. In many photographs, Gillan stands on the high ground as he oversees the "native" workers removing and loading the driftsand into railway wagons (figure 4.9).[50] In a letter to her family, Culwick described her experience in a *haboob* of May 1949 as follows:

> The whole northern and western sky was a mixture of a thundercloud and red sand, rapidly approaching. . . . The storm overtook me and I hastily shut the car windows. Driving, blinding sand. One gust of wind blew my car right across the road, and at one point I had to stop altogether as the visibility was nil. . . . [The next day], I was astounded on the way to see dead animals everywhere. The storm had been so sudden and so violent that sheep and goats, and even cows, had died—those which were already in poor shape due to the seasonal shortage of fodder. The mess in the house after such a storm has to be seen to be believed. Even with the windows shut, it gets in at doors and windows. First of all, the dust, inches deep—then the rain to turn it all to mud.[51]

As a matter of fact, the already challenging impact of a *haboob* was aggravated due to the colonial city plan. The large straight avenues, deceptively designed to capture the breeze for the sake of "white men's" thermal comfort, did not help during the frequent sandstorms that hit Khartoum and its countryside. The day after, it was the Sudanese cleaning professionals employed by British officials as private servants or public workers who cleaned the resulting debris. Culwick's description of the overwhelming sand and mud

Figure 4.8 Karakashian Brothers, A *haboob* (sandstorm) in Khartoum, July 1933. Karakashian Brothers Collection, Sudan Archive Durham (SAD 870/12/2). Reproduced by permission of Durham University Library and Collections.

Figure 4.9 James Angus Gillan, Driftsand the day after a *haboob* in Khartoum, February 18, 1938. J. Gillan Collection, Sudan Archive Durham (SAD A85.10). Copyright. Reproduced by permission of Durham University Library and Collections.

that needed to be cleaned out of living spaces was not an anomaly. To this day, Khartoum residents mention the dust as the most significant problem that they face in their houses. Things could have been different if the colonial planners gave dust its due attention, rather than investing so passionately in their perceived notions of race.

WHITE THERMAL COMFORT, COLONIAL HOUSES, AND THE VERANDA

Both McLean and Sarsfield-Hall extended their views on tropical city planning to architecture. McLean listed climate-specific regulations: walls should be protected from the sun with verandas; timber should be preferred over brick and stone while constructing verandas; roofs should be thick and flat at least in part to enable sleeping outside; rooms should be as far from each other as possible to enable ventilation; green, dark yellow, and brown color should be preferred over white, which produces glare; and kitchens should be separated from the house. Most importantly, McLean differentiated the "crowded native houses" with courtyards from the European ones, and endorsed the veranda as the most appropriate architectural element for the latter, both to protect the walls from the sun and as a covered, ventilated outdoor living space.[52] The veranda became the most identified and designed element of colonial architecture in both residential and public buildings.

Family photographs confirm that almost every British individual occupied a single-family freestanding house in a large garden with at least one veranda (figure 4.10). The architectural design of these verandas varied: they could be built of wood or brick; their ceilings could be lifted with arches, timber posts, or classical columns with capitals. For instance, an inspector of the repression of the slave trade who served in Sudan between 1904 and 1920, F. J. L. Atterbury, lived in a house along the Nile in Khartoum that was elevated from the ground by a few steps, and had a long, deep veranda bordered by brick arches.[53] The senior medical inspector and director of hospitals between 1904 and 1919, J. B. Christopherson, lived in a brick house with an elevated veranda that was finished with elaborate wooden balustrades, narrow timber columns buttressed by triangles, and a wooden lattice screen above eye level.[54] Rudolf Carl von Slatin's house when he was inspector general in Khartoum between 1900 and 1914 (after being held captive by Mahdi in Omdurman in 1884–85) was one of the most elaborate: an elevated veranda that encircled the building and provided extension bays made of timber columns, crossed balustrades, and wooden lattice screens above eye level to break the sun. Stairs inside the veranda carried one to the upper roof

Figure 4.10 Verandas in family photographs of British colonial officers, ca. 1900–1950. *Clockwise from top left*: R. C. von Slatin; Byson family; and N. R. Udal Collections; and Assistant District Commissioner in E. G. Sarsfield-Hall Collection, Sudan Archive Durham (SAD A34/187; SAD D12/8; SAD 778/11/92; SAD A67/194). Copyrights. Reproduced by permission of Durham University Library and Collections.

deck.[55] Some of these houses were as big as to accommodate two-story ornate verandas with monumental stairs that connected them from the outside.[56] Sleeping in these verandas or on roof decks must have been common. In the houses of Nicholas Robin Udal from the Education Department, who served between 1906 and 1930, and George Ronald Storrar, who worked in railways between 1905 and 1927, external stairs from the verandas led to visually distinct sleeping-out platforms on the roof, which must have been specifically designed there to catch the view and the breeze.[57]

Family photographs taken from the interior of verandas illustrate that these shaded outdoor rooms functioned as the main living spaces. Families passed long hours on the verandas and furnished them with comfortable chairs, dining and work tables, sleeping corners, hunting trophies, animal skins, and carpets (figure 4.11).[58] Many photographs capture colonizers next to their servants who wore *jalabiya* that could be unmistakably differentiated from British costumes. The photograph from Christopherson's veranda even captures a child servant, and its caption notes that the boy's name was Hussein, the brother of a "private secretary, cook and body servant" (figure 4.12).[59]

Figure 4.11 Interiors of verandas in family photographs of British colonial officers, ca. 1900–1950. *Clockwise from top left*: R. V. Savile (*mudiriya* [government office]); L. K. Smith; F. J. L. Atterbury; and J. H. Dick Collections, Sudan Archive Durham (SAD A11/22; SAD A72/8; SAD A10/99; SAD 747/2/29). Copyrights. Reproduced by permission of Durham University Library and Collections.

Figure 4.12 J. B. Christopherson's veranda with a child servant. The caption reads, "The boy's name is Hussein, the brother of a private secretary, cook and body servant." J. B. Christopherson Collection, Sudan Archive Durham (SAD 2/2/138). Copyright. Reproduced by permission of Durham University Library and Collections.

The topic of slavery in the Ottoman Empire and its difference from the white European plantation slavery in the Americas exceeds the scope of this book, but suffice it to say that many historians have long acknowledged the slave supply as one of the main motivations behind the Ottoman Egypt's occupation of Sudan. The trade continued informally even after the abolishment of slavery, and became a point of contention during the British rule. As Eve Troutt Powell illustrates, the voice of slaves evaporated between the British abolitionists who foregrounded slavery in Sudan as an example of Egyptian "barbarity and despotism" on one side, and the nationalists who saw British abolitionists as colonial oppressors criminalizing Islam's domestic and multiracial marriage practices that actually enabled the enslaved upward social mobility on the other side. Even though the views of Ottoman elites differed and changed over time, many Egyptian nationalists defined institutions like the British and Foreign Anti-Slavery Society as opportunist invaders who denied them rights to their land, religion, and privacy. The rivalry between Britain and Egypt over the ownership of Sudan mirrored the rivalry about the institution of slavery itself.[60] While the British outlawed slavery at this time and weaponized this decision to justify their allegedly more benevolent and civilized ruling,[61] they continued the same habits with their treatment of the "servant class" in their private spaces—a word that appeared in everyday language—and by denying maintenance professionals chances for upward-class mobility. The ample veranda photographs with servants, sometimes child servants, are the remaining visual documents that allow historians to assess the continuities and discontinuities between the institution of slavery and colonial domesticity. The body language of comfortably sitting British officers and standing Sudanese maintenance professionals exposes the stratification that operated in the colonial society. Diaries and visual documents reveal that many families had multiple non-British individuals working for them, including cleaners, cooks, drivers, security officers, and clerks, most of whom worked in the houses but lived in a separate outbuilding. Toward the 1950s, some British officers lamented that the "servant class" was slowly disappearing at the dawn of independence, as rebellions grew and new generations aspired to take other jobs.[62]

In addition to verandas, large private gardens were supposed to provide ventilation for climate control in colonial residences as opposed to the precolonial houses placed along narrow streets and around courtyards. This was the reason that the Governor Sarsfield-Hall called Khartoum a garden city. Almost all family photographs attest to these large gardens, composed of tennis lawns, flowers, well-maintained grass, carefully sculpted bushes, and ample citrus and neem trees.[63] In a climate threatened by droughts and famine, the colonial gardens were amply irrigated with electricity-driven pumps along the Nile. Most water was provided by the Sudan Light and Power Company, and only a few preexisting water wells were permitted due to the fear of mosquitos. British superintendents trained at Kew Gardens maintained the manicured gardens with a large staff of Sudanese workers.[64] The governor also made a point about having planted six thousand street trees by 1936.

Inside, occupants furnished these houses in ways that projected wealth and permanence (figure 4.13). All family photographs indicate that window shutters throughout the entire house were kept closed for long hours in order to block the sun, which must have augmented the feeling of living in one's own artificial and secluded world that hid the reality of the city beyond the garden walls. Even though the decorating tastes were wide-ranging, all rooms were filled with ample furniture and household objects. These houses did not follow the modern plan conceptions of the time such as open, free, or Raum plan. Instead, rooms were closed, large, and bounded by walls. Some had memorable proportions, such as the Foleys' house with high ceilings and an arched opening where they lived between 1928 and 1940.[65] Each house included a drawing room where government matters must have been handled in elaborate working corners. Ceiling fans and wicker chairs were common, and so were carpets and wooden screens that resembled mashrabiya.[66] Flowery textiles and pillows were fashionable; ample photographs, books, and small objects adorned the spaces and created a microcosm impact. Some governors collected animal skins, hunting trophies, and cultural heritage artifacts that should have been placed in museums.[67] It would be hard to imagine that the colonizers went to such lengths to populate these rooms with so many heavy furniture items and memory artifacts if they were to conceive themselves as temporary residents of Sudan.

Of all the architects and builders who designed these houses, the architect Gordon Brock Bridgman built a local reputation. Born in 1884 as the son of a surveyor of the sewers of London, Bridgman had studied in London and Regent Street Polytechnic, before he was appointed to the Public Works Department in Khartoum in 1906—a post he held till 1930, after which he continued his architectural practice in Sudan till the 1950s. A manuscript about his career stated: "In Brief, Brock [Bridgman] was responsible for almost all modern buildings in Sudan before 1930 when a modern administration

Figure 4.13 Interiors of British colonial officers' houses. *Clockwise from top left*: G. H. and E. M. Barter; D. S. B. Thompson; D. S. B. Thompson; and R. V. Savile Collections, Sudan Archive Durham (SAD 12/10/67; SAD 491/3/3, SAD 491/3/2; SAD/A14/57). Copyrights. Reproduced by permission of Durham University Library and Collections.

was being established: buildings that have attracted appreciative attention."[68] Bridgman's project for the Housing Scheme for British Officials (1920–27) came to be referred to as "Bridgman-type houses" in everyday language, and selected to showcase exemplary residences of British officials in government reports (figure 4.14).[69] These houses were distinguished by virtue of their verandas with neoclassical columns and Ionic column capitals. The molds for casting these Ionic column capitals were initially prepared for the kiosk that Bridgman designed at Port Sudan where King George V visited on his way to Durbar in colonial India in 1911.[70] Mabel Elise and Gertrude Lucy Wolff, who both worked at the Midwifery Training School in Omdurman, resided in one of these houses in the late 1920s and early 30s;[71] so did John F. E. Bloss, who was a medical inspector and director in public health services between 1934 and 1954.[72] Houses in this series reflected some of the contemporary trends in Central and Western Europe, such as the elimination of ornament and the use of flat roofs and cubic masses. "Housing for Officials in Khartoum, 1922" designed by Bridgman was a group of buildings made up of light-colored cubes into which verandas with sloped roofs or arches were carved (figure 4.15). Verandas with classical column capitals

Figure 4.14 Gordon Brock Bridgman, Housing for British Officers, Khartoum, 1920–27. E. M. Barter stands beside a Riley motor car in front of her Bridgman-designed house. G. H. Barter Collection, Sudan Archive Durham (SAD 12/10/68). Reproduced by permission of Durham University Library and Collections.

Figure 4.15 Gordon Brock Bridgman, Housing for Officials in Khartoum, 1922. Bridgman Album, Sudan Archive Durham (SAD 528/24/17–20). Reproduced by permission of Durham University Library and Collections.

combined with flat-roofed houses created a unique hybrid of neoclassicist and modernist architecture, even though they unmistakably symbolized the introduction of European tastes into the colonized city.[73]

Geoffrey Herbert Barter from the Finance Department, who served in Sudan between 1925 and 1949, lived in one of the Bridgman-designed houses with Elise Barter in the mid-1930s.[74] Barter's Riley car (reportedly the only car of its kind in Sudan) reached the veranda that was separated by a drive from the grass lawn with knee-high bushes (see figure 4.14).[75] The family spent ample time in the veranda that they furnished with comfortable garden chairs, dining table, and flower boxes. A tree-lined footpath carried one from the veranda to the bushes at eye level that encircled the entire garden. The exterior walls of the house were perforated with ventilation louvers along the roof line, which, according to Barter, did not function as planned, as birds, cats, and other small animals lived and bred there.[76] Inside, the house was designed so that sitting, dining, and drawing rooms melded into one another, and the family used densely figured thick curtains to open and shut this visual access at will. All windows had both glass frames and wooden shutters that were, judging from photographs, kept closed for long hours to block the sun. The choice of furniture with ornate fabrics, wicker and wooden chairs, armchairs and sofas, wooden tables and desks, elevated shelves, lamps, mirrors, picture frames, and bookshelves projected wealth and a sense of permanent settlement (see figure 4.13, top left). Some of these were indeed collected objects that should have been placed in museums as cultural heritage artifacts. In their second house in Khartoum at Gordon Avenue, Barters displayed a bride's chest from Saudi Arabia, which, they were proud to write in a letter, was similar to a larger version with "royal house pedigree" in the British Museum.[77]

Only a few British officers are reported to have lived in Omdurman, but their houses could be differentiated easily as modernist minimalist boxes with carved-in verandas.[78] In addition to pictures from Khartoum, family photographs taken in Port Sudan, El Obeid, and Wad Medani, and settlements of the Red Sea, Gezira, Sennar Dam, and Kordofan regions give evidence that the veranda had become the most common living space for British colonizers throughout Sudan.[79]

These houses for the British residents differed significantly and intentionally from those of the "native workers." The frequently stated contrast between the European houses in Khartoum and the houses in Omdurman was projected onto government-built residential spaces for all sections of the society. While demonstrating his service in a photo album, Governor Sarsfield-Hall differentiated the Bridgman-type house that represented "a senior British official's residence" from the model house for "a native official's residence" (figure 4.16).[80] In contrast to the classical columns and capitals of the former, the latter was a flat-roofed rectangular brick building with shutters and small square windows in a smaller garden behind a high garden wall. In 1935, the municipality prepared a design for an "African-type dwelling." The designers envisioned a freestanding, single-story house with a pitched roof, approached from a front veranda where an arched gate was added in the middle. Inside, the house was arranged symmetrically around a covered "sala" (central hall) in between a bedroom and a dining room. The *sala* opened up to another veranda at the back, which surrounded a courtyard, where accesses to a dressing room, kitchen, and bath were provided in addition to doors to the bedroom and dining room. Judging from the placement of only one bedroom and dressing room, the municipal officers must have imagined the family would spend the day in the semiopen *sala* and verandas, host visitors in the dining room, and sleep in the same room or outside at night (figure 4.17).[81]

Improving the living conditions of the working class interested the British rulers even less. The 1929 master plan of Khartoum placed the native cantonment for workers in a removed but accessible zone from the European neighborhoods. An aerial photograph around 1930 clearly shows the development inland at a safe distance.[82] Municipal and commercial photographs only capture this housing area from outside or afar, as if it were an inaccessible prison or a camp.[83] Composed of row houses that created a solid wall in the middle of a treeless ground, these units had only a handful of outside features producing a rhythm of symmetrically placed windows on two sides of a door underneath a flat arch, and rainwater-removal pipes jutting out of flat roofs (figure 4.18).[84] In his memoirs, S. R. Simpson, the district commissioner between 1939 and 1943, talks about the Deims as the "native lodging area" in Khartoum and Khartoum North, where the temporary laboring population lived in single rooms without latrine facilities. The squatting rights of these single rooms could be terminated at a month's notice. He notes that the bulk of the Sudanese working population lived in the single rooms of the native cantonment to the south of the railway line in an area that was subject to frequent floods.[85]

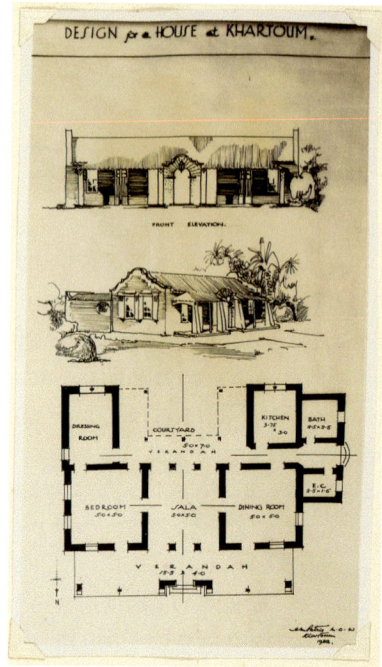

Figure 4.16 (left) Governor Sarsfield-Hall's differentiation of "a senior British official's residence" (*top*) from "a native official's residence" (*bottom*). E. G. Sarsfield-Hall Collection, Sudan Archive Durham (SAD 684/5/43; SAD 684/5/45). Copyright. Reproduced by permission of Durham University Library and Collections.

Figure 4.17 (right) Edwin Geoffrey Sarsfield-Hall and I. G. Watson, "African type dwelling" in "Some African-Type Buildings for Use in the Anglo-Egyptian Sudan," Khartoum, 1934. E. G. Sarsfield-Hall Collection, Sudan Archive Durham (SAD 678/6/36). Copyright. Reproduced by permission of Durham University Library and Collections.

In contrast, the *tukl* (sometimes referred to as "native straw huts") fascinated the British staff in Sudan as an exotic feature. The colonialists frequently photographed the round structures and thatched roofs with habitants. While these photographs that are intentionally not reproduced here are a topic of critical ethnography studies, I am interested in their place as a source of exotic contrast and inspiration for modern architecture in British Sudan. At one point, the government tried to modernize the *tukl* by building collective

Figure 4.18 Native cantonments during the Anglo-Egyptian colonization, Khartoum, 1920–50. E. G. Sarsfield-Hall Collection, Sudan Archive Durham (SAD 678/2/41). Copyright. Reproduced by permission of Durham University Library and Collections.

housing for railway workers where each unit was made of a round brick room and mimicked a sloped thatched roof. The colonial designers must have assumed they were catering to "native laborers" by mimicking their residential culture or putting them in place as workers who lived in essentially different houses than those of European colonizers (figure 4.19).[86]

Curiously, the planners and architects did not consider Suakin as a local heritage site that could have informed the climatization of new residential typology. Suakin had been an elaborate settlement since ancient times. Under Ottoman rule since 1517 and especially under Ottoman Egyptian rule after 1865, and at the eastern end of the pilgrimage route from Shendi, Suakin had already developed into a vivid and rich port at the Red Sea by the time the British arrived. The town was exceptionally memorable due to its unique urban fabric that took its cue from the circular contour of the island and its houses built with coral taken out of the sea (figure 4.20). It was populated with densely placed four- or five-story buildings, adorned

Figure 4.19 Railway workers' housing. The caption reads: "Brick built tukls," 1932. P. T. M. Wells Collection, Sudan Archive Durham (SAD 855/1/53). Copyright. Reproduced by permission of Durham University Library and Collections.

with exquisite extension bays and wooden mashrabiya windows. (Unfortunately, none of these buildings stand today.) Many British officers visited and took ample photographs,[87] but were unwilling to learn from the climate wisdom, know-how, or aesthetic sensibility of Suakin's houses. When the founder and first dean of the Department of Architecture at the University of Khartoum, Alick Potter, visited Suakin in the early 1960s, the city had already been deserted. In his memoirs, Potter wrote: "Suakin was a ghost town . . . we gathered that as the living population had moved out, the ghosts had moved in. . . . So after more than a quarter of a century of neglect the whole town was steadily crumbling, and piles of debris almost blocked some of the lanes down which we ventured."[88] Due to the lack of appreciation and trivialization of the Egypto-Ottoman building culture and as a typical example of agnotology as defined in the introduction, the British officials did not see Suakin as a possible source of inspiration for climate-responsive modern architecture. They thereby contributed to the discontinuation and, in this island's case, erasure of this cultural heritage in today's Africa.

Figure 4.20 Aerial view of the city of Suakin, Sudan, during the Ottoman period. Photo: Charles Brown, ca. 1920.

CLIMATE, COLONIAL PUBLIC BUILDINGS, AND THE VERANDA

In addition to residential buildings, climate control with verandas was the identifying principle in iconic and strategically placed government and religious buildings of the colonial regime. The British Empire's first step after occupying Khartoum was to construct an Anglican church.[89] It needs no repetition that colonialists and missionaries were twin forces, as McLean's and Sarsfield-Hall's muse, Samuel Baker, had put it bluntly: England, he said, "possesses a power that enforces a grave responsibility. She has the force to civilize. She is the natural colonizer of the world. . . . True Christianity cannot exist apart from civilization: thus the spread of Christianity must depend upon the extension of civilization."[90] Khartoum under the British rule continued to be as multireligious as other Ottoman societies. In the 1930s, Anglican, Roman Catholic, Greek, and Coptic cathedrals as well as mosques stood out as major monuments in the city.[91] Despite the existence of churches for Christian communities descending from the Ottoman Empire, the construction of a prestigious All Saints Cathedral in stone (a rare building material) was a matter of pride and presence for the British. Overseen by the architect Robert Weir and the stonemason John Latimer, and constructed by "native" women and men who were labeled "unskilled laborers" in architectural publications, the church was designed to keep away the direct hit of "tropical sunlight."[92] Accordingly, the designers added stone hoods to break the sun for lower windows, an external veranda to set back upper windows, and a double roof to protect the vault from excessive heat.

Of all the colonial enterprises, perhaps the most memorable for the everyday life of colonizers were the spaces for social gatherings, such as the Grand Hotel of Khartoum and the Sudan Clubs. Designed by the British architect G. E. Francis, and supervised by the Public Works Department, the Grand Hotel opened as early as 1902.[93] It was situated in a prestigious location next to government buildings and attracted attention with its two-level wooden veranda that overlooked the Blue Nile. As the resting place for the British in their first days in Khartoum or on their way to other Sudan provinces, the Grand Hotel would have been recognized by anyone in Khartoum (figure 4.21). Another similar icon was the Sudan Club (now demolished).[94] Several clubs had spread to Sudan to provide facilities and a social network for British officers, such as Medani Club and 88 Club in Khartoum's southern countryside (in Gezira), which offered baths and dressing rooms for both sexes so that British staff members could spend the day, play games, and stay for a dance at night.[95] A Sudan Club in the outskirts, photographed and most likely designed by the architect Bridgman, was composed of an open veranda that encircled a large pool. The water extended to the borders of the veranda through which one could see trees and greenery outside. The building created an experience of swimming in an artificial forest in the desert mediated by a veranda with Ionic columns (figure 4.22).

Bridgman designed the Kitchener Memorial School in the early 1920s with his signature columns and Ionic capitals. Built to educate Sudanese doctors to fight epidemics, the Kitchener Memorial School was one of the most visible monuments in the city that attracted attention in bird's-eye view photographs. Four L-shaped buildings (two were built) formed an all-symmetrical public square in between and created a focal point on the Victoria Avenue (today's El Qasr's Avenue). The corners of the square and intersection of building wings were marked by octagonal entrance halls

Figure 4.21 G. E. Francis and Public Works Department, Grand Hotel, Khartoum, opened in 1902. McCorquodale & Co. Collection, Sudan Archive Durham (SAD 843/4/5). Reproduced by permission of Durham University Library and Collections.

Figure 4.22 The Sudan Clubs of the Anglo-Egyptian colonial period. *Top*: Sudan Club of Khartoum in G. N. Morhig postcard, 1906–1910 (handwriting is N. R. Udal's). *Center and bottom*: Sudan Club for Gezira, photographed and possibly designed by Gordon Brock Bridgman, 1920–50. G. N. Morhig and G. B. Bridgman Collections, Sudan Archive Durham (SAD 778/8/12; SAD 508/24/38; SAD 508/24/42). Copyright. Reproduced by permission of Durham University Library and Collections.

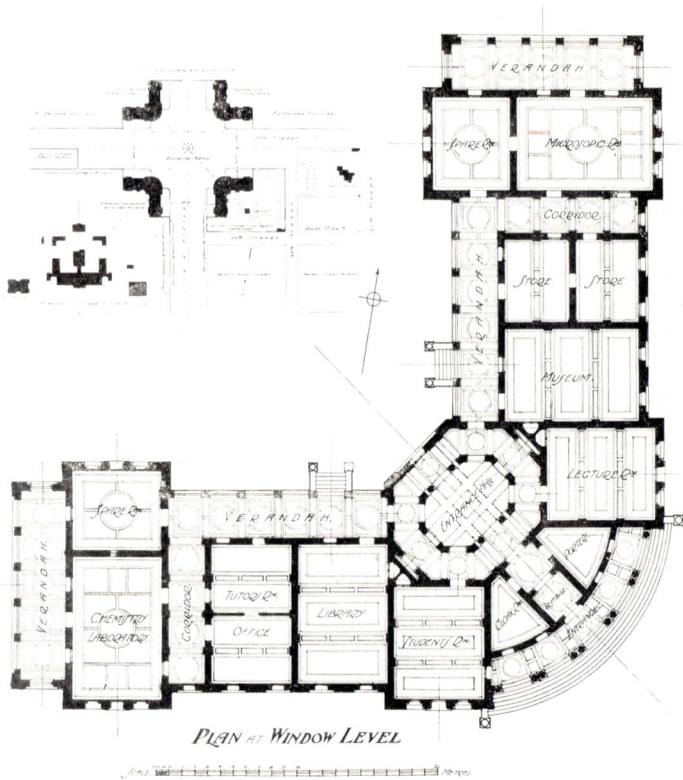

Figure 4.23 Gordon Brock Bridgman, plan for Kitchener Memorial Medical School, Khartoum, 1924. From *Builder*, 1924.

covered with domes. The verandas encircled all facades, both to block the sun and to create monumental entrances. Bridgman designed more verandas to protect side facades from the sun and in-between rooms to provide cross ventilation (figure 4.23; see also figure 4.4).[96]

Monumental government edifices were built out of brick with verandas. On the one hand, the British introduced brick as an industrially produced material to construct their colonial enterprises that carbonized the planet and brought climate change; on the other hand, they kept designing veranda-protected buildings for sun shading and ventilation to mitigate the heat that these buildings kept augmenting. These included the Governor's Palace, the Secretariat, and the post office, placed next to each other along the Blue Nile. The verandas of the Omdurman civic center (1953, today's municipality), designed by Derek Matthews, were protected with concrete brise-soleil, which was presented as a climate-control technique for verandas superior to columns.[97] Hospitals had memorable large verandas, such as the ones in Omdurman, or the memorable civic hospital in Port Sudan where a heavy brick arched veranda on the ground floor was accompanied by a light wooden one overlooking a view on the upper floor.[98]

The official monuments in Khartoum were built after the permission of the governor, medical officer, municipal engineer, and district commissioner, and the aesthetic considerations were under the purview of the Town Planning Committee. The construction was overseen by the Military Works Department of the Egyptian army, and the laborers were men and women of mixed religions. For instance, in a photograph intentionally not reproduced here, Bridgman captured a scene where two women with exposed chests carry construction materials on their heads next to men wearing *jalabiya*.[99] In addition to possible religious tensions one can anticipate, this scene also reflects the hierarchy of labor distribution in architecture, moving from British policymakers and architects to possibly Ottoman mid-level military managers and local and migrant construction workers from West Africa.

The underacknowledged agency of Ottoman architects and builders warrants special mention for the purpose of this book. Among them, the Ottoman builders from the island of Karpathos in today's Greece constructed ample monuments during the making of the British Khartoum (figure 4.24). Evangelia Georgitsoyanni has identified the names and buildings of Karpathian masons and craftspeople in Sudan who constituted a network of builders that passed on their skills and employment opportunities to one another and worked in nearby Mediterranean and Aegean islands, Crete, and Asia Minor between April and October every year. Given that Sudan was technically under the rule of the Anglo-Egyptian Condominium, Ottoman builders continued finding job opportunities in northeast Africa during British colonization and many Karpathians moved permanently to Sudan. Architects, engineers, contractors, and subcontractors built important edifices such as the Ministry for the Army, medical school and state chemical laboratory, Greek Orthodox church and Greek school, Anglican church, observatory, and English banks in Khartoum.[100] They also built the famous bridge over the Blue Nile that connected Khartoum to its north, and government buildings and the Greek school in Port Sudan. The eight hundred Karpathians who worked in Sudan between 1900 and 1920 established an association in 1907.[101] They donated their property to Greece for the advancement of Greek

Figure 4.24 A scene from the Aegean island of Karpathos, whose masons built multiple monuments in Khartoum. Photo: Esra Akcan, 2024.

nationalism in 1912, when Karpathos came under the Italian rule until it became part of modern Greece only in 1947.

These two themes—the climatization with veranda and the convergence of Ottoman and British colonial architecture—is nowhere better exemplified than in one of the first and most visible monuments of the colonial rule: the Gordon College, or the University of Khartoum after independence. The building was originally designed by the Greek-Ottoman architect Dimitri Fabricius after being employed by the Ottoman khedive (figure 4.25).[102] It was completed, reportedly, by Lieutenant George Frederick Gorringe after the Anglo-Egyptian takeover in 1902—the military head who fought for British forces in Palestine a decade later in World War I.[103] The structure portrays typical features of the governmental buildings that were constructed in provinces during the late Ottoman modernization, and stands out along the Blue Nile with its unmistakable brick facades. The institution was established to create a competent "native" artisan and administrative group by educating boys between the age of sixteen and twenty. A tropical research lab was also located on the premises. In 1935, three hundred students were enrolled in the college where the education was in Arabic.[104] In the administration's eyes, the school was meant to educate "self-reliant, more adaptable and more versatile boys," and to embody "the principles and methods of the best English schools, radically adapted to meet local conditions."[105] The building entrance from the garden was mediated by a deep veranda all along, perforated with brick pointed arches, clusters of brick round columns, and brick balustrades. The facades that faced the city had double height perforations with arched windows at the bottom and round openings above. The garden was the platform for numerous events, rituals, and photo shoots. A photograph taken by R. von Slatin of a eurythmics ceremony in 1926 testifies to the use of sports and performance for disciplinary purposes in educational settings.[106] After World War II, the London-supervised Public Works Department commissioned W. G. Newton to prepare a project for the college's extension. Newton added new brick hostel buildings (today's faculties) on two sides of the main pedestrian spine, as well as an open-air theater, library, and mosque. His explanations prove that the veranda continued to be perceived throughout the first half of the twentieth century as the most appropriate space for tropical architecture due to its sun shading and ventilation advantages.[107] In the meantime, Gordon College became a building where ideas of equality and decolonization emerged.[108]

While the colonial officers envisioned houses and public buildings with colonnaded verandas in gardens to be occupied by Europeans in Khartoum, they insisted that an "African" aesthetics be developed across the river in Omdurman. Sarsfield-Hall complained that the new buildings in Omdurman looked too much like those in Khartoum, and wished they were more "African in character and consequently more suitable to the environment of an African city."[109] His office developed designs for what they called "African-type buildings . . . in order to avoid, where possible, the violent imposition

Figure 4.25 Dimitri Fabricius and British Colonial Office, Gordon College, Khartoum, 1900 (renamed the University of Khartoum after Sudan's independence in 1956). *Top*: Pupils of Gordon College, 1904–1914; postcard. *Bottom*: Eurythmic ceremony at Gordon College, 1926. R. C. von Slatin Collection, Sudan Archive Durham (SAD 869/1/1; SAD 138/187). Reproduced by permission of Durham University Library and Collections.

of buildings of purely western design on native environments."[110] Allegedly after doing research in North Sudan, Sarsfield-Hall claimed that "there was practically nothing in existence in the way of distinctive Sudanese architecture."[111] For that reason, the governor declared to have searched for inspiration in the French Colonial Exposition of 1931, and ordered designs for an ablution pavilion, almshouse, butcher's market, blacksmith's shop, dispensary, dwelling, market, market shed for women, and tea pavilion. These structures only had occasional verandas, confirming the racist climate determinism that infiltrated Sudan's planning and architectural design all along. The climate control that verandas provided were allegedly necessary for white Europeans, but the "natives" could live without it. The "African-type" buildings, instead, were designed as mud-brick rectangular volumes with ornamented roof lines. The almshouse was composed of a courtyard surrounded by two rows of units whose facades created a wall of rhythmic mud-brick columns topped with pyramidal finishes.[112] The teahouse was the most decorated, with ornamented columns and mud-brick walls, as well as a dynamic roof line (figure 4.26).[113]

DISMISSAL OF LOCAL CLIMATE KNOWLEDGE AND ENTITLEMENT TO CLIMATE PROFICIENCY

The history of colonial architecture in Khartoum demonstrates the dismissal of local climate wisdom and is another stark example of agnotology. As defined in the introduction, *agnotology* here refers to the trivialization of knowledge in order to claim the superiority of one episteme over another. Even when designing buildings for the "Africans" in opposition to the "Europeans," the British officers never sought to learn some climate know-how from the local builders. Instead, they claimed "Sudanese" had no identifying buildings and that their cultures could be modernized only by learning from the European Expos.

Journals and institutions of "tropical architecture" played a role in the dismissal of local knowledge and the dissemination of Northern comfort standards much beyond Sudan. The journal *Colonial Building Notes (Overseas Building Notes* after 1958), established in 1944 by the Colonial Office and funded by the Colonial Development and Welfare Act, disseminated technical information on housing and construction in British colonies.[114] In 1955, the office listed forty partnering institutions all over the world, and in 1961, the journal's distribution reached 1,400 copies. Many issues defined tropical zones as "hostile climates," where human comfort could be nonetheless provided through environmental science.[115] Articles and manu-

Figure 4.26 Almshouse (*top*) and teahouse (*bottom*), from a Khartoum Municipality portfolio of "African-type buildings," 1935. E. G. Sarsfield-Hall Collection, Sudan Archive Durham (SAD 679/6/10; SAD 679/6/51). Copyright. Reproduced by permission of Durham University Library and Collections.

als developed the science of calculating comfort indexes and the technical know-how for making Northerners more comfortable in Southern and non-Western climates.[116] They drew attention to the improvement of passive climate-control techniques despite progress in mechanized technologies. As one author wrote, comparing tropical to British weather, "We are unable to sweep warmth away by wholesale air-conditioning. Subtler, gentler and cheaper methods are forced on us by circumstances; and of course that is not entirely a bad thing."[117]

The expertise on tropical architecture soon trickled down to London's influential architecture school, the AA (Architecture Association School of Architecture). Indeed, the same governmental institutions that produced expertise about tropical architecture also had educational ambitions. On the suggestion of the Colonial Liaison Officer George Anthony Atkinson (who held the position since June 1948), and as a result the 1953 Conference on Tropical Architecture, organized upon the request of the Nigerian student Adedokun Adeyemi, who demanded an architectural training that would better equip him to build in his home country, the AA started providing a six-month course on tropical architecture.[118] Despite this background, the AA's pedagogical approach, curriculum, and influence in the foundation of other architectural schools in former British colonies made it less a freedom fighter for decolonization than an apparatus for the commissioning of British architects in formerly colonized territories. The AA's Department of Tropical Studies educated architects who used this expertise as their entitlement to build in the Global South, even during postcolonial times. In Jiat-Hwee Chang's words, who wrote on British tropical architecture in East Asia, "the technoscientific clarity and certainty of climatic design facilitated the export of British architectural expertise to the tropical colonies."[119] Postwar architects' overemphasis on the technoscience of climate control and their trivialization of the local know-how helped to depoliticize and flatten out variation in countries collected under the umbrella of the tropics. The reduction of complex contextual issues into scientifically quantifiable climatic conditions augmented British architects' claims to professional credibility in designing for tropical countries without confronting their colonial baggage or having them even set foot in these actual places.

In fact, the British entitlement to climate literacy was embarrassingly mistaken on many fronts. For instance, Sudan's place in the field of tropical architecture was premised on a foundational miscategorization. British colonizers confused all their colonies as tropical lands in an overarching umbrella that spanned from Libya to Malaysia, from Saudi Arabia to Hong

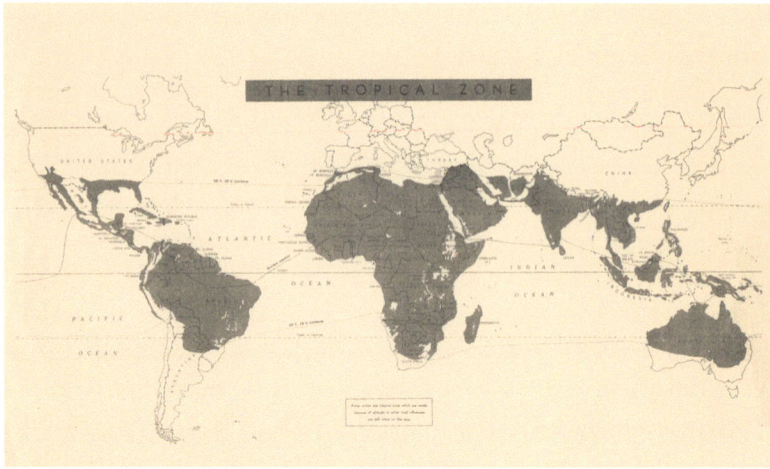

Figure 4.27 "The Tropical Zone," as published in *Colonial Building Notes* 32 (1955): 7.

Kong. A map published in a 1955 issue of *Colonial Building Notes* exposes this colonial epistemology and identifies the "tropical zone" in relation to geopolitical borders rather than Mercator lines. The entire continent of Africa as well as countries in the Middle East, Asia, and South America were identified as tropical areas even though some are situated on the same latitude as European and North American countries (figure 4.27).[120]

Of course, there is nothing inherently colonial about passive climatization in architecture. In fact, local builders and architects had already developed many of these techniques for centuries and continued to improve them after independence. However, the colonial planners either dismissed or gave no due respect to precolonial local wisdom in climate control. For instance, claiming that the veranda was a British invention meant the trivialization of local climate knowledge. Indeed, comparable spaces to what the British called "the veranda" existed in both anonymous and iconic houses in the areas that they found upon conquest. This included the Khalifa's house in Omdurman—where many British officers visited and photographed—Ali Dinar's palace, and some *tukl* structures that were surrounded by semiopen spaces (figures 4.28).[121] When the colonial planners dismissed the local climate knowledge, their alternative town-planning decisions led to severe consequences. Khartoum's large and wind-exposed avenues and expansive urban development is a case in point. The misnaming of tropical lands resulted in mistaken urban decisions.

Figure 4.28 Captain F. C. Poole standing on the veranda of the Khalifa's house in Omdurman, ca. 1905. H. A. MacMichael Collection, Sudan Archive Durham (SAD 587/1/42). Copyright. Reproduced by permission of Durham University Library and Collections.

INDEPENDENCE-ERA CRITIQUE, DOXIADIS ASSOCIATES, AND EX-OTTOMAN PROFESSIONAL NETWORKS

Independence-era professionals did not let these mistakes due to climate determinism go unnoticed. During the process of decolonization in the aftermath of World War II, national authorities invested in city planning according to then-prevalent theories of development and modernization. Soon after Sudan's independence in 1956, a cohort of citizen and noncitizen architects aimed to mark this transition with new planning and stylistic revisions.[122] My book discusses the dissemination of ex-Ottoman professional networks in the making of architecture during the independence era. As mentioned in the introduction, Kavala and Khartoum, two towns in today's Greece and Sudan, had been connected to each other since the first days of the Ottoman presence in Sudan. The Greek-speaking population was in the thousands during the Ottoman governor Mehmet Ali's times, when Greek-Ottoman builders and other urban professionals had established themselves in North Africa.[123] Many ethnically Greek builders of the Ottoman Empire had worked to construct important buildings and structures, and some local Greeks such as Georges Stafinidis designed the earliest modernist public buildings in Khartoum's prestigious locations, including the Abdoulla Commercial Building. Advertisements for architecture jobs and news in periodicals report that Greek and Sudanese architects owned most of the architectural offices in Independent Sudan between 1955 and 1969.[124] Among them, the most relevant for this book are the architects who were part of the dissolution of the Ottoman Empire, such as Constantinos Doxiadis and professionals in his office Hassan Fathy and Kleon Krantonellis, as well as the Omdurman-born architect Abdel Moneim Mustafa.

Born in Asenovgrad in 1913, Doxiadis was among the resettled populations during the dissolution of the Ottoman Empire. His family was subject to the Greek-Bulgarian population exchange in 1919,[125] and his father Apostolos Doxiadis worked as the top government official who was responsible for the settlement of refugees arriving from Turkey to Greece during the Christian-Muslim partition of 1923 (chapter 2). Doxiadis referred to himself as a vulnerable refugee child growing up in a refugee world.[126] He kept his father's documents that related to the resettlement of exchanged populations in the aftermath of the 1923 treaty in the files in his own office, and dedicated the first volume of his magnum opus to him and his mother for "leading their descendants towards human development."[127] Doxiadis Associates soon became the world's most prolific architectural, planning, and consulting office. The locations of the office's clients covered half of the globe, spanning most of North and South America, Europe, West Asia, North and East Africa, and South and Southeast Asia. Doxiadis Associates prepared master plans for almost all of the Ottoman successor states, except for Turkey and countries north of the Black Sea.[128]

Doxiadis was convinced of the power of *ekistics*, a term he coined to denote "the science of human settlements [that] co-ordinates economics, social sciences, political and administrative sciences, technology and aesthetics into a coherent whole and leads to a new type of human habitat."[129] He thought extensive spatial surveys, empirical analyses, and candid diagnoses of contemporary problems would deliver both universal progress and regional specificity. The architectural historian Panayiota I. Pyla has described the office's work in Iraq and Syria as "a corrective to Eurocentric modernism," because it appealed to "post-colonial governments of the time [with] the promise that it would be more amenable to local cultural preferences."[130] Doxiadis's method that promised extensive research on the ground according to the standards of "universal science" must have been attractive to national governments, as it seemingly freed him of "imperial stigma," to use a term from his *New Yorker* profile.[131] This must have referred to the imperialism of both Ottoman and European empires.

Doxiadis may have represented sufficient distance from imperialism, but he was a facilitator of American soft power in the Cold War context.[132] The political backdrop of Doxiadis's involvement in Sudan was the country's acceptance of US aid as a result of the agreement between the two governments in 1957. Doxiadis worked on Sudan during the same years that he was invited to international conferences in India (1954), and received comprehensive projects in Pakistan (1957–73), usually upon the suggestion of US advisers.[133] These included the Korangi master plan for the resettlement of refugees after the India-Pakistan partition, just as his father did after the Greek-Turkish partition. Scholars studying Doxiadis Associates' work in Lebanon (1957–59) and Iraq (1955–60, 1973–75) have revealed his connection to US soft power.[134] The *New York Times* praised Doxiadis for eliminating empty and lonely urban environments that made dwellers susceptible to communist sympathies.[135] Soon after independence, Sudanese cities became a target of the Cold War's two blocs, a condition easily visible in the physical landscape with large, eye-catching buildings that were built either with the "American aid" or as "Chinese gifts" that came out of the New Asian-African Strategic Partnership launched at the 1955 Bandung Conference.[136] Archival documents also reveal that Doxiadis was in communication with the American embassy in Sudan, where he sent reports on Sudan, Pakistan, and Lebanon.[137] The American aid provided funds and assistance for many of the major public buildings in Khartoum, such as the ones built by the Greek-Austrian architect A. O. Petermuller.[138]

While Doxiadis's connections to the United States during the pursuit of his international career has been confirmed by other scholars, my book additionally discusses the office as a meeting place of professionals who descended from the Ottoman Empire. The fact that Doxiadis received commissions in Ottoman successor states early in his career facilitated the office's global reach. In Alexandros-Andreas Kyrtsis's words, the "projects that Doxiadis undertook in the Middle East in less than three years from the founding of his practice were enough to create the reputation of an international company, to which governments and international organizations could entrust large scale projects."[139] The Greek community in Sudan had reached about seven thousand by the time of Doxiadis's arrival.[140] Doxiadis illustrated modern Khartoum with their buildings such as those by Stafinidis,[141] and continued to use his connections with the Greek community in Sudan to ask for their support.[142]

On October 8–17, 1958, two years after Sudan's independence, Doxiadis visited Sudan following the new government's invitation, and undertook the master plan of greater Khartoum whose preliminary report was submitted in May 1959. Additionally, the office prepared reports for Port Sudan, established a branch in the city of El Obeid, and undertook research and projects for land and water in Gezira and Kordofan. The city of Khartoum, Doxiadis later noted in his books *Architecture in Transition* and *Ekistics*, was the first to accept his idea of the dynapolis—"a city that had development built into it."[143] In February and March 1959, Doxiadis gave a lecture titled "The Future of Our Cities" in Port Sudan and at the University of Khartoum. He provided the theoretical framework for the office's master plans and underlined major changes in land settlement around the world due to population increase, uncontrolled growth, industrialization, and the invention of mechanized transportation vehicles. "The most important change, however," Doxiadis said, "resulted from the new social order, generated by development. In the place of old feudal pattern of land ownership . . . of lords and serfs, we now have the rural dweller and the urban dweller, who are both fully recognized as citizens."[144] Doxiadis seems to anticipate that all societies would transform into nation-states with sovereign populations and adopt the property regimes of capitalism in postcolonial times. His proposal for this new global context was the developmental and dynamic dynapolis: "A city that would develop freely and naturally," ironically, "along a planned and predetermined course."[145] Doxiadis positioned Sudan in the second "phase of development,"[146] suggesting that he inherited much of the postwar developmentalist hierarchies that assumed all countries would follow the same path of "developed" (industrial, formerly colonizing) countries.

Recently, architectural historians have critically addressed the continuities between European coloniality and midcentury developmentalism, by building on the ideas of Arturo Escobar.[147] Doxiadis appears frequently in these debates as a consultant associated with development and a frequent recipient of the UN and Ford Foundation funds.[148] While building on these ideas, I look at the zeal of development from the perspective of those who did not necessarily inherit its supremacies from British, French, or German colonization. As explained in the introduction, writing the history of the twentieth century by registering the dissolution of the Ottoman Empire changes some of the established accounts. This book follows the architects of the ex-Ottoman professional networks, after which a more layered global history of midcentury modernization emerges.

Doxiadis Associates proposed significant changes to the British colonial master plan without necessarily exposing its racist and militarist colonial policies. Throughout his career, Doxiadis diagnosed problems of world cities as challenges caused by previous urbanization, but without identifying colonization as an additional historical burden on postcolonial cities.[149] For Khartoum, the office surveyed the existing situation in line with the theory of ekistics, including the city's architectural history, climatic conditions, environmental characteristics, animal life—insofar as it interfered with human life—population analysis, current land use, transportation, conditions and quality of housing, and institutional buildings. Among the long list of problems caused by Khartoum's previous master plan, the worst proved to be the inaugural idea of the colonial grid. The team identified problems to be rectified, such as flooding areas; lack of transportation and communication between the settlements at different banks of the rivers; lack of local community centers and hospitals; overcrowding of schools; wrong placements of the airport, the train station, and the zoo; loss of opportunities using the Nile; and the lack of expansion area due to the municipal boundaries and military zones (figure 4.29). Without naming it, the Doxiadis report identified the British General Kitchener's colonial grid as the major cause of "problems of proper and rational land use."[150] The Sudanese towns, the reports indicated, had very low densities, forcing the formation of "satellite villages" sprawling in an unhealthy and unplanned way across the landscape. This was a factor of "unrealistic calculations" to accommodate rural immigrants, low-income groups, and nomadic populations including those from West Africa who

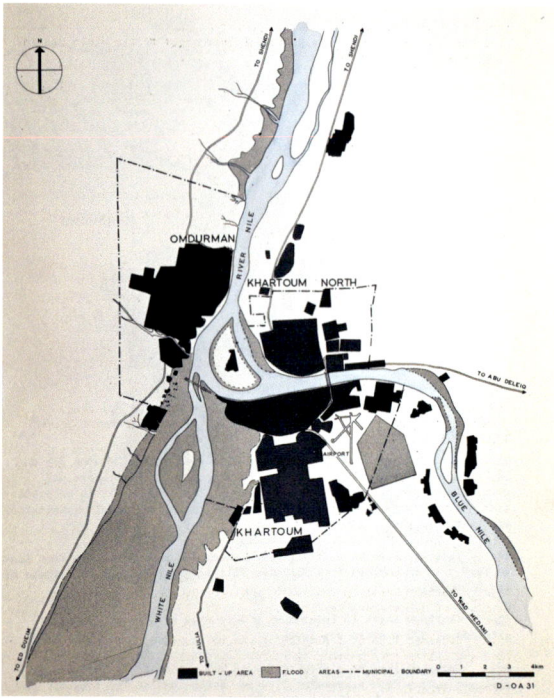

Figure 4.29
Doxiadis
Associates, "Areas
Subject to Floods,"
from Studies for
Preliminary Master
Plan, Greater Plan
of Khartoum, 1959.
Constantinos A.
Doxiadis Archives.
© Constantinos
and Emma
Doxiadis
Foundation.

came to the capital city for work—a situation that was common across the world, the Doxiadis team noted, such as in New Delhi.[151]

The Doxiadis Associates' official narrative obscured colonial military violence, but the collaborators within the office took much more antagonistic tones while writing internal reports and confidential documents. This included Hassan Fathy, the now-famous architect from Egypt who joined Doxiadis Associates between 1957 and 1961. Born in Alexandria in 1900 when Egypt was a legally recognized Ottoman province but a de facto state, Fathy, and his collaboration with Doxiadis, demonstrates the professional networks sustained by the last Ottoman generation. In confidential reports, Fathy explicitly blamed colonization for Khartoum's waste of space and energy. Furthermore, he characterized Kitchener's, McLean's, and Sarsfield-Hall's master plans as a security measure against anticolonial resistance:

> The reason for this is essentially because the city has been developed in a hasty and careless way. No-one has been interested in planning for human convenience. . . . The planners wanted to segregate the native population and the European, so put the natives as far as possible from the European quarter

Doxiadis
Associates.
Preliminary
Master Plan,
Greater Plan of
Khartoum, 1959.
Constantinos A.
Doxiadis Ar-
chives. ©
Constantinos
and Emma
Doxiadis
Foundation.

and the city center; [they] thought of population as something static, and did not have the imagination to allow for future development and change. . . . The planners were military engineers who do not have particular town-planning skills. These engineers, in fact, laid out Khartoum for defense—not against external enemies, like a medieval city, but against an internal rising. Therefore, the roads are straight and wide, . . . not to accommodate motor traffic but to allow a free yield of fire for the authorities' cannon.[152]

Following on-site analyses, Doxiadis Associates made a case for the master plan of the greater Khartoum area, and proposed to combine the colonial town of Khartoum with Khartoum North and Omdurman. They proposed to add new transportation networks, and to construct five arterial roads and two new bridges. Most comprehensively, the Doxiadis Associ-ates proposed the city's sectors—the new module for the dynapolis—in a way that knit the three towns together.[153] In other words, the sector grid would be overlaid on the existing colonial and traditional settlements as a modernizing order that was supposed to glue them together. The midcen-tury modernization grid of the dynapolis would replace both the colonial military grid established by General Kitchener in Khartoum and the Mahdist street pattern in Omdurman (figure 4.30). The Doxiadis team also specified locations for agriculture and for several urban functions within the sector grid's logic. They suggested preventing development in flooding zones, relocating the train station, and moving the zoo to the Tutti Island and the airport to North Khartoum.

There is no indication whether the actual habitants in Khartoum prioritized the problems identified in the Doxiadis Associates' reports in the same way, if at all, or whether they had other complaints. The team members took into account their conversations with national authorities, which allowed more agency to the local population than in a colonial setting. The permanent staff in Doxiadis office, such as Orestis Yakas, who had worked in Pakistan and was the project manager in Sudan, prepared reports of his conversations with local bureaucrats on climate, health conditions, community life, customs and habits, land ownership, symbolic buildings, administrative and educational buildings, open spaces and sports grounds, and more.[154] Nonetheless, the voices and experiences of the majority habitants were absent. The team members must have assumed that the national authority was the legitimate representative of a population that was ethnically, socially, and economically diverse. However, this assumption was oblivious to the fact that the midcentury world order inherited significant baggage from the imperial and colonial times, and that the partitions and the borders of postcolonial nation-states had been established during a set of negotiations between the ex-colonial forces—situations that caused many aftershocks in the upcoming years.[155] That said, the identification of the root cause of problems as the dimensions of the colonial grid was an important professional insight. Above, I demonstrated in hindsight that the spacious colonial grid resulted in an overexpansive city due to the low density and large-sized urban blocks. The straight and wide roads and large distances between blocks additionally increased environmental problems due to a misguided climate determinism.

Doxiadis proposed retaining integrated personnel in both Sudan and Athens, in order to implement the office's proposals.[156] Employees of the office specializing in planning, administration, and housing were to stay in Sudan, conduct surveys with collaborating local professionals, and provide monthly reports to the central office, which would then be integrated into the final master plan and its explanatory reports.[157] Additionally, Doxiadis insisted that students from Sudan receive training in the Center of Ekistics in Athens, at the Sudanese government's expense, to eventually replace Western experts. He proposed that students go to his institute, rather than attend other schools established during British colonization, so as to be better educated in the newly developing science of ekistics. Students would take one year of theoretical training in Athens with courses on the ekistics of architecture, on the theory and practice of ekistics, on the theory and history of civilization, on economics, statistics, sociology, housing management, law, and community facilities and works; and follow that up with a second year of practical training in Sudan, where they would be assigned to government-led ekistics projects.[158] Scholars such as Mohammed Osman El Sammani and El-Sayed El-Bushra continued their involvement with the Center of Ekistics throughout the 1970s.[159]

In 1959, the Doxiadis team made suggestions for a new residential typology in order to rectify the wrong dimensions of the urban blocks in colonial Khartoum. In a report titled "The Size and Shape of Urban Plots," they, too, prioritized climate in urbanism, but foregrounded the need for new plot dimensions, the proper orientation of the houses in their plots vis-à-vis the sun, as well as ventilation created through narrow passages of breeze (unlike colonial planners who advocated for large gardens). Coupled with what the team named as "social factors" (i.e., "Sudanese people like to have privacy in their houses"), this new climatic urbanism pointed toward rectangular plot sizes encircled by high walls: "Elongated plot gives the possibility of creating two compact courtyards in the front and back of the house."[160] Accordingly, the team prepared drawings for three types of houses that ranged between 80 and 160 square meters. All had courtyards in the front and back surrounded by high walls. Bigger houses additionally included covered outdoor spaces named "shelter" but reminiscent of verandas (figure 4.31). A drawing titled "Perspective of a Typical House" depicted a paved veranda in a courtyard that was covered with light wooden beams carried by a wooden column, and surrounded by vertical screens, shutters, and an external wall perforated with ample square openings (figure 4.32).

In the theory of dynapolis, the settlements were organized in relation to a hierarchy of scale that moved from a house to a neighborhood to a sector and eventually to a super sector. Ten to twenty-five families would form a Community Class I and increasing numbers would move up to Community Class V. Each group would share some public facilities, moving from basic neighborhood needs to schools and to cultural facilities. The Doxiadis team prepared a project for Community Class IV for Khartoum in relation to their proposed plot sizes and residential types. The project envisioned a zone for a thousand to sixteen hundred families, and identified a market and shops, a social center, a health center, a secondary school, a religious center, and an administration building, accumulated together and rising as relatively taller

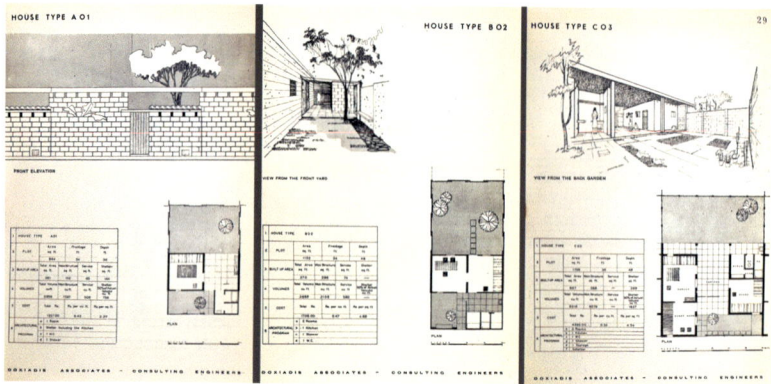

Figure 4.31 Doxiadis Associates, house studies for Preliminary Master Plan, Greater Plan of Khartoum, 1959. Constantinos A. Doxiadis Archives. © Constantinos and Emma Doxiadis Foundation.

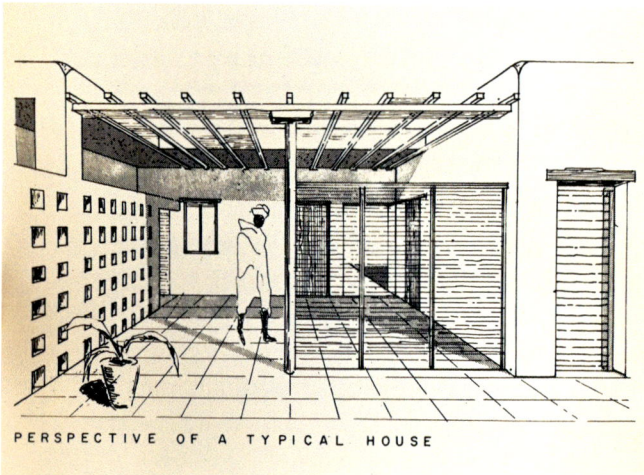

Figure 4.32 Doxiadis Associates. "Perspective of a Typical House," Khartoum, Sudan, 1959. Constantinos A. Doxiadis Archives. © Constantinos and Emma Doxiadis Foundation.

and bigger buildings in the middle of a low-rise residential fabric composed of courtyards (figure 4.33).

In one of the conversations on climatic conditions, the government meteorologist Sayed Ahmet Abdul Haab and his assistant Sayed Mustafa warned the Doxiadis team about the serious *haboob* of Khartoum. There were no known precautions, even though planting would have helped. The local experts pro-

Figure 4.33
Doxiadis
Associates.
"Formation of
the Community
Class IV," from
Study for
Preliminary
Master Plan,
Greater Plan of
Khartoum, 1959.
Constantinos A.
Doxiadis
Archives. ©
Constantinos
and Emma
Doxiadis
Foundation.

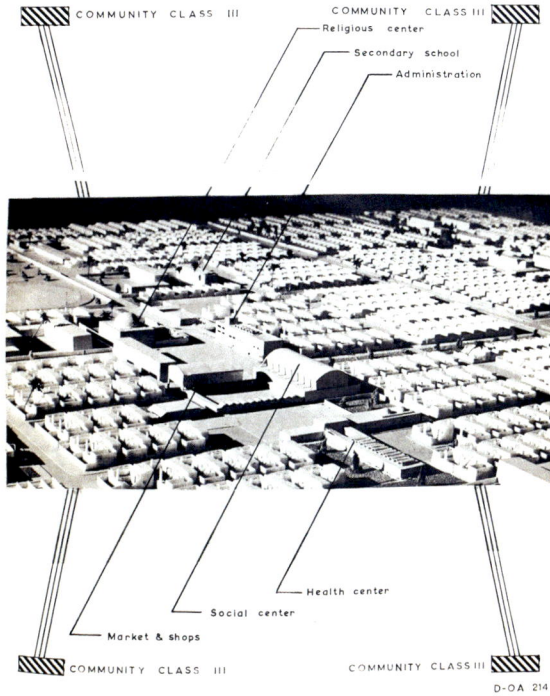

posed to lift the houses above the ground in order to protect the living spaces
from sand and mud that accumulated due to these strong sandstorms.[161] This
residential typology would have indeed been concurrent with modernist aesthetic and functionalist values at the time—use of *pilotis* (stilts) was one of
Le Corbusier's five principles of modern architecture. However, this proposal
from Sudanese officials must have fallen on deaf ears, as there is no indication
in archives that envisioned such a housing type. The Doxiadis Associates did
not receive further commissions to advance the master plan of Khartoum, but
instead shifted their attention to the Gezira region, discussed below.

ABDEL MONEIM MUSTAFA AND CLIMATE CONSCIOUSNESS
AS CORRECTIVE

Where the revision of colonial residential spaces in relation to the ethos of
independence and climate consciousness is concerned, Abdel Moneim Mustafa deserves the utmost attention.[162] Born in 1930 in today's Sudan, Moneim

Mustafa started studying at the University of Khartoum to become a civil engineer (*mühendis*), where there was no department of architecture (*mimar*) at the time. He received a fellowship to continue an architectural education in the United Kingdom, where he became the "first non-British" recipient of the best student of the year award in the Leicester School of Architecture.[163] He was employed in the Ministry of Public Works immediately after his return to Sudan, as well as in the newly inaugurated architecture department at the University of Khartoum in 1964.[164] His office Technocon collaborated with Doxiadis for a second plan of Khartoum in 1990, and implemented some of the suggestions of the 1959 plan, such as a bridge over the Nile (built), and a new airport in North Khartoum (unbuilt, and Moneim Mustafa collaborated with Italian architects Paolo Portoghesi and Vittorio Gigliotti in 1973 for this design).[165]

Moneim Mustafa is one of the most locally admired Sudanese architects of his generation despite the lack of published recognition. His buildings in Khartoum can be easily identified with their recognizable details and climate-control techniques. The private houses, most of which were commissioned by the new statesmen, professionals, and rising elite of Sudanese independence, are modular reinforced concrete frameworks filled with variations of solids and voids, programmed as verandas, terraces, and interior spaces. In these buildings, Moneim Mustafa placed sun and air control at the center of urban and architectural design and intentionally built on the know-how of "tropical architecture," albeit in a corrective way.[166]

There is a significant quality that differentiates Moneim Mustafa from colonial architects and contemporary colleagues, including the Greek-Austrian architect Petermuller with whom he otherwise shared many aesthetic and functionalist sensibilities. Both architects translated verandas and sun-screening devices into a new modern architectural language. While designing private houses, Petermuller placed the buildings in open gardens and provided ample verandas just like the colonial architects but, instead, with highlighted reinforced concrete columns and extended beams. Having designed many private houses, Moneim Mustafa's career also advanced a rich set of variations of verandas, terraces, and sunscreens expressed in modular reinforced concrete frames. They provide a network of open, covered, screened, and closed spaces for the climate control of different activities, including open-air sleeping terraces for the night and shaded verandas and socializing spaces for the day. Unlike Doxiadis's one-story residential types, Moneim Mustafa usually lifted bedrooms and living spaces to the second floor, possibly as a better response to sandstorms. Moneim Mustafa used verandas, clearly named in drawings with this word, both as living areas attached to interior spaces and as circulation paths that were part of the landscaping of gardens. This is the case in the Mahmood Abdelrahim House in Khartoum, which integrates high street walls into the design that create a courtyard behind these walls (figure 4.34). Instead, Bedridi Suleyman House and Haj Al Safi House in North Khartoum are freestanding buildings in large spacious gardens (figure 4.35). His sister's house and Mansour Khalid's house create a hybrid relation with the street due to the lifted veranda from which one can see behind the high garden wall (figure 4.36). The trees consciously planted outside the solid walls of a double house in Omdurman both protect the house from overheating and provide a shaded and paved meeting place on the public street. In his designs for less wealthy collective housing, Moneim Mustafa made sure to provide a veranda for each unit, regardless of the modest means (figure 4.37).

These gestures were carried to public buildings as well. Moneim Mustafa's concerns for climatization provided the most memorable metropolitan structures of Khartoum, such as the El Ikhwa Building (figure 4.38), and translated into signature window details in his larger office buildings such as the Arab Bank for Economic Development, Sudan Development Cooperation, and Sudanese Savings Bank. His campus and neighborhood designs participated in the midcentury modernist transformations in greater Khartoum. In the chemistry laboratory of the Faculty of Science at the University of Khartoum, Petermuller lifted the entire multistory building on *pilotis* to create a shaded public space, and as a possible precaution against mud in interior spaces after a *haboob*. The memorable verandas of this building, with tilted wooden grid latticework, protect the walls and regulate the linear and vertical circulation spaces with impressive shadows (figure 4.39).[167] The veranda-in-the-air, which functioned both as a sun-shading device and a socializing circulation space that knit buildings together, became a repeated pattern during this time, including in the Faculty of Architecture, designed in four phases by different faculty.[168]

There is a significant quality that differentiates Moneim Mustafa from his predecessors and collaborators, and shows his corrective participation in "tropical architecture." This difference can best be illustrated by comparing Petermuller's and Moneim Mustafa's campus designs. In the Khartoum Senior Trade School, Petermuller followed the British colonial planners' assumptions about the need for large, open spaces in between buildings that

Figure 4.34
Abdel Moneim Mustafa, Mahmood Abdelrahim House, Khartoum. Photo: Esra Akcan, 2019.

Figure 4.35
Abdel Moneim Mustafa, Haj Al-Safi House, Khartoum North, 1967–69. Photo: Esra Akcan, 2019.

Figure 4.36
Abdel Moneim Mustafa, the architect's sister's house, Khartoum North, 1960s. Photo: Esra Akcan, 2019.

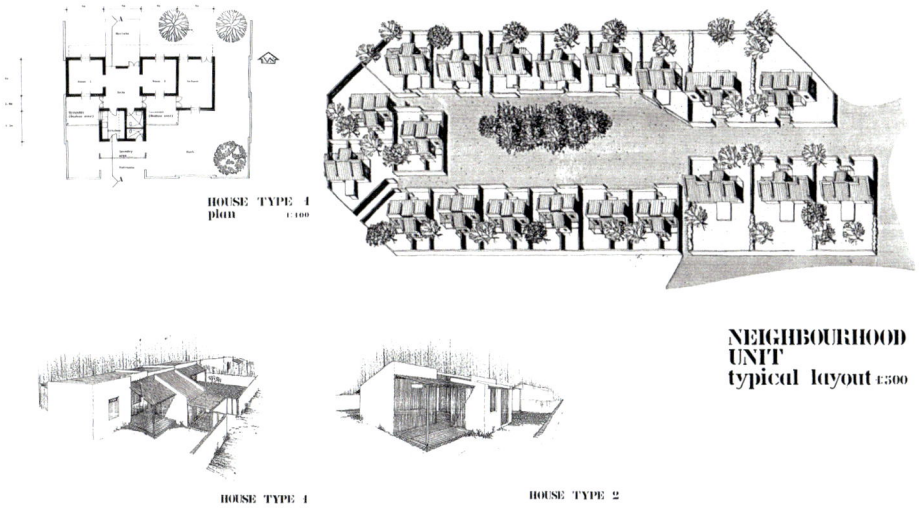

Figure 4.37 Abdel Moneim Mustafa, "Neighborhood Unit, Typical Layout" for Sudan, with plan and drawings for different house types.

Figure 4.38 Abdel Moneim Mustafa, El Ikhwa Tower, Khartoum. Photo: Esra Akcan, 2019.

Figure 4.39 A. O. Petermuller, Chemistry Lab of the Faculty of Science at the University of Khartoum, Khartoum, 1960s. Photo: Esra Akcan, 2019.

were expected to generate wind flow and ventilation.[169] He, thus, considered freestanding modernist blocks as viable solutions (figure 4.40). The tropical architecture discourse with its British connections went through some transformations but continued to inform the architects in Khartoum during this time.[170] In the pages of *Colonial Building Notes*, as well as the tropical architecture program in London's AA School, tropical architecture had become a discipline of scientifically tested climate-control techniques.[171] These venues hosted Sudanese students and included research of examples from Sudan such as Y. A. Mukhar's article, which "scientifically" certified the effectiveness of the double roof system in Petermuller's campus.[172]

Instead, Moneim Mustafa corrected the British nomenclature by defining Khartoum's climate as "hot and dry," and warned additionally against the "strong dust storms that reduce vision and create disagreeable working conditions." In his report for the College of Fine and Applied Arts, in collaboration with Ayoub & Omer Salim, he continued: "Such climate conditions call for maximum efforts to improve micro-climate of the site. Buildings should be

Figure 4.40 A. O. Petermuller, Senior Trade School (now University of Sudan), Khartoum, 1960s. Photo: Esra Akcan, 2019.

oriented in the east-west axis. They should be grouped around courtyards of green lawns and thick trees. Open grounds and fields should be planted and made green to reduce the strong sun glare. Uncovered links between buildings should be as short as possible."[173]

While there were many open-air areas in between buildings in Petermuller's campus design, Moneim Mustafa consciously designed a microcosm in his design for the College of Fine and Applied Arts. He made sure the campus did not repeat the large, wind-exposed open-air areas inherited from colonial and midcentury planning. Instead, he grouped buildings around courtyards and minimized uncovered walkways in a tightly knit network of buildings. Based on programmatic-relation diagrams, he designed shared courtyards and verandas between different art departments that would additionally foster interdisciplinary dialogues. Student hostels were to provide 50 percent outdoor sleeping possibilities in the form of terraces and verandas.[174] Landscaping was to play a vital role in the creation of the microclimate and the shading of cars and courts, and for providing different identity to courts (figures 4.41).

Moneim Mustafa reflected this corrective application of tropical architecture's know-how in the design of building sections as well (figure 4.42): "[This] led to a sectional development running east-west providing north

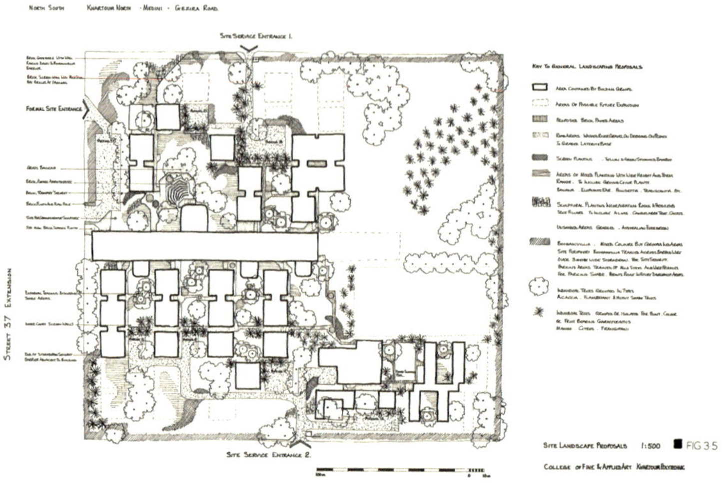

Figure 4.41 Abdel Moneim Mustafa, and Ayoub & Omer Salim, plan for the College of Fine and Applied Art, Khartoum Polytechnic, 1970s.

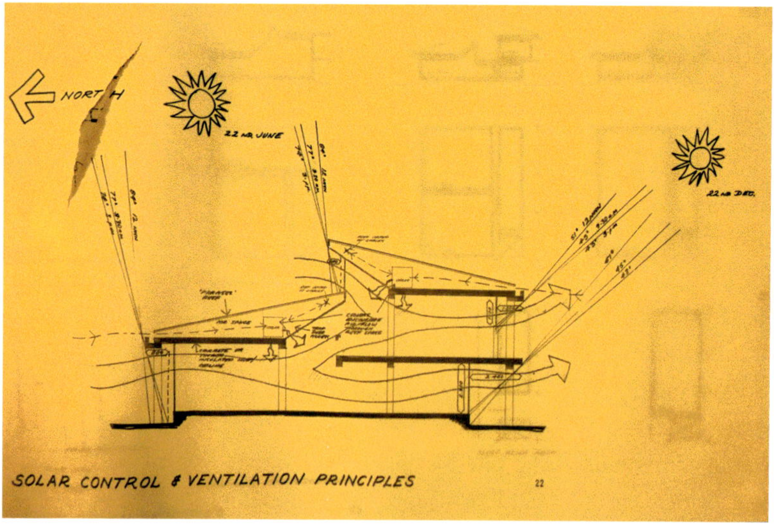

Figure 4.42 Abdel Moneim Mustafa, and Ayoub & Omer Salim, section showing solar control and ventilation principles for the College of Fine and Applied Art, Khartoum Polytechnic, mid-1970s.

light as the major source and supplemented by south light from a deeply shaded walkway area. All windows are totally shielded by overhead and flanking walls from receiving direct rays of the sun. The sectional form uses identical trusses resting on concrete slabs providing a location within a "parasol" roof system for the siting of simple desert coolers which in turn mechanistically assist the roof space ventilation."[175]

Even though Moneim Mustafa used some of the technical know-how that he must have acquired as a student in the United Kingdom, such as solar diagrams, the parasol system, and technical sectional drawings showing sun and wind control, he corrected the colonial expertise on climate control. It was the local know-how found in what the British Orientalists dismissed as the "miserable . . . primitive houses" that guided some of the passive climate control in Moneim Mustafa's buildings. Moneim Mustafa lived during Sudan's transition from the colonial regime into the national one, where many professionals were connected to one another through a network that reached not only the British colonial architects but also those of the last Ottoman generation. Rather than blindly refusing or accepting the colonial heritage or postwar architecture, Moneim Mustafa rationally chose the functioning climate-control techniques and translated them into his own building designs to be inhabited by the new Sudanese citizens. He also rationally chose to disuse some of these techniques in his urban designs, when he assessed their inappropriateness from the viewpoint of climate control. This freedom to choose, I would say, should be called independence or, rather, self-determined interdependence, which redistributes the material and symbolic wealth produced during colonization among the new self-governing citizens, rather than canceling it in the name of decolonization.[176] The standard views of decolonization hardly have explanatory power for this practice, which requires other frameworks such as commitment to translatability in multiple directions, postcolonial cosmopolitanism, or anticolonial worldmaking, which will be discussed in this chapter's conclusion. Such an architectural position, I suggest, can be regarded as an example of climate consciousness that resists colonial inequalities of climate determinism but does not reject international connections and the modern as well as precolonial know-how of climatization.

Water: Used or Abused?

"Scarcity was frequent. Famines were periodical. . . . The Egyptian Government . . . continued, however, indirectly but deliberately, to make money out of [the slave trade]." This is how Winston Churchill described the Ottoman

Egypt's rule in Sudan, in order to justify the British conquest for an allegedly more benevolent and prosperous rule.[177] The people of Sudan have experienced the highest number of droughts and famines in the history of the world, which by no means came to an end with British colonization. Why, one might ask, was this land subject to such a recurrent and continuing disaster, especially being placed between the two Niles and on the world's largest irrigation infrastructure? How do climate disasters and geopolitical conflicts cause and fuel each other? What is the real reason behind the trauma of drought and famine or "the catastrophic convergence of poverty, violence and climate change," as Christian Parenti calls it in his book *Tropic of Chaos?*[178] Famine is often perceived as a lack of development and modernity, and summons conventional humanitarian responses and modern technical solutions, but, as Jenny Edkins argues, it might as well be modernity's symptom rather than its antithesis.[179] As in the case of earthquakes discussed in chapter 3, scrutinizing the historical causes of famines blurs the boundary between natural and man-made disasters, and invites us to see ostensible misfortunes as preventable injustices. The following pages discuss an intersection of architecture with a water infrastructure that claimed to heal cycles of famine.

ARCHITECTURE AS ORDER IN PLANTATIONS

In a black-and-white photograph taken in Khartoum's southern countryside, a few men dressed in white *jalabiya* stand on top of a high pile of sacks (figure 4.43).[180] One is looking straight at the camera, while three are carrying sacks and others seem to be on route to pick up more sacks. Judging from the sweat and posture of their bodies, one can imagine that the load is heavy and they have been laboring for extended hours in hot weather. In the background lies a flat treeless land with a dense agglomeration of objects extending almost till the horizon line. Looking at the height of bodies nearby and the perfect geometric order of the overall landscape, one could confuse this agglomeration with a densely planned city of one-story-high buildings. In fact, it is made up of stacked sacks of cotton seed, eighteen bags high. In a landscape dominated by orderly piles of cotton sacks, two water towers and a factory also fall into the picture frame.

Architectural order was employed for the sake of colonial extraction in Khartoum's countryside. The Gezira Scheme to the immediate south of Khartoum is one of the largest irrigation projects in the world that opened canals between the two Nile rivers in order to maximize fertile soil and use the slope for water's course in canals. With the Gezira Scheme, the British turned millions of acres inhabited by farmers, traders, nomads, and pil-

Figure 4.43 Gezira Plantations, Sudan (opened 1925): cotton workers on top of stacked sacks, 1925–50. A. D. Wesson Collection, Sudan Archive Durham (SAD 1/25/7). Copyright. Reproduced by permission of Durham University Library and Collections.

grims into the world's largest irrigation project dedicated to the production of cotton. With Kitchener's orders and just a year after McLean's master plan of Khartoum, the British District Officers started the Gezira Scheme following the famine of 1913–14. They completed it in 1925 with the opening of the Sennar Dam. The scheme's director, Arthur Gaitskell, blamed famine, disease, warfare, "arbitrary seizure of surplus," and "fifteen years of instability during the Mahdi period" as reasons that had discouraged productivity in the region and had driven "many landowners and cultivators away."[181] In his perception, the Gezira Scheme was meant to change this state of affairs. However, rather than crops to feed the population and prevent the next famine, the British officers used this infrastructure to grow cotton. Given the active world market of cotton and because of its use by the British industry, cotton was deemed more lucrative—for the interest of the British colonizers. The colonial rule threatened farmers with eviction if they failed to produce cotton or disobeyed the protocols of the new agrarian system.[182]

The Gezira Scheme was yet another engine in the "Empire of Cotton," to use Sven Beckert's words. Beckert identifies today's Sudan as the first land in Africa where cotton was cultivated as early as 5000 BCE, from where it must have spread to the North.[183] However, the rise of European domination in the cotton industry soon became the main locomotive of global industrial capitalism. Countries waged wars to access fertile lands, and powerful industrialists made use of colonial expansion and slave labor to produce cotton. "Along the way," Beckert writes, "planters put untold numbers of people into shackles, . . . workers, both slave and free, struggled for freedom and living wage. Men and women who had long sustained themselves through small plots of land, growing cotton alongside their food, saw their way of life end."[184]

The Gezira Scheme is a perfect case in point for the creation of cotton monocultures during colonization, whose slow violence in causing climate disasters and mass extinction is being realized today. When the Kirkuk-born Ottoman traveler Muhammed Mihri visited Sudan in 1910, he chronicled a long list of crops in addition to cotton, including wheat, barley, sesame, melon, watermelon, date, lemon, orange, grape, French fig, pomegranate, peach, apple, pear, banana, and "all sorts of vegetables" he found too many to write down.[185] After the implementation of the Gezira irrigation canals, almost all were replaced by cotton. Not that Mihri was a protector of biodiversity in Sudan—the travelogue is full of photographs of hunted animals with which the Egyptian royal Yousuf Kemal proudly posed as the hunter. Nonetheless, Mihri depicted an environment in 1910 that contrasted with the one that emerged out of the Gezira Scheme. The local farming systems had created three seasonal zones for different crops; the nomads, pilgrims, and traders carrying goods to Omdurman had made the area a multiethnic crossroads. However, the Gezira Scheme disregarded the existing farming and pastoral life, and obliterated many of its practices.

Chronicling the project from 1900 till 1959 as its close observer and eventually director (1923–45), Gaitskell identified the Gezira Scheme as a device to make Sudan "useful" for the British. He was determined to prove General Gordon wrong, who in 1884 had written, "The Sudan is a useless possession ever was so and ever will be so."[186] Lord Edward Cecil had said, "The Sudan is not, and never will be a country suitable for permanent European habitation, it is therefore in the interest of the Government to encourage as far as possible native landowners."[187] In line with Cecil's thinking, the scheme was presented as a partnership between the colonial government, London-based Sudan Plantations Syndicate, and local tenant farmers, where 80 percent of profits were transferred to the government and tenants equally, and the remaining 20 percent to the syndicate. Gaitskell insisted that the land was "predestined" for cotton production as if the existing grain and livestock did not matter. The colonial and cotton officers enticed tribes from nearby lands and pilgrims from West Africa on their way to Mecca to set up settle-

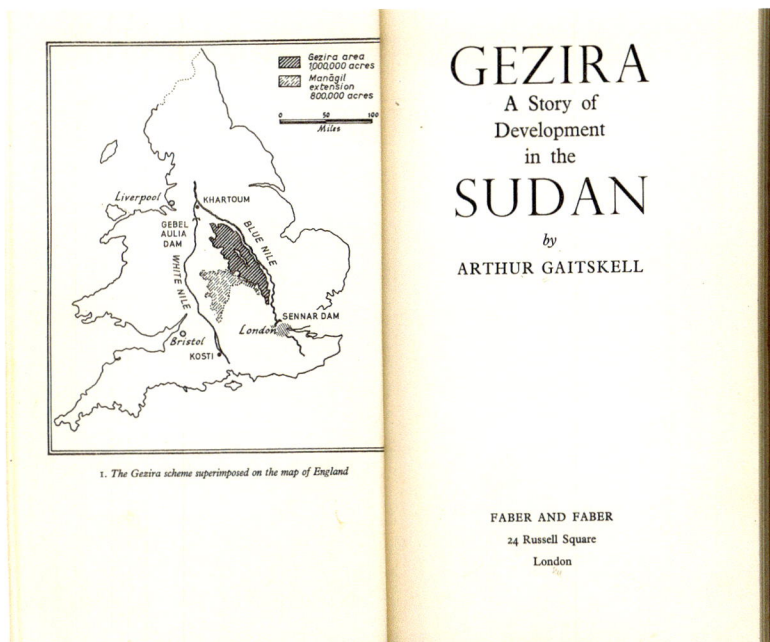

Figure 4.44 Frontispiece with a map of Gezira overlaid on the map of England, in Arthur Gaitskell, *Gezira: A Story of Development in Sudan* (London: Faber and Faber, 1959).

ments and to join the peasant labor force, planting seeds of more conflict for years to come.

On the opening page of his book, Gaitskell juxtaposed Gezira's map over a map of England (figure 4.44). In his eyes, this might have been a demonstration of the Gezira Scheme's large scale so that his fellow citizens would compare its size to Britain's territory. However, this seemingly benevolent act of drawing also projected entitlement to claim a land in Africa as British territory. Gaitskell often wrote about the Sudanese as ignorant, superstitious, and fanatic people as opposed to rational civilized man. He described sedentarization for the sake of increasing farmer labor force as the British government's "responsibility to teach him to do [farming] well. The principle of control and help" come together, he said.[188]

Historians of labor, agriculture, food security, and nomadism would identify multiple book-length research questions in the Gezira Scheme. For the purposes of this book, I am interested in the houses and settlements necessitated by the project, as well as the use of architecture to control laborers.

The scheme made use of architecture and physical planning's symbolic power to create a colonial social structure in the cotton plantations.

Aerial photos of the Gezira cotton fields capture miles and miles of land divided into perfect rectangles with perfect linear lines—much like the logic of the militant grid that Kitchener and McLean fancied to endorse the British Empire in Africa as the true heir of the Roman Empire.[189] The photos occasionally capture small villages that timidly punctuate the strict geometry of the vast cotton fields with low-rise houses (figure 4.45).[190] This was where the laborers of the cotton fields slept at night, and where their children received basic education in crowded schools.[191] Camels and light rails carried sacks of cotton from the fields to the agglomeration centers (figure 4.46).[192] These bales of cotton sacks amounted to sturdy structures as high as three- or four-story buildings in the middle of the flat landscape (figure 4.47).[193]

When Geraldine Mary Culwick arrived in Gezira as a nutritionist in 1949, she wrote about the environment in her letters:[194]

> The landscape is the least inspiring you could possibly imagine. Dead flat, crisscrossed by the most bewildering network of canals, field channels, and drains, so that any journey is sort of jigsaw puzzle to the stranger, as one dodges this way and that to find a bridge. E . . . always seems to be getting lost, for every track looks like every other—at least it does to me at the present. . . . It is most irritating at times, for you may see your destination quite near, and yet be hours finding your way to it. Dotted here and there are mud-colored villages, squat square buildings with satellite settlements of "Westerners" (Nigerians mostly) of round huts with pointed thatched roofs. Seldom a tree of any kind anywhere, except for little islands of cherished vegetation around the SPS [Sudan Plantations Syndicate] houses. . . . In this very hot climate with water very strictly controlled to meet essential needs only, irrigation does not mean a lush land flowing with milk and honey—not by a long way . . . it is a pretty grim stark existence even yet.[195]

In contrast to the monotony of the fields and temporary houses of the tenant farmers, British cotton inspectors of the London-based Sudan Plantations Syndicate lived in "research farms" and in large houses made of durable materials. The surveyors camped in tents when they traveled to the area for feasibility and agricultural research.[196] But once the scheme received the green light, they built large houses and wealthy research farms simultaneously

Figure 4.45 Gezira Plantations: main canal, road to Khartoum, cotton fields, and a farmer village, Sudan, ca. 1914–56. J. F. E. Bloss collection, Sudan Archive Durham (SAD 705/1/2). Copyright. Reproduced by permission of Durham University Library and Collections.

Figure 4.46 Gezira Plantations: cotton workers in the fields, Sudan, ca. 1925–1956. T. H. B. Mynors, Sudan Government collection, Sudan Archive Durham (SAD 778/3/6). Copyright. Reproduced by permission of Durham University Library and Collections.

Figure 4.47 Gezira Plantations: stacked sacks of cotton, 1925–50. A. D. Wesson Collection, Sudan Archive Durham (SAD 1/25/9). Copyright. Reproduced by permission of Durham University Library and Collections.

with the water canals.[197] In Culwick's lively description, one of these houses, which must have been quite typical, had "a terraced garden overlooking [one of the two lakes], *very* attractive (but a damned awful monstrosity of a new house in the latest Public Works Dept. style) . . . one feels somewhat shut in by the tropical luxuriance."[198] Research farms were composed of brick one- to two-story houses in large gardens.[199] District administrator George

Figure 4.48
Gezira Planta-
tions: interior
view of the dis-
trict adminis-
trator George
Gillett Hunter's
house, 1914–56.
G. G. Hunter
Collection,
Sudan Archive
Durham (SAD
784/3/41). Re-
produced by
permission of
Durham Univer-
sity Library and
Collections.

Gillett Hunter's house, for one, was a two-story stone structure perforated with arched gateways, sturdy rectangular windows, and shutters in a large fenced garden on a tree-lined road.[200] Inside, the house was like a cabinet of curiosity packed with sofas, armchairs, pillows, and curtains made up of flowery fabric, and ample plants, wooden cabinets, picture frames, Oriental carpets, and animal skins. Mirrors amplified the visual conglomeration even further (figure 4.48).[201]

These houses had verandas like those in Khartoum, which were additionally covered with mosquito nets.[202] Sanitary inspector E. Jane, who worked in the Gezira cotton plantations between 1929 and 1944, mapped the area and conducted extensive research on malaria prevention.[203] He concluded that the verandas should be covered all over with mosquito nets, guiding the typical houses of junior district government officials and cotton inspectors.[204] The veranda of the Sudan Plantations Syndicate was one of the most memorable spaces in Sudan. The wide and high semioutdoor

Figure 4.49 Gezira Plantations: The veranda of the Sudan Plantations Syndicate, 1914–56. N. R. Syme Collection, Sudan Archive Durham (SAD 2/7/1). Copyright. Reproduced by permission of Durham University Library and Collections.

space was furnished for socializing, sheltered with mosquito nets as an antimalaria measure, and covered with a pitched roof made of dense timber elements (figure 4.49).[205] Many houses were raised on plinths surrounded by deep brick-lined ditches to keep white ants away.[206]

Comparing two photographs, one from the fields, the other from a house in the syndicate's research farm, exposes the social hierarchy that operated between labor and research in the Gezira plantations (figure 4.50).[207] In the first, a group of unnamed agricultural workers are threshing with their elementary tools in a vast landscape with nothing but monocultural crops. They use hard manual labor and seem exhausted. In the second photograph, plant physiologist Frank Crowther's partner, Bunty Crowther, sits and reads comfortably in a garden of the Gezira research farm in Wad Medani. The building behind is made of durable brick and perforated with glass windows and shutters. The veranda is sheltered with a mosquito net, the lawn is landscaped, the grass is mowed, the pram is covered with tulle fabric, and the garden furniture holds ample bottles of water for hydration. These photographs and deduction from the legal and political structure confirm that it was always Black bodies laboring in the cotton fields and white ones ordering from their wealthy residential and research spaces.

Figure 4.50 Gezira Plantations: comparison between a cotton field (*top*) and a research farm (*bottom*), 1925–56. H. C. Jackson, Sudan Government, and F. and B. E. Crowther C oections, Sudan Archive Durham (SAD 302/9/1; SAD 8/51/7). Reproduced by permission of Durham University Library and Collections.

A few visual documents pertaining to the agriculture workers' houses suggest that they sometimes lived in round *tukl* structures with thatched roofs, at other times in mud-brick houses with rectangular shapes and flat roofs. These two types could well be placed next to each other (figure 4.51).[208] Occasionally and only toward the midcentury, these houses were more durable and ornamented.[209] When Culwick arrived in Gezira for nutrition research, she decided to stay in a village rather than a syndicate or government house, to the surprise of many of her coworkers and tenant farmers. This allowed her easier access to the villagers, especially women, of whom she wanted to measure weights, keep food records, and observe cooking methods. Even though there were instances where she was accused of being a "missionary lady" having immoral relations with her male coworkers, she thought women were "very far from regarding [her] as an inquisitive intruder."[210] Her description of her own village house exposes a striking contrast to those of British officers:

> [I live in the] guest house or *diwan* where he [Muslim tenant farmer] entertains his male friends. It is of burnt brick (unusual in this fuelless area), and has one large room, 21 × 15 which will be office and living room, and one about 12 × 12 my private room. A wide veranda goes around 2 sides of the latter. . . . Sanitation will be a pit latrine in a corner of the courtyard out of sight, behind my house up against the wall of his inner courtyard (the family's part of the establishment.) I shall bath in my trek bath in my room, and get a civilized bath when I visit neighboring British (SPS staff houses are about 4 kms apart and the nearest one to me will be the Block Inspector's house about 1 km away.) . . . Everything will be netted in to keep out flies and mosquitos. The flies in the village have to be experienced to be believed.[211]

About other houses, Culwick reported on a cockroach-filled deep-pit latrine to be used as a washroom, where she was occasionally visited by a lion.[212] She appreciated the verandas, the courtyard with a shoulder-height wall, and the fact that her house in the village was cooler "than the more civilized ones" she occupied as part of the government program.[213] In addition to the mixed residential culture of tenant farmers originating from the west and north of the area, Culwick noticed that the Gezira villages were occasionally and seasonally inhabited by "gypsies."[214] She also reported on the gradual transformation from temporary shelters with one room to mud and then brick houses with multiple rooms. "To live in thatched hut is now

Figure 4.51 Gezira Plantations: agriculture workers' houses showing both *tukl* and mud brick houses, 1925–56. G. M. Culwick Collection, Sudan Archive Durham (SAD 428/3/196). Copyright. Reproduced by permission of Durham University Library and Collections.

something to be spoken of deprecatingly and with humility. Houses of new shapes were built either, like the old huts, in puddled clay or else in green brick, with the latter apparently gaining ground. Outside they are plastered with clay and cow dung to make them waterproof, and inside with ash and dust."[215]

Culwick's assessment of the Gezira Scheme differed from that of other colonialists and historians, who celebrated it as a generous gift to the Sudanese with paternalistic certitude. In Holt and Daly's words, the "Gezira Scheme itself was a remarkable experiment in cooperative farming, a tribute to the vision of those British officials who conceived and executed it."[216] Instead, as a result of her research on three villages conducted between 1951 and 1955 at the dawn of independence, Culwick wrote the 295-page manuscript "A Study of the Human Factor in the Gezira Scheme."[217] This document, of a British woman on a mission to help food security in Africa, was not free from the stereotypical Orientalist accounts that characterized the era before British colonization as one of barbarity, exploitation, and incompetence. Nonetheless, Culwick was not hesitant to criticize British bad management either. She reported on conflicts and disasters, such as the cotton monoculture policy that deprived the farmers from growing previous crops includ-ing dura and lubia, the lack of decent living conditions for migrant laborers who settled seasonally, the lack of beauty and appreciation of workmanship, and manipulations such as the discrepancies between the English and Ara-bic versions of the tenant contracts. At the last account, Culwick evaluated the Gezira Scheme as a "great social experiment" whose success depended on the "ordinary people of the Gezira villages." Her warnings were not false anticipations: "Unheeded stresses and strains in the social structure could produce disaster no less destructive though perhaps less spectacular than unheeded stresses and strains in the concrete structure at Sennar."[218]

As the anthropologist Victoria Bernal rightly pointed out, the Gezira Scheme was a matter of symbolic power, even more than it was a matter of economic rationality. "The Gezira Scheme represented the triumph of mod-ern civilization over nature and ignorant tradition, which in practice meant the imposition of colonial order on the Sudanese landscape and society."[219] In other words, the Gezira Scheme was not a settler-colonial project but it devised another form of oppression: a disciplinary managerial system that created controlled farmers within the logic of industrial capitalism.[220] In the summarizing words of Bernal, "If one views the mission of colonialism as that of literally and figuratively creating a world order and ordering the world, the Gezira Scheme is a stunning exemplar. Its miles and miles of irrigation canals and uniform fields stretched out in a huge grid dominate space, its rigid schedules for agricultural operations command time, and above all, its hierarchy of inspectors and bureaucrats supervising, documenting, and disciplining strive to control the people of the Gezira."[221] The Gezira Scheme conceptualized agriculture as a disciplinary institution, rather than one for food security or economic prosperity. It was not necessarily successful eco-nomically,[222] but it used architectural order to symbolize modernization, progress, and power. Architectural order was recruited for the symbolic success of the British cotton plantations.

INDEPENDENCE-ERA CRITIQUE, KLEON KRANTONELLIS, AND EX-OTTOMAN PROFESSIONAL NETWORKS

Reading Gaitskell's memoirs against the grain would suggest that the local farmers were not just helpless crowds who let the British colonizers use them as hidden slaves. A labor historian would write a more detailed analysis and might interpret the negotiations between the Sudan Plantations Syndicate in London, the on-site managers, and the Gezira Tenants Union as benchmarks of anticolonial resistance. According to British officers, "Neglecting cotton or . . . aspiring to be other than a cotton-farming tenant" was not anticolonial activism, but it was "laziness and incompetence" or simply a "moral failing of a race" that needed colonial discipline.[223] In Gaitskell's eyes, the "British paternal administrators were proud of their virtues. They had brought order, justice, some economic advance, and a foreign civil service with a very high code of integrity to a country which had not experienced these benefits before." And so, Gaitskell continued, "when the small educated class first pressed for political independence, the British were genuinely doubtful whether these benefits, so important to the bulk of the population, would continue. They rejected as untrue and prejudicial to their wards the claim of the educated classes to represent the whole country."[224] The colonial administrators saw educated Sudanese who could have taken managerial positions as a threat to the British interest, and resisted the transition of power after independence, claiming that Sudanese elite would oppress Sudanese farmers.

When Sudan became independent, the nationalization of the Gezira Scheme and the redistribution of wealth to new Sudanese citizens therefore took priority. In this context, the new Sudanese government invited Doxiadis Associates to study the Gezira villages and possibly suggest a regional plan of development. In his master plan of Khartoum, Doxiadis proposed to build a water canal between the bifurcating streams of the White Nile and Blue Nile, which would bring water to the town's center. This was indeed an urban analogy of the Gezira Scheme's rural technology in Khartoum's southern countryside.

On April 3–12, 1960, Kleon Krantonellis, a senior planner at Doxiadis Associates, visited Sudan to conduct preliminary research on the Gezira villages.[225] Like his classmate Doxiadis from the School of Architecture in Athens, Krantonellis was personally affected by the dissolution of the Ottoman Empire. He was born in Kavala in 1912—in the same town as the founder of Ottoman Khartoum, Mehmet Ali—when the city was still part of the Ottoman Empire, but was exchanged between Bulgaria and Greece until the end of World War I. One of his elder brothers was killed in Smyrna/İzmir in today's Turkey in 1922. Krantonellis stayed as a Greek citizen after the Greek-Turkish Exchange of Populations of 1923, when his hometown lost 69 percent of its residents, but the population doubled with the influx of exchanged refugees arriving from Turkey. He was twelve years old during this partition, which must have caused him to lose all his Muslim friends. Nearby Komotini, by contrast, was one of the Macedonian villages exempt from the exchange treaty and continued to be a Turkish-speaking settlement.

Krantonellis became an established architect in Greece with canonic works such as his own house in the Plaka district of Athens, but he never lost ties to Macedonia. He designed buildings for cities in the region such as Kavala and Drama, worked for the UN High Commissioner for Refugees, and designed and renovated tourism complexes for the Greek National Tourism Organization as part of the Greek-Turkish Partnership Project (1965–67). He became the director of building studies and residential studies at Doxiadis Associates in 1957, for which he took up posts in Pakistan, Iraq, and Sudan.[226]

Reporting internally to the Doxiadis office on his fieldwork, Krantonellis did not fail to notice the homogenizing and monocultural impact of the cotton plantation grid in Gezira. He wrote, "One gets a very neat picture of the area and how it is settled and organized with the sole object of high agricultural efficiency but without any regard to the human settlement. I see now that this is the sole problem of our regional plan."[227] Krantonellis, along with his collaborators, such as Sudanese town planners and geographers Sayed Mubarak Sinaadah, Sayed Ibrahim Suleiman, and Salah Mezeri, and speaking to Sudan's deputy governor, staff at the Ministry of Local Government, and director of the Gezira Board, identified a set of problems in land use and architectural quality that impaired the farmers' lives in the Gezira Scheme. The villages were unplanned, with no communication or reasoned placement of community buildings. Residential plots were too small, houses and construction substandard. The flat land was abruptly intervened by irrigation canals "on an impeccably standardized pattern,"[228] around which villages were "haphazardly scattered," some squeezed by canals, others sparsely built on wasted land, some on lands suitable for cultivation, and others with no possibility of expansion.[229] Community facilities, drinking-water supplies, and road networks were inadequate. Children had to walk to school taking long detours around irrigation canals. Graves of holy men were dispersed between canals.[230]

When Fathy visited the same area as part of the Doxiadis Associates the same year, he identified similar problems and diagnosed the capitalist pressures for causing the wretched condition of the settlements: "Cotton growing has made Gezira what it is today. For better or worse, every feature of the country has been shaped by the demand of the World's Cotton Markets, from the pattern of the field to the system of work. Virtually this effect is very monotonous."[231]

Additionally, Krantonellis reported on the classist and racist segregation in the plantations: Houses for the Gezira Board were built of solid red brick in an orderly way with carefully planted and maintained gardens, while there was "no sign of green inside or around the villages."[232] Moreover, there were racial tensions between the Arab farmers and the West African pilgrims, tribes, and traders who had been sedentarized by the cotton plantation officers. The Doxiadis Associates mapped their project area onto the Savanna Belt and caravan routes as a visualization of climatic and social pressures as twin problems in the area (figure 4.52). Krantonellis's reports from the ground anticipated the civil wars that were around the corner for Sudan. These documents allow scholars to trace the precise reasons for ethnic conflict rather than blame it on essential and unbridgeable differences. Recording the thoughts of the deputy governor, Krantonellis wrote:

> Among other problems, he said, is that of new comers to Gezira, e.g. West Africans who come from their countries vis. Nigeria, Ghana, French Equatorial Africa, etc. on their way to Mecca. They stay for a while and work as farm laborers, earn some money to enable them to continue to the pilgrimage and on their way home they stay again, in many instances for good. The open frontier and in most cases the absence of passport makes control almost impossible. The readily available jobs make too great a temptation for the West Africans to settle permanently in the Gezira. These people don't mix with the Sudanese, in fact they are rather disliked. They have totally different ways of life and customs, different language, and they don't abide to Government laws, send their children to school, bury dead animals. They live in separate clusters of canonical grass huts built on the West African pattern in some distance from the villages.[233]

For the official report, Doxiadis Associates selectively pulled information from these internal reports and highlighted the architectural problems that the team promised could be healed with a regional plan. However, the official report did not mention the colonial plantation history as a root cause of the pressing settlement problems or continuing racial tensions: "The villages appear to have developed haphazardly either from old villages existing before the irrigation scheme or from labor camps built when the irrigation works were under way. In many cases, the inadequacy of space for the proper development and expansion of the villages is characteristic of this fact. . . . Planning should be human centered based on an effort to establish a physical environment in which human beings can release their potential and families can find optimum conditions of human growth."[234]

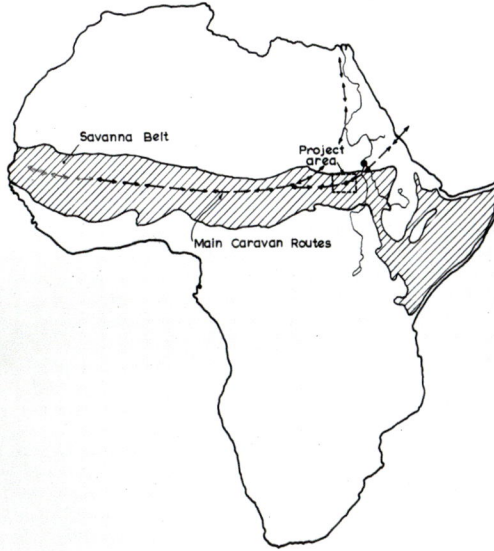

Figure 4.52
Doxiadis Associates, pilgrimage routes from West Africa to Mecca through the Project Area in Gezira, 1963. Constantinos A. Doxiadis Archives. © Constantinos and Emma Doxiadis Foundation.

HASSAN FATHY AND RURAL HABITATION BETWEEN EUROPEAN AND OTTOMAN RACISM

In his correspondence with the new Sudanese government, Doxiadis insisted on the importance of standardized villages. "It is neither sound nor possible for a nation, however rich and whatever wealth, to dispose a large part of its technical and specialized manpower for the individual study of villages, houses and community buildings, considering each as a separate problem. . . . Standardization of village types is therefore a must and can be successfully applied to the design of villages. . . . Villages can have common characteristics . . . that can be applied to a rational and successful regional housing development, in a nationwide scale, for the benefit of the nation and its people."[235] Doxiadis Associates' Gezira plans complicate the team's reputation as thinkers of urbanization alone, as Petros Phokaides also noticed about the office's engagement in Zambia.[236] Given the daunting scale of problems inherited from the colonial regime, the postwar independence thinkers around Doxiadis must have concluded that repair could only be achieved through the repetition of urban solutions such as standardization in the countryside.

Fathy undertook the preliminary project of one such pilot rural settlement in Gezira in 1960. During his research trip to the African continent as part of the Doxiadis Associates' "City of the Future" (see chapter 5), Fathy kept handwritten notes where he communicated his critique of colonization and ideas for decolonization without restraint:

> A people cannot be held down by force forever, to give freedom is the best chance of keeping friendship and getting a share of trade. . . . We Africans are more and more conscious of all that we have in common with each other; we have been long enough in bonds and we have a continent with great resources. Someday, we shall control it ourselves. . . . We shall turn to those who give us the hope of equality, who offer freedom. Please be clear about one thing. We put freedom before gold. You may talk to us for hours about economic advantage, technical assistance and the need for capital, but not a pulse will beat faster. We expect help of that kind, yes,—But we don't see that you have any moral right to make it dependent on our giving a privileged position to a few Europeans.[237]

In confidential reports on the Gezira plantations of Sudan, Fathy spoke about the decolonizing power of architecture.

> Cotton has flattened the countryside and put it into uniform; can we doubt that it has done the same to the minds of the people? As architects we cannot propose changes in the economy of the countryside. It is therefore our duty to alleviate as far as possible the deadening effect of the economic pattern. We must try to create . . . an environment as different as possible from that of the fields. We must give the villages a chance. Give them, instead of the rectangularity of the field, a winding pattern in their village streets and a free patterning of buildings to suit best the requisite of climate and social grouping.[238]

Just like Bernal, who interpreted the Gezira Scheme as a matter of building symbolic power even more than of economic rationality,[239] Fathy understood that the scheme made use of architecture and physical planning's symbolic power to maintain colonial relations. And he intervened with the same tools. If architectural order was used to colonize cotton plantations, it could also be used to build resistance. If the colonial scheme disabled the villagers from aspiring to be other than cotton-farming tenants, Fathy introduced in his design of a typical Gezira village vegetable gardens and cattle and a variety of trades as well as schools so that future generations could escape the cotton fields. If the scheme resulted "in rectangular fields, the same size

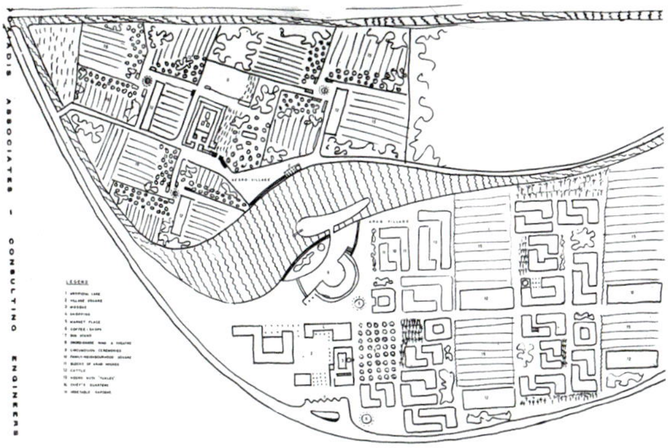

Figure 4.53
Hassan Fathy for
Doxiadis Associ-
ates, village pro-
posal for Gezira,
Sudan, 1960. Has-
san Fathy Papers
and Photographic
Collection, Rare
Books and Spe-
cial Collections
Library, The
American Uni-
versity in Cairo.

and the same color, all growing the same crop and each crop the same stage of growth,"[240] Fathy added an artificial lake and a village square as well as public programs such as a mosque, a marketplace, coffee houses, a theater, and a circumcision-ceremony area (figure 4.53).

However, Fathy maintained some of the racial categories and hierarchies that he must have inherited from Ottoman authors. He acknowledged the conflicts between Arab Sudanese tenant farmers and West African settlers arriving from Nigeria, Cameroon, Congo, and the Sahara on their way to Mecca. He warned that a unified village with standardized houses for both communities, while economical and simpler, would have been inappropriate in this situation. In such an integrated village, the two communities would have "diluted and spoiled" each other, so that instead of "two distinct bright colors of culture, we should be left with a single unlovely gray." Instead, Fathy proposed two distinct quarters, close enough to each other, for the "Arab houses" and "West African huts," where each community would have kept "its own style of architecture and its own communal compactness, and maintain its own cultural integrity."[241]

While he insisted on separating the "Arab" and "African" houses, Fathy also proposed to sedentarize pilgrims from West Africa on their way to Mecca. Just as in the colonial plantation logic, pilgrims from West Africa, whom he called "Negroids," could be enticed to cultivate the cotton fields. In a self-contradicting moment that is at odds with his otherwise decoloniz-ing aspirations, Fathy spoke of tribes and pilgrims as birds to be hunted and "taken advantage of helplessness."[242] In his eyes, this village would be the op-posite of an "extractive labor camp," because pilgrims would build "familiar homes" for themselves, "establish the same kind of society they knew in their homeland," and keep traditional ceremonies and dances.[243] Fathy neglected the diversity of communities and reduced them to two groups based on a conflation of religious, ethnic, and racial categories. He offered courtyards for "Arab houses" in one zone,[244] and freely scattered huts, albeit "more hygienic, weather and insect proof" ones for West African immigrants in the second zone.[245] While explaining a typical "Arab house," Fathy retrieved ideas from his rural rehabilitation project for the New Gourna village in Egypt of 1945. Accordingly, the courtyard had a functional and symbolic significance for the "Arab house" in the harsh climate of the desert, because seeing the sky from the courtyard of an inward-looking secluded house was a matter of peace and divinity.[246] To justify the distinction between "Arab" and "African" houses as two dwelling types, Fathy continued: "If the Arab-Sudanese looks on the sky as his only comfort in a harsh world, the [West African], on the other hand, has a more gentle relationship with the landscape. He is a garden loving person, taking delight in trees, extrovert in the extreme, and would never appreciate being shut up in a courtyard."[247]

Paradoxically, after criticizing the British colonizers for segregating the "native" and the "white" neighborhoods in Khartoum, Fathy proposed to do the same for the "Arab" and the "African" dwellings in the countryside. The difference from the colonial logic, in his eyes, was that the sectors allotted for these two types of dwelling would share the same level of resources and proximity to public programs and common services. "But this equality of treatment should not be taken to mean sameness. . . . Our job is to preserve this variety, not to iron it out," Fathy concluded in his internal report to the Doxiadis Associates.[248] Just as in New Gourna, the villagers would build their own houses in a cooperative manner in accordance with their separate traditional customs.[249]

Fathy's project was a mixture of decolonizing motivation, ethnoracial essentialism, and urban-to-rural gaze, as a reflection of his situatedness between post-Ottoman and postcolonial subjectivity. Fathy's position with respect to Sudanese anticolonial struggles was indeed complicated. The fact that Sudan was technically colonized by an Anglo-Egyptian Condominium between 1898 and 1956 makes Fathy a citizen of the colonizing force. However, many scholars agree that for all practical purposes, Sudan was ruled by the British during this colonization, when the same officers who served in Egyptian colonization also served in Sudan. Fathy's unreserved criticism against the British master plans signifies his anticolonial mindset. However, he inherited some of the Ottoman racial hierarchies when he insisted on separating the Arab and West African houses, and occasionally talked about the latter as "birds to be hunted" and sedentarized to work in the cotton fields for the sake of the cotton plantation's economic success.[250] For example, the Ottoman traveler Mihri had claimed that the Arab was superior to the *zenci* (Black) by virtue of the civilizing impacts of Islam.[251] In "Brown Men Are Called White," the Orientalist Samuel Baker had also used color-based categories of race to distinguish between himself and people of color(s) that he claimed were "uncivilized." He said: "Arabs, being simply brown, are called *white men* by the blacks of these countries. I was called a *very* white man as a distinction."[252] Scholar Eve Troutt Powell collects several texts and popular culture artifacts in Egypt that constantly stereotyped Sudanese as inferior and worthy of slavery.[253] Similarly, Mustafa Minawi shows the construction of ethnic and racial differences during the late Ottoman Empire, called *unsur* in distinction from *millet*, which indicated religious differentiations. Minawi demonstrates that Arab Ottoman imperialists racialized and assumed superiority over locals in Ottoman Africa, as they themselves were being racialized in the imperial capital of Istanbul.[254] Fathy's racial assumptions in the rural habitation projects of Gezira overlapped with a similar mentality.

Fathy based his ideas for the New Gourna village in Egypt and the "Arab houses" in Gezira on traditional climate-control and cooling techniques. While working in Iraq for Doxiadis Associates, he had conducted a similar analysis of the "old Baghdad houses" in 1957. As Pyla finds, Fathy identified the *bagdir* (wind-catchers) in traditional houses as effective passive ventilation devices, and suggested that Doxiadis Associates employ their improved versions in residential communities of Baghdad.[255] Doxiadis's projects in Iraq were indeed comprehensive, spanning several cities from Baghdad to Basra, Kirkuk, and Mosul. His housing schemes impacted over one million people of the six million population.[256] In Iraq, Fathy was also the connector between the Doxiadis team and the Harvard University team who designed the University of Baghdad as a climate-responsive modernist campus, as explained in the introduction. William Polk from the Harvard team introduced Walter Gropius and Fathy to each other, and wrote the foreword for Fathy's book *Architecture of the Poor*. Fathy designed Polk's house in Aspen, Colorado.[257] In these residential zones and campuses in Iraq and Sudan, midcentury architects cited climate as the core criterion for their design decisions. However, while defending the separation of "Arab" and "African" houses in the Gezira village, Fathy prioritized cultural habits and lifestyle in explaining his design decisions, rather than climate specificity. The "Arab" and the "African" houses would be fundamentally different typologically, but placed in the same village with the exact same climatic conditions. This can be interpreted in two ways: either racial difference was more important than climate consciousness in Fathy's mental cosmology or climate consciousness did not necessarily dictate the same architectural form, especially when it was coupled with other cultural considerations. Fathy's ideas in these projects connected four capital cities of Ottoman successor states—Athens, Baghdad, Cairo, and Khartoum—and infiltrated into the work of Greek, German, and American architects. His ideas on passive climate-control techniques and continuation of cultural and climatic heritage were disseminated in professional circles long before the book that made him famous, *Architecture for the Poor*, was published in 1973.

Conclusion: Climate Reparations

In summary, it is fair to say that, during the post-Ottoman British colonization of Khartoum, the dismissal of existing knowledge about the rain caused flooding; the trivialization of local urban fabric's aptness for the wind worsened the effects of sandstorms; the racial presumptions about the impact of the sun resulted in a segregated city and the discontinuation of a building culture; the misuse of the river in agricultural production failed to prevent famines; and the monocultural cotton plantations caused the loss of biodiversity and extinctions. The de-appreciation of one building and farming culture with the entitlement of another is a typical example of climate agnotology in architecture. Climate agnotology here refers to the trivialization of one episteme to claim the superiority of another episteme. Agnotology is not simply ignorance, but the active production of non-knowledge for the interest of one group over the other. Agnotology is the conscious manufacturing of ignorance, the suppression of knowledge production, the disenfranchisement of the existing wisdom.

At the height of European colonialism in Asia and Africa, architecture on lands that were previously part of the Ottoman Empire became a platform to sustain the British Empire's industrial-capitalist and carbonizing power. Architects and planners either exerted the symbolism of order in the plantations, or segregated the city along racial lines, or employed miscalculated passive climate-control techniques with a misguided entitlement to climate literacy. Climate determinists imagined Africa and the Middle East as hostile climates, and maintained the Orientalist conviction against Ottoman lands that the locals needed European civilizing technologies. Colonial architects were perceived as civilizing agents due to their proficiency in tropical architecture that was being advanced in military offices and architecture schools in the United Kingdom. The colonial planners of Khartoum claimed that the grid-plan relied on climate proficiency and fostered thermal comfort in a perceived tropical climate, but it actually did exactly the opposite. The colonial planning decisions resulted in an overexpansive city due to the low density of housing zones to be ventilated in green areas and due to the distances between large urban blocks. The decision to settle on areas that were previously identified as flooding zones in Ottoman-era plans continues to distress the city to this day.[258] The dismissal of local knowledge in microclimate making resulted in neighborhoods and buildings that were neither attuned to climate nor prepared for climate challenges such as floods and sandstorms. The colonial urbanization and plantation logics created controlled cities and homogenized the countryside, by dismissing the previous climate know-how and obliterating pastoral and farming habits. The overall result was the carbonization of the atmosphere and destruction of biodiversity that constantly accelerated climate disasters.

Today, the economic and geopolitical hierarchies of the twentieth century are augmented by climate change, which brings more drought and more famine to this part of the world.[259] There are ten thousand deaths recorded annually due to water-related disasters in the world such as droughts or floods. Water insecurity disproportionately impacts the world. According to the UN summit on water in March 2023, estimated costs of damage due to water-related disasters will be $125 trillion by 2050.[260] Where will reparations or healing from climate disasters start from? This chapter also uncovered the criticism formulated by independence-era figures in confidential and unpublished reports, some of which may serve as ideas for healing from colonial carbonization and monoculturalization. Additionally, this chapter and the introduction focused on three campus designs to discuss climate consciousness as opposed to climate determinism: the University of Baghdad in Iraq (Gropius, TAC, Munir, and a team of experts from Harvard University), the College of Fine and Applied Arts in Khartoum (Moneim Mustafa), and the Rural Settlement in Gezira (Fathy). Residential and academic villages provide appropriate building programs to think about climate consciousness, because architects are bound to reflect on both buildings and outdoor spaces between buildings. The architects in all three projects analyzed anonymous precolonial houses and their neighborhoods in order to distill passive cooling techniques. They resisted agnotology, the conscious production of ignorance, by learning climate wisdom from people's architecture. Yet they did so without supporting local or national isolation. The independence-era figures of the Ottoman successor states discussed in this book, such as Hassan Fathy and Kleon Krantonellis at Doxiadis Associates and Abdel Moneim Mustafa, sought for a new internationalism that respected self-determination.

The story of the veranda uncovered in this chapter is a case in point for the joint history of climate consciousness and self-determination. The colonial history of this space is by no means limited to Sudan. In his foundational book *The Bungalow*, Anthony King studied the worldwide translations of the bungalow as a dwelling form in India, Britain, North America, Africa, and Australia from the seventieth till the mid-twentieth century. The veranda, he argued, "is an essential feature of the 'colonial' bungalow for much of its history. In some respects, it could be seen as a defining one which distinguishes the bungalow from other single-story dwellings."[261] King dates the first recorded use of the term *veranda* in English to India in 1711, after which it was excessively used not only in India but also in England, Australia, United States, and Britain's colonies in Africa. The veranda soon became the signifier of European residences in the tropics, particularly with its widespread use in African colonies. It was a space designed to help its colonial users adopt to hotter climates compared to the temperatures that they moved from. British buildings in Sudan illustrate the monopoly of the veranda in colonial architecture. After racially segregating "white men" from "natives," British municipal officers, architects, and families used the veranda as an architectural device for cooling purposes for the sake of colonizers' comfort in perceived tropical climates, while they did not deem this space necessary for the colonized. For this very reason, the history of the veranda in Sudan gains further relevance given its translations during the independence period. The colonial connotations of the veranda were transformed after Sudanese independence, thanks to its creative use by architects such as Moneim Mustafa, who critically and selectively employed the technical know-how advanced under the field of tropical architecture in the lands of ex-colonizers.

The standard views of decolonization hardly have explanatory power for this practice. These views tend to underestimate architects of midcentury modernism in the newly inaugurated nation-states, as if they were not decolonizing enough, were helpless victims of Western developmentalism, or suffered from Stockholm syndrome.[262] However, giving due acknowledgment to these architects requires other concepts, such as commitment to the project of translatability in multiple directions and postcolonial cosmopolitanism. I tried to advance this framework in *Architecture in Translation* in order to come to terms with the tensions, dilemmas, and contributions of architects in the newly independent Turkey, against the usual view of decolonization as the rejection of foreign ways and the search for the continuation of traditional languages.[263] Similarly, Adom Getachew suggests anticolonial worldmaking as a conceptual framework that allows for an understanding of professionals and intellectuals who seek for a new, more equitable international dialogue, and who struggle for self-determination in order to undo the domination of global empires but not foreclose cosmopolitanism. Getachew acknowledges the work of Black Anglophone intellectuals of the immediate independence period as an example of this type of anticolonial struggle, one that aims to construct the conditions for an egalitarian but still globally connected world order.[264] Some of the postcolonial struggles discussed in this chapter aimed for a similar type of international nondomination, but many forces eroded these aspirations. The forces that cut short an egalitarian postcolonial consciousness included the soft powers of the Cold War, the inherited racial identity categories from the British and Ottoman Empires, and the lingering geopolitical hierarchies of the midcentury developmentalist zeal.

At varying degrees, the architects discussed above moved from climate determinism toward climate consciousness against all odds. The climate reparations movement, on the other hand, is relatively new. Since the mid-1990s, several international commissions such as Pan African, Caribbean, Indigenous, or Latin American coalitions on reparations have made demands to bring the first industrializing countries of the Global North to admit their historical responsibility in causing climate change and to pay their debt to countries that are vulnerable to climate disasters. A precondition for just energy transition is to institute an international climate debt that would restore justice retroactively to those subjugated and extracted. This would not be a loan as it is conceived in mainstream developmentalist framework that puts developing countries in perpetual liability, but it would be reparations, a debt, paid by first industrializing and colonizing countries to their colonies and extracted countries, so that the latter can invest in renewable energies. The People's Agreement of Cochabamba of 2010, for one, suggests to establish an International Climate and Environmental Justice Tribunal, and to institute an Adaptation Fund that would regulate the climate debt. It defines climate debt not only as a matter of monetary compensation, but also as demands that developed countries "decolonize the atmosphere by reducing their emissions"; transfer technology for energy transition to developing countries; assume responsibility for climate refugees by offering them a decent life after migration; and pay "developing countries adaptation debt" so that they can "prevent, minimize and deal with damages arising from their excessive emissions." The declaration conceptualizes climate debt as a "broader debt to Mother Earth [to be paid] by adopting and implementing UN Declaration on the Rights of the Mother Earth."[265] Namely, the petition defined climate reparations as a matter of rights that need to be safeguarded by an international organization. Circling back to the concept of human rights that was discussed in chapter 1, the next and final chapter of this book envisions species' rights beyond humans, by continuing the discussion on the Doxiadis Associates' work in Sudan and by revealing an early de-extinction project in the Middle East that was carried out by an international team of architects.

5 Extinction

GARDENS, PARKS, RUDERAL URBAN SPACES

In the geological time scale, extinction is ordinary to the extent that it is every species' eventual destiny, just as life is a matter of birth and death, and just as life, in some way, is a fatal disease. However, scientists warn that extinction has reached a record speed in recent decades, relative to its rate in the past 500 million years, and comparable to the mass extinctions of the geological past.[1] During the time when this chapter was written, reliable indicators suggested that the built environment is not the main cause of but is nonetheless partially responsible for mass extinction. Could architectural design, then, prevent ecocide and increase biodiversity? Urban planners have long established the need for parks and green spaces from the viewpoint of human health and consumption, but what about their evaluations from the viewpoint of extinction? Should there be more domesticated animals and more agriculture in cities, or more untamed life and ruderal urban spaces that fall outside the formal purview of landscape design and urban planning? What are the ethical concerns in inflicting existential harm to species? Where do international organizations such as the UN stand with respect to species' right to exist? What is an apt balance between the built and the unbuilt environments on Earth, or between human settlements and wildlife, for a just coexistence of humans and nonhumans?

Rob Nixon has famously coined the term *slow violence* for the social impacts of environmental degradation and identified its main characteristics as its invisibility and the delayed effects that make it unnoticeable, its disproportionate impact on poor communities, and the rift it creates between short-term extractors and long-term dwellers who live in the aftermath of extraction.[2] If pollution and environmental degradation are examples of slow violence, the realization of extinction is the sudden recognition of this violence. Extinction is the traumatic moment after which one can no longer unsee the hitherto unnoticeable. Tragically, the invisible slow violence is brought to consciousness with the final disappearance of a species from sight. If extinction is the ultimate harm on species, and if its realization is the moment of sudden trauma for humans, where does architecture stand in the right to heal from this disaster?

In this chapter, I explore some architects' responses to the realization of extinction with projects that sought to heal planetary loss. An architect's claim to reverse extinction rates would raise skepticism at the beginning of the twenty-first century. The more architects intervene and replace nature with designed environment, the more endangered will nonhuman species become, it seems. In the established professional and scholarly literature, only a few architects are recognized for having contributed to the question of extinction directly. A major exception is the founding role of Frederick Law Olmsted in the creation of national parks and the wilderness discourse in the United States.[3] More recently, Bill McDonough's "Hannover Principles: Design for Sustainability" (1992), written in the same year as the UN Rio Summit that warned against threats to biodiversity, criticized architects for harming the biodiversity of the planet and for being ignorant of the interdependence among world organisms. McDonouogh outlined nine design principles that expanded "on the rights of humanity and nature to co-exist."[4] Kate Orff has famously built a career so that humans can cohabit on the planet with other species. Her practice goes beyond the preservation of wildlife but reconceptualizes designers' tasks and adopts local community programs to increase biodiversity. Her project "Oyster-tecture" aims to bring back edible oysters to the New York City harbor by 2050: Designs to support oyster regeneration, such as rope-nets and oyster-raising canals, go hand in hand with community engagement for clean water.[5] Architects such as Jeanne Gang have participated in the nascent discussions about the gradual rewilding of cities.[6] This chapter uncovers the history of and thinks with earlier projects coming from the lands that concern this book.

Protected Areas or Anticolonial Gardens? Current Debates on Ecocide Prevention

Despite the difficulties of precise calculations,[7] scientists today recognize the responsibility of humans who, by changing the environment in the modern era, created a situation that many call *ecocide* or the *sixth mass extinction*:[8] Deforestation to make room for the settlements of increasingly rising human populations, creation of sugar and cotton monocultures during the colonial era, conversion of grasslands into agricultural land, draining wetlands, the fur trade, hunting, commercial whaling, extraction and carbonization during industrialization, and warfare, including the creation of "sacrifice" zones that are reserved for military experimentation, accumulatively created this situation. It is predicted that global warming is causing up to 52 percent of extinctions (the average of predictions is 24 percent).[9] Extinction is a geopolitically charged planetary issue. Extractivism, as in removing minerals from the lands of Indigenous communities and the Global South in the name of technological inventions to be enjoyed predominantly by the affluent settlers and the Global North, and waste colonialism, as in dumping Europe's dirty plastic waste to slowly rot in China, Turkey, and Vietnam, create long-term social, global, and planetary harms.[10]

The history of the discovery and changing explanations of extinction warrants a short summary. Prior to the eighteenth century, philosophers categorized animals but did not imagine them as having a history of appearance and disappearance. Elizabeth Kolbert outlines how the theory of extinction oscillated between paradigms of sudden and slow change, namely between mass extinction and gradual eradication. While Georges Cuvier was the founder of catastrophist extinction theory that had currency in the early nineteenth century, Charles Darwin's theory of evolution suggested slow extinction, because natural selection also meant the annihilation of the unfit. Since 1980, the year Walter Alvarez explained the last mass extinction as ending the era of dinosaurs with an asteroid,[11] scientists have settled on a hybrid explanation, postulating that our planet has witnessed both mass extinctions caused by sudden catastrophes and slow evolutionary changes.[12] While multiple forces, including celestial ones, caused extinctions in the past, scientists recognize the responsibility of humans for the current mass extinction disaster in the age called the Anthropocene.

As discussed in the introduction, this book finds the term *Anthropocene* insufficient for coming to terms with climate change and mass extinction, as long as the word refers to the human species as a whole without differentiating the uneven historical responsibility of the first industrializing and colonizing nations from that of the Global South and non-West. The neglect of social and geopolitical inequalities and the reduction of extinction to a matter of allegedly apolitical science impairs possibilities of healing as well. The mainstream corrective response to extinction has been the planning of large protected areas where human habitation is separated from nonhumans. Upon the near extinction of the American bison, Theodore Roosevelt famously described the Yellowstone National Park, which established a bison reserve, as "a natural breeding ground and nursery for those stately and beautiful haunters of the wilds which have now vanished from so many of the great forests."[13] In North America, the conservation movement has lobbied to set aside national parks and fortress them for natural preservation, in conjunction with the development of wilderness discourse throughout the nineteenth and twentieth centuries. National parks are supposed to conserve nonhuman species by protecting them from the harms of the built environment. Protected areas also emerged in Mongolia, Australia, New Zealand, India, Indonesia, North and sub-Saharan Africa, and the Middle East, and globally exploded between 1985 and 1995.[14] According to the International Union for the Conservation of Nature, protected areas increased from 14.1 to 16.64 percent of land, and from 2.9 to 7.74 percent of oceans between 2010 and 2021.[15]

A large body of literature criticizes the inner contradictions of this environmentalist movement that advances national parks premised on the idea of wilderness. The debates go back to the likes of John Muir and Gifford Pinchot, but, most impactfully, William Cronon's "The Trouble with Wilderness" exposed the intellectual weaknesses of the wilderness debate for claiming to make space for humans to encounter something radically different from themselves while being predicated on the most individualist and humancentric philosophies such as Romanticism, primitivism, and American exceptionalism.[16] Ironically this romanticized idea of wilderness and pristine nature emerged only after modern technologies were sufficient to protect humans from the threat of wild animals. Protected areas locate planetary healing in the perpetuation of the human-nonhuman and the nature-culture divide, assuming that the unbuilt Earth can only be saved from humans through this separation. Moreover, many national parks were instituted in North America during the age of Indigenous dispossession and rural displacement, and thereby created conservation refugees when habitants of lands eligible for natural protection were forcibly moved.[17] In Cronon's words, "The myth of the wilderness as 'virgin' uninhabited land [to be enjoyed by the elites] had always been especially cruel when seen from the perspective of the Indians who had once called that land home."[18] One of the biggest contradictions of the North American conservationists is that, in the name of saving nature, they either had significant conflicts with or turned a blind eye to the dispossession and displacement of Indigenous communities who have a longer and more credible history of land stewardship.

Another contradiction of this "mainstream conservationism"—a term coined by Dan Brockington, Rosaleen Duffy, and Jim Igoe to describe such national parks—is its entanglement with capitalism.[19] Examples abound: The idea of wilderness was supported by privileged hunting networks whose interest was to preserve enough specimens; national parks serve as tourist destinations for the wealthy, even though photographs hide signs of human interventions; the tourism industry supports charismatic animals at the expense of attention to all species and biodiversity; ecotourism perpetuates an idea of natural conservation only as far as nature can be made lucrative (even though some examples have empowered local communities). In other words, the extinction crisis perpetuates the idea of protected parks and coerces them into the logic of capitalism that is responsible for environmental degradation itself, given the privatization and commercialization of nature, as well as fascination with continuous growth. Urban and literary theorist Ashley Dawson, among others, has pinpointed capitalism as the root cause of mass extinction, not only because capitalism has turned nature into a commodity that can be bought and sold for the sake of leisure and culture industries in an exploitative logic on a global scale, but also because it has deprived communities of their rightful access to the commons. "Extinction is the product of a global attack on the commons: the great trove of air, water, plants, and collectively created cultural forms. . . . The destruction of global biodiversity needs to be framed, in other words, as a great, and perhaps ultimate, attack on the planet's common wealth."[20] If continuous growth is both capitalism's first mandate and the environment's major slayer, a capitalist conservation movement is bound to come to terms with its self-contradiction.

The common but contradictory history of the natural conservation movement whose origins are usually attributed to the national parks in North America has prompted alternatives in the twenty-first century. For instance, the disappointment with the hypocrisies of mainstream environmentalism prompts some authors to defend the idea of protected areas much more radically. If the age of powerful humans destroyed the biodiversity of the planet, the best way to heal this wound would be to reinforce the fortress wall that segregates humans and preserves nonhumans, they argue. Activist movements such as Earth First and Dave Foreman's ideas made a considerable impact after the late 1980s, culminating in what Bram Büscher and Robert Fletcher categorize as "neoprotectionism."[21] From the viewpoint of a purist but equally displacement-based defense of protected areas, it would be best if architects restrain themselves, retreat to restricted zones, and leave nature completely to its own devices, as in Liam Young's *Planet City* (2022) and NEOM's *The Line* (projected completion 2039) (figure 5.1). The film that represents Young's project depicts the design of a radically dense and continuous city where the world's population of 10 billion people has surrendered the rest of the planet's land to wilderness.[22] However, the community displacements that this project would inflict in the name of

Figure 5.1 Still from *Planet City* (2022), designed and directed by Liam Young with visual-effects technology. Supervisor Alexey Marfin. Courtesy of Liam Young.

natural conservation suggest a far more vehement intervention than any other neoprotectionist project.

Another trajectory that is more relevant for this chapter is the recognition that it is already too late and too evasive to assume that nature continues to self-heal in protected areas in the age of climate change and mass extinction. It is impossible to study or imagine ecosystems without humans, unrealistic to assume that lands can go back to a baseline without human impact, and intellectually debatable to separate natural and human history. It may be time to disuse terminology such as "invader species vs. native habitat," which disregards that species have been migrating for centuries, or "pristine nature vs. human disturbance," which overlooks that the cult of wilderness was a North American elite construction in the first place. "Our mistake has been thinking that nature is something out there. . . . This dream of pristine wilderness haunts us. It blinds us," Emma Marris wrote in 2011, in order to counteract the nostalgia of healing nature with protected areas. Instead, Marris argues, it is necessary to imagine cohabitation in more-than-human landscapes in a radically different way where the whole earth would be treated as a garden.[23] "Our increasing understanding of history and atmospheric chemistry has left us with no areas at all that have not been altered by humans. And once we do change it, a heretofore unthinkable, exciting, and energizing thought occurs: we can make more nature."[24] In Marris's suggestion, in the "postwild" age, the entire planet can be imagined and constructed as a "rambunctious garden."

Since the 2010s, the idea of garden has returned as a muse for planetary healing.[25] Surely, the garden metaphor predates the realization of mass extinction caused by climate change. The garden image assisted the search for Eden and Paradise, with multiple roots in Christian, Persian, Arabic, Indian, and other philosophical and religious traditions. In his book *Green Imperialism*, Richard Grove thoroughly examines the garden as a conceptual metaphor in the colonialist imagination between 1600 and 1860.[26] Against the general consensus that environmentalism developed as a response to industrialization in the West, Grove shows ample evidence that the ideas developed in the colonies (by both local and imperial figures) constituted, in fact, the foundations for Western modern environmentalism. Confronting deforestation, soil exhaustion, erosion, or famine caused by extractive economies in the colonies prompted thinking about the garden as an analogue of the society, the climate, and the world. The garden as "a designed earth" served as a testing ground for solutions to environmental problems in the colonies. When the colony became the birthplace of both environmental degradation and conservation, the garden served as the ecocide prevention area for both opportunistic and genuine reasons. "The apocalyptic environmental discourses of the colonial scientists frequently articulated a vision and a message of a far less cynical kind, and indeed, one that resonates with us today. In a threatened garden, it appeared, an empirically and experimentally derived awareness of environmental risk could be transformed into a veritable tree of knowledge."[27]

This chapter explores two projects from the 1960s and 1970s, undertaken by international teams and located in Sudan and Iran, when architects intuitively recognized that extinction meant human harm on the planet, and responded to the need for healing with the garden metaphor. It participates in Ramachandra Guha and Juan Martinez-Alier's call to examine examples from the Global South, which go against the consensus that modern environmentalist movements started in the affluent West, while other countries were "too poor to be green." Without covering up the geopolitical tensions and contradicting national policies, the authors foreground the environmentalist movements with different priorities and conceptualizations rising from the Global South.[28] This chapter of *Architecture and the Right to Heal* adds to this list.

World as Garden: Doxiadis Associates and Water Pollution

In his speech during the "Water for Peace" conference in 1967, Constantinos Doxiadis suggested a "universal garden" to heal from the water crisis of the mid-1960s. Water pollution and large-scale disappearance of marine life had reached alarming levels. The organizers asked the architect to give the plenary speech of the international conference with 6,400 participants, including delegates from 94 countries and 24 international organizations.[29] Big companies and polluting nations evade responsibility for slow violence by perpetuating the myth that nature self-heals, and will, with time, return to its harmony that has been disrupted due to extraction. In Max Liboiron's assessment, colonial science gives entitlement to pollute the land and water up to the threshold of assimilative capacity, the most bearable point, because it relies on the conception that "nature is robust with limits."[30] The science of pollution calculates this precise limit beyond which land is registered contaminated, as if harms below the bearable threshold do not matter because nature will supposedly heal them. Human-caused extinction is the moment of no return when the legend that nature heals itself can no longer hold. For many architects of the 1970s, this realization prompted a response that advocated more planning and, ironically, more extensions of the human mind onto the planet.

WATER INSECURITY IN KORDOFAN, AND SEDENTARY AND NOMADIC COEXISTENCE

In chapter 4, I discussed Doxiadis Associates' work on the water infrastructure in Sudan following the newly independent Sudanese government's invitation in terms of both post-Ottoman and postcolonial subjectivity. During the same years, the Food and Agriculture Organization of the UN commissioned the Doxiadis Associates as a consultant for the Kordofan Special Fund Project for Land and Water in Sudan. The office sustained a team on the ground to conduct research and pilot projects between 1961 and 1970.[31] In 1960, Doxiadis Associates also initiated a project titled "The City of the Future," for which they invited professionals from around the world, including Hassan Fathy, who conducted research on African cities, and developed internal reports and pilot projects for Sudan, also outlined in the previous chapter. Following these discussions in chapter 4, I foreground here archival findings that illuminate Doxiadis Associates' work in Sudan for water-catchment systems to heal drought, on the one hand, and for employing spatial planning to organize the cohabitation of humans and animals as well as the coexistence of sedentary and nomadic peoples, on the other hand. While his office worked on land and water in Sudan, Doxiadis suggested the idea of a "universal garden" to fight water pollution and marine life extinction. He continued to comment on the relationship between land, water, and human settlements until he published his final theory on the history, present, and future (along with an action plan) for human settlements in a four-volume series titled *Anthropopolis, Ecumenopolis, Building Entopia and Action* published between 1974 and 1976 (the last two volumes, posthumously).[32]

The project manager in Doxiadis Associates for the UN-funded Kordofan project, M. G. Ionides, reported on the common pessimism that groundwater would ever be found in the water crisis area. "Discussions were almost entirely dominated by fears and apprehensions about over-grazing, over-cultivation, soil erosion and 'creeping desert.' Practical action was conceived, about exclusively in terms of things which must be done if the region were to be saved from destruction by erosion. There were even some who urged that the only solution would be to transfer the population to another region and abandon the Project area."[33] The Doxiadis team soon came to the realization that the water crisis was hardly an environmental problem that could be isolated from its social dimension or addressed with a purely technological solution. In the neglected savanna belt of Africa that was vulnerable to water scarcity, and in an area home to seminomadic camel- and cattle-raising as well as gum-growing populations, the use of land for agricultural and livestock purposes often created conflicts.[34]

The initial ekistics study of 1962 brought together thirty-seven reports on several villages and tribes, surveyed by a variety of researchers, and written mostly in English but also in Greek and Arabic. The researchers sought to collect information on climate, the use of land for agricultural or grazing purposes, the administration of communities, housing types, water supplies and distribution, community buildings, and sedentary and nomadic populations and their occupations.[35] The living conditions were usually alarming. Mohammed O. El Sammani, who surveyed the village of Unn Garku, reported: "Population lives on the verge of subsistence. They cultivate the land and provide themselves with the necessary food crops. The cash crops produce is limited, and the small amount of cash they get every year is spent on a few goods like clothes . . . they have little interest in cotton."[36] About the tribes, El Sammani reported on the history of Ottoman and Mahdi sovereignty, taxation during the British rule, uncontrolled spread of settlements, and social disputes that disintegrated villages.[37] During the nine years of their research, the Doxiadis team continued devising ways of mapping the fluctuating contours of settlements and nomadic movements in the Kordofan region (figures 5.2 and 5.3).

Doxiadis Associates devised technologies of water supply so that the 355 villages in the area had "a chance of progressive development."[38] Each year, they sent reports on the progress of water collecting and storing in arid climates from the fields in Sudan to the main office in Athens. They developed seven prototypes that advanced traditional methods of water catchment and storage, which had capacities that ranged from 5 to 230 cubic meters. They named these prototypes pillared roof tank, bottle tank, interconnected beehive, crisscross honeycomb, multiple separate beehive, and two types of sand bed. Each had an artificial catchment mechanism to collect water, a tank to store it, and a cover to prevent evaporation. Filters could be added for the purification of water depending on the budget. The reports included detailed line drawings (figure 5.4), as well as construction photos for the making, filling, and using of each of the prototypes (figure 5.5). The team sought for criteria that honored local techniques, skills, and materials: They vowed to "give fullest possible stimulus to the indigenous skills and aptitudes of the people; make the smallest possible call on the services of professionals; make the maximum possible use of materials found on the spot; and make the minimum use of materials requiring to be transported to the site or bought for cash, especially imported materials requiring foreign exchange."[39] These were solutions for limited resources, but Doxiadis Associates also suggested that the Sudanese government invest more finances in larger-scale water-catchment tanks, borehole water yards, and networks of piped deliveries.[40]

The team took pride that their prototypes in Kordofan did not import technologies from elsewhere but were built on local skills and methods, and responded to the unique social, physical, and economic circumstances of the region. Similarly, they warned against exporting these prototypes elsewhere without translation.

These prototype tanks . . . have been specifically developed for the particular human and physical circumstances of the Project Area. . . . The people of the area have their own characteristic skills and habits of mind and hand. They have their own traditional methods of getting, carrying, and conserving water, evolved from the local conditions of life, the materials at hand, and the tools they use. The region has its characteristic construction materials. . . . Study of these factors was an essential part

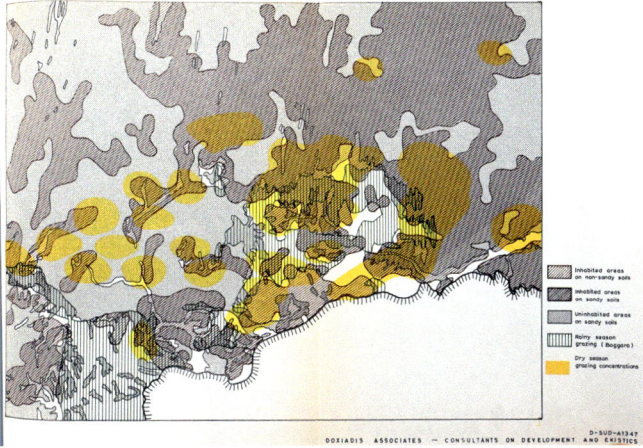

Figure 5.2 Doxiadis Associates, "Combined Patterns of Land Use,"
Kordofan Project, Sudan, 1961–70. The map shows inhabited and
uninhabited areas on sandy and nonsandy soils, and grazing areas
during rainy and dry seasons. Constantinos A. Doxiadis Archives.
© Constantinos and Emma Doxiadis Foundation.

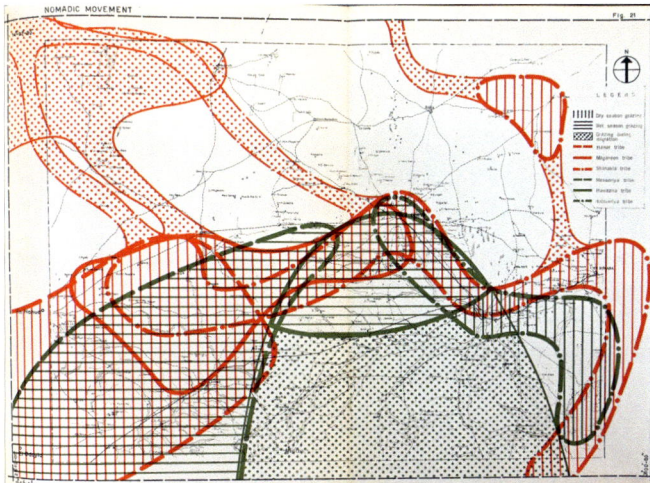

Figure 5.3 Doxiadis Associates, "Nomadic Movement," Kordofan
Project, Sudan, 1961–70. Constantinos A. Doxiadis Archives.
© Constantinos and Emma Doxiadis Foundation.

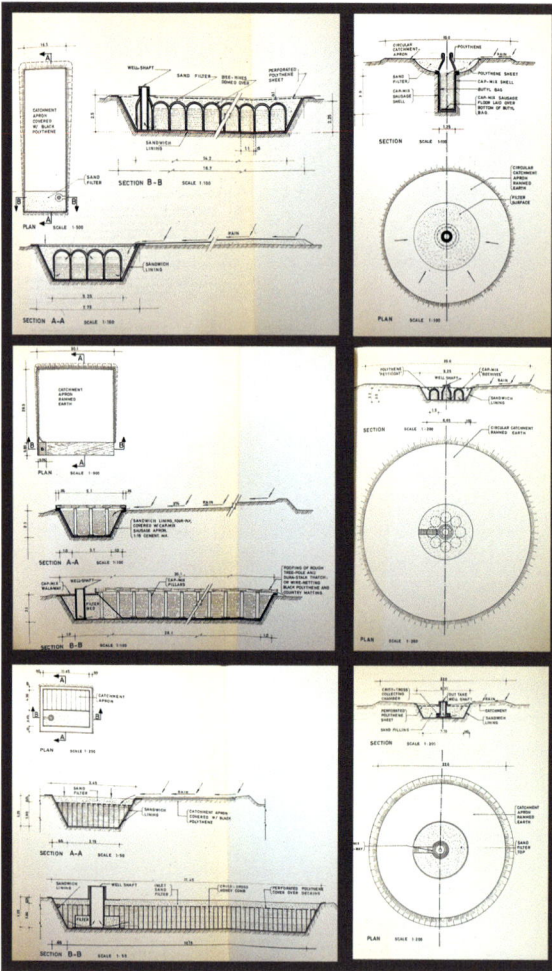

Figure 5.4
Doxiadis Associates, prototypes
that advance traditional methods
of water catchment and storage,
Kordofan Project,
Sudan, 1961–70.
Constantinos A.
Doxiadis Archives. © Constantinos and
Emma Doxiadis
Foundation.

of the programs of research and development. . . . It was a question of finding the best combination of local skills, local material resources, with modern materials and technology.[41]

In other words, these water catchment prototypes turned the conditions of precarity into an ethos of local climate wisdom that the British colonization in Sudan had disrupted (chapter 4). They meant a struggle against agnotology—the conscious production of ignorance about a technology for the ideological or financial sake of another technology.

Doxiadis Associates' water-catchment prototypes were structures that were dug into the land on the scale of buildings, using technical drawings and

Figure 5.5 Doxiadis Associates, prototypes that advance traditional methods of water catchment and storage, illustration of stages, Kordofan Project, Sudan, 1961–70. Constantinos A. Doxiadis Archives. © Constantinos and Emma Doxiadis Foundation.

local construction skills. Additionally, the office suggested a spatial-design logic to avoid conflicts between farmers and cattle- or camel-raising populations. By way of a preliminary diagrammatic sketch titled "New Village Development," the team claimed that an architectural design could heal the rift between sedentary and nomadic populations.[42] The project was composed of a regular grid with zones reserved for grazing, gum, timber, and firewood. The village would be centered on a water well, and encircled by a fence and

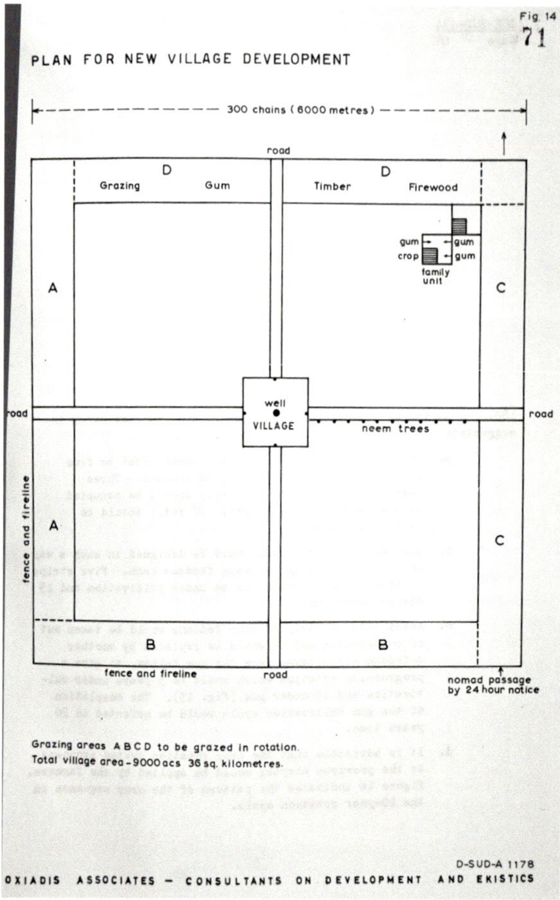

PLAN FOR NEW VILLAGE DEVELOPMENT

Fig. 14

71

300 chains (6000 metres)

road

D — Grazing — Gum — D — Timber — Firewood

A

gum → ← gum
crop
gum → ← gum
family
unit

C

well
VILLAGE — neem trees

road

road

fence and fireline

A

C

fence and fireline — road — B — B

nomad passage
by 24 hour notice

Grazing areas A B C D to be grazed in rotation.
Total village area - 9000 acs 36 sq. kilometres.

D-SUD-A 1178

OXIADIS ASSOCIATES — CONSULTANTS ON DEVELOPMENT AND EKISTICS

Figure 5.6

Doxiadis Associates, "Plan for Village Development," Kordofan Project, Sudan, 1961–70. Constantinos A. Doxiadis Archives. © Constantinos and Emma Doxiadis Foundation.

fire line. At the point of the town center, where a religious, government, or a cultural building is expected, there would be a water supply structure to embody the architectural symbolism. Dwellings would be surrounded by gum and crop areas. Most uniquely, there would be nomad passageways on the periphery of the planned land, which would be reserved for the transition of camel- and cattle-raising nomadic populations on twenty-four-hour notice. Namely, Doxiadis Associates suggested that a good site plan and a spatiotemporal organizational logic could have prevented the conflicts between the agriculture-dependent sedentary and livestock-dependent nomadic communities of the Kordofan region. In their eyes, architectural design could deliver cohabitation and prevent fights between agriculture- and livestock-dependent communities (figure 5.6).

Doxiadis must have considered his UN-supported water management and regional planning projects in Sudan as a contribution to world peace. In the "Water for Peace" conference that took place during the time of the Kordofan project, he promised to define the proper relation between water, land, and humanity in the face of the global water crisis. Starting with a short history of human settlements, Doxiadis narrated how humans settled in areas with available fresh water, and were therefore "forced to live more densely in certain parts of the surface of the Earth," which formed civilizations. Water scarcity led to the technologies of underground water systems, canals, pipes, dams, and artificial ponds, all of which consequently led to the age of what he called "Anthropos": "With the passing of time, man could no longer depend only on 'hunting' for water in rivers and lakes; he had to try and 'domesticate' it."[43] Humanity's ability to engineer water on Earth created more water to use while also producing more sewage to dispose of, which polluted rivers and lakes, Doxiadis's historical narrative continued. Some settlements were therefore in danger of abandonment because of either water scarcity or water pollution. The contemporary water crisis that originated from what Doxiadis described as the "three element system: land-water-man," would only worsen in the future given the increasing population, and the uneven distribution of clean water across the earth. "What should we do in this case?" he asked: "We cannot move the land. Should we move the people and their settlements, or the water?"[44] His solution was the "universal garden":

> Human happiness is our only goal. . . . To face the crisis in the relationship between water and man, we must work towards building a universal city that will guarantee a proper relationship between land, water and man. . . . Such action requires the achievement of two goals. First, we must establish a balanced system between land, water and man; and second, we must develop the best technology for dealing with water. . . . If this is achieved, then the universal city of man will also be the universal garden.[45]

In his report "Water for Human Development" three years later, Doxiadis continued to draw on the metaphor of a garden for healing water-related disasters. He often started his texts during this time with the acknowledgment of an environmental crisis caused by overpopulation.[46] The increasing amount of population and waste, and the historical harms originating from water such as waterborne diseases and floods, continued to distress humanity. Luckily, there were examples in the past that could be reimagined to mitigate these crises. For example, Doxiadis continued, "For many centuries the Deep Gardens were created helping Man to exist within completely unfavorable conditions." Learning from the history of "Deep Gardens," Doxiadis asserted, prompted him to zoom out of the "day to day problems" and envision human settlements "as part of the biological system developed by Nature on the surface of the earth."[47]

Doxiadis believed numerous human crises could be overcome if the world was prepared to store, process, and transport water in the "universal garden."[48] The universal city and garden would be made of three parts: the natural, the agricultural, and the urban. In this earth as one garden, the natural areas would be conserved so that they would cover half of the Earth. Agriculture would be reserved to 45 percent of the usable part of the earth, and organized "like huge mechanized factories rather than present day farms," with water under full human control.[49] Urban areas would cover only 5 percent of the usable Earth, and create a continuous urban environment.[50] Doxiadis concluded, "Although in the beginning there was water—everything will not end with water. In the fourth act of our long history we will have built the great, universal city and garden of man with water running in its arteries bringing life and guaranteeing its inner balance and peace."[51]

For the remaining years of his career, Doxiadis theorized and prepared action plans for this universal city and garden that he named Ecumenopolis.[52] Even though the 469-page book with the same title was published in 1974—a year before the architect's death—the multisited research had already started with the "City of the Future" project in 1960, for which Doxiadis had secured a grant from the Ford Foundation. The questions posed by the planning of world cities that occupied Doxiadis Associates at the time—such as the new capital city Islamabad in Pakistan, Khartoum in Sudan, and Baghdad in Iraq—necessitated a broader ekistics research in order to be able to envision a city that would satisfy the needs of next generations.[53] The settlements of the past and present from the smallest to the megapolitan scale needed to be studied in a systematic manner to make substantiated predictions and plans.[54] This study exposed how recent human settlements created "many problems concerned with pollution and the environment," and how the uneven habitability of earth due to tough climates created conflicts. "We must therefore consider the whole range of problems connected with

Nature, those created by Nature for Anthropos, as well as those created by Anthropos for Nature."[55]

Doxiadis continued to advance research at the Athens Center of Ekistics and collaborated or crossed paths in conferences with an unprecedented number of international experts.[56] These included Jaqueline Tyrwhitt, who edited the *Ekistics* journal for twenty-eight years and made the connection with the British tropical architecture discourse discussed in chapter 4. In his lectures and publications on the "City of the Future," Doxiadis differentiated the "inevitable future" and the "desirable future," and based his argument on what he saw as the unavoidable population rise and urbanization. In his speech to the Nobel Foundation in 1969, he reiterated that his research into settlement precedents and population increase led him to the prediction that the human population would stabilize after a period of transition of a hundred or two hundred years.[57]

Rather than letting the inevitable overcrowding take its course and create environmental crises in unchecked and uneven spread of settlements, Doxiadis suggested to think in reverse and envision the city of the foreseeable future—the ecumenopolis—in a planned way. Archival documents reveal that he had been determined to plan for the universal city and garden all along. In a "strictly confidential" presentation to the research team already in 1961, Doxiadis asked what if they approached planning in reverse:

> Theoretically, we can predict the time at which the whole earth is going to be covered by one human settlement. This time is not very far away. . . . Therefore, when we speak of one big city, we do speak of the moment at which, we will have built such a percentage of this earth that there will be a balance between this percentage of built-up area, the percentage necessary for primary production, and the percentage necessary for the survival of nature on this earth. . . . I think [of] the ultimate goal, the "ecumenopolis" or the city covering the whole earth.[58]

In the next decade, the idea of the universal and perpetual city and garden turned into precise maps and calculated predictions. The team mapped the distribution of metropolitan and megapolitan areas, and population densities across the surface of the earth in the second half of the twentieth century. They also mapped the "habitability of the globe" according to climate, elevation, and water scarcity (figure 5.7).[59] They overviewed the technological and economic trends, and calculated the energy and food capacity of the land. Based on these maps of habitation and habitability, Doxiadis Associates designed the ultimate plan of the planet to be achieved after a

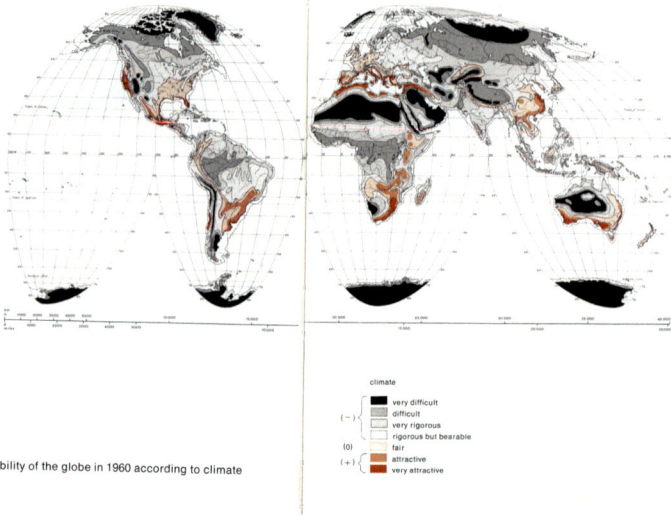

Figure 5.7 Constantinos A. Doxiadis and J. G. Papaioannou. "Habitability of the Globe According to Climate," as published in *Ecumenopolis: The Inevitable City of the Future* (Toronto: McLeod, 1974). Constantinos A. Doxiadis Archives. © Constantinos and Emma Doxiadis Foundation.

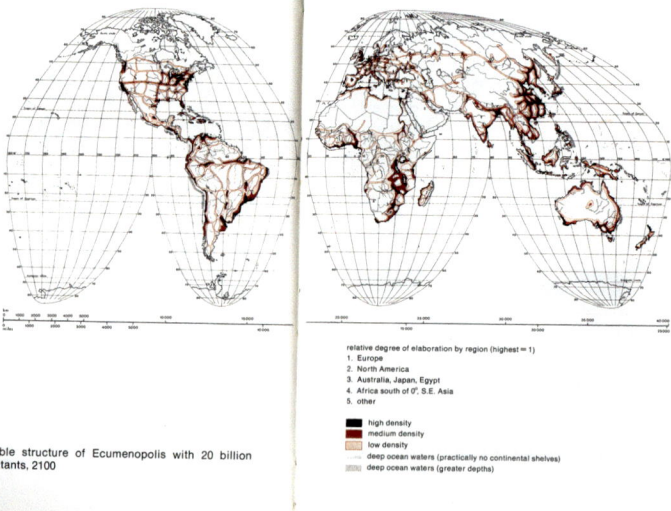

Figure 5.8 Constantinos A. Doxiadis and J. G. Papaioannou, "Probable Structure of Ecumenopolis with 20 Billion Inhabitants," as published in *Ecumenopolis: The Inevitable City of the Future* (Toronto: McLeod, 1974). Constantinos A. Doxiadis Archives. © Constantinos and Emma Doxiadis Foundation.

period of transition. "The present phase is a transitional one," he claimed, "but will be followed by an era in which Anthropos achieves a state of balance and harmony with Nature."[60] In the universal city and garden of the stabilized future, urban zones would be connected to one another and would create an amorphous grid on the surface of the earth, outlining agricultural and natural zones. Doxiadis published maps that represented the probable structure of Ecumenopolis in a spectrum of predictions that ranged from 15 billion inhabitants in year 2100 to 50 billion habitants in year 2200 (figure 5.8).[61] In his utopia, this City of the Future, "if all goes well," would bring balance in all spheres: wealth, social, political, technological, and cultural.[62] "Ecumenopolis is coming: whether we do nothing or whether we take action, it is certain to happen. . . . Should we try to make the future city of Anthropos really happy and safe? . . . We are left with the optimistic belief that . . . a happy Ecumenopolis will be achieved."[63]

To summarize, Doxiadis Associates started with updating local water-catchment tanks in order to resolve conflicts between sedentary and nomadic peoples in water-insecure Sudan, and ended in the planning of the entire earth's surface as one connected city and garden in order to heal from planetary disasters. Even though some of the team members' anticolonial motivations opened space for alternatives to European technologies and epistemologies, Doxiadis never freed himself from the anthropocentric framework that put "human happiness" at the center of the universe, nor abandoned the Cartesian conviction that everything material was an extension of "Man." The naïvely optimistic trust in architecture motivated an imperial impulse, and it led Doxiadis to the conviction that a spatial organization alone could bring peace, no matter if this concerned the planning of a village, an urban-rural network, a nomadic territory, a city, or finally the entire surface of the earth. This imperial ambition to grow bigger, or the still common impulse to scale up in the face of the daunting scale of world problems, resulted in a theory of human settlement that was totalizing. The critique of this position will be continued in this chapter's conclusion.

Garden as World: Pardisan's Multispecies History

HEALING THE EARTH FROM THE EAST: A MULTINATIONAL COLLABORATION

When Doxiadis referred to "Deep Gardens" with underground water systems as an inspiration to heal water scarcity in Sudan, he probably had in mind "Persian Gardens." This section discusses a park designed by professionals

Figure 5.9 WMRT
Ian McHarg, Nader Ardalan, Laleh Bakhtiar, et al., Pardisan Park, designed in Tehran and Philadelphia, 1974–80. Interpretation of a Persian garden; still from *Pardisan* (1977), directed by Charles (and possibly Ray) Eames and Glen Fleck with David Negron and George Spacek. The Architectural Archives, University of Pennsylvania, Ian McHarg Collection.

from Iran and United States, which was envisioned during similar years that Doxiadis developed his theory of the universal garden. Pardisan was designed upon the alarming news that the Persian lion was almost extinct, as a modern Persian Garden that aimed to heal the broken bond between the humans and the environment (figure 5.9).[64] If Doxiadis's vision was to design the entire world as a garden, Pardisan sought to put the entire world in a garden. In some of its proponents' hopes, Pardisan was an invention to bring back the Persian lion, the inspiration for a national symbol that had been hunted to extinction (figure 5.10). It was also the first response to the call for "only one earth" during the UN Conference on the Human Environment in Stockholm in June 1972.[65] In a report about the garden in 1975 and much before Paul Crutzen (and Eugene Stoermer) coined the term *Anthropocene* in 2002,[66] Pardisan's team identified modern humans as "a geological force, able to destroy the environment and himself."[67] Pardisan was codesigned by Eskandar Firouz—the vice chair of the Iranian delegate in Stockholm, the director of Iran's Department of Environmental Conservation, and the conceptual creator of Pardisan—the US design team WMRT (Wallace, McHarg, Roberts, and Todd), the Iranian architect Nader Ardalan, scholar Laleh Bakhtiar, and many other professionals who were consulted or commissioned during the process including Charles and Ray Eames and Buckminster Fuller. For its most committed American designer, the chair of the Department of Landscape Architecture at the University of Pennsylvania, Ian McHarg, who did not give up until the project was brought to the international court of the Iran-US Claims Tribunal at The Hague, Pardisan would be a lifetime

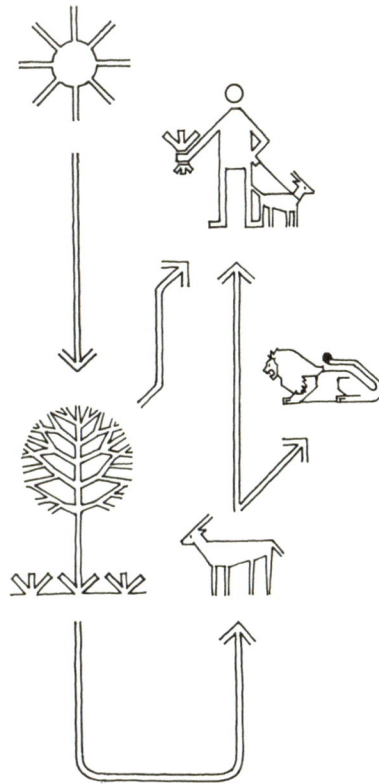

Figure 5.10 WMRT, Ian McHarg, Nader Ardalan, Laleh Bakhtiar, et al., Pardisan Park, designed in Tehran and Philadelphia, 1974–80. Representation of human-nature relations and the Persian lion. "Pardisan: Plan for an Environmental Park in Tehran." Report of 1975. Permission granted by Nader Ardalan.

opportunity to exemplify his theory in *Design with Nature*—a book that he had published in 1969 and that eventually earned him the title of being "the father of ecological planning."[68] Throughout the process, McHarg continued publishing essays on ecological design that he collected in the volume *To Heal the Earth*. These essays undertook a variety of issues including landscape design as a discipline that combines natural sciences and humanities, ecological design as the understanding of biophysical and social processes, design in ecologically damaged environments, critique of the oil lobby and biocide, and calls for a solar energy lobby, housing, and more.[69]

Given the currency of national parks in the United States by the 1970s, the American professionals in the Pardisan team were immersed in the mainstream conservation movement in this country. And yet Pardisan was not

Figure 5.11 WMRT, Ian McHarg, Nader Ardalan, Laleh Bakhtiar, et al. Pardisan Park, designed in Tehran and Philadelphia, 1974–80. Perspective drawing of park. "Pardisan: Plan for an Environmental Park in Tehran." Report of 1975. Permission granted by Nader Ardalan.

planned to be a protected area that separated humans from nature, or one that tried to create an illusion of wilderness and pristine nature. To the contrary, exhibition buildings, geodesic domes, urban squares, monorail systems, and car parks were going to be mixed with wildlife habitats all over Pardisan (figure 5.11). Its conceptual designer Firouz defined it as neither a zoo nor a botanical garden, a natural history museum, a planetarium, or an aquarium in conventional senses, but a garden that combines all of the above and more.[70] From the very early days of the design process, the team identified the park's three "piers" as "education, recreation and conservation."[71] The urban garden would have been easily accessible for the residents of Tehran, and navigated with trains and buses. According to landscape architect and historian Kathleen John-Alder, this dream of modern transportation owed more to the "American shopping mall, Disneyland, and separation of circulation in New York City's Central Park" than pristine national parks.[72] The heavy hand of humans in the entire enterprise and the all-encompassing narrative about the adaptation of plants, animals, and cultures of the world would have framed the environment without any pretension of wilderness.

Namely, through a unique collaboration between American and Iranian professionals, a different idea of natural conservation and extinction prevention emerged in Pardisan between 1972 and 1979.

The Pardisan project was canceled shortly after the topographical design started construction (see figure 5.18) due to the fall of the Shah's regime following the Islamic Revolution in Iran (1978–79). The following text is an imagination of a visitor's experience in the unbuilt Pardisan based on the drawings and documents left behind in the archives, as well as a prediction of the unintended processes that would have been put into motion by Pardisan's more-than-human agents. If plans for Pardisan materialized before 1979, a visitor would have approached the park from a set of terraces. Pardisan was a "rambunctious garden" in Marris's sense in that it also appealed for a shift of mentality that would abolish the myth of pristine nature and put an end to the goal of preserving wilderness that no longer exists and indeed hardly ever did since modernity.[73] The visitor to Pardisan—a constructed environment located on a land of 270 hectares/630 acres—would have taken a vehicle to a high plateau on the northwest of Tehran with views of the city and the desert to the south and the Elburz mountains to the north. Passing through car parks and picnic areas located under trees and next to water channels, she would have approached a gate with large arches. Perhaps she would have already noticed the idea of "adaptive architecture" in this entrance building, one of the many around the park to be designed by the Iranian architectural firm Mandala Collaborative of Nader Ardalan. With Laleh Bakhtiar, Ardalan was the coauthor of *The Sense of Unity* (1973) and the co-organizer of the International Congresses of Architecture in Iran (1974), which was arguably one of the most inclusive venues in bringing influential architects from around the world to discuss the harms of industrialization on the environment.[74] In the orientation pavilion, the visitor would have seen a satellite image of Iran and one of Buckminster Fuller's Dymaxion world maps. She would have watched the films prepared by Charles (and possibly Ray) Eames and Glen Fleck on multiple screens, which would have been lifted high up to create a sense of boundary with moving images, just as in the screening of the Eameses' movie at the American National Pavilion in Moscow in 1959 (see figure 5.9).[75] These orientation movies and a large model of the garden would have prepared our visitor for the long educational and recreational ride she was about to take to the different bioclimatic zones of the world.

The exhibition pavilions and installations at every section throughout Pardisan demonstrate that the designers sought out the hard balance between conservation of wildlife and education of humans. Firouz explained

Figure 5.12 WMRT, Ian McHarg, Nader Ardalan, Laleh Bakhtiar, et al., Pardisan Park, designed in Tehran and Philadelphia, 1974–80. Programmatic scheme of the site plan, showing that the world's bioclimatic zones (*top right, supplementary map*) will be mapped to the site plan (*bottom right, supplementary map*). "Pardisan: Plan for an Environmental Park in Tehran." Report of 1975. Permission granted by Nader Ardalan.

the park's objective as follows: "Exhibits at the environmental park will emphasize that we have reached a stage on the road of destruction of the environment that paying lip service to these ideas is not enough, that it is necessary to take immediate action to protect the environment. . . . It is therefore necessary to stress that in view of existing circumstances, when the exponential increase of populations and the concomitant increase in the pollution of the environment genuinely threatens the very existence of our planet, even commercial common sense should compel the preservation of the environment."[76]

Originally, Firouz aspired to represent two ecosystems and their histories, which sustained the life of two nearly extinct animals: the *arjan* for the Persian lion and the prairie for the American buffalo. This would have shown how animals become extinct when humans disrupt the harmony of ecosystems, and promoted the understanding of extinction in both its environmental and sociocultural aspects.[77] The team members used the term "holistic science of ecology" to describe their commitment to reconnecting multiple fragmented forms of knowledge.[78] Along the process however, ambitions reached such a sense of grandeur that Pardisan was designed to encompass all bioclimatic zones of the world, against Firouz's warnings (figure 5.12).[79]

If the promotional movie by the Eameses and Fleck is of any indication, the visitor would have been presented, already in the first introductory exhibit, with a distillation of Pardisan's basic theme and its architectural design as a modern Persian Garden.[80] The garden would show "the way in which plants by mutation and natural selection, and animals by these means plus behavior, and man by all these plus cultural adaptation, change themselves and their environment in order to survive. The processes of change are continuous. By understanding them, the cultural and natural resources of Iran may be protected, and future problems may be solved."[81]

The park sought to substantiate this argument through multiple display paths. Leaving the entrance building at the southern center of the site, our visitor would have found herself in a tree-shaded and fountain-cooled *meydan*, a plaza, where storytellers and musicians would have recounted and performed narratives that reinforced Pardisan's main message. These would probably have been stories of environmental degradation, extinction, adaptation, survival, and quality of life, and probably some would have reflected nationalist sentiments and the Shah's propaganda about Iran's essential place for saving nature on planet Earth. Choosing the option of discovering the Iranian landscapes first (figure 5.13), the visitor would have walked north and passed a linear aquarium, as if she were underwater, and had a look at the seaweeds, ancestral algae, squid, clams, and oysters as representatives of ancient animals. Perhaps, she would have stopped to watch the sharks and cartilaginous fish that represented the next stage of evolution in maritime species according to the natural history constructed in Pardisan's aquarium. And then she would have walked into the large community tank where she would have been exposed to the fascinating biodiversity of marine life. She would have learned about "the adaptations of protective coloration, schooling, mutualism and stratum feeding" in this spacious room surrounded by water containers and oceanic animals placed there for the sake of her education and pleasure, before she would have moved to the next linear aquarium to see amphibians and reptiles.[82]

At the end of this short trip underwater whose displays transcended 250,000 years, she would have found herself in a fishing village with wading birds, boats, nets, and other fishing equipment. This is where she would have walked into a *bazaar*, a series of exhibits in buildings and on terraces that represented Iran. This architectural metaphor of Iran would have been located between two artificial lakes constructed as symbols of the Caspian Sea and the Persian Gulf. In this bazaar, she would have seen the exhibits of the arts, industries, cultural traditions, and cuisines of different regions in

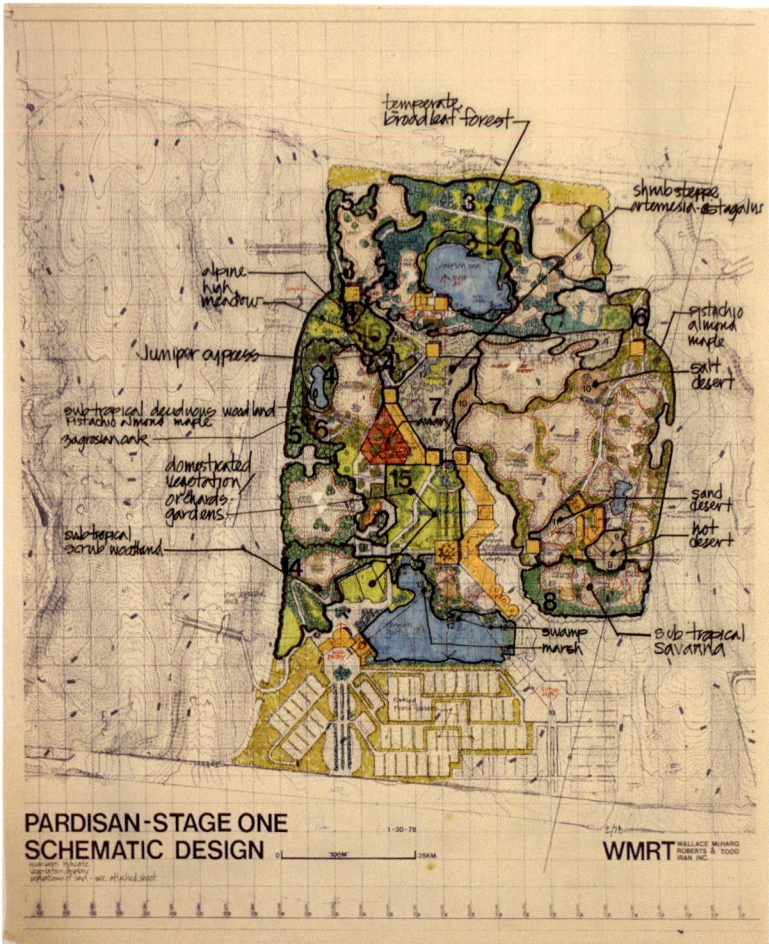

Figure 5.13 WMRT, Ian McHarg, Nader Ardalan, Laleh Bakhtiar, et al., Pardisan Park, designed in Tehran and Philadelphia, 1974–80. Study for the "Iranian corridor." Architectural Archives, University of Pennsylvania, Ian McHarg Collection.

Iran. Bracketing the paradoxical combination of environmentalist activism and commercialist-leisure industry, she would have taken a meal in one of the restaurants, each of which offered a different cuisine corresponding to a different Persian region. Outside this walkway, she would have observed the designed landscapes of Iran with different bioclimatic zones. Along the way, she would have seen onagers, snow leopards, tigers, and, yes, Persian lions, whose near extinction had created a national trauma. She would have

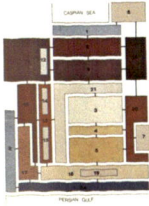

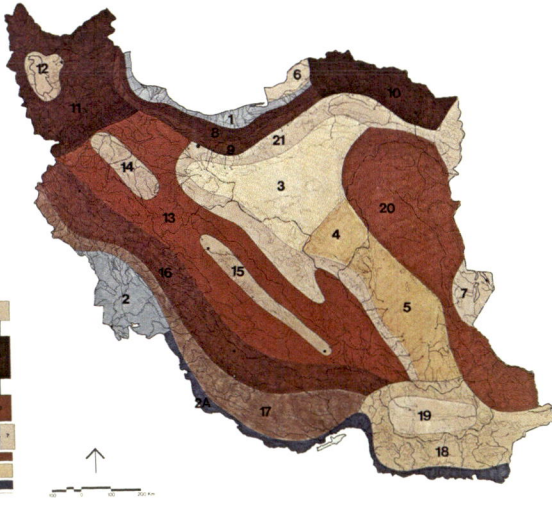

Figure 5.14 WMRT, Ian McHarg, Nader Ardalan, Laleh Bakhtiar, et al., Pardisan Park, designed in Tehran and Philadelphia, 1974–80. The bioclimatic zones of Iran. "Pardisan: Plan for an Environmental Park in Tehran." Report of 1975. Permission granted by Nader Ardalan.

seen birds and rodents of the desert; oak, breech, shrubs, and wildflowers of the Hyrcanian forest; open woodlands of pistachio and oak of the Zagros mountains; stony steppes of the plateau desert; pale greens of Artemisia; and salt deserts and flora of halophytic plants. Unlike in zoos or botanical gardens, none of these would have been located in fenced or closed spaces but in constructed landscapes whose boundaries would have been defined with manufactured topography, ditches, hills, trees, bushes, and buildings (see figures 5.16 and 5.18).

Adjacent to each landscape, our visitor would have entered a pavilion in order to learn about the "biological, behavioral and cultural adaptations" that have been achieved for the survival of species over time. These sets of knowledge would have reflected the ideas of the consultant scientists in Pardisan's team: the biologist David Goddard, anthropologist Yehudi Cohen, ethnographer Solomon Katz, and Iranian studies scholar Brian Spooner.[83] Our visitor would have engaged in "discussions of problems such as zinc and cretinism, goitre, advancing deserts and diminishing forests and methods for their solution."[84] In short, as she walked across Pardisan from south to

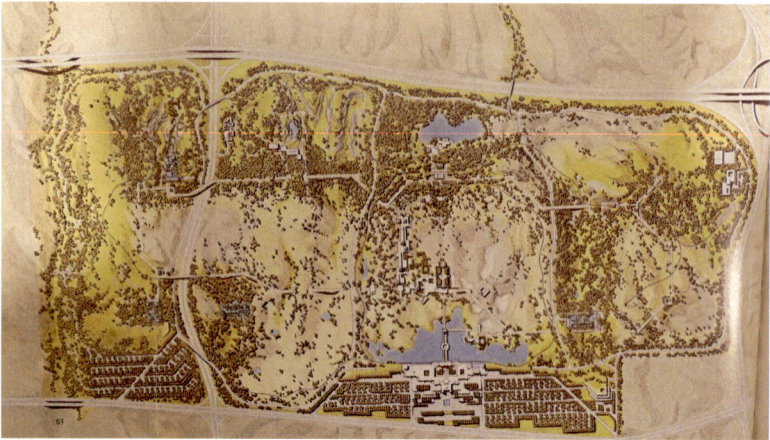

Figure 5.15 WMRT, Ian McHarg, Nader Ardalan, Laleh Bakhtiar, et al., Pardisan Park, designed in Tehran and Philadelphia, 1974–80. Site plan. "Pardisan: Plan for an Environmental Park in Tehran." Report of 1975. Permission granted by Nader Ardalan.

north, she would have metaphorically crossed Iranian landscapes with their plants, animals, and building cultures, and would have experienced the manufactured versions of the six different bioclimatic zones found in Iran: tundra, deciduous forest, grassland, dry scrub and woodland, desert and semidesert, and savanna.[85] Even though the visitor would have seen representations of architectural settlements, she would have been presented a categorization that divided the land into physiognomic clusters, regardless of the ethnic diversity of Arabic-, Kurdish-, or Turkish-speaking towns in Iran.

During this walk, the visitor would have also learned about other places in the world that were analogues to Persian bioclimatic zones. That Pardisan's scientists could find in Iran six out of eight different bioclimatic zones of the world convinced them of the possibility and moral obligation of creating a microcosm of the entire planet Earth in Tehran for the sake of public education and scientific research (figure 5.14). They would have created a garden that contained the entire planet. Even if we assume that this could be a plausible argument, they must have overlooked the fact that the city of Tehran is in only one of these eight bioclimatic zones. In 1973, McHarg's team, WMRT, had prepared a feasibility report for Firouz, where they had concluded that the "concept is valid and exciting with potentially great benefits to the people. The site chosen is sufficient in size and other aspects are suitable for . . . an environmental park of education, recreation and conservation."[86]

Figure 5.16 WMRT, Ian McHarg, Nader Ardalan, Laleh Bakhtiar, et al., Pardisan Park, designed in Tehran and Philadelphia, 1974–80. Sketches of open areas. Architectural Archives, University of Pennsylvania, Ian McHarg Collection.

Leaving the exhibit of Iran, our visitor would have embarked on the second route, a nowhere-to-be-found excursion into the nonhuman species of the entire world (figure 5.15). For that she would have been given a passport that would have also served as a map, a guide, and a ticket to the monorail and minibus system that carried her to the environments of Europe and North America at the northwest of Pardisan, to South America and Africa at the southwest; and on the other side of the spine that represented Iran, to South Asia and Oceania at the southeast, and finally to north Asia at the northeast of the park. After visiting all these lands, she would have returned to the center before she closed the loop (figure 5.15). Selected environments of these lands would have been created in detail in relation to the eight designated bioclimatic zones: tundra, coniferous forest, deciduous forest, grassland, dry scrub and woodland, desert, savanna, and tropical forest.[87]

At every monorail stop, our visitor would have found amenities for food and recreation as well as educational pavilions that would have informed her of the re-created environments, as well as the biological and behavioral adaptations necessary for the survival of species in these environments. For

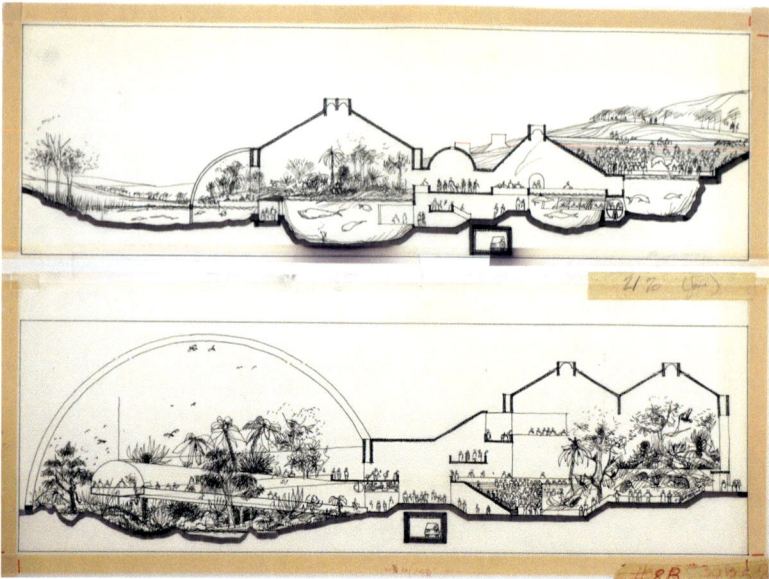

Figure 5.17 WMRT, Ian McHarg, Nader Ardalan, Laleh Bakhtiar, et al., Pardisan Park, designed in Tehran and Philadelphia, 1974–80. Sketches of closed areas with artificially created climatic conditions. Architectural Archives, University of Pennsylvania, Ian McHarg Collection.

instance, during her world tour, she would have passed through five deserts and learned how animals adapt to intense heat. She would have experienced different conditions designed to create "the most attractive, safe and appropriate" human-nonhuman relations "that allow the animals to be viewed in surroundings as similar as possible to their natural habitat and in some cases allow the spectator to experience that environment with the animal."[88] Depending on different climates and human-nonhuman interfaces she would have seen animals across moats, slippery slopes, or horizontal barriers; from viewing bays, islands, and elevated walkways; and behind transparent screens (figures 5.16 and 5.18). In the Alpine regions of North America and Europe, for example, she would have stood on a platform across from the rocky and steep slopes. In the temperate forests, she would have sensed the seasonality and variety of experiences. In the tropical grassland of Africa, she would have experienced a sense of vastness. For the tropical climates with temperature and humidity requirements far different from the ones that can be passively (i.e., without fueled energy) re-created in Tehran, the designers collaborated with Buckminster Fuller.[89] For these environments, the visitor would have entered geodesic domes, experienced the climatic conditions of tropical forests, and viewed the animals from multilevel platforms (figure 5.17).[90]

The circulation design would have made our visitor follow an imaginary silk route that joined China to the Mediterranean. She would have thought about the historical migrations of not only nonhuman species but also humans who thereby hybridized cultures. In North America, she would have seen the beeches, oaks, maples, cherries, dogwoods, rhododendrons, and others. The coniferous forest exhibit would have required refrigeration in another dome, and she would have seen the spruce and fir, pine, birch, and alder along with elk and bear, mink and otter, mountain lion and wolverine. In contrast, she would have enjoyed the temperate climate of deciduous forest outside. A loop in Pardisan through steppe, grassland, prairie, plains, pampas, and savanna would have enabled her see the largest animals of the world, including horse, sheep and goat, bison and buffalo, giraffe, elephant and kangaroo, lion, tiger, leopard, and jaguar. The design of topography would have created ditches, hills, valleys, caves, and tunnels in order to make this animal-human coexistence possible, and would have been a good illustration of Ian McHarg's motto of designing with nature (figure 5.18). Our visitor would have been made conscious that there are many engendered species, but Pardisan would have foregrounded only the charismatic animals, "big mammals with big eyes" as some extinction scholars would say, but not the parasites, the microbes, or the understated species that also need protection. Seeing the domesticated animals in grasslands, she would have been reminded of the agricultural revolution and other myths about the birth of civilization that were taken for granted during the time of Pardisan's design.[91]

Finally, the visitor would have looped back to the entrance building, where she could enjoy the third exhibit, a planetarium of sorts combined with a museum of technology, which would have covered the "evolution of matter and cosmic evolution: galaxies, the sun, the solar system and the earth,"[92] on the one hand, and the growth of technology that allows humans to manage the environment, on the other hand. According to Eames and Fleck's movie, these two were put together so that a visitor would have been reminded of the theme of Pardisan one more time: the evolution and adaptation of life, along which comes the possibility to destroy or save the environment and the awareness that there is "only one earth" where humans are inseparably linked to the environment. Needless to say, nothing less than a colossal and expensive scientific, architectural, landscaping, and engineering production with the enablement of a monarchic ruler in an authoritarian state would have made this excursion possible. Pardisan would not have concealed this

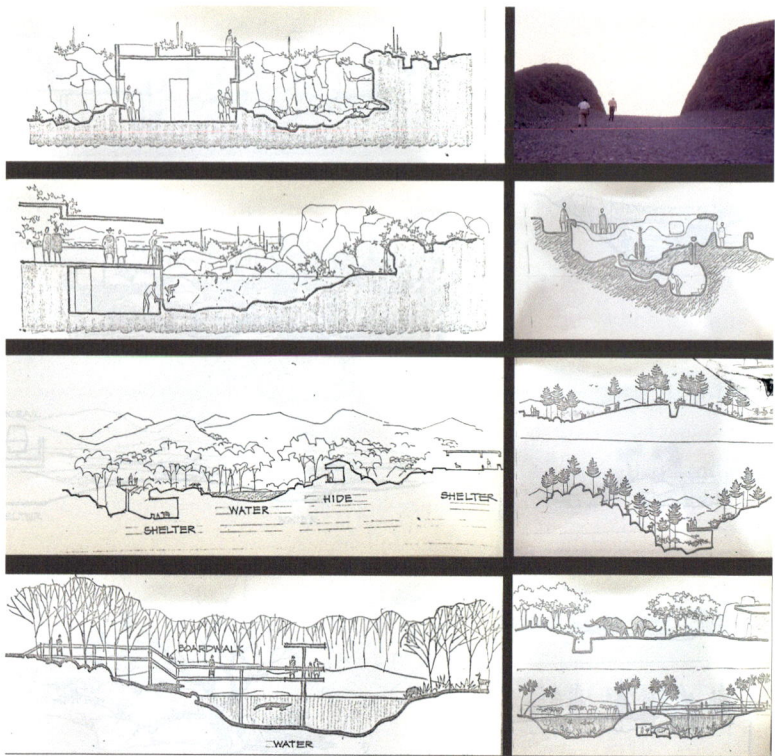

Figure 5.18 WMRT, Ian McHarg, Nader Ardalan, Laleh Bakhtiar, et al., Pardisan Park, designed in Tehran and Philadelphia, 1974–80. Design sketches for the co-existence of humans and animals. Photograph at top right shows the beginning of construction, before the park's cancellation. Architectural Archives, University of Pennsylvania, Ian McHarg Collection.

megaintervention, unlike conventional national parks that artificially construct wilderness and create an illusion of nature without humans.

Pardisan would have been an early experimentation with what Michael Rosenzweig called "reconciliation ecology," an initiative in natural conservation that envisions a humanity that does not cause mass extinction but learns to share spaces with species. Reconciliation ecology "is the science of inventing, establishing, and maintaining new habitants to conserve species diversity in places where people live, work or play."[93] Pardisan would have also experimented with many of the ideas that Emma Marris outlines as examples of the rambunctious garden of the early twenty-first century. First, radical rewilding takes the purist conservationist idea of rewilding to another level, in the sense that it trucks many wild animals into new zones and expects them to perform as keystone species to generate more life. Among the most well-known contemporary examples, Oostvaarders-plassen in Amsterdam is not the result of wilderness but "a garden about wilderness."[94] Second, assisted migration helps animals find new habitats in the age of climate change. At the same time, it acknowledges centuries-long circulation of seeds, plants, and animals, and pacifies the war against "invasive species" by suggesting that it is not migration that causes extinction. It invites us to change our nomenclature and to love the migrant species that move and adapt to their new places in the age of climate change and mass extinction, because they might well become the new keystone species and generators of future biodiversity.[95] Third, designer ecosystems no longer hope to restore nature back to a baseline—which is already indeterminable and whose choice is a value judgment—but embrace "cosmopolitan wilderness." A version of all of these ideas would have been experimented with in Pardisan at a more ambitious level. Pardisan dared an alternative response to extinction, rather than national parks that had been the model for natural conservation according to the general consensus at the time. The team designed a garden for education, conservation, and research, rather than a protected area without humans. Marris's description of a world designed as a rambunctious garden would have fit Pardisan as well: "We may be able to grow nature larger than it currently is. This will not only require a change in our values but a change in our very aesthetics, as we learn to accept both nature that looks a little more lived-in than we are used to and working spaces that look a little more wild than we are used to."[96] But, would Pardisan have achieved reconciliation ecology and reversed extinction rates if it was built? I discuss this question below.

ADAPTATION: A THEORY OF MANY CONVICTIONS

The Pardisan team unambiguously defined their role as the re-creation of a technologically advanced modern Persian Garden that would create the educational and scientific platform for planetary healing:

> The [Persian] Garden itself was a miracle of technology, an irrigation system, air conditioning and cooling method, a habitable enclosure in an arid landscape. The transforming waters emanated from the ground in the fountain of the blessed and parted into four ways, creating a Paradise in the desert. The Persian Garden became the metaphysical symbol of a new technology, a new pattern of settlement, a novel agriculture,

indeed a new way of life. . . . Pardisan is conceived as a continuation of this tradition. . . . The metaphysical view represented in Pardisan is the unity of man and nature. Its purpose is to understand and celebrate this unity and interdependence.[97]

The designers of Pardisan upheld the idea of adaptation as the opposite of extinction. Yet, adaptation proved to serve as a grounding principle for many different, sometimes discordant convictions. The team's biologist Goddard, anthropologist Cohen, and ethnographers Katz and Spooner theorized adaptation to explain the way plants, animals, humans, and societies survive.[98] The team made an inventory of animals that charted their vulnerability and adaptability,[99] and selected animals for Pardisan by using adaptation as the main criterion: "While all animals have adapted—otherwise they won't exist—some adaptations are more conspicuous than others, and some of these can provide striking analogies and contrasts than others."[100] Pardisan would have been a research lab on adaptation so that engendered species could be saved.

Additionally, Ardalan and Bakhtiar advanced a theory that they named "adaptive architecture" and demonstrated it in the design of Pardisan's pavilions. McHarg mirrored these ideas when he spoke about "adaptive architecture" in his book *To Heal the Earth*: "There must be generic form in architecture, which leads us to something which must be called adaptive architecture—not architecture to gratify the muddy psyches of architects but architecture as a device by which man can adapt toward survival and the more distant prospect of fulfillment."[101] If the Persian Garden "symbolizes the transformation of the desert into a habitable and delightful environment," Pardisan would have proved the importance of adaptation for the entire planet so that life could survive.[102] In this approach, architecture was conceived as a major prop for human adaptation. Humans existed on earth by adapting to different climates and different ecologies with different architectural forms. There was no shortage of statements in the internal reports that made eerie analogies between natural and social adaptation, and between biological mutation and cultural transformation. The feasibility report already embodied this postulation in 1973: "If the lesson of adaptation is the central generating conception of Pardisan, then evolutionary adaptation by plants and animals to the environments of Iran must provide the basis of interpretation. Human adaptation through culture and technology must be superimposed upon this base."[103] So did the main report of 1975: "Pardisan is, then, a selective representation of the world in microcosm but because it is faithful to geography, it can permit investigation of innumerable themes. . . . The employment of adaptation as the essential challenge confronting all creatures is itself a powerful integrative device. . . . While adaptation in plants and animals occurs by mutation and natural selection, in man, cultural adaptation is the most significant adaptive strategy."[104]

Despite their shared preoccupation and consensus on the centrality of adaptation, the team members did not share the same theories about adaptation and extinction. Pardisan was designed before the recent consensus shift among the scientific community. Given that Walter Alvarez's article appeared only in 1980, Darwin's theory provided the only scientific explanation for extinction at the time, which was not left unchallenged by the theological experts in the team. In their ideas about extinction and adaptation, some in the Pardisan team had Darwinian persuasions;[105] others believed it was a divine force, God or Allah, who had created the universe where living beings were predestined to adapt. These differences do not seem to have been resolved during the design process, nor did they need to for the professionals to work together.

Scholars have already pointed out the Christian convictions in the beginnings of North American environmentalism. In Guha and Martinez-Alier's words, the "environmental community has examined and reexamined its ethical responsibilities toward nature" against the backdrop of the national parks believed to preserve wilderness. After a common diagnosis of the root cause of ecological crisis as the "Judeo-Christian belief that man was meant to dominate nature, [many Christians tried to revive] their traditions of stewardship that had been suppressed within their own religion; others abandoning Christianity altogether, enthusiastically embraced non-Western religions believed to be more in harmony with nature."[106] Cronon has also explained the myth of wilderness as a metaphor of the original garden, a place out of time, where humans are supposed to have fallen from.[107] In a similar vein, some of Pardisan's protagonists hoped to demonstrate the teachings of Islam, Sufism in particular, for a better human-nature relation that would protect the environment.

Most significantly, Laleh Bakhtiar prepared "Persian Epistemologies" during Pardisan's design as a document that reflected her studies under the Islamic theologian Hossein Nasr.[108] She compiled ideas of Avicenna, Ghazali, Ibn Arabi, and Mulla Sadra as four schools of thought that in her eyes "found a permanent home in the Iranian perspective," and moved toward a synthesis of Sufism.[109] "Intelligence, a divine gift, in the Iranian Islamic perspective is that which leads man to an affirmation of the doctrine of unity. Knowledge or science, both called *ilm*, means that knowledge or science makes man aware of God, of the eternal truths that reside within things."[110] True knowledge meant unity of "reason, revelation and mystical intuition."[111] Nasr was one of the consultants of Pardisan who resisted the idea of adaptation as the ultimate guiding principle, but proposed to find something that preceded it. In Ardalan's summary of Nasr's ideas, "Pardisan can be viewed as a place of symbols, some are universal, some are specific to Iran, in the Islamic context. . . . What can we place in Pardisan as a primordial principle which either precedes or complements adaptation but certainly deals with the aspect of fulfillment? We want to create a place that deals with the concept of totality."[112]

Ardalan and Bakhtiar simultaneously advanced these views in their book *The Sense of Unity*, for which Nasr wrote the foreword. In the book, they drew on the monuments of the Islamic tradition in Isfahan, and sought to translate the teachings of Sufism into practical principles of space, shape, surface, color, and matter.[113] The Mandala Collaborative's simultaneous theorization of the idea of "adaptation" during Pardisan led to the drawing of a matrix that showed the adaptive shapes that could be generated from traditional forms. The traditional forms included a platform, a stair, a courtyard, a gateway, a porch, an integrative space, and a room; each was "adapted" in relation to their square, triangular, and octagonal permutations (figure 5.19). The Mandala Collaborative designed the entrance building of Pardisan as a display of these adaptations (figure 5.20).[114] If Pardisan were constructed, they would have probably undertaken architectural design of pavilions in relation to these ideas of adaptive architecture.

In 1979, when Pardisan was canceled due to the Islamic Revolution whose leaders found it "too fancy and glorious for the present circumstances," McHarg was therefore puzzled.[115] In a letter from the United States to the representative of the Khomeini government, he asserted that the design did not reflect the outgoing Shah regime but "the universal recognition of the necessity to understand the environment as a physical, biological and social system in order to manage it wisely." Referring to Bakhtiar's "Persian Epistemologies" that was undertaken for Pardisan, he continued: "Pardisan is an [environment] with the conceptions of God-Man-Nature in Islam and Iranian cultural identity."[116]

Throughout the process, Pardisan's team intuitively defined three major roles for architects in the struggle for planetary healing under the threat of mass extinction. First, as a profession, architecture was believed to be the primal and most effective medium for humans to adapt to their environ-

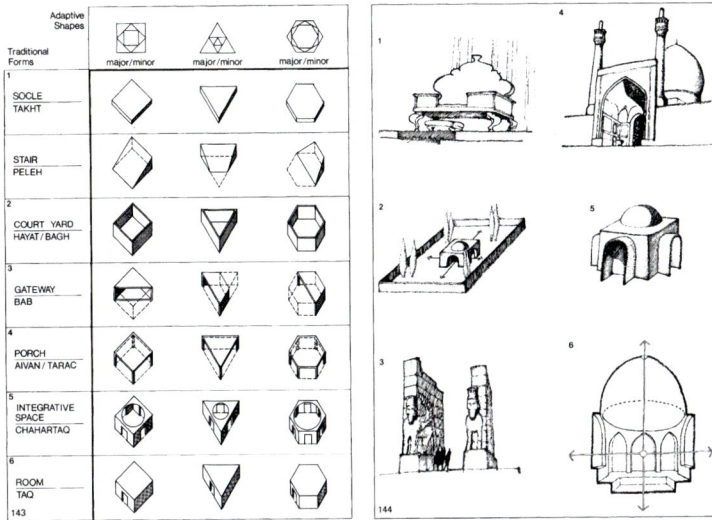

Figure 5.19 Nader Ardalan and Laleh Bakhtiar, Adaptive Architecture, Tehran, 1974–80, in *The Sense of Unity: A Sufi Tradition in Persian Architecture* (Chicago: University of Chicago Press, 1973). Permission granted by Nader Ardalan.

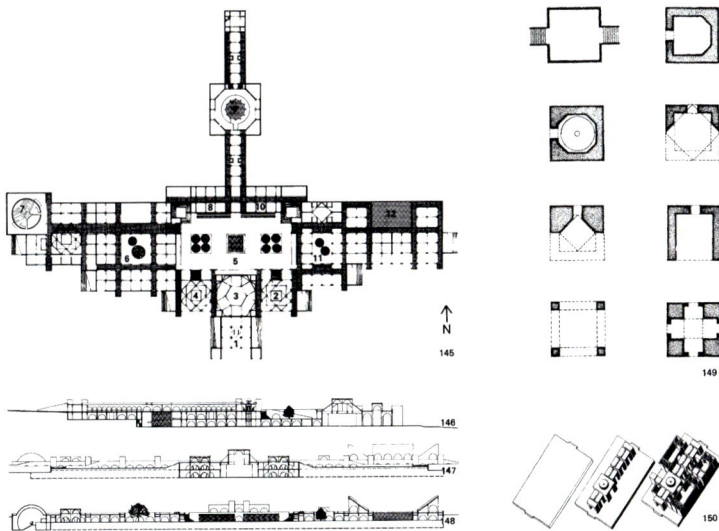

Figure 5.20 Nader Ardalan and Laleh Bakhtiar, Entrance Building to Pardisan Park, Tehran, 1974–80. "Pardisan: Plan for an Environmental Park in Tehran." Report of 1975. Permission granted by Nader Ardalan.

ments. Architecture was seen as the materialization of the scientific and theological concept of adaptation. Second, as a space-making discipline, architecture could employ spatial thinking to recreate the microcosm of the whole earth and thereby enable research, education, and leisure. Third, as a discipline that brings together experts from different fields, architecture could communicate to the public "a holistic science of ecology."

Recent discussions in environmentalism differentiate between adaptation and mitigation as two distinct, sometimes competing, ways of responding to climate change. While the former involves changing projects to get ready for a warmed planet, the latter advocates changing policies to prevent climate change. Climate activists rightly caution against the complacency of climate adaptationists today for construing global warming as an unavoidable fait accompli. However, what is overlooked in this evaluation is the fact that architecture has a long, albeit obliterated, history of climate-adaptation techniques, and that low-carbon architecture has long served as a climate-adaptation technique before fossil fuel–dependent technologies took over. In this context, the theory of architecture as climate adaptation that was advanced by the architects of Pardisan gains newfound relevance. While fighting the extinction of the Persian lion, Pardisan also exhibited world architectures as climate adaptation. It is partially the erasure of these climate-adaptation techniques in favor of generic fossil fuel–dependent technologies that has brought the carbonization of the environment and extinction.

If it was built, would Pardisan have achieved reconciliation ecology and reversed extinction rates? In her book *The Mushroom at the End of the World*, Anna Tsing has aptly called for telling the story of landscapes with both human and nonhuman agents, because these environments are products of "unintentional design, that is, the overlapping world-making activities of many agents, both human and nonhuman. The design is clear in the landscaper's ecosystem. But none of the agents have planned this effect. Humans join others in making landscapes of unintentional design. As sites for more-than-human dramas, landscapes are radical tools for decentering human debris. Landscapes are not backdrops for historical action: they are themselves active."[117] The ecosystem transforms like an unintended design; it is unpredictable. Pardisan's designers never imagined the processes that would have been put into motion by more-than-human agents. In their eyes, it was either "Man" or a divine force beyond humans that could fix the damage in the process of adaptation and return it to a state that prevented extinctions.

Along with Tsing, we may ask: What unintended events could have happened if Pardisan was built? What kind of ecological consequences would the project have put into motion? Would it have been yet another disaster prepared by the human hand, or succeeded in its goals for ecocide prevention? Would it be doomed to failure like Biosphere II in Arizona, an experiment with similar ambitions that was constructed more than a decade later and that officially collapsed in 1995? Biosphere II was a comparable project that contained an artificial rainforest, desert, agricultural zone, and ocean in a sealed glass ziggurat (unlike Pardisan, which would not have been sealed in its entirety), where four men and four women lived to prove that a microcosm of life on earth could be recreated. However, they soon lost control of the artificial atmosphere, spent their time hungry and in altitude sickness, and watched the oxygen levels drop sharply and the fish die.[118]

I asked these questions to botanists and wildlife biologists who agreed to be employed as consultant experts for this book. Christopher Dunn predicted that the wildlife in the Fuller-designed domes would have probably shared the same destiny as those in Biosphere II and died. Species in open areas had more chances of surviving. Amanda Rodewald outlined Pardisan's strengths and weaknesses as follows:

1   Pardisan acts as a demonstration project or model that establishes a new standard, or perhaps even norm, for how parks/open spaces can support biodiversity and be environmentally sustainable. In this case, the lasting impact of Pardisan would scale and be replicated in public and private lands across the region(s), with impacts greatly exceeding the direct and local contributions to conservation.

2   Pardisan would act as a premier education and outreach/engagement facility that would help cultivate awareness and appreciation for nature and biodiversity among students and the general public. . . . Serving that role also would allow the impacts from Pardisan to scale beyond local species/systems.

3   Pardisan could be developed and used, in part, as a breeding facility for certain critically endangered species (just as some of our zoos do now). That would directly augment populations of certain critically endangered species. This is very likely the only path by which Pardisan could directly play a role in preventing extinctions.

4   Pardisan would support native species from the local area and thus contribute at least somewhat to biodiversity.[119]

In other words, Rodewald appreciates Pardisan as an educational garden that could be a catalyst for biodiversity, but raises suspicion that it could prevent extinction or repair the harms to endangered species. "Species are generally listed as critically endangered after decades of inaction or ineffective action. By that time, species distributions have become so restrictive and species so vulnerable to stressors that parkland within human-dominated landscapes is unlikely to play meaningful roles in species recovery."[120]

The protagonists of Pardisan seem to have uncritically accepted the premise that an ecoengineering enterprise where all species are at the disposal of human scientific curiosity and theological conviction would foster nature-culture harmony. This implies a conviction that an anthropocentric garden could be the healer of anthropocentrism. In positing the Persian Garden as an archetype, many in the Pardisan team held sentiments that overlapped with anticolonial approaches. For the Iranian members of the team, such as Ardalan and Bakhtiar, the Persian Garden provided a corrective to the Western domination of nature. However, its anti-Westernness would not have been enough for Pardisan to uphold the idea of an anticolonial garden, because the garden would have continued to foster the colonization of land in another guise. The architects of Pardisan sought to demonstrate that the colossal problems of the planet could be resolved with comparatively ambitious initiatives. However, by imagining an ecoengineering utopia, the designers overtrusted inconclusive findings of bioengineering, and assumed that a big garden could be a testing ground for the entire planet, without calculating the potential harms.

Conclusion: Transitional Imaginary for a Multispecies Right to Heal

The City of the Future designed the entire planet as a garden; Pardisan recreated the entire planet in a garden. The totalizing vision of the City of the Future was mirrored in Pardisan, which would be implemented by a totalitarian regime. Both project teams started small with a strong moral conscience over human-caused harms to nature, but both ended in visions that involved the entire planet. How could taking accountability and responsibility for water pollution and extinction carry such talented planners and architects to such totalitarian visions? They seem to have worked with a basic unchecked premise that bigger environmental problems needed bigger design solutions. McHarg famously widened his site plans to include much larger swaths of land; Doxiadis considered the entire planet as one project site.[121] They assumed that planetary healing was a matter of scaling up, and falsely equated unity and totality as if the unity of the ecosystem necessitates a totality of design and political action.

Pardisan needed an all-powerful ruler for implementation. In handwritten notes, McHarg communicated his fascination with working in a context as if the US president had combined all national parks, natural history museums, conservation centers, zoos, aquariums, botanical gardens, and planetariums under one institution—this seemed possible under the Shah's rule in Iran.[122] Buckminster Fuller also pointed out the role of the Shah for "all the money and energy being concentrated in this part of the world" to make Pardisan possible.[123] It should not be surprising that the project was canceled after the toppling of this monarchic ruler. Doxiadis, in contrast, was optimistic that his vision could be implemented through scientific research and democratic persuasion. In his speech to the Nobel Foundation in 1969, he said:

> We conclude that we must influence the minds of people, inform them of the better ways in which they can live. In order to accomplish this, we will need more knowledge than we have at present, which again means research, education and guided experimentation. . . . We have the obligation to transmit the message in a meaningful, that is scientific way, so that our society and our political leaders will see it as a problem which can be approached in a rational and objective way. When we reach this point the overall solution will be clear and we will not be afraid of the big city to come: instead of fighting it we will build it.[124]

Their delusions of grandeur and political action notwithstanding, the City of the Future and Pardisan bring us to at least one realization that is still relevant. Both teams concluded that planetary healing was a global issue that needed inclusive international engagement and organizations. "The division of global ecosystem into nation states is ecocidal," as Franz Broswimmer aptly stated.[125] Looping back to the introduction and the first chapter of this book, extinction fosters the conceptualization of healing as a matter of rights and the recognition of the rights of all species, the future generations, and the earth as administered by international organizations.

The political and professional backdrop for Pardisan was the government's and architects' intentions to demonstrate Iran's role in ending the environmental crisis. After the UN Conference on the Human Environment in Stockholm in 1972, the government of Iran launched the International

Pahlavi Environment Prize Award, administered by the UN and gifted by the Iranian government in ceremonies usually with the presence of the UN Secretary General Kurt Waldheim.[126] As I write in detail elsewhere, Ardalan and Bakhtiar were among the masterminds for the organization of the Second International Congress of Architects in Persepolis in 1974, from which the *Habitat Bill of Rights* emerged as the Iranian delegate's contribution to the UN Habitat Conference in Vancouver in 1976.[127] Fifty architects from multiple countries that spanned from North America to East Asia presented at the congress, and wrote the Persepolis Declaration: "The threshold of the complete deterioration of the quality of life within our human Habitat has been reached."[128] Following the recommendation of this declaration, *Habitat Bill of Rights* was penned by five influential architects from five countries, Ardalan, Georges Candilis, Balkrishna Doshi, Moshie Safdie, and Josep Louis Sert, who suggested an international human rights code for architecture to be ratified by all participating countries.[129] Doxiadis almost joined as an author of the *Habitat Bill of Rights* as well,[130] but eventually his journal *Ekistics* "abstracted an illustrated digest of each of its major points," where the declaration was presented as the "most sought-after report" in the UN conference, and one that is "unique in that its major thrust puts forth global outlines," despite being "a national document."[131] As one of its seven recommendations to designers, the *Habitat Bill of Rights* posited the "garden" as an archetype for the betterment of the quality of life that had been impaired due to industrialization and environmental degradation (figure 5.21).[132] Finally, in 1982, the UN *World Charter for Nature* declaration acknowledged the accountability of humans in threatening species' existence.[133]

I decided to focus on Pardisan as the last example of this book also because it was one of the last moments when a large group of architects from the "Western" and "Islamic" countries were united in their shared responsibility to find architecture's apt relation to the environment. Less than a decade after the UN's call for only one Earth, this international political will to work together was foreclosed. The cancelation of the multinational collaborative design for Pardisan reflected a bigger divide that dictated the world order after 1980. It signaled the beginning of a new rift between the West and Islam that continued to sabotage global peace and shared commitment to planetary healing. It was the harbinger of the refusal of countries on both sides of the divide to collaborate. This historical episode demonstrates that the nations' right to heal from global war also fosters the species' right to live together.

While the designers of the City of the Future and Pardisan envisioned ways of living together, an imperial mode of thinking infiltrated their minds.

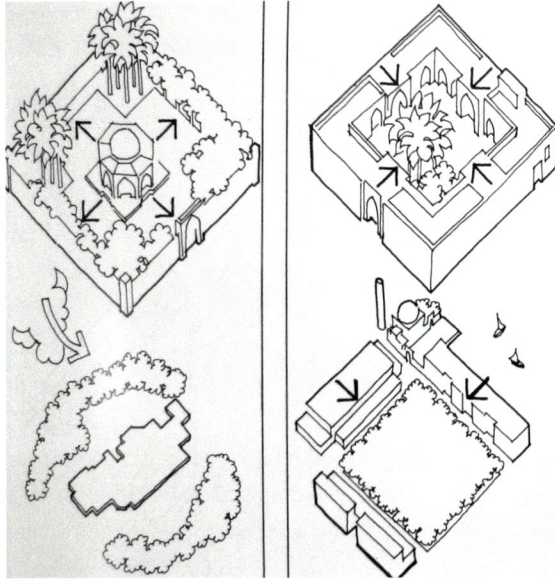

Figure 5.21
Nader Ardalan, Georges Candilis, Balkrishna Doshi, Moshie Safdie, and Josep Louis Sert, "The Principle of 'Garden,'" in *Habitat Bill of Rights* (Tehran: Hamadi Foundation, 1976).

Both projects ended in total solutions, the world as garden and garden as world, despite their designers' different political positions, motivations, and starting points. As if planetary healing could take place under imperial motivations, the architects and planners of these two projects were captured by the ungrounded persuasion that a society, a government, or an institution needs to expand to be successful. But does caring for the entire planet necessarily involve acting on the entire planet with one project? Does acknowledging the whole earth as a unified ecosystem and realizing the interconnectedness between social and environmental issues necessarily call for totalizing designs from above? Do big problems and global challenges really necessitate scaling up to total solutions? What is the relation between unity and totality?

Recent discussions in natural conservation challenge the premise that planetary healing requires hyperopic architects and planners. For instance, after reviewing the strengths and weaknesses of the mainstream and emerging natural conservation movements of the twenty-first century, Büscher and Fletcher proposed "convivial conservation" (*con vivre*—living together) as a bottom-up and collaborative alternative.[134] They proposed concrete political actions, such as instituting a Convivial Conservation Coalition, or securing conservation basic income. Instead of big companies of the private sector, they proposed "collective pooling of resources from state taxation to crowdsourcing."[135] Most relevantly, they advocated for historic reparations that would return land to dispossessed communities and find ways of compensation to pay for environmental degradation. "Acknowledgment of past injuries and redistribution of resources need to go hand in hand."[136]

After a critical review of architectural environmentalism that relies on total and scaled-up solutions, this chapter also invites us to imagine another environmentalism that foregrounds shared responsibility, reciprocity, and resource redistribution for the sake of an environment where humans and nonhumans cohabit the planet rather than being categorized separately. This planetary healing imagines a world where all humans are political actors so that they can protect and promote nature as dwellers and visitors but not invaders or extractors. Rather than spectacular or top-down environmentalism, this promotes everyday and democratic environmentalism. It may put advanced technology to use in collaborative ways: rather than big corporate–driven geoengineering, a world network of professional and amateur builders and gardeners can be established where they can report experimentation in a data system to advance the science of ecocide prevention.[137] This environmentalism also promotes climate reparations as discussed in chapter 4 as the prerequisite of planetary healing.

This chapter explored the possible role of architects and planners in healing the environment, but it also demonstrated the need for withdrawal and restraint of ambitions. These discussions invite a question in reverse. What is the role of nonhuman actors in healing the cities that humans built? Urban nature is a growing scholarly field, where phenomena discussed in this book have inspired some of the basic concepts. Matthew Gandy defines urban nature in opposition to the idea of "pristine first nature," and finds evidence for its prevalence in the growing number of living organisms in cities. Urban biodiversity has proven to be on higher levels than those found in hinterlands that have long been controlled and monoculturalized by industrialized agriculture and plantations.[138] Authors discuss nonnative "new natures" that emerge uninvited in wastelands, accidental gardens, and nonplanned open urban areas. They see alternatives to xenophobic nationalism and examples of cosmopolitan environments in these spaces. Bettina Stoetzer theorizes on nature not as a separate but an integral, albeit unruly, unplanned, and uncontrolled, part of urban environments. She discusses ruderal urban plants (sometimes called invasive species) in conjunction with xenophobic and racist sentiments against immigrants.[139] These studies often go beyond human intentionality in designed natures and record spontaneous urban spaces with ruderal species that emerge with the "independent agency of nature."[140] Others look closer at ghostly landscapes, polluted spaces, nuclear wastelands, and damaged environments at the edge of extinctions, without failing to observe nature's ability to grow back after conflicts and disasters.[141]

Each chapter of this book has already alluded to cosmopolitan urban natures. A list of these locations where nonhuman agents are acting would also reveal the healing spaces from the loss of biodiversity that this book has visited. Chapter 1 foregrounded the disappearing and surviving cemeteries in Istanbul as spaces for truth-telling and accountability after state violence— but cemeteries are also the planet's most active "biodiversity hotspots," where unpredictable and unplanned species emerge and live.[142] Chapter 2 traveled across both sides of a divide, cut by an international treaty between two neighboring communities. Nicosia, Cyprus, remains the last divided city of Europe as a residue of that same conflict, which mandated the Greek-Turkish or Christian-Muslim partition. Today, Nicosia's buffer zone, or Green Line, whose previous dwellers were evicted, has become a thriving area for biodiversity. The UN personnel that controls the zone has discovered that it hosts 358 plant species, thirteen of which are endemic.[143] New natures flourish on the ruined walls of vacated houses, and on streets that have lost their urban functions (figure 5.22). This happened in the buffer zone of divided Berlin as well, a city that inspired the emergence of urban botany as a discipline.[144] Species that emerge in between or on different sides of divided cities cross borders long before humans pull down the separating walls. Thanks to dogs, cats, birds, flowers, plants, and ruderal species that do not need passports to cross urban checkpoints, the two sides of Nicosia may already have been reconnected more than humans are able to see. Chapter 3 wrote the history of a refugee arrival zone in Istanbul that grew into one of the largest *gecekondu* (squatter) neighborhoods, where industrial plants and food gardens existed side by side, and where factory workers engaged in both urban and rural activities. Stoetzer has coined the term "ruderal city" to refer to the same type of urban nature that a Turkish immigrant's *gecekondu* house generated at the border between East and West Berlin.[145] Moreover, chapter 3 revealed the history of the dogs that sustained the world-famous leather industry in the hinterlands of Istanbul, the garden of healing plants that broadcast alternative approaches to medicine, and the urban agricultural land (*bostan*) where farmers continued to grow food for fifteen centuries in one of the world's biggest metropolises. Chapter 4 exposed a brutal murder of biodiversity during the creation of cotton monocultures in the Gezira plantations of British colonizers in Sudan, but one can expect to find cultivated and self-growing

Figure 5.22 Biodiversity in the Green Line, Cyprus. Photo: Esra Akcan, 2021.

plants in the university campuses designed after the country's independence. Needless to say, if these sections had been written from the perspective of landscape or botany, they would have extended to volumes. Ruderal urban spaces demonstrate that life and design continue to unfold after architects and urbanists leave the stage. As consecutive chapters of this book discussed the right to heal of an individual, a village community, an urban borough's residents, and a nation, they also depicted spaces where nonhuman species had been taking agency and doing their part to heal the planet.

Notes

Introduction

1   Coates, "Case for Reparations." The term *reparations* has recently attracted interest in architectural discussions as well. For instance, a recent issue of *Journal of Architectural Education*, the official publication of the Association of Collegiate Schools of Architecture, was themed on reparations. McEwen et al., "Reparations."

2   Wynter, "Unsettling the Coloniality," 260–61. Also see Sharpe, *In the Wake*; McKittrick, *Sylvia Wynter*.

3   Even though many readers may recognize this perception of human rights in numerous countries, the United Kingdom is a good example. See Clapham, *Human Rights*, 133–37.

4   Bentham, *Anarchical Fallacies*.

5   Marx, "On the Jewish Question."

6   Despite Karl Marx's criticism, Henri Lefebvre is invested in the actualization of human rights through social justice: "concrete rights come to complete the abstract rights of man and the citizen inscribed on the front of buildings by democracy during its revolutionary beginnings: the rights of ages and sexes (the woman, the child and the elderly), rights of conditions (the proletarian, the peasant), rights to training and education, to work, to culture, to rest, to health, to housing." Like Marx, Lefebvre posits the working class as the principal "agent, social career or support of" a revolutionary transformation. Yet, unlike Marx, Lefebvre includes the realization of human rights in this transformation as well: "The pressure of the working class has been and remains necessary (but not sufficient) for the recognition of these rights, for their entry into customs, for their inscription into codes which are still incomplete." Lefebvre, *The Right to the City*.

7   The literature on Lefebvre is too extensive to cite here, especially by well-known authors such as David Harvey, Edward Soja, Saskia Sassen, and Manuel Castells. For authors writing in the discipline of architecture, see

McLeod, "Henri Lefebvre's Critique"; Stanek, *Henri Lefebvre on Space*; Feldman, *From a Nation Torn*.

8   De Gouges, "Declaration of the Rights of Woman"; Wollstonecraft, *Vindication*.

9   For a discussion, see Sen, "Culture and Human Rights"; Sen, "Elements of a Theory of Human Rights"; Sen, "Human Rights and Capabilities."

10   For a review, see Tasioulas, "Human Rights."

11   Arendt, "We Refugees," 77; Agamben, "We Refugees." For a revised version, see Agamben, "Biopolitics and the Rights of Man." For more reflections of this on architecture, see Akcan, *Open Architecture*.

12   MacDonald, "Natural Rights," 21.

13   For a discussion of human rights in other disciplines, see Freeman, *Human Rights*.

14   Article 25 of the Declaration reads: "Everyone has the right to a standard of living adequate for the health and well-being of himself and of his family, including food, clothing, housing and medical care and necessary social services." The UN Covenant on Economic, Social and Cultural Rights gives a vague definition of "adequate housing," which involves security, availability of services, habitability, accessibly, location and cultural adequacy. However, the governments' obligations as to what level these standards should be provided are unclear, and the evaluation criteria for states that fail to keep up with these obligations are even less defined.

15   Clapham, *Human Rights*, 133–37. In the sphere of architecture, the most impactful field that brings these issues to the attention of the world is forensic architecture. Weizman, *Forensic Architecture*.

16   Salvioli, *Promotion of Truth*, 22.

17   Teitel, *Transitional Justice*; Teitel, *Globalizing Transitional Justice*; De Greiff, "Theorizing Transitional Justice."

18   Cronon, "Trouble with Wilderness"; Marris, *Rambunctious Garden*; Tsing, *Mushroom at the End of the World*; Haraway, "Tentacular Thinking"; Haraway, "Making Kin"; Tsing et al., *Arts of Living on a Damaged Planet*; Büscher and Fletcher, *Conservation Revolution*.

19   Stoler, *Imperial Debris*.

20   Malm, *Fossil Capital*.

21   Klein, *This Changes Everything*; Demos, *Decolonizing Nature*; Demos, *Against the Anthropocene*; Dawson, *Extreme Cities*.

22   Lowe, *Intimacies of Four Continents*; Walcott, *Long Emancipation*; Liboiron, *Pollution Is Colonialism*.

23   Said, *Orientalism.*

24   For books that are specifically on migrations due to the Ottoman-Russian and Balkan War, see Ladas, *Exchange of Minorities*; Geray, *Türkiye'den ve Türkiye'ye Göçler*; Pentzopoulos, *Balkan Exchange*; İpek, *Rumeli'den Anadolu'ya Türk Göçleri*; Halaçoğlu, *Balkan Harbi Sırasında*; Toumarkine, *Migrations des populations*; Dündar, *Ittihat ve Terakki'nin Müslümanları İskan Politikası*; Dragostinova*, Between Two Mother-lands*; İpek, "Balkans, War and Migration"; Hamed-Troyansky, *Empire of Refugees.*

25   I am using Justin McCarthy's illustration because his mapping and numeric estimations still provide one of the sharpest visualizations of the forced migrations during this time. But his statements about the Armenian killings have been conveniently used by the denialist Turkish nationalists.

26   Hamed-Troyansky, *Empire of Refugees*, 124–34.

27   Dündar, *Ittihat ve Terakki'nin Müslümanları İskan Politikası*, 56, 252.

28   Makdisi, *Age of Coexistence.*

29   Therefore, this book is a continuation of the idea of welcoming, translatability from below, and open architecture that I explored in previous books by theorizing on cosmopolitan ethics. Akcan, *Architecture in Translation*; Akcan, *Open Architecture.*

30   For general histories of Ottoman and British Sudan written during the periods, see Mihri, *Sudan Seyahatnamesi*; Hill, *Egypt in the Sudan*. For more recent scholarship, see Holt and Daly, *History of Sudan*; Daly, *Modernization in the Sudan*; Collins and Deng, *British in the Sudan*; Troutt Powell, *Different Shade of Colonialism.*

31   "Osmanlı Afrikası-Kuzeydoğu, Der Kriegsschauplatz Im Aegyptischen Sudan," Ottoman Archives, Istanbul, Document No. HRT.h._651-_3, Document Location: 651, Document Date: H-03-05-1301.

32   Mazower, *Greek Revolution*, 277.

33   These included Halid Paşa, who was the governor general of Sudan provinces; he hosted European travelers through their travels in the province of Sudan such as John Petherick. Mahu Bey, of Kurdish origin, who was the governor of Berber since 1822, had a habitual residence near Khartoum. When Ali Khurshid Aga took over the office in 1826, he focused on developing the city by attracting families to move and have permanent houses here. During this time, a mosque was built in 1829–30 and replaced with a larger one in seven years; barracks, military storehouses and a dockyard were constructed; commerce and trade routes were encouraged. Ivory trade soon made several Ottoman subjects wealthy, some of whom lived in Khartoum, where the slave market remained open until

1854. Arakil Bey, who was an Armenian, was appointed as the first governor of Khartoum and the Gezira region to its south until 1858. Holt and Daly, *History of Sudan*, 47–82; Petherick, *Egypt, the Soudan and Central Africa*, 127.

34 Deringil, "They Live in a State."

35 Deringil, "They Live in a State," 311.

36 Minawi, *Ottoman Scramble for Africa*.

37 When Mahdi (the awaited one in Muslim faith) passed away a few months after the revolt, the rule was passed on to his successor, Khalifa Abdallah al-Tayushi.

38 P. M. Holt and M. W. Daly identify Lord Curzon as one of the architects of this political equation, who was also one of the masterminds of Greek-Turkish partition treaty. Holt and Daly, *History of Sudan*, 130–31.

39 Troutt Powell, *Different Shade of Colonialism*.

40 See, for example, Hall, *Balkan Wars*.

41 Schurman, *Balkan Wars*, 3, 8.

42 Schurman, *Balkan Wars*, 22. As a result, Prince Otto of Bavaria was designated as the first, and King George (originally a Danish Prince) as the second king of Greece until his assassination in 1913.

43 Schurman wrote: "Of all perplexing subjects in the world few can be more baffling than the distribution of races in Macedonia [where] classified population with religion. Accordingly, Greeks, Serbians and Bulgarians are the same. . . . Race being thus merged in religion—in something that rests on the human will and not on physical characteristics fixed by nature—can in that part of the world be changed as easily as religion. . . . In that land, race is a political party with common customs and religion who stand for a 'national idea' which they strenuously endeavor to force on others. . . . Each 'race' seeks to convert the people to its faith by the agency of schools and churches, which teach and use its own language." He claimed that the "Turkish Sultans are responsible" for the hostility of Slavs and Bulgarians against Greeks, because all Christians were collected under one *millet* in Ottoman Empire, and until 1870, the Greek Patriarch had jurisdiction over Bulgarians. Schurman, *Balkan Wars*, 80–81, 17–18.

44 Blumi, *Ottoman Refugees*, 12

45 The dispute over whether to call the Balkan War genocidal or not continues. One might compare two recent articles, where the first interprets it as the starting point of radicalized warfare, systematic attack on civilians and ethnic cleansing, while the second refrains from calling it ethnic cleansing due to the "legacy of the Ottoman Empire," the impossibility of drawing lines between combatants and civilians, and the "inability or the

unwillingness of the [Ottoman] Porte to impose the rule of law." Biondich, "Balkan Wars"; Delis, "Violence and Civilians During the Balkan Wars," 558.

46   Zürcher, "Balkan Wars and the Refugee Leadership."

47   Against the initial narratives that assumed a break with the Ottoman Empire, the continuities between the late Ottoman elite around the Committee of Union and Progress (CUP) and the Republic of Turkey are now well known. Ahmad, *From Empire to Republic*; Aksakal, *Ottoman Road to War in 1914*; Zürcher, *Young Turk Legacy and Nation Building*; Akçam, *From Empire to Republic*.

48   Recently, scholars have textually analyzed the writings of Yahya Kemal, Ziya Gökalp, Mehmet Akif Ersoy, Ömer Seyfettin, and Halide Edip Adıvar to show the psychological impact of the Balkan War on the Turkish intellectuals. Şirin, "Traumatic Legacy of the Balkan Wars"; Arisan, "Effects of the Balkan Wars."

49   Halide Edib [Adıvar], *Memoirs of Halidé Edib*, 333.

50   Keyder, "Ottoman Empire"; Kieser, Öktem, and Reinkowski, *World War I and the End of the Ottomans*.

51   For example, the following article warns against the assumed consensus that CUP members were involved in a "senseless defeat of imperial self-destruction" immediately after the Balkan War. Instead, the defeat opened an era of debate that included ideas about the imperialist expansion and restoration of Ottoman Empire in Europe, irredentism, and revenge. The Young Turks did not embrace Turkism and the myth of Anatolia as the fatherland immediately, and Ottomanism maintained relevance well into 1920. Öztan, "Point of No Return?"

52   Some scholars take a soft antagonistic tone against ethnic cleansing as if the trauma of Muslim expulsion from the Balkans could serve as an excuse. Among those who unapologetically identify demographic engineering and genocide, see especially Dündar, *Modern Türkiye'nin Şifresi*; Akçam, *Young Turks' Crime Against Humanity*.

53   Kurt and Gürpınar, "Balkan Wars," 350.

54   Ginio, *Ottoman Culture of Defeat*. Eyal Ginio takes the term "culture of defeat" from Wolfgang Schivelbusch, who analyzed the interplay between trauma, mourning, pessimism, and sentiments of glory and power after catastrophes.

55   İpek, *Rumeli'den Anadolu'ya*.

56   For instance, in 1912, the Azerbaijani author Ahmet Agayev (Ağaoğlu) characterized the Balkan War as one between the Cross and the Crescent and reminded his readers that the Ottoman Empire was the only territory for independent Muslims (along with Iran and Morocco), who otherwise

were under European colonization. Ginio, *Ottoman Culture of Defeat*, 100–102, 126.

57   According to Stanford Shaw's survey, "stories of persecution and savagery from Crimea to Belgrade and Sarajevo were mingled with accounts of oppression from India to Algeria, and contrasted with the toleration and good treatment provided for non-Muslims in great Muslim empires including that of the Ottomans. . . . Soon these feelings were translated into a movement to establish contacts with all oppressed Muslims of the world, including those in British India and Egypt, Russian Central Asia and French Algeria and Tunisia." Shaw and Shaw, *History of Ottoman Empire and Modern Turkey*, 259.

58   See Panayi and Virdee, *Refugees and the End of Empire*; Bashir and Goldberg, *Holocaust and the Nakba*; Siddiqi, *Architecture of Migration*.

59   Nichols, *Theft Is Property*.

60   For the translation of property definitions between Russian and Ottoman Empires, and its impact on urban and rural environment, see my doctoral advisee's dissertation: Sarıçayır, "Property in Transition."

61   Çavuşoğlu, "Yugoslavya-Makedonya Topraklarından," 145.

62   Selim Deringil explains the cultural project of the Hamidian regime as follows: "Communication with his people and the outside world had therefore to be made through a world of symbols. These were based almost entirely on Islamic motifs. . . . It was Islam that would provide the store of symbols which could compete with the national symbols of the Greeks and the Serbs." Deringil, *The Well-Protected Domains*, 18.

63   Benjamin, "Theses on the Philosophy of History."

64   Broswimmer, *Ecocide*, 8.

65   These five causes were: human activity has transformed 30–50 percent of the land surface of the planet; most major rivers have been dammed or diverted; fertilizer plants have been producing more nitrogen than terrestrial ecosystems; fisheries have removed more than one third of production of coastal waters; and humans use more than half of world's freshwater runoff. Crutzen, "Geology of Mankind," 108.

66   Chakrabarty, "Climate of History."

67   A series of terms have been offered in search for a more accurate root cause of climate change, such as Capitalocene, Plantationocene, and Plasticene. Malm and Hornborg, "Geology of Mankind," 67; Haraway, "Tentacular Thinking"; Demos, *Decolonizing Nature*; Demos, *Against the Anthropocene*.

68   Edwards et al., *Dark Scenes from Damaged Earth*. In recent years, several architects have imagined utopian projects, such as The Line in Saudi Arabia, or *Planet City*, a film by Liam Young.

69   Nixon, *Slow Violence*.

70   Banham, *Architecture of the Well-Tempered Environment*, 9.

71   Banham, *Architecture of the Well-Tempered Environment*, 13.

72   Frampton, "Towards a Critical Regionalism."

73   Barber, *Modern Architecture and Climate*.

74   Barber, *Modern Architecture and Climate*, 25.

75   Barber, *Modern Architecture and Climate*, 12–13.

76   Uduku, "Modernist Architecture and 'the Tropical'"; Chang, *Genealogy of Tropical Architecture*; Ozaki, "Brazilian Atlantic."

77   Bernal, "Colonial Moral Economy"; Shklar, *Faces of Injustice*; Beckert, *Empire of Cotton*; Parenti, *Tropic of Chaos*; Edkins, *Whose Hunger?*

78   Eyal Weizman and Fazal Sheikh have famously described colonialism as climate change in the Negev Desert in today's Israel, rather than seeing climate change as a consequence. Weizman and Sheikh, *Conflict Shoreline*.

79   Taut, *Mimari Bilgisi*.

80   Bruno Taut suggested that almost all external conditions of architecture were a function of climate, the only basis for all the other real factors. Climate not only gave "a specificity, a tonality, a musical color to the building," but also mirrored the ethnic differences in body proportions and human expressions. Here, Taut came dangerously close to the racial theory where climatic differences in the world were used to claim an argument about racial difference, and subsequently, the superiority of one race over another. Taut, *Mimari Bilgisi*, 62, 65.

81   Akcan, *Architecture in Translation*.

82   McLean, *Regional and Town Planning*, 225.

83   Barber, *House in the Sun*.

84   Borasi and Zardini, *Sorry, Out of Gas*.

85   Basile, *Cool*; Sisson, "How Air Conditioning Shaped Modern Architecture"; Koheji, "Thermal Comfort and (Im)possible Futures."

86   Sultani, "Architecture in Iraq." See also Crinson, *Modern Architecture and the End of Empire*.

87   On architecture in Baghdad during this time, see Fethi, "Contemporary Architecture in Baghdad"; Isenstadt, "Faith in a Better Future"; Nooraddin, "Globalization and the Search"; Azara and Martinez, *Irak Restored*; Isenstadt and Rizvi, *Modernism and the Middle East*; Bernhardsson, "Faith in the Future"; Pieri, *Baghdad*; Al Chalabi, موسوعة العمارة العراقية; Akcan, *Abolish Human Bans*.

88   Akcan, "Democracy and War."

89   Coke, *Baghdad*.

90   William Polk also said, "Our reasons for identifying ourselves with [the former Iraqi government] were three: it existed, it was prepared to agree to join our side in the Cold War, and it was able to assure the flow of oil." Polk, "Lesson of Iraq."

91   Barber, *Modern Architecture and Climate*.

92   "The University of Baghdad: The Master Plan = Jami'at Baghdad, 1981," Rare LG 338.B33/U641X, Frances Loeb Special Collections, Harvard Graduate School of Design, Cambridge.

93   Klein, *Shock Doctrine*, 325–84.

94   "US Military Is a Bigger Polluter."

95   Proctor and Schiebinger, *Agnotology*.

96   Akcan, "North to South"; "Reparations for Colonization/Carbonization."

97   Foucault, *Surveiller et punir*.

98   Zinn, *People's History of the United States*.

99   Provence, *Last Ottoman Generation*.

100   Mazower, *Greek Revolution*.

101   Neglia, "Some Historiographical Notes on the Islamic City."

102   Neglia, "Some Historiographical Notes on the Islamic City," 14–15.

103   This is a list of major books and anthologies that collect scholarship from different countries: Raymond, *Osmanlı Döneminde Arap Kentleri*; Dumont and Georgeon, *Vivre dans l'empire Ottoman*; Yerasimos, "Tanzimat'ın Kent Reformları Üzerine"; Hanssen et al., *Empire in the City*; Raymond, "French Studies"; Eroğlu et al., *Osmanlı Vilayet Salnamelerinde Bağdat*; Çelik, *Empire, Architecture and the City*; Holod et al., *City in the Islamic World*; Arnaud, "Modernization of the Cities"; Ceylan, *Ottoman Origins of Modern Iraq*; Pieri, *Baghdad*; Reilly, *Ottoman Cities of Lebanon*; Flood and Necipoğlu, *Companion to Islamic Art and Architecture*.

Chapter 1. Enforced Disappearance: Urban Squares, Cemeteries, Memorials

1   "Mehmet screamed when he saw a photograph of a body whose face was cut into pieces with a knife, left shoulder burnt, armpits bruised, and neck strangled with metal." Günçikan, *Cumartesi Anneleri*, 134.

2   Hasan Ocak's story of reburial were recorded in articles in the daily newspaper *Milliyet*. "Ocak ailesi İstanbul Valisiyle görüştü," April 24, 1995 ; "Ocak için CHP işgali Sürüyor," April 24, 1995; "Kayıp Ocak Gömülmüş," May 17, 1995; "Ocak'ın Mezarı Belirlendi," May 19, 1995;

"Ocak Sırlarla Gömülü," May 23, 1995; "CHP'de İşgal Sone Erdi," May 24, 1995; Akcan interview with Maside Ocak, November 14, 2019, Istanbul.

3   The first group of families were the relatives of Hasan Ocak, Rıdvan Karakoç, Kenan Bilgin, Hasan Gülünay, Hüseyin Toraman, and Hanım Tosun.

4   The portrait was accompanied with the inscription "The losers are those who caused disappearances in Chile, Argentina and elsewhere" (Şili'de Arjantin'de öteki ülkelerde kaybedenler kaybetti).

5   Due to police violence, the weekly meetings had to be halted in 1999 to resume later. Some mothers were elderly and in bad health, and police violence and two- or three-day detentions were taking a toll on their bodies. The younger relatives and civil right activists offered to continue the demonstrations on behalf of the mothers, but the mothers did not want to leave them alone. As a result, the group decided to put a hold on the meetings for a while. Şanlı, "Yasın Protestoya Dönüşümünü İncelemek."

6   It is hard to determine precise numbers because the disappeared are not officially recorded as deceased—they are living-deads. Nonetheless, the Truth, Justice and Memory Center in Turkey compiled several sources and concluded that 1,353 people disappeared in Turkey between 1980 and 2013, with the highest numbers in regions with a Kurdish majority and in Istanbul. Seven hundred and fifty bodies were recorded disappeared in 1994–95 alone. Additionally, the Sweden-based Stockholm Center for Freedom published a report in June 2017, indicating that there were twelve additional cases of enforced disappearances under the emergency rule established after the 2016 coup attempt in Turkey. Göral et al., *Unspoken Truth*; Stockholm Center for Freedom, "Enforced Disappearances in Turkey."

7   The International Convention for the Protection of All Persons from Enforced Disappearance, adopted in 2006, came into effect in 2010; UN General Assembly, "International Convention." Turkey has still not signed the convention. The working group had started working in 1980.

8   UN General Assembly, *Report of the Working Group*.

9   Agamben, *Homo Sacer*.

10   Mbembe, "Necropolitics."

11   UN General Assembly, "International Convention."

12   For a recent comprehensive work, see Figari Layus, *Reparative Effects of Human Rights Trials*. For a history of Mothers of Plaza de Mayo, see Bouvard, *Revolutionizing Motherhood*. For articles discussing the case of disappearances specifically in Argentina, see Garibian, "Ghosts Also Die"; Montes, "Right to Truth"; Jacqmin, "When Human Claims Become

Rights." For a perspective on the relation between feminism and urban space, see Torre, "Claiming the Public Space."

13 See, for instance, Roht-Arriaza, "Need for Moral Reconstruction."

14 Here is a list of basic anthologies and periodicals: Hesse and Post, *Human Rights in Political Transitions*; Teitel, *Transitional Justice*; Rotberg and Thompson, *Truth vs. Justice*; Williams, *Transitional Justice*; Shaw and Waldorf, *Localizing Transitional Justice*; Teitel, *Globalizing Transitional Justice*; the *International Journal on Rule of Law, Transitional Justice and Human Rights* (2010–18).

15 UN Secretary-General, *Rule of Law and Transitional Justice*.

16 For the role of Inter-American Court of Human Rights, see Dykmann, "Impunity and the Right to Truth." For regional organizations in general, see Klinkner and Davis, *Right to Truth in International Law*.

17 For instance, UN Special Rapporteur Fabian Salvioli issued a report in July 2021 that suggests transitional justice mechanisms should examine the human rights violations committed during colonial times. Salvioli, *Promotion of Truth*.

18 Teitel, *Transitional Justice*.

19 De Greiff, "Theorizing Transitional Justice"; Williams, *Transitional Justice*, 31–77. Also see *Nomos* 51 (2012): 31–77.

20 Göral et al., *Unspoken Truth*, 81–84.

21 Ignatieff, "Human Rights," 313.

22 Especially, see Rotberg and Thompson, *Truth vs. Justice*.

23 Rolston, *Turing the Page*; Hainsworth, "Right to Truth," 28.

24 Hesse and Post, "Introduction," 14.

25 Especially, see Gutmann and Thomson, "Moral Foundation of Truth Commissions."

26 Garibian, "Ghosts Also Die," 518.

27 See several case studies in Williams, *Transitional Justice*; Turgis, "What Is Transitional Justice?"

28 De Greiff, "Theorizing Transitional Justice," 34, 55.

29 See chapters in Shaw and Waldorf, *Localizing Transitional Justice*.

30 Weinstein et al., "Stay the Hand of Justice."

31 "I am suggesting that human rights activism should be supplemented by an education that should suture the habits of democracy onto the earlier cultural formation. . . . the real effort should be to access and activate the tribes' indigenous 'democratic' structures to parliamentary democracy by patient and sustained efforts to learn from below." Spivak, "Righting Wrongs," 548.

32 I am taking the distinction between retrospective and prospective justice from Webber, "Forms of Transitional Justice"; Williams, *Transitional Justice*, 31–77. The Truth Justice and Memory Center's report on enforced disappearances in Turkey suggests architectural and art projects as a form of "compensation program." Göral et al., *Unspoken Truth*, 81.

33 For articles that emphasize the psychoanalytical perspective of grief, see Şanlı, "Yasın Protestoya Dönüşümünü İncelemek"; Şılar, "Bitmeyen yas."

34 Göral et al., *Unspoken Truth*, 54. Berfo Kırbayır's son, Cemil Kırbayır, disappeared on October 8, 1980; his case was taken to court in 2011. Even though she was given promises before she died in 2013, the case of her son was closed without conclusion on December 28, 2021.

35 Günçıkan, *Cumartesi Anneleri*, 135.

36 Crimp, "Mourning and Militancy"; Eng and Kazanjian, *Loss*. See also Akcan, *Architecture in Translation*.

37 Also see Şanlı, "Yasın Protestoya Dönüşümünü İncelemek"; Butler et al., *Vulnerability in Resistance*.

38 Teitel, *Transitional Justice*, 87.

39 According to the numbers compiled by the Truth, Justice and Memory Center in Turkey, the highest number of disappearances are in Diyarbakır (382), Şırnak (211), and Mardin (184). Istanbul is the fifth on the list. Göral et al., *Unspoken Truth*, 25.

40 Esra Akcan, interview with Maside Ocak and Sebla Ercan, November 14, 2019, Istanbul.

41 Testimony of Yıldırım Beğler, http://bianet.org/bianet/toplum/123989 -15-yildir-inanmadiniz-atilla-kiyata-da-mi-inanmayacaksiniz, accessed January 31, 2020.

42 Arendt, *Eichmann in Jerusalem*.

43 While the highest number was 518 in 1994 and 232 in 1995, it dropped to 33 in post-2000 period, with a new wave after the 2016 coup attempt. Göral et al., *Unspoken Truth*, 24.

44 Melek, quoted in Şanlı, "Yasın Protestoya Dönüşümünü İncelemek," 12.

45 The Kazlıçeşme anecdote is recorded in Baydar and İvegen, "Territories, Identities, and Thresholds."

46 Baydar and İvegen, "Territories, Identities, and Thresholds."

47 Also see Ahıska, "Counter-Movement, Space and Politics"; Ahıska, "Memory as Encounter."

48 Emine Rezzan Karaman associates this with a Spivakian strategic essentialism. The image of "traditional mothers with untraditional demands" confused authorities. The "value system, in which mothers are understood

[as] apolitical, initially helped the mothers gain access to public forums." Karaman, "Remember, S/he Was Here Once."

49   Bouvard, *Revolutionizing Motherhood*, 184, 188.

50   Curated by Çelenk Bafra, the artists were Elvan Alpay, biriken (Melis Tezkan, Okan Urun), Hera Büyüktaşçıyan, Antonio Cosentino, Burak Delier, Hasan Deniz, Cemal Emden, Barış Göktürk, Ali Kazma, and Vahit Tuna. In his installation titled "There Is No School on Saturday," Vahit Tuna illustrated the plan of the site as if it had been burned and destroyed. The accompanying images brought memories of conflict, such as police violence against the Saturday Mothers. Antonio Cosentino inserted the names of the disappeared including Hasan Ocak into the symbolic model of the city. Bafra, *Mektep Meydan Galatasaray*. The exhibition marked the 150th anniversary of the Galatasaray Lycee.

51   "I don't remember the first time I entered through the doors of the Galatasaray High School. When I close my eyes and try to relive those years, there is one reoccurring vision—a hazy, dizzying blow to my mind. An image forms out the fog of memory, first noise, then people. Sitting in front of the building, they are spread out over the square with photographs of other people in their hands. I walk through to get in. I know, yet I don't know who they are and why they are there. It is perhaps too much to bear. I read about them, but when I am there, I am not there. I can see, but I am also blinded by the weight of it all. I am a teenager. I can't come to terms with it. I walk on. It is a Saturday. It is every Saturday. I know this and I don't know it at all. They are the Saturday Mothers. I look down and enter the school . . . *Saturday* is a personal exercise in memory. I wish to erase that forced memory from my teenage years by rebuilding it." Artist statement during exhition.

52   The UN, Amnesty International, Turkey's Human Rights Association, and Truth, Justice, and Memory NGO.

53   Bouvard, *Revolutionizing Motherhood*; Gordon, *Ghostly Matters*.

54   Aylin Tekiner, "On the Wall," http://aylintekiner.com/aylin.asp?l=en&kid =4&alt_kid=12&alt_kid1=0&id=47.

55   "Kemikler vurur kıyılarına Kürt denizinin," *Gazete Duvar*; Testimony of Yıldırım Beğler, http://bianet.org/bianet/toplum/123989-15-yildir -inanmadiniz-atilla-kiyata-da-mi-inanmayacaksiniz, accessed January 31, 2020; Taylor, "Traumatic Memes."

56   Butler, *Precarious Life*, 20.

57   Eldem, *İstanbul'da Ölüm*.

58   Kentel, "Assembling 'Cosmopolitan' Pera."

59   A recent exhibition at the Istanbul Research Institute (IAE) illustrated this history with relevant documents and photographs. "Aralıktan Bakmak."

60   Marmara, *Pancaldı*; Demirakın, "Expropriation as a Modernizing Tool"; Ueno, "Urban Politics in 19th-Century Istanbul"; Gölunu, "From Graveyards to the 'People's Gardens.'"

61   Nalci and Dağlıoğlu, "Istanbul Radyosu Arazisi." Also see Parla and Özgül, "Property, Dispossession, and Citizenship in Turkey." For more on the property regime that prevents ex-Ottoman Armenians from reclaiming their property in today's Turkey, see Akçam, "Spirit of the Law."

62   "Cumartesi Anneleri Sabahattin Ali'yi Andı," *Cumhuriyet*.

63   "Cumartesi Anneleri, Kaybedilen Ermeni Aydınları Andı," *Evrensel*.

64   Esra Akcan, interview with Maside Ocak and Sebla Ercan, November 14, 2019, Istanbul.

65   "Mağdurlar İşkencehanenin 5 Yıldızlı Otele." The repurposing of torture spaces as shopping malls or entertainment spaces is quite common. For a critique of the process in Latin America, see Draper, "Business of Memory."

66   Gates-Madsen, "Marketing and Sacred Space"; Huyssen, "Memory Sites in an Expanded Field."

67   Collins, "Moral Economy of Memory."

68   Collins, "Moral Economy of Memory."

69   Read and Wyndham, *Narrow but Endlessly Deep*.

70   Robben, *Argentina Betrayed*.

71   "The major required task for any [modern] society today is to take responsibility for its past. . . . Human activism in the world today depends very much on the depth and breadth of memory discourses in public media." Huyssen, *Present Pasts*, 94–95.

72   See, for example, the *Architectural Review* (1948), *Progressive Architecture* (1948), and *Perspecta* (1953, 1967), *Harvard Architecture Review* 4 (1984), and *Oppositions* 25 (1983). For a review of the modern monumentality debate, see Collins and Collins, "Monumentality."

73   Mumford, *Culture of Cities*, 438.

74   See Sert et al., "Nine Points on Monumentality"; Giedion, " Need for a New Monumentality"; Mock, "Built in USA," 25.

75   For a discussion of Lin's memorial, see Griswold, "Vietnam Veterans Memorial"; McLeod, "Battle for the Monument"; Struken, "Wall, the Screen, and the Image."

76   Gillis, *Commemorations*.

77   Robben, *Argentina Betrayed*.

78   Horkheimer and Adorno, *Dialectic of Enlightenment*.

79   Young, *Texture of Memory*; Huyssen, *Present Pasts*.

80 For my views, see Akcan, "Apology and Triumph."

81 Gates-Madsen, "Marketing and Sacred Space"; Huyssen, "Memory Sites in an Expanded Field"; Levey, "Between Marginalization and Decentralization of Memory"; Friedrich, "The Memoryscape in Buenos Aires"; Robben, *Argentina Betrayed.*

82 Viebach, "Aletheia and the Making of the World."

83 Sodaro, *Exhibiting Atrocity.*

84 Gates-Madsen, "Marketing and Sacred Space"; Bilbija and Payne, *Accounting for Violence*, 157.

85 Collins, "Moral Economy of Memory."

86 Huyssen, *Present Pasts*, 21

87 For a collection of essays discussing the memory market in Argentina, Brazil, Chile, Mexico, Peru, and Uruguay, see Bilbija and Payne, *Accounting for Violence.*

88 The three completed sculptures are William Tucker's *Victoria*, Dennis Oppenheim's *Monument to Escape*, and Nicolas Guagnini's *30000*. Friedrich, "Memoryscape in Buenos Aires."

89 Frequent economic and social crises have halted its functioning and reversed the post-dictatorship confrontation with Argentina's former atrocities. Levey, "Between Marginalization and Decentralization of Memory."

90 Rothberg, *Multidirectional Memory.*

91 Huyssen, *Present Pasts.*

92 Mandel, *Cosmopolitan Anxieties*, 109-40; Yurdakul and Bodemann, "'We Don't Want to Be the Jews of Tomorrow.'"

93 Şenocak, *Gefährliche Verwandtschaft*. See also Adelson, *Turkish Turn*, 79-122; Huyssen, "Diaspora and Nation."

94 Özyürek, "Export-Import Theory," 41.

95 For more discussion, see Akcan, *Open Architecture*; Akcan, "Apology and Triumph."

96 Şenocak, *Gefährliche Verwandtschaft*, 89.

97 For more discussion, see the "Germany to Germany" panel as part of the AY 2020–21 "Repair and Reparations" series. This panel brought together scholars who provided new perspectives on the historical and pending reparations in the eras after colonization, Nazism, and communism in Germany, as well as the significance of these restitutions in serving as a model for transitional justice and international law. We gathered to discuss postwar, post-unification, and pending postcolonial reparations in Germany, not to blur the distinctions between the three, or to rank suffering, but to see if and how this dialogue can build solidarities,

identify double standards, if any, and work toward overcoming them. We explored both material and moral reparations, such as return and the restitution of property that had been confiscated, monetary payments as compensation, and educational steps to take responsibility for the past. The panel not only acknowledged reparations to ex-citizens and refugees, but also questioned the limits of established formulas and the inequality of reparations throughout the history of today's Germany. Akcan, "Germany to Germany."

More panels in the "Repair and Reparations" series can be found at Einaudi Center for International Studies, Institute for European Studies, "IES Migrations Series (up to 2021)," https://einaudi.cornell.edu /programs/institute-european-studies/events/ies-migrations-series-2021.

98   Rozas-Krause, "Apology and Commemoration."

99   See Chicago Torture Justice Center, https://www.chicagotorturejustice .org/.

100   Serrano, "Final Design Picked for Memorial."

101   Democracy Now!, "Angela Davis: Toppling of Confederate Statues."

102   For more discussion, see Akcan, "Belgium to Congo."

103   Coates, "Case for Reparations."

104   See, for instance, King and Page, "Towards Transitional Justice?"; Satz, "Countering the Wrongs of the Past."

105   Meister, "Forgiving and Forgetting," 135.

106   National Park Service, National Register of Historic Places, "National Register Database and Research," https://www.nps.gov/subjects /nationalregister/database-research.htm. Courtesy Sara Bronin.

107   Amnesty International, "Listen to the Saturday Mothers."

108   Mihr, *Regime Consolidation and Transitional Justice*, 359–61, 370–71, 381.

109   Kurban, *Reparations and Displacement in Turkey*.

110   For human rights struggles, organizations, and NGOs in Turkey, see Arat, *Human Rights in Turkey*.

111   Türkmen, "Turkey's Participation in Human Rights Regimes."

112   Mihr, *Regime Consolidation and Transitional Justice*, 375.

113   For more discussion and my views on its impact on architecture, see Akcan, "Translation Theory and the Intertwined Histories."

114   See, for instance, Ishay, *History of Human Rights*. One may also consult Amartya Sen (citations above), who argued that the cultural critique of human rights and the perception of so-called Asian values as different from human rights does not survive critical scrutiny. For a discussion of the encounter between Jesuit thinkers and the Americas' Indigenous

communities, as well as the impact of this encounter in the production of human rights values such as freedom and equality, see Graeber and Wengrow, *Dawn of Everything*,

115   For a map that shows which countries ratified which of the UN's eighteen human rights conventions, see United Nations Human Rights, Status of Ratification Interactive Dashboard, https://indicators.ohchr.org/.

116   UNICEF, "16 children Including Greta Thunberg."

Chapter 2. Partition: Camps, Model Villages, Retrofits

1   "Lausanne Peace Treaty VI"; Pentzopoulos, *Balkan Exchange*, 258–59.

2   Psomiades, *Fridtjof Nansen*.

3   For much of the twentieth century, the histories of the "exchange of populations" have been written from the differing perspectives of Greek and Turkish nationalism. Scholarly books that analyze the event in the context of both countries have started appearing only in the first decade of the twenty-first century, even though nationalist perspectives persisted even to this day. For major book-length treatments, see Pentzopoulos, *Balkan Exchange*; Arı, *Büyük Mübadele*; Hirschon, *Crossing the Aegean*; Cengizkan, *Mübadele*; Yıldırım, *Diplomacy and Displacement*; Kitromilides, "Greek-Turkish Population Exchange"; Psomiades, *Fridtjof Nansen*; Balta, *Exchange of Populations*; Lytra, *When Greeks and Turks Meet*; Özsu, *Formalizing Displacement*; Iğsız, *Humanism in Ruins*; Erdal, *Ulus Devlet Sürecinde*. For a review of the history of accounts on the population exchange, see Tsitselikis, "Convention of Lausanne."

4   Özsu, *Formalizing Displacement*, 125.

5   Iğsız, *Humanism in Ruins*, 5.

6   The international law of minority protection is usually traced back to the 1648 Peace of Westphalia, but it developed in the early nineteenth century and persisted until World War I. Minority protection laws available during World War I were of four kinds: treaties, specific bilateral agreements, statements inserted to peace treaties, and declarations required to be part of the League. See Özsu, *Formalizing Displacement*.

7   Vretu Meneksepulu's testimony at CAMS. Millas, *Göç*, 161.

8   Kasaba, *Moveable Empire*, 15. Also see Freitag et al., *City in the Ottoman Empire*.

9   The literature on nation formation and theories of nationalism is extensive. For foundational works, see especially Anderson, *Imagined Communities*; Chatterjee, *Nationalist Thought and the Colonial World*; Smith, *Theories of Nationalism*; Gellner, *Nations and Nationalism*; Özkırımlı, *Theories of Nationalism*.

10 Kasaba, *Moveable Empire.*

11 Sarkar, *Swadeshi Movement in Bengal.*

12 "Lausanne Peace Treaty VI."

13 Özsu, *Formalizing Displacement,* 79.

14 Nichols, *Theft Is Property.*

15 The calculations of Turkish and Greek wealth in respective countries differed significantly according to the two authorities. The same land could be priced at 5 million by Turkish but sixty-five thousand by Greek authorities in comparable currencies, Belli, *Türkiye ve Yunanistan Arasında,* 46–47.

16 The Soviet Union joined at a later date, and the United States declared that it was "entitled to be present and to be heard in equality" but not vote. Applications by India, Spain, and Denmark to participate were rejected.

17 The archive holds 145,000 pages of data, 4,832 photographs, and 495 manuscripts of which forty-four were written before 1922. Two migrants from today's Turkey provided translation services. Funded by the French state until 1962 (probably because its cofounder Octave Merlier was the director of French Institute in Athens), the archive also made a name as a platform for leftist intellectuals. Merlier, "Présentation du Centre d'Études d'Asie Mineure"; Yiannakopoulos, *Refugee Greece,* 46. Also see Papailias, *Genres of Recollection,* 93–138.

18 The testimonies were published in two volumes as *Exodus* in 1980 and 1982; and translated into Turkish in 2001 by Herkül Millas. Millas, *Göç.*

19 Papailias, *Genres of Recollection,* 110, 111.

20 The chronological marker for this turn is the publication of *Emanet Çeyiz* (Entrusted trousseau). In his interview with scholar Aslı Iğsız, its author Kemal Yalçın declared he preferred to cast his collection of interviews as a literary novel because he thought the public was not ready for facts. Yalçın, *Emanet Çeyiz;* Iğsız, *Humanism in Ruins.*

21 Especially see Güvenç, *Avrupa Kültür Başkenti Mübadele Müzesi; Mübadiller.* For additional testimonial accounts, see Tevfik, *İnsan ve Mekan Yüzüyle Mübadele.*

22 Cappadoccia is the name used in historical sources for the area around today's towns Aksaray, Nevşehir, Kayseri, and Niğde. Its settlement is traced back to the Paleolithic age, but more is known after the region becomes part of the Eastern Roman Empire (later named Byzantium due to the empire's division in 395). The region has been at the crossroads of multiple religions and communities since the medieval period. Almost all locations have a Greek and a Turkish name due to this multicultural existence and the Turkification policies following the population exchange.

While reconstructing residents' stories, I will either use both names or alternate the names, depending on the name used by the relevant community.

23 Between 1952 and 1966, Seraphim Rizos submitted forty-two manuscripts and several photographs about Cappadocia to the Center for Asia Minor Studies in Athens. He was the editor of *Anatoli* (four issues in 1930) and *Phoni tis Istiaias* (eight issues in 1934). He compiled the names of 878 refugees from Sinasos with their occupations. Balta, "Recording of the Settlements"; Balta, "Exchange of Populations," 35–39.

24 Anagnostakis and Balta, *Dècouverte de la Cappadoce*.

25 Benlisoy and Benlisoy, *Hıristiyan Türkler*.

26 The number of Turkish-speaking Orthodox Christians living in Central Anatolia varies between 139,199 and 500,000 according to the 1914 Ottoman census and 1922 British foreign intelligence sources, respectively. Benlisoy and Benlisoy, *Hiristiyan Türkler*, 154. Vasso Stelaku mentions the number of expelled Orthodox Cappadocians as 44,432. Stelaku, "Space, Place, and Identity."

27 Aytaş, *Mübadelenin Hüzünlü Mirası*, 34–35.

28 Seraphim Rizos in the CAMS ethnography project; reprinted in Balta, *Exchange of Populations*, 93–94.

29 Testimony of Aliye Özbay, in Aytaş, *Mübadelenin Hüzünlü Mirası*, 39–40.

30 For instance, see the testimonies of Panayotis Marselis, Nikolas Papanikolau,Vasilas Kuçomitos, and Evripidu Lafazani in Millas, *Göç*; those of Vasili Vasilyadis and Angela Katrini and Çirkince habitants Mustafa Acar and Ismet Altay in Yalçın, *Emanet Çeyiz*; and those of Mürvet Duman and Şükran Ergün in Millas, *Onlar İki Kere Yabancıydılar*.

31 Testimony of Kalistenis Mustakidu, in Millas, *Göç*, 185–86.

32 Testimony of Sofia Devletoğlu, in Millas, *Göç*, 192.

33 He probably produced this booklet in 1924–26. Rizos, *Sinasos*, 1924 [in Karamanlı, i.e., written in Turkish with Greek alphabet], CAMS Archives. I would like to thank Aslı Özbay for providing me with a copy of this original work. Seraphim Rizos later wrote the two-volume book on Sinasos that was reprinted by CAMS in 2007. In his memoirs, he said he took the negatives to Istanbul before leaving for Greece, and asked the Istanbul committee overseeing their transportation to make a hundred reproductions. He also participated in the oral history project later as a Greek citizen in the 1950s. Rizos, *Σινασός*, 2007; Balta, "Recording of the Settlements."

34 This paragraph was reproduced in Balta, *Sinasos*, 30.

35 Balta, *Sinasos*, 151–52.

36   Apart from the testimonies, fiction writers have also imagined immi-
      grants' stories, either through their firsthand experience or based on their
      relatives' accounts. Dido Sotiriou's *Farewell Anatolia* and Yaşar Kemal's
      Fırat Suyu Kan Akıyor Baksana are the foundational novels in Greece
      and Turkey. Recently, there has been a boom of short stories, penned by
      the children and grandchildren of migrants. Sotiriou, *Farewell Anatolia*;
      Kemal, *Fırat Suyu Kan Akıyor Baksana*; Pekin, *Mübadele Öyküleri*; Özsoy,
      Ah Vre Memleket; *Mübadele Öyküleri*. For literary and film narrative
      criticism, see Millas, "Exchange of Populations in Turkish Literature";
      Mackridge, "Myth of Asia Minor"; Lemos, "Early Literature of the Asia
      Minor Disaster"; Süar, "Yunan Sinemasında Türk-Yunan Nüfus Mübade-
      lesi"; Bedlek, *Imagined Communities in Greece and Turkey*.

37   Issopoulos, "Greeks of Sinasos," 175.

38   Halaçoğlu, *Balkan Harbi Sırasında*, 153–57.

39   Yıldırım, *Diplomacy and Displacement*, 157–79.

40   Morgenthau, *I Was Sent to Athens*, 103, 107.

41   Some of these IDs have been donated to the Museum of Exchange of
      Populations in Çatalca, and can be viewed there. See Akcan, "*Antallagi/
      Mübadele* Ships." The bibliography on the disciplinary use of photogra-
      phy would be extensive. For major works pertaining to Britain, colonial
      India, and Ottoman Turkey, see especially Tagg, *Burden of Representa-
      tion*; Pinney, *Camera Indica*; Hight and Sampson, *Colonialist Photogra-
      phy*; Shaw, *Possessors and Possessed*; Akcan, "Society of Political Images."

42   The ships carried the migrants along the following routes to Turkey: from
      Salonica to Tekfurdaği; Kalikratya to Istanbul and Mudanya; from Kavala
      to Istanbul, Zonguldak, Sinop, Samsun, Ordu, Giresun, İzmit, Tekfurdağı,
      Gelibolu, Bandırma, and Burhaniye; from Crete to Mersin, Silifke, Mar-
      maris, Bodrum, Gökabad, Göllük, Ayvalık, Çanakkale, and Erdek. Arı,
      Büyük Mübadele.

43   Morgenthau, *I Was Sent to Athens*, 101.

44   Quoted in Tsitselikis, "Convention of Lausanne," 216.

45   Yıldırım, *Diplomacy and Displacement*.

46   Balta, *Exchange of Populations*, 83–84; Stelaku, "Space, Place, and Iden-
      tity," 179-92. *Nea* means "new." Many towns and urban neighborhoods in
      today's Greece are named in reference to the departure place of the mi-
      grants who arrived with the Exchange of Populations.

47   Aytaş, *Mübadelenin Hüzünlü Mirası*, 18, 46.

48   Yiannakopoulos, *Refugee Greece*, 33.

49   Sharpe, *In the Wake*, 40–41.

50   Testimony of Kamile Yakar, in Aytaş, *Mübadelenin Hüzünlü Mirası*, 39.

51 Sipahioğlu, "Odisseus'u Aramak," 33. Also see Özsoy, *Ah Vre Memleket.*

52 Fatsea, "Migrant Builders and Craftsmen."

53 Morgenthau, *I Was Sent to Athens,* 237–243; Tzonis and Rodi, *Greece,* 76.

54 Leonidas Bonis Papers (1896–1963), ANA _023; Patroklos Karantinos Papers (1903–1976), ANA_108; Kleon Krantonellis Papers (1912–1978), ANA_069, Modern Greek Architecture Archives, Benaki Museum, Athens. For more on Kleon Krantonellis, see chapter 4.

55 Nikos Zoumboulidis Papers (1888–1969), ANA 24, Modern Greek Architecture Archives, Benaki Museum, Athens; L. Sotiriou, Νικόλαος Ζουμπουλίδης.

56 For the Greece-Bulgaria exchange, see Dragostinova, *Between Two Motherlands.*

57 Pentzopoulos, *Balkan Exchange.* The number of refugees was recorded in April 1923, and is believed to be much lower than those who migrated due to deaths during transportation.

58 Yiannakopoulos, *Refugee Greece,* 33.

59 Morgenthau, *I Was Sent to Athens,* 293.

60 Tzonis and Rodi, *Greece,* 76.

61 "Greek Refugee Settlement" (1926). Quoted in Pentzopoulos, *Balkan Exchange,* 101–2.

62 Hirschon, *Heirs of the Greek Catastrophe,* 24.

63 Yiannakopoulos, *Refugee Greece,* 33; see also Colonas, "Housing and the Architectural Expression."

64 Photographs in the Center for Asia Minor Studies Archive.

65 Gerber and Myofa, "Δουργούτι"; Myofa and Papadias, "Development of the Neighborhood of Dourgouti"; "Μαγική πόλις" [Magic city].

66 Koundouros, *Magiki Polis.*

67 Myofa and Papadias, "The Development of the Neighborhood of Dourgouti."

68 Tzonis and Rodi, *Greece,* 76–77.

69 This number was announced in the UN's official newsletter in November 1930, p. 1481. It is repeated in Pentzopoulos, *Balkan Exchange,* and Belli, *Mübadele.*

70 Kontogiorgi, "Economic Consequences Following."

71 See, for instance, Biris, "Founding of Modern Athens"; Theocharopoulou, *Builders, Housewives.*

72 Yerolympos, "Inter-War Town Planning," 142.

73 Colonas, "Housing and the Architectural Expression."

74   Morgenthau, *I Was Sent to Athens*.

75   Balta, "Recording of the Settlements," 132. Also see Issopoulos, "Greeks of Sinasos."

76   See the testimonies of Prokopians, in Balta, *Exchange of Populations*.

77   This was the declaration of the Settlement Ministry's Mustafa Necati (Uğural). Cengizkan, *Mübadele*, 21.

78   According to one assessment, eleven thousand beds were provided in Istanbul as well as in southern and northern port cites. Istanbul: Ahırkapı, 2,000; İplikhane, 1,000; Çatalca, 300; Gelibolu, 500. Menteşe/Muğla: Güllük, 300; Bodrum, 200; Marmaris, 250; Fethiye, 500; Çanakkale, 300; Erdek, 1,000/1,500; Samsun, 3,000; Edirne, 1,000. Erdal, *Ulus Devlet Sürecinde*.

79   "Muhacirin Misafirhaneleri Ta'limatnameleri" (November 1923), TCBCA Türkiye Cumhuriyeti Başbakanlık Arşivleri, 272. 12/40.42.3. Reprinted in Cengizkan, *Mübadele*, 115–16.

80   I have extracted these from individual testimonies, and some of these cases were even discussed in the Parliament. Arı, *Büyük Mübadele*, 109–10.

81   Aytaş, *Mübadelenin Hüzünlü Mirası*, 38, 40, 48.

82   Mustafa Acar's testimony, in Yalçın, *Emanet Çeyiz*, 174.

83   1. Sinop, Samsun, Ordu, Giresun, Trabzon, Gümüşhane, Amasya, Tokat, Çorum; 2. Edirne, Tekfurdağı, Gelibolu, Kırkkilisi, Çanakkale; 3. Balıkesir; 4. İzmir, Manisa, Aydın, Menteşe, Afyon; 5. Bursa; Istanbul, Çatalca, Zonguldak; 6. İzmit, Bolu, Bilecik, Eskişehir, Kütahya; 7. Antalya, Isparta, Burdur; 8. Konya, Niğde, Kayseri, Aksaray, Kırşehir; 9. Adana, Mersin, Silifke, Kozan, Ayıntab, Maraş. Arı, *Büyük Mübadele*.

84   Yıldırım, *Diplomacy and Displacement*, 146.

85   Koker, "Lessons in Refugeehood."

86   Belli, *Mübadele*, 101.

87   Records show that 88,700 houses were distributed to exchanged populations, and 20,797 to refugees. Furthermore, 172,029 houses were given to migrants from Romania, Bulgaria, the Soviet Union, and Yugoslavia. *İskan Tarihçesi*, 137–8.

88   Dündar, *İttihat ve Terakki'nin Müslümanları*, 213–15.

89   The Secretary of Exchange Mustafa Necati declared that one hundred thousand houses were left vacant due to the emigration of Greeks, but only twenty thousand were eligible for the relocated, as the rest were squatted in or looted. Many communities had to be replaced as the previously vacant houses were occupied. The vacated Greek and Armenian houses in big cities such as Istanbul, İzmir, Samsun, and

Bursa were particularly in demand, given the already existing housing shortage. According to a news report, in İzmir, 44 of the vacated Greek houses were occupied by state officers, 27 by disaster refugees, 14 by pseudorefugees, 53 by exchanged migrants, and 13 of the best ones by ministers. Arı, *Büyük Mübadele*, 12–13, 115–16. Many migrants also mentioned that some of the houses were already occupied. Yalçın, *Emanet Çeyiz*.

90   Cengizkan, *Mübadele*, 50.

91   Koyunoğlu, "Merhum Mimar Arif Hikmet," 48.

92   See also Keyder, *Türkiye'de Devlet ve Sınırlar*.

93   Quoted in Arı, *Büyük Mübadele*, 100.

94   See, for example, Arı, *Büyük Mübadele*; Halaçoğlu, *Balkan Harbi Sırasında*; Erdal, *Ulus Devlet Sürecinde*.

95   Bookman, *Demographic Struggle for Power*, 2.

96   Morland, *Demographic Engineering*, 3.

97   Also see McGarry, "Demographic Engineering"; Şeker, "Forced Population Movements."

98   Dündar, *Ittihat ve Terakki'nin Müslümanları*; Dündar, *Modern Türkiye'nin Şifresi*, 194–248.

99   There was a distinction between war-migrant (*mühacir*) and refugee (*mülteci*). The former referred to people who migrated to remaining Ottoman lands due to the loss of land in wars; the latter indicated subjects who wanted to become Ottoman. While war migrants and refugee numbers after the Balkan War required the construction of hundreds of villages, no records show such a massive undertaking, amplifying the housing shortage for the new republic. İpek, *Rumeli'den Anadolu'ya*; Dündar, *Ittihat ve Terakki'nin Müslümanları*, 201–13.

100 Psomiades, *Fridtjof Nansen*.

101 The 1934 Settlement Law was also advertised in the regime's propaganda magazine *La Turquie Kemaliste*. "L'Immigration en Turquie."

102 This was Sadri Maksudi's statement. The Minister of Interior Şükrü Kaya said, "This law will create a country speaking with one language, thinking in the same way and sharing the same sentiment." Both quotations: Kaya, TBMM *Zabıt Ceridesi*, Devre IV, Cilt 23, Ictima: 3, 14/06/1935, p. 71, p. 141, quoted in Ülker, "Assimilation, Security and Geographical."

103 Some of the Balkan immigrants were settled in Diyarbakır with the 1934 settlement law. According to the state journal *La Turquie Kemaliste*, fifteen hundred immigrants were settled in East Anatolia in three hundred houses. Fifteen thousand houses were constructed for the new

immigrants from Romania, Bulgaria, and Yugoslavia, and three thousand were on the way. "Immigration en Turquie," 16. Tekeli, "Osmanlı İmparatorluğu'ndan Günümüze."

104   The numbers and spelling of place names in this case are taken from the RSC's "Ethnographic Map of Greek Macedonia," Pentzopoulos, *Balkan Exchange*, insert between pp. 136–37.

105   Karakasidou, *Fields of Wheat*, 162–73.

106   See Colonas, "Housing and the Architectural Expression."

107   Colonas, "Housing and the Architectural Expression."

108   Quoted in Colonas, "Housing and the Architectural Expression," 174.

109   Hirschon, *Heirs of the Greek Catastrophe*.

110   Colonas, "Housing and the Architectural Expression."

111   Hirschon, "History, Memory and Emotion."

112   Filippidis, *Urban Housing of the 30s*.

113   Tournikiotis, "Public Interest in Modern Architecture"; Karolyi, "Refurbishment or Demolition."

114   "Siedlung in Athen."

115   Eres, "Türkiye'de Çağdaş Köy Kurma."

116   See Cengizkan, *Mübadele*, for drawings.

117   For figures, see Dündar, "Balkan Savaşı Sonrasında"; İpek, *Rumeli'den Anadolu'ya*.

118   Initially, fourteen model villages with fifty dwellings, a mosque, and a school were ordered: 7 in Samsun, 2 in İzmir and Bursa, 1 in İzmit, Antalya, and Adana. Yet orders were placed to construct more villages for two hundred dwellings in İzmit, İzmir, Bursa, and Bilecik on fertile grounds, close to water, next to ruined zones that were impossible for the locals to construct. The number eventually reached sixty-nine. Erdal, *Ulus Devlet Sürecinde*.

119   Selçuk Seçkin has visited and observed the transformation of these villages. Seçkin, "Mübadele Sonrası Kurulan."

120   See Akcan, *Architecture in Translation*.

121   Burhan Arif, "Köy Projesi"; Ünsal, "Sincan Köyü Planı."

122   Kazim Dirlik prepared the "Ideal Republican Village" project in 1937, and gave it to A. Afetinan. Afetinan, *Devletçilik İlkesi ve Türkiye*; Mortaş, "Köy Evi Tipleri."

123   Abdullah Ziya, "Halkevleri Trakya Göçmen Evleri."

124   Burhan Arif, "Köy Projesi," 320.

125 Abdullah Ziya, "Köy Mimarisi"; Abdullah Ziya, "Gün Geçiminde Kerpiç Köy Yapısı"; Hatif Öğe, "Köy Yapılarımız."

126 In a two-part article in 1936, Zeki Sayar introduced the concept of inner colonization (*iç kolonizasyon*), which he translated from French "koloni-sation intérieure," but which was also an explicit reference to Victor Aime Huber's German term *Innenkolonisation*. What Sayar had in mind was immigrant housing. He pointed out the urgency to build new residential neighborhoods (*Siedlungen*) to settle the relocated populations immi-grating to Turkey mostly from the Balkans and Greece after the founda-tion of the republic. Sayar identified the villages built for this purpose in Trakya, Diyarbakır, and Ankara as low-quality settlements that needed to be improved by the standards of European mass housing. "As far as the architecture of the village is concerned, we may categorize the new agri-cultural colonies in Europe built for the unemployed industrial workers, and the settlements for immigrants in our country under the same term. For this reason, it is extremely useful for us to examine European prac-tices"; Sayar, "İç kolonizasyon," 231. In addition to architecture, he listed legal matters, financing, and organization as the three other main institu-tions of inner colonization. Sayar's examples were ideologically mixed: he praised the Jewish colonies in Palestine, the socialist co-ops and the Na-tional Socialist agricultural colonies in Germany with equal levels of en-thusiasm. Sayar introduced "rational house plans," "standardized building parts" (such as doors and windows), and the study of several "types" as opposed to one standard plan as the main architectural considerations for immigrant mass housing. Sayar, "İç kolonizasyon." For more discus-sion, see Akcan, *Çeviride Modern Olan*.

127 Tzonis and Rodi, *Greece*, 115.

128 One can detect the state-built rectangular structure from its white walls, green door, and flat roof, and locate the additions such as the veranda with a red tiled roof and a big room with a sloped ceiling to the left, another room to the back, and two smaller structures to the right.

129 L. Sotiriou, Νικόλαος Ζουμπουλίδης, 17.

130 Nikos Zoumboulidis Papers, ANA 24, Modern Greek Architecture Ar-chives, Benaki Museum, Athens.

131 Balta, *Exchange of Populations*; Stelaku, "Space, Place, and Identity."

132 Kafkoula, "In Search of Urban Reform."

133 L. Sotiriou, Νικόλαος Ζουμπουλίδης.

134 L. Sotiriou, Νικόλαος Ζουμπουλίδης.

135 Benlisoy and Benlisoy, *Hıristiyan Türkler*, 183–225.

136 Kitromilides, "Greek Irredentism."

137 Quoted in Colonas, "Housing and the Architectural Expression," 173.

138 "L'Immigration en Turquie."

139 Sofia Devletoğlu's testimony for CAMS, in Millas, *Göç*, 195.

140 Aliye Özbay's interview, in Aytaş, *Mübadelenin Hüzünlü Mirası*, 42–43.

141 Şefik Kırca's diary, in İhsan Tevfik, *İnsan ve Mekan*, 93.

142 When they first found the void that led to the discovery of the Byzantine church buried under debris, Turgut Cansever used to advise the Argos team. Aslı Özbay acknowledges Serkan Bayram as the on-site architect, and praises the hotel's owner Gökşin Ilıcalı for the results, who took a great deal of economic risks and sacrifices in the tourism industy. The government had curiously assessed the threat of falling rocks as the reason for this zoning. Özbay states that the villagers welcomed the subsidized housing in the newly growing modern part of town, which they were eligible for because of living in a disaster zone. As the state subsidy was not sufficient, they dismantled the stones in their old houses and reused them in new constructions. They piled the construction debris and trash on the ruins of the abandoned village, which slowly overfilled the subterranean living spaces. Özbay, "Yok Edilen Tarihi Bir Mahallenin."

143 See especially Aktar, *Varlık Vergisi ve Türkleştirme Politikaları*; Akar, *Aşkale Yolcuları*; Demir and Akar, *Istanbul'un Son Sürgünleri*.

144 See especially Güven, *Cumhuriyet Dönemi Azınlık Politikaları*; Vryonis, *Mechanism of Catastrophe*; Bali, *Anti-Greek Riots*.

145 For more discussion, see Yannas, "Human Rights Condition."

146 Belli, *Mübadele*, 101.

147 Belli, *Mihri Belli'nin Anıları*, 255–326. For his motivations and conclusions of his thesis on the 1923 exchange of populations, see p. 262.

148 Ediz, "Uyuyan Köyü Uyandırmak."

149 Ediz, "Uyuyan Köyü Uyandırmak"; Köymen, "Kayaköy."

150 Aktüre, "From Greek Town to Turkish Tourism"; Köymen, "Kayaköy."

151 Özbay and Idil, "Settlement We Have Discovered."

152 Özbay and Aytaş, "Mustafapaşa'yı Korumak İçin Bilmemiz Gerekenler" (brochure distributed for Mustafapaşa Yerel Gündem 21. Kent Konseyi, 2006, author's collection).

153 *Common Cultural Heritage*.

154 See especially testimonies of Elefteria and Paulos Staboulidis, Kayserili Anastasiya, Prodromos Vasilyadis, Aleco Ferteklidis, Muhittin and Sabiha Yavuz, Havva Aykan, Ismet Altay, Nejat Atam, and Ilya Akritidis, in Yalçın, *Emanet Çeyiz*; Tevfik, *İnsan ve Mekan Yüzüyle*. Going back has also been a common trope of literary works.

155 Zoumboulidis to Rizos, letter from Sinasos, July 8, 1957, in *Sinasos*, 149.

156 The travelers shared their memories in *Mübadiller: Onlar İki Kere Yabancıydılar.*

157 Ballian, *Relics of the Past*; Güvenç, *Avrupa Kültür Başkenti Mübadele Müzesi.*

158 Ballian, "Relics of the Past," 36–56.

159 Petropoulou, "Voice of the Heirlooms," 28–30.

160 For further critique of this memory boom in Turkey, see Iğsız, *Humanism in Ruins.*

161 Rohidea, "Sinasos."

162 Özbay, "Yok Edilen Tarihi Bir Mahallenin," 125.

163 Özbay, "Yok Edilen Tarihi Bir Mahallenin," 131.

164 Argos Yapı, "Uçhisar'ın Kadınları İçin."

165 I am using the word *cosmopolitan ethics* here in the same sense that I have defined in my previous work. Akcan, *Architecture in Translation*; Akcan, *Open Architecture.*

166 For more discussion and information on my analysis of Hagia Sophia's conversion into a mosque, see Akcan and Christensen, "Hagia Sophia: Perspectives from Cultural Heritage."

167 Besteman, *Militarized Global Apartheid.*

168 The earthquake that impacted Istanbul along with other major cities took place on August 17, 1999, with a magnitude of 7.6. As the largest and by far the deadliest in the world that year, it was part of a sequence of earthquakes on the North Anatolian Fault. 17,127 people died according to official numbers, when approximately 20,000 buildings collapsed and more than 120,000 were damaged beyond repair. The earthquake that affected Athens took place on September 7, 1999, with a magnitude of 6. It was part of the seismic activity in the complex interactions between Euroasian, Anatolian, Aegean Sea and African plates. Despite the smaller casualties due to building collapses, the Athens earthquake has also been characterized as one of the deadliest in Greece's modern history. 143 people died due to the collapse of approximately 100 buildings. Sources say 70,000 buildings were damaged, and 100,000 people rendered homeless during the first days. The damage was mostly in the northern suburbs, and in buildings built according to the seismic codes instituted before 1984, and usually attributed to inappropriate construction and detailing. Elenas, "Athens Earthquake of 7 September 1999"; "Athens Hit by Devastating Earthquake."

169 Since 2006, "Greek-Turkish earthquake diplomacy" (*diplomatia ton seismon*; *deprem diplomasisi*) has a Wikipedia page (accessed July 23, 2022), https://en.wikipedia.org/wiki/Greek%E2%80%93Turkish_earthquake _diplomacy.

1 The earthquake with a magnitude of 7.6 impacted Istanbul along with other major cities such as İzmit, Kocaeli, and Gölcük. It was part of a sequence of earthquakes on the North Anatolian Fault moving from east to west, with earthquakes in Erzincan in 1939, Niksar Erbaa in 1942, Çankırı in 1951, Abant in 1957, and Adapazarı-Mudurnu in 1967. This earthquake was the largest and by far the deadliest in the world that year.

2 "Deprem değil, bina öldürür" (Turkish).

3 Kendrick, *Lisbon Disaster*; Voltaire, *Poem upon the Lisbon Disaster*; Rousseau, *Discourse on Inequality*; Kant, "3 articles."

4 Shklar, *Faces of Injustice* 51, 54.

5 Shklar, *Faces of Injustice*, 58.

6 Klein, *Shock Doctrine*, 327.

7 Kenzo Tange and Skopje City Centre Planning Team, "Skopje Urban Plan S.F.R. Yugoslavia. Report on City Centre Planning," report prepared for United Nations acting as executive agency for the United Nations Special Fund, 1965–66, Document No. 174129, Frances Loeb Library Archives, Harvard University; Ito et al., *Architecture*.

8 For some examples, see Architecture for Humanity, *Design like You Give a Damn*.

9 Siddiqi, *Architecture of Migration*.

10 See the introduction for relevant references.

11 See, especially, Perloff, *Futurist Movement*; Blum, *Other Modernism*; Todorova, "War and Memory."

12 I followed the numbers from the best estimates with the comprehensive set of facts in Hall, *Balkan Wars*, 135–36.

13 Latest Earthquakes List, Disaster and Emergency Management Authority, Ministry of the Interior, Republic of Turkey, https://deprem.afad.gov.tr /tarihteBuAy?id=35.

14 For books that are specifically on migrations due to the Ottoman-Russian and Balkan War, see Ladas, *Exchange of Minorities*; Geray, *Türkiye'den ve Türkiye'ye Göçler*; Pentzopoulos, *Balkan Exchange of Minorities*; İpek, *Rumeli'den Anadolu'ya Türk Göçleri*; Halaçoğlu, *Balkan Harbi Sırasında Rumeli'den*; Toumarkine, *Migrations des populations musulmanes*; Dündar, *İttihat ve Terakki'nin Müslümanları İskan*; Dragostinova, *Between Two Motherlands*; Ipek, "Balkans, War and Migration."

15 Kasaba, *Moveable Empire*, 138.

16 This number was calculated by Justin McCarthy, whose book has been challenged on other grounds, and his statements about the Armenian

killings have been conveniently used by the denialist Turkish nationalists. But his estimation of this number based on Western and Ottoman
sources, military and refugee settlement records in Salonica, Üskü-
dar, Kavala, Biga, İzmir, Edirne, Aydın, Istanbul, Ankara, and Eskişehir
remain cited. Nedim İpek and Alexandre Toumarkine's accounts also
confirm the magnitude of Muslim mass migration from the Balkans to
Anatolia. Pointing out the difference between Muslims in Balkans before
1911 and after 1923 as 1,445,179 people, he calculated that 27 percent of
Muslims died, and 413,922 migrated to Anatolia because of the Balkan
War. McCarthy, *Death and Exile*, 164.

17   İpek, "Balkans, War and Migration."

18   This number has been calculated by Geray, *Türkiye'den ve Türkiye'ye
      Göçler*, 18. I calculated the percentage based on the following numbers.
      The population of Turkey was about 14 million in 1923 and 27 million in
      1960, making the mean about 20 million.

19   For more on this commission and the Ottoman immigration law, see
      Hamed-Troyansky, *Empire of Refugees*.

20   İpek, "Balkans, War and Migration," 651; Yıldırım, *Diplomacy and
      Displacement*. According to some calculations, half of the population
      of Edirne was composed of refugees in the immediate aftermath
      of the Ottoman-Russian War; İpek, "Balkans, War and Migration,"
      642.

21   Kaya, "Immigration into Ottoman Territory."

22   Blumi, *Ottoman Refugees*, see especially pp. 43–65.

23   İpek, "Balkans, War and Migration," 651.

24   Yıldırım, *Diplomacy and Displacement*.

25   Kasaba, *Moveable Empire*.

26   Istanbul's population increased from 722,000 in 1877 to 1.6 million in
      1914–16, largely due to war migrants and refugees. Toumarkine, *Migra-
      tions des populations musulmanes*, 73, 74.

27   İpek, "Balkans, War and Migration," 648.

28   The Iskan-ı Muhacirin and Sevkiyat-ı Muhacirin commissions tried
      to rent apartments first, but soon decided that it would be too expen-
      sive, and settled refugees in *hans* (inns), hostels, military barracks,
      and schools, but mostly mosques and schools. Halaçoğlu, *Balkan Harbi
      Sırasında Rumeli'den*, 102–10. Mosques were the major temporary settle-
      ment area for the migrants of the Russian-Ottoman War as well. İpek,
      Rumeli'den Anadolu'ya Türk Göçleri, 61–62.

29   Quoted in Ginio, *Ottoman Culture of Defeat*, 95.

30   Yıldırım, *Diplomacy and Displacement*.

31 Riza Nuri and Irfan Bey were commissioned as officials to regulate the temporary accommodations outside the city walls, and provided building materials such as wooden frames, glass, tin, and clothes. A refugee hospital was also provided, given that infectious disease including cholera spread as a result of the migration from the wartorn Balkans. Halaçoğlu, *Balkan Harbi Sırasında Rumeli'den*, 110–11, 139–52.

32 This is also the title of the only history book on the district. Evren, *Surların Öte Yanı Zeytinburnu*.

33 Ahmet Tamgüney's and Süleyman Sefer Cihan's testimonies, in Zeytinburnu Oral History Project (hereafter: ZAD), 51, 487.

34 Ortaylı, "Tarihsel Perspektiften Surdışı."

35 For more on the Byzantine period of the area, see Özbayoğlu, "Byzantine Period."

36 Çelebi, *Evliya Çelebi Seyahatnamesi*, 189.

37 Byzantios, *Constantinople*, 471.

38 Byzantios, *Constantinople*, 471.

39 Baykal, "Istanbul During Balkan Wars."

40 Yıldırım, *Diplomacy and Displacement*, 137.

41 Nurten Yenal, ZAD 385–86.

42 Şemsettin Loklar, ZAD 491.

43 Üzeyir Üzüm, ZAD 523.

44 Turgut Soner, ZAD 516.

45 Fikret Dalbeler, ZAD 174.

46 İşli, "Zeytinburnu Tekkeleri"; Öztabak, "Seyyahlar Diyarı Zeytinburnu."

47 Çelebi, *Evliya Çelebi Seyahatnamesi*, 189; Hamdi Ali Baykan's testimony, ZAD 195.

48 Işın, "Yenikapı Mevlevihanesi"; Kaya, "Yenikapı Mevlevihanesinin Tarihçesi"; Tekeli et al., *Mimar Kemalettin'in Yazdıkları*.

49 Almost all travelers and explorers write about the complex. For a concise and comprehensive compilation of several accounts, see Evren, "Balıklı Holy Spring and Church." Also see Kafadar, "Su Gibi Aziz Ayazmalar."

50 Byzantios, *Constantinople*, 460.

51 Yıldırım, "Balıklı Rum Hastanesi"; Yıldırım, "İstanbul Yedikule Göğüs Hastalıkları."

52 Koptaş, "Bir Başka Gözle Surp Pırgiç Ermeni Hastanesi." Also see Günhan, "Displaced Modernities."

53   Göncüoğlu, "Kazlıçeşme Sanayi Bölgesi."

54   Erkal, "Şehrin Boğazı."

55   Byzantios, *Constantinople*, 438.

56   Şahin, "Zeytinburnu'nda Sanayileşme Tarihi."

57   Yıldırım, "Zeytinburnu Hastanesi"; Özvar, "Osmanlı Zamanında Zeytinburnu."

58   Küçükerman and Erdinç, "Osmanlı'dan Cumhuriyet'e."

59   Küçükerman and Erdinç, "Osmanlı'dan Cumhuriyet'e"; Şahin "Zeytinburnu'nda Sanayileşme Tarihi." Also see Ersoy, *Architecture and the Late Ottoman Historical Imaginary*.

60   Galitekin, "Balıklı-Kozlu Panayırı"; Özvar, "Osmanlı Zamanında Zeytinburnu"; Sakaoğlu, "Çırpıcı Çayırı." Also see Hamadeh, *City's Pleasures*.

61   Murat and Ersöz, "Zeytinburnu'nun Sosyo-Ekonomik Yapısı."

62   Özgür, "Bulgaristan Türkleri'ni 1950–51 Yıllarında."

63   Only 4.7 percent of the migrants from Macedonia were settled by the state. Kapan and Sinan, "Makedonya'dan Yapılan Göçlerin Mekansal Analizi."

64   Enver Nehir, ZAD 160.

65   *Resmi Gazate*, no. 12362, July 30, 1966.

66   The scholarly literature on different squatter settlements in Turkey is quite extensive. See Bozdoğan and Akcan, *Turkey*. Also see Karpat, *Gecekondu*; Keleş, *Kentleşme Politikası*; Şenyapılı, "Cumhuriyet'in 75. Yılı, Gecekondunun 50.Yılı."

67   Akçay, *Zeytinburnu gerçek yönleriyle bir gecekondu kenti*.

68   Of those who forcefully or voluntarily migrated to Turkey from the Balkans between 1923 and 1960, 33.9 percent were from Greece, 31.1 percent from Bulgaria, 22.4 percent from Macedonia/Yugoslavia, and 10 percent from Romania. Geray, *Türkiye'den ve Türkiye'ye Göçler*, 7–13.

69   Hart, *Zeytinburnu Gecekondu Bölgesi*.

70   "CIAMS Faculty Talk." And I thank Magnus Fiskesjö for being a consultant for this book. See also Byler, *Terror Capitalism*.

71   After 2017, there have been ample reports on Uyghur detension camps in the Xinjiang region, with documents obtained by International Consortium of Investigative Journalists and others, and GPS tracking. Some of these also analyze the architectural methods of surveillance and discipline. In addition to detention equipment such as barbed wire and security cameras, these settlements also make use of rationalized architectural techniques to control bodies in space. Parallel blocks and orderly out-

door and indoor spaces provide easy surveillance; total elimination of hideouts and intimate outdoor spaces guarantees that all activity happens in plain sight; and watch towers efficiently placed at corners allow guards to control the entire space. Ramzy and Buckley, "'Absolutely No Mercy'"; Ruhoha and Fifield, "She Survived a Chinese Internment Camp"; CBS News, "Rare Look Inside China's Muslim Internment Camps"; CNN, "China Tries to Thwart"; "Hamit Göktürk'le Söyleşi."

72 With a law that passed on March 13, 1952, 1,850 Kazaks and Uyghurs who had escaped through India were legally accepted in Turkey, and settled in Kayseri, Niğde, Aksaray, and Manisa, although many moved to Zeytinburnu shortly after.

73 Gayretullah, "Bir Göç Hikayesi."

74 Saka, quoted in TRT Avaz, "Türkiye'deki Türkistan."

75 Göktürk, Ilham Tohti, 133.

76 Göktürk, "Doğu Türkistan'dan Anadolu'ya Göçler."

77 Kulca, "Bir Göç Hikayesi."

78 Ali Çağrı, "Afganistan'dan Zeyrinburnu'na Yolculuk."

79 Apart from Yusuf Kulca, Abdulvahab Kılıç also mentions the hostel in Zeytinburnu as the first arrival place, ZAD 19.

80 Abdulvahap Kara and Abdulvahab Kılıç, ZAD 17, 20

81 Testimonies of Abdulvahap Kılıç, Abdülhak İmren, Ahmet Esdevlet, Mustafa Kırmızıgül, Orhan Kumandan, and Reşide Yüksel, ZAD 19, 24, 46, 358, 397, 432. Çakırer-Özservet, "Zeytinburnu'nda Doğu Türkistan Türklerinin"; Çakırer-Özservet, "Zeytinburnu Kentsel Mekanında Soydaş Diyasporasının Örgütlenmesi."

82 "Zeytinburnu Anı Defteri." The document compiles 168 testimonies with early residents. Zeytinburnu Municipality Archives.

83 Hatullah Yeniyol, ZAD 204.

84 Ismet Aydın, ZAD 255.

85 Hasan Yılmaz, ZAD 198–99.

86 Mehmet Ali Vatansever, ZAD 280–81.

87 "We built it three times, they destroyed it three times. . . . One week later we gave money to a gendarme, and they did not demolish that house." Ahmet Dildar, ZAD 39.

88 Cemal Aslan, ZAD 133.

89 Muzaffer Çavuşoğlu, ZAD 352.

90 One of the earliest settlers, Nurten Yenal, describes how she and her father dug the ground, laid the foundation, after which the father could

not trust his construction ability and hired a master. Another Balkan migrant, Enver Nehir, says: "There were famous masters who built the houses. . . . They had reputations such as this master would finish the house in two days, that master would have such and such qualities." Nurten Yenal, ZAD 385–6; Enver Nehir, ZAD 163.

91 Enver Sertel, ZAD 164.

92 Mehmet Zeynel, ZAD 299.

93 Akbulut, "Mekansal Dönüşüm."

94 Ayşe Bilgiç, ZAD 98.

95 Akçay, *Zeytinburnu*.

96 Fikret Dalbeler, ZAD 174.

97 Adil Çalışkan, Arif Şahin, Bahriye Bahtir, Cabir Çelik, Enver Sertel, Nimet Ceylan, Orhan Mutlu, Sebahattin Sönmez, and Tacettin Erdem talk about working as a child in Zeytinburnu. ZAD 35, 76, 114, 126, 166, 380, 384, 465, 504.

98 Bahriye Bahtır, ZAD 114.

99 Sebahattin Sönmez, ZAD 465–66.

100 Adil Çalışkan, ZAD 35.

101 In addition to scholarship on Turkey's informal settlements in general, in the only book specific for Zeytinburnu *gecekondu* houses, Faik Akçay characterizes the district as a "place where cultureless, senseless [bilinçsiz] working class exerts its existence." Akçay, *Zeytinburnu*, 144.

102 This is frequently mentioned, but for examples, see ZAD 35, 72, 303, 316,321, 329, 337, 560.

103 Besim Sadıker, ZAD 118.

104 *İktisat Fakültesi Mecmuası*, vol. 14, nos. 1–4 (1952–53): 154.

105 Mehmet Alpay, ZAD 286.

106 Ayşe Ceylan, ZAD 101.

107 Hamdi Ali Baykan, ZAD 197.

108 Cengizhan Mutlu, ZAD 114.

109 Tekeli, *Türkiye'de Yaşam ve Yazında Konut*, 63.

110 Hiçdurmaz, *Çark*.

111 Hiçdurmaz, *Çark*, minutes 54.35–54.46.

112 Akçay, *Zeytinburnu*.

113 Ali Yerli, ZAD 69, 83.

114 Fahriye Efeoğlu, ZAD 167.

115 Akçay, *Zeytinburnu*. Oral histories confirm that carrying water to the house was one of the major challenges for everyone. "Zeytinbunu Anı Defteri."

116 Uzmay, "Expanding Water Geographies."

117 Mennan Çayır, ZAD 308.

118 Muzaffer Çavuşoğlu, ZAD 353.

119 Emine Albayrak, ZAD 154.

120 Doing fieldwork in 1974, Faik Akçay criticized the lack of sufficient health services in the area and mentioned that the Greek and Armenian hospitals did not treat local patients. Akçay, *Zeytinburnu*.

121 Mennan Çayır and Nimet Ceylan, ZAD 308, 380.

122 Liboiron, *Pollution Is Colonialism*.

123 Gökçen, "Zeytinburnu Gecekonduları." Rıfat Akbulut emphasizes February 26, 1957, when sixty-two families were granted the title of their properties in Zeytinburnu. Akbulut, "Mekansal Dönüşüm."

124 Keleş, *Kentleşme Politikası*; Bozdoğan and Akcan, *Turkey*.

125 Inancık, *Ottoman Empire*.

126 Keyder, "Housing Market from Informal to Global." Even though not related to Istanbul, for the impact of different property regimes on architecture at the borderlands between Ottoman and Russian Empires, see Sarıçayır, "Property in Transition."

127 Akçay, *Zeytinburnu*.

128 Gökçen, "Zeytinburnu Gecekonduları," 372.

129 Onan, "Minority Concept and Rights in Turkey."

130 Gökçen, "Zeytinburnu Gecekonduları."

131 The comments to this effect are ubiquitous. For examples, see ZAD 11, 19, 23, 46, 50, 55, 66, 72, 107–8, 117, 121, 129, 174, 177, 190, 238, 260, 262, 289, 295, 308, 350, 388, 417, 457, 460, 479, 528, 543, 554.

132 "When we first came here, people whom we had never met became our maternal and paternal aunts and uncles. We were bonded with love. One made a soup and shared it. The other cooked a halva and offered it. There was such a solidarity, such a brotherhood, such an understanding of neighborliness that I cannot put it into words for you. You had to live it." Besim Sadıker, ZAD 119.

133 For the use of the word *cosmopolitan*, see ZAD 295, 392; for *mosaic*, see ZAD 289.

134 Burhan Eraslan, ZAD 121.

135 Halil Küçük, ZAD 190; Kadir Zincir, ZAD 260.

136 ZAD 308, 438–39.

137 Abdulvahab Kılıç, ZAD 20; Abdülfettah Malkoç, ZAD 23.

138 Süleyman Cindibek, ZAD 479–80; Veysel Topçu, ZAD 528; Yusuf Yonucu, ZAD 543.

139 ZAD 127, 251, 347, 465, 485, 495.

140 For instance, in March 28, 2004, Local Municipality elections, the votes for the Islamic Justice and Development Party (AKP) were 40.3 percent in Turkey, 41.7 percent in Istanbul, and 52.7 percent in Zeytinburnu. For more data, see Murat and Ersöz, "Zeytinburnu'nun Sosyo-Ekonomik Yapısı."

141 ZAD 66.

142 ZAD 72.

143 ZAD 238.

144 "Since the houses were in gardens, there were pergolas and benches to sit and talk. There are migrants here from Bulgaria, Greece, Romania, Albania, and so and so. We are all together anyway. Everyone told stories. I came from Bulgaria in this way, I had these difficulties. I was such a victim of persecution in Greece. I suffered this much and so on. Thank god, Turkey opened the doors for us." Ahmet Tamgüney, ZAD 50.

145 Recep Hakyemez, ZAD 417.

146 Mehmet Zeynel, ZAD 299.

147 Kefayet Sertel, ZAD 263.

148 He explains his parents' choice of Turkey as their asylum destination because they wanted to be together with their "heart, soul and siblings." Abdülhak İmren, ZAD 25.

149 Reşide Yüksel, ZAD 432.

150 The *hodja* of Merkezefendi mosque speaks about the mutual nondiscriminatory relation between him and the Greek grocery store owner. Celalettin Şensoy, ZAD 129. Some talk about discovering wells and underground tunnels while playing as a kid in the Greek hospital's garden. Turgut Soner, ZAD 517.

151 Fikret Dalbeler, ZAD 175.

152 Yusuf Yonucu, ZAD 543.

153 Mustafa Yalçın, ZAD 347.

154 Orhan Aytek, ZAD 388.

155 These were only restored from 1960 to 1969. Vryonis, *Mechanism of Catastrophe*.

156 Kurtoğlu, "Zeytinburnu Ulaşım Tarihi."

157   This information is confirmed by the representatives of the Greek Patri-
       arch on site. Eremya Çelebi Kömürciyan talks about a Karamanlı cem-
       etery along the city walls. Kömürciyan, *Istanbul'un Tarihi XVII Asırda
       Istanbul*. Also see Öztabak, "Seyyahlar Diyarı Zeytinburnu."

158   Keyder, *Istanbul*, 10–12; Aktar, *Varlık Vergisi ve Türkleştirme Politikaları*;
       Akar, *Aşkale Yolcuları*.

159   The pamphlet is quoted in Yelmen, "Kazlıçeşme."

160   Ginio, *Ottoman Culture of Defeat*, 103–9.

161   ZAD 64, 327, 408, 486–87, 508.

162   For more discussion, see Bozdoğan and Akcan, *Turkey*. Also see Ekinci,
       Istanbul'u Sarsan On Yıl; Buğra, "Immoral Economy of Housing in Tur-
       key"; Bilgin, "Anadolu'da Modernleşme Sürecinde Konut ve Yerleşme."

163   "History of Japan's Assistance to Developing Countries (1945–1999),"
       Ministry of Foreign Affairs of Japan. https://www.mofa.go.jp/policy/oda
       /summary/1999/ref8.html. I would like to thank my research assistant
       Sky Russell from Harvard University for her help in guiding me through
       the documents from Japan. One instance of such help involved docu-
       mention relating to a professor from Tokyo University, Takahiro Hagi-
       wara, who had been invited to teach engineering seismology in the newly
       established Seismology Department at the Istanbul Technical University
       in 1952.

164   "Kocaeli (Turkey) Earthquake," Japan Society of Civil Engineers, http://
       www.jsce.or.jp/kokusai/disaster_report/kocaeli_e.htm.

165   Shigeru Ban Architects, "Paper Log House—Turkey." https://
       shigerubanarchitects.com/works/paper-tubes/paper-log-house-turkey/,

166   The UN Special Fund had allocated $1,475,000 for the reconstruction of
       the area. It would include public buildings, university, schools, hospi-
       tals, and dwellings. The first Kenzo Tange team included Arata Isozaki,
       Vojislav Mackic, Radovan Miscevic, Yoshio Taniguchi, Dragan Tamvski,
       Sadao Watanabe, Fedor Senzler, and Stanislaw Furman, but the proj-
       ect prompted the invitation of multiple international and local architects
       afterward. Kenzo Tange Team and Skopje City Centre Planning Team,
       "Skopje Urban Plan S.F.R."; "Design Award Made in U.N. for Recon-
       structing Skopje."

167   The UN reports compiled during the implementation of the project
       till 1970 are extensive, including the international and local archi-
       tects' undertaking afterward. For a condensed analysis, see Lozanovska
       and Martek, "Skopje Resurgent"; Stierli and Kulic, *Toward a Concrete
       Utopia*.

168   Fabio Mattioli states, "Tange thus uses modernist architecture to implant
       a western urban 'soul' in the city, valorizing a heritage, but one that

Skopje never had. Moreover, this valorized heritage was one in which Ottoman/Turkish and Muslim urbanism has no place." Mattioli, "Unchanging Boundaries." See also Tolic, *Dopo il terremoto*.

169 Japan International Cooperation Agency, official website, https://www .jica.go.jp/english/index.html.

170 JICA and Istanbul Metropolitan Municipality, "Study on a Disaster Prevention/Mitigation Basic Plan in Istanbul Including Seismic Microzonation in the Republic of Turkey," report of December 2002, JICA-Pacific Consultants International Archives, Japan.

171 JICA and Istanbul Metropolitan Municipality, "Study on a Disaster Prevention," chapter 8, 8–39.

172 JICA and Istanbul Metropolitan Municipality, "Study on a Disaster Prevention," 3–16.

173 Zeytinburnu Municipality, "Deprem Referanslı Kentsel Dönüşüm," accessed December 12, 2019, http://www.zeytinburnu.istanbul/Imar-ve -Sehircilik-Hizmetleri.

174 "Sümer Mahallesinde Anahtar Teslimi Heyecanı," 2.

175 This number is predicted with an updated report using 2019 data, although the same report's predictions for the death and injury toll is much lower than the one in 1999 (668 dead, 374 heavily injured, and 1,767 hospitalized). Büyükşehir Belediyesi and Kandilli Rasathanesi, "Zeytinburnu Olası Deprem Kayıp Tahminleri Kitapçığı," unpublished report, 2020, IBB archives, Istanbul.

176 These laws included Law 5237, Gecekondu Alanlarının Iyileştirilmesi [Renewal of *gecekondu* areas], 2004; Law 5393, Gecekondu Dönüşüm/ Kentsel Yenileme Projeleri İçin Yerel Belediyelerin Görevlendirilmesi [Authorization of local municipalities for *gecekondu* transformation and and urban renewal], 2005; Law 5366, Tarihi Alanların Yenilemeye ve Ranta Açılması [The renewal and real estate development of historic districts], 2005. According to the official records, twelve thousand houses in squatter settlements were demolished between 2003 and 2011, and their residents were settled in much smaller units away from their original neighborhoods. Squatter removal became a new strategy in integrating citizens into the neoliberal economic policy by forcing them to participate in the state-governed financing for homeownership. Karaman, "Urban Renewal in Istanbul"; Akcan, "*Homo oeconomicus* of the 'New Turkey.'"

177 Aydın, "Kültür Vadisi," 10.

178 Cansever, "Zeytinburnu Sur Dışı."

179 Çelik, "Turgut Cansever ve Zeytinburnu Raporu," 41.

180 Cansever, *İslam'da Şehir ve Mimari*.

181 Cansever, "Zeytinburnu Sur Dışı," 19.

182 Cansever, "Zeytinburnu Sur Dışı," 32.

183 White, *Muslim Nationalism and the New Turks*; Batuman, *New Islamist Architecture and Urbanism*; Gür, ""Political Misuse of Hagia Sophia."

184 Cansever, "Zeytinburnu Sur Dışı," 33.

185 Öğün and Öğün, "Örnek Bir Dönüşüm Projesinin Kısa Hikayesi," 35.

186 Kutsal, "Kültür Vadisi'ni Arındıran Yıkımlar," 66.

187 Halil Amca, quoted in Turan and Ayar, "Kültür Vadisi Projesi ve Merkezefendi'de."

188 Cansever, "Zeytinburnu Sur Dışı," 21.

189 The first book was Evren, *Surların Öte Yanı*, before the execution of the Cultural Valley. The municipality continued commissioning articles that extended especially Merkez Efendi's and Seyyid Nizam's religious teachings, as well as the architectural and material history of the dervish lodges in the area. The following essays were published in volume 1 *Zeytinburnu Kültür Vadisi*, edited by Murat Çekin, 292–453: Murat Çekin and Efsun Sertoğlu, "Merkez Efendi Şahsiyeti ve Külliyesi"; Bayram Ali Kaya, "Yenikapı Mevlevihanesi'nin Tarihçesi"; Ruhi Ayangil, "Musiki Tarihimizde Yenikapı Mevlevihanesi'nin Yeri ve Önemi." The following essays were published in volume 2 of *Zeytinburnu Kültür Vadisi*, edited by Murat Çekin, 468–646: Ahmed Nezih Galitekin, "Seyyid Nizam Hayatı ve Dergahı"; Gül Sarıdikmen, "Zeytinburnu'nun Tarihi Çeşmeleri ve Sebilleri"; Hayri Necdet İşli, "Zeytinburnu Tekkeleri"; Ahmed Nezih Galitekin, "Kazlıçeşme Bektaşi Dergahı"; Orhan Sakin, "Zeytinburnu Kitabeleri."

190 Aydın, introduction to *Surların Öte Yanı*, 11.

191 Yıldırım, "Balıklı Rum Hastanesi"; Yıldırım, "Istanbul Yedikule."

192 Berk, *Zamanı Aşan Taşlar*, 11.

193 Robert Barker received a patent for a painted panorama on June 17, 1787: a painting on a 360-degree circular canvas displayed on the interior walls of a large rotunda usually built for this purpose, with the painting being a realist representation of a place viewed from all angles and from the farthest possible point. Buddemeier, *Panorama, Diorama, Photographie*; Oettermann, *Panorama*; Comment, *Panorama*.

194 For a critical discussion of this building, see Türeli, *Istanbul, Open City*; Gür, "Two Conquerors."

195 This included the inaugural exhibition of the newly redesigned AKM in Taksim Square in summer 2022.

196 Cansever, "Zeytinburnu Sur Dışı," 21–22.

197 Fifteen thousand of the overall 247,000 population. "Zeytinburnu'nda Küçük Türkistan," 374.

198 Özservet, "Zeytinburnu'nda Doğu Türkistan," 73.

199 "Göç Sempozyumu Bildiriler"; Göktürk, *Ben Türkistan Kızıyım*.

200 Kulca, "Bir Göç Hikayesi."

201 Öğün, "Örnek Bir Dönüşüm."

202 For more on the making and use of the typology of the "Turkish house," see Akcan, *Archicture in Translation*.

203 Çekin and Alpınar, "Zeytinburnu Tıbbı Bitkiler Bahçesi."

204 I would like to thank Ayfer Mertler for her guidance when I visited the municipality archives.

205 Cansever, "Zeytinburnu Sur Dışı," 21.

206 The structures built in 1904 of the Balıklı Greek hospital had already been rented to the Turkish Ministry of Heath from 1949 onward. Yıldırım, "Balıklı Rum Hastanesi."

207 Aydemir, *Zeytinburnu Mozaikleri*.

208 For more discussion, see Akcan, "*Homo oeconomicus* of the 'New Turkey.'"

209 "İstanbul'da Kentsel Dönüşüm Skandalı;" Emlak Kulisi, "KIPTAS Locamahal Projesinde Zarar Etti İddiası."

210 Cansever, "Zeytinburnu Sur Dışı," 19; Çekin, *Zeytinburnu Kültür Vadisi*, vol. 1, 122.

211 See esp. Ginio, *Ottoman Culture of Defeat*.

212 Çiçek, "More History than They Can Consume?," 797.

213 "Istanbul'un Zeytinburnu İlçesinde Bir Bina Çöktü."

214 Taylan, "Factors Influencing Homeowners' Seismic Risk."

215 Özçelik, "Istanbul'da Kaç Tane Toplanma Alanı Olduğu Bilinmiyor."

216 Gültekin, "Tımarhanede Deprem Hazırlığı."

217 For more discussion, see Akcan, "*Homo oeconomicus* of the 'New Turkey.'"

218 Gürek, *AKP'nin Müteahhitleri*; Toker, *Kamu İhalelerinde Olağan İşler*.

219 Kuyucu, "Law, Property and Ambiguity"; Akcan, "*Homo oeconomicus* of the 'New Turkey.'"

220 Davis, *Planet of Slums*; Davis, "Who Will Build the Ark?"; Dawson, *Extreme Cities*; Dawson, *Environmentalism from Below*.

1   June 18–19, 2022, were the hottest days in Britain in recorded history until that time, in a country that kept weather reports for the longest time on the planet. The temperatures exceeded all previous record-breaking intervals, not by 1/10 degree but by 1–2 degrees Celsius. June 2022 kept its record of being the hottest June on the planet only for a year, and the hottest day record was broken three times in a week in the first days of July 2023. McKibben, "Record Heat Wave in Europe"; Mishra and Boyle, "Earth Sets Its Hottest Day Record."

2   Winckelmann, *History of the Art of Antiquity*, 186–91.

3   Malm, *Fossil Capital*, 36.

4   For general histories of Sudan, see especially Holt and Daly, *History of Sudan*; Daly, *Modernization in the Sudan*; Collins and Deng, *British in the Sudan*; Trout Powell, *Different Shade of Colonialism*.

5   "Osmanlı Afrikası-Kuzeydoğu, der Kriegsschauplatz im Aegyptischen Sudan." Ottoman Archives, Istanbul, Document No. HRT.h.._651-_3 Document Location: 651, Document Date: H-03-05-1301.

6   Sudan Archives, University of Durham, Durham, UK (hereafter SAD). SAD 646/4/80.

7   Muhammed Mihri, *Sudan Seyahatnamesi*; Petherick, *Egypt, the Soudan and Central Africa*, 128.

8   SAD 679/1/11.

9   SAD 679/1/14–15.

10 McLean, *Regional and Town Planning*, 62. The sections on Sudan were given as a paper as "Town Planning in Khartoum and Omdurman" at RIBA Town Planning Conference in London, October 1910. SAD 679/1/9.

11 Melly, *Khartoum, and the Blue and White Niles*; Petherick, *Egypt, the Soudan and Central Africa*; Baker, *Albert N'Yanza*.

12 Petherick, *Egypt, the Soudan and Central Africa*, 132.

13 "The town as approached from the White River, presents a mass of dirty grey houses, over-topped by a single minaret, and in front lies a sterile sandy plain without trees or bushes. It is entered by a long narrow street . . . dirty in the extreme, and bordered by mud houses." Apart from a few spacious mansions occupied by Turks, Copts, and Arabs, the houses were "of miserable description, consisting of sun-dried clay, cemented with cow-dung and slime." Edwin Geoffrey Sarsfield-Hall, "Memorandum on the Layout and Development of Khartoum, Khartoum North and Omdurman," Manuscript of 1936, SAD 679/1/1–105, with quotation at 679/1/10.

14   Edwin Geoffrey Sarsfield-Hall repeated many sentences in the War Of-
        fice's report while writing the history of Khartoum, and added: "Here and
        there were open spaces, large enough for fields. But there were numer-
        ous low-lying places, which became stagnant pools in the rains. . . . There
        was no hotel or inn, and travelers had either to lodge with friends or ask
        the Governor for a place which was often a large and dirty courtyard sur-
        rounded by rooms. Restaurants and places of refreshments in the ordi-
        nary sense of the word did not exist, though there were numerous shops
        owned by Greeks in which alcoholic liquors could be obtained. Near
        the market place stood the mosque, coffee houses, brandy shops and so
        on. The Coptic School, an infirmary, a prison and barracks also existed."
        Edwin Geoffrey Sarsfield-Hall and E. J. N. Wallis, "Handbook of Khar-
        toum Province," Manuscript of ca. 1936, SAD 678/8/1-347, with quotation
        at 678/8/35–36.

15   McLean, *Regional and Town Planning*, 68.

16   Said, *Orientalism*.

17   Baker, *Albert N'Yanza*, vol. 1, xli.

18   McLean, "Town Planning in the Tropics," 225.

19   Baker, *Albert N'Yanza*, vol. 1, xliii.

20   McLean, "Town Planning in the Tropics," 225.

21   McLean, "Town Planning in the Tropics," 225–26.

22   Here were the results of the 1934 census: The population of Khartoum
        had increased from 14,000 in 1905, to 46,700 in 1934. So did the popula-
        tion of Khartoum North from 20,600 to 21,100; and Omdurman from
        40,000 to 111,000. The demographics were as follows: Khartoum-born
        Sudanese: 3,000 men, 1,740 women, and 2,100 children; Deims (Na-
        tive): 6,250 men, 8,750 women, and 10,000 children; Greek: 870 men,
        420 women, and 590 children; Egyptian: 584 men, 547 women, and 769
        children; Hawaa: 307 men, 259 women, and 127 children; British: 270
        men, 99 women, and 59 children; Cypriot: 205 men, 87 women, and 132
        children; Yemenis: 170 men, 1 woman, and 4 children; Syrians: 121 men,
        96 women, and 111 children; Armenians: 86 men, 78 women, and 80
        children. Other groups with much less than 100 people included Maltese,
        Italian, American, Jewish, Abyssinian, French, Austrian, German, and In-
        dian. Sarsfield-Hall and Wallis, "Handbook of Khartoum Province," with
        quotation at 678/8/313.

23   SAD 679/2/10. Europeans amounted to less than a hundred.

24   Geraldine Mary Culwick to Family, letter of September 5, 1947. SAD
        428/1/36.

25   SAD 679/1/18.

26   SAD 679/1/21.

27 Edwin Geoffrey Sarsfield-Hall, "Khartoum, Today and Tomorrow: A Brief Account of History Planning and Development of Khartoum and the Neighboring Towns of Khartoum North and Omdurman," Manuscript of ca. 1936, SAD 646/4/1–83, with quotation at 646/4/17–18.

28 SAD 679/1/22.

29 SAD 679/1/21.

30 SAD 679/1/22.

31 SAD 646/4/29.

32 SAD 679/1/21.

33 Sarsfield-Hall, "Memorandum on the Layout and Development," with quotation at SAD 679/1/4. The total width of Victoria Street was 45.71 meters, and Gordon Avenue was 36.57 meters. SAD 679/1/34.

34 Edwin Geoffrey Sarsfield-Hall, "Progress Between 1928–1935," Manuscript of ca. 1936, SAD 678/7/1–44.

35 Seth, *Difference and Disease.*

36 Edwin Geoffrey Sarsfield-Hall put it clearly: "Speaking broadly, the principal object of Town Planning is the combination of satisfactory public health and sanitary conditions, with the creation and preservation of amenities in such a way as to secure the highest possible standard of well being for local inhabitants." Sarsfield-Hall, "Khartoum, Today and Tomorrow," with quotation at SAD 646/4/1.

37 F. J. L. Atterbury's photograph taken between 1905 and 1911 depicts a Black woman drawing water from a well with her two children in Omdurman's tightly knit urban fabric composed of flat-roofed mudbrick houses. SAD A10/134.

38 Edwin Geoffrey Sarsfield-Hall and H. Richards, "Memorandum on the Public Health of Khartoum Province," Manuscript of 1935, SAD 679/2/1–88.

39 SAD 679/1/32.

40 Average daily clearance was 4,018 buckets in Khartoum, 1,235 in Khartoum North, and 387 in Omdurman. SAD 679/2/31.

41 SAD 679/2/31–44.

42 SAD 679/1/45.

43 Sarsfield-Hall, "Khartoum, Today and Tomorrow," with quotation at SAD 646/4/31.

44 SAD 679/1/89.

45 SAD 679/1/89–90.

46 On the agglomeration of water in front of the Khartoum mosque, SAD A68/157; on the view of a flooded streets, SAD A68/156; SAD 870/17/11–13.

47   Mihri, *Sudan Seyahatnamesi*, 170–71.

48   SAD 870/12/2.

49   SAD 677/4/9–11.

50   SAD A85/10–13.

51   Geraldine Mary Culwick, letters from Gezira, 1949–52, SAD 428/3/1–262, with quotation for a letter to family dated July 5, 1949 at SAD 428/3/32.

52   McLean, "Town Planning," 230–31.

53   SAD A10/182.

54   SAD 2/2/133.

55   SAD A34/187; SAD 453/698/23; SAD 453/698/24; SAD A15/43.

56   This included Farquharson Lang's house in Khartoum, SAD 729/22/165. Also see SAD A10/122.

57   Udal: SAD 778/11/92; G. R. Storrar: SAD 56/1/28. The photograph of Nicholas Robin Udal's house also shows a tennis lawn in front of the house.

58   SAD 2/12/17; SAD A10/99; SAD/A10/118; SAD 2/2/138.

59   SAD 2/2/138.

60   Trout Powell, *Different Shade of Colonialism*, 2, 135–67. Also see Powell, *Tell This in My Memory*.

61   For an example, see Baker, *Albert N'Yanza*, vol. 2, 516–19.

62   Winifred Johnson's diary, entry between July 9 and September 29, 1947. SAD 751/19/1–50.

63   Civil Secretary James Angus Gillan's house in Khartoum (1932–39), for one, was situated just next to the Blue Nile near the iron bridge and surrounded by tall trees. SAD A84/217-218; SAD A84/30; SAD A85/97.

64   Sarsfield-Hall, "Memorandum on the Layout and Development," with quotation at SAD 679/1/62.

65   SAD 789/3/19.

66   SAD 491/3/2.

67   In his dining room, G. R. Storrar had hunting trophies and a horse bridle from Darfur: SAD 45/1/157. The governor's house in Kassala (1905) had hunting trophies and weapons: SAD A14/57. D. S. B. Thomson's and G. G. Hunter's houses were decorated with animal skins: SAD 475/12/12; SAD 784/3/33.

68   Gordon Brock Bridgman Papers, (Uncategorized). SAD 639/9/2.

69   Caption of a photograph by G. H. Barter of their own house. SAD 12/10/44. Photographs of Bridgeman's houses circulated with caption: "Typical House of a British Official." SAD 637/9/12; SAD 637/9/13; SAD 637/9/14; SAD 637/9/16.

70 Gordon Brock Bridgman Papers, (Uncategorized). SAD 639/9/2.

71 SAD 583/2/71; SAD 583/74.

72 SAD 879/5/9.

73 E. G. Sansfield Hall's photograph: SAD A67/327. Without Ionic column capitals, some verandas adopted the language of abstract classicism. A photograph of the Bryson family in July 1941 shows one such verandah carved into an otherwise brick building with pitched roofs. SAD/D/128.

74 SAD 2/28/12; SAD 12/10/44–79.

75 SAD 12/10/68.

76 SAD 12/10/46.

77 Caption of photograph. SAD 12/10/93.

78 L. K. Smith's house in Omdurman (1914–15) had a thatched roof and wooden stilts for the veranda: SAD A.70/3; G. F. Thomas's house in Omdurman (1950–54) was a modernist white box and carved-in veranda with abstracted columns that must have stood in contrast to the surrounding houses: SAD 747/7/2.

79 District Commissioner John Henry Dick, who served between 1931 and 1955, lived in a house with an elevated deep verandah with brick columns, and wooden roof in an elaborate garden in Shendi (SAD 747/2/29). When he was the deputy governor of Kordofan, Sarsfield-Hall lived in a house with a deep spacious veranda with high ceilings, arched openings, and wooden screens that divided the space into several semiverandas (SAD A67/334). In A. R. C. Bolton's house in Wadi Halfa when he was district commissioner between 1942 and 1944, classical round columns with Corinthian capitals carried the plate over the veranda in front of stone-built walls; elegant tiny timber stilts carried the roof of the upper-level veranda that encircled three facades (SAD 718/39/10–11). The inspector's house in El Obeid and the governor's House in Kassala had clear diagrams: thick brick columns carried the roofs of verandas that encircled the houses from all sides (SAD A79/174, SAD A14/55). Also see SAD 778/5/2–4; SAD 2/25/20; SAD 474/13/9; SAD 766/9/157; SAD 877/18/10; SAD/877/18/17; SAD A21/22; SAD A50/40; SAD A17/14; SAD A82/315; SAD A83/204; SAD A84/30; SAD A85/133; SAD A68/73.

80 "A senior British official's residence": SAD 684/5/43; "A native official's residence": SAD 684/5/45.

81 Edwin Geoffrey Sarsfield-Hall and I. G. Watson, "Some African-Type Buildings for Use in the Anglo-Egyptian Sudan," Manuscript of 1934, SAD 678/6/1–57.

82 SAD 684/3/1.

83   In one of the Morhig postcards taken to show the famous Sudan Club, the cantonment accidentally falls into the frame as a homogenous, one-story-high barrier with an arched gateway at a great distance. SAD 870/16/11.

84   SAD 679/2/37–42.

85   S. R. Simpson also explains his policy to eliminate these living quarters by reserving plots of land in the "Third Class Areas," where casual laborers could gradually build and extend their mud houses in time so that they would find regular employment and settle with their families. Simpson, "Town Planning and Development."

86   The caption read: "Up to date counterparts of the native 'Tukl' (straw hut) Railway laborers' houses." P. T. M. Well's photograph and caption, 1932. SAD 855/1/53–54.

87   Officers who were crucial in determining the urban and architectural culture in British Sudan visited Suakin and took striking photographs of buildings, including G. B. Bridgman, Sansfield-Hall, F. R. Wingate, C. H. Thomson, MacMichael, J. A. Gillan, J. F. E. Bloss, and N. R. Udal.

88   Potter and Potter, *Everything Is Possible*, 147–48.

89   After the conquest of 1898, the church services were temporarily held in the Governor's Palace until the construction of All Saints Cathedral. Newspaper started reporting on the building as early as 1906.

90   Baker, *Albert N'Yanza*, vol. 1, xli–xlii.

91   For pictures of these churches, see SAD 679/1/49–51.

92   "The Cathedral of All Saints."

93   The drawings were prepared by the local staff recruited from Gordon College. "The Grand Hotel, Khartoum."

94   Both buildings were frequent subjects for the two major photography studios of the time: Karakashian Brothers and Mohrig, the latter used frequently in postcards.

95   Geraldine Mary Culwick to Family, letter of 26/4/1949. SAD 428/3/24.

96   "The Kitchener Memorial Medical School, Khartoum."

97   "Current Architecture in the Sudan."

98   Photographs exist from the verandas of the following hospitals: Omdurman's Women's Hospital: SAD 583/2/43; Civic Hospital in Port Sudan: SAD540/153; Midwifery Training School in Omdurman: SAD 742/3/15, SAD 742/3/53.

99   Gordon Brock Bridgman captured a photo of two women carrying materials on their heads for the construction of his buildings. SAD 679/1/58, 637/9/5.

100 These architects included Ioannis Hatziantoniou, Nikolaos Pothitos, Polychronis Zavolas, Constantinos Batis, Polychronis Hiotis, Ioannis Stavrakis, and Ioannis Moulakis. Georgitsoyanni, "Greek Masons in Africa."

101 Georgitsoyanni, "Greek Masons in Africa."

102 "Gordon Memorial College, Khartoum, Scheme for Redevelopment"; "Gordon Memorial College." SAD 1/6/47. Photograph taken in 1908. Also see SAD 1/18/14; SAD A34/177; SAD 7/7/1; SAD 484/1/48; SAD 484/4/8; SAD 840/7/178.

103 Alick Potter mentions that Lieutenant Gorringe turned himself into a civil engineer and even an architect, with General Kitchener's permission, and took charge of the building. Also see Potter and Potter, *Everything Is Possible*, 18–31.

104 SAD 869/1/1. Also see SAD A38/186.

105 Edwin Geoffrey Sarsfield-Hall, and E. J. N. Wallis, "Handbook of Khartoum Province," with quotation at 678/8/218, 678/8/220.

106 SAD A38/186.

107 In two publications of 1946 and 1951, the architect listed several measures. The building was designed in compliance with "the two conditioning factors of most importance: a. the heat and glare from sunshine, b. north to south and south to north currents of air." The extension buildings continued the same principles: "The walls most in danger of heating up [were] shaded with verandas. . . . The rooms in the hostels have windows which open into high porches in such a way that much of the glare is kept out of the rooms. Also these porches canalize the two prevailing air currents. The windows, further, have an arrangement of shutter-scoops, to catch these air currents as they pass." "Gordon Memorial College," 5; "Gordon Memorial College, Khartoum, Scheme for Redevelopment," 36, 38.

108 If one is to infer from the nuanced oral histories conducted by the UN's first Special Representative on the Human Rights of Internally Displaced Persons, Francis Deng (who also served as the UN Special Rapporteur for Disappearances in Turkey—chapter 1), Gordon College (where Deng attended after it was turned into University of Khartoum) was one of the rare buildings that hosted relatively more cooperative relations between the British and the Sudanese professionals, probably due to both parties' elitist convictions and the willingness of colonizers to sustain an educated group among what they called "better class natives." Even though there were different accounts in the society about "whether the English were equals or masters, . . . the teaching profession encouraged a feeling of equality." Deng reports on the "free atmosphere" in the Gordon College Students' Union, with vocal students and professors who were beaten

up by police when they poured into the streets. Deng, "In the Eyes of the Ruled," 229–30.

109   SAD 679/1/98.

110   Sarsfield-Hall and Watson, "Some African-Type Buildings."

111   Sarsfield-Hall and Watson, "Some African-Type Buildings."

112   SAD 678/6/10–13.

113   SAD 678/6/50–57.

114   All issues published in the 1970s wrote that the journal was meant to distribute information to "housing and construction authorities in countries receiving technical assistance from the British government."

115   Henry Sanoff, University of Berkeley—Department of Architecture report, "Low Cost Housing Demonstration," CD 37-018-003/CD 37-S4 014 2/2: Research Material on Low Cost Housing in Canadian Center for Architecture, Montreal (CCA). For a critical interpretation of architects' goal to provide comfort, see Barber, "After Comfort."

116   The textbook on tropical architecture that came out of the British trajectory is Koenigsberger et al., *Manual of Tropical Housing and Building*; Baweja, "Otto Koenigsberger."

117   "Ventilation in Warm Climates," 2.

118   Wakely, "Development of a School"; Chang, *A Genealogy of Tropical Architecture*, 203–44; Akcan, *Abolish Human Bans*.

119   Chang, *Genealogy of Tropical Architecture*, 189.

120   Map of "Tropical Zones," *Colonial Building Notes* 32 (1955): 7.

121   See, for instance, SAD A16/62

122   For the architecture of Sudan during this time, see Osman and Osman, "Modern Heritage of Khartoum"; Osman et al., "Architecture in Sudan"; Osman, "Sudanese Architecture Around Independence"; Akcan, *Abolish Human Bans*.

123   Mazower, *Greek Revolution*, 277.

124   "Taking a Job in Africa."

125   For the Greece-Bulgaria exchange, see Dragostinova, *Between Two Motherlands*.

126   Constantinos Doxiadis, "Human Relations within Ekistic Environment," Address by C. A. Doxiadis at the Hellenic Public Relations Society, January 29, 1970, Doxiadis Archives, Athens. Ref. Code: 6548. On Doxiadis's childhood and father, also see Deane, *Constantinos Doxiadis*; Kyrtsis, *Constantinos A. Doxiadis*, 303–5.

127   Doxiadis, *Anthropopolis*, dedication page.

128 Constantinos A. Doxiadis, *Ekistics* 62, nos. 373, 374, 375 (July–August, September–October, November–December 1995): 164–67.

129 Doxiadis, *Architecture in Transition*, 96; Doxiadis, *Ekistics*.

130 Pyla, "Ekistics, Architecture and Environmental Politics," 21, 57; Pyla, "Baghdad's Urban Restructuring, 1958."

131 Rand, "Ekistic World," 53.

132 Doxiadis's father had already worked in close communication with the American refugee aid institutions in the aftermath of the Exchange of Populations of 1923 (see chapter 2). Doxiadis himself was vocal on the need for Greece's alignment with United States in Cold War bipolarities, during his involvement with reconstruction after World War II. Kyrtsis, *Constantinos A. Doxiadis*, 337–53.

133 Kyrtsis, *Constantinos A. Doxiadis*, 359–62; Karim, "Between Self and Citizenship"; Muzaffar, "Boundary Games."

134 Pyla, "Ekistics, Architecture and Environmental Politics." Hashim Sarkis also interpreted Constantinos Doxiadis's invitation to Lebanon as part of the US policy to intervene on different levels in the Middle East against the threat of communism. Sarkis, "Dances with Margaret Mead."

135 Pyla, "Ekistics, Architecture and Environmental Politics," 63.

136 The House of Friendship in Khartoum was built as a Chinese gift.

137 Doxiadis to Stephen Dorsey, Counselor to American Embassy of Sudan, 11.9.59 (C-OA 120); Doxiadis to Stephen Dorsey, Counselor to American Embassy of Sudan, 12.10.1959 (C-OA 128), Sudan Correspondence C-OA 28–441. Administrative Circulars A-OA 1–4 1959–62, Sudan Reports, vol. 6, Doxiadis Archives, Athens, no. 24827.

138 When he returned to Athens, A. O. Petermuller oversaw the Gibb-Petermuller branch that built buildings for Saudi Arabia and the Gulf States. An advertisement published in *Architects Journal* in November 16, 1988, declares the office was established in Athens in May of the same year. Petermuller's buildings in Sudan included the Khartoum Senior Trade School, College of Engineering, Sudan University of Science and Technology (Khartoum Polytechnic), Industrial Bank, Bata shoe factory, an extension to Sudan Archeology Museum, residential blocks, and houses.

139 Kyrtsis, *Constantinos A. Doxiadis*, 373.

140 Chaldeos, "Sudanese Toponyms Related to Greek Entrepreneurial Activity"; Makris and Stiansen, "Angelo Capato"; "Sudanese Greeks." Most were traders, and some were slave traffickers. They accompanied both the Ottoman Egyptian and the British army for trading goods. Some accompanied the travelers during the heights of archaeological discovery into Sudanese ancient sites.

141 Sudan Reports, vol. 1, p. 273, Doxiadis Archives, Athens, no. 24822.

142 Doxiadis asked the Greek professionals to report on job opportunities and insider government information in Khartoum that they should know about. Antachopoulos to Messrs Conromichalos, 12.1.1961, 2.2.1961 (C-OA 166), Sudan Correspondence C-OA 28–441, Administrative Circulars A-OA 1–4 1959–62, Sudan Reports, vol. 6, Doxiadis Archives, Athens, no. 24827. Kleon Krantonellis from Doxiadis Associates visited the office of Conromichalos when he went on fieldwork for the Gezira Scheme. C. Crantonellis (Kleon Krantonellis), "Diary of a Visit to Khartoum and the Gezira Area," April 3–12, 1960, pp. 1–48, R-OA 15–16, R-OE 1–37, 1962, Sudan Reports, vol. 8, Doxiadis Archives, Athens, no. 24829.

143 Doxiadis, *Architecture in Transition*, 103; Doxiadis, *Ekistics*, 474.

144 We can safely assume that a lecture with the same title given a year later in Oslo provides sufficient information about these presentations in Sudan. C. A. Doxiadis, "Dynapolis: The City of the Future," Lecture at the Oslo Arkitektforening Oslo, March 3, 1960, p. 12, Canadian Center for Architecture Collection, Montreal.

145 Doxiadis, "Dynapolis," 26.

146 Doxiadis, "Dynapolis," 1.

147 Dutta et al., *Architecture in Development*.

148 Constantinos Doxiadis was closely aligned with the UN's developmentalism. He said: "Development is the major task of every nation and every community in our era. The UN has recognized this officially and has proclaimed the decade 1961–1970 as the Development Decade. Doxiadis Associates, realizing the importance of this task, has organized development-minded consulting services qualified to render technical assistance in every development effort." Doxiadis Associates, *Consultants on Development and Ekistics* (office brochure), p. 5, Canadian Centre for Architecture Collection, Montreal.

149 In a typical passage, Doxiadis wrote, "The settlements of the present, then, were born in 1825 and are still developing into new types, with more people, rising incomes, decreasing differences in income levels between urban and rural people, rising energy consumption, expanding territories and much more complex functions." Doxiadis and Papaioannou, *Ecumenopolis*, 151.

150 Doxiadis Associates, "Omdurman" Report, 1959, p. 110. DOX-OA 3 in DOX-OA 1–7, MR-OA 1–6, Nov. 1958—Jun. 1959, Sudan Reports, vol. 1, Doxiadis Archives, Athens, no. 24822.

151 Doxiadis Associates, "The Size and Shape of Urban Plots," Report, 1959, pp. 1–35. DOX-OA 8 in DOX-OA 8–16, MR-OA 7–11, Jul. 1959–Nov. 1959, Sudan Reports, vol. 2, Doxiadis Archives, Athens, no. 24823; Doxiadis

Associates, "Description of Greater Khartoum Area," Report, 3.2.1959, pp. 89–95, R-OA 1–14, R-OK 1–48, Jan.–Aug. 1959, Sudan Reports, vol. 3, Doxiadis Archives, Athens, no. 24824.

152   Hassan Fathy to "The City of the Future" Research Staff, "Report: Information and Comments" R-ERES 15 (2), 3.6.61. p.3. ATO/GSER WF: Omdurman-Khartoum-Lagos, 1961 (Cr-Eres 15 (2), (4). Doxiadis Archives, Athens, no. 19864.

153   Doxiadis, *Architecture in Transition*.

154   Doxiadis Associates, R-OA 1–14, R-OK 1–48, Jan.–Aug. 1959, Sudan Reports, vol. 3, Doxiadis Archives, Athens, no. 24824.

155   Sudan would soon be swept into two civil wars, resulting in the Darfur genocide and the country's separation into two, the highest number of famines in recent world history, and the ongoing struggle between the military dictatorship and democratic forces. Karadawi, *Refugee Policy in Sudan 1967–1984*; Johnson, *The Root Causes of Sudan's Civil Wars*.

156   Doxiadis Associates, "Training Ekistics: Preparation for the Republic of Sudan," 26.6.1959, pp. 509–75, DOX-OA 1–7 MR-OA 1–6, Nov. 1958–Jun. 1959, Sudan Reports, vol. 1, Doxiadis Archives, Athens, no. 24822.

157   My research in the Doxiadis Archives in Athens revealed that the following experts from the Doxiadis office and the local government prepared these surveys in Sudan: planning reports: Orestis Yakas and M. Panagos; administration reports: Grigoratos, Messaris, and Strataki; and housing reports: Iacovou and Simeon. The local authorities named in these reports include Sayed Hassan Subara, Sayed Mamoon Klamin, Sayed Mohamed Hag, Sayed Awadalla Mahgoub, Sayed Halid Abdel Magi, Sayed Ahmed Elhag, Sayed Ahmed Abdul Ruhman El Agib, Sayed Esher Abdel Latif, and Sayed Ibrahim Mohamad Taha El Fahal.

158   Doxiadis Associates, "Training Ekistics: Preparation for the Republic of Sudan," 505; Doxiadis to Ali Hassan Abdalla (Director of Ministry of Local Government), 21.3.1959 (C-OA 71); Doxiadis to Hassan Ali Abdallah. 17.10.1960 (C-OA 160), Sudan Correspondence C-OA 28–441, Administrative Circulars A-OA 1–4, 1959–62, Sudan Reports, vol. 6, Doxiadis Archives, Athens, no. 24827.

159   The scholar Gamal Hamdan also contributed to *Ekistics*. See Hamdan, " Growth and Functional Structure of Khartoum"; El-Bushra, "Sudan's Triple Capital"; El-Bushra and El Sammani, "Water for Human Use"; As-Sammani, "Private Sector and Government."

160   Doxiadis Associates, "Size and Shape of Urban Plots," 24.

161 Doxiadis Associates, "Climatological Data of Greater Khartoum Area," 1959, pp. 75–78, R-OA 1–14, R-OK 1–48, Jan.–Aug. 1959, Sudan Reports, vol. 3, Doxiadis Archives, Athens, no. 24824.

162 Akcan, "Decolonize or Redistribute?" I can't express enough my gratitude for Migdad Bannaga, Mustafa's office Technocon, Adil Mustafa Ahmad, Salah Hassan, Amira Swar-El-Dahab, Osman M. El Kheir, Elamin Osman, and Ilham Abdalla Tagelsir Ali for helping me reach the private sources and archives in Khartoum.

163 Newspaper clip identifying Moneim Mustafa as "first non British student of the year," found in family archive. Source not visible. Author has a copy.

164 Yahya Muhammasalieh and Professor Abu Bakir Abdulrahab (Abdel Moneim Mustafa's partners at Technocon Engineering Group, Khartoum), interview by author, Khartoum, in person, December 22, 2019.

165 Norberg-Schulz, "Locus." Norberg-Schulz does not credit Moneim Mustafa's office, but the drawings can be located in Moneim Mustafa's archive.

166 Among the professionals of early Independence in Sudan, the Omdurman-born architect Abdel Moneim Mostafa relates to one of my proudest by-products of this book. I was happy to initiate the processes, during the window of opportunity immediately after the democratic transition and before the current war, when we digitized the drawings of a previously unknown architect with the architects in Sudan. I eventually featured Moneim Mustafa's work in *Architectural Review's* Reputation series. In 2022, the Canadian Centre for Architecture archived and digitalized Moneim Mustafa's remaining drawings, which can be found at "Category: Buildings by Abdel Moneim Mustafa," Wikimedia Commons, https://commons.wikimedia.org/wiki/Category:Buildings_by_Abdel -Moneim_Mustafa (accessed May 12, 2022). See also Canadian Centre for Architecture, "CCA Find and Tell Elsewhere: Abdel Moneim Mustafa."

167 For photographs, see Akcan, *Abolish Human Bans*, 7.

168 For a memoir on the establishment of the Architecture Department and the design of Examination Hall at the University of Khartoum, see Potter and Potter, *Everything Is Possible*, 31–72.

169 Since 1975, this school is now part of the Khartoum Polytechnic Institute.

170 For an account of these transformations that impacted Southeast Asia, see Chang, *Genealogy of Tropical Architecture*.

171 *Colonial Building Notes* was renamed *Overseas Building Notes* in 1958.

172 For instance, Moneim Mustafa's student, the prominent scholar and teacher Adil Mustafa Ahmad, went to AA to study with Otto Koeningsberger. Mukhar, "Roofs in Hot Dry Climates."

173 Moneim Mustafa and Ayoub & Omer Salim, "College of Fine and Applied Art, Khartoum Polytechnic Sudan," Report 1, 8. Office Archives.

174 Moneim Mustafa and Ayoub & Omer Salim, "College of Fine and Applied Art," Report 2, 6–7.

175 Moneim Mustafa and Ayoub & Omer Salim, "College of Fine and Applied Art," Report 2, 2.

176 Needless to say, the independence of Moneim Mustafa's mind would not necessarily indicate the political independence of a country, or mean he was attentive to continuing hierarchies and inequalities of the age. Sudan would soon be swept with two civil wars that resulted in the genocide of Darfur and the separation into two countries. In the ongoing struggle between the military rule and democratic forces, Moneim Mustafa was personally affected, as he could no longer find public commissions once the Islamist military officer Omar al-Bashir came to power in 1989. His symbolic buildings were also affected, as in the case of the military occupation of Mansour Khalid's house. Many of these buildings may not have survived the war that is still continuing during the publication of this book.

177 Churchill, *River War*, 10–11.

178 Parenti, *Tropic of Chaos*.

179 Edkins, *Whose Hunger?*

180 Photograph taken between 1935–50. A. D. Wesson collection. SAD1/25/7.

181 Gaitskell, *Gezira*, 32, 42.

182 Bernal, "Colonial Moral Economy."

183 Beckert, *Empire of Cotton*, 9–10.

184 Beckert, *Empire of Cotton*, xii.

185 Mihri, *Sudan Seyahatnamesi*, 120.

186 Gaitskell, *Gezira*, 137.

187 Gaitskell, *Gezira*, 46.

188 Gaitskell, *Gezira*, 102.

189 Photograph dated 1928 of the Barakat area of Gezira in Harold Alfred MacMichael's collection. SAD 588/2/72. Also see SAD 588/2/67; SAD 711/2/6; SAD 778/3/5; SAD 705/1/1; SAD 883/5/9.

190 Photograph dated 1934(?) of a village near the main irrigation canal and the road to Khartoum in J. F. E. Bloss's collection. SAD 705/1/2.

191 A photograph dated 1950–59 from inside a village school shows sons of tenant farmers listening to a teacher showing the Arabic numbers in a crowded classroom. Six boys are sitting at a desk probably good for three.

The first intermediary school for girls was opened in 1940. D. M. H. Evans's collection. SAD 711/2/1.

192   Photograph dated 1950–55 showing tenant farmers packing cotton into sacks to be transported by a camel in T. H. B. Mynors's collection. SAD 778/3/6.

193   Photograph (1925–50) in A. D. Wesson collection. SAD 1/25/9.

194   G. M. Culwick is riding on a camel on her trip to Gezira villages as a nutritionist, where the *tukl* structures are visible in the background. SAD 428/3/188.

195   Geraldine Mary Culwick, letter of 26 April 1949. SAD 428/3/22.

196   Photograph dated 1902–7, showing the "survey camp" at Wad Hamid in Gezira in C. W. L. Crompton's collection. SAD 877/10/3.

197   Photograph showing Sudan Plantations Syndicate employees' living quarters (1934–46) in F. B. Hunt's collection. SAD 692/19/7.

198   Geraldine Mary Culwick, letter 4 of May 20, 1947. Original emphasis. SAD 428/1/49.

199   SAD 8/51/9.

200   SAD 784/3/72; SAD 784/3/91.

201   SAD 784/3/34; SAD 784/3/33; SAD 784/3/41.

202   Photograph showing Sudan Plantation Syndicate cotton inspector's house in Gezira (1934–46) in F. B. Hunt's collection. SAD 692/19/6.

203   E. Jane, "Anti-Malaria Work in the Gezira Plantation Area." SAD 403/5/99.

204   Photograph of 1937 in E. Jane's collection. SAD G//S25; SAD 403/5/26. Photograph of 1934–46 in F. B. Hunt's collection. SAD 692/19/6.

205   Photograph of 1935 in N. R. Syme's collection. SAD 2/7/1.

206   Geraldine Mary Culwick, letter of July 4, 1947. SAD 428/1/56.

207   SAD 302/9/1 and SAD 8/51/7.

208   Photograph of 1949–50 in Remeitab Village in G. M. Culwick's collection. SAD 428/3/196 and SAD 428/3/250. The houses and buildings in the background of G. M. Culwick's photographs suggest this complexity. SAD 428/3/188; SAD 428/3/185; SAD 428/3/197; SAD 428/3/207; SAD 428/3/251.

209   Photograph of 1954 of a brick house in Gezira in G. M. Culwick's collection. SAD 428/3/251.

210   Geraldine Mary Culwick, letter of June 30, 1949, and June 5, 1949. SAD 428/3/47; SAD 428/3/37

211   Geraldine Mary Culwick, letter of April 26, 1949. SAD 428/3/24.

212 Geraldine Mary Culwick, letter of July 4, 1947. SAD 428/1/56.

213 Geraldine Mary Culwick, letter of June 30, 1949. SAD 428/3/44.

214 Culwick described their living spaces as follows: "The gypsies have not even got tents, they live entirely in the open, come wind come weather, with a few mats to sit on and lie on. They are a community by themselves, with their own strange ways just as among us, belonging neither to the settled peasantry, not yet to the organized nomad tribes, just appearing and disappearing without warning, their arrival an event and excitement in the quiet village life." Geraldine Mary Culwick, letter of August 21, 1949. SAD 428/3/59.

215 The quotation continues: "Properly maintained, especially as regards to repair of the outside plaster before the rains, the square mud buildings were said to last 20 years and more, this is certainly an exaggeration, except perhaps in the north with its scantier rainfall. . . . The better built ones of green brick often had rooms of good size and carpentered doors and window openings with ill-fitting shutters. The carpentry was usually of a very poor quality." Geraldine Mary Culwick, "A Study of the Human Factor in the Gezira Scheme," unpublished manuscript, 1955. SAD 428/4/1–295, with quotation at SAD.428/5/75–76.

216 Holt and Daly, *History of Sudan*, 140.

217 Geraldine Mary Culwick, "A Study of the Human Factor in the Gezira Scheme," unpublished manuscript, 1955. SAD 428/4/1–295.

218 SAD 428/4/6.

219 Bernal, "Colonial Moral Economy," 451.

220 Bernal, "Colonial Moral Economy," 453. Even Arthur Gaitskell said the Gezira farmers were like "soldiers in a camp" and outside "free as a nomad."

221 Bernal, "Colonial Moral Economy," 447.

222 Victoria Bernal notes that the colonial government in fact made a loss on the Gezira Scheme on one out of every two years between 1925 and 1946.

223 Bernal, "Colonial Moral Economy," 465.

224 Gaitskell, *Gezira*, 321.

225 Doxiadis Associates, "Proposed Regional Planning Services for Gezira Scheme and Managil Extension," 1960, pp. 1–17, DOX-OA 18–19, MR-OA 12–15, 1960–62, Sudan Reports, vol. 5, Doxiadis Archives, Athens, no. 24826.

226 Kardamitsi-Adami, *Architect Kleon Krantonellis*.

227 Crantonellis (Kleon Krantonellis), "Diary of a Visit to Khartoum and the Gezira Area," April 3–12, 1960, pp. 1–48, with quotation on p. 17, R-OA

15–16, R-OE 1–37, 1962, Sudan Reports, vol. 8, Doxiadis Archives, Athens, no. 24829.

228 Krantonellis, "Diary of a Visit," 6, Doxiadis Archives.

229 Krantonellis, "Diary of a Visit," 2, Doxiadis Archives.

230 Krantonellis, "Diary of a Visit," 6, Doxiadis Archives.

231 Hassan Fathy, "Notes on the Planning of the Gezira Cotton-Growing Area," 12.7.60, pp. 250–72, with quotation on p. 250, DA-General, vol. 22, Doxiadis Archives, Athens, no. 24995.

232 Krantonellis, "Diary of a Visit," 6, Doxiadis Archives.

233 Krantonellis, "Diary of a Visit," 18, Doxiadis Archives.

234 Doxiadis Associates, "Proposed Regional Planning Services for Gezira Scheme," 2–3.

235 Doxiadis to Sayed Mirgani El Amin (Deputy Under Secretary Ministry of Interior), 25.9.1959 (C-OA 125), Sudan Correspondence C-OA 28–441, Administrative Circulars A-OA 1–4 1959–62, Sudan Reports, vol. 6, Doxiadis Archives, Athens, No. 24827.

236 Phokaides, "Ruralizing Zambia."

237 Hassan Fathy, City of the Future, Research Notes, Africa Notebooks, 1961; Handwritten notebook, Doxiadis, Box 3 (of 9), Hassan Fathy Papers and Photographic Collection, The American University in Cairo, Rare Books and Special Collections Library.

238 Fathy, "Notes," 250, Doxiadis Archives.

239 Bernal, "Colonial Moral Economy."

240 Fathy, "Notes," 250, Doxiadis Archives.

241 Fathy, "Notes," 254.

242 Fathy, "Notes," 268.

243 Fathy, "Notes," 270.

244 Fathy, "Notes," 258–66.

245 Fathy, "Notes," 270.

246 Fathy extracted pages from his report on Gourna for this purpose. Fathy, "Notes," 256–60, Doxiadis Archives.

247 Fathy, "Notes," 266.

248 Fathy, "Notes," 270.

249 Fathy, "Notes," 254.

250 "These African immigrants provide the only hope of increasing the population to a more desirable manner. The experts complain that the country is under-populated and that the people there already are not

enough even to maintain the existing irrigation system, let alone utilize it to maximum advantage." Fathy, "Notes," 268, Doxiadis Archives.

251 Mihri, *Sudan Seyehatnamesi*, 140.

252 Baker, *Albert N'Yanza*, vol. 1, 255.

253 Trout Powell, *Different Shade of Colonialism*.

254 Minawi, *Losing Istanbul*.

255 Pyla, "Hassan Fathy Revisited."

256 Kyrtsis, *Constantinos A. Doxiadis*, 364–68.

257 Akcan, "Democracy and War."

258 Mahmood et al., "Lessons Learned from Khartoum Flash Flood."

259 Parenti, *Tropic of Chaos*.

260 Water and Climate Coalition, "Water and Climate Coalition."

261 King, *Bungalow*, 265.

262 For instance, Walter Mignolo sees the 1955 Bandung Conference that led to the nonaligned movement as the first but ultimately failed step toward decolonization. He describes it as the first "dewesternizing" movement against the two "westernizing ideologies of the Cold War." Instead, he defines "decolonial thinking and doing" as "delinking from the epistemic assumptions common to all areas of knowledge established in the Western world since European Renaissance and through the European Enlightenment." Mignolo and Walsh, *On Decoloniality*, 106.

263 Akcan, *Architecture in Translation*.

264 Getachew, *Worldmaking After Empire*, 2.

265 World's People's Conference on Climate Change and the Rights of Mother Earth, "People's Agreement of Cochabamba," 4. Also see Táíwò and Bigger. "Debt Justice for Climate Reparations."

Chapter 5. Extinction: Gardens, Parks, Ruderal Urban Spaces

1 According to some estimates, a hundred or more species are becoming extinct per day in the modern era. While David Raup calculated the extinction rate in the past 500 million years as one species every five years, Norman Myers estimates that four species have been going extinct a day in Brazil alone in the last decades. Broswimmer, *Ecocide*, 1–3.

2 Nixon, *Slow Violence*.

3 See especially Spirn, "Legacy of Frederick Law Olmsted."

4 McDonough and Partners, "Hannover Principles," 6.

5 Orff, *Toward an Urban Ecology*.

6　　For example, "Rewilding Cities," a webinar organized by Future of Cities in collaboration with New Cities Foundation, on October 5, 2021; see https://focities.com/rewilding-cities/.

7　　Scientists have pointed out the difficulties that impair precision in the study of extinction. These include calculating the full number of extinct species, finding out the details of mass extinctions in the history of the Earth, identifying the time that recent number of extinctions accelerated, and settling on exact conceptual distinctions between categories such as "critically endangered" and "vulnerable" species. Brockington et al., *Nature Unbound*, 50.

8　　The term *ecocide* was coined by Arthur Galston in 1970. For its relation to recent state of extinction, see Broswimmer, *Ecocide*; Kolbert, *Sixth Extinction*; Dawson, *Extinction*.

9　　Kolbert, *Sixth Extinction*, 167.

10　　Michaelson, "Waste Colonialism.'"

11　　Walter Alverez et al.'s "discovery" that an asteroid caused the fifth mass extinction was published in June 1980. Alvarez et al., "Extraterrestrial Cause for the Cretaceous-Tertiary Extinction."

12　　Elizabeth Kolbert has synthesized the scholarship on the history of the science on extinction from the eighteenth century onwards. Kolbert, *Sixth Extinction*, 23–94.

13　　Quoted in Marris, *Rambunctious Garden*, 23.

14　　Brockington et al., *Nature Unbound*.

15　　Numbers are taken from two reports: IUCN, "Nations Fall Short on Biodiversity"; Protected Planet, *Protected Planet Report May 2020*.

16　　Cronon, "Trouble with Wilderness," in Cronon, *Uncommon Ground*.

17　　Also see Jacoby, *Crimes Against Nature*; Brockington et al., *Nature Unbound*, 113–31.

18　　Cronon, "Trouble with Wilderness," in *Environmental History*, 25.

19　　For a history and critique of current "protected areas" policies, see Brockington et al., *Nature Unbound*.

20　　Dawson, *Extinction*, 12–13.

21　　Bram Büscher and Robert Fletcher identify four distinct positions and map them according to their relations to capitalism and the nature/culture dichotomy. While "mainstream conservation" spreads the idea of national parks around the world within the logic of capitalism and maintains the assumed separation between nature and culture, the authors name three alternatives to the status quo: "neoprotectionism" (anticapitalist but maintains the nature/culture dichotomy), "new conservation" (debunks the nature/culture dichotomy but is capitalist), and their own proposal, "convivial conservation" (both debunks the nature/culture dichotomy and is anticapitalist). Büscher and Fletcher, *Conservation Revolution*.

22 Young, *Planet City*.

23 Marris, *Rambunctious Garden*, 1.

24 Marris, *Rambunctious Garden*, 56.

25 Büscher and Fletcher named this approach as new conservationism of the twenty-first century. They additionally emphasized the work of Peter Kareiva of the Nature Conservancy, but criticized the complicity of new conservationist policies with capitalism and market enthusiasm. For Büscher and Fletcher's critique, see *Conservation Revolution*, 24–25, 54–69. For the Nature Conservancy, see https://www.nature.org/en-us/.

26 Grove, *Green Imperialism*.

27 Grove, *Green Imperialism*, 15.

28 This book also gives due acknowledgment to previously ignored thinkers, including architectural theorists such as Lewis Mumford. Guha and Martinez-Alier, *Varieties of Environmentalism*.

29 Doxiadis, "Water and Environment."

30 Liboiron, *Pollution Is Colonialism*, 60.

31 The contract was signed after a preliminary inspection on December 14, 1961, and the fieldwork started in 1962. This chapter bases the discussion on the UN-funded Kordofan project on the documents kept in Doxiadis Archives, Athens, nos. 24822–24855, 34 volumes.

32 These four volumes built on Doxiadis's theory of ekistics that had already been published in 1968. While the first volume outlined the research on the past and present of human settlements, the second anticipated the future and defined an ideal settlement; the third commented on the combination of goals and reality; and, finally, the fourth was set to define the policies for the implementation of the ideal future settlement. Doxiadis, *Ekistics*; Doxiadis, *Anthropopolis*; Doxiadis and Papaioannou, *Ecumenopolis*; Doxiadis, *Building Entopia*; Doxiadis, *Action for Human Settlements*.

33 M. G. Ionides, "Land and Water Use Survey in Kordofan Province, Sudan," October 1969, pp. 1–127, with quotation on p. 5. DOX-SUD-A 59–60, 1969–70, Sudan Reports, vol. 34. Doxiadis Archives, Athens, no. 24855.

34 "My enquiries revealed with crude clarity that it would be a great mistake to treat the problems of this area if they would respond to technological treatments already well-known and ready to be applied. Diagnosis is essential before cure. It is a dynamic situation which needs to be understood and can only be understood by specific studies oriented

towards the specific problems." M. G. Ionides to UN Special Funds, "Confidential Report on Kordofan Problems Investigation," 1969, pp. 101–20, with quotation on p. 101, DOX-SUD-A 59–60, 1969–70, Sudan Reports, vol. 34, Doxiadis Archives, Athens, no. 24855. Also see "Republic of Sudan Kordofan Problems Investigation (KPI) Revised Request to the U.N. Special Fund," pp. 73–95, DOX-SUD-A 59–60, 1969–70, Sudan Reports, vol. 34, Doxiadis Archives, Athens, no. 24855.

35   M. G. Ionides, "Kordofan Background Study," 1962, pp. 16–55, R-OA 15–16, R-OE 1–37, 1962, Sudan Reports, vol. 8, Doxiadis Archives, Athens, no. 24829.

36   Mohd. O. El Sammani, "Village of Unn Garku," 1962, pp. 56–64, R-OA 15–16, R-OE 1–37, 1962, Sudan Reports, vol. 8, Doxiadis Archives, Athens, no. 24829.

37   Mohd. O. El Sammani, "Preliminary Ekistic Survey in Um Ruaba Area," 1962, pp. 161–99, R-OA 15–16, R-OE 1–37, 1962, Sudan Reports, vol. 8, Doxiadis Archives, Athens, no. 24829.

38   Ionides, "Land and Water Use Survey in Kordofan Province, Sudan," 49.

39   "Village Water Tanks—Report on the 1964 Yard Prototype Program," July 1965. pp. 91–223, with quotation on pp. 93–94, DOX-SUD-A 41–44, MR SUD A 35–37, June–December 1965, Sudan Reports, vol. 26, Doxiadis Archives, Athens, no. 24843.

40   Ionides, "Land and Water Use Survey in Kordofan Province, Sudan," 49.

41   "Village Water Tanks," 96.

42   "Agronomic Investigations Concluding Report on the Crop and Soil Trials," April 1966, pp. 1–87, DOX-SUD-A 54–58, 1966, Sudan Reports, vol. 32, Doxiadis Archives, Athens, no. 24859.

43   Doxiadis, "Water and Environment," 34–35. Constantinos A. Doxiadis usually replaced the English *man* with *Anthropos*, which he thought embodied a more universal meaning after 1974. Doxiadis, "Anthropos."

44   Doxiadis, "Water and Environment," 38.

45   Doxiadis, "Water and Environment," 39, 46.

46   Humanity has "polluted not only those resources close to him, but also those far out such as the oceans." Doxiadis Associates, "Water for Human Development," paper presented at the American Water Works Association 9th Annual Conference, Washington, DC, June 24, 1970, r-gen-a471, Canadian Centre for Architecture Collection, Montreal.

47   "All this must lead to the necessary conclusion that Man can face his present and future problems if he does not concentrate so much as he does on the day to day problems . . . whilst looking at the overall problem of the evolution of Man as part of the biological system developed by Na-

ture on the surface of the earth." Doxiadis Associates, "Water for Human Development," 18.

48 "The answer to our problems lies in the achievement of a proper dynamic balance of land, water and man: first on a local basis, and then on a universal one, with the total universal city." Doxiadis, "Water and Environment," 36, 40.

49 Doxiadis, "Water and Environment," 42.

50 Doxiadis, "Water and Environment," 43.

51 Doxiadis, "Water and Environment," 46.

52 Doxiadis and Papaioannou, *Ecumenopolis*.

53 C. A. Doxiadis, "An Analysis of the Scope and the Design of the Project," 5.10.1960, R-ERES 1, pp. 1–18; Doxiadis, "Questions by Team Members and Answers by D on the Project and Its Contents" 6.12.1960, R-ERES 2, pp. 18–36, ATO ACE COF Reports, R-ERES 1–15, Oct. 1960–June 1961, vol. 5, Doxiadis Archives, Athens, no. 17351.

54 This structure of thinking from the smallest to the largest settlement scale, and from the study of the past to present and the future, dictated the outline of the final publication. Doxiadis, *Ecumenopolis*.

55 Doxiadis, *Ecumenopolis*, 122.

56 See Kyrtsis, "Ekistics and the World of Sciences."

57 "This is the inevitable future of Human Settlements in the next few generations and we can well foresee that assuming we avoid any major catastrophe, we will have to deal with a universal city whose population will tend to be stable in numbers." Constantinos A. Doxiadis, "The Future of Human Settlements," paper prepared for the Nobel Symposium on "The Place of Value in a World of Facts," Stockholm, September 19, 1969, p. 29, Document: R-GEN-A 443, Canadian Center for Architecture, Montreal. In his final study, Constantinos A. Doxiadis predicted that the population would stabilize at 15 to 25 billion. Doxiadis, *Ecumenopolis*, 13–40.

58 C. A. Doxiadis "Towards Ecumenopolis: A Different Approach to the Problem of the 'City of the Future,'" 6. 25.1961, pp. 90–104, With quotation pp. 90–93, CONFIDENTIAL R-ERES. ATO ACE COF Reports, R-ERES 1–15, October 1960–June 1961, vol. 5, Doxiadis Archives, Athens, no. 17351.

59 Doxiadis and Papaioannou, *Ecumenopolis*, 140–50; 188–204.

60 Doxiadis and Papaioannou, *Ecumenopolis*, 338. In Constantinos A. Doxiadis's prediction, the current trends and crises would continue during the transition period. "This is inevitable because we are in the middle of the greatest transitional period of the whole of human history, so Anthropos

must suffer first, and then go through a natural stage of growing pains." Doxiadis and Papaioannou, *Ecumenopolis*, 335.

61   Doxiadis and Papaioannou, *Ecumenopolis*, 356–69.

62   For problems that would continue or remain unresolved, such as wealth inequality, threatened cultures, or nondemocratic governance, Doxiadis assured that situations would be more balanced than in the present. Doxiadis and Papaioannou, *Ecumenopolis*, 382–94.

63   Doxiadis and Papaioannou, *Ecumenopolis*, 394.

64   Pardisan is often mentioned in passing in books and articles about architecture in Iran of the 1970s. This chapter was written after research into the design process in archives, as well as in consultation with experts in wildlife biology and botanical studies, including Amanda Rodewald and Christopher Dunn. A feedback structure was established with the support of a generous grant so that the intellectual labor for this expert consultation gets compensated. This structure acknowledges the need for more collaboration between humanities scholars and scientists to bear on issues of the designed environment, both architectural and natural, in settlements with more-than-human residents. I thank all the scientists who helped me understand the contributions, limits, and dangers of this project if it were built. For the only comprehensive article on Pardisan from the viewpoint of landscape architecture, see John-Alder, "Paradise Reconsidered." While Kathleen John-Alder's article outlines the design process in detail, my chapter imagines the experience of being in Pardisan if it were built and discusses the park from the viewpoint of ecocide prevention and right to heal. The project and terminology changed during the design process, and so, when there was a contradiction or multiple possibilities, I used the version that is in the promotional materials and publications. McHarg Collection #365, Architectural Archives, McHarg Center, School of Architecture, University of Pennsylvania (hereafter McHarg Archives). For architecture in Iran during this time, see Grigor, *Building Iran*; Karimi, *Domesticity and Consumer Culture in Iran*.

65   This is how the team defined it already in the first reports of 1973. Eskandar Firouz, "Description of Objectives," ca. 1973, McHarg Collection #365, box 4, McHarg Archives; "Pardisan: A Feasibility Study for an Environmental Park in Tehran, for the Imperial Government of Iran," Report of 1973, McHarg Archives, 365.II.89-90; Eskandar Firouz, "Introduction," in "Pardisan: Plan for an Environmental Park in Tehran," Report of 1975 by Mandala Collaborative/Wallace, McHarg, Roberts and Todd, McHarg Archives, 365.II.93. Also see Firouz, *Environment Iran*; Firouz, *Complete Fauna of Iran*.

66   Crutzen, "Geology of Mankind."

67 "Pardisan: Plan for an Environmental Park in Tehran," Report of 1975, p. 6.

68 McHarg, *Design with Nature*. The quotation is taken from the biographical blurb of Ian McHarg on the back jacket of this book.

69 McHarg, *To Heal the Earth*.

70 Firouz, "Description of Objectives," 3.

71 "Pardisan: A Feasibility Study," 3.

72 John-Alder, "Paradise Reconsidered," 128.

73 Marris, *Rambunctious Garden*.

74 Ardalan and Bakhtiar, *Sense of Unity*. For more on the International Congress of Architecture in Iran, see Akcan, *Abolish Human Bans*.

75 For a discussion of the Eameses' project, see Colomina, "Enclosed by Images."

76 Firouz, "Description of Objectives," 6.

77 Firouz, "Description of Objectives," 8–9.

78 "This proposes that the earth is unitary, divided by science and language, and that knowledge must be reintegrated to solve human problems. . . . Implicit in this proposition is a commitment to the understanding of whole systems and thus to the holistic science of ecology." "Pardisan: Plan for an Environmental Park in Tehran," 6.

79 "Spatial problems are obviously most critical with respect to the live wildlife exhibits, particularly since we would like to show each species in an environment approximating its natural surroundings. The conflict therefore arises between the numbers of species exhibited and the naturalness of each exhibit. Clearly our basic philosophy will be better served by having a smaller number of specimens and species presented in a reasonable simulation of their respective natural habitants." Firouz to McHarg, 5 October 1975, McHarg Center, School of Architecture, University of Pennsylvania, 109.III.C.13.

80 This chapter examines the idea of Persian Garden according to Pardisan's designers. For the scholarly history of Persian Gardens, see especially Gharipour, *Persian Gardens and Pavilions*; Khansari et al., *Persian Garden*. Pardisan's designers probably referred to Arthur Pope: Pope, *Survey of Persian Art*.

81 Eames and Fleck, dirs., *Pardisan*, Charles Eames Studio, 1977, Architectural Archives, McHarg Center, School of Architecture, University of Pennsylvania, 109.V.B.2.2. While drawings by WMRT and the Mandala Collective was used throughout the movie, the end of the movie also credits the illustrations to David Negron—the storyboard artist and illustrator of *Blade Runner, Jurassic Park, Indiana Jones*—and design to

George Spacek, and music to a James Bond, whose existence could not be confirmed.

82   "Pardisan: Plan for an Environmental Park in Tehran" report, p. 14.

83   "Pardisan: Technical Report" prepared by Mandala/WHRT, report of 1975, McHarg Archives, 365.II.92

84   "Pardisan: Plan for an Environmental Park in Tehran" report, p. 19.

85   I should mention that the terminology of these "bioclimatic zones" shifted during the design process. The early feasibility report mentioned the following as the bioclimatic zones of Iran: tidal marsh, desert, tamarisk, herbaceous steppe, scrub steppe, alpine, and broadleaf forest.

86   "Pardisan: A Feasibility Study for an Environmental Park in Tehran" report, p. 1.

87   "The concept of the bioclimatic zone was employed to facilitate this comparison [of world environments]. Bioclimatic zones or major biome-types are grouping of terrestrial ecosystems which share major features of the environment and are similar in vegetation structure and physiognomy and in some characteristic of their animal communities." "Pardisan: Plan for an Environmental Park in Tehran" report, p. 29.

88   "Pardisan: A Feasibility Study for an Environmental Park in Tehran," p. 38.

89   "Meeting Notes with B. Fuller," in Mandala Collective/WHRT, "Pardisan: Technical Report," 1975, pp. 1–8, McHarg Archives, 365.II.92.

90   Fuller made a comparison between the cooling techniques of his geodesic domes and the mud-brick domes covered with reflective glazed tiles in Iran's vernacular buildings, which allowed the release of hot air from the ceiling. "Meeting Notes with B. Fuller," 3.

91   For a recent book that debunks these myths, see Graeber and Wengrow, *Dawn of Everything.*

92   Fleck and Eames, dirs., *Pardisan*, 00:11.

93   Rosenzweig, *Win-Win Ecology.*

94   Marris, *Rambunctious Garden*, 71.

95   Marris, *Rambunctious Garden*, 109.

96   Marris, *Rambunctious Garden*, 151.

97   "Pardisan: Plan for an Environmental Park in Tehran" report, p. 6.

98   "Meeting Notes with David Goddard," pp. 9–19; "Meeting Notes with Yehudi Cohen," pp. 20–24; "Meeting Notes with Solomon Katz," pp. 25–29; "Meeting Notes with Brian John Spooner," pp. 30–37; in Mandala Collective/WHRT, "Pardisan: Technical Report," 1975, McHarg Archives, 365.II.92.

99 "Worldwide Adaptive Strategies," two separate files, McHarg Archives, 365.II.85, 365.II.86; "Animal Display," McHarg Archives, 365.II.83.

100 "The goal of the overall selection process was to yield an animal inventory which reflects the natural ecological relationships between organisms and their environment and which best represents adaptation to environment." "Animal Selection and Accommodation," McHarg Archives, 365.II.88, pp. 1–2

101 McHarg, "Architecture in an Ecological View of the World," in *To Heal the Earth*, 175–93, with quotation on pp. 182, 193. Also see McHarg, "Ecology and Design," in *To Heal the Earth*, 194–202.

102 "Pardisan: Plan for an Environmental Park," 10.

103 "Pardisan: A Feasibility Study," 8.

104 "Pardisan: Plan for an Environmental Park in Tehran," 9.

105 See, for instance, "Meeting Notes with David Goddard," in Mandala Collective/WHRT, "Pardisan: Technical Report," 1975, pp. 9–19. McHarg Archives, 365.II.92.

106 Guha and Martinez-Alier, *Varieties of Environmentalism*, 77.

107 "Seen as the sacred sublime, it is the home of a God who transcends history by standing as the One who remains untouched and unchanged by time's arrow. . . . Wilderness offers us the illusion that we can escape the cares and troubles of the world in which our past has ensnared us." Cronon, "Trouble with Wilderness," in *Environmental History*, 26.

108 Laleh Bakhtiar, "Persian Epistemologies," n.d., McHarg Archives, 365.II.96.

109 Bakhtiar, "Persian Epistemologies," 8.

110 Bakhtiar, "Persian Epistemologies," 5.

111 Bakhtiar, "Persian Epistemologies," 8.

112 "Meeting Notes with Seyyed Hossein Nasr," in Mandala Collective/WHRT, "Pardisan: Technical Report," 1975, pp. 42–53, with quotation on pp. 47–48, McHarg Archives, 365.II.92. Hossein Nasr also resisted the idea that nature could be a self-generating closed system. "Let us not destroy the sense of miracle in nature," p. 53.

113 Ardalan and Bakhtiar, *Sense of Unity*.

114 Mandala Collaborative Drawings, n.d., McHarg Archives, 365.VII.9.

115 Hossein Bani-Asadi to Russell Ackoff, August 26, 1979, McHarg Archives, 109.III.C.13.

116 McHarg to Shahriar Rouhani, April 10, 1979. Also see McHarg to Hossien Bani Asadi, deputy prime minister, July 6, 1979, McHarg Archives, 109.III.C.13.

117   Tsing, *Mushroom at the End of the World*, 152.

118   Kallipoliti, *Biospheres and the Rise of Botanical Capital*; Kolbert, *Sixth Extinction*, 135.

119   Amanda Rodewald to the author, email correspondence, March 2, 2023.

120   Amanda Rodewald to the author, email correspondence, March 2, 2023.

121   McHarg, "Ecological Determinism," in *To Heal the Earth*, 39–56; Doxiadis and Papaioannou, *Ecumenopolis*.

122   McHarg, "Notes," n.d., McHarg Archives, 109.III.C.19.

123   "Meeting Notes with B. Fuller," 2.

124   Doxiadis, "Future of Human Settlements."

125   Broswimmer, *Ecocide*, 8

126   See press releases and documents for the Pahlavi Prize for the Environment at the UN (1972–78): UN documents, from S-0910-0018-01-00001 to S-0910-0019-004-00001.

127   Akcan, *Abolish Human Bans*, 42–50.

128   Bakhtiar, *Towards a Quality of Life*, xvii.

129   Ardalan et al., *Habitat Bill of Rights*.

130   J. L. Sert to Nader Ardalan, December 23, 1974, E62, Documents in Josep Lluis Sert Collection, Frances Loeb Special Collections, Harvard Graduate School of Design, Cambridge, MA.

131   National Committee of Human Settlements, Government of Iran, "Habitat Bill of Rights."

132   Ardalan, et al., *Habitat Bill of Rights*, 161.

133   UN General Assembly, *World Charter for Nature*.

134   The authors named their approach after Ivan Illich's *Tools of Conviviality* (1973).

135   Büscher and Fletcher, *Conservation Revolution*, 157.

136   Büscher and Fletcher, *Conservation Revolution*, 187.

137   This was also Emma Marris's proposal. Marris, *Rambunctious Garden*.

138   Gandy, *Natura Urbana*.

139   Stoetzer, *Ruderal City*.

140   Gandy, *Natura Urbana*, 33. Following Bettina Stoetzer, I have taken the liberty to call these *ruderal urban spaces* in this chapter's title. Also see Gandy and Jasper, *Botanical City*.

141   Tsing et al., *Arts of Living on a Damaged Planet*.

142   For the role of cemeteries in urban biodiversity, see Kowarik, "Urban Cemeteries in Berlin and Beyond."

143 Public Information Office of the UN Peacekeeping Force in Cyprus, "Untouched Buffer Zone Bursting in Biodiversity," no. 81 (May 2016). I would like to thank Panayiota Pyla for inviting me to Nicosia, which allowed me to explore the Green Line.

144 Botanists reported two thousand wild plants, many emerging as a result of human influence. Zerbe et al., "Biodiversity in Berlin"; Gandy, "Signs of Life."

145 Stoetzer, *Ruderal City*.

Bibliography

Archives and Personal Collections (with Abbreviations)

Abdel Moneim Mustafa Office Personal Collection, Khartoum
Adil Ahmad Personal Collection, Khartoum
Architectural Archives, McHarg Center, School of Architecture, University of
    Pennsylvania, Philadelphia (McHarg Archives)
Asia Minor Collection, Benaki Museum, Athens
Aslı Özbay Personal Collection, Mustafapaşa, Turkey
Canadian Centre for Architecture Collection, Montreal (CCA)
Center for Asia Minor Studies, Athens (CAMS)
Doxiadis Associates Archives, Athens (Doxiadis Archives)
ETH-Bibliothek Zürich, Bildarchiv, Zurich
Frances Loeb Special Collections, Harvard Graduate School of Design,
    Cambridge, MA
Getty Research Institute, Los Angeles
Gropius Archives, Harvard University, Cambridge, MA
Hassan Fathy Papers and Photographic Collection, Rare Books and Special Col-
    lections Library, American University in Cairo
Istanbul Research Institute Collection, Istanbul (IAE)
JICA-Pacific Consultants International Archives, Japan
Lozan Mubadilleri Museum Collection, Istanbul (LMV)
Maside Ocak Personal Collection of Family Photographs, Istanbul
Modern Greek Architecture Archives, Benaki Museum, Athens
Nea Sinasos Museum, Nea Sinasos, Greece
Ottoman Archives, Istanbul
Sudan Archives Durham, Durham University Library and Collections,
    Durham (SAD)
United Nations Digital Library, New York
Water Resources Center Archives, University of California, Berkeley
Zeytinburnu Belediyesi Kültür Yayınları, Zeytinburnu Municipality Archives,
    Istanbul
Zeytinburnu Oral History Project, Istanbul (ZAD)

Abdullah Ziya. "Gün Geçiminde Kerpiç Köy Yapısı." *Ülkü*, no. 3 (1934): 66–70.

Abdullah Ziya. "Halkevleri Trakya Göçmen Evleri Proje Müsabakasında Kazanan Eserin Raporu." *Arkitekt*, nos. 7–8 (1935): 205–6.

Abdullah Ziya. "Köy Mimarisi." *Ülkü*, no. 5 (1933): 370–74.

Acker, Caroline Jean. *Creating the American Junkie: Addiction Research in the Classic Era of Narcotic Control*. Baltimore: Johns Hopkins University Press, 2002.

Adelson, Leslie. *The Turkish Turn in Contemporary German Literature: Towards a New Critical Grammar of Migration*. New York: Palgrave Macmillan, 2005.

Adey, Peter. *Aerial Life: Spaces, Mobilities, Affects*. Malden, MA: Wiley-Blackwell, 2010.

Afetinan, A. *Devletçilik İlkesi ve Türkiye Cumhuriyetinin Birinci Sanayi Planı 1933*. Ankara: Türk Tarih Kurumu, 1972.

Agamben, Giorgio. "Biopolitics and the Rights of Man." In *Homo Sacer: Sovereign Power and Bare Life*, edited by Werner Hamacher and David E. Wellbery, translated by Daniel Heller-Roazen, 126–35. Stanford, CA: Stanford University Press, 1998.

Agamben, Giorgio. *Homo Sacer: Sovereign Power and Bare Life*. Edited by Werner Hamacher and David E. Wellbery. Translated by Daniel Heller-Roazen. Stanford, CA: Stanford University Press, 1998.

Agamben, Giorgio. "We Refugees." Translated by Michael Rocke. *Symposium* 49, no. 2 (1995): 114–19.

Ahıska, Meltem. "Counter-Movement, Space and Politics: How the Saturday Mothers of Turkey Make Enforced Disappearances Visible." In *Space and the Memories of Violence: Landscapes of Erasure, Disappearance and Exception*, edited by Estela Schindel and Pamela Colombo, 162–75. New York: Palgrave Macmillan, 2014.

Ahıska, Meltem. "Memory as Encounter: The Saturday Mothers in Turkey." In *Women Mobilizing Memory*, edited by Ayşe Gül Altınay, Maria Jose Contrera, Marianne Hirsch, Jean Howard, Banu Karaca, and Alisa Solomon, 133–51. New York: Columbia University Press, 2019.

Ahmad, Feroz. *From Empire to Republic: Essays on the Late Ottoman Empire and Modern Turkey*. 2 vols. Istanbul: İstanbul Bilgi University Press, 2008.

Ahmet Halaçoğlu. *Balkan Harbi Sırasında Rumeli'den Türk Göçleri (1912–1913)*. Ankara: Türk Tarih Kurumu, 1995.

Akar, Rıdvan. *Aşkale Yolcuları: Varlık Vergisi ve Çalışma Kampları*. Ankara: Belge Yayıncılık, 1999.

Akbulut, Rıfat. "Mekansal Dönüşüm." In *Surların Öte Yanı—The Other Side of the City Walls: Zeytinburnu*, 3rd ed., edited by Burçak Evren, 376–413. Istanbul: Zeytinburnu Belediyesi Kültür Yayınları, 2006.

Akçam, Taner. *From Empire to Republic: Turkish Nationalism and Armenian Genocide*. New York: Zed, 2004.

Akçam, Taner. "The Spirit of the Law: Following the Traces of Genocide in the Law of Abandoned Property." *International Criminal Law Review* 14 (2014): 377–95.

Akçam, Taner. *The Young Turks' Crime Against Humanity: The Armenian Genocide and Ethnic Cleansing in the Ottoman Empire.* Princeton, NJ: Princeton University Press, 2012.

Akcan, Esra. *Abolish Human Bans: Intertwined Histories of Architecture.* Montreal: Canadian Center for Architecture, 2021.

Akcan, Esra. "*Antallagi/Mübadele* Ships: Visual Documents of Forced Migration Across the Aegean Sea." In *The Seas and the Mobility of Islamic Art*, edited by Sean Roberts, Radha Dalal, and Jochen Sokoly, 234–51. New Haven, CT: Yale University Press, 2021.

Akcan, Esra. "Apology and Triumph: Memory Transference, Erasure and a Re-reading of the Berlin Jewish Museum." *New German Critique* 110 (Summer 2010): 153–79.

Akcan, Esra. *Architecture in Translation: Germany, Turkey and the Modern House.* Durham, NC: Duke University Press, 2012.

Akcan, Esra (organizer and moderator). "Belgium to Congo: Colonialism Reparations and Truth and Reconciliation Commissions." Panel with Amah Edoh, Pablo de Greiff, Pedro Monaville, and Liliane Umubyeyi at Cornell University, February 24, 2021. YouTube, 2 hours, 24 min., 47 sec. https://www.youtube.com/watch?v=PtGaN2A_tC4.

Akcan, Esra. *Çeviride Modern Olan: Şehir ve Konutta Türk-Alman Ilişkileri.* Istanbul, YKY, 2009.

Akcan, Esra. "Decolonize or Redistribute? Abdel Moneim Mustafa and Mid-Century Modernism in Sudan." Canadian Center for Architecture, May 12, 2022. www.cca.qc.ca/en/articles/85227/decolonize-or-redistribute-abdel -moneim-mustafa-an d-mid-century-modernism-in-sudan.

Akcan, Esra. "Democracy and War: The University of Baghdad Between Collaboration and National Competition." In *Architecture Against Democracy: Histories of the Nationalist International*, edited by Reinhold Martin and Claire Zimmerman, 299–320. Minneapolis: University of Minnesota Press, 2024.

Akcan, Esra (organizer and moderator). "Germany to Germany: New Perspectives on Post-War, Post-Unification and Postcolonial Reparations." Panel with Rebecca Boehling, Tiffany Florvil, Nicholas Mulder, and Ruti Teitel, at Cornell University, March 15, 2021. YouTube, 2 hours, 19 min., 30 sec. https://www.youtube.com/watch?v=IlT5e6q4M1M.

Akcan, Esra. "*Homo oeconomicus* of the 'New Turkey': Urban Development of Istanbul in the 2000s." In *Neoliberalism on the Ground: Architecture and Transformation from the 1960s to the Present*, edited by Kenny Cupers, Catharina Gabrielsson, and Helena Mattsson, 383–407. Pittsburgh: University of Pittsburgh Press, 2020.

Akcan, Esra (organizer and moderator). "North to South: Repair and Reparations for Climate Refugees." Panel with Ashley Dawson, Anne McClintock, Bronwyn Leebaw, Anooradha Iyer Siddiqi, and Billy Fleming at Cornell

University, April 2, 2021. YouTube, 2 hours, 42 min., 1 sec. https://www
.youtube.com/watch?v=96KAQHK-ztc.

Akcan, Esra. *Open Architecture: Migration, Citizenship and the Urban Renewal of Berlin Kreuzberg by IBA-1984/87*. Basel: Birkhauser/De Gruyter, 2018.

Akcan, Esra (organizer). "Reparations for Colonization/Carbonization." Symposium at the Institute for Comparative Modernities, Cornell University, March 2, 2023.

Akcan, Esra. "Society of Political Images: Centric and Common Proliferation of Photography." *Journal of Decorative and Propaganda Arts* 28 (2016): 88–111.

Akcan, Esra. "Translation Theory and the Intertwined Histories of Building for Self-Governance." In *Terms of Appropriation*, edited by Ana Miljacki and Amanda Lawrance, 116–38. London: Routledge, 2018.

Akcan, Esra, and Peter Christensen (organizers and moderators). "Hagia Sophia: Perspectives from Cultural Heritage." Webinar at Cornell University, September 19, 2020. YouTube, 3 hours, 3 min., 12 sec. https://www.youtube.com /watch?v=79DACHU4X78.

Akçay, Faik. *Zeytinburnu Gerçek Yönleriyle Bir Gecekondu Kenti*. Istanbul: Çelik-cilt Matbaası, 1974.

Aksakal, Mustafa. *The Ottoman Road to War in 1914: The Ottoman Empire and the First World War*. Cambridge: Cambridge University Press, 2008.

Aktar, Ayhan. *Varlık Vergisi ve Türkleştirme Politikaları*. Istanbul: İletişim, 2000.

Aktüre, Zeynep. "From Greek Town to Turkish Tourism Report: Kayaköy Since Early 20th Century." In *REHAB 2016: 2nd International Conference on Preservation, Maintenance and Rehabilitation of Historical Buildings and Structures*, 361–70. Barcelos: Green Lines Institute, 2015.

Al Chalabi, Ridha. العراقية العمارة موسوعة [Encyclopedia of Iraqi Architecture]. 3 vols. Baghdad: n.p., 2018.

Al-Natour, Ryan. "To Be a Citizen: A Genealogy of Arab American Fiction." *MELUS* 39, no. 4 (2014): 22–44.

Alvarez, Luis, Walter Alvarez, Frank Asaro, and Helen Michel. "Extraterrestrial Cause for the Cretaceous-Tertiary Extinction." *Science* 208, no. 4448 (1980): 1095–108. https://www.science.org/doi/10.1126/science.208.4448.1095.

Amnesty International. "Turkey: Listen to the Saturday Mothers." Amnesty International, Research, Index no. EUR: 44/017/1998, November 1, 1998. https://www.amnesty.org/en/documents/eur44/017/1998/en/.

Anagnostakis, Ilias, and Evangelia Balta. *La dècouverte de la Cappadoce au dix-neuvième siècle*. Istanbul: Eren, 1994.

Anderson, Benedict. *Imagined Communities: Reflections on the Origin and Spread of Nationalism*. New York: Verso, 1983.

Aralıktan Bakmak: Meşrutiyet Caddesi'nden Bir Kesit: 21 Mart–21 Eylül, 2019. Exhibition, Istanbul Araştırmaları Institute. Istanbul Araştırmaları Enstitütsü. Accessed February 23, 2020. https://www.iae.org.tr/Sergi/Araliktan-Bakmak/203.

Arat, Zehra Kabasakal, ed. *Human Rights in Turkey*. Philadelphia: University of Pennsylvania Press, 2007.

Architecture for Humanity. *Design like You Give a Damn: Architectural Responses to Humanitarian Crises.* New York: Metropolis, 2006.

Ardalan, Nader, and Laleh Bakhtiar. *The Sense of Unity: A Sufi Tradition in Persian Architecture.* Chicago: University of Chicago Press, 1973.

Ardalan, Nader, Georges Candilis, Balkrishna Doshi, Moshie Safdie, and Josep Louis Sert. *Habitat Bill of Rights.* Tehran: Hamadi Foundation, 1976.

Arendt, Hannah. *Eichmann in Jerusalem: A Report on the Banality of Evil.* New York: Viking, 1963.

Arendt, Hannah. "We Refugees." *Menorah Journal,* no. 1 (1943): 77.

Argos Yapı. "Uçhisar'ın Kadınları İçin." Pamphlet. Uçhisar: Argos Yapı, 2016.

Arı, Kemal. *Büyük Mübadele: Türkiye'ye Zorunlu Göç (1923–1925).* Istanbul: Tarih Vakfı Yurt Yayınları, 1995.

Arisan, Mehmet. "The Effects of the Balkan Wars on the Construction of Modern Turkish Nationalism." In *War and Nationalism: The Balkan Wars, 1912–1913, and Their Sociopolitical Implications,* edited by M. H. Yavuz and Isa Blumi, 704–26. Salt Lake City: University of Utah Press, 2013.

Arnaud, Jean-Luc. "Modernization of the Cities of the Ottoman Empire." In *The City in the Islamic World,* vol. 2, edited by Renata Holod, Attilio Petruccioli, and André Raymond, 953–75. Boston: Brill, 2008.

Ashcroft, Bill, Gareth Griffiths, and Helen Tiffin. *The Empire Writes Back: Theory and Practice in Post-Colonial Literatures.* London: Routledge, 1989.

As-Sammani, Mohammed Osman. "Private Sector and Government Commercial Fishing in the Sudd Area, Southern Sudan." *Economic Geography* 60, no. 3 (1984): 210–16.

"Athens Hit by Devastating Earthquake." *Greek City Times,* September 7, 2016. https://greekcitytimes.com/2016/09/07/september-9-1999-athens-hit-by -devastating-earthquake.

Aydın, Murat. "Introduction." In *Surların Öte Yanı—The Other Side of the City Walls: Zeytinburnu,* 3rd ed., edited by Burçak Evren, unpag. Istanbul: Zeytinburnu Belediyesi Kültür Yayınları, 2006.

Aydın, Murat. "Kültür Vadisi: Zeytinburnu'ndan Geçen Medeniyet Irmağının Mecrası." In *Zeytinburnu Kültür Vadisi,* vol. 1, edited by Murat Çekin, 10–17. Istanbul: Zeytinburnu Belediyesi Kültür Yayınları, 2018.

Aytaş, Süreyya. *Mübadelenin Hüzünlü Mirası.* Istanbul: YKY, 2020.

Azara, Pedro, and Laura Iglesias Martinez, eds. *Irak Restored: City of Mirages; Baghdad from Wright to Venturi.* Barcelona: Polytechnical University of Catalonia, 2008.

Bafra, Çelenk, curator. *Mektep Meydan Galatasaray: 14 Eylül–25 Kasım, 2018.* Exhibition, Pera Museum, Istanbul. Pera Müzesi. Accessed March 20, 2025. www.peramuzesi.org.tr/Sergi/Mektep-Meydan-Galatasaray-/228.

Baker, Samuel White. *The Albert N'Yanza: Great Basin of The Nile and Explorations of the Nile Sources.* 2 vols. New York: Horizon Press, 1962. Originally published in 1866.

Bakhtiar, Laleh, ed. *Towards a Quality of Life: The Role of Industrialization in the Architecture and Urban Planning of Developing Countries: Report of Proceedings of the Second International Congress of Architects, Persepolis, Iran 1974.* Tehran: Hamdami Foundation, 1976.

Bali, Rıfat N., ed. *Anti-Greek Riots of September 6–7, 1955: Documents from the American National Archives.* Istanbul: Libra Kitapçılık ve Yayıncılık, 2015.

Ballian, Anna. "Relics of the Past: Treasures of the Greek Orthodox Church and the Population Exchange." In *Relics of the Past: Treasures of the Greek Orthodox Church and the Population Exchange*, edited by Anna Ballian, 36–56. Athens: Benaki Museum, 2011.

Ballian, Anna, ed. *Relics of the Past: Treasures of the Greek Orthodox Church and the Population Exchange.* Athens: Benaki Museum, 2011.

Balta, Evangelia. "The Exchange of Populations." In *Crossing the Aegean*, edited by Renée Hirschon, 83–84. New York: Berghahn, 2003.

Balta, Evangelia. *The Exchange of Populations: Historiography and Refugee Memory.* Istanbul: İstos, 2014.

Balta, Evangelia. "The Exchange of Populations: The Case of Sinasos." In *Common Cultural Heritage*, edited by Sefer Güvenç, 35–39. Istanbul: Foundation of Lausanne Treaty Emigrants, 2005.

Balta, Evangelia. "The Recording of the Settlements of Anatolian Refugees in Eubola by the Centre for Asia Minor Studies (1948–1964)." In *The Exchange of Populations: Historiography and Refugee Memory*, edited by Renée Hirschon, 103–54. Istanbul: İstos, 2014.

Balta, Evangelia, ed. *Sinasos: Mübadeleden Önce Bir Kapadokya Kasabası/Sinasos: Images and Narratives.* Translated by Alexandra Doumas. Istanbul: Bir Zamanlar Yayıncılık, 2007.

Balta, Evangelia, and Spyros Issopoulos. "The Greeks of Sinasos, and Their Current Relationship with Their Place of Origin." In *Common Cultural Heritage*, edited by Sefer Güvenç, 175–77. Istanbul: Foundation of Lausanne Treaty Emigrants, 2005.

Banham, Reyner. *The Architecture of the Well-Tempered Environment.* 2nd ed. Chicago: University of Chicago Press, 1984. Originally published in 1969.

Barber, Daniel. "After Comfort." *Log* 47 (2019): 45–50.

Barber, Daniel. *A House in the Sun: Modern Architecture and Solar Energy in the Cold War.* New York: Oxford University Press, 2016.

Barber, Daniel. *Modern Architecture and Climate: Design Before Air-Conditioning.* Princeton, NJ: Princeton University Press, 2020.

Bashir, Bashir, and Amos Goldberg, eds. *The Holocaust and the Nakba: A New Grammar of Trauma and History.* New York: Columbia University Press, 2019.

Basile, Salvatore. *Cool: How Air Conditioning Changed Everything.* New York: Fordham University Press, 2014.

Batuman, Bülent. *New Islamist Architecture and Urbanism: Negotiating Nation and Islam Through Built Environment in Turkey.* London: Routledge, 2018.

Baweja, Vandana. "Otto Koenigsberger and the Tropicalization of British Architectural Culture." In *Third World Modernism: Architecture, Development and Identity*, edited by Duanfang Lu, 236–54. New York: Routledge, 2011.

Baydar, Gülsüm, and Berfin İvegen. "Territories, Identities, and Thresholds: The Saturday Mothers Phenomenon in İstanbul." *Journal of Women in Culture and Society* 31, no. 3 (2006): 689–715.

Baykal, Erol. "Istanbul During Balkan Wars (1912–13): Cholera, Medicine and Press." *Turkish Historical Review* 5 (2014): 141–64.

Beckert, Sven. *The Empire of Cotton: A Global History*. London: Penguin, 2014.

Bedlek, Emine Yeşim. *Imagined Communities in Greece and Turkey: Trauma and the Population Exchanges Under Atatürk*. London: I. B. Tauris, 2016.

Belli, Mihri. *Büyük Mübadele*. Istanbul: Bilgi Üniversitesi Yayınları, 2001.

Belli, Mihri. *Mihri Belli'nin Anıları. İnsanlar Tanıdım*. Vol. 1. Istanbul: Milliyet Yayınları, 1989.

Belli, Mihri. *Türkiye ve Yunanistan Arasında Gerçekleşen Zorunlu Nüfus Mübadelesine Ekonomik Açıdan Bakış*. Translated by Müfide Tekin. Istanbul: Belge Yayınları, 2004. Originally prepared as "Greek-Turkish Compulsory Population Exchange from an Economic Perspective," MA thesis, University of Missouri, 1940.

Benjamin, Walter. "Theses on the Philosophy of History." In *Illuminations*, edited by Hannah Arendt, translated by Howard Zohn, 253–64. New York: Schocken, 1985.

Benlisoy, Foti, and Stefo Benlisoy. *Hıristiyan Türkler ve Papa Eftim*. 2nd ed. Istanbul: İstos, 2022.

Bentham, Jeremy. *Anarchical Fallacies; Being an Examination of the Declaration of Rights Issued During the French Revolution*. Edited by J. Bowring. Vol. 2 of *The Works of Jeremy Bentham*. Edinburgh: William Tait, 1843. Accessed June 21, 2021. https://oll.libertyfund.org/title/bowring-the-works-of-jeremy -bentham-vol-2#lf0872-02_head_ 411.

Berk, Süleyman. *Zamanı Aşan Taşlar: Zeytinburnu'nun Mezar Taşları*. 2 vols. Istanbul: Zeytinburnu Belediyesi Kültür Yayınları, 2016.

Bernal, Victoria. "Colonial Moral Economy and the Discipline of Development: The Gezira Scheme and 'Modern' Sudan." *Cultural Anthropology* 12, no. 4 (1997): 447–79.

Bernhardsson, Magnus T. "Faith in the Future: Nostalgic Nationalism and 1950s Baghdad." *History Compass* 9–10 (2011): 802–17.

Besteman, Catherine L. *Militarized Global Apartheid*. Durham, NC: Duke University Press, 2020.

Bhabha, Homi K. *The Location of Culture*. London: Routledge, 1994.

Bilbija, Ksenija, and Leigh Payne, eds. *Accounting for Violence*. Durham, NC: Duke University Press, 2011.

Bilgin, Ihsan. "Anadolu'da Modernleşme Sürecinde Konut ve Yerleşme." In *Tarihten Günümüze Anadolu'da Konut ve Yerleşme*, edited by Yıldız Sey, 472–90. Istanbul: Tarih Vakfı, 1996.

Biondich, Mark. "The Balkan Wars: Violence and Nation Building in the Balkans." *Journal of Genocide Research* 18, no. 4 (2016): 389–404.

Biris, Manos. "The Founding of Modern Athens: The New City Plan and Urban Development." In *Athens: From the Classical Period to the Present Day*, edited by Charalambos Bouras et al., 373–97. Athens: Kotinos, 2000.

Blumi, Isa. *Ottoman Refugees, 1878–1939: Migration in a Post-Imperial World.* London: Bloomsbury Academic, 2013.

Bookman, Milica Zarkovic. *The Demographic Struggle for Power: The Political Economy of Demographic Engineering in the Modern World.* London: Frank Cass, 1997.

Borasi, Giovanna, and Mirko Zardini. *Sorry, Out of Gas: Architecture's Response to the 1973 Oil Crisis.* Montreal: Canadian Center for Architecture, 2007.

Bouvard, Marguerite Guzman. *Revolutionizing Motherhood: The Mothers of the Plaza de Mayo.* Lanham, MD: SR Books, 2004.

Bozdoğan, Sibel, and Esra Akcan. *Turkey: Modern Architectures in History.* London: Reaktion, 2012.

Brockington, Dan, Rosaleen Duffy, and Jim Igoe. *Nature Unbound: Conservation, Capitalism and the Future of Protected Areas.* London: Earthscan, 2010.

Broswimmer, Franz. *Ecocide: A Short History of the Mass Extinction of Species.* New York: Pluto, 2002.

Brown, Michael F. *The Historiography of Genocide.* New York: Palgrave Macmillan, 2008.

Buddemeier, Heinz. *Panorama, Diorama, Photographie.* Munich: Wilhelm Fink, 1970.

Buğra, Ayşe. "The Immoral Economy of Housing in Turkey." *International Journal of Urban and Regional Research* 22, no. 2 (1998): 303–17.

Burhan Arif. "Köy Projesi." *Arkitekt*, nos. 11–12 (1935): 320.

Büscher, Bram, and Robert Fletcher. *The Conservation Revolution: Radical Ideas for Saving Nature Beyond the Anthropocene.* London: Verso, 2020.

Butler, Judith. *Precarious Life: The Powers of Mourning and Violence.* New York: Verso, 2006.

Butler, Judith, Zeynep Gambetti, and Leticia Sabsay. *Vulnerability in Resistance.* Durham, NC: Duke University Press, 2016.

Büyükerman, Önder, and Jülide Edirne Erdinç. *Osmanlı'dan Cumhuriyet'e Bir Ağır Sanayi Bölgesi Zeytinburnu.* Istanbul: Zeytinburnu Belediyesi Kültür Yayınları, 2021.

Büyükşehir Belediyesi and Kandilli Rasathanesi. "Zeytinburnu Olası Deprem Kayıp Tahminleri Kitapçığı." Unpublished report, June 2020.

Byler, Darren. *Terror Capitalism: Uyghur Dispossession and Masculinity in a Chinese City.* Durham, NC: Duke University Press, 2022.

Byzantios, Skarlatos. *Constantinople: A Topographical, Archeological and Historical Description.* Vol. 1. Translated by Haris Theodorelis-Rigas. Istanbul: İstos, 2019.

Çağrı, Ali. "Afganistan'dan Zeyrinburnu'na Yolculuk." In *Göç Sempozyumu,* 139–40. Istanbul: Zeytinburnu Belediyesi Kültür Yayınları, 2006.

Çakırer-Özservet, Yasemin. "Zeytinburnu Kentsel Mekanında Soydaş Diyasporasının Örgütlenmesi." *FSM İlmî Araştırmalar İnsan ve Toplum Bilimleri Dergisi* 3 (2014): 231–43.

Çakırer-Özservet, Yasemin. "Zeytinburnu'nda Doğu Türkistan Türklerinin Ulusötesi Bellek Eklemlenmesi." *Marmara Üniversitesi Siyasal Bilimler Dergisi* 3, no. 1 (2015): 59–80.

Canadian Centre for Architecture. "CCA Find and Tell Elsewhere: Abdel Moneim Mustafa." *e-flux Architecture*, May 12, 2022. www.e-flux.com/announcements /443946/cca-find-and-tell-elsewhere-abdel-moneim-mustafa/.

Cansever, Turgut. *İslam'da Şehir ve Mimari*. Istanbul: İz Yayıncılık, 1997.

Cansever, Turgut. "Zeytinburnu Sur Dışı Sit Alanı Düzenleme Projeleri Ön Raporu." Report of May 2000. In *Zeytinburnu Kültür Vadisi*, vol. 1, edited by Murat Çekin, 19–33. Istanbul: Zeytinburnu Belediyesi Kültür Yayınları, 2018.

"The Cathedral of All Saints. Khartoum, Sudan." *Builder*, May 19, 1916, 371–72.

Çavuşoğlu, Halim. "Yugoslavya-Makedonya Topraklarından Türkiye'ye Göçler ve Nedenleri." *Bilig* 41 (2007): 123–54.

CBS News. "Rare Look Inside China's Internment Camps Holding More than 1 Million Muslims." YouTube, posted June 18, 2019. 4 min., 51 sec. https:// www.youtube.com/watch?v=ujk8spsLA_Q.

Çekin, Murat, ed. *Zeytinburnu Anı Defteri*. Istanbul: Zeytinburnu Belediyesi Kültür Yayınları, 2018.

Çekin, Murat, ed. *Zeytinburnu Kültür Vadisi*. 2 vols. Zeytinburnu Municipality Documents, No. 54. Istanbul: Zeytinburnu Belediyesi Kültür Yayınları, 2018.

Çekin, Murat, and Kerim Alpınar. *Zeytinburnu Tıbbı Bitkiler Bahçesi*. Istanbul: Zeytinburnu Belediyesi Kültür Yayınları, 2015.

Çelebi, Evliya. *Evliya Çelebi Seyahatnamesi*. Vol. 1. Edited by Seyit Ali Kahraman-Yücel Dağlı. Istanbul: YKY, 2018. Written in 1630–72.

Çelik, Celaleddin. "Turgut Cansever ve Zeytinburnu Raporu." In *Zeytinburnu Kültür Vadisi*, vol. 1, edited by Murat Çekin, 41–47. Istanbul: Zeytinburnu Belediyesi Kültür Yayınları, 2018.

Çelik, Zeynep. *Empire, Architecture and the City: French-Ottoman Encounters 1830–1914*. Seattle: University of Washington Press, 2008.

Cengizkan, Ali. *Mübadele: Konut ve Yerleşimleri*. Ankara: ODTÜ Yayınları, 2004.

Çevik, Necdet Sakaoğlu. "Çırpıcı Çayırı." In *Surların Öte Yanı—The Other Side of the City Walls: Zeytinburnu*, 3rd ed., edited by Burçak Evren, 442–79. Istanbul: Zeytinburnu Belediyesi Kültür Yayınları, 2006.

Ceylan, Ebubekir. *The Ottoman Origins of Modern Iraq: Political Reform, Modernization and Development in the Nineteenth-Century Middle East*. London: I. B. Tauris, 2011.

Chakrabarty, Dipesh. "The Climate of History: Four Theses." *Critical Inquiry* 35, no. 2 (2009): 197–222.

Chaldeos, Antonis. "Sudanese Toponyms Related to Greek Entrepreneurial Activity." *Dotawo: A Journal of Nubian Studies* 4, no. 4 (2017): 183–95.

Chang, Jiat-Hwee. *A Genealogy of Tropical Architecture: Colonial Networks, Nature and Technoscience.* London: Routledge, 2016.

Chatterjee, Partha. *Nationalist Thought and the Colonial World.* Minneapolis: University of Minnesota Press, 1986.

"CHP'de Işgal Sone Erdi." *Milliyet*, May 24, 1995. https://gazetearsivi.milliyet.com .tr/Arsiv/1995/05/24.

Churchill, Winston. *The River War: An Account of the Reconquest of the Soudan.* New York: Scribner, 1933.

Çiçek, Nazan. "More History than They Can Consume? Perception of the Balkan Wars in Turkish Republican Textbooks (1932–2007)." In *War and Nationalism: The Balkan Wars, 1912–1913, and Their Sociopolitical Implications*, edited by M. H. Yavuz and Isa Blumi, 777–804. Salt Lake City: University of Utah Press, 2013.

Clapham, Andrew. *Human Rights.* Oxford: Oxford University Press, 2007.

CNN. "China Tries to Thwart CNN Investigation into Detention Camps." YouTube, posted May 8, 2019. 5 min., 35 sec. https://www.youtube.com/watch?v =nbBsh46aSz4.

Coates, Ta-Nehisi. "The Case for Reparations." *Atlantic*, June 2014. www .theatlantic.com/magazine/archive/2014/06/the-case-for-reparations /361631/.

Coke, Richard, *Baghdad: City of Peace.* London: Thornton Butterworth, 1927.

Collins, Cath. "The Moral Economy of Memory: Public and Private Commemorative Space in Post-Pinochet Chile." In *Accounting for Violence*, edited by Ksenija Bilbija and Leigh Payne, 235–64. Durham, NC: Duke University Press, 2011.

Collins, Christiane C., and George R. Collins. "Monumentality: A Critical Matter in Modern Architecture." *Harvard Architecture Review* 4 (1984): 15–35.

Collins, Robert O., and Francis M. Deng, eds. *The British in the Sudan, 1898–1956.* Stanford, CA: Hoover Institute Press, 1984.

Colomina, Beatriz. "Enclosed by Images: The Eameses Multimedia Architecture." *Grey Room* 2 (2001): 6–29.

Colonas, Vassilis. "Housing and the Architectural Expression of Asia Minor Greeks Before and After 1923." In *Crossing the Aegean*, edited by Renée Hirschon, 163–78. New York: Berghahn, 2003.

Comment, Bernard. *The Panorama.* Translated by Anne-Marie Glasheen. London: Reaktion, 1999.

"Convention Concerning the Exchange of Greek and Turkish Populations." *American Journal of International Law* 18, no. 2 (1924): 84–90.

Crimp, Douglas. "Mourning and Militancy." *October* 51 (1989): 3–18.

Crinson, Mark. *Modern Architecture and the End of Empire*. Aldershot: Ashgate, 2003.

Cronon, William. "The Trouble with Wilderness; or, Getting Back to the Wrong Nature." In *Uncommon Ground: Rethinking the Human Place in Nature*, edited by William Cronon, 69–90. New York: Norton, 1996.

Cronon, William. "The Trouble with Wilderness." *Environmental History* 1, no. 1 (1996): 7–55.

Crutzen, Paul. "Geology of Mankind." *Nature*, January 3, 2002, 23–24.

"Cumartesi Anneleri, Kaybedilen Ermeni Aydınları Andı." *Evrensel*, April 28, 2018.

"Cumartesi Anneleri Sabahattin Ali'yi Andı." *Cumhuriyet*, March 31, 2018.

"Current Architecture in the Sudan: The Civic Centre and a Girls' School, Omdurman." *Builder*, January 4, 1953, 561–63.

Daly, M. W., ed. *Modernization in the Sudan: Essays in Honor of Richard Hill*. New York: Lilian Barber Press, 1985.

Davis, Mike. *Planet of Slums*. New York: Verso, 2006.

Davis, Mike. "Who Will Build the Ark?" *New Left Review* 61, no. 1 (2010): 29–46.

Dawson, Ashley. *Environmentalism from Below: How Global People's Movements Are Leading the Fight for Our Planet*. Chicago: Haymarket, 2024.

Dawson, Ashley. *Extinction: A Radical History*. New York: OR, 2016.

Dawson, Ashley. *Extreme Cities: The Peril and Promise of Urban Life in the Age of Climate Change*. New York: Verso, 2017.

Deane, Philip. *Constantinos Doxiadis: Master Builder for Free Men*. New York: Oceana, 1965.

De Gouges, Olympe. "The Declaration of the Rights of Woman (September 1791)." *Liberté, Égalité, Fraternité: Exploring the French Revolution*. Accessed June 21, 2021. https://revolution.chnm.org/d/293.

De Greiff, Pablo. *Promotion of Truth, Justice, Reparation and Guarantees of Non-Recurrence*. New York: United Nations, 2014. https://digitallibrary.un.org/record/782020?ln=en&v=pdf.

De Greiff, Pablo. "Theorizing Transitional Justice." In *Transitional Justice*, edited by Melissa Williams, 31–77. New York: NYU Press, 2012.

Delis, Panagiotis. "Violence and Civilians During the Balkan Wars." *Journal of Balkan and Near Eastern Studies* 20, no. 6 (2018): 547–63.

Demir, Hülya, and Rıdvan Akar. *Istanbul'un Son Sürgünleri*. Ankara: Belge Yayıncılık, 1994.

Demirakın, Işık. "Expropriation as a Modernizing Tool in the Nineteenth Century Ottoman Empire: The Case of Cemeteries in Beyoğlu." *International Journal of Turkish Studies* 18, nos. 1–2 (2012): 1–15.

Democracy Now! "Angela Davis: Toppling of Confederate Statues Reflects Reckoning with Slavery and Historical Racism." YouTube, posted June 12, 2020. 10 min., 25 sec. https://www.youtube.com/watch?v=pD3wlRJWCxc.

Demos, T. J. *Against the Anthropocene: Visual Culture and Environment Today*. Berlin: Steinberg, 2017.

Demos, T. J. *Decolonizing Nature: Contemporary Art and the Politics of Ecology.* Berlin: Sternberg, 2016.

Deng, Francis. "In the Eyes of the Ruled." In *The British in the Sudan, 1898–1956,* edited by Robert O. Collins and Francis M. Deng, 216–43. Stanford, CA: Hoover Institute Press, 1984.

Deringil, Selim. "'They Live in a State of Nomadism and Savagery': The Late Ottoman Empire and the Post-Colonial Debate." *Comparative Studies in Society and History* 45, no. 2 (2003): 311–42.

Deringil, Selim. *The Well-Protected Domains: Ideology and the Legitimation Power in the Ottoman Empire, 1876–1909.* London: I. B. Tauris, 2011.

"Design Award Made in U.N. for Reconstructing Skopje." *New York Times,* July 25, 1965, 14.

Dirlik, Kazim. "Ideal Republican Village." MA thesis, Istanbul University, 1937.

Doxiadis, Constantinos A. *Action for Human Settlements.* New York: Norton, 1976.

Doxiadis, Constantinos A., ed. *Anthropopolis: City for Human Development.* New York: Norton, 1975.

Doxiadis, Constantinos. "Anthropos." *Ekistics* 37, no. 222 (1974): 305.

Doxiadis, Constantinos A. *Architecture in Transition.* London: Hutchinson, 1963.

Doxiadis, Constantinos A. *Building Entopia.* New York: Norton, 1976.

Doxiadis, Constantinos A. "Dynapolis: The City of the Future." Paper presented at the Oslo Arkitektforening, March 3, 1960. Canadian Center for Architecture Collection, Montreal.

Doxiadis, Constantinos A. *Ekistics: An Introduction to the Science of Human Settlements.* New York: Oxford University Press, 1968.

Doxiadis, Constantinos. "Water and Environment." In *Water for Peace: International Conference on Water for Peace, May 23–31, 1967,* vol. 1, 33–60. Washington, DC: Government Printing Office, 1968.

Doxiadis, Constantinos A., and J. G. Papaioannou. *Ecumenopolis: The Inevitable City of the Future.* Toronto: John McLeod, 1974.

Dragostinova, Theodora. *Between Two Motherlands: Nationality and Emigration Among the Greeks of Bulgaria, 1900–1949.* Ithaca, NY: Cornell University Press, 2011.

Draper, Susana. "The Business of Memory: Reconstructing Torture Centers as Shopping Malls and Tourist Sites." In *Accounting for Violence,* edited by Ksenija Bilbija and Leigh Payne, 127–50. Durham, NC: Duke University Press, 2011.

Dumont, Paul, and Francois Georgeon, eds. *Vivre dans l'empire Ottoman: Sociabilités et relations intercommunautaires/Modernleşme Sürecinde Osmanlı Kentleri.* Istanbul: Tarih Vakfı Yurt Yayınları, 1992.

Dündar, Fuat. "Balkan Savaşı Sonrasında Kurulmaya Çalışılan Mühacir Köyler." *Toplumsal Tarih* 82 (2000): 52–54.

Dündar, Fuat. *Ittihat ve Terakki'nin Müslümanları İskan Politikası 1913–1918*. Istanbul: İletişim, 2001.

Dündar, Fuat. *Modern Türkiye'nin Şifresi: Ittihat ve Terakki'nin Etnisite Mühendisliği (1913–1918)*. Istanbul: İletişim, 2008.

Dutta, Arindam, Ateya Khorakiwala, Ayala Levin, Fabiola Lopez-Duran, and Ijlal Muzaffar, eds. *Architecture in Development: Systems and the Emergence of the Global South*. London: Routledge, 2022.

Dykmann, Klaas. "Impunity and the Right to Truth in the Inter-American System of Human Rights." *Iberoamericana*, n.s., 7, no. 26 (2007): 45–66.

Eames, Charles, and Glen Fleck, dirs. *Pardisan*. Charles Eames Studio, 1977.

Ediz, Özgür. "Uyuyan Köyü Uyandırmak, Sürdürülebilir bir Geçmiş: Kayaköy." *Mimarist*, no. 1 (2013): 101–6.

Edkins, Jenny. *Whose Hunger? Concepts of Famine, Practices of Aid*. New ed. Minneapolis: University of Minnesota Press, 2000.

Edwards, Justin D., Rune Graulund, and Jahan Höglund, eds. *Dark Scenes from Damaged Earth: The Gothic Anthropocene*. Minneapolis: University of Minnesota Press, 2022.

Ekinci, Oktay. *Istanbul'u Sarsan On Yıl (1983–1993)*. Istanbul: Anahtar Kitaplar, 1994.

El-Bushra, El-Sayed. "Sudan's Triple Capital: Morphology and Functions." *Ekistics* 39, no. 233 (1975): 246–50.

El-Bushra, El-Sayed, and Mohammed Osman El Sammani. "Water for Human Use: Urban and Rural Water Supplies in the Sudan." *Ekistics* 43, no. 254 (1977): 36–42.

Eldem, Edhem. *Istanbul'da Ölüm: Osmanlı-İslam Kültüründe Ölüm ve Ritüelleri*. Exhibition catalog. Istanbul: Osmanlı Bankası Arşiv ve Araştırma Merkezi, 2005.

Elenas, A. "Athens Earthquake of 7 September 1999: Intensity Measures and Observed Damages." *ISET Journal of Earthquake Technology: Technical Note* 40, no. 1 (2003): 77–97.

Emlak Kulisi. "KIPTAS Locamahal Projesinde Zarar Etti Iddiası." December 14, 2021. https://emlakkulisi.com/kiptas-locamahal-projesinde-zarar-etti -iddiasi/689865.

Eng, David, and David Kazanjian, eds. *Loss: Politics of Mourning*. Berkeley: University of California Press, 2002.

Erdal, İbrahim. *Ulus Devlet Sürecinde Türkiye ve Yunanistan*. Istanbul: İdeal Kültür Yayıncılık, 2018.

Eres, Zeynep. "Türkiye'de Çağdaş Köy Kurma Çabasının İlk Örnekleri: Mübadil Köyleri." In *Mübadil Kentler: Mekan ve İskan*, 272–86. Istanbul: Lozan Mübadilleri Vakfı Yayınları, 2014.

Erkal, Namık. "Şehrin Boğazı: Yedikule Salhaneleri ve Surönünün Ekolojisi." In *Şehrin Doğası*, edited by Çiğdem Kafesçioğlu and Cemal Kafadar. Forthcoming.

Eroğlu, Cengiz, Murat Babuçoğlu, and Orhan Özdil. *Osmanlı Vilayet Salnamel-erinde Bağdat*. Ankara: Global Strateji Enstitüsü, 2006.

Ersoy, Ahmet. *Architecture and the Late Ottoman Historical Imaginary: Reconfiguring the Architectural Past in a Modernizing Europe*. Aldershot: Ashgate, 2015.

Evren, Burçak. "Balıklı Holy Spring and Church." In *Surların Öte Yanı—The Other Side of the City Walls: Zeytinburnu*, 3rd ed., edited by Burçak Evren, 40–67. Istanbul: Zeytinburnu Belediyesi Kültür Yayınları, 2006.

Evren, Burçak. "Byzantine Period." In *Surların Öte Yanı—The Other Side of the City Walls: Zeytinburnu*, 3rd ed., edited by Burçak Evren, 14–37. Istanbul: Zeytinburnu Belediyesi Kültür Yayınları, 2006.

Evren, Burçak, ed. *Surların Öte Yanı—The Other Side of the City Walls: Zeytinburnu*. 3rd ed. Istanbul: Zeytinburnu Belediyesi Kültür Yayınları, 2006.

Evren, Burçak, ed. *Surların Öte Yanı Zeytinburnu*. Istanbul: Zeytinburnu Belediyesi Kültür Yayınları, 2003.

Fatsea, Irene. "Migrant Builders and Craftsmen in the Founding Phase of Modern Athens." In *The City in the Ottoman Empire: Migration and the Making of Urban Modernity*, edited by Ulrike Freitag, Malte Fuhrmann, Nora Lafi, and Florian Riedler, 190–218. New York: Routledge, 2011.

Feldman, Hannah. *From a Nation Torn: Decolonizing Art and Representation in France*. Durham, NC: Duke University Press, 2014.

Fethi, Ihsan. "Contemporary Architecture in Baghdad." *Process Architecture*, May 1985, 112–32.

Figari Layus, Rosario. *The Reparative Effects of Human Rights Trials: Lessons from Argentina*. London: Routledge, 2019.

Filippidis, Dimitris. "Urban Housing of the 30s: Modern Architecture in Pre-War Athens." *Urban History* 21, no. 1 (1994): 49–60.

Firouz, Eskandar. *The Complete Fauna of Iran*. London: I. B. TauArchitecture, May 1985, andar. *Environment Iran*. N.p.: Iran Publication of National Society for Conservation, 1974.

Fiskesjö, Magnus. "CIAMS Faculty Talk." Paper presented at Cornell University, Ithaca, New York, December 10, 2020.

Flood, Finbarr Barry, and Gülru Necipoğlu, eds. *A Companion to Islamic Art and Architecture*. 2 vols. Hoboken, NJ: Wiley, 2017.

Foucault, Michel. *Surveiller et punir: Naissance de la prison*. Paris: Gallimard, 1975.

Frampton, Kenneth. "Towards a Critical Regionalism: Six Points for an Architecture of Resistance." In *The Anti-Aesthetic: Essays on Postmodern Culture*, edited by Hal Foster, 16–30. Seattle: Bay, 1983.

Freeman, Michael. *Human Rights: An Interdisciplinary Approach*. 2nd ed. Cambridge: Polity, 2011.

Freitag, Ulrike, Malte Fuhrmann, Nora Lafi, and Florian Riedler, eds. *The City in the Ottoman Empire: Migration and the Making of Urban Modernity*. New York: Routledge, 2011.

Friedrich, Daniel. "The Memoryscape in Buenos Aires: Representation, Memory and Pedagogy." *Journal of Curriculum Theorizing* 22, no. 3 (2011): 171–89.

Gaitskell, Arthur. *Gezira: A Story of Development in the Sudan.* London: Faber and Faber, 1959.

Galitekin, Ahmed Nezih. "Balıklı-Kozlu Panayırı." In *Zeytinburnu Kültür Vadisi,* vol. 2, edited by Murat Çekin, 125–67. Istanbul: Zeytinburnu Belediyesi Kültür Yayınları, 2018.

Gandy, Matthew. *Natura Urbana: Ecological Constellations in Urban Space.* Cambridge, MA: MIT Press, 2022.

Gandy, Matthew. "Signs of Life: Interview with Herbert Sukopp." In *The Botanical City,* edited by Matthew Gandy and Sandra Jasper, 18–22. Berlin: Jovis, 2020.

Gandy, Matthew, and Sandra Jasper, eds. *The Botanical City.* Berlin: Jovis, 2020.

Garibian, Sevane. "Ghosts Also Die: Resisting Disappearance Through the 'Right-to-Truth' and the Juicios por la Verdad in Argentina." *Journal of International Criminal Justice* 12 (2014): 515–38.

Gates-Madsen, Nancy. "Marketing and Sacred Space: The Parque de la Memoria in Buenos Aires." In *Accounting for Violence: Marketing Memory in Latin America,* edited by Ksenija Bilbija and Leigh Payne, 151–78. Durham, NC: Duke University Press, 2011.

Gayretullah, Hızırbek. "Bir Göç Hikayesi: Doğu Türkista'dan Göç Hatıraları." In *Göç Sempozyumu,* 136–38. Istanbul: Zeytinburnu Belediyesi Kültür Yayınları, 2006.

Gellner, Ernest. *Nations and Nationalism.* Ithaca, NY: Cornell University Press, 1983.

Georgitsoyanni, Evangelia. "Greek Masons in Africa: The Case of Karpathian Masons of Sudan." *Journal of Hellenic Diaspora* 29, no. 1 (2003): 115–27.

Geray, Cevat. *Türkiye'den ve Türkiye'ye Göçler: Türk İkdisadi Gelişmesi Araştırma Projesi.* Ankara: SBF Maliye Enstitüsü, 1962.

Gerber, Hans, and Nikolina Myofa. "Δουργούτι: Ο αρμενικός συνοικισμός στον Νέο Κόσμο." [Dourgouti: The Armenian Settlement in the New World]. *Documentonews,* October 1, 2020. https://www.documentonews.gr/.

Getachew, Adom. *Worldmaking After Empire: The Rise and Fall of Self-Determination.* Princeton, NJ: Princeton University Press, 2019.

Gharipour, Mohammad. *Persian Gardens and Pavilions: Reflections in History, Poetry and Arts.* London: I. B. Tauris, 2020.

Giedion, Sigfried. "The Need for a New Monumentality." In *New Architecture and City Planning: A Symposium,* edited by Paul Zucker, 549–68. New York: Philosophical Library, 1944.

Gillis, John R. ed. *Commemorations: The Politics of National Identity.* Princeton, NJ: Princeton University Press, 1994.

Ginio, Eyal. *The Ottoman Culture of Defeat: The Balkan Wars and Their After-math*. New York: Oxford University Press, 2016.

Gökçen, Turgay. "Zeytinburnu Gecekonduları." In *Surların Öte Yanı—The Other Side of the City Walls: Zeytinburnu*, 3rd ed., edited by Burçak Evren, 366–73. Istanbul: Zeytinburnu Belediyesi Kültür Yayınları, 2006.

Göktürk, Hamit. "Doğu Türkistan'dan Anadolu'ya Göçler." In *Göç Sempozyumu*, 130–35. Istanbul: Zeytinburnu Belediyesi Kültür Yayınları, 2006.

Göktürk, Hamit, ed. *Ilham Tohti:Yolum ve Gayem: Uygur Türkleri ve Çin Mese-lesi*. Istanbul: Şira Yayınları, 2015.

Göktürk, Nurala. *Ben Türkistan Kızıyım*. Istanbul: Kusak Ofset, 2008.

Gölunu, Berin. "From Graveyards to the 'People's Gardens': The Making of Pub-lic Leisure Space in Istanbul." Paper presented at Cornell University, NYC Humanities Corridor, 2019.

Göncüoğlu, Süleyman Faruk. "Kazlıçeşme Sanayi Bölgesi." In *Zeytinburnu Kül-tür Vadisi*, vol. 2, edited by Murat Çekin, 187–95. Istanbul: Zeytinburnu Belediyesi Kültür Yayınları, 2018.

Göral, Özgür Sevgi, Ayhan Işık, and Özlem Kaya. *The Unspoken Truth: Enforced Disappearances*. Istanbul: Hafıza Merkezi, 2013.

Gordon, Avery. *Ghostly Matters: Haunting and Sociological Imagination*. Minne-apolis: University of Minnesota Press, 2008.

"Gordon Memorial College, Khartoum." *Builder,* July 6, 1951, 4–6.

"Gordon Memorial College, Khartoum, Scheme for Redevelopment." *Builder*, January 11, 1946, 36–38.

Graeber, David, and David Wengrow. *The Dawn of Everything: A New History of Humanity*. New York: Farrar, Straus and Giroux, 2021.

"The Grand Hotel, Khartoum." *Builder,* August 28, 1931, 342.

Grigor, Talinn. *Building Iran: Modernism, Architecture and National Heritage Under the Pahlavi Monarchs*. New York: Periscope, 2009.

Griswold, Charles L. "The Vietnam Veterans Memorial and the Washington Mall: Philosophical Thoughts on Political Iconography." *Critical Inquiry* 12 (1986): 688–719.

Grove, Richard. *Green Imperialism: Colonial Expansion, Tropical Island Edens and the Origins of Environmentalism, 1600–1860*. Cambridge: Cambridge University Press, 1997.

Guha, Ramachandra, and Juan Martinez-Alier. *Varieties of Environmentalism: Essays North and South*. London: Earthscan, 2006.

Gültekin, Levent. "Tımarhanede Deprem Hazırlığı." Medyascope TV. YouTube, posted October 1, 2019. 31 min., 10 sec. https://www.youtube.com/watch?v=a5IuKngRmk4.

Günçıkan, Berat. *Cumartesi Anneleri*. Istanbul: İletişim, 1996.

Günhan, Aslıhan. "Displaced Modernities: Ottoman Empire, Turkey and the Specter of Armenian Architects." PhD diss., Cornell University, 2023.

Gür, Berin. "Political Misuse of Hagia Sophia as the Lost Object of the Istanbul Con-quest." *Space and Culture* (2023): 1–22. https://doi.org/10.1177/12063312231159198.

Gür, Berin. "Two Conquerors Under the Dome of the Panorama 1453 History Museum." *Journal of Architecture* 29, nos. 5–6 (2024): 870–95.

Gürek, Harun. *AKP'nin Müteahhitleri*. Istanbul: Güncel Yayıncılık, 2008.

Gutmann, Amy, and Dennis Thompson. "The Moral Foundation of Truth Commissions." In *Truth vs. Justice: The Morality of Truth Commissions*, edited by Robert Rotberg and Dennis Thompson, 22–44. Princeton, NJ: Princeton University Press, 2000.

Güven, Dilek. *Cumhuriyet Dönemi Azınlık Politikaları ve Stratejileri Bağlamında 6–7 Eylül Olayları*. Istanbul: İletişim Yayınları, 2005.

Güvenç, Sefer, ed. *Avrupa Kültür Başkenti Mübadele Müzesi*. Istanbul: Lozan Mübadilleri Vakfı, 2011.

Güvenç, Sefer, ed. *Common Cultural Heritage: Developing Local Awareness Concerning the Architectural Heritage Left from the Exchange of Populations in Turkey and Greece*. Conference proceedings with translations by Emine Yıldırım and Katerina Kitidis. Istanbul: Foundation of Lausanne Treaty Emigrants, 2005.

Guzman Bouvard, Marguerite. *Revolutionizing Motherhood: The Mothers of the Plaza de Mayo*. Lanham, MD: SR Books, 2004.

Hainsworth, Paul. "The Right to Truth." *Fortnight*, no. 358 (February 1997): 28.

Halaçoğlu, Ahmet. *Balkan Harbi Sırasında Rumeli'den Türk Göçleri (1912–1913)*. Ankara: Türk Tarih Kurumu, 1995.

Halidé Edib. *Memoirs of Halidé Edib*. New York: Century, 1926.

Hall, Richard. *The Balkan Wars 1912–13: Prelude to the First World War*. New York: Routledge, 2000.

Hamadeh, Shirine. *The City's Pleasures: Istanbul in the Eighteenth Century*. Seattle: University of Washington Press, 2007.

Hamdan, Gamal. "The Growth and Functional Structure of Khartoum." *Ekistics* 9, no. 56 (1960): 393–98.

Hamed-Troyansky, Vladimir. *Empire of Refugees: North Caucasian Muslims and the Late Ottoman State*. Stanford, CA: Stanford University Press, 2024.

"Hamit Göktürk'le Söyleşi." *Amerikanın Sesi*, July 7, 2009.

Hanssen, Jens, Thomas Philip, and Stefan Weber, eds. *The Empire in the City: Arab Provincial Capitals in the Late Ottoman Empire*. Wurzburg: Ergon in Kommission, 2002.

Hatif Öğe. "Köy Yapılarımız" (three fragments). *Yapı*, February 15, 1942, 8–9; April 1, 1942, 12; April 15, 1942, 8–9.

Haraway, Donna. "Making Kin." In *Staying with the Trouble: Making Kin in the Chthulucene*, 99–103. Durham, NC: Duke University Press, 2016.

Haraway, Donna. "Tentacular Thinking: Anthropocene, Capitalocene, Chthulucene." In *Staying with the Trouble: Making Kin in the Chthulucene*, 30–58. Durham, NC: Duke University Press, 2016.

Hart, Charles W. M. *Zeytinburnu Gecekondu Bölgesi*. Translated by Nephan Saran. Istanbul: Istanbul Ticaret Odasi, 1969.

Hatif Öğe. "Köy Yapılarımız" (three fragments). *Yapı*, February 15, 1942, 8–9; April 1, 1942, 12; April 15, 1942, 8–9.

Hesse, Carla, and Robert Post. "Introduction." In *Human Rights in Political Transitions: Gettysburg to Bosnia*, 13–36. New York: Zone, 1999.

Hiçdurmaz, Muzaffer, dir. *Çark*. 80 mins. Burak Film, 1987.

Hight, Eleanor M., and Gary Sampson, eds. *Colonialist Photography: Imag(in)ing Race and Place*. New York: Routledge, 2002.

Hill, Richard. *Egypt in the Sudan 1820–1881*. London: Oxford University Press, 1959.

Hirschon, Renée, ed. *Crossing the Aegean: An Appraisal of the 1923 Compulsory Populatiion Exchange Between Greece and Turkey*. New York: Berghahn, 2003.

Hirschon, Renée. *Heirs of the Greek Catastrophe: Social Life of Asia Minor Refugees in Piraeus*. Oxford: Clarendon Press, 1989.

Hirschon, Renée. "History, Memory and Emotion: The Long-Term Significance of the 1923 Greco-Turkish Exchange of Populations." In *When Greeks and Turks Meet*, edited by Vally Lytra, 23–43. London: Ashgate, 2014.

Holod, Renata, Attilio Petruccioli, and André Raymond, eds. *The City in the Islamic World*. 2 vols. Boston: Brill, 2008.

Holt, P. M., and M. W. Daly. *A History of the Sudan: From the Coming of Islam to the Present Day*. London: Routledge, 2019.

Horkheimer, Max, and Theodor Adorno. *Dialectic of Enlightenment* .Translated by John Cumming. London: Verso, 1979.

Huyssen, Andreas. "Diaspora and Nation: Migration into Other Pasts." *New German Critique* 88 (2003): 147–64.

Huyssen, Andreas. "Memory Sites in an Expanded Field: The Memory Park in Buenos Aires." In *Present Pasts: Urban Palimpsests and the Politics of Memory*, 94–109. Stanford, CA: Stanford University Press, 2003.

Huyssen, Andreas. *Present Pasts: Urban Palimpsests and the Politics of Memory*. Stanford, CA: Stanford University Press, 2003.

Ignatieff, Michael. "Human Rights." In *Human Rights in Political Transitions: Gettysburg to Bosnia*, edited by Carla Hesse and Robert Post, 313–24. New York: Zone, 1999.

Iğsız, Aslı. *Humanism in Ruins. Entangled Legacies of the German-Turkish Population Exchange*. Stanford, CA: Stanford University Press, 2018.

Inancık, Halil. *The Ottoman Empire: The Classical Age*. New York: Phoenix, 1973.

İpek, Nedim. "The Balkans, War and Migration." In *War and Nationalism: The Balkan Wars, 1912–1913, and Their Sociopolitical Implications*, edited by M. H. Yavuz and I. Blumi, 621–64. Salt Lake City: University of Utah Press, 2013.

İpek, Nedim. *Rumeli'den Anadolu'ya Türk Göçleri (1877–1890)*. Ankara: Türk Tarih Kurumu, 1994.

Isenstadt, Samuel. "'Faith in a Better Future': Josep Lluis Sert's American Embassy in Baghdad." *Journal of Architectural Education* 50, no. 3 (1997): 172–88.

Isenstadt, Sandy, and Kishwar Rizvi, eds. *Modernism and the Middle East: Architecture and Politics in the Twentieth Century*. Seattle: University of Washington Press, 2008.

Ishay, Micheline. *The History of Human Rights: From Ancient Times to the Globalization Era*. Berkeley: University of California Press, 2004.

Işın, Ekrem. "Yenikapı Mevlevihanesi." In *Surların Öte Yanı—The Other Side of the City Walls: Zeytinburnu*, 3rd ed., edited by Burçak Evren, 266–93. Istanbul: Zeytinburnu Belediyesi Kültür Yayınları, 2006.

İskan Tarihçesi. Istanbul: Hamit Matbaası, 1932.

İşli, Hayri Necdet. "Zeytinburnu Tekkeleri." In *Zeytinburnu Kültür Vadisi*, vol. 2, edited by Murat Çekin, 547–61. Istanbul: Zeytinburnu Belediyesi Kültür Yayınları, 2018.

Issopoulos, Spyros. "The Greeks of Sinasos, and Their Current Relationship with Their Place of Origin." In *Common Cultural Heritage*, edited by Sefer Güvenç, 175–77. Istanbul: Foundation of Lausanne Treaty Emigrants, 2005.

"İstanbul'da Kentsel Dönüşüm Skandalı." *Sözcü Gazetesi*, December 14, 2021. www.sozcu.com.tr/2021/gundem/istanbulda-kentsel-donusum-skandali -6826734/.

"Istanbul'un Zeytinburnu İlçesinde Bir Bina Çöktü." *T24*, May 6, 2021. https://t24 .com.tr/haber/istanbul-un-zeytinburnu-ilcesinde-bir-bina-coktu,950753.

Ito, Toyo, Kumiko Inui, Sou Fujimoto, Akihisa Hirata, and Naoya Hatakeyama. *Architecture: Possible Here? Home-for-All*. Tokyo: Toto, 2013.

IUCN. "Nations Fall Short on Biodiversity Despite Protected Area Growth." October 7, 2020. https://www.iucn.org/news/world-commission-protected -areas/202010/nations-fall-short-biodiversity-despite-protected-area -growth-iucn-co-authored-study.

Jacoby, Karl. *Crimes Against Nature: Squatters, Poachers, Thieves and the Hidden History of American Conservation*. Berkeley: University of California Press, 2014.

Jacqmin, A. "When Human Claims Become Rights. The Case of the Right to Truth over 'Desaparecidos.'" *Oñati Socio-Legal Series* 7, no. 6 (2017): 1247–72. http://ssrn.com/abstract=3051031.

John-Alder, Kathleen. "Paradise Reconsidered: The Early Design History of Pardisan Park in Tehran." In *Contemporary Urban Landscapes of the Middle East*, edited by Mohammad Gharipour, 120–48. London: Routledge, 2016.

Johnson, Douglas. *The Root Causes of Sudan's Civil Wars*. Oxford: James Currey, 2003.

Kafadar, Cemal. "Su Gibi Aziz Ayazmalar." *Z Journal*, accessed April 4, 2022. https://www.zdergisi.istanbul/makale/su-gibi-aziz-ayazmalar-158.

Kafkoula, Kiki. "In Search of Urban Reform: Co-Operative Housing in Inter-War Athens." *Urban History* 21, no. 1 (1994): 49–60.

Kallipoliti, Lydia, dir. *Biospheres and the Rise of Botanical Capital*. 32 min., 16 sec. Rensellaer Polytechnic Institute, 2017. https://vimeo.com/430971877.

Kant, Immanuel. "3 articles." In *Werke*, vol. 1, edited by Ernst Cassirer, 429–84. Berlin: Bruno Cassirer, 1922.

Karadawi, Ahmad. *Refugee Policy in Sudan 1967–1984*. New York: Berghahn, 1999.

Karakasidou, Anastasia. *Fields of Wheat, Hills of Blood: Passages to Nationhood in Greek Macedonia, 1870–1990*. Chicago: University of Chicago Press, 1997.

Karaman, Emine Rezzan. "Remember, S/he Was Here Once: Mothers Call for Justice and Peace in Turkey." *Journal of Middle East Women's Studies* 12, no. 3 (2016): 382–410.

Karaman, Ozan. "Urban Renewal in Istanbul: Reconfigured Spaces, Robotic Lives." *International Journal of Urban and Regional Research* 37, no. 2 (2013): 715–33.

Kardamitsi-Adami, Maro. *The Architect Kleon Krantonellis*. Athens: Benaki Museum, 2009.

Karim, Farhan. "Between Self and Citizenship: Doxiades Associates in Postcolonial Pakistan, 1958–1968." *International Journal of Islamic Architecture* 5, no. 1 (2016): 135–61.

Karimi, Pamela. *Domesticity and Consumer Culture in Iran: Interior Revolutions of the Modern Era*. London: Routledge, 2013.

Karolyi, Elisabeth. "Refurbishment or Demolition: The Fate of a 1930s Housing Complex in Athens Remains Pending." *Docomomo*, no. 37 (2007): 64–67.

Karpat, Kemal. *The Gecekondu: Rural Migration and Urbanization*. Cambridge: Cambridge University Press, 1976.

Kasaba, Reşat. "A Moveable Empire." In *The City in the Ottoman Empire: Migration and the Making of Urban Modernity*, edited by Ulrike Freitag, Malte Fuhrmann, Nora Lafi, and Florian Riedler, 15–28. New York: Routledge, 2011.

Kasaba, Reşat. *A Moveable Empire: Ottoman, Nomads, Migrants and Refugees*. Seattle: University of Washington Press, 2009.

Kaya, Bayram Ali. "Yenikapı Mevlevihanesi'nin Tarihçesi." In *Zeytinburnu Kültür Vadisi*, vol. 1, edited by Murat Çekin, 405–17. Istanbul: Zeytinburnu Belediyesi Kültür Yayınları, 2018.

Kaya, Dilek Akyalcin. "Immigration into Ottoman Territory: The Case of Salonica in the Late Nineteenth Century." In *The City in the Ottoman Empire: Migration and the Making of Urban Modernity*, edited by Ulrike Freitag, Malte Fuhrmann, Nora Lafi, and Florian Riedler, 177–90. New York: Routledge, 2011.

Kaya, Şükrü. *TBMM Zabit Ceridesi* [Official Minutes of the Grand National Assembly of Turkey.] Devre IV, Cilt 23, Ictima: 3. June 14, 1935. https://www5.tbmm.gov.tr/tutanaklar/TUTANAK/TBMM/d04/c023/tbmm04023068.pdf.

"Kayıp Ocak Gömülmüş." *Milliyet*, May 17, 1995. https://gazetearsivi.milliyet.com.tr/Arsiv/1995/05/17.

Keleş, Ruşen. *Kentleşme Politikası*. 10th ed. Istanbul: İmge Yayınları, 2006.

Kemal, Yaşar. *Fırat Suyu Kan Akıyor Baksana*. Istanbul: Adam, 1998.

"Kemikler vurur kıyılarına Kürt denizinin." *Gazete Duvar*, December 2, 2019. www.gazeteduvar.com.tr/forum/2019/12/02/kemikler-vurur-kiyilarina-kurtun-denizini n/.

Kendrick, T. D. *The Lisbon Disaster*. London: Methuen, 1956.

Kentel, Koca Mehmet. "Assembling 'Cosmopolitan' Pera: An Infrastructural History of Late Ottoman Istanbul." PhD diss., University of Washington, 2018.

Keyder, Çağlar. "The Housing Market from Informal to Global." In *Istanbul: Between the Global and the Local*, edited by Çağlar Keyder, 143–59. Lanham, MD: Rowman and Littlefield, 1999.

Keyder, Çağlar, ed. *Istanbul: Between the Global and the Local*. Lanham, MD: Rowman and Littlefield, 1999.

Keyder, Çağlar. "The Ottoman Empire." In *After Empire: Multiethnic Societies and Nation-Building—The Soviet Union and the Russian, Ottoman, and Habsburg Empires*, edited by Karen Barkey and Mark von Hagen, 30–44. Boulder, CO: Westview, 1997.

Keyder, Çağlar. *Türkiye'de Devlet ve Sınırlar*. Istanbul: İletişim, 1989.

Khansari, Mehdi, M. R. Moghtader, and Minouch Yavari. *The Persian Garden: Echoes of Paradise*. Washington, DC: Mage, 2003.

Kieser, Hans Lukas, Kerem Öktem, and Maurus Reinkowski. *World War I and the End of the Ottomans: From the Balkan Wars to the Armenian Genocide*. London: I. B. Tauris, 2015.

King, Anthony. *The Bungalow: The Production of a Global Culture*. London: Routledge, 1984.

King, Desmond S., and Jennifer M. Page. "Towards Transitional Justice? Black Reparations and the End of Mass Incarceration." *Ethnic and Racial Studies* 41, no. 4 (2018): 739–58.

"The Kitchener Memorial Medical School, Khartoum." *Builder,* January 4, 1924, 9, plate.

Kitromilides, Paschalis. "Greek Irredentism in Asia Minor and Cyprus." *Middle Eastern Studies* 26, no. 1 (1990): 3–17.

Kitromilides, Paschalis. "The Greek-Turkish Population Exchange." In *Turkey in the Twentieth Century*, edited by Erik-Jan Zürcher, 255–70. Berlin: Klaus Schwarz Verlag, 2008.

Klein, Naomi. *The Shock Doctrine: The Rise of Disaster Capitalism*. New York: Metropolitan, 2007.

Klein, Naomi. *This Changes Everything: Capitalism vs. the Climate*. New York: Simon and Schuster, 2014.

Klinkner, Melanie, and Howard Davis. *The Right to Truth in International Law: Victims' Rights in Human Rights and International Criminal Law*. London: Routledge, 2020.

Koenigsberger, O. H., T. G. Ingersol, Alan Mayhew, and S. V. Szokolay. *Manual of Tropical Housing and Building. Climatic Design*. Hyderabad: Universities Press, 1975.

Koheji, Marwa. "Thermal Comfort and (Im)possible Futures: The Story of Air-Conditioning in Bahrain." In *Sweating Assets: On Climate Conditioning and Ecology*, unpag. Manama: Bahrain's Authority for Culture and Antiquities, 2023.

Koker, Tolga, with Leyla Keskiner. "Lessons in Refugeehood: The Experience of Forced Migrants in Turkey." In *Crossing the Aegean*, edited by Renée Hirschon, 193–208. New York: Berghahn, 2003.

Kolbert, Elizabeth. *The Sixth Extinction: An Unnatural History*. New York: Henry Holt, 2014.

Kömürciyan, Eremya Çelebi. *Istanbul'un Tarihi: XVII Asırda Istanbul*. Translated by Kevork Pamukciyan and edited by Hrand D. Andreasyan. Istanbul: Eren, 1988.

Kontogiorgi, Elisabeth. "Economic Consequences Following Refugee Settlement in Greek Macedonia, 1923–32." In *Crossing the Aegean*, edited by Renée Hirschon, 63–77. New York: Berghahn, 2003.

Koptaş, Robert. "Bir Başka Gözle Surp Pırgiç Ermeni Hastanesi'nin Tarihi: Kiminin Şefkat Evi Kiminin Dert Yuvası." *Toplumsal Tarih* 148 (2006): 32–39.

Koundouros, Nikos, dir. *Magiki Polis*. 1954.

Kowarik, Ingo. "Urban Cemeteries in Berlin and Beyond: Life in the Grounds of the Dead." In *The Botanical City*, edited by Matthew Gandy and Sandra Jasper, 305–11. Berlin: Jovis, 2020.

Köymen, Esin. "Kayaköy: Barış ve Dostluk Köyünden, Tatil Köyüne." *Mimarlık* 382 (March–April 2015). http://www.mo.org.tr/mimarlikdergisi/index.cfm?sayfa=mimarlik&DergiSayi=396&RecID=3613.

Koyunoğlu, Arif Hikmet. "Merhum Mimar Arif Hikmet Koyunoğlu'nun Anıları 4." *Tarih ve Toplum* 7 (1987): 47–51.

Kulca, Yusuf. "Bir Göç Hikayesi: Zeytinburnu'nda Başlayan Hayatın Öyküsü." In *Göç Sempozyumu*, 249–52. Istanbul: Zeytinburnu Belediyesi Kültür Yayınları, 2006.

Kurban, Dilek. *Reparations and Displacement in Turkey, Lessons Learned from the Compensation Law, Case Studies of Transitional Justice and Displacement, Brookings Report*. New York: International Center for Transitional Justice, 2012.

Kurt, Ümit, and Doğan Gürpınar. "The Balkan Wars and the Rise of the Reactionary Modernist Utopia in Young Turk Thought and the Journal *Turk Yurdu* [Turkish Homeland]." *Nations and Nationalism* 21, no. 2 (2015): 348–68.

Kurtoğlu, Akın. "Zeytinburnu Ulaşım Tarihi." In *Zeytinburnu Kültür Vadisi*, vol. 1, edited by Murat Çekin, 221–69. Istanbul: Zeytinburnu Belediyesi Kültür Yayınları, 2018.

Kutsal, Feruz. "Kültür Vadisi'ni Arındıran Yıkımlar." In *Zeytinburnu Kültür Vadisi*, vol. 1, edited by Murat Çekin, 65–69. Istanbul: Zeytinburnu Belediyesi Kültür Yayınları, 2018.

Kuyucu, Tuna. "Law, Property and Ambiguity: The Uses and Abuses of Legal Ambiguity in Remaking Istanbul's Informal Settlements." *International Journal of Urban and Regional Research* 38, no. 2 (2014): 609–27.

Kyrtsis, Alexandros-Andreas. *Constantinos A. Doxiadis: Texts, Design Drawings, Settlements.* Athens: Ikaros, 2006.

Kyrtsis, Alexandros-Andreas. "Ekistics and the World of Sciences." In *Constantinos A. Doxiadis: Texts, Design Drawings, Settlements,* edited by Alexandros-Andreas Kyrtsis, 449–63. Athens: Ikaros, 2006.

Ladas, Stephen. *The Exchange of Minorities: Bulgaria, Greece and Turkey.* New York: Macmillan, 1932.

"Lausanne Peace Treaty VI. Convention Concerning the Exchange of Greek and Turkish Population Signed at Lausanne January 30, 1923." *League of Nations Treaty Series* 32 (1925): 76–87.

Lefebvre, Henri. *The Right to the City.* In *Writings on Cities,* selected and translated by Eleonore Kofman and Elizabeth Lebas. Oxford: Oxford University Press, 1996. https://theanarchistlibrary.org/library/henri-lefebvre-right-to -the-city.

Lemos, Natasha. "Early Literature of the Asia Minor Disaster and the War of Independence: Where Greek and Turk Have Yet to Meet." In *When Greeks and Turks Meet,* edited by Vally Lytra, 185–208. Farnham: Ashgate, 2014.

Levey, Cara. "Between Marginalization and Decentralization of Memory: Peripheral Palimpsests in Post-Dictatorship Buenos Aires and Montevideo." *Journal of Romance Studies* 14, no. 3 (2014): 67–85.

Liboiron, Max. *Pollution Is Colonialism.* Durham, NC: Duke University Press, 2021.

"L'Immigration en Turquie." *La Turquie Kemaliste,* nos. 23–24 (1938): 15–18.

Lowe, Lisa. *The Intimacies of Four Continents.* Durham, NC: Duke University Press, 2015.

Lozanovska, Mirjana, and Igor Martek. "Skopje Resurgent: The International Confusions of Post-Earthquake Planning, 1963–1967." *Planning Perspectives* 34, no. 3 (2019): 497–513.

Lytra, Vally, ed. *When Greeks and Turks Meet.* Farnham: Ashgate, 2014.

MacDonald, Margaret. "Natural Rights." In *Theories of Rights,* 2nd ed., edited by Jeremy Waldron, 21–40. Oxford: Oxford University Press, 2009.

Mackridge, Peter. "The Myth of Asia Minor in Greek Fiction." In *Crossing the Aegean,* edited by Renée Hirschon, 235–46. New York: Berghahn, 2003.

"Mağdurlar İşkencehanenin 5 Yıldızlı Otele Dönüştürülmesine Tepkili." *Mağduriyetler* (blog), January 19, 2020. https://magduriyetler2.blogspot.com /2020/01/magdurlar-iskencehanenin-5-yldzl-otele.html.

"*Μαγική πόλις*: Ηιστορία της συνοικίας Δουργούτι που σήμερα αποτελεί την περιοχή του Νέου Κόσμου" [*Magic City*: The History of the Dourgouti District That Today Is the Area of the New World]. *Lifo,* February 22, 2020. https://www.lifo.gr/now/athens/magiki-polis-i-istoria-tis-synoikias -doyrgoyti-poy-simera-apotelei-tin-periohi-toy-neoy?amp.

Mahmood, Mohammad Ibrahim, Nadir Ahmed Elagib, Finlay Horn, and Suhair A. G. Saad. "Lessons Learned from Khartoum Flash Flood Impacts: An Integrated Assessment." *Science of the Total Environment,* 601–2 (2017): 1031–45.

Makdisi, Ussama. *Age of Coexistence: The Ecumenical Frame and the Making of the Modern World*. Stanford, CA: Stanford University Press, 2021.

Makris, G. P., and Endre Stiansen. "Angelo Capato: A Greek Trader in the Sudan." *Sudan Studies*, no. 21 (1998): 10–19.

Malm, Andreas. *Fossil Capital: The Rise of Steam Power and the Roots of Global Warming*. New York: Verso, 2016.

Malm, Andreas, and Alf Hornborg. "The Geology of Mankind? A Critique of the Anthropocene Narrative." *Anthropocene Review* 1, no. 1 (2014): 62–69.

Mandel, Ruth. *Cosmopolitan Anxieties: Turkish Challenges to Citizenship and Belonging in Germany*. Durham, NC: Duke University Press, 2008.

"Map of 'Tropical Zones.'" *Colonial Building Notes* 32 (1955): 7.

Marmara, Rinaldo. *Pancaldı. Quartier Levantin du XIXe Siècle*. Istanbul: Les Éditions Isis, 2004.

Marmor, Andrei, ed. *The Routledge Companion to Philosophy of Law*. New York: Routledge, 2015.

Marris, Emma. *Rambunctious Garden: Savage Nature in a Post-Wild World*. New York: Bloomsbury, 2011.

Marx, Karl. "On the Jewish Question." In *The Marx-Engels Reader,* edited by Robert C. Tucker, 26–52. New York: Norton, 1978. Originally published in 1843.

Mattioli, Fabio. "Unchanging Boundaries: The Reconstruction of Skopje and the Politics of Heritage." *International Journal of Heritage Studies* 20, no. 6 (2014): 599–615.

Mazower, Mark. *The Greek Revolution: 1821 and the Making of Modern Europe*. New York: Penguin, 2021.

Mbembe, Achille. "Necropolitics." *Public Culture* 15, no. 1 (2003): 11–40.

McCarthy, Justin. *Death and Exile: The Ethnic Cleansing of Ottoman Muslims, 1821–1922*. Princeton, NJ: Darwin, 1995.

McDonough, William, and Partners. "Hannover Principles: Design for Sustainability. Prepared for EXPO 2000, The World's Fair, Hannover, Germany." Unpublished report, 1992. Accessed January 4, 2023. https://mcdonough .com/wp-content/uploads/2013/03/Hannover-Principles-1992.pdf.

McEwen, Mitch, Cruz Garcia, and Nathalie Frankowski, eds. "Reparations." Special issue, *Journal of Architectural Education* 77, no. 1 (2023).

McGarry, John. "Demographic Engineering: The State-Directed Movement of Ethnic Groups as a Technique of Conflict Resolution." *Ethnic and Racial Studies* 21, no. 4 (1998): 613–38.

McHarg, Ian. *Design with Nature*. 1969. New York: Wiley, 1992.

McHarg, Ian. *To Heal the Earth: Selected Writings of Ian L. McHarg*. Edited by Frederick R. Steiner. Washington, DC: Island, 1998.

McKibben, Bill. "Record Heat Wave in Europe Is Latest Warning That Action on Climate Can't Wait." Democracy Now!, July 18, 2022. www.democracynow .org/2022/7/18/record_heat_wave_europe_north_africa.

McKittrick, Katherine, ed. *Sylvia Wynter: On Being Human as Praxis*. Durham, NC: Duke University Press, 2015.

McLean, W. H. *Regional and Town Planning*. London: Crosby Lockwood, 1930.

McLean, W. H. "Town Planning in the Tropics: With Special Reference to the Khartoum City Development Plan." *Town Planning Review* 3, no. 4 (1913): 225–31.

McLeod, Mary. "The Battle for the Monument: The Vietnam Veterans Memorial." In *The Experimental Tradition: Essays on Competitions in Architecture*, edited by Hélène Lipstadt, 115–37. New York: Princeton Architectural Press, 1989.

McLeod, Mary. "Henri Lefebvre's Critique of Everyday Life: An Introduction." In *Architecture of the Everyday*, edited by Steven Harris and Deborah Berke, 9–29. New York: Princeton Architectural Press, 1997.

Meister, Robert. "Forgiving and Forgetting: Lincoln and the Politics of National Recovery." In *Human Rights in Political Transitions: Gettysburg to Bosna*, edited by Carla Hesse and Robert Post, 135–75. New York: Zone, 1999.

Melly, George. *Khartoum, and the Blue and White Niles*. London: Colburn, 1851.

Merlier, Melpo. *Présentation du Centre d'Études d'Asie Mineure Recherches d'Ethnographie*. Brochure distributed at the 22nd Oriental Congress, Istanbul, 1951. Reprint, Athens: CAMS, 2011.

Michaelson, Ruth. "'Waste Colonialism': World Grapples with West's Unwanted Plastic." *Guardian*, December 31, 2021. www.theguardian.com/environment/2021/dec/31/waste-colonialism-countries-grapple-with-wests-unwanted-plastic.

Mignolo, Walter, and Catherine Walsh. *On Decoloniality: Concepts, Analytics, Praxis*. Durham, NC: Duke University Press, 2018.

Mihr, Anja. *Regime Consolidation and Transitional Justice: A Comparative Study of Germany, Spain and Turkey*. Cambridge: Cambridge University Press, 2018.

Mihri, Muhammed. *Sudan Seyahatnamesi*. 1908–9. Edited by Ahmet Kavas. Istanbul: İletişim, 2016.

Millas, Herkül. "The Exchange of Populations in Turkish Literature: The Undertone of Texts." In *Crossing the Aegean*, edited by Renée Hirschon, 222–34. New York: Berghahn, 2003.

Millas, Herkül, trans. *Göç: Rumların Anadolu'dan Mecburi Ayrılışı (1919–1923)*. Istanbul: İletişim, 2001. Originally published in Greek in 1980–82 as *He Exodos*, 2 vols.

Millas, Herkül. *Onlar İki Kere Yabancıydılar*. Istanbul: Lozan Mübadilleri Vakfı Yayınları, 2015.

Minawi, Mostafa. *Losing Istanbul: Arab Ottoman Imperialists and the End of Empire*. Stanford, CA: Stanford University Press, 2023.

Minawi, Mostafa. *The Ottoman Scramble for Africa: Empire and Diplomacy in the Sahara and the Hijaz*. Stanford, CA: Stanford University Press, 2016.

Mishra, Stuti, and Louise Boyle. "Earth Sets Its Hottest Day Record for Third Time in a Week." *Independent*, July 6, 2023. https://www.independent.co.uk/climate-change/news/hottest-day-of-the-year-2023-earth-b237 1394.html.

Mock, Elizabeth. "Built in USA—Since 1932." In *Built in USA, 1932–1944*, edited by Elizabeth Mock, 25. New York: Museum of Modern Art, 1944.

Montes, Jorge Alberto. "The Right to Truth in the Recent History of Argentina." Translated by Kristin Beamish Brown. In "Human Rights and Latin American Cultural Studies," edited by Ana Forcinito and Fernando Ordonez, special issue, *Hispanic Issues On Line* 4, no. 1 (2009): 137–49.

Morgenthau, Henry. *I Was Sent to Athens*. Garden City, NY: Doubleday, Doran, 1929.

Morland, Paul. *Demographic Engineering: Population Strategies in Ethnic Conflict*. London: Taylor and Francis, 2014.

Mortaş, Abidin. "Köy Evi Tipleri." *Arkitekt*, nos. 1–2 (1940): 8–9.

Mübadele Öyküleri. Tekirdağ: Tekirdağ Büyükşehir Belediyesi, 2017.

Mübadiller: Onlar İki Kere Yabancıydılar. Istanbul: Lozan Mübadilleri Vakfı Yayınları, 2015.

Mukhar, Y. A. "Roofs in Hot Dry Climates with Special Reference to Northern Sudan." *Overseas Building Notes* 182 (1978): 1–15.

Mumford, Lewis. *The Culture of Cities*. New York: Harcourt, Brace, 1938.

Murat, Sedat, and Halis Ersöz. "Zeytinburnu'nun Sosyo-Ekonomik Yapısı." Istanbul: Zeytinburnu Belediyesi Kültür Yayınları, 2005.

Muzaffar, Ijlal. "Boundary Games. Ecohard. Doxiadis and the Refugee Housing Projects Under Military Rule in Pakistan, 1953–1959," In *Governing by Design: Architecture, Economy and Politics in the Twentieth Century*, edited by Aggregate (Architectual History Collaborative), 147–75. Pittsburgh, PA: University of Pittsburgh Press, 2012.

Myofa, Nikolina, and Evaggelos Papadias. "The Development of the Neighborhood of Dourgouti Since 1922." *Athens Social Atlas*, November 2016. www.athenssocialatlas.gr/en/article/dourgouti/.

Nalci, Tamar, and Emre Can Dağlıoğlu. "Istanbul Radyosu Arazisi Bir Zamanlar Ermeni Mezarlığıydı." *Agos*, accessed August 26, 2011. www.bianet.org/biamag/azinliklar/141423-istanbul-radyosu-arazisi-ermeni-mezarligiydi.

National Committee of Human Settlements, Government of Iran. "Habitat Bill of Rights." *Ekistics* 42, no. 252 (1976): 302–8.

Neglia, Giulia Annalinda. "Some Historiographical Notes on the Islamic City with Particular Reference to the Visual Representation of the Built City." In *The City in the Islamic World*, vol. 1, edited by Renata Holod, Attilio Petruccioli and André Raymond, 1–46. Boston: Brill, 2008.

Nichols, Robert. *Theft Is Property: Dispossession and Critical Theory*. Durham, NC: Duke University Press, 2020.

Nixon, Rob. *Slow Violence and the Environmentalism of the Poor*. Cambridge, MA: Harvard University Press, 2013.

Nooraddin, Hoshiar. "Globalization and the Search for Modern Local Architecture: Learning from Baghdad." In *Planning Middle Eastern Cities*, edited by Yasser Elsheshtawy, 59–84. London: Routledge, 2004.

Norberg-Schulz, Christian. "Locus: Opera di Paolo Portoghesi e Vittorio Gigliotti." *Controspazio* 7, no. 4 (1975): 40–79.

"Ocak ailesi Istanbul Valisiyle görüştü." *Milliyet*, April 24, 1995. https://gazetearsivi.milliyet.com.tr/Arsiv/1995/04/24.

"Ocak için CHP Işgali Sürüyor." *Milliyet*, April 24, 1995. https://gazetearsivi.milliyet.com.tr/Arsiv/1995/04/24.

"Ocak'ın Mezarı Belirlendi." *Milliyet*, May 19, 1995. https://gazetearsivi.milliyet.com.tr/Arsiv/1995/05/19.

"Ocak Sırlarla Gömüldü." *Milliyet*, May 23, 1995. https://gazetearsivi.milliyet.com.tr/Arsiv/1995/05/23.

Oettermann, Stephan. *The Panorama: History of a Mass Medium*. Translated by Deborah Lucas Schneider. New York: Zone, 1997.

Öğün, Emine, and Mehmet Öğün. "Örnek Bir Dönüşüm Projesinin Kısa Hikayesi." In *Zeytinburnu Kültür Vadisi*, vol. 1, edited by Murat Çekin, 35–39. Istanbul: Zeytinburnu Belediyesi Kültür Yayınları, 2018.

Onan, Baskın. "The Minority Concept and Rights in Turkey: The Lausanne Peace Treaty and Current Issues." In *Human Rights in Turkey*, edited by Zehra Kabasakal Arat, 35–56. Philadelphia: University of Pennsylvania Press, 2007.

Orff, Kate. *Toward an Urban Ecology*. New York: Monacelli, 2016.

Ortaylı, İlber. "Tarihsel Perspektiften Surdışı." In *Surların Öte Yanı—The Other Side of the City Walls: Zeytinburnu*, 3rd ed., edited by Burçak Evren, 154–65. Istanbul: Zeytinburnu Belediyesi Kültür Yayınları, 2006.

Osman, Omer S. "Sudanese Architecture Around Independence." In *Proceedings: Conference "Modern Architecture in East Africa Around Independence," 27th–29th July, Dar es Salaam, Tanzania*, 53–57. Utrecht: ArchiAfrika, 2005.

Osman, Omer S., and Amira O. S. Osman. "The Modern Heritage of Khartoum." In "New Frames," special issue, *Docomomo Journal* 32 (2005): 68–71.

Osman, Omer S., Amira O. S. Osman, and Ibrahim Z. Bahreldin. "Architecture in Sudan: The Post-Independence Era (1956–1970)." In "Modern and Sustainable," special issue, *Docomomo Journal* 44 (2011): 80–84.

Ozaki, Ana. "The Brazilian Atlantic: New 'Brazils', Plantation Architecture, Race, and Climate in Brazil and Africa, 1910–1974." PhD diss., Cornell University, 2022.

Özbay, Aslı. "Yok Edilen Tarihi Bir Mahallenin, Turizm Bahanesiyle Hayata Dönüşü: Argos Inn Cappadocia Öyküsü." In *Tarihi Çevrede Yapılaşma Deneyimleri*, edited by Aylan Bekleyen and Neslihan Dalkılıç, 115–41. Istanbul: Lord Matbaacılık, 2018.

Özbay, Aslı, and Baran Idil. "The Settlement We Have Discovered via Its Conservation Plan (Cappadoccia's 'Sleeping Beauty' Mustafapaşa)." In *Common*

Cultural Heritage, edited by Sefer Güvenç, 167–68. Istanbul: Foundation of Lausanne Treaty Emigrants, 2005.

Özbayoğlu, Erdeniz. "Byzantine Period." In *Surların Öte Yanı—The Other Side of the City Walls: Zeytinburnu*, 3rd ed., edited by Burçak Evren, 14–37. Istanbul: Zeytinburnu Belediyesi Kültür Yayınları, 2006.

Özçelik, Merve. "İstanbul'da Kaç Tane Toplanma Alanı Olduğu Bilinmiyor." Medyascope TV, September 27, 2019. https://medyascope.tv/2019/09/27/istanbulda-kac-tane-deprem-toplanma-alani-oldugu-bilinmiyor-erdogana-gore-bu-sayi-onbinlerce-imamogluna-goreyse-77/.

Özgür, Ulvi. "Bulgaristan Türkleri'ni 1950–51 Yıllarında Türkiye'ye Göçleri." MA thesis, Istanbul University, 2007.

Özkırımlı, Umut. *Theories of Nationalism: A Critical Introduction*. London: Red Globe, 2000.

Özsoy, Iskender. *Ah Vre Memleket*. Istanbul: Bağlam Yayıncılık, 2014.

Özsu, Umut. *Formalizing Displacement: International Law and Population Transfers*. Oxford: Oxford University Press, 2015.

Öztabak, Murat. "Seyyahlar Diyarı Zeytinburnu." In *Zeytinburnu Kültür Vadisi*, vol. 1, edited by Murat Çekin, 108–23. Istanbul: Zeytinburnu Belediyesi Kültür Yayınları, 2018.

Öztan, Ramazan Hakkı. "Point of No Return? Prospects of Empire After the Ottoman Defeat in the Balkan Wars." *International Journal of Middle East Studies* 50 (2018): 65–84.

Özvar, Erol. "Osmanlı Zamanında Zeytinburnu." In *Surların Öte Yanı—The Other Side of the City Walls: Zeytinburnu*, 3rd ed., edited by Burçak Evren, 70–97. Istanbul: Zeytinburnu Belediyesi Kültür Yayınları, 2006.

Özyürek, Esra. "Export-Import Theory and the Racialization of Anti-Semitism: Turkish- and Arab-Only Prevention Programs in Germany." *Comparative Studies in Society and History* 58, no. 1 (2016): 40–65.

Pamuk, Orhan. *Istanbul: Memories and the City*. Translated by Maureen Freely. London: Faber and Faber, 2006.

Panayi, Panikos, and Pippa Virdee, eds. *Refugees and the End of Empire: Imperial Collapse and Forced Migration During the Twentieth Century*. Basingstoke: Palgrave Macmillan, 2011.

Papailias, Penelope. *Genres of Recollection: Archival Poetics and Modern Greece*. New York: Palgrave Macmillan, 2005.

Parenti, Christian. *Tropic of Chaos: Climate Change and the New Geography of Violence*. New York: Nation Books, 2012.

Parla, Ayşe, and Ceren Özgül. "Property, Dispossession, and Citizenship in Turkey; or, The History of the Gezi Uprising Starts in the Surp Hagop Armenian Cemetery." *Public Culture* 28, no. 3 (2016): 617–53.

Pekin, Müfide, ed. *Mübadele Öyküleri*. Istanbul: Lozan Mübadiller Vakfı, 2009.

Pentzopoulos, Dimitri. *The Balkan Exchange of Minorities and Its Impact upon Greece*. Paris: Mouton, 1962.

Perloff, Marjorie. *The Futurist Movement: Avant-Garde, Avant-Guerre, and the Language of Rupture*. Chicago: University of Chicago Press, 1986.

Petherick, John. *Egypt, the Soudan and Central Africa: With Explorations from Khartoum on the White Nile, to the Regions of the Equator; Being Sketches from Sixteen Years' Travel*. London, 1861.

Petropoulou, Ioanna. "The Voice of the Heirlooms: Their Long Journey Through Time." In *Relics of the Past: Treasures of the Greek Orthodox Church and the Population Exchange*, edited by Anna Ballian, 24–34. Athens: Benaki Museum, 2011.

Phokaides, Petros. "Ruralizing Zambia: Doxiadis Associates' Systems Based Planning and Developmentalism in the Non-Industrialized South." In *Architecture in Development: Systems and the Emergence of the Global South*, edited by Arindam Dutta, Ateya Khorakiwala, Ayala Levin, Fabiola Lopez-Duran, and Ijlal Muzaffar, 279–301. London: Routledge, 2022.

Pieri, Caecilia. *Baghdad: La construction d'une capitale moderne (1914–1960)*. Beirut: Damas, 2015.

Pinney, Christopher. *Camera Indica: The Social Life of Indian Photographs*. Chicago: University of Chicago Press, 1997.

Polk, William. "The Lesson of Iraq." *Atlantic*, December 1958. www.theatlantic.com/magazine/archive/1958/12/the-lesson-of-iraq/306494/.

Pope, Arthur. *A Survey of Persian Art from Prehistoric Times to the Present*. 1938. New York: Oxford University Press, 1967.

Potter, Alick, and Margaret Potter. *Everything Is Possible: Our Sudan Years*. Gloucester: Alan Sutton, 1984.

Proctor, Robert N., and Londa Schiebinger, eds. *Agnotology: The Making and Unmaking of Ignorance*. Stanford, CA: Stanford University Press, 2008.

Protected Planet. *Protected Planet Report May 2020*. Accessed January 1, 2023. https://livereport.protectedplanet.net/.

Provence, Michael. *The Last Ottoman Generation and the Making of the Middle East*. Cambridge: Cambridge University Press, 2017.

Psomiades, Harry J. *Fridtjof Nansen and the Greek Refugee Crisis, 1922–1924*. Athens: Kyklos, 2001. Reprint, Bloomingdale, IL: Asia Minor and Pontos Hellenic Research Center, 2011.

Pyla, Panayiota I. "Baghdad's Urban Restructuring, 1958: Aesthetics and Politics of Nation Building." In *Modernism and the Middle East, Architecture and Politics in the Twentieth Century*, edited by Sandy Isenstadt and Kishwar Rizvi, 97–115. Seattle: University of Washington Press, 2008.

Pyla, Panayiota I. "Ekistics, Architecture and Environmental Politics, 1945–1976: A Prehistory of Sustainable Development." PhD diss., MIT, 2002.

Pyla, Panayiota I. "Hassan Fathy Revisited." *Journal of Architectural Education* 60, no. 3 (2007): 28–39.

Ramzy, Austin, and Chris Buckley. "'Absolutely No Mercy': Leaked Files Expose How China Organized Mass Detension of Muslims." *New York Times*, November 16, 2019.

Rand, Christopher. "The Ekistic World." *New Yorker*, May 11, 1963.

Raymond, Andre. "French Studies of the Ottoman Empire's Arab Provinces." *Mediterranean Historical Review* 19, no. 1 (2004): 54–72.

Raymond, Andre. *Osmanlı Döneminde Arap Kentleri*. Translated by Ali Berktay. Istanbul: Tarih Vakfı, 1995.

Read, Peter, and Marivic Wyndham. *Narrow but Endlessly Deep: The Struggle for Memorialization in Chile Since the Transition to Democracy*. Acton: Australian National Press, 2016.

Reilly, James. *The Ottoman Cities of Lebanon: Historical Legacy and Identity in the Modern Middle East*. New York: I. B. Tauris, 2016.

Rizos, Seraphim. *Sinasos*. Istanbul: n.p., 1924.

Rizos, Seraphim. *Σιναςός* [Sinasos]. Athens: Center for Asia Minor Studies, 2007.

Robben, Antonius C. G. M. *Argentina Betrayed*. Philadelphia: University of Pennsylvania Press, 2018.

Rohidea, Stylianos. "Sinasos: The People and the Houses, Part II." In *Common Cultural Heritage*, edited by Sefer Güvenç, 167–68. Istanbul: Foundation of Lausanne Treaty Emigrants, 2005.

Roht-Arriaza, Naomi. "The Need for Moral Reconstruction in the Wake of Past Human Rights Violations: An Interview with Jose Zalaquett." In *Human Rights in Political Transitions: Gettysburg to Bosnia*, edited by Carla Hesse and Robert Post, 195–213. New York: Zone, 1999.

Rolston, Bill. *Turning the Page Without Closing the Book: The Right to Truth in the Irish Context*. Dublin: Irish Reporter, 1996.

Rosenzweig, Michael. *Win-Win Ecology: How the Earth's Species Can Survive in the Midst of Human Enterprise*. New York: Oxford University Press, 2003.

Rotberg, Robert, and Dennis Thompson. *Truth vs. Justice: The Morality of Truth Commissions*. Princeton, NJ: Princeton University Press, 2000.

Rothberg, Michael. *Multidirectional Memory: Remembering the Holocaust in the Age of Decolonization*. Stanford, CA: Stanford University Press, 2009.

Rousseau, Jean-Jacques. *Discourse on Inequality*. Oxford: Oxford University Press, 2000. Originally published in 1755.

Rozas-Krause, Valentina. "Apology and Commemoration: Memorializing the WWII Japanese American Incarceration at the Tanforan Assembly Center." *History and Memory* 30, no. 2 (2018): 40–78.

Ruhoha, Emily, and Anna Fifield. "She Survived a Chinese Internment Camp and Made It to Virginia. Will the U.S. Let Her Stay?" *Washington Post*, November 17, 2019.

Şahin, Orhan. "Zeytinburnu'nda Sanayileşme Tarihi." In *Zeytinburnu Kültür Vadisi*, vol. 2, edited by Murat Çekin, 169–87. Istanbul: Zeytinburnu Belediyesi Kültür Yayınları, 2018.

Said, Edward. *Orientalism*. New York: Random House, 1978.

Salvioli, Fabián. *Promotion of Truth, Justice, Reparation and Guarantees of Non-Recurrence*. New York: United Nations, 2021. https://digitallibrary.un.org/record/3936552?ln=en&v=pdf.

Şanlı, Ayşem Sezer. "Yasın Protestoya Dönüşümünü İncelemek: Cumartesi Anneleri Hareketi Örneği." *Journal of Human Studies* 1, no. 2 (2018): 97–113.

Sarıçayır, Ecem. "Property in Transition: Architecture, Migration, and the Translation of Land Regimes in the Ottoman South Caucasus Under the Russian Empire, 1877–1921." PhD diss., Cornell University, 2025.

Sarkar, Sumit. *The Swadeshi Movement in Bengal, 1903–1908*. New Delhi: People's Publishing House, 1973.

Sarkis, Hashim. "Dances with Margaret Mead: Planning Beirut Since 1958." In *Projecting Beirut: Episodes in the Construction and Reconstruction of a Modern City*, edited by Peter Rowe and Hashim Sarkis, 187–201. London: Prestel, 1998.

Sartini Blum, Cinzia. *The Other Modernism: F. T. Marinetti's Futurist Fiction of Power*. Berkeley: University of California Press, 1996.

Satz, Debra. "Countering the Wrongs of the Past: The Role of Compensation." In *Transitional Justice*, edited by Melissa Williams, 129–50. New York: NYU Press, 2012.

Sayar, Zeki. "İç Kolonizasyon" (two parts). *Arkitekt*, no. 2 (1936): 46–51; no. 8 (1936): 231–35.

Schurman, Jacob Gould. *The Balkan Wars 1912–1913*. Princeton, NJ: Princeton University Press, 1914.

Seçkin, Selçuk. "Mübadele Sonrası Kurulan Planlı Köy Yerleşimleri." In *Mübadil Kentler: Mekan ve İskan*, 134–50. Istanbul: Lozan Mübadilleri Vakfı Yayınları, 2014.

Şeker, Nesim. "Forced Population Movements in the Ottoman Empire and the Early Turkish Republic: An Attempt at Reassessment Through Demographic Engineering." *European Journal of Turkish Studies* 16 (2013): n.p. https://doi.org/10.4000/ejts.4396.

Sen, Amartya. "Culture and Human Rights." In *Development as Freedom*, 227–48. New York: Knopf, 2000.

Sen, Amartya. "Elements of a Theory of Human Rights." *Philosophy and Public Affairs* 32, no. 4 (2004): 315–36.

Sen, Amartya. "Human Rights and Capabilities." *Journal of Human Development* 6, no. 2 (2005): 152–66.

Şenocak, Zafer. *Gefährliche Verwandtschaft*. Munich: Babel, 1998.

Şenyapılı, Tansı. "Cumhuriyet'in 75. Yılı, Gecekondunun 50.Yılı." In *75 Yılda Değişen Kent ve Mimarlık*, edited by Yıldız Sey, 301–16. Istanbul: Tarih Vakfı, 1998.

Serrano, Alejandro. "Final Design Picked for Memorial to Police Torture Victims Under Jon Burge." *Chicago Tribune*, June 11, 2019. https://www.chicagotribune.com/2019/06/11/final-design-picked-for-memorial-to-police-torture-victims-under-jon-burge/.

Sert, José Luis, Fernand Léger, and Sigfried Giedion. "Nine Points on Monumentality." In *Architecture Culture, 1943–1968: A Documentary Anthology*, edited by Joan Ockman, 29–30. New York: Columbia Architectural Press, 1993.

Seth, Suman. *Difference and Disease: Medicine, Race, and the Eighteenth-Century British Empire.* Stanford, CA: Stanford University Press, 2018.

Sezer Şanlı, Ayşem. "Yasın Protestoya Dönüşümünü İncelemek: Cumartesi Anneleri Hareketi Örneği." *Journal of Human Studies* 1, no. 2 (2018): 97–113.

Sharpe, Christina Elizabeth. *In the Wake: On Blackness and Being.* Durham, NC: Duke University Press, 2016.

Shaw, Rosalind, and Lars Waldorf, eds. *Localizing Transitional Justice: Interventions and Priorities After Mass Violence.* Stanford, CA: Stanford University Press, 2010.

Shaw, Stanford, and Ezel Kural Shaw. *History of Ottoman Empire and Modern Turkey*, vol. 2. Cambridge: Cambridge University Press, 1977.

Shaw, Wendy. *Possessors and Possessed: Museums, Archaeology, and the Visualization of History in the Late Ottoman Empire.* Berkeley: University of California Press, 2003.

Shklar, Judith. *The Faces of Injustice.* New Haven, CT: Yale University Press, 1990.

Siddiqi, Anooradha Iyer. *Architecture of Migration: The Dadaab Refugee Camps and Humanitarian Settlement.* Durham, NC: Duke University Press, 2023.

"Siedlung in Athen—Nach 20 Jahren." *Der Baumeister* 71 (1974): 785–87.

Şılar, Oktay. "Bitmeyen Yas: Faili Meçhul Kayıplara Psikanalitik Bakış." *Bianet*, October 26, 2013. https://bianet.org/biamag/toplum/150814-bitmeyen-yas -faili-mechul-kayiplarapsikanalitik-bakis.

Simpson, S. R. "Town Planning and Development During the Condominium: Two Extracts from a Memoir." In *Modernization in the Sudan*, edited by M. W. Daly, 73–84. New York: Lilian Barber, 1985.

Sinan, Gizem, and Kaan Kapan. "Makedonya'dan Yapılan Göçlerin Mekansal Analizi." In *1st Istanbul International Geography Congress Proceedings Book*, edited by B. Gönençgil, T. A. Ertek, I. Akova, and E. Elbaşı, 431–45. Istanbul: Istanbul University Press, 2019. https://doi.org/10.26650/PB/PS12.2019.002 .043.

Sipahioğlu, Hakan. "Odisseus'u Aramak." In *Mübadele Öyküleri*, 27–34. Tekirdağ: Tekirdağ Büyükşehir Belediyesi, 2017.

Şirin, Funda Selçuk. "The Traumatic Legacy of the Balkan Wars for Turkish Intellectuals." In *War and Nationalism: The Balkan Wars, 1912–1913, and Their Sociopolitical Implications*, edited by M. H. Yavuz and Isa Blumi, 679–703. Salt Lake City: University of Utah Press, 2013.

Sisson, Patrick. "How Air Conditioning Shaped Modern Architecture—And Changed Our Climate." *Curbed*, May 9, 2017. https://archive.curbed.com /2017/5/9/15583550/air-conditioning-architecture-skyscraper-wright-lever -house.

Smith, Anthony D. *Theories of Nationalism.* 2nd ed. London: Duckworth, 1983.

Sodaro, Amy. *Exhibiting Atrocity: Memorial Museums and the Politics of Past Violence.* New Brunswick, NJ: Rutgers University Press, 2018.

Sotiriou, Dido. *Farewell Anatolia.* Translated by Fred A. Reed. Athens: Kedros, 1991.

Sotiriou, Lila Theodoridou. Νικόλαος Ζουμπουλίδης: Ένας σημαντικός αρχιτέκτονας. Ένας πολύπλευρος άνθρωπος [Nicholas Zoumboulidis: An Important Architect, A Versatile Man]. Thessaloniki: Disigma, 2016.

Spirn, Anne Whiston. "The Legacy of Frederick Law Olmsted." In *Uncommon Ground: Rethinking the Human Place in Nature,* edited by William Cronon, 91–113. New York: Norton, 1996.

Spivak, Gayatri. "Righting Wrongs." *South Atlantic Quarterly* 103, nos. 2–3 (2004): 523–81.

Stanek, Lukasz. *Henri Lefebvre on Space: Architecture, Urban Research and the Production of Theory.* Minneapolis: University of Minnesota Press, 2011.

Stelaku, Vasso. "Space, Place, and Identity." In *Crossing the Aegean,* edited by Renée Hirschon, 179–92. New York: Berghahn, 2003.

Stierli, Martino, and Vladimir Kulic, eds. *Toward a Concrete Utopia: Architecture in Yugoslavia, 1948–1980.* New York: Museum of Modern Art, 2018.

Stockholm Center for Freedom. "Enforced Disappearances in Turkey." Stockholm: Stockholm Center for Freedom, 2017. https://stockholmcf.org/wp-content/uploads/2017/06/Enforced-Dissappearences-in-Turkey_22_June_2017.pdf.

Stoetzer, Bettina. *Ruderal City: Ecologies of Migration, Race and Urban Nature in Berlin.* Durham, NC: Duke University Press, 2022.

Stoler, Ann Laura. *Imperial Debris: On Ruins and Ruination.* Durham, NC: Duke University Press, 2013.

Struken, Marita. "The Wall, the Screen, and the Image: The Vietnam Veterans Memorial." *Representations* 35 (1991): 118–42.

Süar, Selin. "Yunan Sinemasında Türk-Yunan Nüfus Mübadelesi." In *Mübadil Kentler: Mekan ve İskan,* 152–208. Istanbul: Lozan Mübadilleri Vakfı Yayınları, 2014.

"Sudanese Greeks." Wikipedia, accessed January 31, 2021. https://en.wikipedia.org/wiki/Sudanese_Greeks.

Sultani, Khalid. "Architecture in Iraq Between Two World Wars, 1920–1940." *UR,* no. 2 (1982): 92–105.

"Sümer Mahallesinde Anahtar Teslimi Heyecanı." *Zeytinburnu Haber,* February 18, 2013.

Tagg, John. *The Burden of Representation: Essays on Photographies and Histories.* Basingstoke: Macmillan, 1988.

Táíwò, Olúfẹmi O., and Patrick Bigger. "Debt Justice for Climate Reparations." Climate and Community Institute, April 2022. https://www.climateandcommunity.org/debt-justice-for-climate-reparations.

"Taking a Job in Africa." *Architects' Journal,* October 22, 1969, 1023–24.

Tandoğan, Emin. *The Urban Transformation Story of Zeytinburnu.* Istanbul: Istanbul Ticaret Odası, 1998.

Tasioulas, John. "Human Rights." In *The Routledge Companion to Philosophy of Law*, edited by Andrei Marmor, 348–63. New York: Routledge, 2015.

Taut, Bruno. *Mimari Bilgisi*. Translated by Adnan Kolatan. Istanbul: Güzel Sanatlar Akademisi, 1938.

Taylan, Arzu. "Factors Influencing Homeowners' Seismic Risk Mitigation Behavior." *International Journal of Disaster Risk Reduction* 13 (2015): 414–26.

Taylor, Diana. "Traumatic Memes." In *Women Mobilizing Memory*, edited by Ayşe Gül Altınay, Maria Jose Contrera, Marianne Hirsch, Jean Howard, Banu Karaca, and Alisa Solomon, 113–32. New York: Columbia University Press, 2019.

Teitel, Ruti. *Globalizing Transitional Justice*. Oxford: Oxford University Press, 2014.

Teitel, Ruti. *Transitional Justice*. Oxford: Oxford University Press, 2000.

Tekeli, İlhan. "Osmanlı İmparatorluğu'ndan Günümüze Nüfusun Zorunlu Yer Değiştirmesi ve İskan Sorunu." *Toplum ve Bilim* 50 (1990): 49–71.

Tekeli, Ilhan. *Türkiye'de Yaşam ve Yazında Konut Sorununun Gelişimi*. Ankara: Başbakanlık Toplu Konut İdaresi, 1996.

Tekeli, Ilhan, Selim Ilkin, and Aslı Özbay, eds. *Mimar Kemalettin'in Yazdıkları*. Ankara: Şevki Vanlı Mimarlık Vakfı, 1997.

Tevfik, İhsan. *İnsan ve Mekan Yüzüyle Mübadele*. Istanbul: İnkılap, 2014.

Theocharopoulou, Ioanna. *Builders, Housewives and the Construction of Modern Athens*. New York: Onasis Foundation, 2017.

Todorova, Maria. "War and Memory: Trotsky's War Correspondence from the Balkan Wars." *Perceptions* 18, no. 2 (2013): 5–27.

Toker, Çiğdem. *Kamu İhalelerinde Olağan İşler*. Istanbul: Tekin Yayinevi, 2020.

Tolic, I. *Dopo il terremoto. La politica della ricostruzione negli anni della guerra fredda a Skopje*. Reggio Emilia: Diabasis, 2011.

Torre, Susana. "Claiming the Public Space: The Mothers of Plaza de Mayo." In *The Sex of Architecture*, edited by Diana Agrest, Patricia Conway, and Leslie Weisman, 241–50. New York: Abrams, 1996.

Toumarkine, Alexandre. *Les migrations des populations musulmanes balkaniques en Anatolie (1876–1913)*. Istanbul: Les Editions Isis, 1995.

Tournikiotis, Panayotis. "Public Interest in Modern Architecture in Athens Between the Wars." In *Athens: From the Classical Period to the Present Day*, edited by Manolis Korres, Charalambos Bouras, and Angelos Delivorrias, 439–59. Athens: Kotinos, 2000.

Troutt Powell, Eve. *A Different Shade of Colonialism: Egypt, Great Britain and the Mastery of Sudan*. Berkeley: University of California Press, 2003.

Troutt Powell, Eve M. *Tell This in My Memory: Stories of Enslavement from Egypt, Sudan and the Ottoman Empire*. Stanford, CA: Stanford University Press, 2012.

TRT Avaz. "Türkiye'deki Türkistan—Zeytinburnu'ndaki Türkistanlılar—7 Bölüm." YouTube, posted March 27, 2017. 30 min., 45 sec. www.youtube.com/watch?v=pkicLhaNOSU&itct=CBIQpDAYACITCNSVnc-smdgCFU8fAwodB4MM1TIHcmVsYXRlZEjG_Je2x8nsjPEB&app=desktop.

Tsing, Anna Lowenhaupt. *The Mushroom at the End of the World: On the Possibility of Life in Capitalist Ruins.* Princeton, NJ: Princeton University Press, 2015.

Tsing, Anna Lowenhaupt, Heather Swanson, Elaine Gan, and Nils Bubandt, eds. *Arts of Living on a Damaged Planet: Ghosts and Monsters.* Minneapolis: University of Minnesota Press, 2017.

Tsitselikis, Konstantinos. "The Convention of Lausanne (1923): Past and Current Appraisals." In *When Greeks and Turks Meet,* edited by Vally Lytra, 211–26. Farnham: Ashgate, 2014.

Turan, Buşra, and Merve Ayar. "Kültür Vadisi Projesi ve Merkezefendi'de Gündelik Hayatın Değişimi." In *Zeytinburnu Kültür Vadisi,* vol. 1, edited by Murat Çekin, 93–105. Istanbul: Zeytinburnu Belediyesi Kültür Yayınları, 2018.

Türeli, İpek. *Istanbul, Open City: Exhibiting Anxieties of Urban Modernity.* London: Routledge, 2018.

Turgis, Noémie. "What Is Transitional Justice?" *International Journal on Rule of Law, Transitional Justice and Human Rights,* no. 1. (2010): 9–15.

Türkmen, Füsun. "Turkey's Participation in Human Rights Regimes." In *Human Rights in Turkey,* edited by Zehra Kabasakal Arat, 249–61. Philadelphia: University of Pennsylvania Press, 2007.

Tzonis, Alexander, and Phoebe Giannisi. *Classical Greek Architecture: The Construction of the Modern.* Athens: Rizarios Foundation, 2003.

Tzonis, Alexander, and Alcestis Rodi. *Greece: Modern Architectures in History.* London: Reaktion, 2013.

Uduku, Ola. "Modernist Architecture and 'the Tropical' in West Africa: The Tropical Architecture Movement in West Africa, 1948–1970." *Habitat International* 30, no. 3 (2006): 396–411.

Ueno, Masayuki. "Urban Politics in 19th-Century Istanbul: The Case of the Armenian Cemetery in Beyoğlu." In *Human Mobility and Multiethnic Coexistence in Middle Eastern Societies,* vol. 1, *Tehran. Aleppo, Istanbul, Beirut,* edited by Hidemitsu Kuroki, 85–102. Tokyo: Research Institute for Languages and Cultures of Asia and Africa Tokyo University, 2015.

Ülker, Erol. "Assimilation, Security and Geographical Nationalization in Interwar Turkey: The Settlement Law of 1934." *European Journal of Turkish Studies* 7 (2008). https://journals.openedition.org/ejts/2123.

Ünal, Mustafa. *Zeytinburnu Gecekondu Gerçeği.* Istanbul: Istanbul Ticaret Odası, 1977.

UN General Assembly. "International Convention for the Protection of All Persons from Enforced Disappearance." Adopted December 20, 2006. https://www.ohchr.org/en/hrbodies/ced/pages/conventioced.aspx.

UN General Assembly. *Report of the Working Group on Enforced or Involuntary Disappearances.* New York: United Nations, 2014. https://docs.un.org/en/A/HRC/27/49.

UN General Assembly. *World Charter for Nature.* New York: United Nations, 1982. https://digitallibrary.un.org/record/39295?ln=en.

UNICEF. "16 Children Including Greta Thunberg, File Landmark Complaint to the United Nations Committee on the Rights of the Child." September 23, 2019. www.unicef.org/press-releases/16-children-including-greta-thunberg -file-landmark-complaint-united-nations.

Ünsal, Behçet. "Sincan Köyü Planı." *Arkitekt*, nos. 1–2 (1940): 15–18.

UN Secretary-General. *The Rule of Law and Transitional Justice in Conflict and Post-Conflict Societies: Report of the Secretary-General.* New York: United Nations, 2004. https://digitallibrary.un.org/record/527647?ln=en&v=pdf.

"US Military Is a Bigger Polluter than as Many as 140 Countries—Shrinking This War Machine Is a Must." *Conversation*, June 24, 2019. https:// theconversation.com/us-military-is-a-bigger-polluter-than-as-many-as-140 -countries-shrinking-this-war-machine-is-a-must-119269.

Uzmay, Asya Ece. "Expanding Water Geographies and Hydropolitics of Istanbul: Disease, Fountains, Blueprints (1933–1971)." Unpublished manuscript.

"Ventilation in Warm Climates." *Overseas Building Notes* 66 (March 1960): 2.

Viebach, Julia. "Aletheia and the Making of the World: Inner and Outer Dimensions of Memorials in Rwanda." In *Memorials in Times of Transition*, edited by Susanne Buckley-Zistel and Stefanie Schaefer, 69–94. Cambridge: Intersentia, 2014.

Voltaire. *Poem upon the Lisbon Disaster.* Translated by Anthony Hecht. Lincoln, MA: Perman Press, 1977.

Vryonis, Speros. *The Mechanism of Catastrophe: The Turkish Pogrom of September 6–7, 1955 and the Destruction of Greek Community of Istanbul.* New York: Greekworks, 2005.

Wakely, Patrick I. "The Development of a School: An Account of the Department of Development and Tropical Studies at the Architecture Association." *Habitat International* 7, nos. 5–6 (1983): 337–46.

Walcott, Rinaldo. *The Long Emancipation.* Durham, NC: Duke University Press, 2021.

Water and Climate Coalition. "Water and Climate Coalition at UN 2023 Water Conference." Accessed January 6, 2024. https://water-climate-coalition.org /road-to-new-york-un-2023-water-conference/.

Webber, Jeremy. "Forms of Transitional Justice." In *Transitional Justice*, edited by Melissa Williams, 31–77. New York: NYU Press, 2012.

Weinstein, Harvey, Laurel Fletcher, Patrick Vinck, and Phuong Pham. "Stay the Hand of Justice: Whose Priorities Take Priority?" In *Localizing Transitional Justice: Interventions and Priorities After Mass Violence*, edited by Rosalind Shaw and Lars Waldorf, 27–49. Stanford, CA: Stanford University Press, 2010.

Weizman, Eyal. *Forensic Architecture: Violence at the Threshold of Detectability.* New York: Zone, 2017.

Weizman, Eyal, and Fazal Sheikh. *The Conflict Shoreline: Colonization as Climate Change in the Negev Desert.* Göttingen: Steidl, 2015.

White, Jenny. *Muslim Nationalism and the New Turks.* Princeton, NJ: Princeton University Press, 2013.

Williams, Melissa, ed. *Transitional Justice*. New York: NYU Press, 2012.

Winckelmann, Johann Joachim. *History of the Art of Antiquity*. Los Angeles: Getty Research Institute, 2006. Originally published in 1763.

Wolf, Matt, dir. *Spaceship Earth*. Impact Partners, 2020.

Wollstonecraft, Mary. *A Vindication of the Rights of Women*. 1792.

World People's Conference on Climate Change and the Rights of Mother Earth. "People's Agreement of Cochabamba." April 24, 2010. https://pwccc .wordpress.com/2010/04/24/peoples-agreement/.

Wynter, Sylvia. "Unsettling the Coloniality of Being/Power/Truth/Freedom: Towards the Human, After Man, Its Overrepresentation—An Argument." *New Centennial Review* 3, no. 3 (2003): 257–337.

Yalçın, Kemal. *Emanet Çeyiz: Mübadele İnsanları*. Istanbul: Belge Uluslararası Yayıncılık, 1998.

Yannas, Prodromos. "The Human Rights Condition of the Rum Orthodox." In *Human Rights in Turkey*, edited by Zehra Kabasakal Arat, 57–71. Philadelphia: University of Pennsylvania Press, 2007.

Yavuz, M. H., and Isa Blumi, eds. *War and Nationalism: The Balkan Wars, 1912–1913, and Their Sociopolitical Implications*. Salt Lake City: University of Utah Press, 2013.

Yelmen, Hasan. "Kazlıçeşme." In *Surların Öte Yanı—The Other Side of the City Walls: Zeytinburnu*, 3rd ed., edited by Burçak Evren, 101–53. Istanbul: Zeytinburnu Belediyesi Kültür Yayınları, 2006.

Yerasimos, Stefan. "Tanzimat'ın Kent Reformları Üzerine." In *Modernleşme Sürecinde Osmanlı Kentleri*, translated by Ali Berktay, edited by Paul Dumont, Francois Georgeon, 1–18. Istanbul: Tarih Vakfı Yurt Yayınları, 1996.

Yerolympos, Alexandra. "Inter-War Town Planning and the Refugee Problem in Greece." In *Crossing the Aegean*, edited by Renée Hirschon, 133–43. New York: Berghahn, 2003.

Yiannakopoulos, Georgios. *Refugee Greece: Photographs from the Archive of the Center for Asia Minor Studies*. Athens: Center for Asia Minor Studies, 1992.

Yıldırım, Nuran. "Balıklı Rum Hastanesi." In *Zeytinburnu Kültür Vadisi*, vol. 2, edited by Murat Çekin, 665–81. Istanbul: Zeytinburnu Belediyesi Kültür Yayınları, 2018.

Yıldırım, Nuran. "İstanbul Yedikule Göğüs Hastalıkları ve Göğüs Cerrahisi Eğitim ve Araştırma Hastanesi." In *Zeytinburnu Kültür Vadisi*, vol. 2, edited by Murat Çekin, 707–13. Istanbul: Zeytinburnu Belediyesi Kültür Yayınları, 2018.

Yıldırım, Nuran. "Zeytinburnu Hastanesi." In *Zeytinburnu Kültür Vadisi*, vol. 2, edited by Murat Çekin, 693–705. Istanbul: Zeytinburnu Belediyesi Kültür Yayınları, 2018.

Yıldırım, Onur. *Diplomacy and Displacement: Reconsidering the Turco-Greek Exchange of Populations, 1922–1934*. New York: Routledge, 2006.

Young, James E. *The Texture of Memory: Holocaust Memorials and Meaning*. New Haven, CT: Yale University Press, 1993.

Young, Liam, dir. *Planet City.* 2021. https://liamyoung.org/projects/planet-city.

Yurdakul, Gökçe, and Michael Bodemann. "'We Don't Want to Be the Jews of Tomorrow': Jews and Turks in Germany After 9/11." *German Politics and Society* 24, no. 2 (2006): 44-67.

Zerbe, Stephen, Ute Maurer, Solveg Schmitz, and Herbert Sukopp. "Biodiversity in Berlin and Its Potential for Nature Conservation." *Landscape and Urban Planning* 62, no. 3 (2003): 139–48.

"Zeytinburnu'nda Küçük Türkistan: İlyaz Saka ile söylesi." In *Surların Öte Yanı— The Other Side of the City Walls: Zeytinburnu,* 3rd ed., edited by Burçak Evren, 374. Istanbul: Zeytinburnu Belediyesi Kültür Yayınları, 2006.

Zinn, Howard. *A People's History of the United States, 1492–Present.* Extended ed. New York: HarperPerennial, 2009.

Zürcher, Erik Jan. "The Balkan Wars and the Refugee Leadership of the Early Turkish Republic." In *War and Nationalism: The Balkan Wars, 1912–1913, and Their Sociopolitical Implications,* edited by M. H. Yavuz and Isa Blumi, 665–78. Salt Lake City: University of Utah Press, 2013.

Zürcher, Erik Jan. *The Young Turk Legacy and Nation Building: From the Ottoman Empire to Atatürk's Turkey.* London: I. B. Tauris, 2010.

Index

Page numbers in italics refer to figures.

Arcan, Sebla, 48

Archaeological Museum (Thessaloniki, Greece), 93

architecture: adaptive architecture, 310–16; Balkan War (1912–13) and, 141–55; climate change and, 24–25, 27–33, 329n80; disasters and responses to, 92–98, 138–40; as dispossession engine, 78–83; Doxiadis's rural settlement plan, 267–72; Gezira Scheme plantations and, 252–63, *258–60,* 265–66; healing and, 1–4; human rights and, 318–22; inner colonization concept and, 346n126; monumentality and, 61–62; Orientalist planning in Khartoum and, 201–9; population transfer and, 82–83; refugee housing projects, 104–21, 345n118; in Sudan, 195–96; tropical architecture, 26, 199–200, 229, 231–32, 245, 248–49; white thermal comfort in Khartoum colonial housing, 209–21, *210–11, 214*

Architecture in Transition and Ekistics (Doxiadis), 236

Architecture in Translation (Akcan), 274–75

Architecture of the Poor (Fathy), 271–72

Architecture of the Well-Tempered Environment (Banham), 25

Ardalan, Nader, 33, 296, 299, 310, 312, 316, 318

Arendt, Hannah, 6, 70

Argos Hotel (Uçhisar, Turkey), 130–31, *133–34,* 347n124

Arif, Burhan, 108

Arkitekt (journal), 109

Armenian Church of Akdamar, restoration of, 74

Armenians: genocide of, 19, 325n25, 349n16; Greek-Turkish population exchange impact on, 95–103; land claims by, 166–67; resettler nationalism in, 22; territorial claims involving, 12; Turkish deportation and enforced disappearance of, 55–58

Armenian Surp Agop cemetery and church (Istanbul), 55–56

art history, Islamic cities and, 37–38

Asia Minor Disaster of 1922–23, 21, 78, 113, 129. *See also* Exchange of Populations Treaty (1923)

Aslan, Cemal, 160

Association of Migrants from East Turkistan, 157

Atatürk, Mustafa Kemal, 19

Athens, Greece: Benaki Museum in, 127–129, *128;* Doxiadis and, 240–41, 264, 286, 293; earthquake in, 137, 348n168; government and refugee housing in, 104–106, *106–107;* Greek-Turkish population exchange refugees in, 14, 84, 92–98, 123; refugee settlements and shelters in, 95–98, *94, 96–97,* 104–21, 146; monument to Exchange of Populations in, 106, *107;* "Royal Seat and Capital City" plan (1834), 98; Zoumboulidis's building in, 113–118, *115, 117, 118*

Athens Opera House, migrant families housed in, 93–95, *94*

Atkinson, George Anthony, 231

Atterbury, F. J. L., 209, 363n37

Attika building (Athens), 93

Avicenna, 311–12

Aydın, Murat, 175–76

Aylwin, Patricio, 61

Ayoub & Omer Salim, 248–49

Aytaş, Süreyya, 76, 84–86, 91–92, 99–101, 121, 124–27, *128,* 130–31

bagdir (wind-catchers) (ventilation device), 271

Baghdad, Iraq, 29–32, 38, 186, 273, 292, 329n87; Doxiadis's housing projects in, 271–72

Bahtır, Bahiye, 161

Baker, Samuel, 198–99, 221, 310

Bakhtiar, Laleh, 33, 296, 299, 311–12, 316, 318

Balıklı Armenian Church (Istanbul), 186, *187*

Balıklı Complex (Istanbul), 150–52, *152,* 165–67, 178, 185–87, *188*

Balkan War (1912–13): arrival cities for refugees after, 146–49; casualty figures for, 141, 349n16; cultural impact of, 85–86, 326n45, 327n56; forced migration after, 144–45; historiography of, 144–45; Ottoman Empire dissolution and, 17–20, 140–55; resettler nationalism and, 140–55; territorial claims during, 12; Turkish-Islamist revision of, 189–93

Doxiadis (*continued*)

Rights and, 318; Khartoum urban planning and, 234–43; Moneim Mustafa's collaboration with, 244–51; planetary healing and work of, 316–17; standardized villages proposal of, 267–72, *269*; UN support for, 237, 370n148; "Water for Peace" conference (1967) and, 284, 291–95; water management initiatives of, 284–90, *287–90*, 380n47

Doxiadis Associates, 234–43, *238–39*, 264–72, 274–76; water pollution and, 284–90

Du Bois, W. E. B., 70

Duffy, Rosaleen, 280

Dündar, Fuat, 19, 102

Dunn, Christopher, 315, 382n64

Dymaxion maps (Fuller), 299

dynapolis, Doxiadis's concept of, 236, 238–43

Eames, Charles, 33, 296, 299, 301

Eames, Ray, 296, 299, 301

Earth First movement, 281

earthquakes: earthquake diplomacy and, 136, 348n168; in Istanbul, 138–40, 171–76, 190–93, 348n1, 358n175; justice and injustice and, 138–40; Kobe disaster, 173; neoliberal urbanization and Japanese expertise and, 171–76; Skopje disaster, 139, 173, *174*; Turkish-Syrian 2023 quake, 2, 191–92

East Turkistan Magazine, 157

ecocide: debates over prevention of, 278–83; resettler nationalism and, 23–33, 328n65

Ecumenopolis: The Inevitable City of the Future (Doxiadis), 292–95, *294*, 370n149, 379n32, 381n54, 381n57, 381n60. *See also* "City of the Future" (Doxiadis)

Edkins, Jenny, 27

Efeoğlu, Fahriye, 164

Eftim (Papa), 84

Egypt, nationalism's rise in, 17

88 Club (Sudan), 222

Eisenman, Peter, 64–65

Ekistics (journal), 293, 318

ekistics, Doxiadis's theory of, 235, 240–41, 285–86, 293–95, 379n32

El-Bushra, El-Sayed, 241

Eldem, Edhem, 54

El Ikhwa Building (Khartoum), 245, *247*

Elise, Mabel, 214

El Sammani, Mohammed Osman, 241, 285–86

Emanet Çeyiz (Entrusted trousseau) (Yalçın), 339n20, 340n30, 344n89, 347n154

energy transition, 1, 26, 33, 38, 193, 195, 275

enforced disappearance: Amnesty International report on, 73; art projects for, 50–54, *51, 53, 54,* 333n32; as human rights violation, 10; memorials to, 59–71, *63, 67*; mothers activism against, 56–59; right to truth and, 42–47; Turkish statistics on, 331n6, 332n39, 332n43

environment: resettler nationalism and, 23–33, 163–65; urban development and, 140

environmentalism: architecture and, 314–16; ecocide prevention debate and, 279–83

environmental justice, 2, 4, 11, 193, 275

Eraslan, Burhan, 168

Erdinç, Jülide Edirne, 153–54

Erdoğan, Recep Tayyip, 73, 175–76, 181–82

Eren, İkbal, 52

Eren, Özkul, 180

Erkal, Namık, 153

Esat Bey, 101

Escobar, Arturo, 237

ethnocentrism: colonialism in Khartoum and, 199–209; Exchange of Populations Treaty (1923) and, 103

Eurocentrism: Balkan War and entrenchment of, 18–19; in human rights regime, 7–8

European Conventions on Human Rights and Fundamental Freedoms, 73

European Court of Human Rights, 44, 73, 126

European Union: Greek-Turkish partition and, 136–37; Turkey's application to, 73–74

Evliya Çelebi, 148, 150, 182

Exchange of Populations Treaty (1923): agricultural settlements for refugees from, 98–103; Athens as refugee

ing developments, 104–21, 345n118; temporary refugee structures for Athens migrants, 95–98, 96–97, 343n89, 344n118; white thermal comfort in Khartoum colonial houses, 209–21, 210–11, 214; workers' housing in Khartoum and, 217–21, 220, 366n85

"Housing for Officials in Khartoum, 1922" (Bridgman), 214

Housing Scheme for British Officials, 214

Howard, Ebenezer, 109

Höweler + Yoon, 63, 65

Huber, Victor Aime, 346n126

human rights: cultural critique of, 337n114; globalization and localization of, 71–75; healing as, 4–11; right to heal, 316–22; Western traditions linked to, 74–75

Hunter, George Gillette, 257–58, 258

Huyssen, Andreas, 61–62, 68, 70

Ibn Arabi, 311–12

Iclal, Fatma, 147

identity politics, transitional justice and, 70–71

Idil, Baran, 124, 130–33

Ignatieff, Michael, 44

Igoe, Jim, 280

IHD (İnsan Hakları Derneği—Human Rights Association), 73

İkizceoba Turkish refugee housing village, 108

immigrants: fictional accounts of, 341n36; war-migrant/refugee distinction, 344n99; xenophobia towards, 70

Imperial Debris (Stoler), 9

imperialism: climate change and imperial urbanism, 196–209; European colonialism and, 16; sedimented violence of, 9

India-Pakistan partition (1947), 20, 82, 235–36

Indigenous communities: colonialism's impact on, 9–10, 337n114; dispossession of, 280; extractivism in, 279

industrial capitalism, healing wounds of, 9–10

Industrial Revolution, fossil fuel emissions and, 195

injury gap, reparations and, 5

inner colonization, population transfers and, 346n126

Inter-American Court of Human Rights, 44

International Climate and Environmental Justice Tribunal, 275–76

international coalitions, climate consciousness advocacy and, 275–76

International Congresses of Architecture in Iran, 299

International Convention for the Protection of All Persons from Enforced Disappearance, 331n7

international law: demographic engineering and, 103; minority protection and, 338n6

International Pahlavi Environment Prize Award, 317–18

International Union for the Conservation of Nature, 280

intertextuality, in memorial architecture, 65–67

Ionides, M. C., 285

Iran: climate change in, 27; Islamic Revolution in (1978–79), 12, 299, 312; Pardisan Park project and, 296–316

Iran-US Claims Tribunal, 296

Iraq: architecture in, 28–30; US-led reconstruction in, 31–32, 271–73

İren, Abdülhak, 168

Irfan Bey, 351n31

irrigation projects, architecture as order in, 252–63

Islamic cities, historiography of, 37–38

Ismāʿīl Bāshā (Khedive Ismail), 15

Israel, 12, 65, 82, 102

Istanbul, Turkey: cemeteries in, 54–60, 56–58; earthquake in, 138–41; Galatasaray and Taksim Squares in, 47–59; Greek refugees in, 147–49; Islamization of, 54–59; refugee housing districts in, 106, 108–21, 343n89, 344n118; refugee populations in, 22, 77–83, 146–49; Saturday Mothers protests in, 40–42; Sixth District of, 54–55, 58

Istanbul Metropolitan Municipality, 172–73

Istanbul Patriarchate, 84

Istanbul Public Exhibition (1863), 154

Istanbul Research Institute (IAE), 334n59

Ito, Toyo, 139
Ittihat ve Terakki (Committee of Union and Progress), 102

Jane, E., 258
Japanese and Japanese Americans internment, memorials to, 71
Japanese expertise, post-earthquake neoliberal urbanization and, 171–76, 355n163, 355n166
Japan International Cooperation Agency (JICA), 173–76, *175*
Japan Society of Civil Engineers, 173
Jerveni, Turkey, 76, 84–86, 91
John-Alder, Kathleen, 298, 382n64
justice, healing and, 1–11, climate and, 24–27, 195. *See also* distributive justice; environmental justice; prospective justice; racial justice; restorative justice; transitional justice
Justice and Development Party (AK Party), 175–76, 180, 188, 356n140

Kalfa, Hadji Komninos, 150
Kant, Immanuel, 138
Kappadokika (Rizos), 84
Karacaoba Turkish refugee housing village, 108
Karaman, Emine Rezzan, 333n48
Karamanlı language, culture and alphabet, 84–85, 91–92, 118–21, 151, 169–70
Karantinos, Patroklos, 93
Kareiva, Peter, 379n25
Karpathos, Greece, Ottoman architects and builders from, 225–26
Kasaba, Reşat, 80
Katz, Solomon, 303, 310
Kavala, Greece: migration and, 37–39; Muslim population decline in, 103; as Ottoman city, 15, 234
Kaya, Şükrü, 19
Kazak migration, to Turkey, 157–58
Kemalettin, Mimar, 150
Kentel, Mehmet, 54–55
Khalifa, 203–4
Khalifa's house (Omdurman), 232, *233*
Khartoum: climate determinism and, 195–96, 272–76; colonial-era public buildings in, 221–29; colonialism and postcolonialism in, 22; colonial maps

of, 196–98, *197, 198*; Doxiadis's master plan for, 236–43, *238–39, 242*; gardens in colonial residences in, 212–13; Gezira plantations in, 27; Greek presence in, 37, 234; Moneim Mustafa's buildings in, 244–51; Ottoman architects and builders in, 225–29; population demographics for, 362n22; postcolonial public buildings in, 245, *247–50,* 249, 251; race and climate determinism in, 199–209; urban and architectural history in, 15, 17; white thermal comfort in colonial housing of, 209–21; workers' housing in, 217–21, *218–19*
Khedive Ismail, 15
Kigali Genocide Memorial Center, 65, 67, *68*
King, Anthony, 275
KIPTAS construction company, 175, 188, 190–91
Kitchener (Lord), 196–99, 201, 237–39, 253, 256
Kitchener Memorial School, 222, *224*
Kılıç, Abdulvahab, 168
Kırbayır, Berfo, 47, 333n34
Kırbayır, Cemil, 47, 333n34
Klein, Naomi, 9, 139
Kokkinia (Athens district), housing in, 104–6, *105–6*
Kolbert, Elizabeth, 279
Konstandinis, Aris, 106
Korangi master plan, India-Pakistan partition refugees and, 235–36
Kordofan Special Fund Project for Land and Water in Sudan, 284–90, *287–90,* 379n31, 379n32
Kosovo: population transfers in, 146; territorial claims involving, 12
Koundouros, Nikos, 95
Koyunoğlu, Arif Hikmet, 101, 108
Krantonellis Kleon, 93, 234, 263–66, 274–76
Küçükakyüz, Hatice, 157
Küçükerman, Önder, 153–54
Kulca, Yusuf, 157, 182
Kurds: demographic engineering and, 103; enforced disappearance in Turkey of, 331n6; resettler nationalism and, 22
Kurt, Ümit, 19

National Museum of Memory in Colombia, 67

national parks: ecocide prevention debate and, 279–83; North American environmentalism and, 311–16

National Register of Historic Places (US), underrepresented minorities in, 72

nation-states: Balkan War and entrenchment of, 18; demographic engineering by, 102–3; human rights regime and, 7–8; Ottoman Empire dissolution and, 81–83; resettler nationalism and, 11–12

natural disaster, building failure or food insecurity, 10–11

Nature Conservancy Institution, 379n25

Nea Philadelphia (Athens migrant housing district), 106, 107

Nea Prokopi, Greece, 91, 99, 113

Nea Sinasos, Greece, 10, 93, 99, 110, 111–12, 113–14, 127–28; wildfires in, 136–37

Nea Sinasos Association, 127

Nea Smyrna, Greece, 95

Nea Ionia, Greece, 95

Neglia, Giula Annalinda, 37

Nehir, Enver, 155, 353n90

Neo Faliro tile workshop (Athens), 116, 118

Neos Kosmos, Greece, 95

neoliberal urbanization, post-earthquake and, 171–76, 188–193

neo-Nazi movement, immigrant attacks by, 70

neoprotectionism, 281–83, 378n21

New Asian-African Strategic Partnership, 235

new conservationism, 281–83, 378n21, 379n25

New Gourna village project (Egypt), 269–71

Newton, W. G., 227

Nichols, Robert, 21, 82

Nicosia, Cyprus, Green Line project in, 321, 322

Niemeyer, Oscar, 30

Night and Fog directive, 42

Nikodimos of Derkos (Terkos), 150

Nixon, Rob, 24, 277–78

nonhuman species rights: adaptation *vs.* extinction and, 310; ecocide prevention and, 279–83; healing and, 4–11, 24–33; right to heal, 316–22; transitional justice and, 8–9

Northern Cyprus, territorial claims involving, 12

Nuri, Roca, 351n31

Ocak, Emine, 40–42, 47

Ocak, Hasan, 40–42, 334n50

Ocak, Maside, 48

Öğün, Emine, 182

Öğün, Mehmet, 182

oil industry, architecture and, 27–33

Olmsted, Frederick Law, 278

Omdurman: African aesthetics in buildings of, 227, 229, 230; colonialism in Khartoum and, 198–209, 206; postcolonial Khartoum master plan incorporation of, 239–43

On the Wall (Tekiner photographic installation), 52–53, 54

Oostvaardersplassen (Amsterdam), 309

Open Architecture (Akcan), 35, 325n29

oral history, architecture and, 35

Orff, Kate, 278

Organization of Petroleum Exporting Countries (OPEC), 28

Orientalism, colonial architecture and, 198–209, 272–76

Orientalism, colonialism and, 10

Orthodox Christians: in Anatolia, 340n26; Ottoman Empire dissolution and, 84–86; population transfers and, 91–92

Ottoman abjection, Islamic Right and, 21

Ottoman architects and builders, agency in Sudan of, 225–29

Ottoman Egypt, 15–16, 200, 212

Ottoman Empire: African colonization and decolonization and, 196; Balkan War (1912–13) and, 17–18; colonization of, 9–10; demographic engineering during, 102–3; dissolution of, 3–4, 36–37, 140–41; Greek culture and identity in, 119–21, 234; Islamization of Istanbul during, 54–59; land ownership during, 166–67; migration and end of, 140–41; racism in, 267–72; resettler nationalism and dissolution of, 11–23; slavery in, 212; Turkish and Greek Christian rivalry in, 84–86;

"A Study of the Human Factor in the Gezira Scheme" (Culwick), 262–63
Suakin (Sudanese heritage site), 219–20, *221*, 366n87
Subcommittee of the Exchange of Prisoners and Populations (Lausanne Treaty), 79
Sudan: absence of architectural scholarship on, 15; architects in, 234, 240–43, 372n166; British colonization of, 16–17, 36–37; civil wars in, 371n155, 373n176; climate determinism and, 195–96; climate disaster in, 26–27; Cold War politics in, 235–36; colonialism in, 28; cotton production in, 252–63; Doxiadis's analysis of, 237–43; drought and water management in, 251–52; independence (1956), 234, 264; Mahdist takeover of, 16; migration to, 325n33; nationalism's rise in, 17; water insecurity in, 284–90
Sudan Clubs, 222, *223,* 366n83
Sudan Development Cooperation, 245
Sudanese Savings Bank, 245
Sudan Light and Power Company, 213
Sudan Plantations Syndicate, 254, 256, 258–59, *259,* 263–66
Suleiman, Sayed Ibrahim, 265
Sultan Beyazit-ı Veli Khan Endowment, 165–67
Surp Pırgiç Armenian Hospital, 151–52, 165
Syria, earthquake in, 2

Takadopoulous, Lazaros, 87–88
Tanforan Assembly Center (California), 71
Tange, Kenzo, 139, 173–74, 176, 355n168
Taut, Bruno, 27–28, 108, 329n80
Technocon, 244–51
Tehcir (relocation) law (1915), 12
Teitel, Ruti, 8, 44, 48
Tekeli, Ilhan, 162
Telford, Thomas, 195
Theological Seminary (Istanbul), closing of, 123
"There Is No School on Saturday" (Vahit Tuna installation), 334n50
Thessaloniki, Greece, 79, 91, 93, 146, 169
Thunberg, Greta, 75
To Heal the Earth (McHarg), 297, 310
Tohti, Ilham, 157

torture spaces, memorialization of, 60–61
tourism: national parks and, 280–83; retrofitting and, 130–33
transitional justice: German models for, 63–65, 69–71; globalization and localization of, 71–75; going back testimonies and, 126–30; healing and, 5; identity politics and, 70–71; memorial spaces and, 59–71; "mother" activism and, 49–59; nation-state manipulation by, 72–75; nonhuman species rights and, 8–9; physical space and right to truth in, 8; as power consolidation tool, 74; reparations debate and, 72–75; right to truth and, 42–47; selective inclusion of victims of, 69–71; UN Definition for, 43–44
Treatise of Friendship and Commerce (1930), 127
Treaty of Berlin (1878), 11, 144
Treaty of Lausanne (1923), 78–86, 113, 127; "movables" in, 127–31, *128*
tropical architecture: climate change and, 26; colonialism and, 199–200; local climate knowledge dismissed in, 229, 231–32; Moneim Mustafa's participation in, 245, 248–49
Tropic of Chaos (Parenti), 252
"Trouble with Wilderness, The" (Cronon), 280
Trump, Donald, Gaza resettlement plan of, 14
truth: monumentality and right to, 71; transitional justice and right to, 43–47
Truth, Justice and Memory Center (Turkey), 44, 331n6, 333n32, 333n39
Truth and Reconciliation Commission (South Africa), 45–46
truth commissions, right to truth and, 48
Tsing, Anna Lowenhaupt, 8, 314–15
tukl (straw structures in Sudan), 218–20, *220,* 232; of Gezira Scheme workers, 261–63, *262*
Tuna, Vahit, 334n50
Tünel (Istanbul subway), 55
Turkey: Balkan Wars of 1912–13 and, 21, 327nn47–48; Central Asian refugee migration to, 14; Christian Greek expulsion from (1964), 12, 20–23, 123–33, 169–70; Cyprus relations with, 73–74; demographic engineering in,

War of Independence (Turkey) (1919–23), 78, 129
"Water for Human Development" (Doxiadis), 291–95
"Water for Peace" conference (1967), 284, 291–95
water management: architecture and, 27; climate change and, 273–76; Doxiadis Associates program for, 284–90, *287–90*; in Sudan, 251–52
Weir, Robert, 222
Western/non-Western divide: human rights policies and, 74–75; population transfers and, 88–89
White, Jenny, 178
white thermal comfort: colonial-era housing in Khartoum and, 209–21, *210–11, 214*, 365nn78–79; dismissal of local climate knowledge and, 231–32; Khartoum urban planning and, 206–9
wilderness ideology: ecocide prevention and, 280–83; North American environmentalism and, 311–16
Wilson, Mabel, 63, 65
Winckelmann, Johann, 194
WMRT (Wall, McHarg, Roberts and Todd), 296–316
Wolff, Gertrude Lucy, 214
Wollstonecraft, Mary, 6
Women's House (Kadın Evi) initiative (Cappadocia), 133
Words in Freedom (Marinetti), 141
World War I, Balkan War (1912–13) linked to, 17–18, 141
Wynter, Sylvia, 5

Yakas, Orestis, 240
Yalçın, Kemal, 339n20
Yapı magazine, 109

Yenal, Nurten, 148–49, 353n90
Yenikapı Mevlevi (Dervish) Lodge, (Istanbul) 150, *151*, 184–85
Yeniyol, Hatullah, 158–60
Yerli, Ali, 163–64
Yerolympos, Alexandria, 98
Yonucu, Yusuf, 169
Young, Liam, 281–82
Young Turks, 18–19, 145, 327n51
Yugoslavia, migration to Turkey from, 12, 155, 168–70
Yüksel, Aydın, 186
Yüksel, Reşide, 168

Zambia, Doxiadis's housing plan for, 267
Zeynel, Mehmet, 160
Zeytinburnu (Istanbul borough): architecture in, 149–55, *151, 152, 154, 155*; building collapse in, 190–93, *191*; Central Asian population in, 181–82; Cultural Valley project in, 176–93, *177*; dispossession in, 165–67; as *gecekondu* (slum) neighborhood, 147, 155–56, *158–59, 158–60*; industrialization in, 152–54, 164–65, *165*; labor exploitation in, 161–62; luxury housing in, 187–88, *189*; pollution in, 163–65; post-earthquake neo-liberal urbanization and, 171–76, *172*; refugee settlements in, 140, *142–43*, 147–49, *149*; resettler nationalism in, 157–70; Soviet and Chinese migrants in, 156–58
Zeytinburnu Turkistan House, 157
Zinn, Howard, 35–36
Ziya, Abdullah, 109
Zoumboulidis, Nikos, 76, 93, 109–18, *111–12, 114–15, 117, 126–27*
Zürcher, Erik Jan, 18